Family Therapy
Concepts and Methods

FOURTH EDITION

Michael P. Nichols, Ph.D.
College of William and Mary

Richard C. Schwartz, Ph.D.
The Family Institute at Northwestern University

Foreword by
Salvador Minuchin, M.D.
Family Studies

Allyn and Bacon
Boston London Toronto Sydney Tokyo Singapore

Series Editor, Social Work and Family Therapy: *Judy Fifer*
Vice President, Social Sciences: *Karen Hanson*
Editorial Assistant: *Sue Hutchinson*
Marketing Manager: *Susan E. Brown*
Sr. Editorial Production Administrator: *Susan McIntyre*
Editorial Production Service: *Ruttle, Shaw & Wetherill, Inc.*
Composition Buyer: *Linda Cox*
Manufacturing Buyer: *Megan Cochran*
Cover Administrator: *Linda Knowles*
Text Design: *Denise Hoffman, Glenview Studios*
Electronic Composition: *Omegatype Typography, Inc.*

A Viacom Company
160 Gould Street
Needham Heights, MA 02194

Internet: www.abacon.com
America Online: keyword: College Online

Library of Congress Cataloging-in-Publication Data

Nichols, Michael P.
Family therapy : concepts and methods / Michael P. Nichols, Richard C. Schwartz ; foreword by Salvador Minuchin.
p. cm.
Includes bibliographical references and index.
ISBN 0-205-26983-4 (alk. paper)
1. Family psychotherapy. I. Schwartz, Richard C. II. Title.
RC488.5.N53 1998
616.89'14—dc21 97-9840
CIP

Text credits appear on page 556, which constitutes an extension of the copyright page.

Printed in the United States of America

10 9 8 7 6 5 4 3 2 RRD 04 03 02 01 00 99 98

To our wives, Melody Nichols and Nancy Schwartz,
and our children, Sandy and Paul Nichols,
Jessie, Sarah, and Hali Schwartz

Contents

4 The Fundamental Concepts of Family Therapy 109

Part II The Classic Schools of Family Therapy

5 Bowen Family Systems Therapy 141

6 Experiential Family Therapy 177

11 From Strategic to Solution-Focused: The Evolution of Brief Therapy 355

12 Narrative Therapy 397

13 Integrative Models 423

Part IV The Evaluation of Family Therapy

14 Comparative Analysis 447

Foreword

In this volume Mike Nichols and Dick Schwartz tell the story of family therapy—and tell it very well. It's hard to imagine a more readable and informative guide to the field.

Born in the late 1950s, family therapy seemed to spring fully formed out of the heads of a group of seminal thinkers and practitioners. Nearly four decades later both theory and practice show the uncertainties and doubts that define maturity. But in the beginning—as the storytellers say—there was Gregory Bateson on the West Coast, a tall, clean-shaven, angular intellectual, who saw families as systems, carriers of ideas. On the East Coast was Nathan Ackerman, short, bearded, portly, the quintessential charismatic healer, who saw families as collections of individuals struggling to balance feelings, irrationalities, and desires. Bateson, the man of ideas, and Ackerman, the man of passion, complemented each other perfectly, the Don Quixote and Sancho Panza of the family systems revolution.

For all the diversity of the 1960s and 1970s that saw the new clinical practice called family therapy take a variety of names—systemic, strategic, structural, Bowenian, experiential—there was also a remarkable solidarity in the shared beliefs that defined the field. The pioneers were united in their rejection of psychoanalysis and embrace of systems thinking, however much they might have differed in their therapeutic techniques.

From the mid 1970s on, as family therapy succeeded and expanded, it was extended to encompass different client populations, with specific interventions for various special groups; with drug addiction, hospitalized psychiatric patients, the welfare population, family violence. . . . All posed their own challenges. Practitioners responded to this expanded family therapy with an array of new approaches, some of which even challenged the fundamental allegiance to systems thinking.

The challenge to systems theory (the official science of the time) took two forms. One was purely theoretical: a challenge to the assumption that systemic thinking was a universal framework, applicable to the organization and functioning of all human collectives. A major broadside came from feminists who questioned the absence of concepts of gender and power in systems thinking, and pointed to the distorting consequences of genderless theory when focusing on family violence. The other concerned the connection between theory and practice: a challenge to the imposition of systems theory as the basis for therapeutic practice. The very techniques that once defined the field were called into question. Inevitably, the field began to recover specificity and to reopen for examination its old taboos: the individual, intrapsychic life, emotions, biology, the past, and the particular place of the family in culture and society.

As is always characteristic of an official science, the field tried to preserve established concepts while a pragmatic attention to specific cases was demanding new and specific responses. As a result, today we have an official family therapy that claims direct descendence from Bateson, and a multitude of excellent practitioners doing sensitive and effective work that is frequently quite different from what systems theory prescribes. The result has often produced conflict and controversy. One such controversy centers on the power of the therapist.

From the perspective of today, with its many challenges to the therapist's authority and responsibility, the early family therapists were all "conductors"—forceful advocates for change, with committed positions about how that change should occur. Therapy was always a joint endeavor, but the responsibility for leading the way was the therapist's.

A number of schools of family therapy now seek to protect the family from the intrusiveness of the therapist. They are concerned that a forceful therapist's interventions might dominate and disempower families. Starting with the Milan Associates' concern with neutrality, this stance has reappeared recently in the constructivists who propose that therapy can only be a dialogue between two coconstructors of a story that is not rooted in any testable reality. (Academic fashion being what it is, the story of family therapy is sometimes told in such a way that the contributions of Ackerman, Bowen, Boszormenyi-Nagy, Fleck, Haley, Lidz, Minuchin, Satir, Whitaker, and Wynne, among others, disappear in favor of a straight and narrow line from Bateson to the Milan group to the narrative constructivists.) The contemporary constructivists' emphasis on language and meaning and their caution to restrain the power of the therapist was presented as radically new. But in some way this concern that therapists not intrude on patients is a throwback to the Freudian concept of the therapist as a tabula rasa onto whom patients projected transferential fantasies.

Lurking between the lines in many recent family therapy articles and books is a straw man, a power-hungry therapist who measures patients against the Procrustean bed of his or her own biases and then stretches or diminishes them to fit. It is to save families from the misguided intrusiveness of this kind of expertise that many of the new modalities of therapy have been constructed. But equating expertise with domination is false mathematics. Besides, control doesn't disappear from family therapy by changing the language from "intervene" to "cocreate." All that happens is that the influence of the therapist goes underground. Made invisible, it may remain unexamined.

Narrative constructivism is an interesting way of looking at human experience—emphasizing as it does one important aspect of the thinking, feeling, and acting beings we all are. But such a philosophical point of view imported unmodified into an interventionist enterprise like family therapy (which is, after all, about reducing suffering) constructs a fairy tale ogre: a therapist unaware of the effect of his interventions, operating from a power base invisible to him. The only way to avoid wielding such a sledgehammer, many now believe, is to intervene only as a coconstructor of stories—as though people were not only influenced by but were nothing but the stories they tell about themselves.

But there is another way of thinking about families and their problems, one held by a group who believes that therapy is a field of human transactions and that it is impossible for the therapist not to influence that field. Therapists in this group tend to be proximal, inventive, committed, interventive, and optimistic that their involvement with families will help family members solve their problems. Positioned in this group, I think that only a clear recognition of the idiosyncrasies of the individual therapist and the partialities of any therapeutic approach offers the possibility of true respect for each family's unique and individual character. I see the therapeutic process as an encounter between distinct interpersonal cultures. Real respect for clients and their integrity can allow therapists to be other than fearfully cautious, can encourage them to be direct and authentic—respectful and compassionate—but also at times honest and challenging. Such a therapist accepts that family members have their own experience and their own integrity, and also that they project their own wishes and fantasies into the therapeutic area, which then becomes a field of forces in which all the participants pull each other in different directions.

The advantage of this position is that the therapist, as a repository of multiple "transferences," experiences varying pulls of behavior. As the therapist, a discreet self, his or her own person, experiences those pulls, he or she responds by creating contexts in which family members encounter themselves in new positions that foster the exploration of novelty and alternative choices.

This conception of the therapist as an active knower—of himself or herself *and* of the different family members—is very different from the neutral therapist of the constructivists. But, of course, these two prototypes are entirely too simplified. Most practitioners fall somewhere between these two poles of neutrality and decisiveness.

The choice between action and interventionism, on the one hand, and meaning and conversation, on the other, is but one of the questions the field is grappling with today; there are many others. Are there useful models of human nature and of functional families, or must every situation be responded to de novo? Are the norms of human behavior and family function universal, or are they culturally constructed products of political and ideological constraint? How do we become experts? How do we know what we know? If we become experts, are we creating the fields that we then discover? Can we influence people? Can we not influence them? How do we know that we are not simply agents of social control? How do we know that we are accomplishing anything at all? What right do we have to constrain diversity, imposing ways of being on others? Are questions better than statements?

These questions and the rich history and contemporary practice of family therapy are explored magnificently in *Family Therapy: Concepts and Methods.* It is a thorough and thoughtful, fair and balanced guide to the ideas and techniques that make family therapy such an exciting enterprise. Nichols and Schwartz have managed to be comprehensive without becoming tedious. Perhaps the secret is the engaging style of their writing, or perhaps it is how they avoid getting lost in abstraction while keeping a clear focus on clinical practice. In any case, this superb book has long set the standard of excellence as the best introduction and guide to the practice of family therapy.

Much has changed in the field in the last few years, and this new edition brings readers right up to date. Considerably improved over the previous edition, this one describes the latest approaches and continues to offer insightful and balanced commentary. The inclusion of a separate chapter on research is also a welcome addition. Without a doubt the definitive textbook of family therapy, this volume offers a wealth of information presented with refreshing clarity and a total absence of cant. It all adds up to an exciting, highly readable book. It is a fascinating journey. Enjoy it.

Salvador Minuchin, M.D.
Boston, Massachusetts

Preface

One thing that tends to get lost in academic discussions of family therapy is the tremendous excitement of sitting down with an unhappy family and being able to help them. Beginning family therapists are understandably so anxious about how to proceed that they aren't sure they'll know how to be helpful. ("How do you get *all of them* to come in?") Veterans often speak in abstractions. They have opinions and discuss big issues—social constructionism, the postmodern degeneration of certainty, managed care. While it's tempting to use this space to say Important Things, I prefer to be a little more personal. Treating troubled families has given me the deepest satisfaction imaginable, and I hope that the same is, or will be, true for you.

In this fourth edition of *Family Therapy* we've tried to describe the full scope of family therapy—its rich history, the classic schools, the latest developments. There are lots of changes in this edition: more up-to-date descriptions of the latest models, a greatly expanded treatment of the cognitive-behavioral approach, a richer description of the research literature, and a more thorough and consistent emphasis on clinical techniques throughout.

When you read about therapy it can be hard to see past the jargon and political packaging to the essential ideas and practices. So, in preparing this edition, we've traveled widely to visit and observe the actual sessions of the leading practitioners. The result is a more pragmatic, clinical focus. We hope you like it.

So many people have contributed to my development as a family therapist and to the writing of this book that it's impossible to thank them all. But I would like to single out a few. To the people who taught me family therapy—Rodney Shapiro, Lyman Wynne, Murray Bowen, Michael Kerr, and Salvador Minuchin—thank you.

Myrna Friedlander did an absolutely marvelous job of reviewing the research literature and putting it into perspective. Bless you, Micki.

Once again I count myself lucky to have Dick Schwartz as a coauthor. Collaborating with another writer is easy, just like making a marriage work. All you have to do is expose your soul to the critical eyes of another person and hope for the best. Well, more than hope, I guess. Find some way to make it work out—somehow remaining true to your own vision while also taking the other person's into account. Maybe the respect and affection Dick and I feel for each other has something to do with making this possible.

Some of the people who went out of their way to help us prepare this fourth edition were Jay Efran, Frank Dattilio, George Simon, Ema Genijovitch, Rich Simon, Insoo Berg, Bill Pinsof, Cheryl Rampage, Kathy Weingarten, Vicki Dickerson, Jeff Zimmerman, Jim Keim, Cloe Madanes, Jay Haley, and Salvador Minuchin. To paraphrase John, Paul, George, and Ringo, we get by with *a lot* of help from our friends—and we thank them one and all.

We are especially grateful to Judy Fifer and Susan McIntyre at Allyn and Bacon for making a hard job easier.

Finally, I would like to thank my postgraduate instructors in family life: my wife, Melody, and my children, Sandy and Paul. In the brief span of twenty-nine years, Melody has seen me grow from a shy young man, totally ignorant of how to be a husband and father, to a shy middle-aged man, still bewildered and still trying. Sandy and Paul never cease to amaze me. My little red-haired girl (who can bench press like a football player) is about to graduate from college and head off to the Peace Corps. Proud of her? You bet I am! And my son, Paul, to whom (masculine reticence being what it is) maybe I haven't always shown the depth of my love, has grown to young manhood true to himself, true to his friends, and true to his mother and me. If in my wildest dreams I had imagined children to love and be proud of, I wouldn't even have come close to any as fine as Sandy and Paul.

Michael P. Nichols
Williamsburg, Virginia

Even though I see my kids every day, occasionally I find myself stepping back and looking at them as if I hadn't seen them for years. I'm always shocked at how much they have changed right under my nose, and I always have mixed emotions. I feel proud of their growth but nostalgic for aspects of our earlier relationships, concerned about their future but excited about sharing it.

Working on this fourth edition of *Family Therapy* has been a similar experience. I have passionate and protective feelings for family therapy similar to those that I have for my children. Since I exist in the field, I hadn't noticed how much it had changed until this new edition forced Mike and me to step outside and look at it from a distance. Not surprisingly, I've experienced the same mixture of concern and excitement, pride and nostalgia. The 1990s have produced so many challenges to and breaks from family therapy traditions that I sometimes feel the way my parents must have felt in the 1960s when they kept telling me that not all of the established culture had to be rejected or rebelled against. Yet, no doubt like my parents back then, I am also intrigued by some of the new ideas and live vicariously through the adventures of those pursuing them.

This year has been particularly nostalgic because I left the Institute for Juvenile Research (IJR), where I had been for 17 years. Through the 1980s and until the early 1990s, IJR was a wonderful place to work; an intellectual incubator in which the best of my perspectives and those of many others were born and nurtured. The faculty of the Family Systems Program of IJR (which at times included Doug Breunlin, Betty Mac Kune-Karrer, Howard Liddle, Celia Falicov, and Rocco Cimmarusti) had the time to think, converse, write, and construct quality training programs. The program will end this year, a casualty of the shift in priorities ushered in by managed care. Its demise is symbolic of a troubling trend. At a time when we need healing perspectives more than ever, everyone is being forced to scramble to survive and no one has energy or time for exploring. The family systems programs of the world are gone, and that is a tragedy.

I'll confess to still another parentlike emotion. I feel sorry for the beginning family therapy student. When I was smitten by the field in the early 1970s, things were much simpler and a student had far fewer choices. There were a handful of models, and all you had to do was pick one and then idolize and impersonate its creator. The field was adequately covered in one semester, and therapy was so straightforward that you could work right from a book.

Now there is so much more detail about different kinds of families, so many different, rapidly evolving approaches and perspectives, and so few charismatic leaders to impersonate or clear-cut techniques to employ. The novice facing all these choices and all this information is understandably daunted. The task of those teaching courses in (or writing texts about) family therapy has increased enormously. The field has become impossible to digest quickly—it must be savored over many years.

Yet, while all this diversity and change has increased the challenge we face, it also represents a welcome new approach to learning. There's less of the closed-minded fervor and chauvinism of those earlier, simpler days and more humility and openness both within the field and toward other disciplines. Family therapy became more complex once we recognized that having simple answers was not always useful. Perhaps it's good that we all have to work harder to grasp the complexity of the human condition.

I remain eternally grateful to Mike Nichols for inviting me to accompany him on this periodic perspective-taking. In addition to enjoying our collaboration, which is always highly stimulating and enriching, I have come to value our friendship a great deal. It is nice that every three years we have an excuse to strengthen it.

As with previous editions, Mike and I have tried to provide a fair representation of the concepts and methods of the approaches we cover, but also to openly discuss our opinions of them, rather than pretending to be totally objective. This book therefore is a perspective on family therapy, not *the* truth about family therapy. I have my biases (and a model, described in Chapter 13, in which these biases are evident), and Mike has his. Our collaboration produces a binocular view that is richer than either would be alone.

Once again I want to express my gratitude to the current and former faculty of the Family Systems Program within the Institute for Juvenile Research. I'm excited to reconnect with Doug Breunlin by joining him at the Family Institute at Northwestern University and looking forward to collaborating with others there, such as Bill Pinsof. Special thanks are also due to several other of my teachers, including Doug Sprenkle, Rich Simon, Mary Jo Barrett, Debbie Gorman-Smith, and Ted and Gen Schwartz.

Finally, I thank my wife, Nancy, and our daughters, Jessie, Sarah, and Hali, for their sacrifice, support, and instruction. Each time I step back and look, my heart fills with joy.

Richard C. Schwartz
Chicago, Illinois

The authors and the publisher wish to express their gratitude to the reviewers of this text, throughout its four editions, and to those who reviewed the Instructor's Manual in this edition; their comments have greatly enriched and contributed to our work: Richard J. Bischoff, University of San Diego; Faith Bonecutter, University of Illinois, Chicago; Kathleen Briggs, Oklahoma State University; Philip M. Brown, Tulane University; Joe Eron, Catskill Family Institute, Kingston, N.Y.; Robert-Jay Green, California School of Professional Psychology; Jim Keim, Family Therapy Institute, Rockville, Md.; Edith C. Lawrence, University of Virginia, Charlottesville; Howard A. Liddle, Temple University; Kaye Nelson, Texas A&M University; Thorana S. Nelson, Utah State University; Bill O'Hanlon, Possibilities, Omaha, Nebr.; and Otha L. Wright, Jr., Norfolk State University.

1

The Foundations of Family Therapy

There wasn't much information on the intake sheet. Just a name, Holly Roberts, the fact that she was a senior in college, and her presenting complaint: "trouble making decisions."

The first thing Holly said when she sat down was, "I'm not sure I need to be here. You probably have a lot of people who need help more than I do." Then she started to cry.

It was springtime. The tulips were up; the trees were turning light, leafy green; and purple clumps of lilacs perfumed the air all over town. Life and all its possibilities stretched out before her, but Holly was naggingly, unaccountably depressed.

The decision Holly was having trouble making was what to do after graduation. The more she tried to figure it out, the less able she was to concentrate on anything. She started sleeping late, missing classes. Finally, her roommate talked her into going to the Health Service. "I wouldn't have come," Holly said. "I can take care of my own problems."

I was into cathartic therapy back then. Most people have stories to tell and tears to shed. Some of the stories, I suspected, were dramatized to compel sympathy and attention. We seem to give ourselves permission to cry only with some very acceptable excuse. Of all the human emotions we're ashamed of, feeling sorry for ourselves tops the list.

I didn't know what was behind Holly's depression, but I was sure I could help. I felt comfortable with depressed people. Ever since my senior year in high school, when my friend Alex died, I'd been a little depressed myself.

After Alex died, the rest of the summer was a dark blur. I cried a lot. And I got mad whenever anybody suggested that life goes on. Alex's minister said that his death wasn't a real tragedy, because now "Alex was with God in heaven." I wanted to scream, but I numbed myself instead. In the fall I went off to college, and, even though it seemed somehow disloyal to Alex, life did go on. I still cried from time to time, but with the tears came a painful discovery. My grief wasn't all for Alex. Yes, I loved him. Yes, I missed him. But his death also provided me the justification to cry about the everyday sorrows in my own life. Maybe grief is always like that. At the time it struck me as a betrayal. I was using Alex's death to feel sorry for myself.

What, I wondered, was making Holly so sad? In fact, Holly didn't have a dramatic story. Her feelings weren't focused. After those first few moments in my office, she rarely cried. When she did, it was more of an involuntary leakage than a sobbing release. She talked about the future and not knowing what she wanted to do with her life. She talked about not having a boyfriend—in fact, she rarely ever had any dates. She never said much about her family. If the truth be told, I wasn't much interested. Back then I thought home was the place we have to leave in order to grow up, to become ourselves.

Holly was vulnerable and needed someone to lean on, but something made her hold back, as though she didn't feel safe and didn't quite trust me. It was frustrating. I wanted very badly to help her.

A month went by and Holly's depression only got worse. I started seeing her three times a week, but we weren't really getting anywhere. One Friday afternoon Holly was feeling so despondent that I didn't think she should go back to her dorm alone. I asked her instead to lie down on the couch in my office and, with her permission, I called her parents.

Mrs. Roberts answered the phone. I told her that I thought she and her husband should come to Rochester and meet with me and Holly to discuss the advisability of Holly taking a medical leave of absence and going home. Unsure as I was of my authority back then, I steeled myself for an argument. Mrs. Roberts surprised me by agreeing to come at once.

The first thing that struck me about Holly's parents was the disparity in their ages. Lena Roberts looked like a slightly older version of Holly; she couldn't have been much over thirty-five. Her husband looked sixty. It turned out that he was Holly's stepfather. They had gotten married when Holly was sixteen.

Looking back, I don't remember much being said in that first meeting. Both parents were very concerned about Holly. "We'll do whatever you think best," Mrs. Roberts said. Mr. Morgan (that was Holly's stepfather's name) said they could arrange for a good psychiatrist "to help Holly over this crisis." But Holly said she didn't want to go home, and she said this with more energy than I'd heard from her in a long time. That was on Saturday. I suggested that there was no need to rush into a decision, so we arranged to meet again on Monday.

When Holly and her parents sat down in my office on Monday morning it was obvious that something had happened. Mrs. Roberts's eyes were red from crying. Holly glowered at her and looked away, her mouth tight and grim. Mr. Morgan turned to me. "We've been fighting all weekend. Holly heaps abuse on me, and when I try to respond, Lena takes her side. That's the way it's been since day one of this marriage."

The story that came out was one of those sad histories of jealousy and resentment that turn ordinary love into bitter, injured feelings and, all too often, tear families apart. Lena Roberts was a stunning woman of thirty-four when she met Tom Morgan. He was a robust fifty-six. Apart from their ages, the second obvious difference between them was money. He was a successful stockbroker who'd retired to run a horse farm. She was waitressing to support herself and her daughter. It was a second marriage for both of them.

"First comes love, then comes marriage," children jumping rope used to chant. But in this case, instead of the baby carriage, then came Lena with a teenage daughter.

Lena looked to Tom to be the missing role model and source of discipline in Holly's life. Unfortunately, she couldn't accept the strict rules Tom felt she invited him to enforce. And so Tom became the wicked stepfather. He made the mistake of trying to take over and, when the predictable arguments ensued, Lena sided with her child. Things got bad and then worse. There were tears and midnight shouting matches. Twice Holly ran away to a friend's house for a few days. The triangle nearly proved Lena and Tom's undoing, but things calmed down when Holly went off to college.

Holly expected to leave home and not look back. She would make new friends at college. She would study hard and make a career for herself. She would *never* depend on a man to support her. Unfortunately, she left home with a lot of unfinished business. She hated Tom for the way he picked on her and for the way he treated her mother. He was always demanding to know where her mother was going, who she was going with, and when she would be back. If her mother was the least little bit late, there would be a scene. Why did her mother put up with it?

Blaming Tom was simple and satisfying. But there was another set of feelings, harder to face, eating at Holly. She hated her mother for marrying Tom and for letting him be so mean to her. What had her mother seen in him in the first place? Had she sold out for a big house and a fancy car? Holly didn't have an answer to these questions; she didn't even dare allow them into full awareness. Unfortunately, repression doesn't work like locking something away in a closet and forgetting about it. It takes a lot of energy to keep unwelcome emotions at bay.

Holly found excuses not to go home much during college. It didn't feel like her home anymore. She buried herself in her studies. But rage gnawed at her, and bitterness fed on her, slowly sapping her strength until, finally, in her senior year, facing an uncertain future, knowing only that she couldn't go home again, she gave in to hopelessness. No wonder she was depressed.

I found the whole story sad. Not knowing much about family dynamics and never having lived in a stepfamily, I wondered why they couldn't just get along better. The worst of it was that they had so little sympathy for each other. Why couldn't Holly accept her mother's right to find love a second time around? Why couldn't Tom respect the priority of his new wife's relationship with her daughter? And why couldn't Holly's mother listen to her daughter's adolescent anger without getting so defensive?

That session with Holly and her parents was my first lesson in family therapy. Family members in therapy talk, not about actual experiences, but about reconstructed memories that resemble the original experiences only in certain ways. Holly's memories resembled her mother's memories very little, and her stepfather's not at all. In the gaps between their truths there was little room for reason and no desire to pursue it.

Although that meeting may not have been terribly productive, it certainly put Holly's unhappiness in perspective. No longer did I think of her as a tragic young woman, all alone in the world. She was that, of course, but she was also a daughter torn between running as far away as possible from a home she no longer felt part of and being afraid to leave her mother alone with a man she didn't trust. I think that's when I became a family therapist. To say that I didn't know much about families, much less about techniques for helping them reason together, would be an understatement. But family therapy isn't just a new set of techniques; it's a whole new approach to understanding human behavior—as fundamentally shaped by its social context.

The Myth of the Hero

Ours is a culture that celebrates the uniqueness of the individual and the search for an autonomous self. Holly's story could conveniently be told as a coming of age drama: a young person's struggle to break away from childhood and provincialism, to take hold of adulthood and promise and the future. If she fails, we're tempted to look inside the young adult, the failed hero.

We are raised on the myth of the hero: the Lone Ranger, Robin Hood, Wonder Woman. When we get a little older we search out real-life heroes and put them on a pedestal. Eleanor Roosevelt, Martin Luther King, Nelson Mandela. Even in troubled times, amid a background of timidity and moral indifference, these were men and women who actually stood for something. If only we could be a little more like these larger-than-life individuals who seem to rise above their circumstances.

Only later do some of us begin to realize that the "circumstances" we want to rise above are part of the human condition—our inescapable connection to our families. The romantic image of the hero is based on the illusory idea that authentic selfhood can be achieved as a proud, autonomous individual. We do many things alone, including some of our most heroic acts, but we are defined and sustained by a network of human relationships. Our need to worship heroes is partly a need to rise above littleness and self-doubt, but perhaps equally a product of imagining a life unfettered by all those pesky relationships that somehow never quite go as we would wish.

When we do think about families, we often think of them in negative terms—as forces of dependency holding us back or as destructive elements in the lives of our patients. What catches our attention in families are differences and discord. The harmonies of family life—loyalty, tolerance, mutual aid and assistance—often slide by unnoticed, part of the taken-for-granted background of family life. If we would be heroes, then we must have villains.

There's a lot of talk these days about "dysfunctional families" as a source of human unhappiness. Unfortunately, some of this amounts to little more than parent bashing. We suffer because of what *they* did: Our mother's drinking, our father's brutish or cold ways—these are the cause of our unhappiness. Perhaps this is an advance on stewing in guilt and shame, but it's a long way from understanding what really goes on in families.

One reason for blaming family sorrows on the personal failings of parents is that it's very hard for the average person to see past individual personalities to the structural patterns that make them a family—a system of interconnected lives governed by strict but unspoken rules.

People feel controlled and helpless not because they are victims of parental folly and deceit, but because they don't understand the forces that hurl husbands and wives and parents and children together. Plagued by anxiety and depression, or merely troubled and uncertain, some people turn to psychotherapy for help and consolation. In the process, they turn away from the irritants that propel them into therapy. Chief among these aggravations are unhappy relationships—with friends and lovers *and* with the family. Their disorders are private ailments. When they retreat to the safety of a synthetic relationship, the last thing they want is to take our families with us. Is it any wonder, then, that when Freud ventured to explore the dark forces of the mind, he deliberately locked the family outside the consulting room?

Psychotherapeutic Sanctuary

Psychotherapy was once a private enterprise, conducted in isolation from everyday pressures and routines. The consulting room was a place of healing, yes, but it was equally a sanctuary, a refuge from a troubled and troubling world.

Buffeted about in love and work, unable to find comfort and solace elsewhere, adults came to therapy looking to find lost satisfaction and meaning. Parents, worried about their children's misbehavior, shyness, or lack of achievement, sent them for guidance and direction. In many ways psychotherapy displaced the family's function of solving the problems of everyday life. Once they hid inside their family shells from the harshness of the outside world; later, psychotherapy provided their haven in a heartless world.[1]

It's tempting to look back on the days before family therapy and see those who insisted on segregating patients from their families as naive and wrongheaded, exponents of a fossilized view of mental disorder, according to which psychiatric maladies were firmly embedded in the heads of individuals. Considering that clinicians didn't begin treating whole families together until the mid 1950s, it is tempting to ask, "What took them so long?" In fact, there are very good reasons for conducting psychotherapy in private, isolated from distressed and distressing relationships.

The two most influential approaches to psychotherapy in the twentieth century, Freud's psychoanalysis and Rogers's client-centered therapy, were both predicated on the assumption that psychological problems arose from unhealthy interactions with others and could best be alleviated in a private relationship between therapist and patient.

Freud's discoveries indicted the family, first as a breeding ground of childhood seduction and later as the agent of cultural repression. Since the natural child is oriented toward pure pleasure, the family must be antipleasure. Ideally, this dialectic tames the animal underside of human nature, making us fit to live in society, able to gratify our needs without stepping too hard on each other's toes. All too often, however, repression is excessive; instead of learning to express needs in moderation, they are buried, sacrificing satisfaction for security. If people grow up a little bit neurotic—afraid of their own natural instincts—who should we blame but their parents?

Given that neurotic conflicts were spawned in the family, it seemed only natural to assume that the best way to undo the family's influence was to isolate relatives from treatment, to bar their contaminating influence from the psychoanalytic operating room.

Freud discovered that the less he revealed of his own personality and feelings, the more his patients reacted toward him as though he were a significant figure from their families. At first these *transference* reactions seemed a hindrance, but Freud soon realized that they provided an invaluable glimpse into the past. Thereafter, fostering and analyzing transference became the cornerstone of psychoanalytic treatment. This meant that since the analyst was interested in the patient's memories and fantasies about the family, the real family's presence would only obscure the subjective truth of the past. Freud wasn't interested in the living family; he was interested in the family-as-remembered, locked away in the unconscious.

By conducting treatment in private, Freud safeguarded patients' trust in the sanctity of the therapeutic relationship and thus maximized the likelihood that the patients would repeat, in relation to the analyst, the understandings and misunderstandings of early childhood.

Carl Rogers also believed that psychological problems stemmed from destructive early interactions. Each of us, Rogers said, is born with an innate tendency toward *self-actualization*, an idea that became the premise of all humanistic psychotherapies. Left to our own devices, we tend to follow our own best interests. Because we are curious and intelligent, we explore and learn; because we have strong bodies, we play and exercise; and because being with others brings us joy, we are outgoing, loving, and affectionate.

[1]Christopher Lasch (1977) described a massive erosion by public schools of the family's educative function and an appropriation of parental functions by the "helping professions" in the first twenty-five years of the twentieth century. His was a telling analysis of the American family besieged by "the guardians of public health and morality."

Unhappily, said Rogers, our healthy instinct toward actualization gets warped and subverted by our craving for approval. We learn to do what we think others want, even though it may not be what's best for us. Little boys act tough to please daddies who wish they were tougher themselves; little girls tame their own free spirits to conform to what they think their parents want.

Gradually, this conflict between self-fulfillment and need for approval leads to denial and distortion of our inner promptings—and even of the feelings that signal them. We swallow our anger, stifle our exuberance, and bury our lives under a mountain of expectations.

The therapy Rogers developed was designed to help patients uncover their real feelings and honest impulses. Given his faith in people discovering their own best interests, Rogers's image of the therapist was like that of a midwife—passive, but supportive. The Rogerian therapist didn't *do* anything *to* patients, but offered support to help them discover what needed to be done, primarily by providing *unconditional positive regard.* The therapist listened carefully and sympathetically, offering understanding, warmth, and respect. In the presence of such an accepting listener, patients gradually got in touch with their own feelings and inner promptings. Although this sounds simple, it is a unique relationship. Try telling someone about a problem you're having and see how long it takes them to interrupt with a story of their own or to give advice—advice more likely to suit them than it does you.

Like the psychoanalyst, the client-centered therapist maintained absolute privacy in the therapeutic relationship to avoid any possibility that patients' real feelings might be subverted to win approval. Only an objective outsider could be counted on to provide the unconditional acceptance to help patients rediscover their real selves. That's why family members had no place in the work of client-centered therapy.

Family versus Individual Therapy

As you can see, there were, and continue to be, valid reasons for conducting psychotherapy in the context of a private and confidential relationship. But although there is a strong claim to be made for individual psychotherapy, there are equally strong claims to be made for family therapy.

Keep in mind that individual psychotherapy and family therapy each offer two things: an approach to treatment and a way of understanding human behavior. As approaches to treatment, both individual and family therapies have their particular virtues. Individual therapy can provide the concentrated focus to help people face their fears and learn to become more fully themselves. Individual therapists have always recognized the importance of family life in shaping personality, but they assumed that these influences were internalized and that intrapsychic dynamics became the dominant forces controlling behavior. Treatment could and should, therefore, be directed at the person and his or her personal makeup. Family therapists, on the other hand, believe that the dominant forces in our lives are located externally, in the family. Therapy based on this framework is directed toward changing the organization of the family. When family organization is transformed, the life of each family member is altered accordingly.

This last point—that changing a family changes the life of each of its members—is important enough to elaborate. Family therapy isn't simply predicated on changing the individual patient in context. Family therapy exerts change on the entire family; therefore, improvement can be lasting because each and every family member is changed *and* continues to exert synchronous change on each other.

Almost any sort of human difficulty can be treated with either individual or family therapy. But certain problems are especially suited to the family approach, among them problems with children (who must, regardless of what happens in therapy, return home to the influence of their parents), complaints about a marriage or other intimate relationship, family feuds, and symptoms that develop in an individual around the time of a major family transition.

If problems that arise around family transitions make a therapist think first about the role of the family, individual therapy may be especially useful when people identify something about themselves that they've tried in vain to change *and* their social environment seems to be stable. Thus, if a woman gets depressed during her first year at college, the therapist might wonder if her sadness is related to leaving home, and leaving her parents alone with each other. But if the same woman were to get depressed in her forties, say, during a long period of stability in her life, we might wonder if there's something about the way she approaches life, something about the way she hasn't fulfilled herself, that's responsible for her unhappiness. Examining her life in private—away from troubled relationships—doesn't mean that she should believe that she can fulfill herself in isolation from other people in her life

The view of persons as separate entities, with families acting on them, is consistent with the way we experience ourselves. We recognize the influence of intimates—especially as obligation and constraint—but it's hard to see that we are embedded in a network of relationships, that we are part of something larger than ourselves.

Psychology and Social Context

Ordinarily, the question of individual versus family therapy is posed as a technical one: Which approach works best with a given problem? But the choice between individual and family therapy also reflects a philosophical understanding of human nature. Although most therapists are too busy to raise philosophical questions about their work, they are nevertheless shaped by the context in which they work, an important aspect of which is the prevailing climate of opinion about the place of the individual and the role of the family.

The rise of individualism and the legitimization of selfhood led many people to place the needs of the individual above those of the group. "Authenticity" was equated with radical individualism, just as it often is among adolescents struggling to define identities independent of their families. Family therapy has flourished at the close of the twentieth century, not only because of its proven clinical effectiveness, but also because we are rediscovering the interconnectedness that characterizes our human community.

Finally, although psychotherapy can succeed by focusing on either the psychology of the individual or the organization of the family, both perspectives—psychology and social context—are indispensable for a full understanding of individuals and their problems.

For years, psychotherapy split human problems into one of two categories: intrapsychic or interpersonal—individual or family. Therapists were encouraged to learn modes of treatment that focused on one of these two domains to the exclusion of the other, because they were considered different enterprises. In case staffings the question was, "Is this a family or an individual case?" In the early days, if the case was deemed a family case, that meant that all members of the family would be included in therapy sessions. If it was an individual case, the family was never to be consulted.

Since then, as the polarization between individual and family therapists has decreased, these distinctions have become less rigid and less politicized. Many family therapists treat individuals and recognize the impact of psychopathology and psychodynamics. They see family therapy as an orientation rather than a technique, so there's no contradiction in doing family therapy with just one person in the room. For their part, most individual therapists recognize the importance of family dynamics and direct their efforts to helping their patients understand and change the patterns of their relationships. In short, a good therapist looks at the whole picture—the barriers that exist in the environment as well as those that exist only in the patient's mind.

Consider, for example, how limited a therapist treating a shy adolescent would be if she weren't aware of the mother's suffocating influence on the boy. Whether it be an obvious case to look for family influence, such as a child's school phobia, or a less obvious instance, like an adult's depression or excessive drinking, problems that seem to be located in one person often turn out to reflect the dynamics of a triangle. As you'll see throughout this book, understanding the abstraction called "the family context" often boils down to broadening the focus from the psychology of one person to the interactional dynamics of three people.

Family therapists teach us that the family is more than a collection of separate individuals; it is a system, an organic whole whose parts function in a way that transcends their separate characteristics. But even as members of family systems, we do not cease being individuals, with hearts and minds and wills of our own. Although it isn't possible to understand people without taking into account their social context, notably the family, it is misleading to limit the focus to the surface of interactions—to social behavior divorced from inner experience.

Working with the whole system means not only considering all the members of the family, but also taking into account the personal dimensions of their experience. Consider a father who smiles despite himself during a discussion of his son's delinquent behavior. Perhaps the smile reveals the father's secret pleasure at the boy's rebelling in a way the father is afraid to. Or take the case of a husband who complains that his wife won't let him do anything with his friends. The wife may indeed restrict him, but the fact that the husband surrenders without a fight suggests that he may be conflicted about having fun. Will negotiating with his wife clear up this man's inner anxieties about doing things on his own? Probably not. If he resolves his own inner constraints, will his wife suddenly start encouraging him to go out and have a good time? Not likely. These impasses, like most human problems, exist in the psychology of individuals *and* are played out in their interactions. The point is this: To provide effective and lasting psychological help, a therapist needs to understand and motivate individuals and influence their interactions.

The Power of Family Therapy

Family therapy was born in the 1950s, grew up in the 1960s, and came of age in the 1970s. The initial wave of enthusiasm for treating the whole family as a unit was followed by an increasing diversification of schools, each vying for a corner of the truth, and of the market for services.

The most widely talked about approach in the 1960s was the Palo Alto Group's communications therapy. Gregory Bateson, Don Jackson, and Jay Haley were the dominating figures, and *Pragmatics of Human Communication* was the most popular book. The 1970s belonged to structural family therapy. Salvador Minuchin was the most admired therapist of the time, and his *Families and Family Therapy* was the book of the decade. In the 1980s, strategic and systemic family therapies dominated the scene—Jay Haley and Cloe Madanes, the brief therapy group at the Mental Research Institute (MRI) in Palo Alto, including Paul Watzlawick, John Weakland, and Richard Fisch; and the Milan Associates, Mara Selvini Palazzoli, Gianfranco Cecchin, Luigi Boscolo, and Guiliana Prata. The book that excited the most interest was *Paradox and Counterparadox*, and its authors, the Milan Associates, were the intellectual darlings of the period. But, as shown in the next chapter, it was Milton Erickson whose clinical wizardry inspired much of the clinical innovation in strategic therapy.

Some day we may look back on the years from 1975 to 1985 as family therapy's golden age. Those years saw the full flowering of the most imaginative and vital approaches to treatment. It was a time full of enthusiasm and confidence. Family therapists may have had their differences about technique, but they shared a sense of optimism and common purpose. Since then several upheavals have shaken the field out of its zealousness and overconfidence. The pioneering models were challenged (on both clinical and sociocultural grounds) and their boundaries blurred to the point where today far fewer family therapists identify themselves exclusively with any one particular school. Even the distinction between individual and family therapy is less clear-cut, as more and more therapists practice both forms of treatment.

While it's comforting to see change as progress, especially if you're part of it, it may be that not all the changes seen in the field of family therapy are progressive.

The dominating trends of the 1990s are social constructionism (the idea that our experience is a function of the way we think about it), narrative therapy, integrative approaches, and a growing concern with social and political issues. The chapters that follow explore these and other developments. Here, we simply want to suggest that as you read about these developments you consider the possibility that, like all new developments, these have pluses and minuses.

The animating idea of family therapy is that because most human behavior is interactive, problems can often best be addressed by helping people change the way they interact. To what extent are the innovations of the 1990s useful corrections and extensions of family therapy's original focus, and to what extent do these new developments take us away from our expertise or back to linear thinking?

Does the constructivist notion that we invent rather than discover reality correct a positivist bias of family therapists, or does it merely revert back from action to insight? Is narrative therapy a way of empowering families to reauthor their lives, or is it just a fancy version of cognitive behavior therapy—wishing away problems with the power of positive thinking? Do integrative therapies combine the strengths of their component elements or simply muddy their distinctive features? And, finally, is family therapy's current emphasis on social issues—notably, sexism and multiculturalism—a logical extension from the system of the family to the systems of culture in which families are embedded, or is it a knee-jerk version of "identity politics" leading to separate and warring factions of men and women, gays and straights, and various racial and ethnic groups?

You'll notice that these questions are posed in simple, either/or terms. As H. L. Mencken once said, most complex questions turn out to have simple answers—and they're usually wrong. While there is undeniable satisfaction in reducing issues to simple polarities, we urge you to stop and search this impulse. Don't be too quick to assume that the latest approach is the best one—or that the old ways are the best ways. Don't be beguiled by charismatic authors or teachers into automatically buying what they're selling.[2] Instead of accepting or rejecting on visceral reactions, we suggest that you begin by looking to see what there is of value in the models and methods presented in this book, and then consider their shortcomings. We'll try to present the material in such a way that you can draw your own conclusions.

The chapters that follow show how family therapy was invented in the 1950s, struggled for legitimacy in the 1960s, and spawned a proliferation of competing models that flowered in the 1970s and 1980s; in the 1990s family

[2]The obvious logical extension of this point is not to accept uncritically the points of view expressed in this book.

therapy has become more collaborative and less competitive. Like all stories, the rise of family therapy can be described from numerous perspectives.

Taking a historical perspective, you will see how family therapy was shaped by being discovered at the same time in several contexts and how it was partly defined against the reigning paradigm, psychoanalysis, and the medical psychiatric establishment. For those of you who think of history as a dead-letter repository of outdated developments, we have news: The most radical and far-reaching shifts in family therapy are taking place right now, at the close of the millennium.

Contemporary Cultural Influences

In this, the only industrialized country in the world other than South Africa without national health care, private insurance corporations and their managed care affiliates are now dictating the shape of clinical practice. Decisions once made by patients and their therapists are now made by managed health care companies hired to keep insurance costs down by limiting services. As a result, mental health treatment is now usually limited to crisis intervention. A therapist who petitions to extend treatment beyond the authorized ten sessions will trigger a utilization review, necessitating an onerous amount of paperwork and a plague of phone calls—and costing an average of $800 (often more than the cost of the treatment itself). In addition to micromanaging day-to-day clinical decisions, managed care has led to a breakdown of patient confidentiality. It's no longer unusual for employers to learn about an employee's psychological treatment, and it isn't rare for such information to have a prejudicial impact on the employee's standing. Therapists, unaccustomed to bureaucratic intrusion into what most consider a private relationship and reluctant to engage in the necessary hucksterism, have responded with outrage and exasperation. Some have even been driven into retirement.

As is true of many changes, managed care hits hardest those therapists accustomed to practicing under the old rules. Therapists entering clinical practice in the twenty-first century, on the other hand, are better equipped to deal with the realities of the marketplace. While many managed care companies have made life difficult for therapists and patients alike, some have taken a reasoned approach, asking only for a certain amount of accountability. Family therapy tends to be appealing to these managers because it's generally briefer than individual therapy and, as insurance regulators are now realizing, treating the whole family together is more cost-effective than paying for separate individual therapies. Finally, family therapists have always been aware of the desirability of working for concrete practical changes in order to help families get back on their feet and on their way again.

The second great revolution in the contemporary history of family therapy is a product of postmodern skepticism. No longer is the field rigidly divided into competing camps, each with its own corner on the Truth. Instead it enjoys a rich cross-fertilization of ideas and integrated models of treatment. Few accomplished family therapists still tie themselves exclusively to one school of thought.

Similarly, family therapists in the 1990s are learning to tailor their approaches to fit clients rather than the other way around. Therapists, of course, have always claimed to consider the uniqueness of their clients. But until recently there was a tendency to try to fit patients onto Procrustean beds of purist models. If, say, a structural or Bowenian therapist were called in to consult at an agency treating drug-abusing delinquents, the therapist would likely try to employ his or her standard approach—bring in the family and see who was doing what to whom. If the fit wasn't good, there was a tendency to think that the families somehow "lacked motivation" or weren't "good therapy candidates." There were, after all, plenty of suitable cases to be seen back at the clinic. Now, however, family therapists are grappling with the need to design approaches to deal with a variety of formerly neglected predicaments, including schizophrenia, depression, drug addiction, delinquency, foster care, behavioral medicine, borderline personality disorders, sexual abuse, domestic violence, and a host of other messy, real-world problems. One-size-fits-all therapies are a thing of the past.

Thinking in Lines; Thinking in Circles

The dynamic group of creative thinkers who invented family therapy orchestrated a momentous shift from linear to recursive thinking about human events. Mental illness has traditionally been explained in linear terms, either medical or psychoanalytic. Both paradigms treat emotional distress as a symptom of an internal dysfunction with historical causes. The medical model assumes that clustering symptoms into syndromes will lead to biological causes and solutions for psychological problems. In psychoanalytic explanations, symptoms are said to arise from trauma or conflict that originated in the patient's past. In both models, treatment focuses on the individual.

Linear explanations take the form of *A* causes *B*. Recursive, or circular, explanations take into account mutual interaction and influence. Linear causality is the way we're used to thinking, and it works fine in some situations. If you're driving along and your car suddenly sputters to a stop, go ahead and look for a simple cause. Maybe you're out of gas. If so, there's a simple solution. Hike to the nearest gas station and try to talk the attendant into lending you a container in which to lug back the gas. Human unhappiness, however, is a bit more complicated.

When things go wrong in relationships, most people are pretty generous in giving credit to the other person. "The reason we're not happy is that *he* doesn't share his feelings with me." "Our love life is lousy because *she's* frigid." Since people peer out at the world from inside their own skins, they see best other people's contributions to their mutual problems most clearly. Blaming is only natural. The illusion of unilateral influence tempts therapists too, especially when they hear only one side of the story. But once they understand that reciprocity is the governing principle of relationship, therapists can help people get past thinking in terms of villains and victims.

Suppose, for example, that a father complains about his teenage son's behavior.

FATHER: "It's my son. He's rude and defiant."

THERAPIST: "Who taught him that?"

Instead of accepting the father's perspective that he's a victim of his son's villainy, the therapist's provocative question invites him to look for patterns of mutual influence. The point isn't to shift blame from one person to another but to get away from blame altogether. As long as he sees the problem as his son's doing, the father has little choice but to hope that the boy will change. (Waiting for other people to change is a little like planning your future around winning the lottery.) Learning to think in circles rather than lines empowers the father to look at the half of the equation he can control. Maybe if he showed his son more respect, or was less restrictive, the boy would be less defiant. And, since patterns of influence frequently involve triangles, he may discover that his son's door-slamming defiance is covertly fueled by his wife's unexpressed anger.

Although it isn't possible to understand family therapy without an appreciation of its historical context and intellectual underpinnings, family therapy is ultimately a clinical enterprise. This book explores the historical, cultural, and intellectual developments that shaped the field of family therapy, but the emphasis throughout will be on clinical matters—on families struggling with adversity and on therapists' efforts to help them.

The power of family therapy derives from bringing men and women and parents and children together to transform their interactions. Instead of isolating individuals from the emotional origins of their conflict, problems are addressed at their source. The great advantage of family therapy is that it works directly on the unhappy relationships that propel people into treatment. Bringing together all the members of a family with problems makes it possible for a therapist to see all their contributions—but bringing the family together does nothing to diminish resistance to change. The sad truth is, it's hard to change, with therapy or without.

What keeps people stuck is their great difficulty in seeing their own participation in the problems that plague them. With their eyes fixed firmly on what those recalcitrant others are doing, it's hard for most people to see the patterns that bind them together. Part of the family therapist's job is to give them a wake-up call. When a husband complains that his wife nags, and the therapist asks him how he contributes to her for doing that, the therapist is challenging the husband to see the hyphenated him-and-her that is the product of their interactions.

When Bob and Shirley came for help with marital problems, her complaint was that he never shared his feelings; his was that she always criticized him. This, of course, is a classic trading of complaints that keeps couples stuck as long as they fail to see the reciprocal pattern in which each partner provokes in the other precisely the behavior he or she cannot stand. So the therapist said to Bob, "If you were a frog, what would you be like if Shirley changed you into a prince?" When Bob countered by saying that one reason he doesn't talk more with her is that she's so critical, it seemed to the couple like the old argument. But the therapist saw this as the beginning of a change—Bob speaking up more. One way to create an opening for change in rigid families is to support the blamed person and help bring him back into the fray.

When Shirley criticized Bob for complaining, he tried to retreat, but the therapist said, "No. Continue. You are still a frog."

Bob tried to shift responsibility back to Shirley. "Doesn't she have to kiss me first?" But the therapist said, "No, in real life that comes afterwards. You have to earn it."

In the opening of *Anna Karenina*, Tolstoy wrote: "All happy families resemble one another; each unhappy family is unhappy in its own way." Each unhappy family may be unhappy in its own way, but they all stumble over the same familiar challenges of family life. It's no secret what these challenges are—learning to live together, dealing with difficult relatives, chasing after children, coping with adolescence—but what not everyone realizes is that there are a relatively small number of systems dynamics that, once understood, illuminate these challenges and enable families to move through the predictable dilemmas of life successfully. Like all healers, family therapists sometimes deal with bizarre and baffling cases, but much of their work is with ordinary human beings learning life's painful lessons. Their stories, and the stories of the men and women of family therapy who have undertaken to help them, make up the theme of this book.

References

Lasch, C. 1977. *The culture of narcissism.* New York: Norton.

Minuchin, S. 1974. *Families and family therapy.* Cambridge, MA: Harvard University Press.

Selvini Palazzoli, M., Boscolo, L., Cecchin, G., and Prata, G. 1978. *Paradox and counterparadox.* New York: Jason Aronson.

Watzlawick, P., Beavin, J., and Jackson, D. 1967. *Pragmatics of human communication.* New York: Norton.

2

The Evolution of Family Therapy

We were going to call this chapter the "birth of family therapy"—an apt metaphor when you consider that the fierce pride new parents feel in the miracle of their own creation was mirrored by what the founding parents of family therapy felt. But "evolution" is a more useful concept for two reasons. First, although family therapy was born as recently as about 1956, the field has a long history. The first family therapists were justly proud of the revolutionary advances made possible by the clinical application of cybernetics and systems theory. But, as you shall see, these and many other concepts held dear by family therapists were borrowed from other fields.

The second reason the term evolution is more appropriate here is that it reminds us that while some things are adaptive at the time they emerge, when the environment changes they may no longer be functional. Take aggressiveness, for example. Surely the level of innate violence in the human species was more adaptive for hunting bison and fighting for territory than it is in today's close-quarters existence. So, too, with family therapy. As we take a careful look at the field's roots and early developments, be alert for ideas that may have been adaptive in the past but no longer seem useful, similar to evolutionary misdirections or false starts. At the same time, however, you may discover that some ideas now deemed passé may be worth hanging on to.

In this chapter we will examine the antecedents and early years of family therapy. There are two fascinating stories here, one of personalities, one of ideas. You will read about the pioneers, iconoclasts, and great originals who somehow broke the mold of seeing life and its problems as a function of individuals and their psychology. Make no mistake about it: The shift from an individual to a systemic perspective is a revolutionary one, providing those who grasp it with a profoundly powerful tool for understanding and resolving human problems.

Some of the leading lights of the systemic revolution continue to be justly famous, their genius and courage preserved and passed on in their writings and through their students. The names of Gregory Bateson, Jay Haley, and Salvador Minuchin will not be new to most of you. But there are other important figures in the evolution of family therapy who, for one reason or another, have been neglected. Among these are brilliant clinicians like Nathan Ackerman and Virginia Satir, whose names may be known but whose contributions have been underappreciated because the power and wisdom of their work was never really distilled in writing. But what about Don Jackson and John E. Bell, two of the most thoughtful pioneers of our movement whose wonderful writings are rarely read these days? Why? Simply because the publication dates aren't recent?

The second story in the evolution of family therapy is one of ideas. The restless curiosity of leading family therapists led them to a variety of ingenious new ways to conceptualize the joys and sorrows of family life. But is it really necessary to study the history of these ideas? Weren't the best and brightest notions sifted and winnowed into contemporary family theories? Unfortunately, no. Family therapy has been blessed and cursed with a fascination for intellectual novelty, which has led to remarkable innovations but also to a romance with the abstruse and the abstract, and to a neglect of some of the most original and practical ideas of family systems theory.

As you read this history of family therapy, you might want to consider what's been lost as well as what's been gained. Perhaps you'll decide that someone like Don Jackson, Virginia Satir, or Nathan Ackerman had something worth keeping alive, something worth learning more about. You may also discover that systems theory is richer and more complex than contemporary practice might suggest, or that the cybernetic metaphor isn't quite ready for the junk heap after all.

We'll do our best to tell the story of family therapy with enough coherence for you to see how the field got to where it is today, but also with enough detail for you to discover a few things worth not losing sight of along the way. Because the stories of the innovators and their innovations are inextricably woven together, we will follow the fate of the most important ideas and the practitioners with the greatest lasting impact in subsequent chapters.

As you read this history, stay open to surprises and ready to reexamine easy assumptions—including the presumably obvious assumption that family therapy started out as a benevolent effort to support the institution of the family. The truth is, therapists first encountered the family system as a powerful adversary.

The Undeclared War

Although we came to think of asylums as places of cruelty and detention, they were originally built to rescue the insane from persecution by their relatives, from being locked away and tortured in the family attic. Accordingly, except for purposes of footing the bill, hospital psychiatrists have long kept families at arm's length. Twentieth-century clinicians recognized the family's role in causing psychiatric problems but believed that excluding them from treatment was necessary to undo their destructive influence. In the 1950s, however, two puzzling developments forced therapists to recognize the family's continuing power to influence the course of treatment.

Therapists began to notice that when the patient got better, someone else in the family got worse, almost as though the family *needed* a symptomatic member. As in the children's game of hide-and-seek, it didn't seem to matter who was "It" as long as someone played the part so the game could continue. In onc case, Don Jackson (1954) was treating a woman for intractable depression. When at last she began to improve, her husband complained that her condition was getting worse. When she continued to improve, the husband lost his job. Eventually, when she was completely well, her husband killed himself. Apparently this man's stability was predicated on having a sick wife.

In another of Jackson's cases, a husband urged his wife to seek treatment for "frigidity." When, after several months of psychotherapy, she grew sexually responsive, he became impotent.

The other strange story of shifting disturbance was that patients frequently improved in the hospital only to get worse when they went home. In a bizarre case of Oedipus revisited, Salvador Minuchin treated a young man hospitalized multiple times for trying to scratch out his own eyes. The man functioned normally in Bellevue but returned to self-mutilation each time he went home. He could be sane, it seemed, only in an insane world.

It turned out that the young man was extremely close to his mother, a bond that grew even tighter during the seven years of his father's mysterious absence. The father was a compulsive gambler who disappeared shortly after being declared legally incompetent. The rumor was that the Mafia kidnapped him. When, just as mysteriously, the father returned, his son began his bizarre attempts at self-mutilation. Perhaps he wanted to blind himself so as not to see his obsession with his mother and hatred of his father.

But this family was neither ancient nor Greek, and Minuchin was more pragmatist than poet. So he did what he always did with profound enmeshment. He challenged the father to protect his son by beginning to deal directly with his wife, and then challenged the man's demeaning attitude toward her, which made her feel all the more in need of her son's proximity and protection. The therapy was a challenge to the family's structure and, in Bellevue, working with the psychiatric staff toward easing the young man back into the family, into harm's way.

Minuchin confronted the father, saying, "As a father of a child in danger, what you're doing isn't enough."

"What should I do?" asked the man.

"I don't know," Minuchin replied. "Ask your son." Then, for the first time in years, father and son began talking to each other. Just at they were about to run out of things to say, Dr. Minuchin commented to both parents: "In a strange way, he's telling you that he prefers to be treated like a young child. When he was in the hospital he was twenty-three. Now that he's returned home again, he's six."

What this case dramatized was how parents sometimes use their children—to give them a sense of purpose or as a buffer to protect them from intimacy they can't handle—*and* how some children accept that role.

To the would-be Oedipus, Minuchin said, "You're scratching your eyes for your mother, so that she'll have something to worry about. You're a good boy. Good children sacrifice themselves for their parents."

What these and other cases like them demonstrated was that families are made of strange glue—they stretch but never let go. Few blamed the family for outright malevolence, yet there was an invidious undercurrent to these observations. The official story of family therapy is one of respect for the institution of the family, but maybe none of us ever quite gets over the adolescent idea that families are the enemy of freedom. And so, regardless of their rhetoric, therapists often revert to a sense of mission in rescuing innocent victims from the clutches of their families.

The impact of a patient's improvement on the family isn't always negative. Fisher and Mendell (1958) reported a spread of positive changes from patients to other family members. However, whether the influence patients and their families have on each other is benign or malignant isn't the point. The point is, change in one person changes the system.

The validity of these observations was first corroborated in a study conducted at the Maudsley Hospital, in which a group of schizophrenic patients discharged to live either with their parents or spouses was compared to a similar group who lived alone. A significantly higher relapse rate was observed in the patients who returned to their families (Brown, 1959). At least in this sample, the disrupting influence of family life outweighed any positive effects of family support. The assumption that family visits are likely to disturb psychiatric patients is so widely accepted that to this day many hospitals don't allow patients to have family visitors, at least during the initial period of a hospital stay.

The shortsightedness of isolating patients from their families in psychiatric hospitals was recently documented in *Institutionalizing Madness.* Through the stories of four disturbed young people, Joel Elizur and Salvador Minuchin (1989) explored the consequences of labeling people as sick and then treating them as such—"a mode of therapy based on seclusion and forced contact with an insane world"—instead of supporting families in caring for their own. In one case, a sixteen-year-old boy tragically deteriorated into a chronically mentally ill patient following a progression of institutional foul-ups. "Although he could act competently in many ways, the diagnosis of madness organized a rocklike reality that constrained possibilities, restricting his life so that the most morbid expectations were fulfilled" (p. 61).

Today, over forty years after the advent of family therapy, most psychiatric hospitals still segregate patients from their families. True, some hospitals offer brief family crisis counseling, and some patients (battered women, sexually molested children) may need shelter from the pernicious influence of their families. But in the vast majority of hospitals the pressure to stabilize patients on medication and return them as quickly as possible to the community means that patients are released into the same chaotic environment that precipitated hospitalization in the first place.

Small Group Dynamics

Those who first sought to understand and treat families found a ready parallel in small groups. One reason group dynamics are relevant to family therapy is that group life is a complex blend of individual personalities and superordinate properties of group structure.

During the 1920s social scientists began studying natural groups in society in the hope of learning to solve political problems by coming to understand social interaction in organized groups. In 1920 the pioneering social psychologist William McDougall published *The Group Mind,* in which he described how a group's continuity depends in part on the group being an important idea in the minds of its members; on the need for boundaries and structures in which differentiation and specialization of function could occur; and on the importance of customs and habits, so that member-to-member relations could be fixed and defined. A more scientific and empirical approach to group dynamics was ushered in during the 1940s by Kurt Lewin, whose *field theory* (Lewin, 1951) guided a generation of researchers, industrial psychologists, group therapists, and agents of social change.

Drawing on the Gestalt school of perceptual psychology, Lewin developed the notion that the group is more than the sum of its parts. This transcendent property of groups has obvious relevance to family therapists, who must work not only with individuals but also with family systems—and with their famous resistance to change.

Another of Lewin's discoveries was that group discussions are superior to individual instruction or lecturing for changing ideas and behavior. This finding suggests that conjoint family meetings may be more effective than separate meetings with individuals. Trying to coach a wife alone to be more assertive, for example, is less likely to succeed than working together with her and her husband. By meeting with both partners, the therapist can help the wife deal with her spouse's counterreactions and make the husband more aware of the indignity—to both of them—of failing to treat his partner as an equal.

Analyzing what he called *quasi-stationary social equilibrium,* Lewin pointed out that all change in group behavior requires "unfreezing" and "refreezing." Only after something shakes up and unsettles a group's accustomed beliefs will its members be prepared to accept change. In individual therapy the unfreezing process is initiated by the disquieting experiences that lead a person to seek help. Once he or she accepts the status of patient and meets with a therapist, the individual has already begun to unfreeze old habits. When families come for treatment, it's quite a different matter.

Many family members aren't sufficiently unsettled by the symptomatic member's predicament to be prepared to change their own ways. Furthermore, family members bring their primary reference group with them, with all its traditions, mores, and habits. Consequently, more effort is required to unfreeze, or shake up, families before therapeutic change can take place. Examples of unfreezing maneuvers include Minuchin's promotion of crises in family lunch sessions, Jay Haley's deliberate use of ordeals, and Peggy Papp's family choreography. The need for unfreezing foreshadowed early family therapists' great concern over disrupting family *homeostasis,* a notion that dominated family therapy for decades.

Wilfred Bion was another major figure in the study of group dynamics who emphasized the group as a whole, with its own dynamics and structure. According to Bion (1948), most groups become diverted from their primary tasks by engaging in patterns of *fight–flight, dependency,* or *pairing.* Bion's "basic assumptions" are easily extrapolated to family therapy: Some families are so afraid of conflict that they skirt around hot issues like a cat circling a snake. Others use therapy just to vent their spleen, preferring to fight endlessly rather than contemplate compromise, much less change. Dependency masquerades as therapy when overly active therapists subvert families' autonomy in the name of problem solving. Pairing is seen in families when one parent colludes with the children to mock and undermine the other parent.

Lewin's and Bion's influences continue to be felt through their students, their wonderful writings, and two major centers for analysis and change of small group behavior, which bear the mark of their inspiration—The National Training Laboratory (NTL) in the United States, and the Tavistock Institute of Human Relations in Britain.

Warren Bennis (1964), a student of Lewin's, described group development as going through a series of standard phases, an idea put to use by family therapists who plan therapy in stages, and later in notions about predictable changes as families move through the life cycle. Bennis's conception of interdependence as the central problem in group life antedates similar notions among family therapists, including Minuchin's description of enmeshment and disengagement and Bowen's concepts of fusion and differentiation.

The *process/content* distinction in group dynamics has likewise had a major impact on family treatment. Experienced therapists learn to attend as much to *how* families talk as to the content of their discussions. For example, a mother might tell her daughter that she shouldn't play with Barbie dolls because she shouldn't aspire to an image of bubble-headed beauty.

The *content* of the mother's message is: respect yourself as a person, not as an ornament. But if the mother expresses her point of view by attacking or negating the daughter's feelings, then the *process* of her message would be: your feelings don't count.

Unfortunately, the content of some discussions is so compelling that even good therapists get sidetracked from the process dimension. Suppose, for example, that a therapist invites a teenage boy to talk with his mother about wanting to drop out of school. Say that the boy mumbles something about school being stupid, and his mother responds with a forceful statement of the need for an education. A therapist who gets drawn in to support the mother's position may be making a serious mistake. In terms of content, the mother might be right, a high school diploma does sometimes come in handy. But maybe it's more important at the moment to help the boy learn to speak up for himself—and to help his mother learn to listen.

Most teenagers are strong-willed, not oppositional. They struggle, not to defy their parents but to achieve a measure of self-determination, and they struggle however hard it takes. How far they carry that struggle, how extreme their behavior, is determined largely by how tenaciously parents resist in an effort to retain control. A therapist who ignores the process of this struggle may end up joining the forces against which young people rebel.

Role theory, explored in the literatures of psychoanalysis and group dynamics, had particularly important applications to the study of families. The expectations that roles provide bring regularity to complex social situations. According to role analysis, multiple roles and multiple group affiliations are keys to understanding individual motives. We often describe family members in terms of a single role (wife or husband), but we need to remember that a wife may also be a mother, a friend, a daughter, and an employee. (Husbands should remember this too.) Even roles that aren't currently being performed are potential and therefore important. A mother who is a single parent is also potentially a friend or lover. Her neglect of these potential roles may impoverish her life and cause her to smother her children. When members of unhappy families get bogged down in few and rigid roles, they develop interpersonal arthritis, a disease that leads to family rigidity and the atrophy of unused life.

While a narrowing of roles shrinks the possibilities of group (and family) life, group members required to play too many roles are subject to overload and to conflicting loyalties (Sherif, 1948). Among the potential roles in a family, for example, are parent, housekeeper, breadwinner, cook, and chauffeur. These roles can be divided—one partner is the breadwinner, the other cooks and cleans—or shared—both work outside the home and divide the other chores. But one partner can be caught in a role conflict if she's forced to choose between staying late for a staff meeting and going home to cook dinner and drive the kids to soccer practice—because, even though she has a partner, he doesn't play those roles.

Roles tend to be stereotyped in most groups and so there are characteristic behavior patterns of group members. Bales (1950) described twelve broad categories of group behavior, including "shows solidarity" (raises others' status, gives help); "shows tension-release" (jokes, laughs); "agrees" (passive-accepting compliance); "gives suggestions"; and "asks for suggestions." Similar role patterns also characterize family members, most of whom learn roles in the family that become more or less fixed.

Virginia Satir (1972) described family roles such as the placator or the disagreeable one in her book *Peoplemaking.* If you think about it, you may realize that you played a fairly predictable role growing up in your family. Perhaps you were "the helpful child," "the quiet one," "the comedian," "the counselor," "the rebel," or "the successful one." The trouble is, such roles, once learned, can be hard to put aside. Dutifully doing what you're told and patiently waiting for recognition may work for "the helpful child," but it may not work in a professional career, where more assertive action is called for.

One thing that makes role theory so useful in understanding families is that roles tend to be reciprocal and complementary. Say, for example, that a woman is slightly more anxious to spend time together with her boyfriend than he is. Maybe, left to his own devices, he'd call twice a week. But if she calls three times a week, he may never get around to picking up the phone. If their relationship progresses and this pattern is played out, she may always be the pursuer and he the distancer. Or take the case of two parents, both of whom like their children to behave at the dinner table. But let's say that the father has a slightly shorter fuse—he tells them to quiet down ten seconds after they start getting rowdy, whereas his wife would wait half a minute. But if he always speaks up first, she'll never get a chance. Eventually these parents may become polarized into complementary roles of strictness and leniency. What makes such reciprocity resistant to change is that the roles reinforce each other—and each one wishes the other would change.

The encounter group movement, which had enormous clinical and social consequences, was a direct offshoot of studies of group dynamics. T-groups, forerunners of encounter groups, were developed in 1964 by Kurt Lewin and his colleagues Leland Bradford, Kenneth Benne, and Ronald Lippit (Benne, 1964). These groups used participant observation to study small group dynamics. The aim gradually shifted from simply understanding group behavior to helping members clarify their goals and learn methods by which to realize these goals in group interactions. These modest aims proved successful in increasing effectiveness and satisfaction; as a result, T-groups evolved into encounter groups, the main purposes of which were personal growth and enrichment. Influential as the encounter group movement was (Nichols & Zax, 1977), it came too late to have an impact on the early history of family therapy. However, as we shall see later, the experiential school of family therapy was inspired by the encounter group movement.

Psychoanalytic group therapists regarded the group as a re-creation of the family, with the therapist as an object of transference and other group members as sibling figures. Thus, ironically, analytic group therapy, which later became one of the prototypes for family treatment, began by treating the group as an ersatz family. Analytic groups were designed to be frustratingly unstructured in order to arouse latent unconscious conflicts and revive problems from the original family group. Group members' basic motives were considered to be conflicting combinations of love and hate, pain and pleasure, and strictures of the superego versus demands of primitive impulses. Notice that the emphasis was on the individual, rather than on the group as a whole.

In the group dynamics approach, developed by Foulkes, Bion, Ezriel, and Anthony in Great Britain, the focus shifted from individuals to the group itself, seen as a transcendent entity with its own inherent laws. These therapists studied group interactions not only for what they revealed about individual personalities, but also to discover themes or dynamics common to all group members. This *group process* was considered a fundamental characteristic of social interaction and a major vehicle for change.

Another clear departure from psychoanalytic group therapy was the existential or experiential model. Experiential group therapy, stimulated by existential psychiatrists Ludwig Binswanger, Medard Boss, and Rollo May in Europe and by Carl Rogers, Carl Whitaker, and Thomas Malone in the United States, emphasized deep personal involvement with patients as opposed to dissection of people as objects. Phenomenology took the place of analysis, and immediate experience, especially emotional experience, was seen as the royal road to personal growth.

Moreno's psychodrama, in which patients act out their conflicts instead of discussing them, was one of the earliest approaches to group treatment (Moreno, 1945). Psychodramas are dramatic enactments from the lives of participants, using techniques to stimulate emotional expression and clarify conflicts. Because the focus is on interpersonal action, psychodrama is a direct and powerful means of exploring family relationships and resolving family problems. Although psychodrama remained tangential to the mainstream of group therapy, Moreno's role-playing techniques were widely adopted by group leaders and family therapists.

Fritz Perls's Gestalt therapy aims to enhance awareness to increase spontaneity, creativity, and personal responsibility. Even though it's frequently used in groups, Gestalt therapy discourages group members from interacting while one person at a time works with the therapist. Although more widely used in individual than in group or family treatment, Gestalt techniques have been borrowed by encounter group leaders and some family therapists to stimulate emotional interaction (e.g., Kempler, 1974; Schwartz, 1994).

Given the extensive and diverse procedures for exploring interpersonal relationships developed by group therapists, it was natural that some family therapists would apply group treatment models to working with families. After all, what are families but collective groups with various subgroups?

Before examining the question of how suitable the group treatment model is for family therapy, we must mention one more historical fact. Even before John Elderkin Bell and Rudolph Dreikurs began to apply group psychotherapy to families in the early 1950s, a number of workers had used the group format to enlist cooperation from family members in planning treatment for individual patients. L. Cody Marsh, for instance, lectured to groups of relatives at Worcester State Hospital (Marsh, 1935), and A. A. Low also used this technique in his work (Low, 1943). Other therapists concentrated on group meetings with mothers whose children were in treatment (Amster, 1944; Burkin, Glatzer, & Hirsch, 1944; Lowrey, 1944). Some, including Ross at McGill, held weekly discussion groups for families of adult patients (Ross, 1948). In all these group meetings, relatives were treated like helpers who were not themselves in need of therapy. The "real" patients weren't included. This work was similar to the long tradition of group counseling with parents, especially in child welfare agencies (Grunwald & Casell, 1958), and is still the way most adolescent inpatient units try to "involve" families.

One step closer to family therapy was "family group counseling" (Freeman, Klein, Riehman, Lukoff & Heisey, 1963), a sociological, problem-solving approach. Family counselors facilitated communication but deemphasized individual goals and change. Conflicts were avoided. Family counselors fostered understanding and mutual support rather than tackle deeper problems in the family or its members. Although improvement in the social climate of a family can effect profound changes in its members, Freeman and his colleagues didn't try or claim to achieve anything more than superficial support.

By the 1970s, when family therapy had become thoroughly sophisticated and thoroughly systemic, these early group counseling approaches seemed naive, treating individuals as the real patients and relegating families to a supportive role in patients' recovery. However, in the 1980s, long after the systemic revolution had been fought and won, there dawned a growing recognition that some problems may, in fact, be primarily problems of individuals—or at least best treated that way. Carol Anderson and her colleagues at the University of Pittsburgh and Michael Goldstein and his associates at UCLA developed programs of *psychoeducation* for families of schizophrenics (Anderson, Reiss,

& Hogarty, 1986; Goldstein, Rodnick, Evans, May, & Steinberg, 1978). Consistent with mainstream psychiatry, this approach treats schizophrenia as a disease, best dealt with using medication for the individual and providing counseling for families faced with the ordeal of coping with a schizophrenic member. Alcohol and drug abuse is another area where many believe that treatment must be directed primarily at individuals and only secondarily at families (Kaufman & Kaufmann, 1979; Steinglass, 1987). Where once family group counseling, which preserved the primacy of the individual patient, seemed naive, today treating schizophrenia or alcohol and drug abuse exclusively as byproducts of family stress seems equally naive.

All these approaches to group treatment were available to be applied in family therapy. Some of the techniques were useful, others were not. It was a short step from observing a patient's reactions to other members of a group—some of whom might be similar to siblings or parents—to observing interactions in real families.

Furthermore, from a technical viewpoint, group and family therapies are similar: Both involve several people. Both are complex and amorphous, more like everyday social reality than individual therapy. In groups and families each patient must react to a number of people, not just to the therapist, and therapeutic use of this interaction is the definitive mechanism of change in both settings. Consequently, many group and family therapists endeavor to remain relatively inactive and decentralized so that patients in the room will relate to each other.

In individual treatment the therapist is a safe but artificial confidant. Patients expect therapists to be understanding and accepting, an audience of one friendly person. Not so with groups and families. In both, the situation is more natural, more threatening perhaps, but also more like everyday experience. Transfer to life outside the consulting room is therefore more direct.

On closer examination, however, we can see that the differences between families and groups of strangers are so many and so significant that the group model has only limited applicability to family treatment. Family members have a long history and—more important—a future together. Groups are composed of strangers, families of intimates. Revealing yourself to strangers is easier and safer than exposing yourself to members of your own family. In fact serious harm can be done by therapists who are so naive as to push family members to always be "completely honest and open" with each other. Once blurted out, there's no taking back rash disclosures that might have better remained private—the affair, long since over, or the admission that a woman *does* care more about her career than about her children. Continuity, commitment, and shared distortions all mean that treatment for families has to differ from therapy for groups.

In one of the few small group studies using families, Strodtbeck (1954) tested a variety of propositions derived from groups of strangers and found major differences, which he ascribed to the enduring relationship of family members. Strodtbeck (1958) later substantiated the opinion that family interactions, unlike those in ad hoc groups, can be understood only in terms of the history of the family group.

Therapy groups are designed to provide an atmosphere of warmth and support. Patients feel less alone in a group. They may have felt isolated before, but they come to see the group as a place where they can be helped and where they can help others. This feeling of safety among sympathetic strangers cannot be part of family therapy, for instead of separating treatment from a stressful environment, the stressful environment itself is brought into treatment. Furthermore, in group therapy, patients can have equal power and status, whereas democratic equality isn't appropriate in families. Someone has to be (or should be) in charge. Furthermore, the official patient in the family is likely to feel isolated and stigmatized. After all, he or she is "the problem." The sense of protection in being part of a therapeutic group of strangers, who won't have to be faced across the dinner table, doesn't exist in family therapy, where it *isn't* always safe to speak openly. (There won't be a therapist to act as referee on the ride home.)

Another basic therapeutic mechanism of groups is that they stimulate typical patterns of social interaction that can then be analyzed and changed. This function of groups has been likened to a "laboratory for social change" (Nichols & Zax, 1977). Groups are designed to provide opportunities for reality testing in a relatively nonthreatening atmosphere (Handlon & Parloff, 1962) so that distorted perceptions may be corrected and new ways of behaving tried out. Families are less flexible and less open to experimentation. They have a complex, shared mythology that dictates certain roles and ways of behaving. These highly developed and patterned communications make families far less able to experiment with new responses.

Therapy groups also provide opportunities for members to resolve transference distortions, played out with a variety of group members (Handlon & Parloff, 1962). In families the real figures are actually present. Transference still occurs but is less amenable to exploration and correction. Parents may see their adolescent children in ways that fit the past better than the present. Children may see their parents accurately as unsympathetic but transfer these perceptions onto the therapist. Therapists are often hamstrung by powerful countertransference reactions when dealing with families. Furthermore, transference distortions are often supported by family mythology. "Daddy is an ogre" is a myth that pervades many mother–child coalitions. (That he isn't is a myth in others.) Such distortions and misperceptions are certainly available as grist for the therapeutic mill, but they're more difficult to deal with in families.

Although group therapy was used as a model for family therapy by some early practitioners, only the process/content distinction and role theory had any lasting impact on the mainstream of family therapy. One application of group methods that has persisted in family therapy are couples groups, and we will examine this form of treatment in later chapters.

The Child Guidance Movement

The usual history of family therapy underemphasizes the contributions of the child guidance movement in favor of the more colorful story of research on schizophrenia. There is a lesson here. Because scholars are more concerned with publishing than are clinicians, students may get a distorted idea of what's going on in the field. Today, for example, cognitive behavior therapy may appear to be the predominant approach to psychological problems because behavior therapy has always been prominent in academia. However, the fame that comes to scholars shouldn't distract us from the contributions of seasoned clinicians who aren't concerned with publication. Certainly it could be argued that the actual clinical practice of family therapy owes less to the innovative ideas of researchers on schizophrenia than it owes to child guidance clinicians laboring in the trenches to treat the emotional problems of children and their families.

The child guidance movement was founded on the belief that since emotional problems begin in childhood, treating children is the best way to prevent mental illness. It was Freud who introduced the idea that psychological disorders of adulthood were the consequence of unsolved problems of childhood. Alfred Adler was the first of Freud's followers to pursue the implication that treating the growing child might be the most effective way to prevent adult neuroses. To this end Adler organized child guidance clinics in Vienna, where not only children but also families and teachers were counseled. Adler's approach was to offer encouragement and support in an atmosphere of optimism and confidence. His technique helped alleviate children's feelings of *inferiority* so they could work out a healthy *life style*, achieving competence and success through *social usefulness*.

In 1909 the psychiatrist William Healy founded the Juvenile Psychopathic Institute (now known as the Institute for Juvenile Research) in Chicago, and this was a forerunner among child guidance clinics. In 1917 Healy moved to Boston and there established the Judge Baker Guidance Center, devoted to diagnostic evaluation and treatment of delinquent children.

When the child guidance movement in the United States expanded in the 1920s, under a grant from the Commonwealth Fund (Ginsburg, 1955), Rudolph Dreikurs, one of Adler's students, was one of its most effective proponents. In 1924 The American Orthopsychiatric Association was organized to work toward the prevention of emotional disorders in children. Although child guidance clinics remained few in number until after World War II, they now exist in every city in the United States, providing a setting for the study and treatment of childhood psychological problems and of the complex social and family forces contributing to these problems. Treatment was carried out by psychiatrist–psychologist–social worker teams, who focused much of their attention on the child's family environment.

Gradually, child guidance workers concluded that the real problem wasn't the obvious one brought to the clinic, the child's symptoms, but rather the tensions in the family that were the source of the symptoms. At first there was a tendency to blame the parents, especially the mother, for the child's problems.

Researchers focused on parental psychopathology throughout the 1940s and 1950s. David Levy (1943) was among the first to establish a relationship between pathogenic traits in parents and psychiatric disturbance in their offspring. The chief cause of childhood psychological problems, according to Levy, was *maternal overprotectiveness*. Mothers who had themselves been deprived of love while growing up became overprotective of their children. Some did so in a domineering manner, others were overly indulgent. Children of domineering mothers were submissive at home but had difficulty making friends; children with indulgent mothers were disobedient at home but well-behaved at school.

During this period, Frieda Fromm-Reichmann (1948) coined one of the most damning phrases in the history of psychiatry, the *schizophrenogenic mother*. These domineering, aggressive, rejecting, and insecure women, especially when they were married to inadequate, passive, and indifferent men, were thought to provide the pathological parenting that produces schizophrenia. Adelaide Johnson's description of the transmission of *superego lacunae* was another example of how parents were blamed for causing their children's problems (Johnson & Szurek, 1954). According to Johnson, antisocial behavior in delinquents and psychopaths was due to defects in their superegos passed on to them by their parents.

The tendency to blame parents, especially mothers, for problems in the family was an evolutionary misdirection that continues to haunt the field. It's important, however, to recognize that by paying attention to what went on between parents and children, Fromm-Reichmann and Johnson helped pave the way for family therapy.

Although the importance of the family was recognized, mothers and children were still treated separately, and discussion between therapists was discouraged on the grounds that it might compromise the individual therapeutic relationships. Under the reigning influence of psychoanalysis, there was a heavy emphasis on the individual psyche, with its unconscious conflicts and irrational motivations. Attempts to apply a social approach to disturbances in family life were dismissed as "superficial"— the ultimate indictment from psychoanalytic clinicians.

The usual arrangement was for a psychiatrist to treat the child while a social worker saw the mother. Counseling the mother was secondary to the primary goal of treating the child. The major purposes for seeing the mother were to reduce emotional pressure and anxiety, redirect hostility away from the child, and modify child-rearing attitudes. In this model, the family was viewed as an extension of the child, rather than the other way around.

It was assumed that resolution of the child's problems would also resolve family problems. Occasionally this happened, but more often it didn't. Characterological problems of individuals are only one problem in relationships; the others are interactional. Unfortunately, individual therapy may cause people to increase their preoccupation with themselves, exclusive of others in the family. After analysis, the patient may be wiser but sadder—and lonelier.

Eventually, the emphasis in the child guidance movement changed from seeing parents as noxious agents to the view that pathology was inherent in the relationships among patients, parents, and significant others. This shift had profound consequences. No longer was psychopathology located within individuals; no longer were parents villains and patients victims. Now the nature of their interaction was seen as the problem. The goal shifted from weaning child patients from their families to improving relationships between parents and children. Instead of trying—in vain—to separate children from their families, child guidance workers began to help families support their children.

John Bowlby's work at the Tavistock Clinic exemplified the transition from an individual to a family approach. Bowlby (1949) was treating a child psychoanalytically and making slow progress. Feeling frustrated, he decided to see the child and his parents together for one session. During the first half of this two-hour session, the child and parents took turns complaining, each blaming the other. During the second half of the session, Bowlby interpreted to each of them what he thought their contributions to the problem were. Eventually, by working together, all three members of the family developed some sympathy for each other's point of view.

Although he was intrigued by the possibilities of these conjoint interviews, Bowlby remained wedded to the one-to-one format. Family meetings might be a useful catalyst, Bowlby believed, but only as an adjunct to the *real* treatment, individual psychoanalytic therapy. Nevertheless by breaking down the strict isolation of the child's treatment from the mother's, and introducing conjoint family interviews, Bowlby began the transition from what had been individual therapy to what would become family therapy.

What Bowlby began as an experiment, Nathan Ackerman carried through—family therapy as the primary form of treatment in child guidance clinics. As early as 1938, Ackerman went on record as suggesting the value of viewing the family as a whole entity when dealing with disturbance in any of its members (Ackerman, 1938). Subsequently he recommended studying the family as a means of understanding the child—instead of the other way around (Ackerman & Sobel, 1950). Once he saw the need to understand the family in order to diagnose problems, Ackerman soon took the next step—family treatment. Before we get to that, however, let us examine parallel developments in social work and research on schizophrenia that led to the birth of family therapy.

The Influence of Social Work

No history of family therapy would be complete without mentioning the enormous contribution of social workers and their tradition of public service. Since the beginning of the profession social workers have been concerned with the family, both as the critical social unit and as the focus of intervention (Ackerman, Beatman, & Sherman, 1961). Indeed, the core paradigm of social work—treating the person-in-the-environment—anticipated family therapy's ecological approach long before systems theory was introduced.

That the importance of social workers and their ideas have been shamefully underemphasized in the history of family therapy says something about how opinions are formed in our field. Social caseworkers have been less visible than the trendsetters in family therapy because they've been busy, working in the trenches and delivering service, rather than in academia, writing books and making speeches. Ours is a field in which great and gifted therapists who don't happen to write books are less well known than a host of others with little or no clinical experience or expertise who happen to write well. (It's tempting to cite a few examples—but we are not that brave.)

In their excellent history of family therapy, Broderick and Schrader (1991) point out that the orthopsychiatry movement, which helped define the professional landscape of family therapy, was dominated by psychiatrists, who grudgingly recognized psychologists but devalued social workers and their contributions. Why this historical lack of respect for the profession of social work? One reason may be that "the early social caseworkers were mostly women writing for a field primarily populated by women . . ." (Braverman, 1986, p. 239) at a time when male voices dominated in our culture.

The field of social work grew out of the charity movements in Great Britain and the United States in the late nineteenth century. Then, as now, social workers were dedicated to improving the condition of society's poor and underprivileged. In addition to ministering to clients' basic needs for food, clothing, and shelter, social workers tried to relieve emotional distress in their client families and to redress the social forces responsible for extremes of poverty and privilege.

The *friendly visitor* was a caseworker who visited clients in their homes in order to assess their needs and offer help. By bringing helpers out of their offices and into the homes of their clients, these visits broke down the artificiality of the doctor–patient model that prevailed for so long. (Family therapists in the 1990s are relearning the value of getting out of the office and meeting clients were they live.) Friendly visitors were directly involved in treating problems of troubled marriages and difficulties of child-rearing. Workers at *settlement houses* offered social services not only to individuals but to family groups as well.

Family casework was the most important focus of early social work training. In fact, the first course taught by the original school of social work in the United States was "The Treatment of Needy Families in Their Own Homes" (Siporin, 1980). Friendly visitors were taught the importance of interviewing both parents at the same time to get a complete and accurate picture of a family's problems—this at a time when mothers were considered responsible for family life, and long before traditional mental health workers began experimenting with conjoint family sessions.

These turn-of-the-century caseworkers were well aware of something it took psychiatry fifty more years to discover—that families must be considered as units. Thus, for example, Mary Richmond (1917), in her classic text, *Social Diagnosis*, prescribed treatment of "the whole family" and warned against isolating family members from their natural context. Richmond's concept of *family cohesion* had a strikingly modern ring, anticipating as it did later work on role theories, group dynamics research, and, of course, structural family theory. According to Richmond, the degree of emotional bonding between family members was critical to their ability to survive and flourish.

Richmond anticipated developments that family therapy became concerned with in the 1980s by viewing families as systems within systems. As Bardhill and Saunders pointed out (1988, p. 319),

> She recognized that families are not isolated wholes (closed systems), but exist in a particular social context, which interactively influences and is influenced by their functioning (i.e. they are open). She graphically depicted this situation using a set of concentric circles to represent various systemic levels from the individual to the cultural. Her approach to practice was to consider the potential effect of all interventions on every systemic level, and to understand and to use the reciprocal interaction of the systemic hierarchy for therapeutic purposes. She truly took a systemic view of human distress.

Ironically, social workers, who pioneered in treating the family as the unit of intervention, retreated to a more traditional individual-as-patient approach when they came under the sway of psychiatry in the 1920s. Social workers in the mental health wing of the profession were strongly influenced by the prevailing psychoanalytic model, which emphasized individuals, not families.

When the family therapy movement was launched, social workers were among the most numerous and important contributors. Among the leaders who came into family therapy through social work training are Virginia Satir, Ray Bardhill, Peggy Papp, Lynn Hoffman, Froma Walsh, Insoo Berg, Jay Lappin, Richard Stuart, Harry Aponte, Michael White, Doug Breunlin, Olga Silverstein, Lois Braverman, Steve de Shazer, Peggy Penn, Betty Carter, Braulio Montalvo, and Monica McGoldrick. (Incidentally, even starting such a list is difficult because unless it went on for pages it would have to omit a host of important names.)

Research on Family Dynamics and the Etiology of Schizophrenia

Families with schizophrenic members proved to be an especially fertile area for research because their strange patterns of interaction were so dramatic and striking. Human nature is exaggerated under stress. However, as we shall see, the fact that family therapy emerged from research on schizophrenia led to an overly optimistic hope that family therapy might be the way to cure this baffling form of madness. Moreover, because abnormal families are so resistant to change, early family therapists tended to exaggerate the homeostatic properties of family life.

Family therapists didn't discover the role of the family in schizophrenia but, by actually observing families interacting, they witnessed patterns that their predecessors had only speculated about. Family influences on schizophrenia had been recognized at least as early as Freud's famous account (1911) of Dr. Schreber. In this first psychoanalytic formulation of psychosis, Freud discussed psychological factors in paranoia and schizophrenia, and also suggested how the patient's bizarre relationship with his father played a role in his fantastic delusions.

Harry Stack Sullivan focused on interpersonal relations in his brilliant work with schizophrenics. Beginning in 1927, he emphasized the importance of the "hospital family"—physicians, nurses, and aides—as a benevolent substitute for the patient's real family. Sullivan did not, however, take his ideas one step further and directly involve families in treatment. Frieda Fromm-Reichmann also believed that the family played a part in the dynamics of schizophrenia and considered the hospital family crucial in the resolution of schizophrenic episodes; however, she also failed to recommend family treatment. Although these interpersonal psychiatrists recognized the importance of family life in schizophrenia, they continued to treat the family as a pathogenic environment from which patients must be removed.

In the 1940s and 1950s, research on the link between family life and schizophrenia led to the pioneering work of the first family therapists.

Gregory Bateson—Palo Alto

One of the groups with the strongest claim to originating family therapy was Gregory Bateson's schizophrenia project in Palo Alto, California. A scientist in the classic mold, Bateson did research on animal behavior, learning theory, evolution, and ecology, as well as in hospital psychiatry. He worked with Margaret Mead in Bali and New Guinea; then, becoming interested in cybernetics, he wrote *Naven* and worked on synthesizing cybernetic ideas with anthropological data.[3] He entered the psychiatric field when, together with Jurgen Ruesch at the Langley Porter Clinic, he wrote *Communication: The Social Matrix of Psychiatry*. In 1962, Bateson shifted to studying communication among animals and from 1963 until his death in 1980 worked at the Oceanographic Institute in Hawaii.

The Palo Alto project began in the fall of 1952 when Bateson received a grant from the Rockefeller Foundation to study the nature of communication in terms of levels. All communications, Bateson had written (Bateson, 1951), have two different levels or functions—*report* and *command*. Every message has a stated content, as, for instance, "Wash your hands, it's time for dinner"; but in addition, the message carries how it is to be taken. In this case the second message is that the speaker is in charge. This second message—*metacommunication*—is covert and often goes unnoticed. If a wife scolds her husband for running the dishwasher when it's only half full, and he says OK but turns around and does exactly the same thing two days later, she may be annoyed that he doesn't listen to her. She means the message. But maybe he didn't like the metamessage. Maybe he doesn't like her telling him what to do as though she were his mother.

Even animals, Bateson observed (1951), metacommunicate. Notice, for example, how two dogs or cats play-fight. One leaps at the other, they tussle, nip each other, and growl, but neither fights seriously or inflicts damage. How do they know they're playing? Clearly they must have some way of metacommunicating, of indicating that the attack is only playful. Humans achieve considerable complexity in framing and labeling messages. Typically, qualifying metamessages are conveyed through nonverbal signals, including gesture, tone, posture, facial expression, and intonation. "I hate you," may be said with a grin, with tears, or with a fixed stare and clenched teeth. In each case, the metacommunication alters the message.

Bateson was joined in early 1953 by Jay Haley and John Weakland. Haley was primarily interested in social and psychological analysis of fantasy; Weakland was a chemical engineer who'd become interested in cultural anthropology. Later that same year a psychiatrist, William Fry, joined them; his major interest was the study of humor. This group of eclectic talents and catholic interests studied otters at play, the training of guide dogs, the meaning and uses of humor, the social and psychological significance of popular movies, and the utterances of schizophrenic patients. Bateson gave the project members free rein, but although they investigated many kinds of complex human and animal behaviors, all their studies had to do with possible conflicts between messages and qualifying messages.

In 1954, Bateson received a two-year grant from the Macy Foundation to study schizophrenic

[3]Norbert Weiner (1950) coined the term "cybernetics" for the emerging body of knowledge about how feedback controls information-processing systems. Applied to families, the cybernetic metaphor focused attention on how families become stuck in repetitive loops of unproductive behavior.

communication. Shortly thereafter the group was joined by Don Jackson, a brilliant psychiatrist who served as clinical consultant and supervisor of psychotherapy.

The group's interests turned to developing a communication theory that might explain the origin and nature of schizophrenic behavior, particularly in the context of families. Worth noting, however, is that in the early days of the project none of them thought of actually observing schizophrenics and their families.

Bateson and his colleagues hypothesized that family stability is achieved by feedback that regulates the behavior of the family and its members. Whenever the family system is threatened—that is, disturbed—it moves toward balance or *homeostasis.* Thus, apparently puzzling behavior might become understandable if it were perceived as a homeostatic mechanism. For example, if whenever two parents argue one of the children exhibits symptomatic behavior, the symptoms may be a way to interrupt the fighting by uniting the parents in concern. Thus symptomatic behavior serves the cybernetic function of preserving the family's equilibrium. Unhappily, in the process, one of the family members may have to assume the role of "identified patient."

Speculating that schizophrenia might be a result of family interaction, Bateson's group tried to identify sequences of exchange that might induce symptomatology. Once they agreed that schizophrenic communication must be a product of what was learned inside the family, the group looked for circumstances that could lead to such confused and confusing patterns of speech.

In 1956 Bateson and his colleagues published their famous report, "Toward a Theory of Schizophrenia," in which they introduced the concept of the *double bind.* They assumed that psychotic behavior might make sense in the context of pathological family communication. Patients weren't crazy in some autonomous way; they were an understandable extension of a crazy family environment. Consider someone in an important relationship where escape isn't feasible and response is necessary; when he or she receives two related but contradictory messages on different levels, but finds it difficult to detect or comment on the inconsistency (Bateson, Jackson, Haley, & Weakland, 1956), that person is in a double bind.

Because this difficult concept is often misused as a synonym for paradox or simply contradictory messages, it's worth reviewing each feature of the double bind as the authors listed them. The double bind has six characteristics:

1. Two or more persons in an important relationship;
2. Repeated experience;
3. A primary negative injunction, such as "Don't do *X* or I will punish you";
4. A second injunction at a more abstract level conflicting with the first, also enforced by punishment or perceived threat;
5. A tertiary negative injunction prohibiting escape and demanding a response. Without this restriction the "victim" won't feel bound;
6. Finally, the complete set of ingredients is no longer necessary once the victim is conditioned to perceive the world in terms of double binds; any part of the sequence becomes sufficient to trigger panic or rage.

Most examples of double binds in the literature are inadequate because they don't include all the critical features. Robin Skynner, for instance, cited (1976): "Boys must stand up for themselves and not be sissies"; but "Don't be rough . . . don't be rude to your mother." Confusing? Yes. Conflict? Probably. But these two messages don't constitute a double bind; they're merely a contradiction. Faced with two such statements, a child is free to obey either one, alternate, or even complain about the contradiction. This and many similar examples neglect the specification that the two messages are conveyed on different levels. A better example is the one given in the original article by Bateson, Jackson, Haley, and Weakland (1956). A young man recovering in the hospital from a schizophrenic episode was visited by his mother. When he put his arm around her, she stiffened. But when he withdrew, she asked, "Don't you love me anymore?" He blushed, and she said, "Dear, you must not be so easily embarrassed and afraid of your feelings." Following this exchange, the patient became upset; after the visit was over he assaulted an aide and had to be put in seclusion.

Notice that all six features of the double bind were present in this exchange, and also that the young man was obviously caught. There is no bind if the subject is not bound. The concept is interactional.

We might assume that this mother was made anxious by intimacy with her son but couldn't accept her feelings; consequently she behaved overtly as a loving mother who always does the right thing. Typically, in such a family, there is no one else, such as a strong father, to intervene and support the child. The mother tries to control her anxiety by controlling the closeness between herself and her child. But because she can't admit her anxiety, even to herself, she has to hide important aspects of her communication—namely, her own discomfort or hostility. In addition she forbids comment about her messages. Hence the child grows up unskilled in the ability to communicate about communication, unskilled in determining what people really mean, and unskilled in the ability to relate.

Another example of a double bind would be a teacher who urges his students to participate in class but gets impatient if one of them actually interrupts with a question or comment. Then a baffling thing happens. For some strange reason that professors have yet to decipher, students tend not to speak up in classes where their comments are dismissed or ridiculed. When the professor finally does get around to asking for questions, and no one responds, he gets angry. ("Students are so passive!") If any of the students has the temerity to comment on the professor's demonstrated lack of receptivity, he'll probably get even angrier. Thus the students will be punished for accurately perceiving that the professor really wants only his own ideas to be heard and admired. (This example is, of course, purely fictitious.)

Although it may sound esoteric, people need to metacommunicate in order to get along. It's often necessary to ask "What do you mean?" or "Are you serious?" In the double-binding family, however, such questions aren't allowed; comment and questioning are threatening to the parents, and the contradictory messages are obscure, occurring on different levels of communication.

We're all caught in occasional double binds, but the schizophrenic has to deal with them continually—and the effect is maddening. Unable to comment on the dilemma, the schizophrenic responds defensively, perhaps by being concrete and literal, perhaps by speaking in disguised answers or in metaphors. Eventually the schizophrenic, like the paranoid, may come to assume that behind every statement is a concealed meaning.

This 1956 double-bind paper proved to be one of the most influential and controversial in the history of family therapy. The discovery that schizophrenic symptoms made sense in the context of some families may have been a scientific advance, but it had moral and political overtones. Not only did these investigators see themselves as avenging knights bent on rescuing "identified patients" by slaying family dragons, they were also crusaders in a holy war against the psychiatric establishment. Outnumbered and surrounded by hostile critics, the champions of family therapy challenged the orthodox assumption that schizophrenia was a biological disease. Psychological healers everywhere cheered. Unfortunately, they were wrong.

The observation that schizophrenic behavior seems to *fit* in some families doesn't mean that families *cause* schizophrenia. In logic, this kind of inference is called "Jumping to Conclusions." Sadly, as we shall see, families of schizophrenic members suffered for years under the assumption that they were to blame for the tragedy of their children's psychoses.

Members of the Bateson group continued to clarify the concept of double bind and document its occurrence in schizophrenic families. Other researchers created laboratory analogues of the double bind to test its effects under controlled conditions. The problem with these studies was that they failed to include one or more of the essential ingredients. A genuinely crucial relationship such as child/parent or patient/therapist must be involved; otherwise the victim can simply ignore the situation or walk away from the relationship. Laboratory experiments rarely re-create anything like a critical relationship. The atmosphere tends to be one of gamesmanship and skepticism. Even if all the conditions seem to be met, what's being studied is merely a potential bind, because a bind isn't a bind unless it binds.

There are four possible ways to respond to double binds, or indeed to disqualifying messages of any kind: comment, withdrawal, acceptance, or counterdisqualification (Sluzki, Beavin, Tarnopolsky, & Veron, 1967). The first two avoid or offset the double bind, and if these responses are able to circumvent the bind, they may lead to a creative solution (Bateson, 1978). The reason for this is that an adaptive solution to a double bind involves stepping out of the frame, recognizing the different logical types. The ability to step back like this is a creative act, based on the rare capacity to take an objective view of one's own situation.

Bateson's original paper focused on two-person interactions, especially between mothers and children. Fathers were described only in a negative way, as being unable to help their children resist being caught in double binds. Family analyses limited to two persons, although frequent (notably among child behavior therapists and couples therapists), are inadequate. A mother's relationship with her child is shaped by her relationship with her husband, and in turn reshapes that relationship. So too, a therapist's relationship with a patient is mutually defined by and defines the therapist's relationship with supervisors and administrators.

In 1960, John Weakland attempted to extend the double bind from two to three-person interactions (Weakland, 1960), and he discussed the fact that three people are usually involved in a double bind, even though one may not be immediately apparent. However, in general, the Bateson group was more concerned with broad applications than with the intricacies of three-person systems. Thus, they suggested that the double-bind concept might be useful for analyzing three-person systems in the family, clinic, business, government, and organized religion; but they dealt with the father's effect on the mother–child dyad only in passing. Indeed, the Bateson group, as well as their strategic therapy offspring, consistently underemphasized the importance of three-person interactions.

After the publication of the double-bind paper, members of the project began interviewing parents together with their schizophrenic offspring. These meetings were exploratory rather than therapeutic, but they did represent a major advance: actually observing family interactions rather than speculating about them. These conjoint family sessions helped launch the family therapy movement, and we'll see what they revealed in the next section.

All the discoveries of the Bateson group were united on one point, the centrality of communication to the organization of families. What makes families pathological, they concluded, was pathological communication. They disagreed about the underlying motivation for the obscurant messages they observed. Haley believed that a covert struggle for interpersonal control was the motivating force for double binding; Bateson and Weakland thought it was the urge to conceal unacceptable feelings. But they all agreed that even unhealthy behavior may be adaptive in the family context. The two great discoveries of this talented team's output were (1) multiple levels of communication and (2) that destructive patterns of relationship are maintained by self-regulating interactions of the family group.

Theodore Lidz—Yale

Theodore Lidz's investigations of the family dynamics of schizophrenia focused on two traditional psychoanalytic concerns: overly rigid family roles and faulty parental models of identification.

Lidz began his explorations of the families of schizophrenics in 1941 while he was completing his residency at Johns Hopkins. In his original study (Lidz & Lidz, 1949) surveying fifty case histories, Lidz found a prevalence of broken homes and seriously disturbed family relationships. Forty percent of the young schizophrenic patients in the sample had been deprived of at least one parent by death, divorce, or separation; 61 percent of the families exhibited serious marital strife; 48 percent contained at least one extremely unstable parent (psychotic, seriously neurotic, or psychopathic); and 41 percent exhibited bizarre or unusual patterns of childrearing. In all, only five of fifty randomly selected schizophrenic patients appeared to have come from stable homes and were raised by two well-adjusted and compatible parents.

Lidz challenged the then current belief that maternal rejection was the major distinguishing feature of schizophrenic families and, in one of his most notable findings, observed that frequently the more destructive influence was that of the fathers.

Lidz followed this initial exploration with an extensive longitudinal study of sixteen families containing a schizophrenic member. These intensive studies on a small number of cases over the course of several years yielded an intimate glimpse of the environment in which young schizophrenics grew up. Using in-depth interviews, family observations, and projective testing, the investigators found consistent and striking patterns of severe family disruption and widespread psychopathology throughout the families of schizophrenic patients.

Although Lidz was firmly rooted in the traditional psychoanalytic way of thinking about families, and many of his concepts focused on individuals and their roles, some of his observations went beyond ideas about identification and ego development to consideration of two- and three-person interactions and even to the whole family as a unit. Thus Lidz bridged earlier theories about the impact of individual parents' personalities on their children and the more modern interest in families as systems.

Lidz rejected Freud's idea that schizophrenia was due to fixation at an early oral level and subsequent regression in the face of stress during young adulthood. Nor did he find overt rejection of children by any of the mothers he studied; consequently he also rejected the idea propounded by Frieda Fromm-Reichmann and John Rosen that maternal rejection was the primary cause of schizophrenia.

Early in his studies Lidz's attention was drawn to the fathers in schizophrenic families who, as previously mentioned, were as frequently and severely disturbed as the mothers (Lidz, Parker, & Cornelison, 1956). In a landmark paper entitled "Intrafamilial Environment of the Schizophrenic Patient II: The Father" (Lidz, Cornelison, Fleck, & Terry, 1957a), Lidz and his colleagues described five patterns of pathological fathering in families of schizophrenics.

The first group was domineering and rigidly authoritarian, constantly in conflict with their wives. Having failed to establish intimate relationships with their wives, they sought to win over their daughters, who thus abandoned their mothers as objects of identification and tried to follow their fathers' inconsistent, unrealistic demands.

The second group of fathers were hostile toward their children rather than toward their wives. These men rivaled their sons for the mother's attention and affection, behaving more like jealous siblings than parents. They strutted and bragged, belittling their sons' achievements and sabotaging their self-confidence.

The third group of fathers exhibited frankly paranoid grandiosity. They were aloof and distant. The sons of these men were too weak to be like their fathers but continued desperately to emulate their bizarre characteristics.

The fourth group of fathers were failures in life and nonentities in their homes. Children in these families grew up as though fatherless. They could hardly look up to the pathetic figures who were treated with such disdain by their wives.

The fifth group of fathers were passive and submissive men who acted more like children than parents. They were pleasant, almost motherly, but offered weak models of identification. These submissive fathers failed to counterbalance the domineering influence of their wives. Lidz concluded that it might be better to grow up without a father than with one who is too aloof or weak to serve as a healthy model for identification.

After describing some of the pathological characteristics of fathers in schizophrenic families, Lidz turned his attention to defects in the marital relationships. The theme underlying his findings was an absence of *role reciprocity*. The partners in these marriages rarely functioned cooperatively as a unit. In a successful relationship, it's not enough to fulfill your own role—to be an effective person; it's also necessary to balance your role with your partner's—to be an effective pair. In the schizophrenic families Lidz studied, the spouses were inadequate to fulfill their own roles and disinclined to support that of their mates.

Lidz followed Parsons and Bales in saying that a father's role is primarily *adaptive-instrumental* while a mother's is primarily *integrative-expressive*. If each parent fulfills a version of one of these roles, they can fit together harmoniously. However, if fathers fail in their instrumental roles, or mothers reject expressive nurturing, difficulties will arise in the relationship.

(Notice how wedded to traditional sex roles these assumptions were: Fathers should be "masculine," not "motherly," and a good marriage is rigidly complementary—fathers were forceful and made their way in the world; mothers were soft and selfless, they stayed home, serving their children, and their men.)

Lidz found highly disturbed marital relationships in all the cases he studied (Lidz, Cornelison, Fleck, & Terry, 1957b). In focusing on the failure to arrive at reciprocal, cooperative roles, Lidz identified two general types of discord. In the first, *marital schism*, there is a chronic failure of spouses to accommodate to each other or to achieve role reciprocity. These husbands and wives chronically undercut each other's worth and compete openly for their children's loyalty and affection. Their marriages are combat zones. The second pattern, *marital skew*, involves serious psychopathology in one partner who dominates the other. Thus one parent becomes extremely dependent while the other appears to be a strong parent figure, but is, in fact, a pathological bully. The weaker spouse, in Lidz's cases usually the father, goes along with the pathological distortions of the dominant one. In all these families, unhappy children are torn by conflicting loyalties and weighted down with the pressure to balance their parents' precarious marriages.

Lyman Wynne—National Institutes of Mental Health

None of the leaders of family therapy has had as long and distinguished a career as Lyman Wynne. His impeccable scholarship and passionate concern for the unfortunate have been guiding inspirations for forty years of hard-nosed and enormously productive research.

Like others before him, Wynne examined the effects of communication and family roles. What distinguished his work was his focus on how pathological thinking is transmitted in families.

After completing his medical training at Harvard in 1948, Wynne went on to earn a Ph.D. in the Department of Social Relations. There he encountered the work of leading figures in sociology, social psychology, and social systems, including Talcott Parsons, from whom he came to see personality as a subsystem within a larger family system. For Wynne, the notion that we are part of something larger than ourselves has been the hallmark of his professional approach to troubled individuals and to his personal commitment to the problems of society. In these twin concerns, Lyman Wynne stands as a model for the entire field.

Wynne saw his first families in 1947 when he was working with Erich Lindemann at Massachusetts General Hospital as part of the treatment of patients with severe mental and physical disorders. Lindemann's understanding of the importance of working with the whole family in dealing with crisis and grief was the perfect practical complement to what Wynne was learning academically.

In 1952, Wynne joined John Clauson's Laboratory of Socioenvironmental Studies at the National Institutes of Mental Health (NIMH), where he first began working intensively with the families of mental patients (Broderick & Schrader, 1991). In 1954, when Murray Bowen came to NIMH as head of a research project on schizophrenics and their families, Wynne found a colleague who shared his belief that the family should be the unit of treatment (even if the two didn't quite agree about the nature of that treatment). When Bowen left NIMH in 1959, Wynne took over as chief of the family research section, where he remained until the early 1970s.

During his tenure at NIMH, Wynne studied at the Washington Psychoanalytic Institute and was on the faculty of the Washington School of Psychiatry. From the 1950s through the 1970s, Wynne published many research reports; he also trained several talented researcher clinicians, including Shapiro, Beels, and Reiss. In 1972, Wynne left NIMH to become Professor and Chair of the Department of Psychiatry at the University of Rochester. He is still actively pursing his research at Rochester, although he stepped down from department chair in 1978.

Wynne's studies of schizophrenic families began in 1954 when he started seeing the parents of his hospitalized patients in twice-weekly therapy sessions. He was fascinated by the chaos he observed in these families and sought to make sense out of it by extending psychoanalytic concepts and role theory to the systems level. What struck Wynne most forcefully about disturbed families were the strangely unreal qualities of both positive and negative emotions, which he labeled *pseudomutuality* and *pseudohostility,* and the nature of the boundaries around them—*rubber fences*—apparently yielding, but actually impervious to outside influence (especially from therapists).

Pseudomutuality (Wynne, Ryckoff, Day, & Hirsch, 1958) is a facade of togetherness that masks conflict and blocks intimacy. Such families have an unnatural dread of separateness. They are so preoccupied with fitting together that there's no room for separate identities or for divergent self-interests. The family cannot tolerate either deeper, more honest relationships or independence. This surface togetherness submerges deep affectionate and sexual feelings and keeps both conflict and greater intimacy from emerging.

Pseudohostility is a different guise for a similar collusion to obscure *alignments* and *splits* (Wynne, 1961). Sequences of splits and alignments may be observed during family sessions; they are used to maintain a kind of dynamic equilibrium in which change in any part of the system, either an alignment or a split, reverberates to produce change in other parts of the system. A typical situation might be an alignment between one parent and the patient, with a split between the parents. But the truth of these coalitions is threatening and therefore often covered up.

Pseudohostility is a self-rescuing operation. Although noisy and intense, it signals only a superficial split. Like pseudomutuality, it blurs intimacy and affection as well as deeper hostility; and, like pseudomutuality, pseudohostility distorts communication and impairs realistic perception and rational thinking about relationships.

In disturbed families, various mechanisms are employed to quell any sign of separateness, either inside or outside the family. The *rubber fence* is an invisible barrier that stretches to permit obligatory extrafamilial involvement, such as going to school, but springs back tightly if that involvement goes too far. The family's rigid role structure persists, protected by the family's isolation. The most damaging feature of the rubber fence is that precisely those who most need outside contact to correct family distortions of reality are the ones allowed it least. Instead of being a subsystem of society (Parsons & Bales, 1955), the schizophrenic family becomes a sick little society unto itself, with a rigid boundary and no openings.

In a context where togetherness is everything and outside relationships are discouraged, recognition of personal differences may be impossible short of the blatantly bizarre behavior seen in schizophrenic reactions. The person may thus finally achieve the status of separateness but is then labeled schizophrenic and extruded from the family; and like mud oozing back over where a rock has been removed from a swamp, the family's pseudomutuality is restored. Acute schizophrenia may be a desperate attempt at individuation that not only fails but also costs the person membership in the family. If acute schizophrenia becomes chronic, the now defeated patient may later be reaccepted into the family.

Wynne linked the new concept of *communication deviance* with the older notion of *thought disorder.* He saw communication as the vehicle for transmitting thought disorder, which is the defining characteristic of schizophrenia. Communication deviance is a more interactional concept than thought disorder, and more readily observable than double binds. By 1978 Wynne had studied over 600 families and gathered incontrovertible evidence that disordered styles of communication are a distinguishing feature of families with young adult schizophrenics. Similar disorders also appear in families of borderlines, neurotics, and normals, but are progressively less severe (Singer, Wynne, & Toohey, 1978). This observation—that communication deviance isn't confined solely to schizophrenic families, but exists on a continuum (greater deviance with more severe pathology)—is consistent with other studies that describe a "spectrum of schizophrenic disorders."

Role Theorists

While it's tempting to skip over some of the lesser known antecedents of family therapy, there is a reason not to. The founders of family therapy gained momentum for their fledgling discipline by concentrating narrowly on verbal communication. Doing so may have been adaptive at the time, but focusing too exclusively on this one aspect of family life neglected both individual intersubjectivity and broader social influences. While integrating models is now all the rage, our history is one in which we forged a distinctive professional identity—"family therapist"—partly by ignoring the collaborative, multidisciplinary base of family studies. The danger of having a short memory and a sense of exclusivity is of professional constriction and isolation, being left outside the mainstream of health care, like psychoanalysts.

Role theorists, like John Spiegel, described how individuals were differentiated into social roles within family systems. This important fact was obscured by oversimplified versions of systems theory, according to which individuals were treated like cogs in a machine. As early as 1954, Spiegel pointed out that the system in therapy includes the therapist as well as the family (an idea reintroduced much later as "second-order cybernetics"). He also made a valuable distinction between "interactions" and "transactions." Billiard balls *interact*—they collide and alter each other's course, but remain essentially unchanged. People *transact*—they come together in ways that not only alter each other's course, but also affect internal changes.

In 1934, Kasanin, Knight, and Sage suggested that family role relationships were an important factor in schizophrenia. In forty-five cases of schizophrenia, they found *maternal overprotection* in twenty-five and *maternal rejection* in two. Kasanin described a pair of identical twins discordant for schizophrenia and suggested that differences in their relationships with family members were responsible for the difference in their fates (Kasanin, Knight, & Sage, 1934).

David Levy (1943) found *maternal overprotection* more frequently associated with schizophrenia than *rejection*. While the mother's overprotection was generally more obvious, Levy also found many cases of paternal overpro tection. Moreover, he observed that overpro tection wasn't simply imposed by parents on their children; children in these families met their overprotecting parents more than halfway. Thus, Levy introduced an interactional dimension to what had previously been regarded as another way that parents harm their children.

Ironically for a field in which circular causality was to become a favorite concept, the unfortunate evolutionary misdirection of describing negative influences in families as linear—blaming parents for rejecting or overprotecting or double binding their children—was not only unfair, but also did lasting damage to the reputation of family therapy. Families of mentally ill persons had reason to be on guard against being blamed for the misfortunes of their children.

In 1951 the Group for the Advancement of Psychiatry (GAP) decided that families had been neglected in psychiatry and therefore appointed a committee, chaired by John Spiegel, to survey the field and report their findings. The GAP committee's report (Kluckhohn & Spiegel, 1954) emphasized roles as the primary structural components of families. They concluded that healthy families contained relatively few and stable roles, and that this pattern was essential to teach children a sense of status and identity. There were norms for every role, and children learned these norms by imitation and identification.

Family roles don't exist independently of each other; every role is circumscribed by other, reciprocal roles. You can't have a domineering spouse, for example, without a submissive partner. Role behavior on the part of two or more people involved in a reciprocal transaction defines and regulates their interchange. A common example is that in many families one parent is stricter than the other. Their differences may start out to be slight, but the stricter one is, the more lenient the other is likely to become. The GAP committee explained roles as a function, not only of external social influences, but also of inner needs and drives. Thus role theory served as a link between *intra*personal and *inter*personal structures.

Spiegel went on to Harvard Medical School in 1953, where he followed up his interests in role theory and family pathology. He observed that symptomatic children tend to be involved in their parents' conflicts; nonsymptomatic children may also have parents in conflict, but these children don't get directly involved. Spiegel (1957) described his observations in psychoanalytic terms: The child identifies with the unconscious wishes of the parents and acts out their emotional conflict. The child's acting out serves as a defense for the parents, who are thereby able to avoid facing their own conflicts—and each other.

R. D. Laing's analysis of family dynamics was often more polemical than scholarly, but his observations helped popularize the family's role in psychopathology. Laing (1965) borrowed Marx's concept of *mystification* (class exploitation) and applied it to the "politics of families." Mystification refers to the process of distorting children's experience by denying or relabeling it. One example of this is a parent telling a child who's feeling sad, "You must be tired" (*Go to bed and leave me alone*). Similarly, the idea that "good" children are always quiet breeds compliant, but spiritless, children.

According to Laing, labeling behavior as pathology, even "family pathology," tends to mystify it. The prime function of mystification is to maintain the status quo. Mystification contradicts perceptions and feelings and, more ominously, reality. When parents continually mystify a child's experience, the child's existence becomes inauthentic. Because their feelings aren't accepted, these children project a *false self* while keeping the *real self* private. In mild instances, this produces a lack of authenticity, but if the real self/false self split is carried to extremes, the result is madness (Laing, 1960).

Murray Bowen at NIMH and Ivan Boszormenyi-Nagy at the Eastern Pennsylvania Psychiatric Institute also studied family dynamics and schizophrenia, but since they are better known for their clinical contributions, their work will be considered in the following discussion.

Marriage Counseling

The history of professional marriage counseling is a less well known contributory to family therapy because much of it took place outside the mainstream of psychiatry. For many years there was no apparent need for a separate profession of marriage counselors. People with marital problems were—and still are—more likely to discuss them with their doctors, clergy, lawyers, and teachers than to seek out mental health professionals. The first professional centers for marriage counseling were established in about 1930. Paul Popenoe opened the American Institute of Family Relations in Los Angeles, and Abraham and Hannah Stone opened a similar clinic in New York. A third center was the Marriage Council of Philadelphia, begun in 1932 by Emily Hartshorne Mudd (Broderick & Schrader, 1981). Members of this new profession started meeting annually in 1942 and formed the American Association of Marriage Counselors in 1945.

At the same time these developments were taking place, a parallel trend among some psychoanalysts led to conjoint marital therapy. Although the majority of psychoanalysts have always followed Freud's prohibition against contact with the patient's family, a few have broken the rules and experimented with concomitant and conjoint therapy for married partners.

The first report on the psychoanalysis of married couples was made by Clarence Oberndorf at the American Psychiatric Association's 1931 convention (Oberndorf, 1938). Oberndorf advanced the theory that married couples have interlocking neuroses and that they are best treated in concert. This view was to be the underlying point of agreement among those in the analytic community who became interested in treating couples. "Because of the continuous and intimate nature of marriage, every neurosis in a married person is strongly anchored in the marital relationship. It is a useful and at times indispensable therapeutic measure to concentrate the analytic discussions on the complementary patterns and, if necessary, to have both mates treated" (Mittleman, 1944, p. 491).

In 1948, Bela Mittleman of the New York Psychoanalytic Institute became the first to publish an account of concurrent marital therapy in the United States. Previously, Rene LaForgue had reported in 1937 on his experience analyzing several members of the same family concurrently. Mittleman suggested that husbands and wives could be treated by the same analyst, and that by seeing both it was possible to reexamine their irrational perceptions of each other (Mittleman, 1948). This was truly a revolutionary point of view from an analyst: that the reality of object relationships may be at least as important as their intrapsychic representations. Nathan Ackerman (1954) agreed that the concomitant treatment of married partners was a good idea and also suggested that mothers and children could profit from being treated together.

Meanwhile in Great Britain, where object relations were the central concern of psychoanalysts, Henry Dicks and his associates at the Tavistock Clinic established a Family Psychiatric Unit. Here couples referred by the divorce courts were helped to reconcile their differences (Dicks, 1964). Subsequently, the Balints affiliated their Family Discussion Bureau with the Tavistock Clinic, adding the clinic's prestige to their marital casework agency and, indirectly, to the entire field of marriage counseling.

In 1956, Victor Eisenstein, Director of the New Jersey Neuropsychiatric Institute, published an edited volume, entitled *Neurotic Interaction in Marriage.* In it were several articles describing the state of the art in marital therapy. Frances Beatman, Associate Executive Director of Jewish Family Services in New York, described a casework treatment approach to marital problems (Beatman, 1956); Lawrence Kubie wrote a psychoanalytic analysis of the dynamics of marriage (Kubie, 1956); Margaret Mahler described the effects of marital conflict on child development (Mahler & Rabinovitch, 1956); and Ashley Montague added a cultural perspective to the dynamic influences on marriage (Montague, 1956). In the same volume, Mittleman (1956) wrote a more extensive description of his views on marital disorders and their treatment. He described a number of complementary marital patterns, including aggressive/submissive and detached/demanding. These odd matches are made, according to Mittleman, because courting couples distort each other's personalities through the eyes of their illusions: She sees his independence as strength; he sees her dependency as sexy and giving. Mittleman also pointed out that the couple's reactions to each other may be shaped by their relationships with their parents. Without insight, unconscious motivation may dominate marital behavior, leading to reciprocal neurotic actions and reactions. For treatment, Mittleman believed that 20 percent of the time one therapist could handle all members of the family, but in other cases separate therapists for the members may be better.

At about this time Don Jackson and Jay Haley were also writing about marital therapy within the framework of communications analysis. As their ideas gained prominence among marital therapists, the field of marital therapy was absorbed into the larger family therapy movement.

From Research to Treatment: The Pioneers of Family Therapy

We have seen how family therapy was anticipated by clinical and research developments in hospital psychiatry, group dynamics, interpersonal psychiatry, the child guidance movement, research on schizophrenia, and marriage counseling. But who actually started family therapy? Although there are rival claims to this honor, the distinction should probably be shared by John Elderkin Bell, Don Jackson, Nathan Ackerman, and Murray Bowen. In addition to these founders of family therapy, Jay Haley, Virginia Satir, Carl Whitaker, Lyman Wynne, Ivan Boszormenyi-Nagy, Christian Midelfort, and Salvador Minuchin were also significant pioneers of family treatment. Of these, Don Jackson, Jay Haley, and Virginia Satir in Palo Alto; Murray Bowen in Washington, DC; and Nathan Ackerman in New York probably had the greatest influence on the first decade of the family therapy movement.

John Bell

John Elderkin Bell, a psychologist at Clark University in Worcester, Massachusetts, who began treating families in 1951, occupies a unique position in the history of family therapy. Although he may have been the first family therapist, he is mentioned only tangentially in two of the most important historical accounts of the movement (Guerin, 1976; Kaslow, 1980). The reason for this is that although he began seeing families in the 1950s, he didn't publish his ideas until a decade later. Moreover, unlike the other parents of family therapy, he had few offspring. He didn't establish an important clinical center, develop a training program, or train well-known students.

Bell's approach (Bell, 1961, 1962) was taken directly from group therapy. "Family group therapy" relied primarily on stimulating an open discussion in order to help families solve their problems. Like a group therapist, Bell intervened to encourage silent participants to speak up, and he interpreted the reasons for their defensiveness.

Bell believed that family group therapy goes through certain phases just as do groups of strangers. In his early work (Bell, 1961), he carefully structured treatment in a series of stages, each of which concentrated on a particular segment of the family. Later, he became less directive and allowed families to evolve through a naturally unfolding sequence of stages. As they did so, he would tailor his interventions to the needs of the moment. For a more complete description of family group therapy, see Chapter 3.

Palo Alto

The Bateson group stumbled onto family therapy while conducting their landmark studies of family dynamics and schizophrenia. Once the group began to meet with schizophrenic families in 1954, hoping to better understand their patterns of communication through unobtrusive, naturalistic observation, project members found themselves drawn into helping roles by the pain of these families (Jackson & Weakland, 1961). While Bateson was the undisputed scientific leader of the group, Don Jackson and Jay Haley were most influential in developing family therapy.

Jackson's work offers a rare example of the development of psychotherapy following the development of a theory—and secondary to theory. As a therapist, Jackson rejected the intrapsychic role theory and psychoanalytic concepts he learned in training and focused instead on the dynamics of interchange between persons. Analysis of communication was his primary instrument. Like Bateson, Don Jackson believed that behavior and communication were synonymous.

Jackson's thinking about family therapy was first stimulated by encounters with patients' relatives in his practice and by occasional visits to the homes of schizophrenic patients (Jackson & Weakland, 1961). Observing the impact of families on patients—and vice versa—wasn't new, but Jackson's conclusions were. Since Freud, the family was understood to be the critical force in shaping personality, for better or worse. But the family was dealt with by segregation, physical and emotional, like removing a sick person from a germ-ridden environment. Jackson began to see the possibility of treating families instead of trying to eliminate their influence.

By 1954 Jackson had developed a rudimentary family interactional therapy, which he reported in a paper "The Question of Family Homeostasis," delivered to the American Psychiatric Association convention in St. Louis. His main emphasis was still on the effect of patients' therapy on their families, rather than on the prospect of family treatment (Jackson, 1954).

Borrowing ideas from biology and systems theory, Jackson described families as homeostatic units that maintain relative constancy of internal functioning.

Jackson's concept of *family homeostasis*—families as units that resist change—was to become the defining metaphor of family therapy's first three decades. In hindsight, we can say that the emphasis on homeostasis overestimated the conservative properties of families and underestimated their flexibility. But at the time the recognition that families resist change and act as a constraining influence was enormously productive for understanding what keeps people stuck.

Although in practice Jackson and his colleagues probably oversimplified the homeostatic nature of families, their theoretical papers became increasingly sophisticated. Consistency, they realized, doesn't necessarily mean rigidity. (As far back as 1939, the physiologist Walter Cannon said that, like the physiological systems of the body, "even social and industrial organizations maintain a relatively steady state in the face of external perturbations.") Family homeostasis is a dynamic state of, as Cannon said, *relative* stability. Families seek to maintain or restore the status quo; family members function as governors, and the family is said to act in error-activated ways (Haley, 1963). The result is not invariance, but stability in variance of behavior. A clinical illustration of homeostasis can be found in families in which the symptomatic behavior of children serves to restore the status quo. Frequently, parental argument is interrupted by disturbed behavior from one of the children, after which the parents stop arguing and become concerned about the now "identified patient's" symptoms.

In "Schizophrenic Symptoms and Family Interaction" (Jackson & Weakland, 1959) Jackson illustrated how patients' symptoms preserve stability in their families. In one such case a young woman diagnosed as a catatonic schizophrenic had as her most prominent symptom a profound indecisiveness. However, when she did behave decisively, her parents fell apart. Her mother became helpless and dependent; her father became, literally, impotent. In one family meeting her parents failed to notice when the patient made a simple decision. Only after listening to a taped replay of the session *three times* did the parents finally hear their daughter's statement. The patient's indecision was neither crazy nor senseless; rather it protected her parents from facing their own difficulties. This case is one of the earliest published examples of how even psychotic symptoms can be meaningful in the family context. The paper also contains the shrewd observation that children's symptoms were often an exaggerated version of their parents' problems. Adults simply have better social covers than children.

In moving away from mentalistic inference to behavioral observation of sequences of communication, Jackson found that he needed a new language of interaction. His basic assumption was that all people in continuing relationships develop set patterns of interaction. He called this patterning "behavioral redundancy" (Jackson, 1965).

The term *redundancy* not only captures an important feature of family behavior, but also reflects Jackson's phenomenological stance. Traditional psychiatric terms like *projection, defense,* and *regression* imply far more about inner states of motivation than the simple descriptive language of early family therapists. Even when using concepts that imply prescription, Jackson remained committed to description. Thus, his *rules hypothesis* was simply a means of summarizing the observation that within any committed unit (dyad, triad, or larger group) there were redundant behavior patterns. Rules (as any student of philosophy learns when studying determinism) can describe regularity, rather than regulation. A second part of the *rules hypothesis* was that family members use only some of the full range of behavior available to them. This seemingly innocent fact is precisely what makes family therapy possible.

Families who come to therapy can be seen as stuck in a narrow range of options, or unnecessarily rigid rules. Since the rules in most families aren't spelled out, no one ratifies them and they're hard to change. The therapist, however, as an outsider can help families see—and reexamine—the rules they live by.

By 1963 Jackson had delineated three types of family rules: (1) norms, which are covert; (2) values, which are consciously held and openly acknowledged; and (3) homeostatic mechanisms, which are rules about how norms and values are enforced (*metarules*). Many of these rules are inculcated by families of origin, but Jackson and his Palo Alto colleagues rarely looked beyond the nuclear family.

Since families operate by rules and by rules about rules (metarules), Jackson concluded that family dysfunction was due to lack of rules for change. Therefore, he sought to make rules explicit and to change those that did more harm than good. This is, in fact, a fancy way of describing interpretation, a technique used by communications therapists far more than their writings suggest.

Although they denied that pointing out family patterns of interactions was useful (Jackson & Weakland, 1961), this technique was, in fact, frequently used by the early MRI therapists. Perhaps one reason they later came to rely almost exclusively on strategic and indirect influence is that there's a big difference between telling family members that they're doing something wrong—"I notice that whenever I ask Johnny a question, he looks to mother for the answer"—and pointing out the consequences of what they're doing—"As long as you keep relying on your mother to speak for you, you'll never learn to speak for yourself."

Jackson's therapeutic strategies were based on the premise that psychiatric problems resulted from the way people behave with each other in a given context. He saw human problems as interactional *and* situational. Problem resolution involves shifting the context in which problems occur. Although Jackson wrote more about understanding families than about treating them, many of his explanatory concepts (*homeostatic mechanisms, quid pro quo, double bind, symmetry*, and *complementarity*) informed his strategies and became the early language of systems-oriented family therapists. He sought first to distinguish interactions (*redundant behavior patterns*) that were functional from those that were dysfunctional (*problem-maintaining*). To do so, he observed when problems occurred and in what context, who was present, and how people responded to the problem. Given the assumption that symptoms are homeostatic mechanisms, Jackson often inquired how a family might be worse off if the problem got better. The individual might want to get better, but the family may need someone to play the sick role. Improvement can be a threat to the defensive order of things.

Jackson's model of the family as a homeostatic system emphasized the equilibrium-maintaining qualities of symptomatic behavior. This led directly to the idea that deviation or deviance, including symptomatic and irrational behavior, wasn't necessarily negative, at least not from the point of view of those who learned to live with it. A father's drinking, for example, might keep him from making demands on his wife and from enforcing discipline on his children. Unfortunately, following Jackson, some family therapists jumped from the observation that symptoms may serve a purpose to the assumption that some families *need* a sick member, which, in turn, often led to a view of parents victimizing *scapegoated* children. Despite the fancy language, this was part of the time-honored tradition of blaming parents for the failings of their children. If a six-year-old boy misbehaves around the house, perhaps we should look to his parents. But a husband's drinking isn't necessarily his family's fault, and certainly it wasn't fair to imply that families were responsible for the psychotic behavior of their schizophrenic members.

Looking back, we can see how the early emphasis on homeostasis, as well as the cybernetic metaphor of the family as machine, led to a view of the therapists as more mechanic than healer. In their zeal to rescue "family scapegoats" from the clutches of their "pathological" families, early family therapists provoked some of the resistance they complained of. Therapists who think of themselves as rescuing innocent victims from their families and who take up an adversarial stance are not unlike the person who whacks a turtle on the back and then notices that the creature doesn't want to come out of its shell.

But we should recognize that these perspectives—like all perspectives—were a product of the context in which they emerged. Seriously disturbed families, like the schizophrenic families that Jackson and his colleagues studied, understandably feel more threatened and are therefore more protective than most.

Among Jackson's most trenchant and influential papers was "Family Rules: Marital Quid Pro Quo" (Jackson, 1965). The role divisions in a marriage are not, according to Jackson, simply a matter of gender differences; instead they result from a series of *quid pro quos,* worked out in any long-term relationship. The traditional view that marital roles stem from sex-role differences ascribes behavior to individual personalities, instead of recognizing the extent to which relationships depend on the interactions and the rules for interaction worked out between people. Jackson's view wasn't that sexual differences don't exist, but that they were relatively unimportant. The major differences in a marriage, as in any other relationship, are worked out, not given.[4] The fact that many marital *quid pro quos* aren't conscious or overt means that family therapists can play a useful role in ferreting out those arrangements that don't work or aren't fair.

Another construct important to Jackson's thinking was the dichotomy between *complementary* relationships and *symmetrical* ones. (Like so many of the seminal ideas of family therapy, this one was first articulated by Bateson). *Complementary* relationships are those in which people are different in ways that fit together: If one is logical, the other is emotional; if one is weak, the other is strong. *Symmetrical* relationships are based on equality and similarity. Marriages between two people who both have careers and share housekeeping chores are symmetrical. (Incidentally, if you actually find a married couple who both have careers and share housekeeping chores equally, you'll know you're not in Kansas, Dorothy!)

Once, the complementary, Ozzie-and-Harriet marriage was the norm in this country, giving families stability if not equality. The most profound change in family life in the second half of the twentieth century has been the advent of the symmetrical two-paycheck family. Unfortunately, the process of transition from complementarity toward symmetrical equality has rearranged the American family like a tornado rearranges the furniture in a trailer park.

Most of Jackson's descriptive concepts (*complementary/symmetrical, quid pro quo, double bind*) describe relationships between two people. Although his intent was to develop a descriptive language of whole family interactions, Jackson's major success was in describing relationships between husbands and wives. This narrow focus on the marital dyad has always been one of the limits of the Palo Alto group. Their sophisticated interest in communication led to an adult-centered bias, and they tended to neglect the children as well as the various triads that make up families. As a consequence, many of their students tended to reduce family problems to marital problems, even or especially

[4]In their enthusiasm for newly discovered interactional forces, early family therapists may have underestimated the importance of gender and the effect of gender bias on families.

where small children were presented as the patients.

The great discovery of the Bateson group was that there's no such thing as a simple communication; every message is qualified by another message on a higher level. In *Strategies of Psychotherapy* Jay Haley explored how covert messages are used in the struggle for control that characterizes all relationships. Symptoms, he argued, represent an incongruence between levels of communication. The symptomatic person does something, such as touching a doorknob six times before turning it, while at the same time indicating that he isn't *really* doing it—he can't help it; it's just his condition. Meanwhile, the person's symptoms—over which he has no control—have consequences for himself and for others. A person who "has a compulsion" of such proportions can hardly be expected to get himself out of the house in the morning, can he?

Psychoanalysts describe the interpersonal gain patients get from their symptoms as "secondary gain." For Haley, "secondary gain" was primary. Or, as he put it, "From the point of view offered here, the crucial aspect of the symptom is the advantage it gives the patient in gaining control of what is to happen in a relationship with someone else" (Haley, 1961, p. 151). Symptomatic behavior is an ingenious way of controlling people while denying that one is doing so.

The cybernetic metaphor behind this analysis is that neurotic symptoms work like a governor that controls the speed of a car—both keep things from going beyond certain limits, and both protect the status quo. Since symptomatic behavior wasn't "reasonable," Haley didn't rely on reasoning with patients to help them. Instead, therapy became a strategic game of cat-and-mouse in which therapists conspired to outwit patients for their own good.

Haley (1963) defined his therapy as a directive form of treatment and acknowledged his debt to Milton Erickson, with whom he studied hypnosis from 1954 to 1960. Indeed, in Haley's early writings it's difficult to know where Erickson leaves off and Haley begins. In what he called "brief therapy," Haley zeroed in on the context and possible function of the patient's symptoms. His first moves were often designed to gain control of the therapeutic relationship. Haley cited Erickson's device of advising patients that in the first interview there will be things they may be willing to say and other things they'll want to withhold, and that these, of course, should be withheld. Here, of course, the therapist is directing patients to do precisely what they would do anyway, and thus the therapist is subtly gaining the upper hand.

Even while gathering initial information, the brief therapist angles for leverage. Accordingly, a history is taken in such a way as to suggest that progressive improvement has and will continue to occur. Alternatively, with a pessimistic patient, the therapist might accept the pessimism but say that since things have gotten so bad, it's time for a change.

The decisive technique in brief therapy has always been the use of *directives.* As Haley put it, it isn't enough to explain problems to patients; what counts is getting them to *do* something about them. However, as he also pointed out, psychiatric patients are famous for not always doing exactly what you tell them to do (Haley, 1963, p. 45). Haley's solution was to use directives so cleverly that patients couldn't help but do what's wanted. Typical of this procedure is to prescribe symptomatic behavior but to slip something into the instructions so that the symptoms fall under therapeutic control.

One of Haley's patients was a freelance photographer who compulsively made silly blunders that ruined every picture. Eventually the patient became so preoccupied with avoiding mistakes that he was too nervous to take pictures at all. Haley instructed the patient to go out and take three pictures, making one deliberate error in each. The paradox here is that you can't make a mistake accidentally if you're doing so deliberately.

In another famous case, Haley told an insomniac that if he woke up in the middle of the night he should get out of bed and wax the kitchen floor. Instant cure! The cybernetic principle illustrated here is: Most people will do anything to get out of housework.

Haley believed that if psychiatric symptoms arise out of attempts to avoid defining one's relationship with other people, therapy could succeed by forcing patients to accept the therapist's definition of the relationship. Moreover, since pathological families bind their members in malignant paradoxes, therapists could unbind them with benign paradoxes. Haley cited John Rosen as a master of authoritarian paradoxes and Frieda Fromm-Reichmann as an expert of the iron paradox in a velvet glove. In one famous case, Rosen dealt with a young schizophrenic who claimed to be God by having the ward attendants force the patient to his knees before Rosen, thus demonstrating vividly that he, Rosen, was in charge. The patient faced a paradoxical dilemma. He could no longer deny that he was relating to the therapist; yet once on his knees, he had to acknowledge either that God was subservient to the therapist or that he was not indeed God.

Frieda Fromm-Reichmann's gentler approach is described in *Principles of Intensive Psychotherapy* (Fromm-Reichmann, 1950). She once treated a patient who said that everything she did occurred in relation to her own private and powerful God, not in relation to other people. This, of course, provided a convenient excuse for refusing to relate to the doctor. Here's what Fromm-Reichmann said to the patient: "Tell him [God] that I am a doctor and you have lived now with him in his kingdom from [the age of] 7 to [the age of] 16—that's nine years—and he has not helped you. So now he must permit me to try and see whether you and I can do that job." This patient, too, was caught in a bind: whatever she did, she had to respond to the therapist. She could either go to her God and repeat what she was told, thereby conceding that the doctor was in charge; or she could rebel against the doctor, which meant she was being influenced by her, which would also render the existence of her God questionable.

What Haley saluted in these examples was the use of *therapeutic paradox*—maneuvering patients to own their actions and take a stand in relationship to the therapist, instead of obfuscating their actions in psychiatric denial.

Most of the ideas that came out of the Palo Alto group—double bind, complementarity, quid pro quo—focused on dyads, but Haley also became interested in triads or, as he called them, "coalitions." Coalitions should be distinguished from alliances, cooperative arrangements between two parties that are not formed at the expense of a third. In the symptomatic families Haley observed, most coalitions were "cross-generational," one parent ganging up with a child against the other parent. For example, a mother might speak for a child in a way that discredited the father. In other cases, a child might insinuate himself between bickering parents by being "helpful" or getting "sick."

In "Toward a Theory of Pathological Systems," Haley described what he called "perverse triangles," which often lead to violence, psychopathology, or the break up of a system. A perverse triangle is a hidden coalition that undermines generational hierarchies. Examples include a child running for comfort to his grandmother every time his mother tries to punish him, or one parent complaining about the other to the children. Perverse triangles also occur in organizations when, for example, a supervisor joins with one subordinate against another, or when a professor complains to his students about the department chair. In looking beyond cybernetics and dyads to triads and hierarchies, Haley was to become an important bridging figure between strategic and structural approaches to family therapy.

Another member of the Palo Alto group who played a leading role in family therapy's first decade was Virginia Satir, one of the great charismatic originals. Known more for her clinical artistry than for theoretical contributions,

Satir's impact was most vivid to those lucky enough to see her in action. Like her confreres, Satir was interested in communication, but she added a dimension of feeling that helped counterbalance what was otherwise a somewhat intellectualized approach.

Satir saw troubled family members as trapped in narrow family roles, like *victim, placator, defiant one,* or *rescuer,* that constrained relationships and sapped self-esteem. Her concern with identifying such life-constricting roles and freeing family members from their grip was consistent with her major focus, which was always on the individual. Thus, Satir was a humanizing force in the early days of family therapy, when many were so enamored of the systems metaphor that they neglected the emotional life of families.

In her work with families, Satir concentrated on clarifying communication, expressing feelings, and fostering a climate of mutual acceptance and warmth. Her great strength was to connect with families not in terms of anger and resentment, but in terms of hopes and fears, yearnings and disappointments. A therapist who can bring out the loneliness and longing behind an angry outburst is a therapist who can bring people together.

One of the things for which Satir was justly famous was her ability to turn negatives into positives. What makes this such an important skill for a family therapist is that most families have at least one member whose faults or failings have cast him in the role of an outsider. Unless these less favored ones can be brought into the family circle, neither healing nor cooperation is very likely.

In one case, cited by Lynn Hoffman (1981), Satir interviewed the family of an adolescent boy, son of the local minister, who had gotten two of his classmates pregnant. On one side of the room sat the boy's parents and siblings. The boy sat in the opposite corner with his head down. Satir introduced herself and said to the boy, "Well, your father has told me a lot about the situation on the phone, and I just want to say before we begin that we know one thing for sure: We know you have good seed." The boy looked up in amazement as Satir turned to the boy's mother and asked brightly, "Could you start by telling us your perception?"

The 1964 publication of Satir's book *Conjoint Family Therapy* did much to popularize the family therapy movement. This book, along with *Pragmatics of Human Communication* (Watzlawick, Beavin, & Jackson, 1967), helped spread the influence of the Palo Alto group's brand of systemic thinking. Eventually, Satir went on to become a leader in the human potential movement, and we will consider her work more fully in Chapter 6.

Murray Bowen

Like many of the founders of family therapy, Murray Bowen was a psychiatrist who specialized in schizophrenia. Unlike others, however, he emphasized theory in his work, and to this day Bowen's theory is the most thoughtful and thoroughgoing system of ideas family therapy has produced.

Bowen began his clinical work at the Menninger Clinic from 1946 to 1954, where he studied mothers and their schizophrenic children who lived together in small cottages. His major interest at the time was mother–child symbiosis, which led to the formation of his concept of *differentiation of self* (autonomy from others and separation of thought from feeling). From Menninger, Bowen moved to NIMH, where he developed a project to hospitalize whole families with schizophrenic members. It was this project that expanded the concept of mother–child symbiosis to include the role of fathers, and led to the concept of *triangulation* (diverting conflict between two people by involving a third). In 1959, Bowen left NIMH for Georgetown Medical School where he was a professor of psychiatry and director of his own training program until his death in the fall of 1990.

In the first year of the NIMH project (1954), Bowen provided separate therapists for individual family members. What he discovered, however, was that these efforts tended to fractionate families. Instead of trying to work out their mutual problems together, family members had a tendency to think, "I'll take up my problems with *my* therapist" (Bowen, 1976). (Of course this never happens when nice people like you and me go to *our* individual therapists.) After a year, concluding that the family was the unit of disorder, Bowen began treating the families together. Thus, in 1955, Bowen became one of the first to invent family therapy.

Beginning in 1955 Bowen began holding large group therapy sessions for the entire project staff and all the families. In this early form of network therapy, Bowen assumed that togetherness and open communication would be therapeutic—for problems within families and between families and staff.

At first Bowen employed four therapists to manage these large multifamily meetings, but he became dissatisfied when he noticed that the therapists tended to pull in different directions. So he put one therapist in charge and consigned the others to supporting roles. However, just as multiple therapists tended to pull in different directions, so did multiple families. As soon as a hot topic was broached in one family, someone from another family would become anxious and change the subject. Finally, Bowen decided that families would have to take turns—one family became the focus for each session, with the others as silent auditors.

At first Bowen's approach to single families was the same one he used in the large meetings. He did what most people new to family therapy do: he brought family members together and just tried to get them talking. He reasoned that families would improve simply by coming together and discussing mutual concerns. He soon rejected this idea. Unstructured family chats are about as productive for therapy as an unrefereed boxing match between several combatants of various sizes. Bowen soon realized this, and he developed a carefully orchestrated approach that paralleled the evolution of his theory.

When Bowen brought family members together to discuss their problems, he was struck by their intense *emotional reactivity*. Feelings overwhelmed thinking and drowned out individuality in the chaos of the group. Bowen felt the family's tendency to pull him into the center of this *undifferentiated family ego mass*, and he had to make a concerted effort to remain neutral and objective (Bowen, 1961). The ability to remain neutral and attentive to the process, rather than the content, of family discussions is what distinguishes a therapist from a participant in a family's drama.

Bowen believed that if families were urged to solve their own problems, they would be forced to become more responsible and competent. So Bowen sat with them, staying neutral and nondirective, while families struggled to sort out their own difficulties. His major active effort during these sessions was to discourage scapegoating by pointing out when family members were using the patient as an excuse to avoid other problems. At the end of each session Bowen summed up what he'd observed, emphasizing the process by which the family went about trying to solve their problems.

Bowen found that observing whole families was invaluable as a source of information, but he was disappointed with the results of therapy. Beginning in 1960 he began meeting with just the parents of symptomatic children. His purpose was to block scapegoating and help parents focus on their own problems, without being distracted by the children.

In order to control the level of emotion, Bowen encouraged spouses to talk to him, not to each other. He found that it was easier for spouses to listen without becoming reactive when their partners spoke to the therapist instead of directly to them.

Bowen discovered that therapists themselves weren't immune from being sucked into family conflicts. This awareness led to his greatest insight. Whenever two people are struggling with a conflict they can't resolve, there is an automatic tendency to draw in a third party. In fact, as Bowen came to believe, the triangle is the smallest stable unit of relationship.

Any two-person emotional system will form a three-person system under stress. A husband who can't stand his wife's habitual lateness, but who also can't stand up and tell her so, may start complaining about her to one of his children. His complaining may relieve some of his tension, but the very process of complaining to a third party makes him less likely to address the original problem at its source. We all complain about other people from time to time, but what Bowen realized was that this "triangling" process is destructive when it becomes a regular feature of a system.

Another thing Bowen discovered about triangles is that they spread out: If relationship tension doesn't remain localized in the original pair, it's likely to activate more and more triangles. In the following case, seen by Michael Nichols, a family had become entangled in a whole labyrinth of triangles.

The story had a simple beginning. One Sunday morning "Mrs. McNeil," who was anxious to get the family to church on time, yelled at her nine-year-old son to hurry up. When the boy told his mother to "quit bitching," she lost her temper and slapped him. At that point her fourteen-year-old daughter, Megan, grabbed her, and the two of them started wrestling. Then Megan ran out and went next door to her friend's house. The friend's parents noticed that Megan had a cut lip, and when she told them what had happened, the friend's parents called the police. One thing led to another, and by the time the family came to see me, the following triangles were in place: Mrs. McNeil, who'd been ordered out of the house by the family court judge, was allied with her lawyer against the judge; she also had an individual therapist who joined her in thinking she was being hounded unfairly by the child protective workers. The nine-year-old was still mad at his mother, and his father supported him in blaming her for flying off the handle. Mr. McNeil, who was a recovering alcoholic, formed an alliance with his sponsor, who felt that Mr. McNeil was on his way to a breakdown unless his wife started being more supportive of his handling of the kids. Meanwhile Megan had formed a triangle with the neighbors, who thought her parents were awful people who shouldn't be allowed to have children. In short, everyone had an advocate—everyone, that is, except the family unit.

When he found himself repeatedly going over the same issues with couple after couple, Bowen decided that he might save time by working with several at once. This seemed appropriate because Bowen's therapy was relatively didactic. So beginning in 1965, he began treating couples in groups. What made Bowen's use of multiple family therapy paradoxical was his emphasis on avoiding the fusion inherent in social and emotional togetherness. But by minimizing emotional interaction between families and forbidding contact outside the group, Bowen was able to teach families about how emotional systems function. The couples in these groups made rapid progress. Families were apparently able to learn about processes of emotional systems, with less anxiety, when they listened to discussions of *other people's* problems.

In addition to couples and couples groups, Bowen also worked with individual family members. This was a unique approach, challenging easy assumptions about family therapy.

Family therapy is both a method and an orientation. As an orientation, it means understanding people in context of significant emotional systems; as a method, it usually means working with whole families. But Bowen's work with individual family members was probably more focused on family systems issues than was the work of most other family therapists, even when they did meet with whole families.

In 1966 there was an emotional crisis in Bowen's family that led him to initiate a personal voyage of discovery that turned out to be as significant for Bowen theory as Freud's self-analysis was for psychoanalysis.

As an adult, Bowen, the oldest of five children from a tightly knit rural family, kept his distance from his parents and the rest of his extended family. Like many of us, he mistook avoidance for emancipation. But as he later realized, unfinished emotional business stays with us, making us vulnerable to repeat conflicts we never got around to working out with our families.

Bowen's most important achievement was detriangling himself from his parents, who'd been accustomed to complaining to him about each other. Most of us are flattered to receive these confidences, but Bowen came to recognize this triangulation for what it was, and when his mother complained about his father, he told his father: "Your wife told me a story about you; I wonder why she told me instead of you." Naturally, his father discussed this with his mother and, naturally, she was annoyed.

Although his efforts generated the kind of emotional upheaval that comes of breaking family rules, Bowen's maneuver was effective in keeping his parents from trying to get him to take sides—and made it harder for them to avoid discussing things between themselves. Repeating what someone says to you about someone else is one way to stop triangling in its tracks.

Through his efforts in his own family Bowen discovered that *differentiation of self* is best accomplished by developing an individual, person-to-person relationship with each parent and with as many members of the extended family as possible. If visiting is difficult, letters and phone calls can help reestablish relationships, particularly if they're personal and intimate. Differentiating one's self from the family is completed when these relationships are maintained without emotional fusion or triangulation. The details of Bowen's personal work on his family relationships are complex but make rewarding reading for the serious student (Anonymous, 1972).

After Bowen told his trainees about his success with his own family, many of them began to return to their families and work on differentiating themselves. When Bowen noted how productive these trainees became as therapists, he decided that one of the best ways to learn about family therapy was to work on emotional issues in your own family. Thus, beginning in 1971, studying one's own family became one of the cornerstones of Bowen's approach to training. The goal is to return to your family of origin, make contact, develop an honest personal relationship with every member of the family, and learn to discuss family issues without becoming emotionally reactive or taking part in triangles.

Nathan Ackerman

Nathan Ackerman was a psychoanalytically trained child psychiatrist whose pioneering work with families remained faithful to his psychoanalytic roots. Although his focus on intrapsychic conflict may have seemed less innovative than the Palo Alto group's attention to communication as feedback, he had a keen sense of the overall organization of families. Families, Ackerman said, may give the appearance of unity, but underneath they are emotionally split into competing factions. This you may recognize as similar to the psychoanalytic model of individuals who, despite apparent unity of personality, are actually minds in conflict, driven by warring drives and defenses. Just as an individual expresses the dynamic conflicts of id, ego, and superego, so too are families dynamic coalitions, sometimes of mothers and daughters against fathers and sons, sometimes of one generation against another.

After completing his psychiatric residency during the Depression, Ackerman joined the staff at the Menninger Clinic in Topeka, Kansas. In 1937 he became chief psychiatrist of the Child Guidance Clinic. At first he followed the child guidance model of having a psychiatrist treat the child and a social worker see the mother. But by the mid 1940s he began to experiment with having the same therapist see both. Unlike Bowlby, Ackerman did more than use these conjoint sessions as a temporary expedient; instead, he reevaluated the whole conception of psychopathology and began to see the family as the basic unit for diagnosis and treatment.

In 1955 Ackerman organized and led the first session on family diagnosis at a meeting of the American Orthopsychiatric Association. There Jackson, Bowen, Wynne, and Ackerman learned about each other's existence and joined in a sense of common purpose. Two years later, in 1957, Ackerman opened the Family Mental Health Clinic of Jewish Family Services in New York City and began teaching at Columbia University. In 1960 he founded the Family Institute, which was renamed the Ackerman Institute following his death in 1971.

In addition to his clinical innovations, Ackerman also published several important articles and books. As early as 1938, he wrote "The Unity of the Family," and some consider his article "Family Diagnosis: An Approach to the Preschool Child," (Ackerman & Sobel, 1950) as the beginning of the family therapy movement (Kaslow, 1980). In 1962 Ackerman, with Don Jackson, cofounded the field's first journal, *Family Process.* Under the editorial leadership of Jay Haley (1962–1969), Donald Bloch (1969–1982), Carlos Sluzki (1983–1990), and Peter Steinglass (1990–present), *Family Process* has for many years been the leading scholarly vehicle through which family therapists communicate their ideas.

While other family therapists downplayed the psychology of individuals, Ackerman was always concerned with what goes on inside people as well as between them. He never lost sight of feelings, hopes, and desires. In fact, Ackerman's model of the family was like the psychoanalytic model of an individual writ large; instead of conscious and unconscious issues, Ackerman talked about how families confront some issues while avoiding and denying others, particularly ones involving sex and aggression. He saw his job as a therapist as one of stirring things up, bringing family secrets into the open.

In *Treating the Troubled Family,* Ackerman (1966a) illustrated his irreverence for politeness and pretense with a clinical vignette. A family of four came for treatment when the fighting between the eleven-year-old daughter and sixteen-year-old son started getting out of hand. The girl had recently threatened her brother with a butcher knife. The father sighed as he sat down. Ackerman asked him why he was sighing and refused to be put off by the father's excuse that he was tired, suggesting that perhaps he had another reason to sigh. Then his wife broke in to announce that she'd been keeping a journal of everyone's misdeeds during the week. Her stridency perfectly complemented her husband's mild-mannered evasiveness. Ackerman's bemused response was: "You come armed with a notebook. Fire away!"

As the mother began to read out her bill of particulars, Ackerman, who sensed that this was just business as usual, commented on the father's nonverbal behavior. "You're picking your fingers." This triggered a discussion about who does what, which the mother gradually took over and turned into an indictment of the father's many nervous habits. At this point the son broke in with an accusation. Pointing to his mother, he said, "She belches!" The mother acknowledged this little embarrassment, then tried to change the subject. But Ackerman wasn't about to let her off the hook.

It turned out that the mother's belching occurred mostly when she was lying down. The father said he was upset by her belching in his face, but he was interrupted by the children, who started bickering. Ackerman said, "Isn't it interesting that this interruption occurs just as you two are about to talk about your love life?" The father then described how it felt when he wanted to kiss his wife and she belched in his face. "You need a gas mask," he said. The daughter tried to interrupt, but Ackerman asked her to move her seat so that her parents could talk.

A few minutes later the children left the session and Ackerman reopened the door to the parents' bedroom. At first the couple played out their familiar pattern: She complained and he withdrew. Specifically, the wife complained that her husband wasn't romantic and that she was the one who had to take care of birth control by using a diaphragm. Meanwhile the husband retreated into meek silence. They were a perfectly matched pair: She was up, he was down. But Ackerman unbalanced them by playfully teasing the wife and provoking the husband to stand up for himself.

Although there's always room in after-the-fact descriptions to accuse a therapist of taking sides, it's worth noting that in this instance the wife didn't seem to feel criticized or put down by Ackerman. Nor did the husband seem to get the idea that Ackerman was trying to elevate him over his wife. Rather, by the end of the session, this grim, angry couple were beginning to laugh and appreciate each other. They saw how they'd drifted apart and had allowed the children to distract them. Thus, although Ackerman's work has been described as essentially psychoanalytic, we see here beginning efforts to reorganize the structure of families.

Ackerman recommended that everyone living under the same roof be present in all family interviews. As he put it, "It is very important at the outset to establish a meaningful emotional contact with all members of the family, to create a climate in which one really touches them and they feel they touch back" (Ackerman, 1961, p. 242). Once contact was made, Ackerman encouraged open and honest expression of feeling. He was an *agent provocateur,* prompting revelations and confrontations with his wit and willingness to stick his nose into personal family issues.

Ackerman pointed out that each person's identity has various aspects: as an individual, as a member of various family subsystems, and as a member of the family as a whole. In order to pinpoint these various components of identity, he was alert to the coalitions revealed in family interviews. One clue was found in the seating arrangement. When family members enter the consulting room they tend to pair off in ways that reveal alignments. To see these alliances more clearly, Ackerman recommended mobilizing conversations among family members. Once family members start talking among themselves, it's easier to see how they are emotionally divided and what problems and prohibitions are present. Ackerman also paid close attention to nonverbal cues, because he believed that disguised feelings were conveyed in body language far more eloquently than in words.

To promote honest emotional interchange, Ackerman "tickled the defenses" of family members—his phrase for provoking people to open up and say what's really on their minds. The playfulness of this phrase nicely reflects Ackerman's style.

What are thought to be family secrets, Ackerman said, generally turn out to be common knowledge but simply not spoken of. Children usually know more than their parents think they do. They also know what they're not supposed to talk about. However, as long as a family is confident of the therapist, they feel freer to speak more plainly about matters they usually avoid.

Ackerman himself was spontaneous, lively, and outspoken, which put him in the center of things. He didn't hesitate to confront, provoke, challenge, or even argue with family members. And if someone should take offense? According to Ackerman, it's more therapeutic for the therapist to become a target for anger and hostility rather than other family members.

In order to encourage families to relax their emotional restraint, Ackerman himself was unrestrained. He freely sided first with one part of the family and later with another. He didn't think it was necessary—or possible—to always be neutral and objective; instead, he believed that an impartial balance was achieved in the long run by moving back and forth, giving support now to one, later to another family member. At times he was unabashedly blunt. If he thought someone was lying, he said so. To critics who suggested this directness might generate too much anxiety, Ackerman replied that people get more reassurance from honesty than from pious politeness.

Ackerman saw family problems as the product of conflict. He said that conflicts within individuals, among family members, and between families and the larger community must be identified and resolved if psychological hurts are to be mended. Conflicts between and within family members are related in a circular feedback system; that is, intrapsychic conflict promotes interpersonal conflict and vice versa (Ackerman, 1961). To reverse symptomatic disturbances, the therapist must bring conflicts into the open, into the field of family interaction, where new solutions can be found. As long as conflicts remain locked within individuals, Ackerman believed, psychopathology remains fixed.

While it's impossible to neatly summarize Ackerman's freewheeling approach, there were consistent themes. One was the necessity for depth of therapeutic commitment and involvement. Ackerman himself became deeply emotionally involved with families, in contrast, for example, to Murray Bowen, who cautioned therapists to remain somewhat distant to avoid being triangulated. Depth also characterized the issues on which Ackerman focused—family analogues of the kinds of conflicts, feelings, and fantasies that lie buried in the individual unconscious. His psychoanalytic orientation sensitized him to hidden themes in the interpersonal unconscious of the family, and his provocative style enabled him to help families bring these themes into the light of day.

Ackerman's contributions to family therapy were extensive and important: He was one of the first to envision whole family treatment *and* he had the inventiveness and energy to actually carry it out. As far back as the late 1940s, he pointed out that treating family members individually without considering the configuration of the family was often futile. Very early, Ackerman (1954) recommended that family groups be evaluated as wholes and that these evaluations be followed by therapy of the family group and individual therapy for selected family members.

Ackerman's second major impact was as a peerless artist of therapeutic technique. He was one of the great geniuses of the movement. Those who studied with him all attest to his clinical wizardry. He was a dynamic catalyst—active, open, and forthright, never rigid or shy. He was passionate *and* effective. Nor was he always content to remain in the office, for he recommended and made frequent home visits (Ackerman, 1966b).

Finally there were Ackerman's contributions as a teacher, which may be his most important legacy. On the East Coast his name was synonymous with family therapy throughout the 1960s. Among those fortunate enough to study with him was Salvador Minuchin, who openly acknowledges his debt to Ackerman's genius.

Ackerman consistently urged therapists to become emotionally engaged with families and to use confrontation to transform dormant conflicts into open discussion. How does a therapist provoke candid disclosures? Ackerman did it by calling attention to avoidance and emotional dishonesty ("tickling the defenses"), challenging cliches, and interrupting fruitless bickering over unimportant matters. Ackerman's techniques suggest that he was somewhat more concerned with the content of family conflicts than with the process by which family members dealt with them, and more interested in family secrets (particularly those involving sex and aggression) than in family structure or patterns of communication. Perhaps his most enduring contribution was his consistent stress on individual persons and whole families; he never lost sight of the self in the system.

Carl Whitaker

Even among the many strong-willed and colorful founders of family therapy, Carl Whitaker stands out as the most irreverent. His view of psychologically troubled people was that they are alienated from feeling and frozen into devitalized routines (Whitaker & Malone, 1953). Whitaker turned up the emotional temperature. His "Psychotherapy of the Absurd" (Whitaker, 1975) was a blend of warm support and unpredictable emotional goading, designed to loosen people up and help them get in touch with their experience in a deeper, more personal way.

Given his bold and inventive approach to individual therapy, it wasn't surprising that Whitaker became one of the first who broke with psychiatric tradition to experiment with family treatment. In 1943 he and John Warkentin, working in Oakridge, Tennessee, began including spouses and eventually children in their patients' treatment. Whitaker also pioneered the use of cotherapy, in the belief that a supportive partner helped free therapists to react spontaneously without fear of unchecked countertransference.

In 1946 Whitaker became Chairman of the Department of Psychiatry at Emory University, where he was joined by Warkentin and Thomas Malone. Together they continued to experiment with family treatment with a special interest in schizophrenics and their families. During this period Whitaker organized a series of conferences that eventually led to the first major meeting of the family therapy movement. Beginning in 1946, Whitaker, Warkentin, and Malone began twice-yearly conferences during which they observed and discussed each other's work with families. The group found these sessions enormously helpful, and mutual observation, using one-way vision screens, has since become one of the hallmarks of family therapy.

In 1953 Whitaker invited John Rosen, Albert Scheflen, Gregory Bateson, and Don Jackson to participate in the semi-annual conference on families, held that year on Sea Island, Georgia. Each took turns demonstrating his own approach with the same family while the others observed and afterward joined in group discussion and analysis. This kind of cross-fertilization of ideas was to become an important characteristic of the family therapy movement. The same openness that brought families into the treatment room also prompted family therapists to share their work with colleagues through videotapes and live demonstrations.

Whitaker resigned from Emory in 1955 and entered private practice with Warkentin, Malone, and Richard Felder. He and his partners at the Atlanta Psychiatric Clinic developed an "experiential" form of psychotherapy, utilizing a number of highly provocative techniques, combined with the force of their own personalities, in the treatment of families, individuals, groups, and couples (Whitaker, 1958).

In 1965 Whitaker left Atlanta to become a Professor of Psychiatry at the University of Wisconsin, where he worked until his retirement in 1982. After that he devoted himself full time to treating families and traveling all over the world conducting workshops. During the late 1970s Whitaker seemed to mellow and also to add a greater understanding of family dynamics to his shoot-from-the-hip interventions. In the process, the former wild man of family therapy became one of the elder statesmen of the movement. Whitaker's death in April 1995 left the field with a piece of its heart missing.

At the beginning of the family therapy movement, Whitaker was less well known than many of the other first-generation family therapists. Perhaps this was due to his atheoretical position. Whereas Jackson, Haley, and Bowen developed theoretical concepts that were intriguing and easy to grasp, Whitaker always eschewed theory in favor of creative spontaneity. His work has therefore been less accessible to students than that of his colleagues. Nevertheless, he always had the respect of his peers. Those who really understood what went on in families could see that there was always method to his madness.

Whitaker deliberately created tension by teasing and confronting families because he believed that stress is necessary for change. He never seemed to have an obvious strategy, nor did he use predictable techniques, preferring, as he said, to let his unconscious run the therapy (Whitaker, 1976). Although his work seemed totally spontaneous, even outrageous at times, there was a consistent theme. All of his interventions had the effect of promoting flexibility. He didn't so much push families to change in a particular direction as he challenged and cajoled them to open up—to become more fully themselves and more fully together.

Ivan Boszormenyi-Nagy

Ivan Boszormenyi-Nagy, who came to family therapy from psychoanalysis, has been one of the seminal thinkers in the movement since its earliest days. In 1957 he founded the Eastern Pennsylvania Psychiatric Institute (EPPI) in Philadelphia as a center for research and training. Because he was a respected scholar-clinician and an able administrator, Boszormenyi-Nagy was able to attract a host of highly talented colleagues and students. Among these were James Framo, one of the few psychologists in the early family therapy movement; David Rubenstein, a psychiatrist who later launched a separate family therapy training program; and Geraldine Spark, a social worker who worked with Boszormenyi-Nagy as cotherapist, codirector of the unit, and coauthor of *Invisible Loyalties* (Boszormenyi-Nagy & Spark, 1973). This group was joined by Gerald Zuk, a psychologist who developed a "triadic-based" approach to family therapy (1971). In triadic-based family therapy, the therapist begins as a mediator but then takes sides in order to shift power alignments in the family. According to Zuk (1971, p. 73), "By judicious siding, the therapist can tip the balance in favor of more productive relating, or at least disrupt a chronic pattern of pathogenic relating."

In 1960 Albert Scheflen moved from Temple University to EPPI and joined with Ray Birdwhistell to study body language in psychotherapy. Ross Speck, who did his psychiatric residency in the early 1960s, developed, along with Carolyn Attneave, "network therapy," which broadened the context of treatment far beyond the nuclear family. In this approach, as many people as possible who are connected to the patient are invited to attend therapy sessions. Often as many as fifty people, including extended family, friends, neighbors, and teachers, are brought together for approximately three 4-hour sessions led by a minimum of three therapists to discuss ways to support and help the patient change (Speck & Attneave, 1973).

In addition to his sponsorship of these students and associates, Boszormenyi-Nagy himself has made major contributions to the study of schizophrenia (Boszormenyi-Nagy, 1962) and family therapy (Boszormenyi-Nagy, 1966, 1972; Boszormenyi-Nagy & Spark, 1973). Boszormenyi-Nagy described himself as a therapist who went from being an analyst, prizing secrecy and confidentiality, to a family therapist, fighting the forces of pathology on an open battlefield. One of his most important contributions was to add ethical accountability to the usual therapeutic goals and techniques. According to Boszormenyi-Nagy, neither the pleasure–pain principle nor transactional expediency is a sufficient guide to human behavior. Instead, he believes that family members have to base their relationships on trust and loyalty, and that they must balance the ledger of entitlement and indebtedness.

In 1980, after thousands of professionals had been trained at the EPPI, the Commonwealth of Pennsylvania abruptly closed it down. Boszormenyi-Nagy and some of his colleagues continue to be associated with nearby Hahnemann University Medical School, but the critical mass was lost. Since then Boszormenyi-Nagy has continued to refine his own approach, contextual therapy, which is among the most thoughtful and underappreciated approaches to family therapy.

Salvador Minuchin

When Minuchin first burst onto the scene, it was the drama of his brilliant clinical demonstrations that people found so captivating. This compelling man with the elegant Latin accent would seduce, provoke, bully, or bewilder families into changing—as the situation required. But even Minuchin's legendary dramatic flair didn't have the same galvanizing impact of the elegant simplicity of the structural model.

Born and raised in Argentina, Minuchin began his career as a family therapist in the early 1960s when he discovered two patterns common to troubled families: Some families are "enmeshed"—chaotic and tightly interconnected; others are "disengaged"—isolated and seemingly unrelated. Both types lack clear lines of authority. Enmeshed parents are too entangled with their children to maintain a position of leadership and exercise control; disengaged parents are too distant to provide effective support and guidance.

Family problems are tenacious and resistant to change because they're embedded in powerful but unseen structures. Take, for example, a mother futilely remonstrating with a willful child. The mother can scold, punish, reward with gold stars, or try leniency; but as long as she's "enmeshed" (overly involved) with the child, her efforts will lack force because she lacks authority. Moreover, because the behavior of one family member is always related to that of others, the mother will have trouble stepping back as long as her husband (the child's father) is disengaged.

Once a social system such as a family becomes structured, attempts to change the rules constitute what family therapists call "first-order change"—change within a system that itself remains invariant. For the mother in the previous example to start practicing stricter discipline would be an example of first-order change. The enmeshed mother is caught in an illusion of alternatives. She can be strict or lenient; the result is the same because she remains trapped in a triangle. What's needed is "second-order change"—a change in the system itself. How such changes are brought about was what family therapists from all over the world flocked to Minuchin's workshops to find out.

Minuchin first worked out his ideas while struggling with the problems of juvenile delinquency at the Wiltwyck School for Boys in New York. Family therapy with urban slum families was a new development, and publication of his ideas (Minuchin, Montalvo, Guerney, Rosman, & Schumer, 1967) led to his being invited to become the director of the Philadelphia Child Guidance Clinic in 1965. Minuchin brought Braulio Montalvo and Bernice Rosman with him, and they were joined in 1967 by Jay Haley. Together they transformed a traditional child guidance clinic into one of the great centers of the family therapy movement.

Minuchin's first notable achievement at the Philadelphia Child Guidance Clinic was a unique program for training members of the local black community as paraprofessional family therapists. The reason for this special effort is that cultural differences can make it hard for white middle-class therapists to understand and relate successfully to urban blacks and Latinos.

In 1969 Minuchin received a training grant that helped launch an intensive two-year program in which Minuchin, Haley, Montalvo, and Rosman developed a highly successful approach to training as well as one of the most important systems of family therapy. According to Haley, one of the advantages to training people with no previous experience as clinicians to become family therapists is that they have less to unlearn and therefore are less resistant to thinking in terms of systems. Minuchin and Haley sought to capitalize on this by developing an approach with the least possible number of theoretical concepts. Conceptual elegance became one of the hallmarks of "structural family therapy."

The major features of the training were hands-on experience, on-line supervision, and extensive use of videotapes. Minuchin believes that therapists are best taught by experience. Only after they've seen a few families, he finds, are therapists ready to appreciate and apply the finer points of systems theory.

The techniques of structural family therapy fall into two general strategies. First the therapist must accommodate to the family in order to "join" them. To begin by challenging a family's preferred mode of relating is to ensure that they will resist. If, instead, the therapist starts by trying to understand and accept the family, they'll be more likely to accept treatment. (No one is eager to accept advice from someone they feel doesn't really understand them.) Once this initial *joining* is accomplished, the structural family therapist begins to use *restructuring* techniques. These are active maneuvers designed to disrupt dysfunctional structures by strengthening diffuse boundaries and loosening rigid ones (Minuchin & Fishman, 1981).

In the 1970s, under Minuchin's leadership, the Philadelphia Child Guidance Clinic became the world's leading center for family therapy and training. The clinic itself is located in a large and well-equipped building with excellent facilities for videotaping, live supervision, workshops, and conferences; the clinic even has small apartments for hospitalizing whole families. Stepping down as director in 1975 left Minuchin free to pursue his special interest in treating families with psychosomatic illness, especially those with anorexia nervosa (Minuchin, Rosman, & Baker, 1978).

In 1981 Minuchin moved to New York and established Family Studies, Inc., where he pursued his dedication to teaching family therapists from all over the world and his commitment to social justice by working with the foster care system. He also continued to turn out a steady stream of the most influential books in the field. His 1974 *Families and Family Therapy* is deservedly the most popular book in the history of family therapy, and his 1993 *Family Healing* contains among the most thorough and moving descriptions of therapy ever written by a family therapist. In 1996 Dr. Minuchin retired and now lives with his wife Patricia in Boston.

Other Early Centers of Family Therapy

In New York, Israel Zwerling (who had been analyzed by Nathan Ackerman) and Marilyn Mendelsohn (who was analyzed by Don Jackson) organized the Family Studies Section at Albert Einstein College of Medicine and Bronx State Hospital. Andrew Ferber was named Director in 1964, and later Philip Guerin, a protege of Murray Bowen's, joined the section. Nathan Ackerman served as a consultant, and the group assembled an impressive array of family therapists with diverse orientations. These included Chris Beels, Betty Carter, Monica Orfanidis (now McGoldrick), Peggy Papp, and Thomas Fogarty.

Philip Guerin became Director of Training of the Family Studies Section in 1970 and in 1972 established an extramural training program in Westchester. Shortly thereafter, in

1973, he founded the Center for Family Learning, where he developed one of the finest family therapy training programs in the nation.

In Galveston, Texas, Robert MacGregor and his colleagues developed "multiple impact therapy" (MacGregor, 1967). It was a case of necessity being the mother of invention. MacGregor's clinic served a large population scattered widely over southeastern Texas, and many of his clients had to travel hundreds of miles. Because they had to come such distances, most of these people were unable to return for weekly sessions. Therefore, to have maximum impact in a short time, MacGregor assembled a large team of professionals who worked intensively with the families for two full days. The team of psychologists, social workers, psychiatric residents, and trainees met with families together and in various subgroups; between sessions the treatment team discussed their findings and refined their intervention strategies. Although few family therapists have used such marathon sessions, the team approach continues to be one of the hallmarks of the field.

In conservative and proper Boston the two most significant early contributions to family therapy were both in the existential–experiential wing of the movement. Norman Paul developed an "operational mourning" approach designed to uncover and express unresolved grief. According to Paul, this cathartic approach is useful in almost all families, not just those who've suffered an obvious recent loss.

Also in Boston, Fred and Bunny Duhl set up the Boston Family Institute, where they developed "integrative family therapy." Along with David Kantor and Sandy Watanabe, the Duhls combined ideas from several family theories and added a number of expressive techniques, including *family sculpting*.

In Chicago, the Family Institute of Chicago and the Institute for Juvenile Research were important centers of the early scene in family therapy. At the Family Institute, Charles and Jan Kramer developed a clinical training program, which was later affiliated with Northwestern University Medical School. The Institute for Juvenile Research also mounted a training program under the leadership of Irv Borstein, with the consultation of Carl Whitaker.

The work of Nathan Epstein and his colleagues, first formulated in the department of psychiatry at McMaster University in Hamilton, Ontario, was a problem-centered approach (Epstein, Bishop, & Baldarin, 1981). The "McMaster Model of Family Functioning" goes step by step, from elucidating the problem to gathering data, considering alternatives for resolution, and assessing the learning process, to help families understand their own interaction and build on their newly acquired coping skills. Epstein later relocated to Brown University in Providence, Rhode Island.

Important early developments in family therapy outside the United States included Robin Skynner's (1976) use of psychodynamic family therapy at the Institute of Family Therapy in London; British psychiatrist John Howells's (1971) system of family diagnosis as a necessary step for planning therapeutic intervention; West German Helm Stierlin's (1972) integrative efforts, bringing together psychodynamic and systemic ideas to bear on understanding and treating troubled adolescents; in Rome, Maurizio Andolfi's work with families early in the 1970s, and his founding, in 1974, of the Italian Society for Family Therapy; and the work of Mara Selvini Palazzoli and her colleagues, who founded the Institute for Family Studies in Milan in 1967.

We conclude this section by mentioning the contributions of Christian Midelfort. Even more than was the case with John Bell, Midelfort's pioneering work in family therapy was slow to gain recognition. He began treating families of hospitalized patients in the early 1950s, delivered what was probably the first paper on family therapy at a professional meeting in 1952 at the

American Psychiatric Association Convention, and published one of the first complete books on family therapy in 1957. Nevertheless, as a staff psychiatrist in LaCrosse, Wisconsin, he remained isolated from the rest of the family therapy movement. Only recently are his pioneering efforts being recognized (Broderick & Schrader, 1991). Midelfort's method of treating families was based on the group therapy model, and it combined psychoanalytic insights with techniques of support and encouragement. At first his concern was to counsel family members on the best ways to help the identified patient, but gradually he evolved a systems viewpoint and conceived of the family as the patient. His technique, which is described in Chapter 3, was to encourage family members to give each other the love and support that was initially provided by the therapist.

Now that you've seen how family therapy emerged in several different places at once, who the pioneering figures were, and what were some of ideas that transformed not just how we treat patients but our whole approach to understanding human behavior, we hope you haven't lost sight of one thing: There is a tremendous excitement to seeing how people's behavior makes sense in the context of their families. Meeting with a family for the first time is like turning on a light in a dark room. That excitement is what inspired the creation of family therapy forty years ago, and that same excitement is available to you when you sit down with a family today. Some things become very clear very fast.

The Golden Age of Family Therapy

In their first decade family therapists had all the enthusiasm and bravado of new kids on the block. "Look at this!" Haley and Jackson and Bowen and others seemed to say when they discovered the amazing extent to which the whole family was implicated in the symptoms of individual patients. These new-style healers were pioneers, busy opening up new territory and staking their claim against unfriendly elements in the psychiatric establishment. Who could blame them if they seemed to mock their psychoanalytic elders, whose response to their innovation had been, "You can't do that!"

While they were struggling for legitimacy, family clinicians emphasized their common beliefs and downplayed their differences. Troubles, they agreed, came in families. But if the watchword of the 1960s had been "Look at this!"—emphasizing the shared leap of understanding made possible by seeing whole families together—the rallying cry of the 1970s was "Look what I can do!" as the new kids carved out their own turf and flexed their muscles.

The period from 1970 to 1985 saw the flowering of the famous schools of family therapy as the pioneers established training centers and worked out the implications of their models. Three of the leading paradigms—experiential, psychoanalytic, and behavioral family therapies—were derived from approaches to treating individuals, whereas the other three, the most celebrated approaches to family therapy—structural, strategic, and Bowenian—were unique products of the systemic revolution.

The leading approach to family therapy in the 1960s was the communications model developed in Palo Alto. The book of the decade was *Pragmatics of Human Communication*, the text that introduced people to the idea of family therapy (and led some to believe that reading it would make them family therapists). The model of the 1980s was strategic therapy, and the books of the decade described its three most vital approaches: *Change* by Watzlawick, Weakland, and Fisch[5]; *Problem-Solving Therapy* by Jay

[5]Although actually published in 1974, this book and its sequel, *The Tactics of Change*, were most widely read and taught in the 1980s.

Haley; and *Paradox and Counterparadox* by Mara Selvini Palazzoli and her Milan associates. The 1970s belonged to Salvador Minuchin. His *Families and Family Therapy* and the simple yet compelling model of family structure it described dominated the decade.

Structural theory seemed to offer just what the would-be family therapist was looking for: a simple, yet meaningful way of describing family organization, and a set of straightforward steps to treatment. So compelling and so clear were the ideas described in *Families and Family Therapy* that for a while it seemed that all you had to do to transform families was join them, map their structure—and then do what Salvador Minuchin did to unbalance them. That was the rub.

Although the opening moves of structural family therapy are, indeed, easily described, it turns out that even after you join families and figure out their structure, altering the structure may be easier said than done. In hindsight we might ask whether the impressive power of Minuchin's approach was a product of the method or of the man? (The answer is, probably a little of both.) But in the seventies the widely shared belief that structural family therapy was something that could be easily learned drew people from all over the world to study at what for a decade was the Mecca of family therapy: the Philadelphia Child Guidance Clinic.

In its heyday (from the late 1960s to the early 1980s) the Philadelphia Child Guidance Clinic was one of the largest and most prestigious mental health clinics in the world. In addition to Minuchin, the training faculty included Braulio Montalvo, Jay Haley, Bernice Rosman, Harry Aponte, Carter Umbarger, Marianne Walters, Charles Fishman, Cloe Madanes, and Stephen Greenstein, with a clinical staff of over three hundred. If you wanted to become a family therapist, it was the place to be.

Although it's hard to imagine that a large organization's success can depend on one or two key people, the Philadelphia Child Guidance Clinic lost its preeminence in the 1980s after Minuchin stepped down as director and Haley and Montalvo left. Toward the end of that decade, structural family therapy, which by then represented the establishment in family therapy, came under attack from a series of challenges to the family therapy establishment, challenges that we'll discuss in Chapter 10. But even before the feminist and postmodernist critiques had their greatest impact, a new brand of treatment took center stage in family therapy. The 1980s became the decade of strategic family therapy.

The strategic therapy that flourished in the 1980s was centered in three unique and creative groups: MRI's brief therapy group, including John Weakland, Paul Watzlawick, and Richard Fisch; Jay Haley and Cloe Madanes, codirectors of the Family Therapy Institute of Washington, DC; and Mara Selvini Palazzoli and her colleagues in Milan. But the leading influence on the decade of strategic therapy was exerted by Milton Erickson, albeit from beyond the grave.

Erickson's genius was much admired and much imitated. Family therapists came to idolize Erickson the way we as children idolized Captain Marvel. We may have been little and the world big, but we could dream of being heroes—strong enough to overpower or clever enough to outwit all that we were afraid of. We'd come home from Saturday matinees all pumped up, get out our toy swords, put on our magic capes—and presto! *We* were superheroes. We were just little kids and so we didn't bother translating our heroes' mythic powers into our own terms; we just copied them directly. Unfortunately, many of those who were star struck by Erickson's legendary therapeutic tales did the same thing. Instead of grasping the principles on which they were predicated, too many therapists just tried to imitate his "uncommon techniques." To be any kind of competent therapist we must keep our psychological distance from the supreme artists—the Minuchins, the Milton

Ericksons, the Michael Whites. Otherwise we end up mimicking the magic of their techniques, rather than grasping the substance of their ideas.

Erickson's emphasis on common, even unconscious, natural abilities is illustrated in his *utilization principle*—using clients' language and preferred ways of seeing themselves to minimize resistance. Instead of analyzing and interpreting dysfunctional dynamics, the idea was to get clients active and moving. Erickson believed that the movement that counted occurred in people's lives outside the consulting room, so he made great use of assignments to be carried out between sessions. Such assignments, or "directives," were to become the hallmark of Jay Haley's strategic approach.

Part of what made Haley's strategic directives so attractive was that they were a wonderful way to gain power and control over people—for their own good—without the usual frustration of trying to convince them to do the right thing. (Part of the problem is, of course, that most people already know what's good for them. The hard part is *doing* it.) So, for example, in the case of a bulimic, a strategic directive might be for the bulimic's family to set out a mess of fried chicken, french fries, cookies, and ice cream. Then, with the family watching, the bulimic would mash up all the food with her hands, symbolizing what goes on in her stomach. After the food was reduced to a soggy mess, she would stuff it in the toilet. Then when the toilet clogged, she would have to ask the family member she resented most to unclog it. This task would symbolize not only what the bulimic does to herself, but also what she puts the family through (Madanes, 1981).

So compelling were such clever interventions that they were much imitated, unfortunately often with little appreciation of the basic principles underlying them. People were so taken by the creative directives that they often lost sight of Haley's developmental framework and emphasis on hierarchical structure.

What the strategic camp added to Erickson's creative approach to problem-solving was a simple framework for understanding how families get stuck in their problems. According to the MRI model, problems develop and persist from mismanagement of ordinary life difficulties, not necessarily by dysfunctional persons or systems. The original difficulty becomes a problem when mishandling leads people to get stuck in more-of-the-same solutions. It was a perverse twist on the old adage, "If at first you don't succeed, try, try again."

The therapist's job was to figure out what people were doing about their difficulties that kept them going, then devise a strategy to get them to act differently. Problems were resolved by interrupting problem-maintaining interactions and getting people back on course. The idea was simply to engineer a 180-degree shift from the client's attempted solution.

The interventions that attracted the most attention were symptom prescriptions, or *paradoxical injunctions*. Why not? They were fun (and their undercurrent of condescension wasn't immediately obvious). The point wasn't really to enact the symptom, but to reverse the attempted solution. If an overweight man had tried unsuccessfully to diet, the idea behind telling him to stop denying himself the foods he craved would be just to do something different; it's making a 180-degree shift in the attempted solution. Whether or not the intervention is a paradox was irrelevant. The technique was to change the attempted solution. Keeping the underlying principle in mind, rather than being captured by the alleged novelty of what was after all only reverse psychology, one might come up with a more effective alternative. Instead of trying to stop eating, perhaps the man could be encouraged to start exercising. (It's always harder to *stop* doing something than it is to *start* doing something else.)

Although cases were conceptualized and treated primarily in behavioral terms, strategic therapists also introduced a cognitive dimension in the technique of "reframing." As the Shakespearean aphorism had it, "There is nothing good or bad, but thinking makes it so." Reframing meant relabeling a family's description to make problems more amenable to solution. It is, for example, easier to deal with a child who "refuses to go to school" than one with a "school phobia."

The Milan group built on the ideas pioneered at MRI, especially the use of the therapeutic double bind, or what they referred to as "counterparadox." Here's an example from *Paradox and Counterparadox* (Selvini Palazzoli, Boscolo, Cecchin, & Prata, 1978). The authors describe using a counterparadoxical approach with a six-year-old boy and his family. At the end of the session a letter from the observing team was read to the family. Young Bruno was praised for acting crazy to protect his father. By preoccupying his mother's time with fights and tantrums, the boy generously allowed his father more time for work and relaxation. Bruno was encouraged to continue doing what he was already doing, lest this comfortable arrangement be disrupted.

The appeal of the strategic approach was pragmatism. Complaints that brought people to therapy were treated as *the* problem, not symptoms of some underlying disorder. Making good use of the cybernetic metaphor, strategic therapists zeroed in on how family systems were regulated by negative feedback. They achieved remarkable results simply by disrupting the interactions that surrounded and maintained symptoms. What eventually turned therapists off to these approaches was their gamesmanship. Reframing was often transparently manipulative. The result was sometimes like watching a clumsy magician—you could see him stacking the deck. "Positive connotation" (ascribing positive motives) was often as sincere as a car salesman's smile, and the way "paradoxical interventions" were employed was usually nothing more than the rote application of reverse psychology.

Meanwhile, as structural and strategic approaches rose and fell in popularity, four other models of family therapy flourished quietly. Though they never really took center stage, experiential, psychoanalytic, behavioral, and Bowenian models grew and prospered. Although these schools never achieved the cachet of family therapy's latest fads, each of them produced powerful clinical advances, which will be examined at length in subsequent chapters.

Looking back from soberer times, it's difficult to convey the excitement and optimism that energized family therapy in its golden age. Training centers sprouted up all over the country, workshops were packed, and the leaders of the movement were as celebrated as rock stars. Active and forceful interveners, their self-assurance was infectious. Minuchin, Whitaker, Haley, Madanes, Selvini Palazzoli—they seemed to rise above the limitations of ordinary forms of talk therapy. Young therapists needed inspiration, and they found it. They learned from the masters, and they legendized them.

Somewhere in the mid 1980s a reaction set in. Despite optimistic assumptions to the contrary, these activist approaches didn't always work. And so the field took revenge on those they'd idealized by cutting them down to size. Maybe it was Haley's manipulativeness that turned them off, or that Minuchin sometimes seemed more bossy than brilliant. Family therapists had marveled at their creativity and tried to copy it, but creativity can't be copied.

By the end of the decade the leaders of the major schools were growing older, their influence waning. What once seemed heroic now seemed aggressive and overbearing. A series of challenges—feminist and postmodern critiques, the reemergence of analytic and biological models, the magic bullet Prozac, the success of recovery programs like Alcoholics Anonymous, the ugly facts of wife beating and child abuse that challenged the notion that domestic problems were always a product of relationship—all shook our confidence in the models we knew to be true, knew would work. We'll take a close look at these challenges in subsequent chapters.

Summary

As we have seen, family therapy has a short history but a long past. For many years therapists resisted the idea of seeing members of a patient's family, in order to safeguard the privacy of the patient–therapist relationship. (That this arrangement also preserved the shame associated with psychological problems as well as the myth of the individual as hero was not noticed, or at least not mentioned.) Freudians excluded the real family in order to uncover the unconscious, introjected family; Rogerians kept the family away in order to provide unconditional positive regard; and hospital psychiatrists discouraged family visits because they might disrupt the benign milieu of the ersatz hospital family.

Several converging developments in the 1950s led to a new view, namely that the family is a living system, an organic whole. Hospital psychiatrists noticed that often when a patient improved, someone else in the family got worse. Moreover, despite good reasons for keeping family members isolated from an individual's therapy, there were also distinct disadvantages to doing so. Individual treatment is predicated on relative stability in the patient's environment; otherwise, trying to change the individual but then returning him or her to a destructive environment wouldn't make sense. When families are undergoing crisis and conflict, a patient's improvement can actually make the family worse. Thus it became clear that change in any one person changes the whole family system. Eventually it also became apparent that changing the family might be the most effective way to change the individual.

Although practicing clinicians in hospitals and child guidance clinics prepared the way for family therapy, the most important breakthroughs were achieved in the 1950s by workers who were scientists first, healers second. In Palo Alto, Gregory Bateson, Jay Haley, Don Jackson, and John Weakland, studying communication, discovered that schizophrenia made sense in the context of pathological family communication. Thus schizophrenics weren't crazy in some meaningless way; their apparently senseless behavior did make sense in the context of their families. At Yale, Theodore Lidz found a striking pattern of instability and conflict in the families of schizophrenics. *Marital schism* (open conflict) and *marital skew* (pathological balance) had profound effects on the development of children. Murray Bowen's observation of how mothers and their schizophrenic offspring go through cycles of closeness and distances was the forerunner of the *pursuer–distancer* dynamic. Behind these cycles, Bowen believed, were cycles of separation anxiety and incorporation anxiety. By hospitalizing whole families for observation and treatment, Bowen implicitly located the problem of schizophrenia in an *undifferentiated family ego mass* and even extended it beyond the nuclear family to three generations. Lyman Wynne linked schizophrenia to the family by demonstrating how communication deviance contributes to thought disorder. *Pseudomutuality* described the maddening unreality of some families, and the *rubber fence* described the psychological membrane that surrounds them, like a thick skin surrounding a living organism.

These observations launched the family therapy movement, but the excitement they generated blurred the distinction between what the research teams observed and what they concluded. What they observed was that the behavior of schizophrenics *fit* with their families; what they concluded was far more momentous. First it was implied that since schizophrenia fit (made sense) in the context of the family, then the family must be the *cause* of schizophrenia. A second conclusion was even more influential. Family dynamics—double binds, pseudomutuality, undifferentiated family ego mass—began to be seen as products of a "system," rather than features of persons who share certain qualities because they live together. Thus was born a new creature, "the family system."

Once the family became the patient, there was a need for new ways to think about and treat human problems. The systems metaphor was the pivotal concept in this endeavor. And, although neither could be considered the founder of family therapy, no one had greater influence on how we think about families than Gregory Bateson and Milton Erickson, the anthropologist and the alienist.

Erickson's legacy was the pragmatic, problem-solving approach. He helped us learn to figure out what keeps families stuck, how to get them unstuck—using creative, sometimes counterintuitive ideas—and then get out, letting families get on about their business, rather than incorporating a therapist into the family as an expensive crutch. But Erickson's mesmerizing artistry also promoted a tradition of the quick fix, done *to* rather than *with* families.

Inspired by Bateson's scientific commitment to observation and study, early family therapists spent a good deal of time watching and listening. They were willing to observe and learn because they knew they were in *terra incognita*. Unfortunately, many family therapists have gotten away from this receptive openness. So much has been written about family dynamics and technique that therapists too often approach families with a set of precooked techniques and generic preconceptions that they impose on a family's unique experience.

Bateson was also the patron saint of the intellectual wing of family therapy. His ideas were so profound that they're still being mined by the most sophisticated thinkers in the field. Unfortunately, Bateson also set an example of overly abstract theorizing and importing ideas from other—"more scientific"—disciplines. In the early days of family therapy, perhaps we needed models from fields like cybernetics to help us get started. But when so many family therapists continue to lean so heavily on the intellectual underpinnings of physics and biology, one wonders, why this physics envy? Perhaps, after all this time, we are still insecure about the legitimacy of psychology and about our own ability to observe human behavior in human terms, without losing our objectivity.

Another reason family therapists gravitated to abstract theories from mechanics and the natural sciences is that they totally rejected the major body of literature about human psychology: psychoanalysis. The psychoanalytic establishment was none too enthusiastic about this new challenge to their way of thinking, and in many quarters family therapists had to fight to win a place for their beliefs. Perhaps it was this resistance that pushed family therapists into a reactive position. The animosity between family therapists and psychodynamic therapists cooled off in the 1970s after family therapy won a place for itself in the mental health establishment. One reason family therapy gained acceptance was that it carved out its domain in areas traditionally neglected by the psychiatric establishment; services to children and the poor. An unfortunate legacy of this early antagonism, however, was a prolonged period of ignorance and neglect. Now, in the 1990s, the pendulum is beginning to shift. Family therapists are beginning to discover that, while we're trying to understand hidden forces in the family, it may also be useful to pay attention to the hidden forces in the individuals who make up the family. Perhaps the fullest appreciation of human nature lies in the fullest understanding of self *and* system.

Obvious parallels between small groups and families led some therapists to treat families as though they were just another form of group. They were well served in this endeavor by a large volume of literature on group dynamics and group therapy. Some even saw therapy groups as models of family functioning, with the therapist as father, group members as siblings, and the group collectively as mother (Schindler, 1951). While group therapists experimented with married couples in groups, some family therapists began to conduct group therapy with individual families. John Bell was preeminent among these; and his family group therapy was one of the most widely imitated of the early models (see Chapter 3).

As therapists gained experience with families, they discovered that the group therapy model wasn't entirely appropriate. Therapy groups are made up of unrelated individuals, strangers with no past or future outside the group. Families, on the other hand, consist of intimates who share the same myths, defenses, and points of view. Moreover, family members aren't peers who relate democratically as equals; generational differences create hierarchical structures that should not be ignored. For these reasons family therapists eventually abandoned the group therapy model, replacing it with a variety of systemic models.

The child guidance movement contributed the team approach to family therapy. At first members of interdisciplinary teams were assigned to different family members but, gradually, as they came to appreciate the interlocking behavior patterns of their separate clients, they started integrating and later combining their efforts. The child guidance movement began in this country in 1909 as a creation of the juvenile courts in order to treat delinquent children who were considered disturbed. Soon these clinics broadened their scope to include a wide range of disorders, and at the same time they broadened the unit of treatment from the child to include the family. At first family therapy was seen as a better means of helping the patient; later it was conceived as a way to serve the needs of the entire family.

Who was the first to practice family therapy? This turns out to be a difficult question. As in every field, there were visionaries who anticipated the recognized development of family therapy. Freud, for example, occasionally saw "Little Hans" together with his father as early as 1909. However, such experiments weren't sufficient to challenge the hegemony of individual therapy until the climate of the times was receptive. In the early 1950s family therapy was begun independently in four different places: by John Bell at Clark University (Chapter 3), by Murray Bowen at the Menninger Clinic and later at NIMH (Chapter 5), by Nathan Ackerman in New York (Chapter 7), and by Don Jackson and Jay Haley in Palo Alto (Chapters 3 and 11).

These pioneers had distinctly different backgrounds and clinical orientations. Not surprisingly, therefore, the approaches they developed were also quite different. This diversity still characterizes the field today. Had family therapy been started by a single person, as was psychoanalysis, it's unlikely that there would have been so much creative competition so soon.

In addition to those just mentioned, others who made significant contributions to the founding of family therapy include Lyman Wynne, Theodore Lidz, Virginia Satir, Carl Whitaker, Ivan Boszormenyi-Nagy, Christian Midelfort, Robert MacGregor, and Salvador Minuchin. Even this list leaves out a number of important figures, for what began after a long period of incubation quickly grew and spread. By the 1960s there were literally hundreds of family therapists. Today the field is so large and complex that it will take an entire chapter (Chapter 10 and Appendix C) just to provide an overview.

What we've called family therapy's golden age—the flowering of the schools in the 1970s and 1980s—may not have been the ultimate expression of our potential, but it was the high-water mark of our self-confidence. Armed with Haley's or Minuchin's latest text, therapists pledged allegiance to one school or another and set off with a sense of mission. What drew them to activist approaches was certainty and charisma. What soured them was hubris. To some, structural family therapy—at least as they had seen it demonstrated at workshops—began to seem like bullying. Others saw the shrewdness of the strategic approach as calculated, distant, manipulative. The tactics were clever but cold. Families were described as stuck rather than sick, but they were stubborn, couldn't be reasoned with. You don't tell a cybernetic machine what you really believe. Therapists got tired of that way of thinking.

In the early years family therapists were animated by a tremendous sense of enthusiasm and conviction. Today, in the wake of postmodern critiques, managed care, and a resurgence of biological psychiatry, we're less sure of ourselves. But on realizing that the founders we grew up with weren't all that we'd hoped and needed them to be, family therapy in the 1990s responded like the kid who discovers that his parents aren't perfect and reacts by rejecting everything they stand for. In subsequent chapters we'll see how today's family therapists have managed to synthesize creative new ideas with some of the best of the earlier models. But as we explore each of the famous models in depth, we'll also see how some good ideas have been unwisely neglected.

All the complexity of the family field should not, however, obscure its basic premise: The family is the context of human problems. Like all human groups, the family has emergent properties—the whole is greater than the sum of its parts. Moreover, no matter how many and varied the explanations of these emergent properties, they all fall into two categories: structure and process. The structure of families includes triangles, subsystems, and boundaries. Among the processes that describe family interaction—emotional reactivity, dysfunctional communication, and so on—the central concept is *circularity*. Rather than worrying about who started what, family therapists understand and treat human problems as a series of moves and countermoves, in repeating cycles.

References

Ackerman, N. W. 1938. The unity of the family. *Archives of Pediatrics. 55:*51–62.

Ackerman, N. W. 1954. Interpersonal disturbances in the family: Some unsolved problems in psychotherapy. *Psychiatry. 17:*359–368.

Ackerman, N. W. 1961. A dynamic frame for the clinical approach to family conflict. In *Exploring the base for family therapy.* N. W. Ackerman, F. L. Beatman, and S. N. Sherman, eds. New York: Family Services Association of America.

Ackerman, N. W. 1966a. *Treating the troubled family.* New York: Basic Books.

Ackerman, N. W. 1966b. Family psychotherapy—theory and practice. *American Journal of Psychotherapy. 20:*405–414.

Ackerman, N. W., Beatman, F., and Sherman, S. N., eds. 1961. *Exploring the base for family therapy.* New York: Family Service Assn. of America.

Ackerman, N. W., and Sobel, R. 1950. Family diagnosis: An approach to the preschool child. *American Journal of Orthopsychiatry. 20:*744–753.

Amster, F. 1944. Collective psychotherapy of mothers of emotionally disturbed children. *American Journal of Orthopsychiatry* 14:44–52.

Anderson, C. M., Reiss, D. J., and Hogarty, G. E. 1986. *Schizophrenia and the family.* New York: Guilford Press.

Anonymous. 1972. Differentiation of self in one's family. In *Family interaction,* J. L. Framo, ed. New York: Springer.

Bardhill, D. R., and Saunders, B. E. 1988. In *Handbook of family therapy training and supervision,* H. A. Liddle, D. C. Breunlin, and R. C. Schwartz, eds. New York: Guilford Press.

Bateson, G. 1951. Information and codification: A philosophical approach. In *Communication: The social matrix of psychiatry,* J. Ruesch and G. Bateson, eds. New York: Norton.

Bateson, G. 1978. The birth of a matrix or double-bind and epistemology. In *Beyond the double-bind,* M. M. Berger, ed. New York: Brunner/Mazel.

Bateson, G., Jackson, D. D., and Weakland, J. 1956. Toward a theory of schizophrenia. *Behavioral Sciences. 1:*251–264.

Beatman, F. L. 1956. In *Neurotic interaction in marriage,* V. W. Eisenstein, ed. New York: Basic Books.

Bell, J. E. 1961. *Family group therapy.* Public Health Monograph #64. Washington, DC: U.S. Government Printing Office.

Bell, J. E. 1962. Recent advances in family group therapy. *Journal of Child Psychology and Psychiatry. 3:*1–15.

Benne, K. D. 1964. History of the T-group in the laboratory setting. In *T-group theory and laboratory method,* L P. Bradford, J. R. Gibb, and K. D. Benne, eds. New York: Wiley.

Bennis, W. G. 1964. Patterns and vicissitudes in T-group development. In *T-group theory and laboratory method,* L P. Bradford, J. R. Gibb, and K. D. Benne, eds. New York: Wiley.

Bion, W. R. 1948. Experience in groups. *Human Relations. 1*:314–329.

Boszormenyi-Nagy, I. 1962. The concept of schizophrenia from the point of view of family treatment. *Family Process. 1*:103–113.

Boszormenyi-Nagy, I. 1966. From family therapy to a psychology of relationships; fictions of the individual and fictions of the family. *Comprehensive Psychiatry. 7*:408–423.

Boszormenyi-Nagy, I. 1972. Loyalty implications of the transference model in psychotherapy. *Archives of General Psychiatry. 27*:374–380.

Boszormenyi-Nagy, I., and Spark, G. L. 1973. *Invisible loyalties: Reciprocity in intergenerational family therapy.* New York: Harper & Row.

Bowen, M. 1961. Family psychotherapy. *American Journal of Orthopsychiatry. 31*:40–60.

Bowen, M. 1976. Principles and techniques of multiple family therapy. In *Family therapy: Theory and practice,* P. J. Guerin, ed. New York: Gardner Press.

Bowlby, J. P. 1949. The study and reduction of group tensions in the family. *Human Relations. 2*: 123–138.

Braverman, L. 1986. Social casework and strategic therapy. *Social Casework.* April, 234–239.

Broderick, C. B., Schrader, S. S. 1981. The history of professional marriage and family therapy. In *Handbook of family therapy,* A. S. Gurman and D. P. Kniskern, eds. New York: Brunner/Mazel.

Broderick, C. B., Schrader, S. S. 1991. The history of professional marriage and family therapy. In *Handbook of family therapy,* Vol. II, A. S. Gurman and D. P. Kniskern, eds. New York: Brunner/Mazel.

Brown, G. W. 1959. Experiences of discharged chronic schizophrenia patients in various types of living groups. *Milbank Memorial Fund Quarterly. 37*:105–131.

Burkin, H. E., Glatzer, H., and Hirsch, J. S. 1944. Therapy of mothers in groups. *American Journal of Orthopsychiatry. 14*:68–75.

Dicks, H. V. 1964. Concepts of marital diagnosis and therapy as developed at the Tavistock Family Psychiatric Clinic, London, England. In *Marriage counseling in medical practice* E. M. Nash, L. Jessner, and D. W. Abse, eds. Chapel Hill, NC: University of North Carolina Press.

Elizur, J., and Minuchin, S. 1989. *Institutionalizing madness: Families, therapy, and society.* New York: Basic Books.

Epstein, N. B., Bishop, D. S., and Baldarin, L. M. 1981. McMaster Model of Family Functioning. In *Normal family problems,* F. Walsh, ed. New York: Guilford Press.

Fisher, S., and Mendell, D. 1958. The spread of psychotherapeutic effects from the patient to his family group. *Psychiatry. 21*:133–140.

Freeman, V. J., Klein, A. F., Richman, L., Lukoff, I. F., and Heisey, V. 1963. Family group counseling as differentiated from other family therapies. *International Journal of Group Psychotherapy. 13*:167–175.

Freud, S. 1911. Psycho-analytical notes on an autobiographical case of paranoia. *Standard edition. 12*:3–84. London: Hogarth Press.

Fromm-Reichmann, F. 1948. Notes on the development of treatment of schizophrenics by psychoanalytic psychotherapy. *Psychiatry. 11*:263–274.

Fromm-Reichmann, F. 1950. *Principles of intensive psychotherapy.* Chicago: University of Chicago Press.

Ginsburg, S. W 1955. The mental health movement and its theoretical assumptions. In *Community programs for mental health,* R. Kotinsky and H. Witmer, eds. Cambridge: Harvard University Press.

Goldstein, M. J., Rodnick, E. H., and Evans, J. R., May, P. R., and Steinberg, M. 1978. Drug and family therapy in the aftercare treatment of schizophrenia. *Archives of General Psychiatry. 35*:1169–1177.

Grunwald, H., and Casell, B. 1958. Group counseling with parents. *Child Welfare. 1*:1–6.

Guerin, P. J. 1976. Family therapy: The first twenty-five years. In *Family therapy: Theory and practice,* P. J. Guerin, ed. New York: Gardner Press.

Haley, J. 1961. Control in brief psychotherapy. *Archives of General Psychiatry. 4*:139–153.

Haley, J. 1963. *Strategies of psychotherapy.* New York: Grune & Stratton.

Handlon, J. H., and Parloff, M. B. 1962. Treatment of patient and family as a group: Is it group therapy? *International Journal of Group Psychotherapy. 12:*132–141.

Hoffman, L. 1981. *Foundations of family therapy.* New York: Basic Books.

Howells, J. G. 1971. *Theory and practice of family psychiatry.* New York: Brunner/Mazel.

Jackson, D. D. 1954. Suicide. *Scientific American. 191:* 88–96.

Jackson, D. D. 1965. Family rules: Marital quid pro quo. *Archives of General Psychiatry. 12:*589–594.

Jackson, D. D., and Weakland, J. H. 1959. Schizophrenic symptoms and family interaction. *Archives of General Psychiatry. 1:*618–621

Jackson, D. D., and Weakland, J. H. 1961. Conjoint family therapy, some considerations on theory, technique, and results. *Psychiatry. 24:*30–45.

Johnson, A. M., and Szurek, S. A. 1954. Etiology of anti-social behavior in delinquents and psychopaths. *Journal of the American Medical Association. 154:*814–817.

Kasanin, J., Knight, E., and Sage, P. 1934. The parent-child relationships in schizophrenia. *Journal of Nervous and Mental Diseases. 79:*249–263.

Kaslow, F. W. 1980. History of family therapy in the United States: A kaleidoscopic overview. *Marriage and Family Review. 3:*77–111.

Kaufman, E., and Kaufman, P., eds. 1979. *Family therapy of drug and alcohol abuse.* New York: Gardner Press.

Kempler, W. 1974. *Principles of Gestalt family therapy.* Salt Lake City: Desert Press.

Kluckhohn, F. R., and Spiegel, J. P. 1954. *Integration and conflict in family behavior.* Group for the Advancement of Psychiatry, Report No. 27. Topeka, Kansas.

Kubie, L. S. 1956. Psychoanalysis and marriage. In *Neurotic interaction in marriage,* V. W. Eisenstein, ed. New York: Basic Books.

Laing, R. D. 1960. *The divided self.* London: Tavistock Publications.

Laing, R. D. 1965. Mystification, confusion and conflict. In *Intensive family therapy,* I. Boszormenyi-Nagy and J. L. Framo, eds. New York: Harper & Row.

Levy, D. 1943. *Maternal Overprotection.* New York: Columbia University Press.

Lewin, K. 1951. *Field theory in social science.* New York: Harper.

Lidz, R. W., and Lidz, T. 1949. The family environment of schizophrenic patients. *American Journal of Psychiatry. 106:*332–345.

Lidz, T., Cornelison, A., and Terry, D. 1957a. Intrafamilial environment of the schizophrenic patient. I: The father. *Psychiatry. 20:*329–342.

Lidz, T., Cornelison, A., and Terry, D. 1957b. Intrafamilial environment of the schizophrenic patient. II: Marital schism and marital skew. *American Journal of Psychiatry. 114:*241–248.

Lidz, T., Parker, B., and Cornelison, A. R. 1956. The role of the father in the family environment of the schizophrenic patient. *American Journal of Psychiatry. 113:*126–132.

Low, A. A. 1943. *The technique of self-help in psychiatry after-care.* Vol. 3, *Lectures to relatives of former patients.* Chicago: Recovery, Inc.

Lowrey, L. G. 1944. Group treatment for mothers. *American Journal of Orthopsychiatry. 14:* 589–592.

MacGregor, R. 1967. Progress in multiple impact theory. In *Expanding theory and practice in family therapy,* N. W. Ackerman, F. L. Bateman, and S. N. Sherman, eds. New York: Family Services Association.

Madanes, C. 1981. *Strategic family therapy.* San Francisco: Jossey-Bass.

Mahler, M. S., & Rabinovitch, R. 1956. The effects of marital conflict on child development. In *Neurotic interaction in marriage,* V. W. Eisenstein, ed. New York: Basic Books.

Marsh, L. C. 1935. Group therapy and the psychiatric clinic. *American Journal of Nervous and Mental Diseases. 82:*381–393.

Minuchin, S. 1974. *Families and family therapy.* Cambridge, MA: Harvard University Press.

Minuchin, S., and Fishman, H. C. 1981. *Family therapy techniques.* Cambridge, MA: Harvard University Press.

Minuchin, S., Montalvo, B., Guerney, B. G., Rosman, B. L., and Schumer, F. 1967. *Families of the slums.* New York: Basic Books.

Minuchin, S., and Nichols, M. P. 1993. *Family healing.* New York: The Free Press.

Minuchin, S., Rosman, B. L., and Baker, L. 1978. *Psychosomatic families: Anorexia nervosa in context.* Cambridge, MA: Harvard University Press.

Mittleman, B. 1944. Complementary neurotic reactions in intimate relationships. *Psychoanalytic Quarterly. 13:*474–491.

Mittleman, B. 1948. The concurrent analysis of married couples. *Psychoanalytic Quarterly. 17*:182–197.

Mittleman, B. 1956. Analysis of reciprocal neurotic patterns in family relationships. In *Neurotic interactions in marriage.* V. W. Eisenstein, ed. New York: Basic Books.

Montague, A. 1956. Marriage—A cultural perspective. In *Neurotic interaction in marriage,* V. W. Eisenstein, ed. New York: Basic Books.

Moreno, J. L. 1945. *Psychodrama.* New York: Beacon House.

Nichols, M. P., and Zax, M. 1977. *Catharsis in psychotherapy.* New York: Gardner Press.

Oberndorf, C. P. 1938. Psychoanalysis of married people. *Psychoanalytic Review. 25*:453–475.

Parsons, T., and Bales, R. F. 1955. *Family socialization and interaction.* Glencoe, IL: Free Press.

Richmond, M. E. 1917. *Social diagnosis.* New York: Russell Sage.

Ross, W. D. 1948. Group psychotherapy with patient's relatives. *American Journal of Psychiatry. 104:* 623–626.

Satir, V. 1964. *Conjoint family therapy.* Palo Alto, CA: Science and Behavior Books.

Satir, V. 1972. *Peoplemaking.* Palo Alto, CA: Science and Behavior Books.

Schindler, W. 1951. Counter-transference in family-pattern group psychotherapy. *International Journal of Group Psychotherapy. 1*:100–105.

Schwartz, R. 1994. *Internal family systems therapy.* New York: Guilford Press.

Selvini Palazzoli, M., Boscolo, L., Cecchin, G., and Prata, G. 1978. *Paradox and counterparadox.* New York: Jason Aronson.

Sherif, M. 1948. *An outline of social psychology.* New York: Harper and Brothers.

Singer, M. T., Wynne, L. C., and Toohey, M. L. 1978. Communication disorders and the families of schizophrenics. In *The nature of schizophrenia,* L. C. Wynne, R. L. Cromwell, and S. Matthysse, eds. New York: Wiley.

Siporin, M. 1980. Marriage and family therapy in social work. *Social Casework. 61*:11–21.

Skynner, R. 1976. *Systems of family and marital psychotherapy.* New York: Brunner/Mazel.

Sluzki, C. E., Beavin, J., Tarnopolsky, A., and Veron, E. 1967. Transactional disqualification. *Archives of General Psychiatry. 16*:494–504.

Speck, R., and Attneave, C. 1973. *Family networks: Rehabilitation and healing.* New York: Pantheon.

Spiegel, J. P. 1957. The resolution of role conflict within the family. *Psychiatry. 20*:1–16.

Steinglass, P. 1987. *The alcoholic family.* New York: Basic Books.

Stierlin, H. 1972. *Separating parents and adolescents.* New York: Quadrangle/New York Times Books.

Strodtbeck, F. L. 1954. The family as a three-person group. *American Sociological Review. 19*:23–29.

Strodtbeck, F. L. 1958. Family interaction, values, and achievement. In *Talent and society,* D. C. McClelland, A. L. Baldwin, A. Bronfenbrenner, and F. L. Strodtbeck, eds. Princeton, NJ: Van Nostrand.

Watzlawick, P. A., Beavin, J. H., and Jackson, D. D. 1967. *Pragmatics of human communication.* New York: Norton.

Whitaker, C. A. 1958. Psychotherapy with couples. *American Journal of Psychotherapy. 12*:18–23.

Whitaker, C. A. 1975. Psychotherapy of the absurd: With a special emphasis on the psychotherapy of aggression. *Family Process. 14*:1–16.

Whitaker, C. A. 1976. A family is a four-dimensional relationship. In *Family therapy: Theory and practice,* P. J. Guerin, ed. New York: Gardner Press.

Whitaker, C. A., and Malone, T. P. 1953. *The roots of psychotherapy.* New York: Balkiston.

Wiener, N. 1948. *Cybernetics, or control and communication in the animal and the machine.* New York: Wiley.

Wynne, L. C. 1961. The study of intrafamilial alignments and splits in exploratory family therapy. In *Exploring the base for family therapy,* N. W. Ackerman, F. L. Beatman, and S. N. Sherman, eds. New York: Family Services Association.

Wynne, L. C., Ryckoff, I., Day, J., and Hirsch, S. I. 1958. Pseudomutuality in the family relationships of schizophrenics. *Psychiatry. 21*:205–220.

Zuk, G. H. 1971. *Family therapy: A triadic-based approach.* New York: Behavioral Publications.

3

Early Models and Basic Techniques: Group Process and Communications Analysis

Most people who practiced family therapy in the early years used some combination of a group therapy approach and the communications model that came out of Bateson's schizophrenia project. In this chapter, we will explore those two models and see how they had to be modified to fit the unique challenges of treating troubled families. We will conclude with a section on the basic techniques of family therapy, as they are applied from the first telephone contact through the various stages of treatment to termination.

Those of us who practiced family therapy in the 1960s could often be seen engaged in a strange ritual. When a family filed in for their first session, all anxious and uncertain, the therapist, all smiles, would kneel in front of one of the small children. "Hi! And what's your name?" Then, often as not, "Do you know why you're here?" meanwhile ignoring the parents. The most common answers to this question were: "Mommy said we were going to the doctor's," in a frightened voice, or, confused, "Daddy said we were going for . . . a ride." Then the therapist, trying not to sound scornful, would turn to the parents and say, "Perhaps you could explain to Johnny why you *are* here."

The reason for this little charade was that before they understood how families were structured, many therapists treated the family as a group, in which the youngest members were presumed to be the most vulnerable and, therefore, in need of "expert" help to express themselves—

as though the parents weren't in charge, as though everybody's opinion was equal.

Another common scene was therapists making solemn comments about patterns of communication: "I notice that when I ask Suzie a question, she first turns to Mom to see if it's okay to answer. . . ."

Very clever. Not only did we expect families to be impressed by such bright remarks, we imagined that they'd somehow instantly start communicating according to some ideal model in *our* heads—"I-statements" and all the rest. *And* we thought that such clear communication would solve all their problems.

Are we being a little condescending here? Absolutely. The first family therapists turned somewhat naively to models from group therapy and communications analysis because there were no other models available.

Early family therapists availed themselves of the techniques of group therapy because, after all, families are groups, aren't they? It was certainly convenient to have a ready-made set of principles to rely on, and for a long time the group therapy model was the most widely used approach to families. Even today, therapists with little understanding of systems dynamics or family structure often treat families as though they were a group of equals.

The communications model that emerged from Palo Alto in the 1950s had an enormous impact on the entire field. Communications family therapy was no mere application of individual psychotherapy to families; it was a radically new conceptualization that altered the very nature of imagination. What was new was the focus on the *process*, the form of communication, rather than its *content*.

Bateson's observations led to the conclusion that the interchange of messages between people defined their relationships and that these relationships were stabilized by homeostatic processes in families. His interest was scientific, not therapeutic, and his goal was to develop a general model of human behavior. When Jay Haley and Don Jackson began interviewing families, they were more interested in studying them than in treating them. Gradually, however, they began to intervene in order to help these families overcome their problems. At first they used interpretations because they still believed that awareness would bring about change. But, finding that this didn't work, they developed new techniques to fit their new ways of thinking. Directives replaced interpretations as the major technique to change the way family members communicate with one another.

The paradigms of communications theory were so well received that they were adopted by other schools of family therapy. Virtually every approach now treats communication as synonymous with behavior, and concepts like the *double bind* and *family homeostasis* have been absorbed in the literature. In fact it might be said that communications family therapy died of success.

Sketches of Leading Figures

Not only did many of the early family therapists turn to the group therapy literature for guidance in treating families, many of the pioneers of family therapy were themselves products of group therapy training. By far the most influential of these was John Elderkin Bell.

Bell (1975) credited his start as a family therapist to a fortunate misunderstanding. When he was in London in 1951, Bell heard that Dr. John Bowlby of the Tavistock Clinic was experimenting with group therapy for families. This caught Bell's interest and inspired him to try this approach as a means of dealing with behavior problems in children. As Bell later put it, if so eminent an authority as John Bowlby was using family therapy, it must be a good idea. It turned out that Bowlby had only interviewed one family as an adjunct to treating a troubled child, but Bell didn't learn this until years later.

While none of the early pioneers of family group therapy were as well known as John E. Bell, their work had a direct impact on many of those who took up family therapy in the early 1960s, among them Rudolph Dreikurs, Christian Midelfort, S. H. Foulkes, and Robin Skynner.

Rudolph Dreikurs was a student of Alfred Adler's who put Adler's theories into practice in child guidance clinics in Chicago. Dreikurs translated Adler's ideas about the need to overcome *feelings of inferiority* by developing *social interest* in a variety of formats, including children's groups, community groups, parents' groups, and family therapy groups. His techniques with families combined emotional support and encouragement with interpretations and suggestions about modifying unhappy interactions. He encouraged families to discuss their mutual problems in an open, democratic spirit; and he urged them to institute regular "family councils" in order to incorporate the model of family group therapy into their daily lives.

Christian Midelfort is another figure in early family therapy whose influence was largely restricted to his own place and time. He practiced at the Lutheran Hospital in LaCrosse, Wisconsin. Charged with responsibility for treating fairly seriously disturbed patients, Midelfort decided that the only way to achieve lasting results was to include patients' families in treatment. Although he still considered the patient as the focus of treatment, Midelfort (1957) developed an array of family therapy techniques that anticipated many later developments.

S. H. Foulkes, an English psychoanalyst, was one of the organizers of the group therapy movement in Great Britain. Although he began conducting conjoint family therapy interviews early in the 1940s, his work was little known to family therapists because his major interest and publications were in analytic group therapy. Among Foulkes's students was Robin Skynner, whose work overlaps the psychoanalytic (Chapter 7) and group approaches to families. More of a synthesizer than an innovator, Skynner's (1976) group analytic orientation to families is revealed in the following remark: "The family, like the small group of strangers, is seen as possessing inherent potential for constructive understanding and for facilitating growth and positive change, as well as for creating confusion and blocking development" (p. 192).

Communications therapy was one of the earliest and certainly most influential approaches to family therapy. The leading characters who created and popularized the communications approach to treating families were the members of Bateson's schizophrenia project and the Mental Research Institute in Palo Alto, most notably Don Jackson and Jay Haley.

Nothing in Jackson's traditional psychiatric background portends his radical departure from conventional psychotherapy. He graduated in 1943 from Stanford University School of Medicine, where the major influences were Freudian and Sullivanian. He completed his residency training at Chestnut Lodge in Rockville, Maryland, in 1949 and remained there as a member of the staff until 1951. During this period he was also a candidate at the Washington-Baltimore Psychoanalytic Institute. In 1951 Jackson moved to Palo Alto, where he maintained a private practice and worked as Chief of the Psychiatric Department of the Palo Alto Medical Clinic. He also was a candidate at the San Francisco Psychoanalytic Institute until 1954 and was associated with the Department of Psychology at Stanford University from 1951 until 1960. He became a consultant to the Palo Alto Veterans Administration Hospital in 1951, which led to his association with the Bateson project.

Jackson established the Mental Research Institute in November 1958 and received his first grant in March 1959. The original staff consisted of Jackson, Jules Riskin, and Virginia Satir. They were later joined by Jay Haley, John Weakland, and Paul Watzlawick. Gregory Bateson served as a research associate and teacher.

When Jackson died tragically in 1968 at the age of 48, he left behind a legacy of seminal papers, the leading journal in the field, *Family Process* (which he cofounded with Nathan Ackerman), and a great sadness at the passing of such a vibrant and creative talent.

Jay Haley was always something of an outsider. He entered the field without clinical credentials and first established his reputation as a commentator and critic. His initial impact came from his writing, in which he infused biting sarcasm with incisive analysis of psychotherapy. In "The Art of Psychoanalysis" (reproduced in Haley, 1963), Haley redefined psychoanalysis as a game of one-upmanship rather than as a search for insight:

> By placing the patient on a couch, the analyst gives the patient the feeling of having his feet up in the air and the knowledge that the analyst has both feet on the ground. Not only is the patient disconcerted by having to lie down while talking, but he finds himself literally below the analyst and so his one-down position is geographically emphasized. In addition, the analyst seats himself behind the couch where he can watch the patient but the patient cannot watch him. This gives the patient the kind of disconcerted feeling a person has when sparring with an opponent while blindfolded. Unable to see what response his ploys provoke, he is unsure when he is one-up and when one-down. Some patients try to solve this problem by saying something like, "I slept with my sister last night," and then whirling around to see how the analyst is responding. These "shocker" ploys usually fail in their effect. The analyst may twitch, but he has time to recover before the patient can whirl fully around and see him. Most analysts have developed ways of handling the whirling patient. As the patient turns, they are gazing off into space, or doodling with a pencil, or braiding belts, or staring at tropical fish. It is essential that the rare patient who gets an opportunity to observe the analyst see only an impassive demeanor. (pp. 193–194)

In the same paper, Haley (1963) also tossed a few barbs at other popular forms of psychotherapy:

> There is, for example, the Rogerian system of ploys where the therapist merely repeats back what the patient says. This is an inevitably winning system. When the patient accuses the therapist of being no use to him, the therapist replies, "You feel I'm no use to you." The patient says, "That's right, you're not worth a damn." The therapist says, "You feel I'm not worth a damn." This ploy, even more than the orthodox silence ploy, eliminates any triumphant feelings in the patient and makes him feel a little silly after a while (a one-down feeling). Most orthodox analysts look upon the Rogerian ploys as not only weak but not quite respectable. They do not give the patient a fair chance. (p. 198)

Haley saw patients and families during the years he worked on the Bateson project, but he retired from direct clinical practice in 1962 when the project disbanded. After that he concentrated on teaching and supervising. His writing continued to be witty and critical, and his relationship with the rest of the field continued to be iconoclastic, even adversarial. Recently, for example, writing about what he called "the plague of drugs in psychiatry," Haley said that today psychotic people are "routinely medicated into a state of zombydom" (Haley, 1986, p. 98).

Haley was studying for a master's degree in communication at Stanford when he met Bateson, who hired him to work on the schizophrenia project. Haley began to interview schizophrenic patients in order to analyze the strange style of their communication. As a therapist Haley was greatly influenced by Milton Erickson, with whom he began studying hypnosis in 1953. Then, after the Bateson project broke up in 1962, Haley worked in research at the Mental Research Institute until 1967 when he joined Salvador Minuchin at the Philadelphia Child Guidance Clinic. It was there that Haley became especially interested in training and supervision, areas in which he may have made his greatest contribution. In 1976 Haley moved to Washington, DC, where with Cloe Madanes he founded the Family Therapy Institute. In 1995 Haley retired and moved back to California.

Bateson himself had a superbly analytic mind, nurtured from an early age in a variety of scientific disciplines, and his scientific background shaped the character of the group's approach to families. Under Bateson's influence the orientation of the project was anthropological. Their goal was to observe, not change, families. They stumbled onto family therapy more or less by accident. When Bateson developed the double-bind hypothesis in 1954 he had never actually interviewed a family. It wasn't until 1956 or 1957 that the group began seeing families. At first they merely wanted to observe patterns of communication; only later were they moved to try to help the unhappy people they'd been studying.

Virginia Satir was also a prominent member of the Mental Research Institute group, but because her emphasis shifted to emotional experiencing, we will consider her in Chapter 6.

Theoretical Formulations

Although he's better known for studying the psychology of individuals, Freud was also interested in interpersonal relations, and many would consider his *Group Psychology and the Analysis of the Ego* (Freud, 1921) the first major text on the dynamic psychology of the group. According to Freud, the major requirement for transforming a collection of individuals into a group is the emergence of a leader. In addition to manifest tasks of organization and direction, the leader also serves as a parent figure on whom the members become more or less dependent. Members *identify* with the leader as a parent surrogate and with other group members as siblings. *Transference* occurs in groups when members repeat unconscious attitudes formed in the process of growing up. Freud's concept of *resistance* in individual therapy also applies to groups, because group members, seeking to ward off anxiety, may oppose the progress of treatment with silence or hostility and by missing sessions and avoiding painful topics. Family groups resist treatment by scapegoating, superficial chatting, prolonged dependency on the therapist, refusing to follow therapeutic suggestions, and allowing difficult family members to stay home.

Like Freud, Wilfred Bion (1961) also attempted to develop a group psychology of the unconscious and described groups as functioning on *manifest* and *latent* levels. The group's official task is on the manifest level, but people also join groups to fulfill powerful, but unconscious, primal needs. At the latent level, groups seek a leader who will permit them to gratify their needs for *dependence, pairing,* and *fight–flight.*

Freudian concepts, extrapolated from the individual to the group, remain part of group dynamics theory, but most of the working concepts focus less on individuals than on the interactions among them. Whole groups, including families, are usually defined by structure; subgroups, by function. Most of the time groups, including families, operate as subgroups. The Family doesn't clean the house—Mom and the kids do. The Family doesn't plan a move—Dad and Mom do.

According to Kurt Lewin's (1951) *field theory,* conflict is an inevitable feature of group life, as members vie with one another for adequate *life space.* Just as animals need their own territory, people seem to need their own "space" (or turf), and for this reason there is an inherent tension between the needs of the individual and those of the group. The amount of conflict generated by this tension depends upon the amount of restriction imposed by the group, compared with the amount of mutual support it gives in exchange. (People who give up a lot for their families expect a lot in return.)

What distinguished Lewin's model of group tensions from earlier theories is that it was *ahistorical.* Instead of worrying about who did what to whom in the past, Lewin concentrated on what was going on in the *here-and-now.* This focus on *process* (how people talk), rather than *content* (what they talk about), is one of the keys to understanding the way a group (or family) functions.

Role theory, which influenced so many branches of psychology, also had a prominent place in theories of group functioning. Every position in a group structure has an associated role, which consists of expected and prohibited behavior for the occupant of that position. In family groups some roles are biologically determined, whereas others depend on the specific dynamics of the group. Sex roles; kinship roles of mother, father, son, and daughter; and age roles of infant, child, teenager, and adult are obvious but not necessarily more significant than such assigned roles as "the strong one," "the scapegoat," or "the baby."

In families, role conflicts can occur within or between roles. *Intra-role* conflict exists when a single role calls for contradictory performances, such as when a child is expected to be both independent and obedient. *Inter-role* conflict exists when two or more roles are incompatible, as, for example, when a woman is expected to be strong as a mother but helpless as a wife. Notice that the notion of role conflict makes no reference to personalities. The problem isn't in the person but in the design of the system.

There can also be problems in how well roles and personalities fit each other. An introverted, narcissistic man may have trouble filling the role of a warm and loving father. Thus personality and role are mutually determinative. Talcott Parsons (1950), speaking as an analytically oriented sociologist, emphasized the internalization of family roles as a determining influence on the formation of character. Over time, roles tend to become stereotyped, and thus limit flexibility in individuals and in the group (Bales, 1970).

Communications therapists adopted the *black box* concept from telecommunications and applied it to the individuals within the family. This model disregards the internal complexities of individuals in order to concentrate on their input and output—that is, communication. It isn't that these clinicians denied the phenomena of mind—thinking and feeling—they just found it useful to ignore them. By limiting their focus to what goes on between, rather than within, family members, communications theorists qualify as "systems purists" (Beels & Ferber, 1969).

Communications theorists also disregarded the past, leaving that to psychoanalysts, while they searched for patterns with which to understand behavior in the present. They considered it unimportant to figure out what's cause and what's effect, preferring to use a model of circular causality in which chains of behavior are seen as effect-effect-effect.

Families were treated as error-controlled, goal-directed systems, and their interactions were analyzed using cybernetic theory, general systems theory, and games theory. For example, interactions can be described using a games analogy. Someone who doesn't know how to play chess could discover the rules by watching the game and noting the pattern of moves. This is precisely the strategy used by communications theorists in their analyses of family communications.

Human communication can be analyzed according to *syntax, semantics,* and *pragmatics*

(Carnap, 1942; Morris, 1938). *Syntax* refers to the way words are put together to form phrases and sentences; it is the manner in which information is transmitted. Errors of *syntax* are particularly likely in persons learning a new language. This is the domain of the information theorist, who is concerned with who speaks to whom, the percentage of speaking time for each member, the parsimony of speech, and the ratio of information to noise. Thus *syntax* is concerned with the stylistic properties of language, not with its meaning. Meaning is the realm of *semantics.* In families, *semantics* refers to the clarity of language, the existence of private or shared communicational systems, and concordance versus confusion of communication. Finally there is the *pragmatics,* or behavioral effect, of communication. In order to evaluate the effects of communication, it's necessary to take into account nonverbal behavior and the context of communication, as well as the words used. The *pragmatics* of communication was the primary concern of communications therapists and was their basis for understanding behavior in any family system.

In *Pragmatics of Human Communication,* Watzlawick, Beavin, and Jackson (1967) sought to develop a calculus of human communication, which they stated in a series of axioms about the interpersonal implications of communication. These axioms are an aspect of *metacommunication,* which means communicating about communication. The first of these axioms is that people are always communicating. Since all behavior is communicative, and one cannot *not* behave, then it follows that one cannot *not* communicate. Consider the following example.

> Mrs. Snead began the first family therapy session by saying, "I just don't know what to do with Roger anymore. He's not doing well in school, he doesn't help out around the house; all he wants to do is hang around with those awful friends of his. But the worst thing is that he refuses to communicate with us."
>
> At this point, the therapist turned to Roger and said, "Well, what do you have to say about all of this?" But Roger said nothing. Instead he continued to sit slouched in a chair at the far corner of the room, with an angry, sullen look on his face.

Roger isn't "not communicating." He's communicating that he's angry and that he refuses to negotiate. Communication also takes place when it isn't intentional, conscious, or successful—that is, in the absence of mutual understanding.

A second major proposition is that all messages have a *report* and a *command* function (Ruesch & Bateson, 1951). The report (or content) of a message conveys information, while the command is a statement about the definition of the relationship. For example, the message, "Mommy, Sandy hit me!" conveys information but also suggests a command—*Do something about it.* Notice, however, that the implicit command is ambiguous. The reason for this is that the printed word omits nonverbal and contextual clues. This statement shrieked by a child in tears would have a different command value than if it were spoken by a giggling child.

The relationship between speakers is another factor that significantly affects how the command aspects of communication are responded to. For example, a therapist whose aim is to help patients express their feelings would likely respond to a husband who was crying by listening sympathetically and encouraging him to continue. The man's wife, on the other hand, might be upset by his display of "weakness," and try to "cheer him up" by telling him that the problem doesn't really exist or by suggesting ways to solve it. In this instance, the therapist can listen to the man's feelings without hearing (or responding to) a command to *do something about them.* The wife feels threatened and obligated by the inferred command, and so cannot simply listen.

The command aspect of communications functions to define relationships. "Mommy, Sandy hit me!" suggests that the speaker accepts a one-down relationship with Sandy, and insists that mother will intercede to settle any problems. This defining is often obscured because it's usually not deliberate or done with full awareness, and, as we have seen, it depends on how it's received. In healthy relationships this aspect recedes into the background. Conversely, problematic relationships are characterized by frequent struggles about the nature of the relationship: "Don't tell me what to do!"

In families, command messages are patterned as *rules* (Jackson, 1965). The regular patterning of interactions stabilizes relationships. These patterns, or rules, can be deduced from observed redundancies in interaction. Jackson used the term *family rules* as a description of regularity, not as a causal or determining concept. Nobody "lays down the rules." In fact, families are generally unaware of them.

The rules, or regularities, of family interaction operate to preserve family *homeostasis* (Jackson, 1965, 1967), an acceptable behavioral balance within the family. Homeostatic mechanisms bring families back to a previous balance in the face of any disruption, and thus serve to resist change. Jackson's notion of family homeostasis describes the conservative aspect of family systems and is similar to the general systems theory concept of *negative feedback*. Thus, according to a communications analysis, families operate as goal-directed, rule-governed systems.

Communications theorists found in *general systems theory* (von Bertalanffy, 1950) a number of ideas useful in explaining how families work. But while they (Watzlawick, Beavin, & Jackson, 1967) described families as *open systems* in their theoretical statements, they tended to treat them as *closed systems* in their clinical work. Thus they concentrated their therapeutic efforts on the nuclear family, with little or no consideration of inputs from the community or extended family.

Relationships between communicants are also described as being either *complementary* or *symmetrical*. *Complementary* relationships are based on differences that fit together. A common complementary pattern is where one person is assertive and the other submissive, with each mutually reinforcing and sustaining each other's position. It's important to understand that these are descriptive, not evaluative, terms. Moreover, it's a mistake to assume that one person's position *causes* the other's or that one is weaker than the other. As Sartre (1964) pointed out, it is the masochist as well as the sadist who creates the possibility of a sadomasochistic relationship.

Symmetrical relationships are based on equality; the behavior of one mirrors that of the other. Symmetrical relationships between husbands and wives, where both are free to pursue careers and share housekeeping and child-rearing, are often thought of as ideal by today's standards. However, from a communications analysis, there's no reason to assume that such a relationship would be any more stable or functional for the system than a traditional, complementary one.

Another aspect of communication is that it can be *punctuated* in various ways (Bateson & Jackson, 1964). An outside observer may hear a dialogue as an uninterrupted flow of communication, but each of the participants may believe that what he or she says is caused by what the other says. Thus punctuation organizes behavioral events and reflects the bias of the observer. Couples therapists are familiar with the impasse created by each spouse saying, "I only do *X*, because he (or she) does *Y*." A common example is the wife who says she only nags because her husband withdraws, while he says he only withdraws because she nags. Another example is the wife who says she'd be more in the mood for sex if her husband was more affectionate; to which he counters that he'd be more affectionate if she'd have sex more often.

As long as couples punctuate their interactions in this fashion, there is little likelihood of change. Each insists that the other causes the impasse, and each waits for the other to change. The impasse is created by the universal tendency for people to punctuate a sequence of interactions so that it appears the other one has initiative, dominance, or dependency—in other words, power. Children illustrate this when they have a fight and run to a parent, both crying, "He started it!" Their mutual illusion is based on the mistaken notion that such sequences have a discrete beginning, that one person's behavior is caused by another's in linear fashion.

Communications theory doesn't accept linear causality or look for underlying motives for behavior; instead, this model assumes circular causality and analyzes specific behaviors occurring at the present time. Considerations of underlying causality are treated as conceptual noise, with no practical therapeutic value. The behaviors that the communications theorist observes are patterns of communications linked together in additive chains of stimulus *and* response. This model of sequential causality enables therapists to treat behavioral chains as *feedback loops.* When the response to one family member's problematic behavior exacerbates the problem, that chain is seen to be a *positive feedback loop.* The advantage of this formulation is that it focuses on interactions that perpetuate problems, which can be changed, instead of inferring underlying causes, which aren't observable and often not subject to change.

Normal Family Development

Now that we have rich literatures on child development and the family life cycle, it doesn't seem particularly fruitful to turn to the group dynamics literature to help us understand normal family development. Nevertheless, in the early days of family therapy, many therapists borrowed concepts of group development and applied them to families. Among the most notorious of these was Talcott Parsons' idea (1950) that groups needed an *instrumental* leader and an *expressive* leader to look after the *social-emotional* needs of the group. Guess who was elected to which roles—and consider how that helped to legitimize an artificial and unfair division of labor.

William Schutz's (1958) discussion of three phases of group development—*inclusion, control,* and *affection*—was more useful. Other studies in the group dynamics literature called attention to the critical need for *cohesiveness.* One factor that helps determine cohesiveness is *need compatibility* (Shaw, 1981). If members of a group have compatible needs, they tend to function well together; if not, not. Likewise, compatible needs—compatible, not identical—make good marriages. This assumption has been supported by studies demonstrating that need compatibility predicts marital choice (Winch, 1955) and marital adjustment (Meyer & Pepper, 1977).

As "systems purists," communications family therapists treated behavior as ahistorical. Whether they were describing or treating family interactions, their attention was on the here-and-now, with very little interest in development. Normal families were described as functional systems, which like all living systems depend on two important processes (Maruyama, 1968). First, they must maintain constant integrity in the face of environmental vagaries. This is accomplished through *negative feedback,* often illustrated by the example of the thermostat on a home heating unit. When the heat drops below a set point, the thermostat activates the furnace until the room returns to the desired temperature.

No living system can survive without a regular pattern or structure. On the other hand, too rigid a structure leaves a system ill-equipped to adapt to changing circumstances. This is why normal families must also have mechanisms of *positive feedback.* Negative feedback minimizes change to maintain a steady state; positive feedback alters the system to accommodate to novel inputs. As children grow older, they change the nature of their input to the family system. The most obvious instance of this is adolescence, at which time children seek more involvement with peers and demand more freedom and independence. A family system limited to negative feedback can only resist such changes. Normal families, on the other hand, also have positive feedback mechanisms and can respond to new information by modifying their structure.

Normal families become periodically unbalanced (Hoffman, 1971) during transition points in the family life cycle. No family passes through these changes in a totally harmonious fashion; all experience stress, resist change, and develop vicious cycles. But normal families aren't trapped in these cycles; they're able to engage in positive feedback to modify themselves. Symptomatic families remain stuck, using a symptomatic member to avoid change.

Concepts from general systems theory, such as positive feedback, have the virtues of wide applicability and theoretical elegance, but often seem esoteric and abstract. When we recognize that the channel for positive feedback is communication, it's possible to state the case more plainly. Healthy families are able to change because they communicate clearly and are flexible. When their children say they want to grow up, healthy parents listen.

Development of Behavior Disorders

From a group theory perspective, symptoms were considered products of disturbed and disturbing group processes. But groups weren't thought to *cause* disturbance in their members; rather, the behavior of the members was part of the disturbance of the group. Thus group researchers and therapists rejected linear causality in favor of a form of circular causality that they called "group dynamics." Family group therapists were less concerned with the origins of psychopathology than with the conditions that support and maintain it. These include stereotyped roles, breakdowns in communication, and blocked channels for giving and receiving support.

Rigidity of roles forces group interactions to occur in a narrow, stereotyped range. When options are reduced for individuals, their flexibility as a group is constrained. Groups stuck with inflexible roles and unvarying structures tend to malfunction when called upon to handle changed circumstances. Moreover, if flexibility is threatening, such groups don't risk communicating about unmet needs; the result is often frustration and sometimes symptomatic disturbance in one of the group's members. If the needs that generate acute disturbance continue to go unmet, the symptoms themselves may be perpetuated as a role, and the group organizes itself around a "sick" member.

According to communications therapists, the essential function of symptoms is to maintain the homeostatic equilibrium of family systems. (As we shall see, the notion that symptoms are functional—implying that families *need* their problems—was to become controversial.) Pathological families were considered to be trapped in dysfunctional, but very strong, homeostatic patterns of communication (Jackson & Weakland, 1961). Their interactions may seem odd, and they may be unsatisfying, yet they are powerfully self-reinforcing. These families cling to their rigid and inflexible structures and respond to signs of change as negative feedback. That is, change is treated not as an opportunity for growth but as a threat and a signal to change back. Changes that threaten stability are labeled as "sick," as the following example illustrates.

> Tommy was a quiet, solitary boy, the only child of East European immigrant parents. The parents left their small farming com-

munity and came to the United States, where they both found factory work in a large city in the Northeast. Although they were now safe from religious persecution and their standard of living improved, the couple felt alien and out of sympathy with their new neighbors. They kept to themselves and took pleasure in raising Tommy.

Tommy was a frail child with a number of peculiar mannerisms, but to his parents he was perfect. Then he started school. He began to make friends with other children and, eager to be accepted, he picked up a number of American habits. He chewed bubble gum, watched cartoons, and rode his bicycle whenever he had the chance. His parents were annoyed by the gum chewing and by Tommy's fondness for television, but they were genuinely distressed by his eagerness to play with his friends. They began to feel that he was rejecting their values, and that "something must be wrong with him." By the time they called the child guidance clinic, they were convinced that Tommy was disturbed, and they asked for help to "make Tommy normal again."

In their theoretical papers, communications theorists maintained the position that pathology inheres in the system as a whole (Hoffman, 1971; Jackson, 1967; Watzlawick, Beavin, & Jackson, 1967). The *identified patient* was considered a role with complementary counterroles, all of which contributed to the maintenance of the system. The identified patient may be the victim, but in this framework "victim" and "victimizer" are seen as mutually determined roles—neither is good or bad, and neither causes the other. However, although this circular causality was a consistent feature of their theorizing, communications therapists often lapsed into demonizing parents.

The foundations for a family theory of the etiology of schizophrenia, focusing on disturbed patterns of communication, were laid down by Gregory Bateson (Bateson, Jackson, Haley, & Weakland, 1956), Theodore Lidz (Lidz, Cornelison, Terry, & Fleck, 1958), and Lyman Wynne (Wynne, Ryckoff, Day, & Hirsch, 1958). All of these researchers emphasized the pathological effect of parents' irrationality on their offspring, suggesting that the disordered thinking of schizophrenic children was caused by their parents.

Despite the enthusiastic response to the idea that schizophrenia might be caused by disordered communication in the family, the fact is that it isn't. Communication deviance isn't found in all schizophrenic families, nor is it limited to families so diagnosed. Wynne's view (1968, 1970) is that communications patterns can be regarded as building on attention-response deficits that probably have an innate, genetically determined component.

It's difficult to judge a single communication as normal or pathological. Instead the judgment must be made on a series or sequence of communications. One can look at syntax and semantics, that is, the content of speech, for clarity or confusion. This approach is exemplified by Lyman Wynne's studies in which he found that schizophrenics' speech could be differentiated from that of normals or delinquents (Wynne & Singer, 1963). Alternatively one can look at the pragmatics of communication, as did the members of the Palo Alto group. Here the emphasis wasn't on clarity or content, but on the *metacommunication* or command aspects of language.

Symptoms were seen as messages. The nonverbal message of a symptom is: "It is not I who does not (or does) want to do this, it is something outside my control—my nerves, my illness, my anxiety, my bad eyes, alcohol, my upbringing, the Communists, or my wife" (Watzlawick, Beavin, & Jackson, 1967, p. 80). As the group became more sophisticated, they tried to get past blaming parents for victimizing their children. Symptoms were no longer considered to be *caused* by communication problems in the family; they were seen as embedded in a pathological context, within which they may be the only possible reaction. Among the forms of pathological communication identified by the Palo Alto group were denying that one is communicating, disqualifying the other person's message, confusing levels of communication, discrepant punctuation of communication sequences, symmetrical escalation to competitiveness, rigid complementarity, and paradoxical communication.

The most pervasive feature of pathological family communications is the use of *paradox.* A paradox is a contradiction that follows correct deduction from logical premises. In family communications, paradoxes usually take the form of *paradoxical injunctions.* A frequent example of a paradoxical injunction is to demand some behavior that by its very nature can be done only spontaneously—"Be spontaneous!" "You should have more self-confidence." "Tell me you love me." A person exposed to such paradoxical injunctions is caught in an untenable position. To comply—to act spontaneous or self-confident—means to be self-consciously deliberate or eager to please. The only way to escape the dilemma is to step outside the context and comment on it, but such metacommunication rarely occurs in families. (It's difficult to communicate about communication.)

Paradoxical communications are a frequent feature of everyday life. They are relatively harmless in small doses, but when they take the form of double binds the consequences are malignant. In a double bind the two contradictory messages are on different levels of abstraction, and there is an implicit injunction against commenting on the discrepancy. A common example of a double bind is the wife who denounces her husband for not showing feelings but then attacks him when he does.

Continual exposure to paradoxical communication is like the dilemma of a dreamer caught in a nightmare. Nothing the dreamer tries to do in the dream works. The only solution is to step outside the context by waking up. Unfortunately, for people who live in a nightmare, it isn't easy to wake up.

Goals of Therapy

The goal of treating family groups was the same as treating stranger groups: individuation of group members and improved relationships. Individual growth is promoted when unmet needs are verbalized and understood and when overly confining roles are explored and expanded. When family members are released from their inhibitions, it was assumed that they would develop greater family cohesiveness. Notice the difference in emphasis between this—considering families as groups of individuals, each of whom must be helped to develop—and the systemic view of the family as a unit. Treating families as though they were like any other group failed to appreciate the need for hierarchy and structure.

Improved communication was seen as the primary way to meet the goal of improved group functioning. The aims of this approach reflected the fairly simple view of families and their problems that was prevalent among practitioners before they learned to think systemically. While Bateson and his colleagues were laboring with their complex systems analyses, the average therapist still thought that the way to help troubled families was simply to have them sit down and talk to one another. In fact, as most families begin to converse, they have enough communication problems to keep therapists busy for a long time correcting their "mistakes," without getting to the individual and systems dynamics that generate them.

The goal of communications family therapy was to take "deliberate action to alter poorly functioning patterns of interaction . . ." (Watzlawick, Beavin, & Jackson, 1967, p. 145). Because "patterns of interaction" are synonymous with communication, this meant changing patterns of communication. In the early days of communications family therapy, especially in Virginia Satir's work, this translated into a general goal of improving communication in the family. Later the goal was narrowed to altering those specific patterns of communication that maintained problems. By 1974 Weakland wrote that the goal of therapy was resolving symptoms, not reorganizing families: "We see the resolution of problems as primarily requiring a substitution of behavior patterns so as to interrupt the vicious, positive feedback circles" (Weakland, Fisch, Watzlawick, & Bodin, 1974, p. 149).

The goal of the communications therapist was, like that of the behavior therapist, to interdict behavior that stimulated and reinforced symptoms. These two models also shared the assumption that once pathological behavior was blocked, it would be replaced by constructive alternatives, instead of by other symptoms. The limitation of the behavioral model was that it treated the symptomatic person as the problem, and conceived of the symptom as a response rather than as both a response and a stimulus in a chain of interaction. The limitation of the communications model was that it isolated sequences of behavior that maintained symptoms and focused on two-person interactions without considering triangles or other structural problems. If, for example, a child is fearful because her overinvolved father yells at her, and her father yells at her because his wife isn't emotionally involved, then changing the father's behavior might result in a different form of a symptomatic behavior in the child, unless the relationship with the wife is addressed.

Conditions for Behavior Change

As we've already indicated, group family therapists thought the way to bring about change was to help family members open up and talk to each other. The therapist encourages them to talk openly, supports those who seem reticent, and then critiques the process of their interaction. It is the power of the therapist's support that helps family members open up where they once held back, and this, in turn, often shows them in a new light, which enables others in the family to relate to them in new ways. For example, children who aren't accustomed to being listened to by grown-ups tend to make themselves "heard" by disruptive behavior. But if a therapist demonstrates willingness to listen, the children may learn to express their feelings in words rather than in actions. As they begin to interact with someone who takes them seriously, they may suddenly "grow up."

Group-oriented therapists promoted communication by concentrating on *process* rather than *content* (Bion, 1961; Yalom, 1985; Bell, 1975). This is an important point, and one easy to lose sight of. The minute a therapist gets caught up in the details of a family's problems or thinks about solving them, he or she may lose the opportunity to discover the process of what family members are doing that prevents them from working out their own solutions.

One of the ways therapists influence the process of family dialogue is to model listening. As the family members talk, the therapist listens intently, demonstrating to the speaker what it feels like to be heard and understood, and to other family members how not to interrupt, argue, or blame. After expression comes analysis. Once members of the family have a chance to express their feelings—and to be listened to—the family group therapist begins to explore why those feelings are present and why they were held back. The assumption was that what families can understand they can change.

If behavior is communication, then the way to change behavior is to change communication. According to the communications theorists, all events and actions have communicative properties: Symptoms can be considered as covert messages, commenting on relationships (Jackson, 1961). Even a headache that develops from prolonged tension in the occipital muscles is a message, since it is a report on how the person feels and also a command to be responded to. If a symptom is seen as a covert message, then by implication making the message overt eliminates the need for the symptom. Therefore one of the important ways to change behavior is to bring hidden messages out into the open.

As we pointed out above, an essential ingredient of the double bind is that it is impossible to escape or look at the binding situation from the outside. But no change can be generated from within; it can only come from outside the pattern. So, according to communications theorists (Watzlawick, Beavin, & Jackson, 1967), the paradigm for psychotherapy is an intervention from the outside to resolve relational dilemmas. The therapist is an outsider who supplies what the relationship cannot: a change in the rules.

From the outside position a therapist can either point out problematic sequences or simply manipulate them to effect therapeutic change. The first strategy relies on the power of insight and depends on a willingness to change, but the second does not; it's an attempt to beat families at their own games, with or without their cooperation. Included in the second strategy are many of the most clever and interesting tactics of communications therapy, and much more was written about these than about simple interpretation. Nevertheless, in the early days of family therapy, therapists relied more on the pointing out of communicational problems than on any other technique.

The first strategy, simply pointing out communicational problems, was represented in Virginia Satir's work and widely practiced by those new to family therapy. The second, less direct, approach was characteristic of Haley and Jackson and eventually became the predominant strategy. By the time they wrote *Pragmatics of Human Communication*, Watzlawick, Beavin, and Jackson (1967) believed that:

> Therapeutic communication, then, must necessarily transcend such counsel as is customarily but ineffectually given by the protagonists themselves, as well as their friends and relatives, [because] bona fide patients—by which we simply mean persons who are not deliberately simulating—usually have tried and failed in all kinds of self-discipline and exercises in will power long before they revealed their distress to others and were told to "pull themselves together." It is in the essence of a symptom that it is something unwilled and therefore autonomous. (pp. 236–237)

Therefore they recommended interventions to *make* people change. These manipulative strategies formed the basis of strategic family therapy (Chapter 11), which was an offshoot of communications theory.

Jackson and Haley's early work with families was influenced by the hypnotherapy they learned from Milton Erickson. The hypnotherapist works by giving explicit instructions whose purpose is often obscure. However, before patients will follow directions the therapist must gain control of the relationship. Jackson sometimes began by giving patients advice about their symptoms. He did so to point up the problem area, just as interpretation would do; but at the same time his comments made the patient focus on the relationship with the therapist—regardless of whether the patient accepted or rejected the advice. Haley (1961) recommended asking certain kinds of patients to do something in order to provoke a rebellious response, which served to make them concede that they were relating to the therapist. He mentions, as an example, directing a schizophrenic patient to hear voices. If the patient hears voices, then he is complying with the therapist's request; if he doesn't hear voices, then he can no longer claim to be crazy.

Haley's (1961) direction to hear voices illustrates the technique of *prescribing the symptom.* By instructing the patient to enact a symptomatic behavior the therapist is demanding that something "involuntary" be done voluntarily. This is a paradoxical injunction that forces one of two changes. Either the patient performs the symptom and thus admits that it isn't involuntary, or the patient gives up the symptom. Prescribing the symptom is a form of what the communications theorists called *therapeutic double binds* (Jackson, 1961). The same technique that drives people crazy was used to drive them sane.

Actually "therapeutic double bind" is somewhat loose usage because it doesn't necessarily involve two levels of message, one of which denies the other. To illustrate what he meant by a therapeutic double bind, Jackson (1961) cited the following case report.

> The patient was a young wife with a martyr complex, who felt that despite her best efforts to please her husband he just would not be satisfied. Jackson sensed that she was probably just "acting nice" in order to cover her intense, but unacceptable, rage at her husband. But the patient bridled when he even suggested that she might be "dissatisfied." In the face of this resistance, Jackson suggested that since her marriage was so important and since her husband's mood had such a profound effect on her, that she should learn to be *really* pleasing.
>
> By accepting the therapist's suggestion, the patient was admitting that she wasn't *really* pleasing. Moreover, she was forced to change.

In the above example, the patient was directed to change by doing more of the same. The object was to force the patient to step outside the frame set by her dilemma, with or without her awareness. In order to succeed, therapeutic double binds, or paradoxical injunctions, must be so cleverly designed as to leave no loopholes through which patients can escape.

According to Jackson's notion of family homeostasis, family systems regulate themselves by using symptoms as negative feedback to maintain their equilibrium. In this way, symptomatic families become caught in an increasingly inflexible set of patterns. The task of therapy was to loosen them up by introducing positive feedback to break up stability and equilibrium. The goal was to change the family system so that deviance was no longer necessary to preserve homeostasis. Timing was considered to be an important factor in how the family would respond to attempts to change them. At a period of steady-state equilibrium, families will resist change; at times of crisis, they are more likely to accept change.

The tactics of change employed by the communication therapists focused on altering discrete sequences of interaction that perpetuate symptomatic behavior. Despite their claims to include triadic sequences in their analyses (Sluzki, 1978), most of their interventions were limited to dyadic interactions.

Techniques

The techniques of family group therapy were similar to those of analytic and supportive group therapy. The role of the therapist was that of a *process leader.* The model of the family was a democratic group, and the therapist related to the family members democratically, just as the members were expected to do with each other. The therapist saw them as people with something to say, often in need of help saying it. There was little concern with structure and few attempts to reinforce the parents' hierarchical position. If anything, there was a tendency to give extra support to children and encourage them to assume a more equal role in family interactions.

John Bell's original approach (1961) was orchestrated in a series of stages. First was a *child-centered phase,* in which children were helped to express their wishes and concerns. Bell was so anxious to help children participate that he held preliminary meetings with parents to encourage them not only to listen but also to go along with some of the children's requests as a means of gaining their cooperation.

After the children spoke up and were rewarded with some additional privileges, it was the parents' turn. In the *parent-centered stage,* parents usually began by complaining about their children's behavior. During this phase, Bell was careful to soften the harshest of parental criticisms and to focus on problem-solving. In the final, or *family-centered,* stage, the group family therapist equalized support for the entire family while they continued to improve their communication and work out solutions to their problems. The following vignette illustrates Bell's (1975) directive style of intervening.

> After remaining silent for a few sessions, one father came in with a great tirade against his son, daughter, and wife. I noticed how each individual in his own way, within a few minutes, was withdrawing from the conference. Then I said, "Now I think we should hear what Jim has to say about this, and Nancy should have her say, and perhaps we should also hear what your wife feels about it." This restored family participation without closing out the father. (p. 136)

It also kept the therapist in charge, preventing him from seeing how the family handled their own confrontations and from possibly being in a position to point out problems in their way of handling things.

Anything that interfered with balanced self-expression was considered resistance and dealt with accordingly. Often this meant confronting nonverbal signs of unexpressed feeling. "Mr. Brown, you've been silent, but I wonder if your drumming your fingers is trying to tell us something."

Three specialized applications of group methods to family treatment were *multiple family group therapy, multiple impact therapy,* and *network therapy.*

Peter Laqueur began *multiple family group therapy* in 1950 at Creedmore State Hospital in New York and refined this approach at Vermont State Hospital (Laqueur, 1966, 1972a, 1972b, 1976). Multiple family group therapy involved the treatment of four to six families together for weekly sessions of ninety minutes. Laqueur and his cotherapists conducted multiple family groups like traditional therapy groups with the addition of encounter-group and psychodrama techniques. Structured exercises were used to increase the level of interaction and intensity of feeling; families were used as "cotherapists" to help confront members of other families from a more personal position than therapists could take.

Although multiple family therapy lost its most creative force with Peter Laqueur's untimely death, it is still occasionally used, especially in hospital settings, both inpatient (McFarlane, 1982) and outpatient (Gritzer & Okum, 1983).

Robert MacGregor and his colleagues at the University of Texas Medical Branch in Galveston developed *multiple impact therapy* as a way to have maximum impact on families who came from all over Texas to spend several days in intense therapy with a large team of professionals (MacGregor, Richie, Serrano, Schuster, McDonald, & Goolishian, 1964; MacGregor, 1967, 1972). Team members met with several combinations of family members and then assembled in a large group to review findings and make recommendations. Although multiple impact therapy is no longer practiced, its intense but infrequent meetings were a powerful stimulus for change and prefigured later developments in experiential therapy (Chapter 6) and the Milan model (Chapter 11).

Network therapy was an approach developed by Ross Speck and Carolyn Attneave for assisting families in crisis by assembling their entire social network—family, friends, neighbors—in gatherings of as many as fifty people. Teams of therapists were used with these large groups, and their emphasis was on breaking up destructive patterns of relationship and mobilizing support for new options (Speck & Attneave, 1973; Ruevini, 1975).

Therapeutic teams meet with networks in meetings lasting from two to four hours; groups typically meet three to six times. Encounter group techniques are used to alleviate defensiveness and foster a climate of warm involvement. After five or ten minutes of shaking hands, jumping up and down, shouting, huddling together, and swaying back and forth, the group experiences a release of tension and a sense of cohesiveness.

The polarization phase begins when the leader identifies and activates conflicting points of view in the network. These may be dramatized by arranging people into concentric circles and inviting them to confront their differences. Under the guidance of the leaders, confrontation is moved toward compromise and synthesis. During the mobilization phase, tasks are presented, and subgroups of involved and active members are asked to develop plans for solving concrete problems. If the identified patient needs a job, a committee might be formed to help; if young parents are stuck at home fighting over who's going to take care of the baby, a group might be asked to develop babysitting resources and allow the couple to get out together.

After the initial enthusiasm wears off, network groups often fall into exhaustion and despair as members begin to realize just how entrenched certain problems are and how difficult it is to resolve them. Uri Ruevini (1975) described one case in which a period of depression set in and the problem family felt isolated and abandoned by the network. Ruevini broke through this impasse by prescribing a cathartic encounter group exercise, "the death ceremony." Family members were asked to close their eyes and imagine themselves dead. The rest of the network were asked to share their feelings about the family: their strengths, their weaknesses, and what each of them meant to their friends. This dramatic device produced an outpouring of feeling that roused the network out of depression.

Speck and Attneave (1973) described breaking the network into problem-solving subgroups, using action instead of affect to move beyond despair. In one case they assigned a group of friends to watch over an adolescent who was abusing drugs and another group to arrange for him to move out of his parents' house. Breakthrough is achieved when the network's energies are unleashed and directed toward active resolution of problems. Network sessions often produce what Speck and Attneave called the "network effect"—a feeling of euphoric connectedness and the satisfaction of solving problems once thought to be overwhelming. Once a network has been activated, there's always someone to call when the need arises.

Communications therapists wrote a great deal about theory before they began applying their ideas to treatment, and even after they began to describe their work with families, most of their publications had a distinctly theoretical flavor. As a result, communications family therapists appear to have had more emotional distance from the families they worked with than other early family therapists. Communications therapy seems to have been done *to* families, more than *with* them.

Formal assessment was typically not used by communications therapists, although Watzlawick (1966) did introduce a *structured family interview.* In this procedure, families were given five tasks to complete, including:

1. Deciding their main problem
2. Planning a family outing
3. The parents discussing how they met
4. Discussing the meaning of a proverb
5. Identifying faults and placing the blame on the correct person

While the family worked on these tasks, the therapist, watching behind a one-way mirror, observed the family's patterns of communication, methods of decision making, and scapegoating. Although it was useful for research, the structured family interview never gained wide acceptance as a clinical tool.

Most of the actual techniques of communications family therapy consisted of teaching rules of clear communication, analyzing and interpreting communicational patterns, and manipulating interactions through a variety of strategic maneuvers. The progression of these three strategies from more straightforward to more strategic reflected the growing awareness of how families resist change.

In their early work (Jackson & Weakland, 1961), communications therapists opened by indicating their belief that the whole family was involved in the presenting problem. Then they explained that all families develop habitual patterns of communication, including some that are problematical. This attempt to convert families from seeing the identified patient as the problem to accepting mutual responsibility underestimated families' resistance to change. Later these therapists were more likely to begin by asking for and accepting a family's own definition of their problems (Haley, 1976).

After the therapists made their opening remarks, they asked family members, usually one at a time, to discuss their problems. The therapist listened but concentrated on the process of communication, rather than on the content. When someone in the family spoke in a confused or confusing way, the therapist would point this out and insist on certain rules of clear communication. Satir (1964) was the most straightforward teacher. When someone said something that was unclear, she would question and clarify the message, and as she did so she impressed on the family basic guidelines for clear speaking.

One rule is that people should always speak in the first person singular when saying what they think or feel. For example:

HUSBAND: We always liked Donna's boyfriends.

THERAPIST: I'd like you to speak for yourself; later your wife can say what she thinks.

HUSBAND: Yes, but we've always agreed on these things.

THERAPIST: Perhaps, but you are the expert on how you think and feel. Speak for yourself, and let her speak for herself.

A similar rule is that people should make personal statements ("I-statements") about personal matters. Opinions and value judgments should be acknowledged as that, not passed off as facts or general principles. Owning opinions, as such, is a necessary step to discussing them in a way that permits legitimate differences of opinion, much less the possibility of changing opinions.

WIFE: People shouldn't want to do things without their children.

THERAPIST: So you like to bring the kids along when you and your husband go out?

WIFE: Well yes, doesn't everybody?

HUSBAND: I don't. I'd like to go out, just the two of us, once in a while.

Another rule is that people should speak directly to, not about, each other. This avoids ignoring or disqualifying family members and prevents the establishment of destructive coalitions. For example:

TEENAGER: (To therapist) My mother always has to be right. Isn't that so, Dad?

THERAPIST: Would you say that to her?

TEENAGER: I have, but she doesn't listen.

THERAPIST: Tell her again.

TEENAGER: (To therapist) Oh, okay. (To mother) Sometimes I get the feeling . . . (Shifts back to therapist) Oh, what's the use!

THERAPIST: I can see how hard it is, and I guess you've kind of decided that it's no use try-

> ing to talk to your mom if she isn't going to listen. But in here, I hope we can all learn to speak more directly to each other, so that no one will give up on having his or her say.

As this exchange illustrates, it's difficult to teach people to communicate clearly just by telling them how. It seemed like a good idea, but it didn't work very well. The reason a directive approach to family therapy persists at all is that, with enough insisting, most people will follow therapeutic directions, at least as long as the therapist is there to insist.

In the early days of communications family therapy, Virginia Satir was probably the most transparent and directive therapist, and Jay Haley was the least; Don Jackson occupied a position somewhere in between.

When he began treating families of schizophrenics, Jackson thought he needed to protect patients from their families (Jackson & Weakland, 1961) but came to realize that parents and children were all bound together in mutually destructive ways. Even now those who are new to family therapy, especially if they themselves haven't yet become parents, tend to identify with the children and see the parents as the bad guys. Not only is this wrong, as Jackson himself later realized, it alienates parents and drives them out of treatment. Young therapists often begin "knowing" that parents are to blame for most of their children's problems. Only later, when they become parents themselves, do they achieve a more balanced perspective—namely, that family problems are all the children's fault.

Jackson emphasized the need for structure and control in family meetings. He began first sessions by saying, "We are here to work together on better understanding one another so that you all can get more out of your family life" (Jackson & Weakland, 1961, p. 37). Not only does this remark structure the meeting, it also conveys the idea that all members of the family are to become the focus of discussion. Furthermore it reveals the therapist's intentions and may, therefore, precipitate a struggle with parents who have come only to help the patient and may resent the implication that they are part of the problem. Thus we see that Jackson was an active therapist who set the rules right at the outset and explained openly what he was doing in order to anticipate and disarm resistance. Today most family therapists find it more effective to be subtler, meeting families' resistance not with psychological karate but with jujitsu—using their own momentum for leverage, instead of opposing them head on.

Jackson may have found it so difficult to deal with schizophrenic families that he became active and intrusive to avoid being caught up in their craziness. In any case, there is a suggestion of combativeness in his writings, as though he saw himself battling families, beating them at their own game (Jackson & Weakland, 1961), using dual or multiple messages, provoking them to do something in defiance of therapeutic directives whose real purpose may be concealed (therapeutic double binds).

If Jackson was subtly combative with families, Jay Haley wasn't subtle about it. He was clear and explicit in defining therapy as a battle for control.[1] Haley believed that therapists need to maneuver into a position of power over their patients in order to manipulate them into changing. Although the notion of manipulation may have unpleasant connotations, moral criticism should be reserved for those who use patients covertly for their own ends, rather than used against those who seek the most effective means of helping patients achieve their goals.

In *Strategies of Psychotherapy*, Haley (1963) described the marital relationship in terms of conflicting levels of communication. Conflicts occur not only over what rules a couple will follow in dealing with each other, but also over who sets the rules. Couples may be complementary in some spheres and symmetrical in others.

[1]Haley has continued to develop and revise his thinking and, today, he is far from this blunt and provocative. See Chapter 11 on strategic family therapy for a description of Haley's contemporary work.

But the complexity goes still further; although it may appear that a wife dominates a dependent husband, the husband may, in fact, provoke the wife to be dominating, thus himself controlling the type of relationship they have. Sometimes it takes a coward to make a bully.

Although Haley's analysis of human relations was highly intellectual and rational, he believed that family members can't be rational about their problems. He probably exaggerated people's inability to understand their own behavior. His therapy therefore tended to be done *to* patients rather than *with* them. Although Haley criticized to the point of ridicule the idea that insight is curative, he put a lot of faith in simple openness of communication as a way of dealing with family problems.

According to Haley the mere presence of a third person, the therapist, helps couples solve their problems. By dealing fairly with each spouse and not taking sides, the therapist disarms the usual blaming maneuvers; in other words, the therapist acts as a referee. In addition to being a referee, the communications therapist relabeled or redefined the activity of family members with each other. One strategy was to redefine what family members say, stressing the positive aspects of their relationship. "For example," Haley (1963) said, "if a husband is protesting his wife's constant nagging, the therapist might comment that the wife seems trying to reach her husband and achieve more closeness with him. If the wife protests that her husband constantly withdraws from her, the husband might be defined as one who wants to avoid discord and seeks an amiable relationship" (p. 139). This technique was later to be called *reframing* and to become a central feature of strategic therapy.

One of Haley's strategies was to make explicit the implicit rules that govern family relationships. Dysfunctional rules made explicit become more difficult to follow. For example, some wives berate their husbands for not expressing themselves, but the wives talk so much and criticize so loudly that the husbands hardly have a chance. If the therapist points this out, it becomes more difficult to follow the implicit rule that the husband should not talk. Haley believed that disagreements about which rules to follow are relatively easily solved through discussion and compromise. Conflicts about who is to set rules are stickier and require that the therapist be less straightforward. Because the issue of control is too explosive to be dealt with openly, Haley recommended subtle directives.

Haley's directives were of two sorts: suggestions to behave differently and suggestions to continue to behave the same. Straightforward advice, he said, rarely works. When it does, it's likely that the conflict is minor or that the couple is moving in that direction anyway. Some of Haley's directives are for changes that seem so small that the full ramifications aren't immediately apparent. In a couple, for example, where the wife seems to have her own way most of the time, the husband is asked to say "no" on some minor issue once during the week. This seems trivial, but it accomplishes two things: It makes the husband practice speaking up for himself, and it makes the wife aware that she's been domineering. (Unfortunately, it also seems to blame the wife for problems in the relationship.) This small beginning gives both partners a chance to work on changing their part of the interaction. The fact that they're doing so under therapeutic direction often, though not always, makes them more likely to follow the advice.

Haley's suggestion that family members continue to behave in the same way was, in fact, a therapeutic paradox. When a rebellious teenager is instructed to "continue to rebel," he or she is caught in a paradoxical position. Continuing to rebel means following the direction of an authority figure (and admitting that what you're doing is "rebellious"). Only by giving up this behavior can the teenager maintain the illusion of freedom. Meanwhile the problematic behavior ceases. Sometimes it's effective to have one partner suggest that the other continue symptomatic behavior. This may produce a major shift because it alters who defines the nature of the relationship.

Lessons from the Early Models

The most important contribution from group studies to family therapy was the idea that all groups, including families, have emergent properties. When people join together to form a group, relational processes emerge that reflect not only the individuals involved but also their collective patterns of interaction, known as *group dynamics*. Family therapists used systems theory to elaborate the nature of these interpersonal forces. Among the group dynamics that family therapists deal with are triangulation, scapegoating, alignments, coalitions, and splits.

Group theorists also taught us the importance of roles, official and unofficial, and how roles organize behavior in groups. Family therapists draw on role theory when they support and enhance parents in their role as leaders or point out how covert roles can detract from group functioning, such as how a father who constantly plays the role of jokester undermines his wife and distracts the family group from discussing and solving problems. Family therapists also help family members realize how certain rigid roles trap them into narrow and inflexible performances, such as when teenagers play counterconformist and are so busy *not* being their parents that they never figure out how to be themselves.

The process/content distinction was also profoundly important to family therapists. When families seek help, they expect expert information and help solving their problems. They might want to know how to encourage a shy youngster to make friends or how to get a defiant teenager to show more respect. But what the family therapist tries to figure out is: Why hasn't the family been able to solve their own problems? What about the way they've been going about it isn't working? Therefore, when the family discusses their problems, the therapist listens as much to the process of the discussion—who speaks to whom and in what way—as to the content of what they're saying.

The shift from attending to what people say to how they say it—openly or defensively, cooperatively or competitively—is one of the important strategies of all forms of therapy. Another way of saying this is that most family therapists focus on the here-and-now, bringing problems into the consulting room in the form of the way family members relate to one another.

The primary group therapy technique—promoting free and open discussion—helped family therapists encourage dialogue and mutual understanding in families. But although helping families talk over their problems may enable them to resolve a minor crisis, mere conversation is rarely sufficient to solve more difficult problems. Moreover, the model of a democratic group on which this technique is predicated overlooked the unique structural properties of families. Unlike therapy groups, families are *not* made up of equals. Every member of a family may have an equal right to his or her feelings and point of view, but someone has to be in charge. Therapists who speak first to children or who invite everyone in the family to have an equal say fail to respect the family's need for leadership and hierarchy.

The other major technique used by group therapists is the process interpretation, of which Bell (1961) delineated four varieties: *Reflective interpretations* describe what's going on at the moment: "I notice that when your wife says something critical, you just hang your head, as if to say 'Poor me.' " *Connective interpretations* point out unrecognized links between different actions among family members: "Have you noticed that Jenny starts to misbehave the minute you two start to argue?" *Reconstructive interpretations* explain how events in the family's history provide the context for current experience. *Normative interpretations* are remarks designed to support or challenge a family member by comparing that person to what most people do: "Big deal, most teenagers are sassy with their parents. It's part of growing up."

The most obvious comment we can make about process interpretations is that simply pointing out what family members are doing may not help them to see that their behavior isn't productive, or to change it. Therapists make interpretations to be helpful, but the people at whom the interpretations are directed often feel such comments as hurtful, as if the therapist were saying, "Look what you're doing; it's wrong—*you're* wrong."

The real reason people don't usually change when something is pointed out to them isn't that they are mindless puppets of a family system, but that even constructive criticism often feels more critical than constructive. Family therapists, already inimical to the analytic approach, came to doubt the usefulness of interpretation, even to mock insight in favor of action. They did so because they believed that individuals were often powerless over the systemic forces of their families. In hindsight it seems that, although individual change is often complicated by the actions of others, it isn't true that family members lack the capacity to reflect on the consequences of their behavior—depending on how it is pointed out to them. Perhaps the same respect for people's capacity to understand and change their behavior might lead therapists to rephrase interpretative comments so that they sound more like permission to be honest than like an attack. Maybe people *can* learn hard truths, when they're told with respect.

Group family therapists were directive to the extent of encouraging people to speak up when they appeared to have something to say; otherwise they were relatively passive and confined themselves to describing the interactional motifs they saw in families. In therapy groups of strangers, with contrasting defenses and personality styles, therapists can act as catalysts to prompt members to confront and challenge each other. Families, however, share defenses and pathological attitudes, and therapists can't rely on other group members to challenge family norms. That's why contemporary family therapists, who treat families more actively, confront family patterns of interaction (rather than individual reticence) and look for ways to circumvent defenses that are more powerful in families than in groups of strangers.

The three specialized applications of group methods considered in this chapter—multiple family group therapy, multiple impact therapy, and network therapy—were experiments of the 1960s. Treating more than one family at the same time allows members of one family to see how others deal with similar problems. However, when there are other families present to serve as distractions, it's hard to focus on entrenched or anxiety-arousing problems for any length of time or depth. What works in group therapy may not work with families.

Both multiple impact therapy and network therapy brought tremendous resources to bear on families stuck in crisis. Although family therapists in clinics often work in teams, today we usually rely on one therapist to treat a family. Perhaps there are times when it makes sense to launch the all-out effort that multiple impact therapy represented. The additional advantage of network therapy was that the resources it mobilized were the natural resources of a family's community. Perhaps this model is still useful: It uses community resources that are still available after treatment is over, and it's a useful antidote to the isolation of many families.

Communications family therapy was one of the first and most influential forms of family treatment. Its theoretical development was closely tied to general systems theory, and the therapy that emerged was a systems approach *par excellence.* Communication was the detectable input and output therapists used to analyze the black box of interpersonal systems. Communication was described as feedback, as a tactic in interpersonal power struggles, and as symptoms. In fact, all behavior was considered communication. The trouble is, when all actions are treated as communication, then communications analysis may be taken to mean everything, and therefore nothing. Human relations aren't all a matter of communication; communication may be the matrix in which interactions are embedded, but human interactions have other attributes as well—love, hate, fear, conflict.

The Bateson group may be best remembered for the concept of the double bind, but their enduring contribution was that of applying communications analysis to a wide range of behavior, including family dynamics. In fact, the idea of *metacommunication* is a much more useful concept than that of the double bind, and it has been incorporated not only by family therapists but also by the general public. Whether or not they are familiar with the term metacommunication, most people understand that all messages have both report and command functions.

Another of the most significant ideas of communications therapy is that families are rule-governed systems, maintained by homeostatic, negative feedback mechanisms. Negative feedback accounts for the stability of normal families and the inflexibility of dysfunctional ones. Because such families don't have adequate positive feedback mechanisms, they're unable to adjust to changing circumstances.

Communications theorists borrowed the open systems model from general systems theory, but their clinical interventions were based on the closed systems paradigm of cybernetics. This is another example of how this approach was more useful theoretically than pragmatically. In their clinical descriptions, relationships were portrayed as struggles for power and control. Haley emphasized the power struggle between spouses; Watzlawick said that the major problem of control in families is cognitive. Therapy was conceived as a power struggle in which the therapist takes control to outwit the forces of symptom maintenance.

When communication takes place in a closed system—an individual's fantasies or a family's private conversations—there's little opportunity for adjusting the system. Only when someone outside the system provides input can correction occur. This is the premise on which communications family therapy was based. Because the rules of family functioning are largely unknown to the family, the best way to examine and correct them is to consult an expert in communications.

While there were major differences among the therapeutic strategies of Haley, Jackson, Satir, and Watzlawick, they were all committed to altering self-reinforcing and mutually destructive patterns of communication. They pursued this goal by direct and indirect means. The direct approach, favored by Satir, sought change by making family rules explicit and by teaching clear communication. This approach could be described as establishing ground rules, or metacommunicational principles, and included such tactics as telling people to speak for themselves and pointing out nonverbal and multileveled channels of communication.

The trouble is, as Haley noted, "One of the difficulties involved in telling patients to do something is the fact that psychiatric patients are noted for their hesitation about doing what they are told." For this reason, communications therapists began to rely on more indirect strategies, designed to provoke change rather than to foster awareness. Telling family members to speak for themselves, for example, may challenge a family rule and therefore meet with strong resistance. With this realization, communications therapy began a treatment of resistance.

Resistance and symptoms were treated with a variety of paradoxical directives, known loosely as "therapeutic double binds." Milton Erickson's technique of prescribing resistance was used as a lever to gain control, as, for example, when a therapist tells family members not to reveal everything in the first session. The same ploy was used to prescribe symptoms, an action that made unrecognized rules explicit, implied that such behavior was voluntary, and put the therapist in control.

Eventually communications therapy became symptom-focused, brief, and directive. The focus on symptoms is consistent with the general systems concept of *equifinality*, which means that no matter where systems change begins, the final result is the same. Moreover, even when they convened whole families, communications therapists focused on the marital pair; they were always more adept with dyadic than triadic thinking.

Today the theories of communications therapy have been absorbed into the mainstream of family therapy and the symptom-focused interventions became the basis of the strategic and solution-focused models. Unfortunately, when group and communications therapists were confounded by the obdurate inflexibility of families, they may have exaggerated the irrational power of the family system.

System's Anxiety[2]

Therapists first encountered the family as a powerful adversary. Freud's discoveries indicted families as seducers of innocent children and, later, as agents of cultural repression, the source of all guilt and anxiety. Hospital psychiatrists also saw patients as victims of their families and, except for purposes of footing the bill, kept the family at arm's length. Child guidance workers approached domestic life with a built-in prejudice. Their vision that flawed relations in the family held the key to psychopathology was blurred by their loyalty to their child patients, with whom they identified. Bent on saving the child, they saw mothers as enemies to be overcome and fathers as peripheral figures to be ignored.

Communications family therapists rescued schizophrenics from psychiatric invalidation by demonstrating that their crazy conversation made sense as a desperate solution to desperate family situations. It wasn't the patient but the family system that was deranged. Family therapy aimed to humanize mental illness, but it created a nonhuman, mechanistic entity—the system—to do so.

In their efforts to make individual family members unrepressed agents in their own right, practicing therapists ran smack into powerful family opposition to personal autonomy. The individual may want to get better, but the family may need someone to play the sick role. Some families apparently require a "scapegoat" to maintain their equilibrium; the patient's sickness becomes necessary for the family's precarious health. This led Don Jackson to characterize families as "rule-governed homeostatic systems." Little noticed at the time was how this description portrayed patients as helpless and passive victims, while attention (as well as blame) was shifted to the family.

The Bateson group's observations were meant to be scientific, yet their language for describing family systems was combative and bellicose, often suggesting not just resistance, but willful opposition to change. The idea that families were oppositional put family therapists in an adversarial stance. Because families were seen as mindless systems, at once rigid (holding fast to their own ways) and slippery (hard to pin down), interviewing them became a struggle for strategic advantage.

Even when family therapists got past the naive idea that patients were innocent victims of malevolent kinfolk, they felt themselves in opposition to families who stubbornly resisted well-meaning efforts to change them.

The shift from working with individuals to working with families was discontinuous and required new ways of thinking. Therapists, unused to seeing whole families interacting, eagerly imported nonclinical models to help them conceptualize patterned interactions.

Cybernetics and general systems theory provided useful metaphors to help clinicians

[2]The ideas in this section were adapted from *The Self in the System* (Nichols, 1987).

organize some of the patterned interactions of family life. Describing the family as a system helped them see that a group of interacting personalities can function like a composite entity, a unit. Families were said to be like systems in that the behavior of every member is related to and dependent on the behavior of all the others.

The great advance of systemic thinking was the recognition that people's lives are linked together such that behavior in families becomes a product of mutual influence. The danger of forgetting that systems metaphors are just that is the danger of overestimating their influence—and of dehumanizing individual family members. One myth of the system is that it is determinative rather than influential. Thus, for example, an overinvolved mother who steps back makes room for her husband to become more involved, but this shift in the system doesn't *make* him get involved. By the same token, while it may be difficult for a disengaged parent to spend more time with the children as long as they are enmeshed with the other parent, it isn't impossible.

The systems metaphor was thought to have the advantage of shifting blame away from individuals who were seen as caught up in the systemic structure of their families. Avoiding blame and fault-finding is all to the good, but denying the possibility of self-determination may not be so good. The danger here is the danger of mechanism.

Systems thinking deals with action—really behavior—but often with little distinction between human action and physical movement. An act is seen as the causal outcome of a mechanistic interaction of elemental "systemic forces." Therapy, therefore, can and should be arational. The truth is that action is also rational, mediated by individuals and their creation of meaning—and responsibility. Much of what we do is automatic and channeled by patterns of interaction. But although we don't always reflect and act rationally, we sometimes do. We aren't just links in a circular chain of events; we are people with names who experience ourselves as centers of initiative. Certainly we are linked to others. Much of what we do is with other people in mind, some of what we do is with others, and once in a while for others. But the "we" who are the authors of the doing are single organisms, with hearts and minds and bodies all encased within our skin.

Family therapists taught us that our behavior is controlled in unseen but powerful ways by the actions of those around us. Family rules and roles operate as invisible constraints influencing all that we do. The idea that people behave as they do because they are induced to live out defined roles can have a liberating effect; if one is playing a role, it's possible to play a new one. For example, modifying roles of manhood and womanhood that were based on sexual stereotypes permits a broader and more authentic definition of self. If overextended, however, this kind of thinking implies that the role is everything.

Systems thinking in the extreme dismisses selfhood as an illusion. The problem is when roles become reified and rigidified as prescribed determinants of behavior *and* as independent of personal agency. Systems thinkers unfortunately implied that the role plays the person, rather than the other way around. But whether they act in concert or separately, it is finally the selves in the system who must act to bring about change.

Early family therapists treated the family as a *cybernetic system* that governs itself through feedback. Perhaps they overemphasized negative feedback, which makes families resist change and maintain homeostasis, in part because they were studying schizophrenic families, who tend to be particularly rigid, and in part because they were reacting against the prevailing psychodynamic focus on the mental life of the individual. Nevertheless, as we came to realize, although systems thinking alerts us to our interconnections, the metaphor of an inanimate system is not an adequate model for human systems. When we think systemically, we realize that individuals are systems within systems, and that although they respond to forces outside themselves, they are also initiators, with imagination, abstract reasoning, creativity, memory, and desire.

The Stages of Family Therapy[3]

The Initial Telephone Call

The goal of the initial contact is to get a minimal amount of information and arrange for the entire family to come for a consultation. Listen briefly to the caller's description of the presenting problem and then identify all members of the household and others who might be involved (including the referral source and other agencies). Then arrange for the first interview, specifying who will attend (usually everyone in the household) and the date, time, and place.

The reason for speaking only briefly to the caller is to avoid becoming caught up in one person's point of view about the problem (which is usually linear and blaming). The only uncomplicated calls are those explicitly requesting family therapy, such as a husband or wife asking for couples therapy or worried parents who expect to participate in the treatment of their child. In most cases, however, people calling for help think of one person as "the problem" and expect treatment to be focused on that person.

While there are things you can learn to say to convert requests for individual therapy into family cases, the most important consideration is attitudinal. First, understand and respect that the parent who wants you to treat his or her child individually or the partner who wants to talk to you alone has a perfectly legitimate point of view, even if it doesn't happen to agree with yours. Second, if you expect to meet with the whole family, your intention to do so and calm insistence that that is necessary, at least for the initial session, will get most families to agree to a consultation. It's not so much not knowing what to say as being anxious and uncertain about the need to meet with the entire group that makes beginning therapists have a hard time convincing families to come in together. (One way to decrease the no-show rate is to help novice therapists avoid feeling relief when the family doesn't show up.)

When the caller presents the problem as limited to one person, a useful way to broaden the complaint is to ask how it affects other members of the family. If the caller balks at the idea of bringing in the whole family or says that a particular family member won't attend, say that you'll need to hear from everyone, at least initially, in order to get as much information as possible. Most people accept the need to give their point of view; what they resist is any implication that they're to blame for the problem—or in some cases, even that they are involved.

When a child is the identified patient, parents may be willing to come but reluctant to bring siblings whom they consider well-adjusted. Like the "uninvolved husband" who's "too busy" to attend, nonsymptomatic brothers and sisters may be important to help broaden the focus from the identified patient's failings to relationship issues in the entire family.

Broadening the focus does not, however, mean broadening the blame. Family members can often acknowledge a role in problematic family patterns if they sense that the therapist genuinely respects them and isn't looking to pin all the responsibility on one person. And it certainly isn't necessary or useful to get family members to openly admit their involvement in the problem; what's important is getting everyone to work together toward a solution.

Although the goal of the first telephone contact is primarily to arrange for a face-to-face meeting with the family, the clinician needs to find out if there are any circumstances that might preclude his or her ability to work with the family. Although many young therapists are equally expert on every imaginable problem, experienced therapists learn that there are some problems they aren't equipped to deal with, for example, severe eating disorders or active alcohol or drug abuse.

[3]The following attempt to describe how family therapists typically conduct treatment at times reflects the senior author's background in structural family therapy.

(Not all family therapists routinely meet with the entire family. Some find they have more room to maneuver by meeting with individuals or subgroups in the initial meeting and then gradually involving others. Others attempt to work with what the late Harry Goolishian called the "problem-determined system," not necessarily the family but everyone intimately affected by the problem. Still others try to determine who are the "customers"—namely, those people who seem most concerned. If the therapist suspects violence or abuse, confidential individual sessions may enable family members to reveal what they might not dare to discuss in front of the whole family. The point to remember is that family therapy is more a way of looking at things than a treatment technique based on seeing families.)

Finally, because *most* families are reluctant to sit down together and face their conflicts, a reminder call before the first session helps cut down on the no-show rate.

The First Interview

The goal of the first interview is to build an alliance with the family and develop a hypothesis about what's maintaining the presenting problem. It's a good idea to come up with a tentative hypothesis (in technical terms, a "hunch") after the initial phone call, and then to test it in the first interview. (In order to avoid imposing pet theories on patient families, recreating them in the image of one's own bias, it's important to remain open to refuting, not just confirming, one's initial hypothesis.) The point isn't to jump to conclusions, but to start actively thinking.

The first objective of a consultation is to establish rapport. Unlike people who request individual psychotherapy, family members often don't think that they are part of the problem, and many don't want to be there. The key to building an alliance is to accept people where they are, to listen respectfully to their points of view and appreciate their attitudes. Few people will put up with anyone's attempt to change them before they feel understood and accepted as they are.

Introduce yourself to the contact person and then to other adults in the household. Ask parents to introduce their children. Shake hands and greet everyone present. Orient the family to the room (e.g., observation mirrors, videotaping, toys for children) and to the format of the session (length and purpose). Repeat *briefly* (a sentence or two) what the caller told you over the phone (so as not to leave others wondering), and then ask for elaboration. Once you've heard and acknowledged that person's point of view ("So what you're saying is . . . ?"), ask each succeeding member of the family for their viewpoint.

At this stage, the objective is to hear from each person one at a time, and therefore arguments or interruptions should be politely but firmly blocked ("Excuse me, but I need to hear from each of you one at a time"). By listening to each person's perspective on the presenting problem, the therapist gathers information and establishes rapport.

While most of the session should be taken up with a discussion of the major problem, this negative focus can have a disheartening effect, and therefore spending some time exploring family members' interests, accomplishments, and strengths is never wasted and sometimes changes the emotional energy of sessions dramatically.

Strive for a balance between warmth and professionalism. Being friendly and accepting doesn't, however, mean spending a great deal of time making small talk, as though this were a social visit. Respectful interest in the family's problems and individual members' points of view is the best way to build trust.

In gathering information, some therapists find it useful to take a family history, and many use *genograms* to diagram the extended family network. Others believe that whatever facts are essential will emerge in the natural course of events and prefer to concentrate on the family's presenting concerns and the circumstances surrounding them. (Why search history for an answer that only the living expression of it can give?)

Family therapists develop hypotheses about how family members might be involved in the presenting problem by asking them how they've attempted to solve it, and by watching how they interact as they discuss it among themselves.

Two kinds of information *(content)* that are particularly important are solutions that don't work and transitions in the life cycle to which the family hasn't yet adjusted. If whatever the family has been doing to solve their problems hasn't worked, then it may be that those attempts are part of the problem. A typical example would be overinvolved parents trying to help a shy child make friends by spending a lot of time coaxing, criticizing, and controlling her. Sometimes family members will say they've "tried everything" to solve their problems and then list the full gamut of possible responses. In this case, the problem may be inconsistency. They try everything but give up too quickly in the face of opposition.

Despite the natural tendency to focus on problems and what causes them, it is a family's strengths, not their weaknesses, that will be most important in successful therapy. Therefore the therapist should search for resilience, accentuating the positive and hope. What have these people been doing well? How have they successfully handled difficulties in the past? What would a hopeful future look like? Even the most discouraged families have had times where they were successful, even though those positive episodes are obscured by the frustration they feel over their current difficulties. By simply asking about family successes and what was different about those occasions, therapists may find that clients have more resources than they give themselves credit for. Successful therapy isn't so much about finding out what's wrong as it is about discovering and releasing unused human potential.

Although it isn't always immediately apparent (especially to them), most families seek treatment because they have failed to adjust to changing circumstances. If a husband or a wife develops problems within the first few months after a baby's birth, it may be because the couple hasn't shifted effectively from being a unit of two to being a unit of three. A young mother may be depressed because she doesn't have enough support (from her husband or extended family or friends) for meeting the consuming demands of caring for a new baby. A young father may feel neglected, jealous of all the time and attention his wife now lavishes on the baby and hurt that she seems too tired to do anything with him when they do have time.

Although the strain on a couple of having a new baby seems obvious, you'd be amazed at how often depressed young mothers are treated by therapists as though there were something wrong with them—"unresolved dependency needs," perhaps, or maybe a Prozac deficiency. The same is true when families develop problems around the time a child enters school or reaches adolescence, or any other developmental shift: The transitional demands on the family are obvious, *if* you think about them.

Novice family therapists may be in their twenties or thirties and have no personal experience with some of the life transitions their clients are struggling with. Where this is the case, it underscores the need for the therapist to remain curious and respectful of a family's predicament rather than jump to uninformed conclusions. For example, as a young single man Richard Schwartz couldn't understand why so many client couples with young children rarely went out on dates together any more. He assumed that they were overly focused on their children and afraid of being alone together. Subsequent events in his own life taught him differently. With small children of his own, he now wonders how those couples got out so often!

Family therapists explore the *process* of family interaction by asking questions to get at how family members relate to each other and by inviting them to discuss their problems with one another in the session. The first strategy, asking "process" or "circular" questions, is favored by Bowenians and systemic therapists; the second, by structural therapists. In either case, the key question for the therapist is: What's keeping the family stuck? What is the force keeping them from adapting to the pressures of development and change? What's interfering with their natural problem-solving abilities?

Once they have met the family, learned about the problem that brings them to treatment, made an effort to understand the family's context, and developed a conjecture about what needs to be done to resolve the problem, therapists should make a recommendation to the family. This may include consulting another professional (a therapist who specializes in the problem the family presents with, a learning disability expert, a medical doctor, a lawyer) or even suggesting that the family doesn't need—or doesn't seem ready to profit from—treatment. Most often, however, the recommendation will be for a course of family therapy. Although most therapists try to make their recommendation at the end of the first interview, this may be hasty. If it takes two sessions to form a bond with the family, understand their situation, and find out if you can work with them, then take two sessions.

If you think you can help the family solve their problem, then offer them a treatment contract. Acknowledge why they came in, say that it was a good idea, and say that you can help. Then negotiate a regular meeting time, the frequency and length of sessions, who will attend, the presence of observers or use of videotape, the fee, and how insurance is handled. Remember that family resistance doesn't magically disappear after the first (or fourteenth) session: So stress the importance of regular meetings and the need for everyone to attend. Finally, don't forget to emphasize the family's goals and the strengths you have observed in people to meet them.

First Session Checklist

1. Make contact with each member of the family and acknowledge his or her point of view about the problem and feelings about coming to therapy.
2. Establish leadership by controlling the structure and pace of the interview.
3. Develop a working alliance with the family by balancing warmth and professionalism.
4. Compliment family members on specific positive actions and family strengths.
5. Maintain empathy with individuals and respect for the family's way of doing things.
6. Focus on specific problems and attempted solutions.
7. Develop hypotheses about unhelpful interactions around the presenting problem. Be curious about why these have persisted.
8. Don't overlook the possible involvement of family members, friends, or helpers who aren't present.
9. Negotiate a treatment contract that acknowledges the family's goals and specifies the therapist's framework for structuring treatment.
10. Ask if family members have any questions.

The Early Phase of Treatment

The early phase of treatment is devoted to refining the therapist's hypothesis into a formulation about what's maintaining the problem and beginning to work on resolving it. Now the strategy shifts from an emphasis on alliance building and accommodating the family to challenging them to produce change. Most therapists are able to figure out what needs to change. Once you have the whole family present, their inadvertent mistakes are often glaringly obvious. What sets good therapists apart is their ability to push for change forcefully.

Some therapists prefer to avoid confrontation and find it more effective to work indirectly. However, regardless of whether they work directly (and at times use confrontation) or indirectly (and avoid it), good therapists are finishers. Strategies and techniques may vary, but what sets the best therapists apart is their personal commitment to do what it takes to see families through to successful resolution of their problems.

Effective family therapy addresses interpersonal conflict, and the first step (especially in structural family therapy) is to bring it into the consulting room and put it between family members. Often this is not a problem. Couples in conflict or parents feuding with their children will usually speak right up about their disagreements. If the family is in therapy not because they want to be but because someone sent them (the court, the school, the Department of Protective Services), the therapist begins by addressing the family's problem dealing with these outside agencies. How must the family change so as to resolve their conflict with these agencies? How must the family change so that its members won't be in trouble?

When one person is presented as the problem, the therapist challenges linearity by asking others how they are involved (or affected). What was their role in creating (or managing) the problem? How have they responded to it?

For example: "The problem is Johnny. He's disobedient." "Who taught him to be disobedient?" Or, "How does he get away with that?"

Less confrontive therapists might ask: "When do you notice this?" "What does he do that seems disobedient?" "How does this disobedience affect you?"

Or: "It's me, I'm depressed." "Who in the family is contributing to your depression?" "No one." "Then who's helping you get over being depressed?"

These challenges can be blunt or gentle, depending on the therapist's preferred style and assessment of the family. The point, incidentally, is not to switch from blaming one person (the disobedient child, say) to another (a parent who lacks authority and doesn't discipline effectively), but to broaden the problem as a triangular, interactional one. Maybe the mother is too lenient with Johnny because she finds father too strict, and moreover she may be overinvested in the boy because of emotional distance in the marriage.

The best way to challenge inappropriate interactions is to point out the patterns that are keeping people stuck. A useful formula for this is: "The more you do *X*, the more he does *Y*—and the more you do *Y*, the more she does *X*." (For *X* and *Y*, try substituting nag and withdraw, or punish and indulge.) Incidentally, when therapists point out what people are doing that isn't working, it's a tactical error to then tell them what they should be doing. Once a therapist shifts from pointing something out to giving advice, the family's attention shifts from themselves and their behavior to the therapist and his or her advice.

"When you criticize your son for feeling upset, he feels misunderstood and hurt. What you're saying may be true, but he doesn't feel supported." "What should I do?" "I don't know, ask your son."

Even though family therapists challenge assumptions, they continue to listen to family members' feelings and points of view. Listening is a silent activity, rare at times, even among therapists. Family members often don't listen to each other for long without become defensive and reactive. Therapists don't listen, either, when they're too anxious to jump in to disagree or give advice. But remember that people aren't likely to change or even reconsider their assumptions until they feel they've been heard and understood.

Homework assignments can be used to test flexibility (simply seeing if they are carried out measures willingness to change), make family members more aware of their role in problems (telling people just to notice something, without necessarily trying to change it, is very instructive), and to suggest new ways of relating. Typical homework assignments include: Suggesting that overinvolved parents hire a babysitter and go out together, having argumentative partners take turns talking about their feelings while the other just listens without saying anything (but noticing tendencies to become reactive that make it hard to listen), and having dependent family members practice spending more time alone (or with someone outside the family) and doing more things for themselves. Homework assignments likely to generate conflict, such as negotiating house rules with teenagers, should be avoided, and such difficult discussions should be saved for when the therapist can act as referee.

Early Phase Checklist

1. Identify major conflicts and bring them into the consulting room.
2. Develop a hypothesis and refine it into a formulation about what the family is doing to perpetuate or fail to solve their presenting problem. Formulations should consider process and structure, family rules, triangles, and boundaries.
3. Keep the focus of treatment on primary problems and the interpersonal conditions supporting them.
4. Homework assignments should address both problems and the underlying conditions supporting them.
5. Challenge family members to see their own role in the problems that plague them.
6. Push for change, in the session and between sessions at home.
7. Seek and make effective use of supervision and consultation to test the validity of formulations and effectiveness of interventions.

The Middle Phase of Treatment

When therapy is anything other than brief and problem-focused, much of the middle phase is devoted to helping family members express themselves and achieve mutual understanding. If the therapist plays too active and central a role in this process—filtering all conversation between family members and him- or herself—family members won't learn how to deal with each other, and will continue to manage only as long as they keep coming in for therapy sessions. For this reason, in the middle phase of therapy, the therapist takes a less active role and encourages family members to talk and interact with each other. As they do so, the therapist steps back and observes the process. When dialogue bogs down, the therapist either points out what went wrong, or simply encourages them to keep talking—but with less interruption and criticism.

When family members address their conflicts directly, they tend to become anxious and reactive. Anxiety is the enemy of listening. Some therapists (Bowenians, for example) make every effort to control and minimize anxiety by having family members talk mostly to the therapist. Others prefer to let family members deal with their own anxiety by helping them learn to talk with each other less defensively (by saying how they feel, and listening to and acknowledging what the other one says). However, even therapists who work primarily with family dialogue need to interrupt when anxiety starts to escalate and conversations become defensive and destructive.

Thus in the middle phase of treatment the therapist takes a less directive role and encourages the family to begin to rely on their own resources. The level of conflict and anxiety is balanced by alternating between having family members talk among themselves or with the therapist. In either case, the therapist encourages family members to get beyond criticism and blaming to talking directly about what they feel and what they want—and to learn to see their own part in unproductive patterns of interaction.

Middle Phase Checklist

1. Use intensity to challenge family members (or ingenuity to get around resistance; or empathy to get underneath defensiveness).

2. Avoid being so directive and controlling that the family doesn't learn to rely on and improve their own ways of relating to each other.
3. Foster individual responsibility and mutual understanding.
4. Make certain that efforts to improve relationships are having a positive effect on the presenting complaint.
5. Even if you meet with subgroups, don't lose sight of the whole family picture, and don't neglect any individuals or relationships—*especially* not those "difficult" ones that are so tempting to avoid.
6. Is therapy stuck on a plateau? Have sessions taken on a sameness and predictability? Does the therapist assume too active a role in choosing what to talk about? Have therapist and family developed a friendly relationship that has become more important than addressing conflicts? Has the therapist assumed a regular role in the family (an empathic listener to the spouses or a firm parent figure to the children), substituting for a missing function in the family (the spouses aren't listening to each other, the parents aren't nurturing and controlling their own children)?

Termination

Termination comes for brief therapists as soon as the presenting problem is resolved. For psychoanalytic therapists, therapy is a long-term learning process and may continue for a year or two, or longer. For most therapists termination comes somewhere between these two extremes and has to do both with the family feeling that they've gotten what they've come for and the therapist's sense that treatment has reached the point of diminishing returns. One clue that it may be time to terminate is when the family comes in with nothing to say but small talk (assuming, of course, that they aren't avoiding conflict).

In individual psychotherapy, where the relationship to the therapist is often the primary vehicle of change, termination focuses on reviewing the relationship and saying goodbye. In family therapy, the focus is more on what the family has been doing that doesn't work. Termination is therefore a good time to review and consolidate what they've learned. Although some strategic therapists are content to manipulate change without necessarily being concerned that the family understands it, most family therapy has some kind of teaching function, and termination is the time to make sure the family has learned something about how to get along.

It can be helpful at this point to ask the family to anticipate upcoming changes or challenges that might cause setbacks and discuss with them how they will handle those challenges. The question "How will you know when things are heading backwards and what will you do?" is useful in this regard. Families can also be reminded that their present harmony can't be maintained indefinitely and that people have a tendency to overreact to the first sign of relapse, which can trigger a self-fulfilling vicious cycle. To paraphrase Zorba the Greek, life *is* trouble. To be alive is to encounter difficulties. The real test is how you handle them.

Although there are cases in which it seems likely that a family will run into additional problems and perhaps need additional treatment, at termination it may be best to recognize that the current relationship has come to an end—and to expressly support the family's strengths and coping skills.

Finally, although in the business of therapy, no news is usually good news, it might be a good idea to check in with the family to see how they're doing some months after termination. This can be done with a letter, phone call, or brief follow-up session. The family will appreciate the therapist's continued interest and concern, and the therapist will feel a greater sense of closure. The therapeutic relationship is, of necessity, somewhat artificial or at least constrained. But there's no reason to make it less than human—or to forget about families once you terminate with them.

Termination Checklist

1. Is the presenting problem resolved or greatly improved?
2. Is the family satisfied that they have gotten what they came for or are they interested in continuing to learn about themselves and improve their relationships?
3. Does the family have an understanding of what they were doing that wasn't working, and how to avoid the recurrence of similar problems in the future?
4. Do minor recurrences of problems reflect lack of resolution of some underlying dynamic or merely that the family has to readjust to function without the therapist?
5. Have family members developed and improved relationships outside the immediate family context as well as within it?

Family Assessment

Family therapists vary widely in the extent to which they make formal assessments. Bowen systems therapists usually complete detailed genograms before beginning treatment, psychoanalysts often start out by taking thorough personal histories, and behavioral therapists routinely rely on a variety of structured questionnaires, checklists, and inventories to obtain baseline data on couples and families. At the other extreme, structural, solution-focused, and narrative therapists do very little in the way of formal evaluation. But regardless of their approach's official posture on assessment, it's probably true that most therapists spend too little time making careful evaluations of families before launching into treatment.

Rather than attempt an exhaustive comparison of the assessment procedures of the different schools or list and evaluate the many available formal assessment devices, we will instead simply describe some of the dimensions of family and individual functioning that therapists should consider before embarking on a course of treatment. This summary is designed to be illustrative rather than exhaustive, and therefore you are quite likely to think of at least one or two important issues we've neglected to cover.

In mentioning some of the major issues that should be considered in evaluating families for treatment, we don't mean to suggest that clinicians should always inquire formally into each of these areas. Rather, our intent is to describe some of the variety of issues that therapists should have some background understanding and awareness of. The decision to delve more deeply into any of these areas is one that therapists must make when they deem it appropriate. Consider, for example, how standard psychiatric interviews are conducted. Medical students are often taught to routinely ask if the patient hears voices or is considering suicide. While this may be fine for a patient who seems disturbed or depressed, such questions may feel jarringly inappropriate to someone complaining of mild anxiety. By the same token, although it could be disastrous to embark on a course of couples therapy without knowing that one of the partners is addicted to cocaine, it's probably neither necessary nor wise to ask everyone who walks into your office if they snort cocaine or smoke crack.

The Presenting Problem

It may seem obvious that the first consideration in evaluating a family for treatment should be the presenting complaint. Nevertheless it's worth stressing that inquiry into the presenting problem should be both detailed and empathic. The minute some therapists hear that a family's problem is, say, a misbehaving child or poor communication between a couple, they're ready to jump into action. Their experience and training have prepared them to deal with misbehaving children or communication problems, and they're raring to go. They know what needs to be done. But before they get started they should realize that they're *not* dealing with "misbehaving children" or "communication problems," they're dealing with a very particular instance of one of those problems.

Exploring the presenting problem begins with simply hearing the family's account, in their own words. Every member of the family should have a chance to express his or her perspective—and both their description and their feelings should be acknowledged. This open-ended inquiry should be followed by specific and detailed questions to find out more about the precise nature of the problem. If a child misbehaves, what exactly does he do? How often? Under what circumstances? Does he misbehave at school or at home, or both?

The next thing to explore are the family's attempts to deal with the problem. What have they tried? What's been helpful? What hasn't? Has anyone other than those present been involved in trying to help (or hinder) the family in dealing with the problem?

Understanding the Referral Route

Beginning with the initial phone call and following through in the first session, it's important to understand who referred your clients to you and why. What were their expectations? What expectations did they communicate to the family?

In many cases the referral process is routine and of no major import. However, it's important to know whether a family's participation is voluntary or coerced, whether all or only some of them recognize the need for treatment, and whether other professionals or agencies will have some kind of continuing involvement with your clients.

When individual therapists make a family referral, they often have a particular agenda in mind. A college student's counselor once referred him and his family for treatment. It turned out that the young man had uncovered a repressed memory of sexual abuse by his father, and the family therapist was somehow supposed to mediate between the young man, who couldn't imagine who else might have been responsible for this vaguely remembered incident, and his parents, who absolutely denied that any such thing ever happened. Did the individual therapist expect confrontation, confession, and atonement? Some sort of negotiated agreement? It's best to find out.

It's also important to find out if clients have been in treatment before. If so, what happened? What expectations or concerns or sources of resistance did previous therapies generate?

Identifying the Systemic Context

Regardless of who the therapist elects to work with, it's imperative to have a clear understanding of the interpersonal context of the problem. Who's in the family? Are there important figures in the life of the problem who aren't present? A live-in boyfriend? A grandparent who lives next door? Are other social agencies involved with the family? What is the nature of their input? Does the family see them as helpful or unhelpful?

Remember that family therapy is an approach to people in context. The most immediately relevant context is often the immediate family. But families don't exist in a vacuum. The system also includes the extrafamilial context. It may be important to meet with the teachers and counselors of a child who misbehaves at school to find out what's really going on. There are even times when the nuclear family may not be the most important social context of a person's problems. Sometimes, for example, a college student's depression has more to do with what's going on in the classroom or dormitory than with what's happening back home.

Stage of the Life Cycle

A family's context has temporal as well as interpersonal dimensions. Most families come to treatment not because there's something inherently wrong with them, but because they've gotten stuck between stages in the family life cycle. Sometimes this will be immediately apparent. Parents may complain, for example, that they don't know what's gotten into Janey.

She used to be such a good girl, but now that she's fourteen she's become sullen and argumentative. (One reason parenting remains an amateur sport is that just when you think you've got the hang of it, the kids get a little older and throw you a whole new set of curves.) Adolescence is that stage in the family life cycle when young parents have to grow up and relax their grip on their children.

Sometimes it isn't so obvious that a family is having trouble adjusting to a new stage in the life cycle. Couples who marry after living together for years may not realize that matrimony can stir up a number of unconscious expectations related to what it means to be part of a family. More than one couple has been surprised to discover a sharp falling off in their love life after formally tying the knot. At other times significant life-cycle changes occur in the parents' generation, and you won't always learn of these influences unless you ask.

Family Structure

The simplest systemic context for a problem is a dynamic process between two parties. She nags and he withdraws; restrictive parental control provokes adolescent rebellion, and vice versa. But sometimes, often, a dyadic perspective doesn't take in the whole picture.

Family problems often become entrenched because they're embedded in powerful but unseen structures. Regardless of what approach a therapist takes, it's wise to understand something about the family's structure. What are the actual functioning subsystems and what is the nature of the boundaries between them? What is the nature of the boundary around the couple or the family? What active triangles are present? What dormant triangles?

Who plays what roles in the family? Are these individuals and subsystems protected by boundaries that allow them to operate without undue interference—but with access to affection and support?

Here, too, there is a temporal dimension. If a wife goes back to work after years of staying home with the children, the parental subsystem is challenged to shift from a complementary to a symmetrical form. Whether or not family members complain directly about these strains, they're likely to be relevant to wherever their distress happens to be focused.

Communication

Although some couples still come to therapy saying they have "communication problems" (usually meaning that one won't do what the other one wants), working on communication has become somewhat of a cliché in family therapy. Because communication is the vehicle of relationship, all therapists deal with communication. Moreover, it turns out that clarifying communication is rarely sufficient to solve family problems.

However, although conflict doesn't magically disappear after family members start to listen to each other, it's unlikely that conflicts will get solved *before* people start to listen to each other. If, after a session or two and the therapist's "encouragement," family members still seem unwilling to listen to each other, talking therapy is going to be an uphill battle.

One other point to be made about listening falls under the technical category of What's Good for the Goose is Good for the Gander. Some therapists encourage family members to listen to each other, but they don't practice what they preach. A family member will start to protest or explain and the therapist cuts that person off to direct him or her to listen to someone else's point of view. The person who gets cut off may grudgingly listen, but no one is really interested in hearing what anyone else has to say until he or she feels heard and understood.

Family members who learn to listen to each other with understanding and tolerance often discover that they don't need to change each other. Many problems can be solved, but the problem of living with other people who don't always see things the way you do, or want what you want, isn't one of them.

Drug and Alcohol Abuse

Although it may not be necessary to ask every client about drug and alcohol consumption, it's critical to inquire carefully if there is any suspicion that this may be a problem. Don't be too polite. Ask straightforward and specific questions. If a member of a family who's seeking couples or family therapy seems to be abusing drugs or alcohol, think twice about assuming that talk therapy alone will be the answer to the family's problems.

Domestic Violence and Sexual Abuse

If there is any hint of domestic violence or sexual abuse, the clinician should look into it. The process of questioning can start with the whole family present, but when there is a strong suspicion of abuse or neglect, it may be wise to meet with family members individually to allow them to talk more openly. While there's room for disagreement about the advisability of a conjoint approach in cases of mild domestic violence, such as slapping or pushing, it's imperative that the therapist consider whether the inevitable stress of seeing a couple together will expose a woman to greater danger from retaliation by her disgruntled partner.

As you know, most states require professionals to report any suspicion of child abuse to child protective services. Any clinician who considers not reporting suspected child abuse based on his or her own clinical judgment should also consider the consequences of this failure to report becoming known if someone else does report it. It's called losing your license.

Extramarital Involvements

The discovery of an affair is a crisis that will strike the majority of couples some time in their relationship. Infidelity is common, but it's still a crisis. It can destroy a marriage. Extramarital involvements that don't involve sexual intimacy, although less obvious, can sabotage treatment if one or both partners regularly turns to a third party to deal with issues that should be worked out in the couple. (One clue that a third-party relationship is part of a triangle is that the relationship isn't openly talked about.) Helpful but unhelpful third parties may include family members, friends, and therapists.

A couple once came to therapy with both partners complaining that the intimacy had gone out of their relationship. It wasn't so much a matter of conflict, it was just that they never seemed to spend any time together anymore. After a few weeks of slow progress, the wife revealed that she'd been seeing an individual therapist. When the couples therapist asked why, she replied that she needed to have someone to talk to.

Gender

Unrecognized gender inequalities can contribute to family problems in a variety of ways. A wife's dissatisfaction may have deeper roots than the family's focal problems. A husband's reluctance to become more involved in the family may be as much a product of cultural expectations and rewards for career achievement as of anything missing in his personality.

Every therapist must work out for him- or herself how to balance between the extremes of naively ignoring the existence of gender inequality and imposing one's personal point of view on clients. However, it's not reasonable to assume that both partners enter marriage with equal power, or that complementarity between spouses is the only dynamic operating on their relationship.

Conflict over gender expectations, whether it's directly talked about or not, is especially common given the enormous shifts in cultural expectations over the last few years. Is it still considered a woman's duty to follow her husband's career, moving whenever and wherever necessary for his advancement, regardless of how this affects her (and the children's) interests? Is it still true that women are expected to be the primary (which often turns out to be a euphemism for only) caregivers for infants and young children?

Regardless of the therapist's values, do the gender roles established in a couple seem to work for them? Or do unresolved differences, conflict, or confusion appear to be sources of stress? Perhaps the single most useful question to ask about gender inequality is, "How does each of the partners experience the fairness of give-and-take in their relationship?"

Cultural Factors

In assessing families for treatment a therapist should consider and respect the unique subculture a family is from as well as the effect of unquestioned assumptions from the larger culture that may have an impact on their problems.

In working with clients from other cultures it's probably more important to be respectful of differences and curious about other ways of doing things than to attempt to become an expert on ethnicity. However, while it's important to respect other people's differences, it can be a problem to accept uncritically statements to the effect that "We do these (counterproductive) things because of our culture." Unfortunately, it's difficult for a therapist from an alien culture to assess the validity of such claims. Perhaps the best advice is to be curious, stay open, but ask questions.

Even, or especially, when working with clients from your own culture, it's important to consider the possible impact of destructive cultural assumptions. How do cultural expectations and aspirations affect the family you're planning to work with? One patient recently complained that his wife expected family life to be like "The Cosby Show." His wife's reply was: "It isn't always 'China Beach,' either."

Among common cultural assumptions you may want to be alert for are that getting married means living happily ever after, that sexual satisfaction is something that just comes naturally, that adolescence is always a time of turmoil, and that teenagers only want freedom and no longer need their parents' love and understanding.

The Ethical Dimension

Most therapists are aware of the ethical responsibilities of their profession: Therapy should be for the client's benefit, not to work out unresolved issues for the therapist. Clients are entitled to confidentiality, and so limits on privacy imposed by requirements to report to probation officers, parents, or managed care companies should be made clear from the outset. Professionals are obligated to provide the best possible treatment, and if they aren't qualified by training or experience to meet the needs of a particular client, they should refer the case to someone else.

But, although most therapists are aware of their own responsibilities, many think less than they might about the ethical dimensions of their clients' behavior. This is another area where there are no hard and fast rules. However, a complete and conscientious assessment of every family should include some consideration of family members' entitlements and obligations. What loyalty obligations do members of the family have? Are there invisible loyalties that seem to be constraining their behavior? If so, are these just and equitable? What is the nature of the partners' commitment to each other? Are these commitments clear? Balanced? What obligations do family members have with regard to fidelity and trustworthiness? Are these obligations being met?

In reading over our topics for family assessment, you may have noticed that there was no section on individual dynamics. This was deliberate. The distinction between individual and systemic levels of experience is useful but artificial. Regardless of whether they're treating individuals or family groups, competent therapists should always keep in mind that there are both interactional and personal dimensions to all human experience. An individual therapist who fails to consider the impact of the therapeutic relationship (as well as relationships outside the office) on a patient's material is missing a most important contribution. Therapists are never blank screens.

By the same token, a family therapist who fails to consider the psychology of a family member's behavior is dealing with only half a deck. Families were never black boxes. Sometimes when family interactions get stuck, it's important to consider the contributions of psychopathology, psychodynamics, or just plain failures of nerve.

Working with Managed Care

Rarely has a profession undergone such upheaval as mental health providers in this country have experienced with the advent of managed care. The suddenness of this transformation has made a difficult transition even more difficult. Practitioners, used to making decisions based on their own clinical judgment, are now being told by the managed care industry which patients they can see, which kinds of treatment are preferred, what they can charge, and how many sessions they should offer. Professionals taught to maintain absolute privacy and confidentiality in their dealings with patients now abruptly find themselves negotiating treatment arrangements with anonymous strangers over the telephone.

The managed care industry itself has been slow to get its act together. Some of the horror stories we've all heard about care being disallowed or abruptly terminated stem from the early days of managed care when the industry tended to manage by denial rather than mediation. Given the mandate to stem the flow of hemorrhaging health care costs, when asked to approve any but the most stringently limited forms of treatment, the industry's first impulse was to just say no.

Now ten years into its existence the managed care industry is coming to terms with two important facts: first, that although their mandate is still to contain costs, their ultimate responsibility is to see that patients receive effective treatment; and second, although there seems to be an almost built-in adversarial relationship to practitioners, industry case managers are discovering something that clinicians should also come to terms with—that both sides profit when they begin to work in partnership.[4]

That's why we titled this section "Working with" managed care, rather than something that might better describe how many therapists feel, such as "Coping with" or "Surviving" managed care. The key to succeeding in a managed care environment is learning to work within the system and getting over the sense that the case manager at the other end of the line is your enemy. Actually, for those who learn to collaborate effectively with managed care, case managers can be the best source of referrals.

For students, learning to work with managed care should begin as early as planning their education. Most managed care companies accept licensed practitioners with graduate degrees in nursing, social work, psychology, and psychiatry. Some, but by no means most, accept other degrees—though not usually on their preferred provider lists. So, just as it's prudent to take state licensing requirements into account when planning a post-graduate education, it's also wise to consider the requirements of the major managed care companies. Moreover, because most companies require at least three years of post-degree experience, it's a good idea to plan on beginning your career in a supervised agency.

In areas with a high concentration of mental health providers it may be necessary to mar-

[4]Increased competition among managed care companies has increased pressure to build trust and loyalty among providers and to reduce internal costs by spending less administrative time managing providers.

ket your skills in order to be selected for managed care providers. Even where managed care panels are already crowded, case managers are always looking for competent professionals who can make their jobs easier. The willingness to accept crisis referrals and to work with difficult cases (e.g., borderlines, chronic and multiproblem clients), accessibility, and having specialized expertise help make therapists attractive to managed care companies.

Once you have the opportunity to become a managed care provider, remember to work *with* case managers, not against them. The regulations and paper work can be frustrating, but keep in mind that case managers have feelings, too—and they have memories. They're just trying to do the job they were hired to do. The biggest mistake practitioners make is to allow themselves to become surly or oppositional when talking to case managers.

Case managers appreciate succinct and informative verbal and written reports. When challenged, many therapists eventually fall back on justifying their requests by saying, "It's my clinical opinion." Being asked to justify their conclusions makes many established practitioners angry. We *are* doing the best we can for patients. We *are* practicing efficiently. But we're not used to being held accountable. We're not used to someone looking over our shoulder, checking up on us. Get used to it. If you use sound clinical judgment, you should be able to provide reasons for your recommendations.

If you can't reach agreement with a case manager, don't lose your temper. If you can't be friendly, don't be hostile. Follow the grievance procedure.

Do the required paper work and submit it on time. Write sharp, well-defined treatment plans. Be available and accessible. Return phone calls promptly. Make arrangements with a colleague to provide back-up if you're out of town or unable to accept a referral.

In addition to maintaining a positive, constructive attitude, being successful in the current health care climate means developing a results-oriented mindset. If you're trained in solution-focused therapy, by all means say so, but don't try to pass yourself off as something you're not.[5] Calling yourself "eclectic" is more likely to sound fuzzy than flexible. The important point is to get a reputation for working within established time limits—and getting results.

[5]We regret to say that one specialty with which you're probably better off not attempting to win the hearts of managed care companies is psychodynamic psychotherapy.

References

Bales, R. F. 1970. *Personality and interpersonal behavior.* New York: Holt, Rinehart and Winston.

Bateson, G., and Jackson, D. D. 1964. Some varieties of pathogenic organization. *Disorders of Communication. 42:*270–283.

Bateson, G., Jackson, D. D., Haley, J., and Weakland, J. H. 1956. Toward a theory of schizophrenia. *Behavioral Science. 1:*251–264.

Beels, C. C., and Ferber, A. 1969. Family therapy: A view. *Family Process. 8:*280–318.

Bell, J. E. 1961. *Family group therapy.* Public Health Monograph No. 64. Washington, DC: U.S. Government Printing Office.

Bell, J. E. 1975. *Family group therapy.* New York: Jason Aronson.

Bion, W. R. 1961. *Experiences in groups.* New York: Tavistock Publications.

Carnap, R. 1942. *Introduction to semantics.* Cambridge, MA: Harvard University Press.

Freud, S. 1921. *Group psychology and the analysis of the ego.* Standard Edition. Vol. 18. London: Hogarth Press, 1955.

Gritzer, P. H., and Okum, H. S. 1983. Multiple family group therapy: A model for all families. In *Handbook of family and marital therapy,* B. B. Wolman and G. Stricker, eds. New York: Plenum Press.

Haley, J. 1961. Control in psychotherapy with schizophrenics. *Archives of General Psychiatry. 5:* 340–353.

Haley, J. 1963. *Strategies of psychotherapy.* New York: Grune and Stratton.

Haley, J. 1976. *Problem-solving therapy.* San Francisco: Jossey-Bass.

Haley, J. 1986. *The power tactics of Jesus Christ,* 2nd ed. Rockville, MD: The Triangle Press.

Hoffman, L. 1971. Deviation-amplifying processes in natural groups. In *Changing families,* J. Haley, ed. New York: Grune & Stratton.

Jackson, D. D. 1961. Interactional psychotherapy. In *Contemporary psychotherapies,* M. T. Stein, ed. New York: Free Press of Glencoe.

Jackson, D. D. 1965. Family rules: The marital quid pro quo. *Archives of General Psychiatry. 12:* 589–594.

Jackson, D. D. 1967. Aspects of conjoint family therapy. In *Family therapy and disturbed families,* G. H. Zuk and I. Boszormenyi-Nagy, eds. Palo Alto: Science and Behavior Books.

Jackson, D. D., and Weakland, J. H. 1961. Conjoint family therapy: Some consideration on theory, technique, and results. *Psychiatry. 24:*30–45.

Laqueur, H. P. 1966. General systems theory and multiple family therapy. In *Handbook of psychiatric therapies,* J. Masserman, ed. New York: Grune & Stratton.

Laqueur, H. P. 1972a. Mechanisms of change in multiple family therapy. In *Progress in group and family therapy,* C. J. Sager and H. S. Kaplan, eds. New York: Brunner/Mazel.

Laqueur, H. P. 1972b. Multiple family therapy. In *The book of family therapy,* A. Ferber, M. Mendelsohn, and A. Napier, eds. Boston: Houghton Mifflin.

Laqueur, H. P. 1976. Multiple family therapy. In *Family therapy: Theory and practice,* P. J. Guerin, ed. New York: Gardner Press.

Lidz, T., Cornelison, A., Terry, D., and Fleck, S. 1958. Intra-familial environment of the schizophrenic patient: IV. The transmission of irrationality. *Archives of Neurology and Psychiatry. 79:* 305–316.

MacGregor, R. 1967. Progress in multiple impact theory. In *Expanding theory and practice in family therapy,* N. W. Ackerman, F. L. Beatman, and S. N. Sherman, eds. New York: Family Service Association.

MacGregor, R. 1972. Multiple impact psychotherapy with families. In *Family therapy: An introduction to theory and technique,* G. D. Erickson and T. P. Hogan, eds. Monterey, CA: Brooks/Cole.

MacGregor, R., Richie, A. M., Serrano, A. C., Schuster, F. P., McDonald, E. C., and Goolishian, H. A. 1964. *Multiple impact therapy with families.* New York: McGraw-Hill.

Marayuma, M. 1968. The second cybernetics: Deviation-amplifying mutual causal processes. In *Modern systems research for the behavioral scientist,* W. Buckley, ed. Chicago: Aldine.

McFarlane, W. R. 1982. Multiple-family therapy in the psychiatric hospital. In *The psychiatric hospital and the family,* H. T. Harbin, ed. New York: Spectrum.

Meyer, J. P., and Pepper, S. 1977. Need compatibility and marital adjustment among young married couples. *Journal of Personality and Social Psychology. 35:*331–342.

Midelfort, C. F. 1957. *The family in psychotherapy.* New York: McGraw-Hill.

Morris, C. W. 1938. Foundations on the theory of signs. In *International encyclopedia of united science,* O. Neurath, R. Carnap, and C. O. Morris, eds. Chicago: University of Chicago Press.

Nichols, M. P. 1987. *The self in the system.* New York: Brunner/Mazel.

Parsons, T. 1950. Psychoanalysis and the social structure. *Psychoanalytic Quarterly. 19:*371–380.

Ruesch, J., and Bateson, G. 1951. *Communication: The social matrix of psychiatry.* New York: Norton.

Ruevini, U. 1975. Network intervention with a family in crisis. *Family Process. 14:*193–203.

Ruevini, U. 1979. *Networking families in crisis.* New York: Human Sciences Press.

Sartre, J. P. 1964. *Being and nothingness.* New York: Citadel Press.

Satir, V. 1964. *Conjoint family therapy.* Palo Alto, CA: Science and Behavior Books.

Schutz, W. C. 1958. *FIRO: A three-dimensional theory of interpersonal behavior.* New York: Holt, Rinehart and Winston.

Shaw, M. E. 1981. *Group dynamics: The psychology of small group behavior.* New York: McGraw-Hill.

Skynner, A. C. R. 1976. *Systems of family and marital psychotherapy.* New York: Brunner/Mazel.

Sluzki, C. E. 1978. Marital therapy from a systems theory perspective. In *Marriage and marital therapy,* T. J. Paolino and B. S. McCrady, eds. New York: Brunner/Mazel.

Speck, R. V., and Attneave, C. A. 1973. *Family networks.* New York: Pantheon.

Von Bertalanffy, L. 1950. An outline of general system theory. *British Journal of the Philosophy of Science. 1:*134–165.

Watzlawick, P. A. 1966. A structured family interview. *Family Process. 5:*256–271.

Watzlawick, P., Beavin, J. H., and Jackson, D. D. 1967. *Pragmatics of human communication.* New York: Norton.

Weakland, J., Fisch, R., Watzlawick, P., and Bodin, A. M. 1974. Brief therapy focused problem resolution. *Family Process. 13:*141–168.

Winch, R. F. 1955. The theory of complementary needs in mate selection: A test of one kind of complementariness. *American Sociological Review. 20:*52–56.

Wynne, L. C. 1968. Methodologic and conceptual issues in the study of schizophrenics and their families. *Journal of Psychiatric Research. 6:* 185–199.

Wynne, L. C. 1970. Communication disorders and the quest for relatedness in families of schizophrenics. *American Journal of Psychoanalysis. 30:*100–114.

Wynne, L. C., Ryckoff, I. M., Day, J., and Hirsch, S. 1958. Pseudomutuality in the family relations of schizophrenics. *Psychiatry. 21:*205–220.

Wynne, L., and Singer, M. 1963. Thought disorder and family relationships of schizophrenics: I. Research strategy. *Archives of General Psychiatry. 9:*191–198.

Yalom, I. D. 1985. *The theory and practices of group psychotherapy,* 3rd ed. New York: Basic Books.

4

The Fundamental Concepts of Family Therapy

Family therapy, like most of the social sciences, has struggled to find metaphors to organize its observations and practices. Over the years a variety of conceptual frameworks from other fields have been borrowed and adapted by family therapy theorists. Consequently, trends in the field often parallel trends in academia. In this chapter the evolving conceptual foundations of family therapy are presented, with an emphasis on those principles that have endured through the decades and those emerging as prominent in the 1990s.

Conceptual Influences on the Evolution of Family Therapy

If family therapists were polled as to the most important conceptual influence on the development of the field, the winner by a landslide would be "systems theory." If therapists were then asked to describe this systems theory, most would mumble something about "the whole is greater than the sum of its parts" or words like *equifinality* and *homeostasis,* while feeling uneasy about their inability to explain the theory they believe to be so essential.

This inarticulateness isn't surprising. Systems theory isn't really a well-defined doctrine, but more like a way of thinking, and there are many variations on the systemic theme. This lack of coherence has been reflected in much of the writing about the application of systemic principles in family therapy. Systemic ideas are abstract enough to permit a wide variety of interpretations. What we describe here is no less an interpretation, but one we hope will provide some clarity.

Many of the concepts family therapists hold dear were borrowed from other fields of study, all of which were changing in a similar direction at the time family therapy was emerging. Some of these fields included biology (systems), physiology (homeostasis), cybernetics (feedback), psychosomatic medicine (the social context of illness), community mental health (the therapeutic community), anthropology (structuralism, functionalism, the participant observer), and social work (the social context of problems). In biology, for example, where the concept of "systems" was coined by Paul Weiss in 1925, the focus was on the interrelation of biopsychosocial systems, concentric rings of organization from the microbiological level to organs to organ systems to the organism, and so on. All these fields were shifting from studying isolated elements of a system to trying to understand how those elements interrelated. Jay Haley (1971a) summarized some of those changes:

> The idea of trying to change a family appeared in the 1950s at the same time as other happenings in the social sciences in America. At midcentury the social sciences became more social: the study of small groups flourished, animals were observed in their natural environments instead of in the zoo or laboratory, psychological experiments were seen as social situations in experimenter-bias studies, businesses began to be thought of as complex systems, mental hospitals were studied as total institutions, and ecology developed as a special field, with man and other creatures looked upon as inseparable from their environments. (p. 1)

Functionalism

Changes within anthropology most closely paralleled the innovations brought to psychotherapy by family therapy. That shouldn't be surprising considering that the person most responsible for bringing systems ideas into psychotherapy was Gregory Bateson, an anthropologist.

Until the turn of the century, anthropology was dominated by cultural evolutionists who applied Darwinian theory to culture and theorized about the various stages through which humankind evolved from primitive societies to modern civilization. Their theories were based on artifacts brought back by archaeologists as well as tales of travelers and merchants, and these were studied outside of their original contexts.

Beginning around 1900, but not dominating the anthropological scene until the 1930s, an approach known as *functionalism* emerged as a reaction against the evolutionist tendency to take cultural traits out of their context and disregard cultures as meaningful wholes. British anthropologists Bronislaw Malinowski and A. R. Radcliffe-Brown took the position that historical studies were futile because the data were scant and unverifiable. They were interested in studying cultures as social systems in the present and had little concern for their history. Thus they studied cultures ethnographically, as "participant observers," and tried to understand cultural ceremonies and customs in context, looking for the function that cultural practices served for the larger social network.

These functionalists were as affected by Darwin's theory as the historical evolutionists against whom they reacted, only in a different way. Functionalists believe that the adaptive value of any activity can be found if the behavior is viewed in the context of its environment. They speculated about the function that certain kinds of social behavior served for the larger group in much the same way Darwinians speculated about the survival value of animal traits.

The parallels between this shift in anthropology and a later shift in psychotherapy are striking. Psychoanalysts tried to reconstruct a personal history by studying, out of context, memories and fantasies. Like evolutionary anthropology, psychoanalysis was based on historical speculation. Indeed, Freud compared his psychological explorations to archaeological excavations.

Family therapy's reaction against the historical and decontextualized theorizing of psychoanalysis was similar to the reaction of anthropological functionalists against the same historical and decontextualized qualities of evolutionism. Like the functionalists, systems-oriented family therapists weren't interested in history and instead tried to become participant observers of families in the present. They were interested in understanding the function that the behavior of family members served for the family system.

One of the hazards of family therapy's functionalist inclination is to view any behavior as potentially adaptive. As Deborah Luepnitz (1988) observed, "Functionalist explanations can justify almost anything in terms of some putative social need. Functionalist historians have even argued that lynchings and witch hunts serve a social need, i.e., a cathartic or 'therapeutic' need. Therapeutic for whom? one might well ask" (p. 65).

An example relevant to family therapy is the assumption by Talcott Parsons (Parsons & Bales, 1955), probably the most influential functionalist sociologist, that a mother's proper role in a family is *expressive*, whereas the father's is *instrumental*. The *expressive role* involves emotional support, management of tensions, and care and support of the children. The *instrumental role* involves managerial decisions, solution of group tasks, and discipline of the children. In this case, Parsons took an observation of the sex-role polarity that existed in many families in the 1950s and used functionalism to imply that this division was adaptive, serving the needs of the family and society.

As family therapist Lynn Hoffman (1971, 1981) pointed out, this functionalist bent entered sociology through the work of Emile Durkheim. Durkheim studied modern society and speculated that many kinds of behavior society considers deviant or pathological may serve a socially useful role in bringing the larger group together. Later, sociologists who studied social deviance, such as Erving Goffman, took Durkheim's ideas even further and suggested that social groups may *need* deviants for their stability or survival.

Before moving on, another sociological study bears mentioning because its findings supported the function-of-the-symptom thinking of family therapists. Alfred Stanton and Morris Schwartz (1964) studied the interactions among patients and staff in a mental hospital. The hospital was Chestnut Lodge, where one of the founders of family therapy, Don Jackson, came into contact with Harry Stack Sullivan and his interpersonal theory of psychiatry. They noticed that patients were often caught in triangles in which one staff member tried to uphold the rules of the institution, while another staff member resented this rigidity and wanted to bend rules to accommodate individual needs. A patient who stumbled into this polarization became the battlefield over which this staff conflict played out, and this patient immediately had a permissive ally pitted against a restrictive antagonist. The more protective one staff member was, the more punitive the other would become, and the whole unit might be pulled into the escalating polarization and forced to take sides. As tension mounted, such patients became increasingly disturbed on the unit. Stanton and Schwartz's description of this triangular process is remarkably similar to the process of *triangulation* or *cross-generational coalition* that family therapists were reporting.

Functionalist Influence in Family Therapy. Family therapists took the functionalist notion that deviant behavior may serve a protective function for a social group and applied it to the symptoms of family members. Initially their view of a family's identified patient was similar to Stanton and Schwartz's view of the patient in the hospital. The family's "identified patient" was a scapegoat, a victim on whom other family members focused and with whom they fought to avoid having to deal with each other. Later, family therapists suspected that most of these "scapegoats" were active volunteers. It was thought that these symptom-bearers willingly sacrificed their own welfare for the greater good. For example, a teenage boy, when his parents began to argue, would pick a fight with his brother, thereby inducing his parents to shift their wrath from each other to him. Salvador Minuchin's case of Oedipus revisited, described in Chapter 1, is another example.

To summarize functionalism's influence on family therapy, families were viewed as living organisms that had to adapt to their environment. The behavior and traits of the family organism were examined in this context to see how they helped families adapt or better meet their needs. Symptoms were viewed as signs that the family wasn't adapting well to its environment or was, for some reason, unable to meet its needs. Descriptions and techniques based on these assumptions are found throughout the family therapy literature.

Functionalism proved useful in understanding how families adapt. Like Darwin, however, functionalists saw the environment as a given that the organism must fit into, and, consequently, they avoided questioning whether the environment families were trying to adapt to was healthy. Thus, functionalism could be used to support a conservative political agenda. Also, functionalist assumptions can lead family therapists to become "pathology detectives" who interrogate family members to find the putative function the symptoms are serving. The difference between assuming that parents might be getting something out of their child's depression or troubles at school and assuming that they don't is the difference between thinking of them as conspirators, albeit unwitting, or allies. Considering the possibility that symptoms might serve some function may occasionally uncover a hidden conflict. The danger of assuming that families profit from their troubles is more than failed compassion; it sets up an us-against-them mentality.

General Systems Theory

Ludwig von Bertalanffy was a prominent biologist who began to wonder if the laws that applied to biological organisms might also apply to other domains, from the human mind to the global ecosphere. Originally investigating the interrelationships among the organs of the endocrine system, he began extrapolating from these observations to more complex social systems. He developed a model that was mistranslated from the German as General Systems Theory (GST), the last word of which he intended to have been "teaching," because it is not so much a theory as an approach, a way of thinking or a set of assumptions that can be applied to all kinds of systems.

Bertalanffy published widely and had some influence on all the social sciences, but, unlike Bateson, he had no extended direct contact with the pioneers of family therapy. In addition, as will be discussed later, Bertalanffy had a life-long disdain for mechanism and was highly critical of cybernetics, the mechanistic model that came to dominate family therapy. Consequently, although many of the concepts of GST seem to have seeped into the family therapy literature, Bertalanffy's work is rarely cited, and, where it is noted, it is often described as being basically the same as cybernetics (Bateson, 1971; Becvar & Becvar, 1988).

Part of Bertalanffy's obscurity may be because he was a generalist, spreading his ideas over the fields of medicine, psychiatry, psychology, sociology, history, education, philosophy, and biology, and also because GST is not a clear-cut theory with a list of testable hypotheses. Until Mark Davidson's thoughtful biography, *Uncommon Sense* (1983), there was no overview or summary of Bertalanffy's voluminous work to help us recognize the immensity of his contribution. Davidson (1983) summarized Bertalanffy's definition of a system as:

> . . . any entity maintained by the mutual interaction of its parts, from atom to cosmos,

> and including such mundane examples as telephone, postal, and rapid transit systems. A Bertalanffian system can be physical like a television set, biological like a cocker spaniel, psychological like a personality, sociological like a labor union, or symbolic like a set of laws. . . . A system can be composed of smaller systems and can also be part of a larger system, just as a state or province is composed of smaller jurisdictions and also is part of a nation. Consequently, the same organized entity can be regarded as either a system or a subsystem, depending on the observer's focus of interest. (p. 26)

His last point is an important one. Every system is a subsystem of larger systems. When they adopted the systems perspective, family therapists forgot about this spreading network of influence. They regarded the family as a system but ignored larger systems of community, culture, and politics in which families are embedded.

Bertalanffy pioneered the idea that a system was more than the sum of its parts, in the same sense that a watch is more than a collection of cogs and springs or a symphony is more than a cluster of notes. There's nothing mystical about this, just that when things are organized into a system, something else emerges: the relationship of the component parts that is more or different, the way water emerges from the interaction of hydrogen and oxygen. Thus, Bertalanffy conveyed the importance of focusing on the pattern of relationships within a system rather than on the substance of its parts.

Bertalanffy believed that science had become *reductionistic* in its tendency to analyze phenomena by dissecting whole systems and studying their parts in isolation. While reductive analysis has a place in science, he believed the study of whole systems had been grossly neglected, and he urged scientists to learn to "think interaction."

Applied to family therapy, these ideas—that a family system should be seen as more than just a collection of people and that therapists should focus on interaction among family members rather than individual personalities—became central tenets of the field.

Like the functionalists, Bertalanffy used the metaphor of an organism for social groups, but an organism that was an *open system*, continuously interacting with its environment. Open systems, as opposed to closed systems (which are nonliving), sustain themselves by continuously exchanging material—for example, taking in oxygen and expelling carbon dioxide—with their environment.

One difference between Bertalanffy's view of organisms and the functionalist perspective was his emphasis on the interrelationship between an organism and its environment, which, of course, includes other organisms. The mechanists forgot that organisms don't just react to stimuli, they actively initiate efforts to flourish.

Bertalanffy was a life-long crusader against the mechanistic view of living systems, particularly those living systems called people. He believed that, unlike machines, living organisms demonstrate *equifinality*, the ability to reach a given final goal in a variety of ways. (In nonliving systems, the final state and the means to that state are fixed.) He and other biologists used that term to identify the organism's inner-directed ability to protect or restore its wholeness, as in the human body's mobilization of antibodies and its ability to repair skin and bone (Davidson, 1983).

Thus, living organisms are creatively, spontaneously active and use many methods to maintain their organization, but aren't solely motivated to maintain the status quo. Family therapy picked up on the concept of *homeostasis*, the tendency of systems to regulate themselves to maintain cohesion in response to changes in the environment. This term, coined by French physiologist Claude Bernard in the nineteenth century to describe the regulation of such conditions as body temperature or blood sugar level, fits some of the behavior of organisms, but

Bertalanffy believed that an overemphasis on this conservative aspect of the organism reduced it to the level of a machine. Bertalanffy wrote that "If [this] principle of homeostatic maintenance is taken as a rule of behavior, the so-called well-adjusted individual will be [defined as] a well-oiled robot . . ." (quoted in Davidson, 1983, p. 104). "In the sense of homeostasis, Michelangelo should have followed his father's advice and gone into the stonecutting business. He would have had a much happier life than the one he led painting the Sistine Chapel in a very uncomfortable position" (quoted in Davidson, 1983, p. 127).

As we shall discuss later, homeostasis is more central in cybernetics, the study of self-regulating systems like thermostats, endrocrine systems, or guided missiles, than it is in GST. Homeostasis was introduced to family therapy by Don Jackson (1957) as a way to explain the tendency of families to resist change. While it remains an important concept in family therapy, its limited ability to account for the wide variety of human behavior has been repeatedly acknowledged by family therapists in ways that echo Bertalanffy's concerns (Hoffman, 1981; Speer, 1970; Dell, 1982). The cyberneticians had to propose new concepts like "morphogenesis" (Speer, 1970) to account for what Bertalanffy believed was simply a property of organisms—to seek, in addition to resisting, change.

One of Bertalanffy's chief quarrels with the mechanistic view of people was that it led to valuelessness, a concern that foreshadowed the feminist critique of family therapy. If families are like machines, then therapists simply study how they work, determine how they become "dysfunctional," and repair the dysfunction. None of this requires an evaluation of the family's functional state or, for that matter, the culture in which it exists, in terms of inequity or violence.

If a family mechanic (therapist) encountered a rebellious adolescent daughter in a striving American family in which the father is never at home and mother hassles the girl about her friends and her appearance, the mechanic might try to break the covert coalition between the father and daughter and encourage the father to support the mother's attempts to discipline the girl. This structural repair might calm the situation and decrease the girl's defiance so that the family could become more "functional." But the therapist would have failed to question the effect of the father's absenteeism on the health of the family members. A Bertalanffian therapist might encourage the family to weigh the economic benefits of the father's long hours at work against the effects of his lack of involvement with the family and high level of stress.

If you think ecologically, you can't avoid values because it becomes clear that certain values are ecological and others are not, whether they're held by an individual, a family, a community, or a nation. A balance must exist among the parts of a system, and whenever one part strives for unrestrained influence, the system and those systems above and below it will lose this healthy balance. Until the 1990s, family therapists by and large tried to remain value-free mechanics.

Bertalanffy's insistence on the importance of human belief systems predated the recent shift in family therapy's focus from behavior to belief. His emphasis on values and beliefs was the result in part of his understanding of the inadequacies of *logical positivism*, the philosophy that has dominated western science since the nineteenth century. Logical positivism holds that the only valid data are those derived from observations that can be empirically verified. This paradigm divorced science from philosophy and ethics with the assumption that only through empiricism can we arrive at the truth. Logical positivism was shaken by the discovery in physics earlier this century that subatomic particles didn't really exist in the sense that we are used to thinking about things existing. Fritzjov Capra (1982), whose book *The Turning Point* provides a good overview of systems thinking in the sciences, describes the discovery this way. "At the subatomic level, matter does not exist with certainty at definite places, but rather shows 'tendencies to exist' . . . subatomic particles have no meaning as isolated entities but can be understood only as interconnections, or correlations, between various processes of observation and measurement" (p. 80). Thus it seems that there are no elementary particles to be found and analyzed. This discovery, captured by the famous Heisenberg uncertainty principle, led theorists in many fields to question absolutist positions on the nature of things.

To counter positivism, Bertalanffy (1968) used the term "perspectivism" to characterize his belief that while reality exists, we can never be fully objective about it, because our view is filtered through our particular perspective. To a man with a hammer, everything looks like a nail. To a physicist, a table is a collection of electrons. A chemist sees the same table as organic compounds, the biologist sees a set of wood cells, and the art historian sees a baroque object. To Bertalanffy, all those views have some validity, but each is incomplete and none should be seen as more authentic than the others.

Bertalanffian perspectivism is similar to a philosophy, derived from Kant, known as *constructivism*, which had a major impact on family therapy in the 1980s and early 1990s. Therapists began to recognize that the way people interpret events largely determines the way they interact with each other. Therapy became an exercise in changing meanings, and constructivism gave therapists a philosophy that justified that meaning-focused practice. The following Bertalanffian quote might just as well have come from Paul Watzlawick or any of the other constructivist writers who have influenced, in particular, the strategic or brief family therapies.

> There are no facts flying around in nature as if they are butterflies that you put into a nice orderly collection. Our cognition is not a mirroring of ultimate reality but rather is an active process, in which we create models of the world. These models direct what we actually see, what we consider as fact. (Quoted in Davidson, 1983, p. 214)

Bertalanffy also recognized that the act of observation has an effect on the observed. This awareness strengthened his perspectivist conviction that we should be humble about our observations and theories rather than search for absolute truth; we should keep our minds open to new ideas.

Some family therapists have interpreted constructivism to mean that since no one has a corner on absolute reality, any interpretation is as valid as any other, and, therefore, therapists are free to "reframe" reality in any way they want as long as the family buys it (Duncan & Solovey, 1989). Bertalanffy would have objected. He believed that our inability to know absolute reality implied that we should be more rather than less concerned with our basic values and assumptions because some perspectives are ecologically destructive. Thus, therapists should carefully scrutinize their values and those of their theories in terms of their ecological impact. Also, if therapists are co-creating new perspectives with clients rather than revealing truths to them, therapists should be more, not less, concerned with the impact of those perspectives. Bertalanffy had this to say to the theorists and philosophers of the world: "It is we who, in the last resort, manufacture the glasses through which people look at the world and at themselves—little as they may know it . . . I dare say we are the great spectacle makers in history" (quoted in Davidson, 1983, p. 69).

To summarize, Bertalanffy brought up many of the issues that have shaped and still are shaping family therapy:

- A system as more than the sum of its parts
- Emphasis on interaction within and among systems versus reductionism
- Human systems as ecological organisms versus mechanism

- Concept of equifinality
- Homeostatic reactivity versus spontaneous activity
- Importance of ecological sound beliefs and values versus valuelessness
- Perspectivism (or constructivism) versus logical positivism

Many of these issues will reappear in the ensuing discussion of cybernetics and throughout the book.

Cybernetics of Families

Cybernetics was developed and named (from the Greek word for helmsman) by Norbert Weiner, a mathematician at MIT. During World War II, Weiner was asked to work on the problem of how to get guns to hit moving targets. From that work he expanded his ideas about cybernetic systems—that is, systems that are self-correcting—to the way people or animals operate. At MIT he collaborated on this project with another famous mathematician, John Von Neumann, but the ideas quickly spread to theorists in other disciplines who refined or expanded cybernetics. Other well-know contributors include physiologist Warren McCulloch, psychologist Kurt Lewin, and anthropologists Gregory Bateson and Margaret Mead (Becvar & Becvar, 1996). These thinkers, as well as others from anatomy, engineering, neuropsychology, and sociology, were communicating with one another in a remarkable multidisciplinary network. It's interesting to contrast this level of multidisciplinary cross-fertilization with the insular way that family therapy developed and, for the most part, remains today.

At the core of cybernetics is the concept of the *feedback loop*, the process by which a system gets the information necessary to self-correct in its effort to maintain a steady state or move toward a preprogrammed goal. This feedback includes information about the system's performance relative to its external environment as well as the relationship among the system's parts. Feedback loops can be *negative* or *positive*. This distinction refers to the effect they have on deviations from a steady, homeostatic state within the system, not to whether they are beneficial. *Negative feedback* reduces deviation or change; *positive feedback* amplifies it.

Because cybernetics developed from the study of machines, where positive feedback loops led to destructive "runaways" in which the machinery breaks down, the emphasis was on negative feedback and the maintenance of homeostasis in the face of change. The system's environment would change—the temperature outside a house would go up or down exceeding a certain temperature range—and this change would trigger the negative feedback mechanisms to bring the system back to homeostasis—the air conditioning or heat would go on.

As applied to families, cybernetics focused attention on several phenomena: (1) *family rules*, which govern the range of behavior a family system can tolerate (i.e., the family's homeostatic range), (2) *negative feedback* mechanisms that families use to enforce those rules (e.g., guilt, double messages, symptoms), (3) *sequences of family interaction* around a problem that characterize a system's reaction to it (i.e., the feedback loops around a deviation), and (4) what happens when a system's accustomed negative feedback is ineffective, triggering *positive feedback loops*.

For example, in a family with a low threshold for the expression of anger, Johnny, the adolescent son, blows up at his parents over their insistence that he not stay out past midnight. Mother is shocked and begins to cry. Father is outraged and responds by grounding Johnny for a month. Rather than reducing Johnny's deviation—bringing his anger back within homeostatic limits—this negative feedback from the parents produces the opposite effect: Johnny explodes and challenges their authority. The parents respond with more crying and punishing, which further escalates Johnny's anger, and so on. In this way the parents' original negative feedback (crying and punishing) becomes positive feedback. It amplifies rather than diminishes Johnny's deviation. The family is caught in a positive feedback "runaway," otherwise known as a vicious cycle.

Later, cyberneticians like Walter Buckley and Ross Ashby recognized that positive feedback loops aren't all bad and can help systems adjust to changed circumstances if they don't get out of hand. Johnny's family needed to recalibrate their rules for anger to accommodate an adolescent's increased assertiveness. The crisis that this positive feedback loop produced could lead to a reexamination of the family's rules, if the family could step out of the loop long enough to get some perspective. In so doing they would be *metacommunicating*, communicating about their ways of communicating, a process that can lead to a change in the system's rules (Satir, 1972). Recognition that positive feedback can lead to change was the conceptual foundation for some of the crisis-inducing forms of family therapy. As Haley (1971a) suggested, "If a treatment program subdues and stabilizes the family, change is more difficult. . . . To change a stabilized, miserable situation and create space for individual growth of family members, the therapists often must induce a crisis which creates instability" (p. 8).

Today, many family therapists have moved away from this kind of crisis-inducing therapy, believing that calmer and more reasoned conversations produce a safer environment for change. It is a mistake, however, to confuse calmer with the absence of challenge to a family's rules or structure. It's possible to encourage family members to bring up secrets or deal with conflict openly without letting sessions turn into unproductive shouting matches. Regardless of the level of emotion in the therapy office, effective therapists will find ways to stretch families to reexamine and change the rules governing them.

Such a change in family rules is what cybernetically oriented family therapists call *second-order change*, to distinguish it from *first-order change*, in which a family changes some behaviors but those behaviors are still governed by the same rules (Watzlawick, Weakland, & Fisch, 1974). For example, Johnny's family might shift the focus of their disagreements from his curfew to his sister's boyfriend (first-order change), yet their patterns around the issues wouldn't change significantly because their repressive rules about anger (second-order) remain unchanged. Unclear communication results in inaccurate feedback, so the system cannot self-correct (change its rules) and, consequently, overreacts or underreacts to change.

Cybernetics was introduced to family therapy by Gregory Bateson. Bateson encountered Wiener and cybernetics shortly after World War II during the Macy Conferences, a series of gatherings of high-level thinkers from diverse disciplines who tried to apply their theories to problems in a variety of fields. Bateson became interested in the feedback processes of systems and pioneered a conceptual shift that was pivotal to family systems thinking, the shift from linear to *circular causality*.

Before the advent of family therapy, explanations of psychopathology were based on linear medical, psychodynamic, and behavioral models. In all of these, etiology was conceived in terms of prior events—disease, emotional conflict, or learning history—which caused symptoms in the present. Using the concept of circularity, Bateson helped us change the way we think about psychopathology, from something caused by events in the past to something that's part of ongoing, circular feedback loops.

The concept of linear causality is based on a Newtonian model, in which the universe is like a billiard table where the balls act unidirectionally on each other. Bateson believed that while linear causality was useful for describing the nonliving world of forces and objects, it was a poor model for the world of living things, because it neglects to account for communication and relationships as well as force.

To illustrate this difference, Bateson (1979) used the example of a man kicking a stone versus kicking a dog. The effect of kicking a stone can be precisely predicted by measuring the force and the angle of the kick and the weight of the stone. If the man kicks a dog, on the other hand, the effect is far less predictable. The dog may respond to a kick in any number of ways, from cringing and running away to turning and biting the man, depending on the temperament of the dog and how it interprets the kick. In response to the dog's reaction, the man may modify his behavior in various ways, and so on, so that the number of possible outcomes is immense.

In addition to observable circular feedback loops, Bateson was also quite interested in how messages are interpreted by those receiving them. Mechanistic cyberneticians believed one could understand systems simply by studying their behavioral inputs and outputs, and in that sense, as Bertalanffy asserted, they were basically behaviorists but with the addition of the feedback loop. Bateson, however, rather than limiting his interest to behavioral sequences, studied the meaning that people derived from communication and its context.

When they began to study families directly, the Bateson group split into two camps (Haley, 1981; Simon, 1982). On one side was Bateson, continuing to focus on the way the receiver of communication processed it and interested in the way individuals perceive and learn. On the other side, Haley and Weakland were taken by the cybernetic metaphor and wanted to focus exclusively on the observable interaction patterns among family members.

The Bateson project ended in 1962 and Bateson shifted his interests away from psychiatric phenomena. The legacy of the project to psychotherapy was left to the other Bateson project and Mental Research Institute members, who (with the exception of Satir) advanced the mechanistic notions of homeostasis and feedback loops, keeping a logical positivistic focus on observable behavior sequences and ignoring Bateson's concerns about the individual's perception and learning (Breunlin, Schwartz, & Karrer, 1992). These theorists adopted a "black box" metaphor to justify their mechanistic position:

> The impossibility of seeing the mind "at work" has in recent years led to the adoption of the Black Box concept from the field of telecommunication . . . the concept is more generally applied to the fact that electronic hardware is by now so complex that it is sometimes more expedient to disregard the internal structure of a device and concentrate on the study of its specific input–output relations. . . . This concept, if applied to psychological and psychiatric problems, has the heuristic advantage that no ultimately unverifiable intrapsychic hypotheses need be invoked, and that one can limit oneself to observable input–output relations, that is, to communication. (Watzlawick, Beavin, & Jackson, 1967, pp. 43–44)

Viewing people as black boxes seems the ultimate expression of the mechanistic tendencies that Bertalanffy lamented. But this metaphor had the advantage of simplifying the field of study by eliminating speculation about the mind and emotions of the individual as well as the history of the family. In addition, one could judge the outcome of therapy equally simply—if the problem was solved and the system returned to a functional state, the outcome was positive, and therapy could end. Hence the evolution of brief, strategic therapy.

Power and Control. Another fundamental disagreement split this group, which by the early 1960s was theorizing from the Mental Research Institute (MRI) in Palo Alto. Haley believed that communication was motivated by people's desire to control each other. His first law of relationships was that "when one person indicates a change in relation to another, the other will act upon the first so as to diminish and modify that change" (Haley, 1963, p. 189). Bateson strongly objected to the use of power and control metaphors, and the other family cyberneticians at the MRI strove to avoid imputing any motivation to people's behavior and instead to simply observe feedback loops (Haley, 1981).

Haley's view of social behavior as attempts to control others led him, more than any other family therapy pioneer, to maintain the functionalist legacy. He now believes that the underlying motive for attempts to control others is love rather than power. He also became less attached to his functionalist assumptions and now sees them as potentially useful hypotheses rather than as factual explanations. Nonetheless, therapists who use the brand of strategic therapy developed by Haley and Cloe Madanes continue to consider the function a symptom serves, not only for the symptom-bearer, but also for the family.

In view of his interest in interpersonal control, it's not surprising that Haley was also drawn to hypnosis. During the years of the Bateson project, as the emphasis shifted from research to therapy, he and John Weakland traveled periodically to Phoenix to study with the well-known hypnotherapist Milton Erickson. Haley (1985) reports, "As we sought consultation and supervision, Dr. Erickson was the only person who could advise us on interview technique with couples and families" (p. 32).

Bateson had reservations about psychotherapy and was wary that the impulse to change systems would supercede that of understanding them. Haley remembers that:

> Bateson was an anthropologist to his soul and an anthropologist doesn't believe you should tamper with the data or change it in any way. . . . After I met Erickson and began to go into a very directive style of therapy in which you produce a change, Bateson got more and more uncomfortable, particularly when I began describing the therapy relationship as a struggle for control or power. (Simon, 1982, p. 22)

Thus, with the exception of Bateson himself, the interests of Bateson Project members shifted from studying people's behavior in context to using that interpersonal context to influence their behavior, and Erickson was a master at manipulating interpersonal contexts.

Haley (1985) again explains, "At that time we were studying communication, focusing on how messages are classified and the paradoxes that occur when levels of messages conflict. Erickson's work was replete with deliberate use of paradox" (p. 32) (see Chapter 11 for more on using paradox and Erickson's influence on technique). Thus, through Erickson, these researchers-cum-therapists were introduced to a wide array of powerful and unorthodox techniques, including such famous maneuvers as paradoxical directives, reframing, and using the client's language, that they applied to families. Indeed, the MRI model (see Chapter 11) of brief therapy could be seen as essentially an elaboration of Erickson's techniques (Bogdan, 1983).

Erickson's beliefs about people had a strong impact on family therapy, countering some of the pessimistic assumptions of cybernetics. Haley (1985) relates that "As we applied the notion [of homeostasis] to families in therapy, it took the form of resistance to change. When we offered these ideas to Dr. Erickson, he responded with polite irritation. He thought, correctly I believe, that a theory that encouraged the notion that people resist change was a noxious theory for a therapist, since expecting resistance encourages it" (p. 32). Erickson's optimistic view of people—that they wanted to change and possessed the resources to do so—was perhaps his most important contribution to family therapy. At a time when the psychotherapy establishment was pessimistic about change, and therapy was long term, interpretive, nondirective, and suspicious of symptom-removal, Erickson's approach was optimistic, brief, directive, problem-focused, and, at times, included the client's family or others in treatment. Erickson offered Haley, Weakland, and their colleagues in Palo Alto an antidote to all the things they didn't like about psychoanalysis as well as an antidote to the pessimism of the homeostatic model.

From Cybernetics to Structure

Haley's interest in power led him to focus on the hierarchy, or generational power structure, of families. He pioneered the understanding of child problems as being the result of coalitions that cross the boundary between children and parents, much like the coalitions that crossed the line of authority between patients and staff in Stanton and Schwartz's mental hospital. With these concepts of hierarchy and boundary, Haley's interest moved toward the structure of families rather than just their communication circuits. In 1967 he left the MRI and joined the architects of structural family therapy, Salvador Minuchin and Braulio Montalvo at the Philadelphia Child Guidance Clinic.

In contrast to the cybernetic model of the MRI, structural family theory owes a debt to the organismic (Bertalanffy and cellular biology) and structural–functional (Malinowski, Radcliffe-Brown, Levi-Strauss, Parsons) trends in the social sciences, mentioned earlier. The family is viewed as an organism, an open system made up of subsystems, each of which is surrounded by a semipermeable *boundary*, which is really a set of rules governing who is included within that subsystem and how they interact with those outside it.

To appreciate structural family therapy's functionalist heritage, consider this passage by Talcott Parsons (Parsons & Bales, 1955):

> That the [nuclear family] is itself a subsystem of a larger system is of course a sociological commonplace. But to break it in turn down into subsystems is a less familiar way of looking at it. Yet we will treat the family in this way and say that, in certain crucially important respects, the very young child does not participate in, is not fully a "member," of his whole family, but only of a subsystem of it, the mother–child subsystem. The marriage pair constitute another subsystem as may, for certain purposes, also the child with all his siblings, all the males in the family, all the females, etc. In fact, any combination of two or more members as differentiated from one or more other members may be treated as a social system which is a subsystem of the family as a whole. (p. 37)

Thus, as early as 1955, families were viewed in this structural way—as having subsystems with boundaries separating them.

According to structural theory, a healthy structure for the family organism requires clear boundaries, particularly generational boundaries. Unclear boundaries (overly rigid or overly diffuse) create a dysfunctional family structure, one manifestation of which is a symptomatic family member. If the structural flaw is corrected, the family organism will return to health (Bertalanffian equifinality).

Thus, where the cyberneticians saw circular interactions maintaining problems, structural therapists saw boundary violations resulting in inappropriate alliances and coalitions. Where cyberneticians were interested in the temporal (tracking sequences over time), structural family therapists were interested in the spatial (the proximity of family members to one another).

The structural perspective can be best characterized by this premise: The key to changing individuals is to change their structural context—the network of relationships in which they are embedded. A related assumption is that, no matter how incompetent a family member appears to be, an improvement in family structure will elicit a more competent self, which, in turn, will reinforce family change. Thus, the structural view of people is actively optimistic.

In his efforts to find a model effective with a disadvantaged population, Salvador Minuchin borrowed the Bertalanffian view of systems as open and flexible and the Parsonian concepts of structure and emphasis on generational boundaries, concepts that were used in social science at that time and had been adopted to varying degrees by more psychoanalytically oriented family theorists, such as Theodore Lidz and Nathan Ackerman. Minuchin, however, discarded the psychoanalytic aspects of their theories and techniques, and, in the process of experimenting with action-oriented techniques, discovered the power of an individual's external context as well as ways to harness that power.

In so doing, Minuchin provided the first clear map to understanding and reorganizing families, a map received as a godsend by legions of bewildered therapists lost amid a confusing jungle of family entanglements. As a therapist and a speaker, Minuchin was charismatic and authoritative at a time when the field was hungry for leadership. He was the street fighter who stood up to the psychiatric establishment, eventually armed with outcome data that could not be dismissed. For all these reasons, structural family therapy became the most popular and influential brand of family therapy in the 1970s.

Satir's Humanizing Effect

Family therapy is often associated with the concept of hierarchy because of its emphasis on encouraging parents to become effective disciplinarians. Through the work of Minuchin and Haley, that disciplinary aspect of hierarchy has been the primary focus of systems-based family therapists, including the MRI family cyberneticians. Virginia Satir focused on the other face of hierarchy. She was devoted to getting parents to be more affectionate and loving to each other and to their children, in addition to being more firm.

As an early member of the MRI, Satir was exposed to the same functionalist and cybernetic influences that produced the MRI model of Watzlawick and Weakland and Haley's version of strategic therapy. Thus, her theorizing included the idea that children's symptoms can serve the function of distracting from an unhappy marriage and that communication is key in family process. Satir's philosophy of therapy, however, was very different. She added yin to what was becoming an overly yang field through her involvement with the human potential movement, pioneered by Abraham Maslow and Carl Rogers.

In contrast to the MRI model's view of people as cybernetic black boxes, Haley's power-game players, and Minuchin's context reactors, Satir saw people as longing for self-esteem, that is, to feel good about themselves, and to get close to others. "The critical factor in what happens both inside and between people is the picture of individual worth that each person carries around with him" (Satir, 1972, p. 21). Her interest in promoting self-esteem kept her focused on the humanity of individuals at a time when her contemporaries were actively ignoring individual feelings in their struggle to understand families.

Her humanistic orientation led Satir to try to change families into incubators for the positive, loving qualities she believed to be at the core of human nature. Her interest in communication wasn't so much to break up dysfunctional interactions but to encourage family members to drop the protective masks they show each other and to discover and express their real feelings.

To illustrate the differences between Satir and the other models, suppose a father says angrily to his teenaged daughter "You can't go out tonight!" MRI cyberneticians might see this as the start of an escalating positive feedback loop, Haley might hear the command message of "I am in control of you" beneath the father's outburst, and Minuchin might hear the father's anger as a reaction to a mother–daughter coalition that leaves him out. Satir, on the other hand, might hear the father wanting but afraid to say "I want you to stay home tonight because I miss you and feel you slipping away."

The father doesn't speak openly about his love because he's afraid of being rejected, which would be a blow to his self-esteem. If, however, the father could be honest, his daughter would have a chance to express her mixed feelings about growing up and away from him, and they'd both feel better for having leveled with each other. Thus, Satir believed that the relationship between self-esteem and communication was circular. Low self-esteem begets defensive, incongruent communication, which elicits similarly defensive responses from others, which, in turn, engender low self-esteem, and so on. Fortunately, however, the cycle can be virtuous as well as vicious: honest communication engenders high self-esteem, which encourages more honesty, and so on (Satir, 1972, 1988).

The key to increasing self-worth is straight-from-the-heart communication. To achieve this, therapists must create an atmosphere that allows family members to feel safe and accepted enough to risk openness. The therapist must be able to challenge people's defensiveness without threatening their self-esteem, and so must be a model of honesty and acceptance.

To summarize, Satir deviated from the mechanistic aspects of the Palo Alto model. Instead of control, she focused on nurturance. She was concerned with the experience of individual family members, whereas the others believed that such a focus distracted from seeing interactional patterns. She worked to improve communication and self-esteem, whereas her male colleagues remained problem-focused. She fostered close, collaborative relationships with clients where the others maintained an air of distant authority. While Satir was seen by many of these theorists as naive and a fuzzy thinker, it may be that she was ahead of her time.

Bowen and Differentiation of Self

Up to this point all of the seminal thinkers described—the MRI group, Haley, Minuchin, Satir—had at least indirect contact with Bateson and his cybernetic perspective. Despite their differences, they all shared an interest in changing the current interactional patterns of the nuclear family system rather than the family of origin. Murray Bowen, the last family therapy pioneer we will consider here, evolved a version of systems theory apart from this cybernetic influence, and his ideas were quite different from these other models. What influenced Bowen's ideas were the biological sciences. In describing his reasons for looking to biology, Bowen (1978) said:

> On the premise that psychiatry might eventually become a recognized science, perhaps a generation or two in the future, and being aware of the past conceptual problems of psychoanalysis [that used metaphors from literature and hydraulics] . . . I therefore chose to use only concepts that would be consistent with biology and the natural sciences. It was easy to think in terms of the familiar concepts of chemistry, physics, and mathematics, but I carefully excluded all concepts that dealt with inanimate things. . . . The concept of differentiation was chosen because it has specific meaning in the biological sciences. When we speak of "differentiation of self," we mean a process similar to the differentiation of cells from each other. The same applies to the term fusion. (p. 354)

Bowen was struck by the fusion of schizophrenic patients and their mothers; that is, that they were so exquisitely reactive to each other. He later noticed that this was the case with the whole family and coined the phrase *undifferentiated family ego mass* to suggest that, because of their emotional reactivity, the whole family was like one chaotic conglomerate. Similarly, he found an absence of *differentiation of self*—emotions overwhelmed intellect to the point that everyone reacted automatically and impulsively. The goal of Bowen's therapy became the differentiation of self of key family members, so they could help the whole family differentiate.

This emphasis on differentiation, meaning control of reason over emotion, betrays Bowen's psychoanalytic roots. Freud's famous dictum "where id is, there ego shall be," is very much like differentiation. Indeed, Bowen (1978) saw the emotional system as "an intimate part of man's phylogenetic past which he shares with all lower forms of life," while the intellectual system was "a function of the cerebral cortex which appeared last in man's evolutionary development, and is the main difference between man and the lower forms of life" (p. 356).

In contrast to the antideterministic position taken by other family therapy pioneers, Bowen saw a person's level of differentiation as a relatively fixed trait that took a long time to change. He also believed that about 90 percent of the population was not well differentiated. Here, too, we hear Freud's echo.

The theory of evolution reappears in Bowen's speculations about how people arrive at their level of differentiation. He called this the *multigenerational transmission process* and believed that most children emerge from their families with the same level of differentiation as their parents, and only a few emerge with lower or higher levels. Thus the transmission of differentiation follows a "genetic-like pattern" across generations (Bowen, 1978, p. 410).

Given these beliefs, it's understandable that Bowen was less interested in trying to repair family communication patterns than were the other theorists. He saw the quality of communication in a family as a product of each family member's level of differentiation. Consequently, communication is unlikely to improve lastingly until differentiation improves. Bowen (1978) asserted that while approaches that work with the whole family to improve their communication "can produce dramatic shifts in the feeling system, and even a period of exhilaration . . . I have not been able to use this as a long-term method for resolving underlying problems" (p. 151).

Like the other family therapy pioneers, Bowen believed that child problems were related to the parents' marriage. In his theory the concept of triangles is central. He saw the forming of triangles as a natural human tendency in the face of anxiety. Whenever a two-person relationship, particularly two people not highly differentiated, experiences stress, a third person will be dragged in. "The twosome might 'reach out' and pull in the other person, the emotions might 'overflow' to the third person, or the third person might be emotionally programmed to initiate the involvement. With the involvement of the third person, the anxiety level decreases" (Bowen, 1978, p. 400). From this we can see that Bowen made many of the same function-of-the-symptom observations that became the centerpieces of other models; but, like the psychoanalysts, he saw these patterns as manifestations of an underlying process that had to be changed, rather than as direct targets of change.

Instead he believed that if people became aware of the existence of the triangling process in their nuclear and extended families, and learned to avoid being pulled into it, they would gradually differentiate. Bowen's interest in the evolution of levels of differentiation made him one of the few pioneers who paid much attention to a family's history. Other family therapy leaders believed that family problems could be solved by focusing on present interactions, so family histories were irrelevant. Bowen contended that to understand and improve one's family life, it was crucial to examine the mulitgenerational patterns in which one was embedded. By seeing how they are just one link in a long dysfunctional family chain, clients gained the perspective necessary to break the chain in their generation and begin the differentiation process.

Family Life Cycle

The concept of the *family life cycle* was borrowed from sociology to become the explanatory background to the structural and strategic approaches. Sociologists Evelyn Duvall and Reuben Hill began applying a developmental framework to families in the 1940s by dividing family development into discrete stages with different tasks to be performed at each stage (Duvall, 1957; Hill & Rodgers, 1964). Duvall's eight stages of family development laid the groundwork (Table 4.1), although later theorists have come up with different frameworks by adding or subtracting stages (Solomon, 1973; Barnhill & Longo, 1978).

TABLE 4.1 Duvall's Stages of the Family Life Cycle

Stage	Developmental tasks
1. Married couples without children.	Establishing a mutually satisfying marriage. Adjusting to pregnancy and the promise of parenthood. Fitting into the kin network.
2. Childbearing families (oldest child birth–30 months).	Having, adjusting to, and encouraging the development of infants. Establishing a satisfying home for both parents and infants.
3. Families with preschool children (oldest child 2 ½–6 years).	Adapting to the critical needs and interests of preschool children in simulating, growth-promoting ways. Coping with energy depletion and lack of privacy.
4. Families with children (oldest child 6–13 years).	Fitting into the community of school-age families. Encouraging children's educational achievement.
5. Families with teenagers (oldest child 13–20 years).	Balancing freedom with responsibility. Establishing postparental interests and careers.
6. Families launching young adults (first child gone to last child's leaving home).	Releasing young adults with appropriate rituals and assistance. Maintaining a supportive home base.
7. Middle-aged parents (empty nest to retirement).	Rebuilding the marriage relationship. Maintaining kin ties with older and younger generations.
8. Aging family members (retirement to death of both spouses).	Coping with bereavement and living alone. Closing the family home or adapting it to aging. Adjustment to retirement.

Family therapists Betty Carter and Monica McGoldrick (1980) enriched this framework by adding a *multigenerational point of view* and by considering stages of divorce and remarriage. That is, they extended the life cycle beyond the normative stages of a nuclear family's development to include unpredictable but common events and to consider a longer time frame. Their book, *The Family Life Cycle*, with chapters on the various stages, popularized the family life cycle concept, reminding therapists of the importance of history. Their second edition (Carter & McGoldrick, 1989) updates the developments in this area over the decade. Other family therapists injected systems ideas into the family life cycle framework so that the transitions between stages are not so discrete and the family as a whole can be characterized. Lee Combrinck-Graham (1983, 1985, 1988) views the three-generational family as alternating between centrifugal and centripetal states as events in their life cycle alternately call for more interdependence or individuation among family members. Douglas Breunlin's (1983, 1988; Breunlin, Schwartz, & Karrer, 1992) oscillation theory provides a sophisticated understanding of the transitions among family or individual life cycle stages. Breunlin demonstrates how such transitions are never discontinuous shifts but instead occur as gradual oscillations between stages or levels of functioning.

Like so many other new ideas, the concept of the family life cycle was first introduced to family therapy by Jay Haley (1973) in his book *Uncommon Therapy*. Haley saw symptoms as the result of a family becoming stuck at a transition between life cycle stages because of the inability or fear of making the transition. Later Haley (1980) focused on one particular life cycle stuck-point in his book *Leaving Home*, which provided strategies for working with families having difficulty launching their young adults.

The formulations of Minuchin (1974; Minuchin & Fishman, 1981) were also influenced by the life cycle concept. The structural model contained many of the ideas from sociology regarding stages and tasks, but couched in terms of the development of various subsystems within the family system and changes in hierarchy and parenting style as children mature. Problems develop when a family encounters a challenge—environmental or developmental—and is unable to adjust their structure to accommodate to the changed circumstances. Thus, problems are usually assumed to be a sign, not of a "dysfunctional family," but simply one that's failed to readjust its structure at one of life's turning points.

The MRI group (Watzlawick et al., 1974) also used the life cycle in their theory of problem formation. Life cycle transitions present a family with predictable difficulties which become problems because of the family's ill-fated attempted solutions. They used this life cycle understanding as a way to reframe the family's problem as normal rather than pathological.

This use of historical life cycle material to reframe current family problems was expanded by Mara Selvini Palazzoli and her Milan associates, who would explore a family's history in some detail to find information with which to develop a "positive connotation" of each family member's behavior. In addition, the Milan associates pioneered in the use of family rituals for facilitating the transitions between life cycle stages. The use of ritual in family therapy was later elaborated on and has become a prominent interest of many family therapists (Imber-Black, Roberts, & Whiting, 1989).

For reasons discussed above, Bowen was less interested in the life cycle of a nuclear family than the longer-term development of the extended family. Other psychodynamically oriented family therapists, however, proposed family life cycle models that were influenced by models of individual development. According to these theorists the development of families can become fixated or arrested at earlier stages, just as it can with individuals (Wachtel & Wachtel, 1986; Skynner, 1981; Paul, 1969; Barnhill & Longo, 1978). The goal becomes to help families recognize and work through these developmental arrests by, for example, mourning unresolved loss.

In summary, most of the early schools of family therapy paid at least lip service to the concept of the family life cycle, in their theorizing if not in their therapy. Strategic therapists, who didn't look much beyond who was doing to whom to keep an unhappy situation going, didn't see much value in accompanying the family on historical investigations, other than to find life cycle information with which to "normalize" the problems. Structural therapists, on the other hand, drew heavily on the family life cycle in their assessments of families. When faced with a family in distress, the first thing they consider is whether they might somehow be stuck in an organizational state that hasn't adjusted to meet a change in the life cycle.

Others have refined and improved the thinking about the family life cycle and, while there remains little consensus as to the best way to use the concept, it has received renewed interest and more sophisticated treatment (Falicov, 1988; Pittman, 1987; Carter & McGoldrick, 1989).

The newer models, like solution-focused and narrative ones, also have little use for the family life cycle framework because neither is interested in exploring historical antecedents of family dilemmas. While narrative therapists do ask about a family's or individual's history, their goal isn't to uncover stuck-points in the past, but rather to find episodes in which clients transcended their troubles.

Miscellaneous Contributions

In the preceding section we tried to summarize the major contextual and conceptual influences on family therapy during its formative years. In focusing this summary on only a few of the most influential theorists, we haven't done justice to the contribution of several other theorists whose work had an impact but didn't develop into a distinct school of family therapy. John E. Bell treated families as groups, helped parents learn to negotiate with their children, and introduced the idea that therapy can be conducted in planned stages. Christian Midelfort worked with families to help them mobilize latent forces of love and support. Norman Paul's technique of *operational mourning* was another attempt to stimulate healing emotional experiences in families.

Ivan Boszormenyi-Nagy's work initially drew little attention outside the scholarly wing of family therapy. Recently, however, his combination of psychoanalytic, systems, and ethical principles has become more influential as increasing numbers of family therapists are becoming interested in integrating psychoanalytic theory and family therapy.

Carl Whitaker is one of the major figures in the field, but his impact has been more personal than conceptual, in part because he argues against therapists having a preconceived theory that might interfere with their intuitions. His contributions include emphasizing the value of cotherapy, and teaching—by example—that family therapy can be a spontaneous and provocative experience. Theodore Lidz and Lyman Wynne also made early conceptual contributions derived from their work with schizophrenic families, which are described in Chapter 2.

Finally, no summary of influences would be complete if it didn't include the impact of the *one-way mirror* and *videotaping.* Originally used by Minuchin and Haley in a project to train people indigenous to the population they were treating to be therapists, the one-way mirror opened a window to the world of family process and therapy that had never existed before. It and the videotaping of sessions offered the ability to directly observe families in action, an ability that accounts in part for the rapid conceptual and technical strides that family therapy has made.

In addition, these technologies allowed students to observe and emulate the technique of master therapists and allowed supervisors to give direct and immediate feedback to students struggling with families. So-called "live" and video supervision have become standard training practices in institutes around the country. These technologies have also promoted the more recent "team work" approaches to family therapy, in which a team of therapists watch a session from behind the mirror and work with the therapist in treating the family (see Liddle, Breunlin, & Schwartz, 1988, for more on how training influences family therapy).

Summary of Conceptual Influences

To summarize the conceptual influences on the field, each of the family therapy pioneers was faced with the same set of questions for which there were no previous answers:

How do families operate?
How do families develop?
What is the difference between healthy and pathological families?
What is the relationship between a family member's symptom and the family's operation?
How can families change the way they operate?
Why do families sometimes resist taking steps toward improvement?

As we have seen, despite the similarity of many of their initial observations, the pioneers' answers to these questions varied enormously, and the therapeutic techniques derived from their answers varied even more. This variation was due in part to differences among the metaphors or conceptual traditions to which each pioneer turned for help. We have seen the influence of a panoply of disparate ideas on the development of the field: functionalism and structuralism, general systems theory, Ericksonian hypnotherapy, cybernetics and Bateson's interpretation of it, communication theory, the humanistic movement, cell biology and evolutionary theory, family life cycle theory from sociology, and psychoanalysis.

Each of these traditions conveys a different view of the nature of people and how they can change. We agree with Bertalanffy's assertion that a theory's basic assumptions regarding the human personality will dictate, to a large degree, the practices of its adherents. Those who view people as mechanistic black boxes will try anything to alter the communications among those boxes, and do so from a distance, like expert repairmen. Those who understand people through a lens of power and see symptoms as control operations also work from a distance and develop strategies to diffuse the power of the symptom or the power arrangements in the family that made it necessary.

Those who see people as chameleon-like in the degree to which they change when family relationships change use their own relationship with the family to change its structure and, consequently, work from a position of proximity. Those who believe people basically want intimacy and love will get close to family members to help them feel and share tender feelings. Those who see people as dominated by irrational emotionality will create a reflective atmosphere in which clients learn to stay rational in the face of family upset.

In family therapy's attempt to focus on the system rather than on the individuals who compose it, these fundamental assumptions about people, at times, have not been clearly articulated. Given the degree to which the methods of each model of family therapy are driven by its basic view of people, we recommend that those assumptions be carefully examined when evaluating a model.

Enduring Concepts and Methods

With the preceding discussion of family therapy's conceptual heritage as a backdrop, we will present below the concepts that seem most enduring and most useful.

Interconnectedness. The idea that change in any one part of a system will affect all the other parts seems like common sense. Yet it's often a lack of awareness of the connections between their actions that creates problems for family members. Much of family therapy is about helping people make those connections.

For example, Brian is the ten-year-old son of Emily Williams, an African-American single parent with a full-time job. When Brian began picking fights with his younger brother and challenging his mother's authority, Emily responded an escalating series of punishments, without success. Finally she concluded that her son was just a belligerent troublemaker. The pace of her life was so hectic that there was no time to reflect long enough to get more perspective on Brian's behavior.

By asking what other things were happening in the family when Brian became disruptive, their family therapist created the space Emily needed to realize that Brian's behavior may have been related to her father's death and her ensuing depression. Brian revealed how frightened he was to see his mother sitting and staring into space, sometimes for hours. When he made her angry, at least she wasn't paralyzed.

Ours is an individualistic culture in which people are assumed to be responsible for their behavior. Pregnant teenagers are judged to be immoral; unemployed people, lazy; drug addicts, hedonistic. We rarely look for connections and often consider any that are suggested as excuses for irresponsible behavior. The more out of control we feel as a society, the more we look for someone to blame. It shouldn't be surprising that family members adopt similarly blaming and simplistic views of one another. We are conditioned to see life as a series of unrelated events and, as a result, we become event-activated—caught off guard by unanticipated problems, we go into action to counter them without considering their larger context, their interconnectedness. This event orientation is often accompanied by what family therapists call *linear thinking*, looking for one specific cause of a particular problem, often a cause unrelated to family processes. Emily thought Brian was "just like his father—a bad seed."

The essence of systems thinking is seeing patterns of connection where others see only isolated events. These patterns of connection are often not obvious to those caught up in them, particularly when those people are besieged by the incessant demands of family life. Systems thinking requires the time and space to reflect and gain perspective. This perspective is what good family therapy provides.

Sequences of Interaction. But exactly what kinds of patterns do family therapists look for in helping people make these connections? As Jay Haley (1980) wrote years ago, "The chief merit of systems theory is that it allows the therapist to recognize repeating sequences and so make predictions. . . . There remains the problem of how to simplify the sequences so they become recognizable and useful." In their attempts to simplify the enormous complexity that families present, various models of family therapy have focused on different kinds of sequences.

Some of these differences can be explained by the various models' different goals for tracking particular sequences. Strategic therapists, for example, believe that families often react to problems in ways that only make them worse. Therefore, strategic therapists are interested in interactions around the presenting problem. They would want to know what Emily was doing when Brian acted up, and then how she responded to his behavior. How he reacted to her. Then what happened next; and so on. They might also want to know if Emily's mother gets involved in these interchanges and how that might affect the outcome.

Triangles. Family therapists are often concerned about third-party interference because they are interested in *triangles*. A variety of theorists have noted that when two people are in conflict they often pull in a third. Understanding the triangular nature of human interaction expands the therapist's lens, allowing for more possibilities. For example, it turned out that Emily's mother often criticized Emily's parenting style shortly after one of Brian's tantrums. This led Emily to be even more impatient with Brian and quick to attack him.

Without considering this triangle the therapist might get some improvement by changing things between Emily and Brian, but as long as Grandma was chronically needling Emily it's unlikely that this improvement would last. When triangles exist, the consequences of not exploring them, limiting the focus of therapy to the monadic or dyadic level, can be the failure of treatment. Whenever therapy isn't progressing as one expects, one should look for triangles.

Circular Sequences. Problematic patterns of interactions are usually repetitive and circular, so that assigning beginning and end points is entirely arbitrary. Brian acts up. Mom scolds him. Brian acts worse. Mom screams. Grandma scolds mom. Mom retreats to her room. Brian calms down. Mom comes out, seeming depressed. Brian acts up—and so on, round and round in repeating circles. Ask any one of them who started it and each will be generous in giving credit to the others. Who started it? It rarely matters. A better question is, what can each do differently now? The repeating sequences between Brian, Mom, and Grandma represent what is called *circular causality* (as opposed to linear causality) in the sense that every act in the circle is caused by and is causing every other. Rather than search for underlying causes, family therapists usually just try to interrupt these circular patterns of interaction.

It was also noted that many of these circles tend to be vicious. Sometimes, the more you do to try to solve the problem, the worse it becomes, which leads you to try more of the same, resulting in things getting still worse, and so on. The more Emily scolded Brian, the more he rebelled, leading her to shout and sometimes hit him, which led him to become even more aggressive and antagonistic to his brother, and so on. Event-oriented, linear types of attempted solutions tend to generate vicious circles (positive feedback loops) because they ignore the interconnectedness of people's actions.

The shifts from dyadic to triangular thinking and from linear to circular causality are some of the early and enduring advances in family therapy. These conceptual shifts distinguished family therapy from behavior therapy, which was concerned with patterns of dyadic reinforcement and psychodynamic approaches where the emphasis was monadic. Thus, contemporary family therapists still track (ask questions about) sequences related to the circular and triangular patterns that surround problems, and they also try to clarify communication.

Indirect Communication. Escalating vicious circles also are often related to the fact that family members don't receive the feedback they need to appreciate the effects of their actions. Feedback is delayed or distorted because families are plagued by *indirect communication.* When someone's angry at you, it's hard to tell that person about vulnerable feelings that are behind your protectiveness. In the face of Emily's wrath, Brian wasn't about to reveal his worry about her sadness or his own grief over the loss of his grandfather. So, instead of sad, he acted mad.

Emily's attempted solution made sense based on the feedback she was getting. She didn't know that her scolding of Brian was, in his mind, helping both of them avoid despondency. In other situations, feedback is delayed to the point where it's hard to connect it to the original action. This is often the case with environmental problems, where we may not reap what we sow for decades and even then not recognize the connection to our original actions. So we continue to pollute, oblivious to the consequences. Similarly, if a father's slapping of his son temporarily stops the boy's misbehavior, reinforcing dad's assumption that physical punishment works, it's unlikely that dad will connect his son's fighting with a playmate the following week to the original punishment. Much of family therapy involves creating an atmosphere in which it is safe for family members to divulge what's really going on for them—that is, to communicate directly—which provides the necessary corrective feedback that can turn vicious circles into virtuous ones.

Family Structure. Other models of family therapy, particularly the structural school of Salvador Minuchin (see Chapter 8), track sequences of family interaction not only because they maintain problems, but also because they are manifestations of the family's *structure.* Structure is generally defined by the rules that govern a set of relationships. In assessing families, for example, therapists are often interested in how close or distant various relationships are and what are the (often covert) rules that keep them that way. Another way of saying this is that family therapists assess a family's *boundaries,* which are thought to be like invisible membranes surrounding each set of relationships (or *subsystem*) within a family. Just as a biological organism is composed of cells with membranes that vary in permeability, allowing certain elements to enter or exit, so too the boundaries around various family relationships allow more or less interaction with other family members and with the extrafamilial world.

Healthy boundaries are neither too open nor too closed, neither too diffuse nor too rigid. They're open enough for a subsystem to receive the resources it needs, yet closed enough to protect its integrity. When boundaries are too open, family relationships are *enmeshed* (or fused), such that each person has trouble differentiating his or her own feelings and thoughts from those of others. When boundaries are too closed, relationships are *disengaged* (and could become cut off). For example, the boundary between Emily and Brian was impermeable to warm exchanges, and the two of them were avoidant to the point of disengagement. On the other hand, the boundary between Emily and her younger son, eight-year-old Nathan, was diffuse—she often spoke for him and had trouble letting him out of the house to play with friends because she felt the constant need of his company.

Grandma usually sided with Brian against Emily, so the boundary *around* Emily and Brian was too open in that there was not enough protection from Grandma's frequent intrusions. This illustrates another important aspect of family structure—the existence of *alliances* and *coalitions,* particularly those that cross generations. The coalition between Brian and Grandma made Emily feel rejected and resentful, which fueled the vicious cycle of her interactions with Brian. The family's *hierarchy* (the way leadership is organized), another key aspect of structure, was in a shambles. Emily's authority was undermined by the alliance between the other two. In addition, Brian's worrying about and covert protectiveness of his mother, which led him to distract her from her depression, made for an *incongruent hierarchy* in which he was caring for his parent rather than vice versa.

Another of family therapy's major contributions to the understanding of human nature, then, is the notion that extremes of behavior are often maintained by unaddressed structural problems. Dysfunctional boundaries, alliances and coalitions, and problematic hierarchies are powerful determiners of our actions and emotions, though we often are unaware of their influence. Instead, we generally feel compelled to act in certain ways, oblivious to the invisible forces pulling our strings.

This isn't just true in families. For example, you might find yourself in a work situation where you enthusiastically participate in conversations with your boss that put down one of your colleagues behind his back, despite the fact that you're usually careful not to engage in that kind of backstabbing. It wasn't until you were telling a friend about the situation at work who then remarked that she was surprised you would collude with your boss in that way that you realized she was right.

You were part of an unhealthy triangle in which there were issues between you and your boss that neither of you wanted to face, and there were things about your colleague that aggravated both of you but your boss was reluctant to confront. As a result, you and your boss formed a secret alliance, a form of cross-generational coalition, in which the two of you could avoid the tensions in your relationship by agreeing that the other guy was a jerk. Also, you so feared losing your job that you were happy to know that your colleague was viewed as worse than you, and you were glad to contribute to that perception.

Experiences like that one profoundly affected our understanding of the power of unhealthy structures to produce extremes in behavior and how difficult these structures are to change from the inside, even when one becomes aware of them. We all find ourselves trapped in structural ruts that we're afraid to leave. Fortunately, many of us actually can leave once we decide to take the risk. Unfortunately, many of the family members in therapy, particularly the children, are not so lucky. They are the reason it is so important to help family members reorganize their relationships.

Not only did family therapy discover the power of unhealthy structures to create problems, it also discovered that improving a structure can heal problems even when the problems aren't addressed directly. If you and your boss had been able to resolve your issues directly, you wouldn't have needed to scapegoat your colleague, whose difficult behavior only increased during this period. And perhaps your colleague's performance would have improved once he was no longer the target of your alliance.

Therapists interested in changing a family's structure track the sequences of interaction that are manifestations of that structure, rather than just the immediate events that revolve around the presenting problem. For example, in addition to learning about Emily's and Brian's relationship, they would ask about other relationships in the family (Emily and her mother, Emily and Nathan, Grandma and Nathan, Brian and Nathan). Through this questioning process, they gradually obtain a map of the family's internal politics. Once some sense of the family's organization has been gleaned, structural therapists set about reorganizing this arrangement by adjusting boundaries and hierarchy and by dissolving coalitions.

For example, a therapist might have Emily and her mother talk about the problems in their relationship, while keeping the two boys from interfering. Although this maneuver may not seem directly related to Brian's behavior problem, by improving the functioning of the family leaders (executive subsystem) such that they work together rather than undermining each other, a major structural flaw can be corrected.

When the therapist encouraged Emily and her mother to talk to each other rather than to him, he was creating an *enactment*. In keeping the boys from interfering in that enactment, he was using a technique called *boundary-making*. This same set of techniques could be used with Emily speaking to Brian (enactment), while keeping Grandma from interfering (boundary-making). The simple act of strengthening a boundary around a subsystem, while the members of the subsystem remain engaged with one another, is often enough to begin a powerful healing process.

Function of the Symptom. Unfortunately, structural problems in families are easier to spot than to resolve. Families face enormous stresses and go through disruptive changes that trigger event-oriented reactions and vicious circles of problem-maintaining behavior. Over time these patterns congeal into rigid relationship structures.

Some structural problems threaten a family's survival more than do others. For example, Emily's incapacitating grief and fights with her mother during which she often declared that she wanted to die were more frightening than were Brian's spats with Nathan. To avoid and distract themselves from highly consequential structural issues, families often accentuate innocuous ones. When Emily was paralyzed with grief, Brian provoked her. When Emily began to argue with Grandma, Brian pounded on Nathan. This isn't to suggest that Brian's behavior and Emily's distraction were necessarily conscious attempts to protect the family. More likely they were automatic reactions to the threatening sense of tension that surrounded certain interactional sequences. In this way, symptomatic behavior sometimes can be viewed as an adaptive response when a family cannot identify or resolve threatening structural problems.

Circumventing Resistance. Because families often fear what might happen if their conflicts were brought into the open, they resist focusing on their most sensitive problems. Early family therapists misinterpreted resistance—fear—as stubbornness—opposition to change (homeostasis). More recently, however, therapists have recognized that all human systems are reluctant to make changes they perceive to be risky. Families *should* resist change—even change that to outsiders seems obviously beneficial—until it's clear that the consequences of those changes are safe and that the therapist is trustworthy. Thus, it's possible to see resistance as prudent rather than bull-headed. Therapists who respect the protective function of resistance realize that it's better to make families feel safe enough to lower their walls than to try to batter down the walls or sneak around them. In sessions, they try to create a warm, nonblaming environment that engenders the hope that healing of even the most threatening issues is possible. In such an atmosphere, family members often spontaneously find the courage to face their difficult issues because, once they believe it is safe and possible, they want to change.

Emily avoided taking on her mother because she didn't believe it would do any good. She was afraid that if challenged, her mother would become even more critical of her and make her feel more depressed. These fears weren't unrealistic. In the past when Emily had said anything critical of her mother that's just what had happened. Other people's defenses look unreasonable only because we can't see their memories. Given Emily's history with her mother, it made sense for her to resist the therapist's urging that she let her mother know about her feelings.

For Emily to be convinced to try again, the therapist needed to build up credibility that working with him would improve things with her mother. To achieve this credibility, the therapist had to respect Emily's pace and listen to and address her fears, rather than confront or manipulate her resistance. Therapists encounter far less resistance when they approach families with an attitude of respectful curiosity, as collaborators who are trying help them identify what constrains them from relating in the way they want to, rather than as experts who point out their flaws and give them sage advice.

The Nonpathological View of People. As you imagine doing family therapy, you may wonder how, as a nice, respectful therapist, you can keep angry family members from screaming at one another or glaring in stony silence as the minutes tick by. Creating a safe atmosphere involves more than just establishing credibility and hope. A therapist must also show that he or she can prevent family members from hurting each other so they know that they can drop their protective armor without fear of attack. In family therapy's early years, it was thought that pushing family members into emotional crises was necessary to unfreeze their homeostatic patterns. Over time, however, therapists learned that while conflict is real and shouldn't be feared—as the old saying goes, "you can't make an omelet without cracking open some eggs"—change is still possible when family members interact in respectful and, if possible, compassionate ways. It's in those moments that they feel safe enough to be real with each other.

When working with family members who seem constantly at odds—screaming, stonewalling, belittling, distracting—it's hard to imagine getting them to treat each other with compassion. Such tolerance is particularly difficult to imagine if you view their anxiety as evidence of serious pathology, because you won't believe they have it in them. Thus, your fundamental beliefs about the nature of people will have a profound impact on what you can do in therapy.

One of family therapy's distinguishing features is its optimistic view of people. A number of family therapy models subscribe to the assumption that behind people's protective fortresses of anger or anxiety lies a healthy core self that can be reasonable, respectful, empathic, and compromising and that wants to change. When family members interact in this state, they often find that they can solve their problems themselves. It's their protective emotions that produce impasses and vicious circles.

But how does one help clients release their resourceful selves from the grip of fear and mistrust that burdens them as they enter therapy? How does one make them tolerant at times when they want to kill each another? Various approaches try to do this in different ways. Some therapists impose rules of communication to minimize the chance that interactions will turn ugly. These therapists ask family members to use only "I-statements," in which each person begins sentences with I feel/think/want, rather than by blaming the others. It's the difference between saying "You don't help out around here enough," and "I'd like you to help out a little more." Family members are also asked to repeat what they heard the other say to ensure that the message sent is the message received. When communication is structured in this way, family members often feel safe enough to disarm and let their unguarded selves emerge.

Another approach to fostering differentiation is to simply stop the action when communication seems destructively emotional and ask each family member to separate from extreme feelings and beliefs so they can return to a calmer state. If the therapist is firm and persistent, people often have a remarkable ability to put aside those interfering parts of themselves and shift into a more productive and compassionate stance, especially when they see other family members doing the same—a form of mutual disarmament.

Regardless of the therapist's technique, the key to generating productive interactions even in acrimonious sessions is the belief that such constructive potential exists within all clients. With that belief, therapists are able to take a collaborative role with clients because they trust that clients have the resources they need. Without that belief, therapists are pushed into the role of the expert who supplies the missing ingredients, whether those ingredients are insight, reparenting, educating, or medication. This isn't to suggest that family therapists who hold this competent self view never provide any of those ingredients; they just don't make presumptions about what is needed and work with clients to figure out what to provide.

Family-of-Origin. Other family therapists, particularly followers of Murray Bowen (see Chapter 5), actively discourage family members from talking directly to one another, at least until they achieve more self-differentiation (that is, more separation of their rational selves from their extreme emotions). The therapist speaks to family members one at a time and tones down emotionality by asking about what they think rather than feel. People are asked to reflect on their feelings rather than to react impulsively to what others say. As clients examine their reactions to one another, the therapist steers toward a discussion of unresolved issues from their families-of-origin. While many family therapists concentrate on problems in the current family, extended family systems therapists see current reactions as being magnified by extreme feelings or beliefs derived from growing up in their families-of-origin.

In other words, if you felt rejected by them, you will overreact when your spouse shows any signs of rejecting you. If you were caught up in a triangular relationship in which you protected your mother from your father, you're likely to recreate elements of that relationship in your family. Extended family system therapists watch for signs of these kinds of transference reactions as they observe family members interacting with each other. Some therapists then try to help clients gain insight into where their overreaction originated. Others, like the Bowenians, coach clients to remain their differentiated selves when they're with members of their original families, which they believe will translate into more differentiation in their current families.

When parents describe, in the presence of other family members, the experiences they endured as children, often the others are better able to understand the parents' extreme reactions and thus can empathize with rather than attack them. As Emily's mother recounted the brutal tongue-lashing she received from her own mother, Emily had a different view of why her mother was so protective of Brian when Emily scolded him. In addition, as Grandma continued to explore her past, she was better able to recognize that her protectiveness was not entirely rational and instead was embedded in a historical pattern going back several generations in which mothers attacked their children and protected their grandchildren.

In this way, taking emotional journeys into family members' pasts, often using *genograms* (schematic drawings of family trees, described in Chapter 5) in which family relationships are plotted over many generations, allows people to recognize the long-term patterns in which they are caught. Often the result is less blame and recrimination in the family and more determination to work together so that their generation will be the one to break the pattern.

Focusing on Solutions. Most family therapists are trained to focus attention on family problems and the interactions around those problems. The optimistic idea that people are basically competent—that they already possess the solutions to their problems—led some therapists to shift from tracking sequences around problems to those related to solutions. Steve de Shazer and Insoo Berg (see Chapter 11) pioneered this movement toward tracking solution-focused sequences that involves, for example, asking about what's happening in the family when the problem *isn't* occuring and encouraging family members to do more of what they do when the problem is absent. In other words, these therapists highlight and build on *exceptions* to the problem, which nearly always exist in family life but are often obscured by the family's preoccupation with and distress over the problem.

Thus, rather than listening to Emily complain about how often Brian misbehaves or even suggesting new parenting skills to her, a solution-focused therapist would explore what she and Brian do differently when he's pleasant and compliant. Emily reported that Brian could be delightful when he had his mother's undivided attention (for example, when Nathan was with his Grandma) and she was in a good mood. Unfortunately, these conditions were rare because Emily's moods were so labile. She was either upset about her father's death or angry at Brian. She thought that Brian should act better during this mourning period to help her out and she bitterly resented that he seemed to do just the opposite. The solution-focused therapist might simply ask Emily to expand the amount of pleasant time they spend alone together.

Changing a Family's Narrative. If at the outset of therapy you were to ask Emily about the story of her life, her narrative would be filled with a sense of powerlessness. She felt victimized by both Brian and her mother and by her economic predicament. She was also overwhelmed by the fear, sadness, and resentment that accompanied the loss of her father. This story of powerlessness and resentment colored all her experiences and interactions. Spending more pleasant time with Brian was difficult as long as she viewed him through the lens of that narrative.

Over the past decade, family therapists began to realize that overlying many of the problematic sequences or structures in families was a set of interpretations or expectations—a narrative about the family, derived from its history, that powerfully governed its functioning. As they began to ask clients about their stories, these therapists came to recognize how much stories affected which past events clients remembered and how they interpreted present events. Life stories function as filters to screen out experiences that don't fit the plot line or, if they can't be screened out, to distort events until they somehow fit. Families with problems come to therapy with pessimistic narratives that often keep them from acting effectively. Narrative therapists help people identify these oppressive narratives and co-create with them new, more productive stories about their lives.

Many of those who have adopted the narrative metaphor for therapy have argued that it isn't complementary to the systems approach, but rather represents a new paradigm that doesn't look at a family's or an individual's inner structure for flaws, instead it simply focuses on changing personal or family narratives. Consequently they reject most of the concepts and techniques described earlier in this chapter. They're not interested in the family dynamics or history that might have created or is maintaining the problem, nor are they concerned with the function that the problem might be serving for the system. Instead, they have ushered in a new set of techniques that help family members reconstitute their concepts of themselves and how powerless they are relative to the problem, regardless of family dynamics. This, then, is a poststructural (perhaps more accurately an antistructural) movement within family therapy that parallels poststructural revolutions in other fields. These revolutionary new ideas and techniques are discussed in detail in Chapter 12.

The Influence of Culture. By now the reader may be waiting impatiently for some discussion of the fact that Emily is a poor, African-American woman struggling to survive in American society and that she and all the members of her family are facing a host of daunting cultural attitudes and practices. (Other readers may have forgotten that Emily is black, just as some therapists overlook race as a key issue with their clients.) Since we're presenting family therapy's concepts and methods somewhat chronologically, it's fitting that this discussion of cultural influences comes at the end of the chapter, because for many years the field was relatively blind to the impact of the larger culture in which families are embedded.

While many family therapists cared about and worked with poor, minority families, their blindness in this regard was related to the belief that therapists shouldn't impose their values on clients and, consequently, shouldn't raise issues that families don't present as a problem. Also, they were so taken with the power of family therapy that they overestimated its ability to overcome extrafamilial obstacles. At some point, however, it became clear to many therapists that not raising cultural issues was itself an imposition of values—remaining "neutral" suggested they implicitly subscribed to the reigning belief system.

The feminist critique of the field in the early 1980s opened the door to broader social issues, and since then the field has increasingly looked beyond the boundaries of individual families. Therapists have recognized that many of the toxic narratives that constrain families are extreme versions of the narratives that permeate our society. Thus, interest has turned toward the impact on families of our culture's attitudes toward women, people of other races, people who are different (e.g., fat, foreign, physically or mentally handicapped, gay or lesbian), and people who are poor. In addition, families are encouraged to examine the impact of our society's striving materialism on their time together and their life choices. Just as family therapy made it unacceptable to consider an individual out of the context of his or her family, it is no longer valid to consider a family in isolation from patriarchy, racism, homophobia, classism, poverty, crime, work pressures, and materialism.

Toxic cultural narratives are inevitably absorbed into the stories family members have about themselves and reflected in the ways they interact with one another. These cultural narratives affect families differently, depending on where they reside in the social pecking order, and will affect individual family members differently, depending on where they are in the family hierarchy, but the effect is always insidious. By helping family members examine the effects of these external belief systems on their lives, therapists provide the perspective from which families can choose how much they want to buy into many assumptions they had previously taken for granted. Such discussions can have the effect of lifting families out of the pool of shame and recrimination about their problems that comes from being unaware of the social forces stacked against them. People shift their view of themselves and of one another from victims or culprits to survivors or heroes, nobly struggling against powerful constraints.

Emily welcomed the opportunity to separate from and reexamine a variety of narratives she had internalized from the American middle-class mainstream about being black, a woman (particularly a heavy woman), and a single parent. She also became aware of beliefs about the dangerousness of young black males that colored her view of Brian when he was aggressive and came not only from the media but also from her own peer group of African-American women. She took another look at the roots of her intense drive for financial success that had her working a full-time job and going to school while trying to raise two boys. She found that drive grounded not so much in American materialism as in a strong fear of poverty and the racial stereotypes that would accompany it. As she began looking at these narratives, rather than unconsciously living them, Emily was better able to decide what she believed and how she wanted to behave.

Conclusions

After reading this chronology of family therapy's concepts and methods, the reader may feel overwhelmed at the number of seemingly discontinuous shifts the field has undergone in the four decades of its existence. It may help to point out a pattern in this apparent chaos. The focus of therapy has continually expanded toward ever-wider levels of phenomena. This revolutionary process started when therapists looked beyond individuals to their families. Suddenly, unexplainable behavior in clients began to make more sense. Then, early family therapists concentrated on assessing and altering the sequences of behavioral interaction surrounding problems. Next, it was recognized that those sequences were manifestations of the family's underlying structure, and structure became the target of change. Then a family's structure was seen to be a snapshot of a long-term, multigenerational process that was governed by extreme belief systems, and therapists aimed their interventions at these underlying beliefs. Most recently it dawned on therapists that these belief systems did not arise in a vacuum, and hence the current interest in cultural narratives.

Another reason for the many discontinuous shifts in the field's history is that, beginning with their rebellion against the psychoanalytic and medical models, family therapists have long tended to be mavericks who have trouble with established wisdom. Whenever family therapy begins to congeal around a certain paradigm or practice such that it becomes the dominant narrative, the field reinvents itself. A new metaphor is proposed to replace the dominant one, which is rejected as totally passé. A new minority of therapists becomes the progressives on the cutting edge, relegating the leaders of the former revolution to the status of reactionary has-beens.

Currently, many therapists are rejecting systems thinking, referring to it as modernist and mechanistic and, consequently, much less useful than the new narrative metaphor. Decades of study, conceptual refinement, and technical development are blithely discarded for the new, improved way of thinking. While we believe that it's important for the field to try on new metaphors and practices and to continuously reexamine the old concepts and methods, it may not be necessary for each advance to be accompanied by a total rejection of the old. Our goal is to capture the exciting spirit of the new but maintain respect for the contributions of the giants on whose shoulders we all stand.

References

Ackerman, N. 1958. *The psychodynamics of family life.* New York: Basic Books.

Auerswald, E. H. 1969. Interdisciplinary versus ecological approach. In *General systems theory and psychiatry,* W. Gray, F. J. Duhl, and N. D. Rizzo, eds. Boston: Little, Brown & Co.

Barnhill, L., and Longo, D. 1978, Fixation and regression in the family life cycle. *Family Process. 17:* 469–478.

Bateson, G. 1956. *Naven.* Stanford, CA: Stanford University Press.

Bateson, G. 1972. *Steps to an ecology of mind.* New York: Ballantine.

Bateson, G. 1979. *Mind and nature.* New York: E. P. Dutton.

Bateson, M. C. 1984. *With a daughter's eye.* New York: William Morrow.

Bateson, G., Jackson, D. D., Haley, J., and Weakland, J. H. 1956. Towards a theory of schizophrenia. *Behavior Science. 1:*251–264.

Bateson, G., Jackson, D. D., Haley, J., and Weakland, J. 1963. A note on the double bind. *Family Process.* *2*(1):154–161.

Becvar, D. S., and Becvar, R. J. 1988. *Family therapy: A systemic integration.* Boston: Allyn and Bacon.

Becvar, D. S., and Becvar, R. J. 1996. *Family therapy: A systemic integration,* 3rd edition. Boston: Allyn and Bacon.

Bertalanffy, L. von. 1968. *General system theory.* New York: George Braziller.

Bogdan, J. 1983. The Ericksonian Rorshach. *Family Therapy Networker.* *7*(5):36–38.

Bogdan, J. 1987. "Epistemology" as a semantic pollutant. *Journal of Marital and Family Therapy.* *13*(1): 27–36.

Boszormenyi-Nagy, I., and Spark, G. 1973. *Invisible loyalties: Reciprocity in intergenerational family therapy.* New York: Harper & Row.

Bowen, M. 1978. *Family therapy in clinical practice.* New York: Jason Aronson.

Breunlin, D. 1983. Therapy in stages: A life cycle view. In *Clinical implications of the family life cycle,* H. Liddle, ed. Rockville, MD: Aspen.

Breunlin, D. 1988. Oscillation theory and family development. In *Family transitions,* C. Falicov, ed. New York: Guilford Press.

Breunlin, D. C., Cornwell, M., and Cade, B. 1983. International trade in family therapy: Parallels between societal and therapeutic values. In *Cultural perspectives in family therapy,* C. J. Falicov, ed. Rockville, MD: Aspen.

Breunlin, D. C., and Schwartz, R. C. 1986. Sequences: Toward a common denominator for family therapy. *Family Process. 25:*67–87.

Breunlin, D. C., Schwartz, R. C., and Karrer, B. M. 1992. *Metaframework: Transcending the models of family therapy.* San Francisco: Jossey-Bass.

Capra, F. 1982. *The turning point.* New York: Simon & Shuster.

Carter, E., and McGoldrick, M., eds. 1980. *The family life cycle: A framework for family therapy.* New York: Gardner Press.

Carter, E., and McGoldrick, M., eds. 1989. *The changing family life cycle: A framework for family therapy.* 2nd ed. Boston: Allyn and Bacon.

Combrinck-Graham, L. 1983. The family life cycle and families with young children. In *Clinical implications of the family life cycle,* H. Liddle, ed. Rockville, MD: Aspen.

Combrinck-Graham, L. 1985. A model for family development. *Family Process. 24*:139–150.

Combrinck-Graham, L. 1988. Adolescent sexuality in the family life cycle. In *Family transitions*, C. Falicov, ed. New York: Guilford Press.

Davidson, M. 1983. *Uncommon sense*. Los Angeles: J. P. Tarcher.

Dell, P. F. 1982. Beyond homeostasis: Toward a concept of coherence. *Family Process. 21*(1):21–42.

Duncan, B. L., and Parks, M. B. 1988. Integrating individual and systems approaches: Strategic-behavior therapy. *Journal of Marital and Family Therapy. 14*(2):151–162.

Duncan, B. L., and Solovey, D. 1989. Strategic-brief therapy: An insight-oriented approach. *Journal of Marital and Family Therapy. 15*(1):1–10.

Duvall, E. 1957. *Family development*. Philadelphia: Lippincott.

Falicov, C. J., ed. 1983. *Cultural perspectives in family therapy*. Rockville, MD: Aspen.

Falicov, C. J., ed. 1988. *Family transitions*. New York: Guilford Press.

Goldner, V. 1987. Instrumentalism, feminism & the limits of family therapy. *Journal of Family Psychology. 1*(1):109–116.

Goldner, V. 1988. Generation and gender: Normative and covert hierarchies. *Family Process. 27*(1): 17–33.

Haley, J. 1963. *Strategies of psychotherapy*. New York: Grune & Stratton

Haley, J. 1971a. Family therapy: A radical change. In *Changing families: A family therapy reader*, J. Haley, ed. New York: Grune & Stratton.

Haley, J., ed. 1971b. *Changing families: A family therapy reader*. New York: Grune & Stratton.

Haley, J. 1973. *Uncommon therapy: The psychiatric techniques of Milton H. Erickson*. New York: Norton.

Haley, J. 1976. *Problem-solving therapy*. San Francisco: Jossey-Bass.

Haley, J. 1980. *Leaving home*. New York: McGraw Hill.

Haley, J. 1981. *Reflections on therapy and other essays*. Chevy Chase, MD: The Family Therapy Institute of Washington, DC.

Haley, J. 1985. Conversations with Erickson. *Family Therapy Networker. 9*(2):30–43.

Hill, R., and Rodgers, R. 1964. The developmental approach. In *Handbook of marriage and the family*, H. T. Christiansen, ed. Chicago: Rand McNally.

Hoffman, L. 1971. Deviation-amplifying processes in natural groups. In *Changing families: A family therapy reader*, J. Haley, ed. New York: Grune & Stratton.

Hoffman, L. 1981. *Foundations of family therapy*. New York: Basic Books.

Imber-Black, E., Roberts, J., and Whiting, R. 1989. *Rituals in families and family therapy*. New York: Norton.

Jackson, D. 1957. The question of family homeostasis. *Psychiatric Quarterly Supplement. 31*:79–90.

Keeney, B. P., and Sprenkle, D. H. (1982). Ecosystemic epistemology: Critical implications for the aesthetics and pragmatics of family therapy. *Family Process. 21*(1):1–20.

Liddle, H. Breunlin, D., and Schwartz, R., eds. 1988. *The handbook of family therapy training and supervision*. New York: Guilford Press.

Lidz, T. 1963. *The family and human adaptation*. New York: International Universities Press.

Luepnitz, D. A. 1988. *The family interpreted: Feminist theory in clinical practice*. New York: Basic Books.

McGoldrick, M., Pearce, J. K., and Giordano, J. 1982. *Ethnicity and family therapy*. New York: Guilford Press.

Minuchin, S. 1974. *Families and family therapy*. Cambridge: Harvard University Press.

Minuchin, S., and Fishman, H. C. 1981. *Family therapy techniques*. Cambridge: Harvard University Press.

Parsons, T., and Bales, R. F. 1955. *Family, socialization & interaction process*. New York: Free Press.

Paul, N. 1969. The role of mourning and empathy in conjoint marital therapy. In *Family therapy and disturbed families*, G. Zuk and I. Boszormenyi-Nagy, eds. Palo Alto: Science and Behavior Books.

Pittman, F. 1987. *Turning points: Treating families in transition and crisis*. New York: Norton.

Satir, V. 1972. *Peoplemaking*. Palo Alto: Science and Behavior Books.

Satir, V. 1988. *The new peoplemaking*. Palo Alto: Science and Behavior Books.

Schwartz, R. C. 1985. Has family therapy reached the stage where it can appreciate the concept of stages? In *Stages: Patterns of change over time*, D. C. Breunlin, ed. Rockville, MD: Aspen.

Selvini-Palazzoli, M., Boscolo, L., Cecchin, G., and Prata, G. 1978. *Paradox and counterparadox*. New York: Jason Aronson.

Simon, R. 1982. Reflections on family therapy: An interview with Jay Haley. *Family Therapy Networker.* 6(5):18–26.

Simon, R. 1984. Stranger in a strange land: An interview with Salvador Minuchin. *Family Therapy Networker.* 8(6):51.

Simon, R. 1987. Good-bye paradox, hello invariant prescription: An interview with Mara Selvini Palazzoli. *Family Therapy Networker.* 11(5):16–33.

Skynner, R. 1981. An open systems, group analytic approach to family therapy. In *Handbook of family therapy*, A. Gurman and D. Kniskern, eds. New York: Brunner/Mazel.

Solomon, M. 1973. A developmental, conceptual premise for family therapy. *Family Process.* 12: 179–188.

Speer, D. C. 1970. Family systems: Morphostasis and morphogenesis, or "Is homeostasis enough?" *Family Process.* 9(3):259–278.

Stanton, A., and Schwartz, M. 1964. *The mental hospital.* New York: Basic Books.

Wachtel, E. F., and Wachtel, P. L. 1986. *Family dynamics in individual psychotherapy.* New York: Guilford Press.

Watzlawick, P., Beavin, J. H., and Jackson, D. D. 1967. *Pragmatics of Human Communication.* New York: Norton.

Watzlawick, P., Weakland, J., and Fisch, R. 1974. *Change: Principles of problem formation and problem resolution.* New York: Norton.

5

Bowen Family Systems Therapy

The pioneers of family therapy recognized that people are products of social context, but they usually limited their attention to the nuclear family. They had the same kind of fervor as the first behavior therapists, who discovered the power of reinforcement to modify behavior, and they had the same kind of narrowness. Yes, our actions are powerfully influenced by what goes on in our immediate families, and often one person's symptoms can be resolved by altering interactions in the nuclear family. But what about the forces, past and present, that generate those patterns? What makes a husband distance himself from the emotional demands of family life? And what makes a wife neglect her own life to manage her children's lives? Murray Bowen sought answers—and solutions—to such questions in the larger network of family relationships.

Bowen family systems therapy has by far the most comprehensive view of human behavior and human problems of any approach to family treatment. It extends the focus deeper—into the hearts and minds of family members—and broader—into the wider family context that shaped, and continues to shape, the life of the family.

While no one doubts the formative influence of family on molding personality, many people imagine that once they leave home they are grown up: independent adults, free at last of their parents' influence. Some people prize individuality and take it as a sign of growth to separate from their parents; others wish they could be closer to their families but find visits home too painful, and so they stay away to protect themselves from disappointment and hurt. Once out of range of the immediate conflict, they forget and deny the discord. But as Bowen discovered, the family remains within us. Wherever we go, we carry unresolved emotional reactivity to our parents, in the form of vulnerability to repeat the same old patterns in every new relationship we enter into. As we shall see, unresolved issues with our original families is the most important unfinished business of our lives.

Sketches of Leading Figures

Bowen family systems therapy is a theoretical–clinical model that evolved from psychoanalytic principles and practice. Murray Bowen, its originator and major contributor, was a dominant force in the family therapy movement since the early 1950s. His preeminent position was due not only to the fact that he was one of the parent figures in the field, but also to the innovative and comprehensive nature of his ideas.

Bowen was the oldest child in a large, cohesive family living in rural Tennessee. After medical school and internship, he served for five years in the military. There he saw widespread psychopathology, matched by equally widespread ignorance about how to deal with it, which inspired him to seek a career in psychiatry. Here, Bowen felt, he could chart a course through largely unknown territory.

Once in psychiatry Bowen turned his attention to the enigma of schizophrenia. Thoroughly trained in psychoanalysis, including undergoing thirteen years of personal analysis, Bowen, not surprisingly, sought to apply psychoanalytic concepts to schizophrenia. He began by expanding his focus from the schizophrenic patient to the mother–child dyad. The goal of this work was to further the understanding of "mother–child symbiosis." These studies began at the Menninger Clinic where Bowen trained and remained on staff until 1954. From Menninger he moved to the National Institute of Mental Health (NIMH) where he became the first director of the Family Division. One of the major observations to come out of the "mother–child symbiosis" research was the observation of repetitive relationship patterns: alternating cycles of closeness and distance, exquisitely sensitive to shifts in emotional tension within either mother or child, or the relationship between them. Separation anxiety coupled with incorporation anxiety was believed to be the underlying dynamic. From these observations Bowen focused on the notion of "anxious attachment," a pathological form of attachment driven by anxiety that subverted reason and self-control. Anxious attachment is the opposite of "functional attachment," which is a central aspect of *differentiation.*

When Bowen moved to NIMH he expanded the scope of his studies to include fathers, and began to work out the concept of *triangle* as the central building block of relationship systems. From NIMH Bowen moved to Georgetown University's Department of Psychiatry in 1959. During his thirty-one years at Georgetown, Bowen developed his comprehensive theory of family therapy, inspired an entire generation of students, and became an internationally renowned leader of the family therapy movement. He died after a long illness in October 1990.

Among the most prominent and influential of Bowen's students are Philip Guerin and Thomas Fogarty. Both trained by Bowen, they joined together on the faculty of the Einstein Family Studies Section where Israel Zwerling and Andrew Ferber attempted to bring together a faculty representative of the diversity of thinking and practice in the field of family therapy. While at Einstein they trained Betty Carter, Monica McGoldrick (then Orfanidis), Ed Gordon, Eileen Pendagast, and Katherine Guerin, all of whom, along with Peggy Papp, joined Guerin and Fogarty in 1973 to form the Center for Family Learning in New Rochelle, New York. Under Guerin's leadership, the Center for Family Learning has become one of the major centers of family therapy training and practice.

While working on her M.S.W. at Hunter College, Elizabeth (Betty) Carter was unable to find a field placement in group therapy and so settled for something new called "family therapy" at the Ackerman Institute. There, with fellow student Olga Silverstein, she learned about technique from Nathan Ackerman, but not much about how families function. Then she read Murray Bowen and felt a whole new world of understanding open up. From that moment she became an avid student of Bowen's approach, attending as many workshops as she could find, and then studying with Phil Guerin and Marilyn Mendelsohn at Einstein.

In 1977 Carter left the Center for Family Learning to become the founding director of the Family Institute of Westchester. She was joined by Monica McGoldrick, Fredda Herz, Ken Terkelson, and others. An ardent and articulate feminist, she is also Codirector of the Women's Project in Family Therapy with Peggy Papp, Olga Silverstein, and Marianne Walters. Today, in addition to being a respected leader in the field of family therapy and a popular teacher, Betty Carter is an active clinician who specializes in marital therapy and therapy with remarried couples.

Monica McGoldrick is another therapist in the Bowenian tradition who, like her friend and colleague Betty Carter, has become one of the most respected voices in the field. McGoldrick is the founding director of the Family Institute of New Jersey and Associate Professor of Psychiatry, UMDNJ–Robert Wood Johnson Medical School. She is a popular teacher, writer, and leader in the field of family therapy. Among her clinical special interests are ethnicity, genograms, family therapy with one person, remarried families, and dual-career families.

Many of Bowen's students continued to work with him for a long time, among them Michael Kerr, Edward Beal, Edwin Friedman, Jack Bradt, Joseph Lorio, Charles Paddock, and Daniel Papero. Each is an important representative of the extended family systems tradition, and all have helped transmit Bowen's ideas in their teaching and through papers presented at the annual Georgetown Family Symposium.

Edwin Friedman, who works in the Washington, DC area, is both a rabbi and a family therapist. Trained by Murray Bowen, he brings an extended family systems perspective to bear on religious life. One of his most important contributions has been introducing a sophisticated understanding and competence in family systems theory to ancillary professionals, especially pastoral counselors.

Michael Kerr, M.D., was a long-time student and colleague of Bowen's, and since 1977 the director of training at the Georgetown Family Center. Kerr is probably the most scholarly, informed, and faithful to the original theory of all Bowen's students, as his brilliant account of Bowen theory in the book *Family Evaluation* (Kerr & Bowen, 1988) richly demonstrates.

Finally, we should mention James Framo, for many years one of the leading figures in family therapy. Although Framo is often thought of either as an independent practitioner or as a colleague of Ivan Boszormenyi-Nagy, he incorporated many of Bowen's ideas in his work. Framo is perhaps best known for his steadfast advocacy of couples groups.

Several key publications over the years are markers in the development of Bowenian family systems theory. Bowen's first major paper outlining the concepts of his new theory was "The Use of Family Theory in Clinical Practice," published in 1966. A year later at a Philadelphia conference organized by James Framo, Bowen delivered his first organized presentation of the application of his theory to his own personal family system (Anonymous, 1972). In 1976 Guerin edited a classic anthology of original papers, one of the most valuable books in the family therapy literature (Guerin, *Family Therapy: Theory and Practice*). In 1978 Bowen assembled all of his own papers from various professional journals and published them in *Family Therapy in Clinical Practice.* In 1987 Guerin and his colleagues at the Center for Family Learning published *The Evaluation and Treatment of Marital Conflict*, one of the best and most useful books ever written in family therapy. In the following year Carter and McGoldrick (1988) published a revised edition of their acclaimed book on the family life cycle. Finally, the publication of *Family Evaluation* by Michael Kerr and Murray Bowen in 1988 represents the mature and comprehensive flowering of Bowen's ideas while Guerin and his colleagues' recent (1996) *Working with Relationship Triangles* is an extremely useful guide to the clinical application of these ideas.

Theoretical Formulations

Most of the early family therapists were pragmatists, more concerned with action than insight, more interested in technique than theory. Murray Bowen was the exception to this rule. Bowen, among the most cerebral of all family therapists, was always more committed to family as an orientation rather than a method, and more interested in theory than technique. From his point of view most mental health professionals are too caught up in narrow questions of technique to ever fully grasp what systems theory is all about. Bowen's own theory is among the most carefully worked out and influential of family systems.

Although Bowenian theory has evolved and expanded, it has always centered around two counterbalancing life forces: *togetherness* and *individuality*. Ideally these two forces are in balance. Unbalance in the direction of togetherness is called variously "fusion," "stuck-togetherness," and "undifferentiation" (Kerr & Bowen, 1988). *Differentiation*, the capacity for autonomous functioning, helps people avoid getting caught up in reactive polarities. Otherwise emotional reactivity results in polarized positions: *pursuer–distancer, overfunctioning–underfunctioning*, and so on. The concepts Bowen used to express this central tension of the human condition evolved from *mother–child symbiosis*, to *undifferentiated family ego mass*, to *fusion/differentiation*. However phrased, the central premise is that unresolved emotional attachment to one's family must be resolved, rather than passively accepted or reactively rejected, before one can differentiate a mature, healthy personality.

Bowen articulated the core concepts of his theory in two major papers: "The Use of Family Theory in Clinical Practice" (1966) and "Theory in the Practice of Psychotherapy" (1976). In the 1966 paper Bowen cited six interlocking concepts that make up his theory: *differentiation of self, triangles, nuclear family emotional process, family projection process, multigenerational transmission process*, and *sibling position*. He added two additional concepts in the 1970s (Bowen, 1976): *emotional cutoff* and *societal emotional process*.

Differentiation of Self

Differentiation of self, the cornerstone of Bowen's theory, is both an intrapsychic and interpersonal concept. Intrapsychic differentiation is the ability to separate feeling from thinking. Undifferentiated people hardly distinguish thoughts from feelings; their intellects are so flooded with feelings that they are almost incapable of objective thinking. Their lives are governed by an accretion of feelings from those around them, either blindly adhered to or angrily rejected. The differentiated person isn't a cold fish who only thinks and never feels. Instead, he or she is able to balance thinking and feeling: capable of strong emotion and spontaneity, but also capable of the restraint and objectivity that comes with the ability to resist the pull of emotional impulses.

Lack of differentiation between thinking and feeling occurs in concert with lack of differentiation between oneself and others. Because they're less able to think clearly, undifferentiated people react emotionally—positively or negatively—to the dictates of family members or other authority figures. These people have little autonomous identity. Instead they tend to be fused with others. They find it difficult to separate themselves from others, particularly on important issues. Asked what they think, they say what they feel; asked what they believe, they echo what they've heard. They either conform or assume pseudo-independence through counterconformity. In contrast, differentiated people are able to take definite stands on issues because they're able to think things through, decide what they believe, and then act on those beliefs. This enables them to be in intimate contact with others without being reflexively shaped by them.

Guerin defines differentiation as the process of partially freeing oneself from the emotional chaos of one's family. Getting free takes analyzing one's own role as an active participant in relationship systems, instead of blaming problems on everyone but oneself (Guerin, Fay, Burden, & Kautto, 1987). Guerin uses the concept of *adaptive level of functioning* to define and evaluate the ability to continue functioning in the face of stress. Adaptive level of functioning is the capacity to make the conscious effort to be objective and behave rationally in the face of pressures of emotionality.

Triangles

Take a minute to think about the most difficult relationship in your family. Actually, that relationship is almost certainly between the two people you thought of and one or more third parties. Virtually all emotionally significant relationships are shadowed by third parties—relatives, friends, even memories.

To understand triangles, it's helpful to remember that relationships aren't static. Any two people in a relationship go through cycles of closeness and distance; it's when they're distant that triangles are most likely to develop. These cycles reflect not only good times and bad in relationships, but also people's needs for autonomy and connectedness. Guerin describes two basic processes that operate in the formation of marital triangles. In the first, the spouse experiencing the most discomfort connects with someone else as a way of gaining an ally. Thus, a wife upset with her husband's distance may increase her involvement with one of the children. In the second process, a third person (perhaps a friend or a child), who is sensitized either to one spouse's anxiety or to the conflict between them, moves in to offer reassurance or calm things down. "For example, an older daughter may attempt to reduce intense marital conflict by talking individually to each parent or to the parent with whom she has the most influence. Meanwhile, her younger brother may absorb the tension of his parents or handle it by acting in an antisocial way. The acting-out behavior also serves the function of pulling the parents together to try to solve the common problem of the son's acting out" (Guerin et al., 1987, p. 62).

Some forms of triangulation seem so innocent that we hardly notice their destructive effect. Most parents who have pretty good relationships with their children can't seem to resist complaining to them once in a while about their spouses. "Your mother's *always* late!" "Your father *never* lets anyone else drive!" These interchanges seem harmless enough. But whenever you hear a story in which one person is victim and the other villain, you're being invited into a triangle.

When we listen too long or too often to someone complaining about someone else, the flattering feeling of being confided in gives way to a nagging suspicion that maybe we should give the two people back to each other. Similarly, when we gripe to one friend about another's unfairness, we know we should talk to the person with whom we have the conflict. And we would, too, except—well, it's too awkward. The average person is about as able to resist emotional triangles as the average cat is able to resist birds.

If something's really bothering you and you're afraid to talk about it—afraid you won't be listened to—the urge to confide in someone else is overwhelming. Unburdening yourself to a friend will make you feel better. It will also lessen the likelihood that you'll engage the problem at its source. Triangulation lets off steam, but it freezes conflict in place. The trouble with triangles isn't so much that complaining or seeking solace is wrong, but rather that many triangles become chronic diversions that corrupt and undermine family relationships.

Most family problems are triangular, which is why working only on a twosome may have limited results. Teaching a mother better techniques for disciplining her son won't resolve the problem that she is overinvolved with the boy as a result of her husband's emotional distance.

Nuclear Family Emotional Process

This concept deals with the emotional forces in families that operate over the years in recurrent patterns. Bowen originally used the term "undifferentiated family ego mass" to describe emotional oneness or fusion in families. Lack of differentiation in the family of origin leads to an emotional cutoff from parents, which in turn leads to fusion in marriage. The less the differentiation of self prior to marriage, the greater the fusion between spouses. Since this new fusion is unstable, it tends to produce one or more of the following: (1) reactive emotional distance between the spouses; (2) physical or emotional dysfunction in one spouse; (3) overt marital conflict; or (4) projection of the problem onto one or more children. The intensity of these problems is related to the degree of undifferentiation, extent of emotional cutoff from families of origin, and level of stress in the system.

Family Projection Process

This is the process by which parents transmit their immaturity and lack of differentiation to their children. Emotional fusion between spouses creates tension that leads to marital conflict, emotional distance, or reciprocal over- and under-functioning. A common case is one in which the husband, who is cut off from his family of origin, relates only in a very cool and distant way to his wife. This predisposes her to a relatively intense focus on the kids. Kept at arm's length by her husband, she devotes her emotional energy to the children, usually with greatest intensity toward one particular child. This child may be the oldest son or daughter, the youngest son or daughter, or perhaps one who looks like one of the parents. Projection is different from caring concern; it's anxious, enmeshed concern.

The child who is the object of the projection process becomes the one most attached to the parents (positively or negatively) and the one with the least differentiation of self. Since it relieves his own anxiety, the husband supports his wife's overinvolvement with the children. He may do so directly, or indirectly by virtue of his own lack of involvement.

The emotional fusion between mother and child may take the form of a warm, dependent bond or an angry, conflictual struggle. As the mother focuses her anxiety on the child, the child's functioning is stunted. This underdevelopment enables the mother to overcontrol the child, distracting her from her own anxieties but crippling the child emotionally. Thus infantilized, the child eventually develops symptoms of psychological impairment, necessitating further parental concern and solidifying the family pattern.

Multigenerational Transmission Process

This concept describes the transmission of the family emotional process through multiple generations. In every generation the child most involved in the family's fusion moves toward a lower level of differentiation of self, while the least involved child moves toward a higher level of differentiation.

We like to think that after we leave home we will marry someone who will make us happy. We expect to keep the good stuff from our families and get rid of the bad. It doesn't work that way. We may fight against our inheritance, but it catches up with us.

Bowen's multigenerational transmission concept takes emotional illness not only beyond the individual to the family, but also beyond the nuclear family to several generations. The problem in the identified patient is a product of the relationship of that person's parents, which is a product of the relationship of their parents, continuing back for several generations. The problem doesn't reside in the child and it's not the child's fault; nor are the parents to blame. Instead the problem is the result of a multigenerational sequence in which all family members are actors and reactors.

Sibling Position

This concept is similar to Toman's (1969) ten personality profiles of children who grow up in different sibling positions. Bowen concurs that children develop certain fixed personality characteristics based on the sibling position in their families. So many variables are involved that prediction is complex, but knowledge of general characteristics plus specific knowledge of a particular family is helpful in predicting what part a child will play in the family emotional process, and in predicting family patterns in the next generation.

Bowen's theory offers an interesting perspective with which to reconsider the familiar notion of sibling rivalry by recognizing the triangular complications of the siblings' relationship with their parents. Say that a mother is anxious that her children should never feel jealous and that she takes responsibility for ensuring that they feel equally loved. (As though she had reason to worry that the truth might be otherwise.) Her anxiety is translated into action by making a show of treating them exactly equally—an attempt at perfect fairness that usually betrays the anxiety behind it. In response, the siblings grow up feeling that their mother *is* responsible for making them feel equally important and for alleviating any fears of inequality. Each child then becomes highly sensitive to the amount of attention he or she receives in relation to his or her siblings. This can result in the siblings continually fighting and resenting one another—just what the mother tried to prevent. Moreover, since the mother is anxious to control how the children feel, she may step in to settle their fights, thus depriving them of the opportunity to do so, and giving them additional reason to feel unequally treated by her. ("How come *I* have to go to my room? *He* started it!")

Thus, sibling conflict, which is often explained as an outcome of inevitable rivalry (as though rivalrousness were the only natural relationship between brothers and sisters), is actually just one side of a triangle. (Of course the intensity of a mother's preoccupation with her children is related to other triangles—the quality and satisfaction of her relationships with her friends, career, and husband.)

Support for this triangular way of looking at sibling relationships comes from studies by Frits Boer and his colleagues at the University of Leiden in the Netherlands. They found that: siblings were aware of partiality not only toward their siblings, but also toward themselves; first-born children reported more positive behavior toward themselves from their second-born siblings than did second-born children with regard to their older siblings; siblings with brothers reported more competition than did siblings with sisters, regardless of their own sex; and perception of parental care by the children was highly correlated with their perception of the sibling relationship—a more negatively judged parent–child relationship coincided with a more negatively judged sibling relationship (Boer, 1990).

The importance of birth order recently received powerful support in a provocative and compelling book, *Born to Rebel*, by Frank Sulloway (1996). Culling biographical data from five hundred years of history, Sulloway's conclusions are supported by a sophisticated multivariate analysis of more than a million biographical data points. Personality, he argues, is the repertoire of strategies that siblings use to compete with one another, secure a place in the family, and survive the ordeal of childhood.

Firstborns in the family identify more strongly with power and authority than do their siblings: They employ their superior size and strength to defend their status and try to minimize the cost of having siblings by dominating them. They also tend to be more self-confident and are well represented among Nobel Prize winners and political leaders. (In the 1920s, Alfred Adler suggested that firstborns become "power-hungry conservatives" as they struggle against siblings to restore their lost primacy within the family.) Winston Churchill, George Washington, Ayn Rand, and Rush Limbaugh are illustrative examples.

As underdogs in the family, laterborns are more inclined to indentify with the oppressed and to question the status quo. They're more open to experience, because this openness aids them, as latecomers to the family, in finding an unoccupied niche. From their ranks have come the bold explorers, the iconoclasts, and the heretics of history. Joan of Arc, Marx, Lenin, Jefferson, Rousseau, Virginia Wolf, Mary Wollstonecraft, and Bill Gates are representative laterborns.

What developmentalists once thought was a shared family environment turns out not to be shared at all. Although the family may seem to be one environment, it's actually a multiplicity of microenvironments, a collection of niches, consisting of distinct vantage points from which siblings experience the same events in very different ways.

Emotional Cutoff

Emotional cutoff describes the way people manage undifferentiation (and emotional intensity associated with it) between the generations. The greater the emotional fusion between generations, the greater the likelihood of cutoff. Some people seek distance by moving far away from their parents; others do so emotionally by, for example, avoiding personal subjects of conversation or always insulating themselves with the presence of third parties.

Mike Nichols (1986) describes how some people mistake emotional cutoff for emotional maturity: "We take it as a sign of growth to separate from our parents, and we measure our maturity by independence of family ties. Yet many of us still respond to our families as though they were radioactive and capable of inflicting great pain. Only one thing robs Superman of his extraordinary power: kryptonite, a piece of his home planet. A surprising number of adult men and women are similarly rendered helpless by even a brief visit to or from their parents" (p. 190).

Societal Emotional Process

This is a concept Kerr and Bowen discuss in their 1988 book, *Family Evaluation*. But they don't discuss it much. The term refers to the fact that the emotional process in society influences the emotional process in families—like a background influence affecting all families. The concept of social emotional process describes how a prolonged increase in social anxiety can result in a gradual lowering of the functional level of differentiation in families. Kerr and Bowen cite the example of the high crime rate that results in communities with great social pressure. Bowen acknowledges that sexism and class and ethnic prejudice are examples of unhappy social emotional process, but he tends to downplay the importance of these concerns for family evaluation and therapy. Feminists don't agree; they believe passionately that sexism is a societal emotional process that infects families—and one that should be fought, and fought hard.

Fogarty (1976a) has described individuals as having four dimensions, and relating to others in three channels. The four dimensions of self are: depth, movement toward objects, movement toward persons, and time. The depth dimension includes much that we generally think of as intrapsychic, including thoughts, feelings, dreams, and aspirations. In addition to these attributes of personality, people vary according to the nature and degree of their proclivity for involvement with things—such as possessions, work, or games—as opposed to other people. Finally, Fogarty says, people vary in being fast or slow to think, act, and feel, and in being committed to the status quo or to change. This is the time dimension.

Fogarty's four-dimensional people are linked to one another by three systems: the thinking system, the emotional system, and the operating system. The thinking system of facts, judgments, and opinions functions in proportion to knowledge and information; it dysfunctions in proportion to which fact is confused with feeling. The emotional system provides color and vitality to relationships. Neither good nor bad, right nor wrong, the emotional system either works effectively or it doesn't. The third system by which people are connected is the operating system. This defines the ways in which people communicate their thoughts and feelings. Silence, withdrawal, talking, or yelling may all be used to convey essentially the same thought or feeling.

To the theoretical concerns of Bowenian therapists, Monica McGoldrick and Betty Carter have added gender and ethnicity. Their point is that to open closed systems it isn't possible to ignore gender inequalities without ignoring some of the primary forces that keep men and women trapped in inflexible roles. Moreover, they might point out that the previous sentence itself is naive in implying that men and women alike are victims of gender bias. Women live with limiting social conditions *and* with men who perpetuate them—men who may not notice their advantage or feel powerful with their wives and mothers, but who live with, and take for granted, social conditions that make it easier for men to get ahead in the world.

McGoldrick has also been a leader in calling attention to ethnic differences in families. Her book *Ethnicity and Family Therapy* (McGoldrick, Pearce, & Giordano, 1982) was a landmark in family therapy's developing sensitivity to this issue. Without understanding how cultural norms and values differ from one ethnic group to the next, the danger is of therapists imposing their own ways of looking at things on families whose perspectives aren't "dysfunctional" but legitimately different. Some readers might be concerned that lengthy descriptions of how families of various ethnic groups differ (e.g., McGoldrick, Preto, Hines, & Lee, 1990: "Trying to talk the Irish out of their sense of guilt and need to suffer is a futile effort") fosters ethnic stereotyping. McGoldrick believes that it's important to sensitize family therapists to ethnic diversity, and that the most important thing is not to learn what characterizes one group or another, but rather to be open to differences.

Normal Family Development

In Bowen's system there is no discontinuity between normal and abnormal family development. When he began studying normal families in the late 1950s, he discovered many of the same mechanisms he had previously observed in schizophrenic families. This convinced him that there are no discrete categories of families (schizophrenic, neurotic, or normal), but that all families vary along a continuum from emotional fusion to differentiation. The fact that most of Bowen's clinical contact in later years was with families of professionals probably reinforced his belief that families are more alike than different.

Optimal family development is thought to take place when family members are relatively differentiated, when anxiety is low, and when the parents are in good emotional contact with their own families of origin. Most people leave home in the midst of transforming relationships with their parents from an adolescent to an adult basis. Thus the transformation is incomplete, and most of us, even as adults, continue to react with adolescent sensitivity to our parents—and to anyone else who pushes the same buttons. Normally, but not optimally, people reduce contact with their parents and siblings to avoid the anxiety and conflict of dealing with them. Once out of contact with their families, people assume they've put the old difficulties behind them. However, they carry around unfinished business in the form of unresolved sensitivities that flare up in intense relationships wherever they go. Having learned to ignore their own role in family conflicts, they're unable to prevent recurrences in new relationships. Therefore people with greater differentiation who remain in contact with previous generations are more stable than people from enmeshed or splintered families. Although problems may not surface immediately in cut-off families, they will eventually occur in future generations.

Another heritage from the past is that the emotional attachment between spouses comes to resemble that which each had in the family of origin. People who were relatively undifferentiated in their original families will continue to be undifferentiated when they form a new family. Those who handled anxiety by distance and withdrawal will do the same in their marriages. Therefore Bowen is convinced that differentiation of autonomous personalities, accomplished primarily in the family of origin, is both a description of normal development and a prescription for therapeutic improvement. This inescapable link to the past, stressed more strongly in Bowen's approach than in any other, is the prevailing feature of functional family development.

In "Systems Concepts and the Dimensions of Self," Fogarty (1976a) elaborates the characteristics of well-adjusted families: (1) They are balanced and can adapt to change; (2) Emotional problems are seen as existing in the whole group, with components in each person; (3) They are connected across generations to all family members; (4) They use a minimum of fusion and a minimum of distance to solve problems; (5) Each dyad can deal with problems between them; (6) Differences are tolerated, even encouraged; (7) Each person can deal on thinking and emotional levels with the others; (8) They are aware of what each person gets from within and from others; (9) Each person is allowed his or her own emptiness; (10) Preservation of a positive emotional climate takes precedence over doing what is "right" or what is popular; (11) Each member thinks it's a pretty good family to live in; and (12) Members of the family use each other as sources of feedback and learning, not as emotional crutches.

In Bowen's system the hallmark of the well-adjusted person is rational objectivity and individuality. A differentiated person is able to separate thinking from feeling, and remain independent of, though not out of contact with, the nuclear and extended family. The degree of differentiation of self depends largely on the course of one's family history, which is a relatively deterministic position. However, as we shall see, it's possible to achieve higher levels of differentiation through the process of family treatment.

Betty Carter and Monica McGoldrick have done as much as anyone in family therapy to study and disseminate information about normal family development (Carter & McGoldrick, 1980). They are also in the vanguard of those calling for sensitivity to and corrective action for the inequality between men and women in American families (Carter & McGoldrick, 1988). Like others in the Bowenian tradition, Carter and McGoldrick stress that to understand the family it is necessary to understand what's going on in at least three generations. This is the operative emotional field at any one time.

Following on the work of Rodgers (1960), Hill (1970), Solomon (1973), and Duvall (1977), Carter and McGoldrick have described the *family life cycle* as a process of expansion, contraction, and realignment of the relationship system to support the entry, exit, and development of family members in a functional way. Transitions from one stage of the family life cycle to the next require *second-order change*—change in the system itself—while problems within stages can usually be handled with *first-order change*—rearranging without restructuring the system.

In the *leaving home* stage the primary task for young adults is to separate from their families without cutting off or fleeing reactively to a substitute emotional refuge. This is a time to become an autonomous self before joining with another person to form a new family. In the *joining of families through marriage* stage the primary task is commitment to the new couple, but it is not simply a joining of two individuals; it is rather a changing of two entire systems and an overlapping to develop a third. While problems in this stage may seem to be primarily between the couple, they may also reflect a failure to separate from families of origin or an extreme cutoff that puts too much pressure on the twosome. *Families with young children* must adjust to make space for children, cooperate in the tasks of parenting, keep the marriage from being submerged in parenting, and realign relationships with the extended family. Both parents are challenged to fulfill the children's needs for nurture and control—and they are challenged to work together as a team. As anyone who's been through it knows, this is an extremely stressful stage, especially for young mothers, and it is the life cycle phase with the highest divorce rate.

The reward for those parents who survive the preceding stages is to have their children turn into adolescents. *Adolescence* is a time when children no longer want to be like Mommy and Daddy; they want to be themselves. They struggle to become autonomous individuals, and they struggle to open family boundaries. And they struggle however much it takes. Parents with lives of their own and a certain amount of flexibility welcome (or at least tolerate) the fresh (pun intended) air that blows through the family at this time. Those who insist on controlling their children as though they were still little ones, provoke painful escalations in the rebelliousness that's normal for this period. In the *launching children and moving on* stage, parents must let their children go, and they must take hold of their own lives. This may be a liberating time of fulfillment, but it is also notoriously the time of the *midlife crisis* (Nichols, 1986). Parents must not only deal with changes in their children's and their own lives, but also with changes in their relationship with their own parents who may need increasing support—or at any rate don't want to act like parents anymore. *Families in later life* must adjust to retirement, which not only means a sudden loss of vocation but also a sudden increase in proximity of the couple. With both husband and wife home all day, the house may suddenly seem a lot smaller. Later in life families must cope with declining health, illness, and then death, the great equalizer.

The one major variation in the life cycle, too common to still be considered a deviation, is *divorce.* With the divorce rate at 50 percent and the rate of redivorce at 61 percent (Glick, 1984), divorce now strikes the majority of American families. The major tasks of the divorcing couple are to end the marriage but maintain cooperation as parents. Some post-divorce families become single-parent families—consisting in the majority of cases of mothers and children, and in the vast majority of those cases facing terrible financial strain. The other alternative is remarriage and the formation of stepfamilies, in which, often, loneliness is swapped for conflict.

Carter and McGoldrick's work on the life cycle bridges Bowen's emphasis on multigenerational emotional processes and various ahistorical approaches to the family (e.g., structural and strategic) that emphasize the developmental stage of the moment. Guerin's clinical model emphasizes stress more than stages of development. Life-cycle changes within individuals, dyadic relationships, and the family as a whole are seen as producing an increasing demand on both functioning and vulnerability. For purposes of clinical work Guerin suggests that developmental stress be viewed as "transition times." Transition times are defined as any addition, subtraction, or change in status of a family member. In this paradigm, a piling up of transition times is "cluster stress." Periods of cluster stress are by their nature times of increased vulnerability for individual family members and the family as a whole. It is during these times that symptom formation is most likely to occur.

Development of Behavior Disorders

In the Bowenian system, symptoms are thought to result from stress that exceeds a person's ability to handle it. The ability to handle stress is a function of differentiation: The more well-differentiated the person, the more resilient he or she is and the more flexible and sustaining his or her relationships. The less well-differentiated the person, the less stress it takes to produce symptoms.

If "differentiation" were oversimplified to "level of maturity," the Bowenian formula for symptom development wouldn't differ from the usual diathesis–stress model that says disease develops when an individual's predisposition is sufficiently taxed. The difference is that differentiation isn't just a quality of individuals, but of relationships. Thus a relatively immature person who manages to create a reasonably healthy marriage will be at less risk than an equally immature person who's alone or in an unhealthy relationship. Symptoms develop when the level of anxiety exceeds the *system's* ability to bind or neutralize it.

But even the quality of two-person relationships is insufficient to explain symptom-development, because when anxiety builds in the twosome, the relationship will automatically involve a third person. If the third person stays in contact with the twosome but remains neutral, anxiety will be reduced and symptom-development will be less likely. However, if the third person does become emotionally involved—taking sides (which prevents the twosome from working out their difficulties) or becoming the focus of displaced emotion (which results in an overload of anxiety)—the likelihood of symptom development increases (Guerin, Fogarty, Fay, & Kautto, 1996).

The most vulnerable individual (in terms of isolation and lack of differentiation) is most likely to develop symptoms or be at the center of relationship conflict. The mechanism for this selectivity is the multigenerational transmission process. For example, a child of ten who presents with a conduct disorder is considered in the context of a three-generational genogram. From the theory it's assumed that the symptomatic child is the most triangled child in the family and, thereby, the one most emotionally caught up in the tension between the parents or affected most by the external tension in a particular parent. The multigenerational process behind this symptom complex is viewed as a byproduct of the parental level of differentiation from their own families, played out and exacerbated first within the marriage, then transmitted through the relationship between the parents (according to Bowen, usually the mother) and symptomatic child.

The clinical methodology tied to this formulation calls for: (1) increasing the parents' ability to manage their own anxiety and thereby being better able to handle their child's problematic behavior; and (2) fortifying the parents' level of emotional functioning by increasing their ability to operate with less anxiety in their families of origin. In this approach the child may or may not be seen. Calming down the parents and coaching them to deal more effectively with the problem was the primary approach taken by Bowen.

In the modification of these methods taken by Guerin and Fogarty, more emphasis is put on establishing a relationship with the symptomatic child, and working with the dysfunctional struggle and reactive emotional process in the nuclear family triangles. Extended family work is put off unless it's directly and explicitly linked to symptom formation and maintenance. In other words, where Bowen generally went straight for the family of origin, second-generation Bowenians pay more attention to the nuclear family, and are likely to wait to institute work on the family of origin as a way to reinforce gains and to enhance individual and family functioning.

Behavior disorders in adults—such as repeated job loss, uncontrollable anger, and compulsions of substance, sex, or acquisition—are viewed in the context of either dysfunctional spouse– or adult–child triangles, and clinical interventions are planned accordingly.

According to Bowen, behavior disorders, mild or severe, result from *emotional fusion* transmitted from one generation to the next. Emotions flood the intellect, impairing rational functioning and competence. The greater the degree of fusion, the more life is programmed by primitive emotional forces, despite rationalizations to the contrary (Bowen, 1975). Furthermore the greater the fusion between emotions and intellect, the more one is fused to the emotional reactions of other people. Emotional fusion consists of anxious attachment, overtly expressed or reactively rejected. Both the clinging, dependent person and the aloof, isolated one are equally caught up in emotional fusion; they merely manifest it in different ways.

Emotional fusion is the reciprocal of differentiation. The fused person has few firmly held convictions and beliefs; he or she seeks acceptance and approval above any other goal, and makes decisions based primarily on feelings rather than rational thought. Creating a good impression is all important, and the undifferentiated person is likely to be either dogmatic or compliant.

Symptoms are a product of emotional reactivity, acute or chronic. They can be generated by an anxiety-driven togetherness pressure to conform, or by disruption of a fused relationship that has sustained someone's functioning (Kerr & Bowen, 1988). In undifferentiated people, symptoms can be relieved (though not necessarily resolved) by retreat to the safety of a dependent relationship, or by fleeing intimacy through distancing. The symptom patterns that develop from emotional fusion are: unhappy marriages, either combative or emotionally distant; dysfunction in one of the spouses (with reciprocal overfunctioning in the other); or projection of problems onto one or more children. The following clinical vignette illustrates how emotional fusion in the family of origin is transmitted.

> After his father died, Mr. Klein and his older sister were reared by their mother. This woman was a relatively mature and thoughtful person, but following the death of her husband she increasingly devoted all her attention to her children. They were her chief preoccupation, and shaping their lives became the major project of her life. She insisted that they conform to her standards; she was persistent in correcting their manners, energetic in demanding high performance in school, and highly critical of anything they sought to do outside the home. She discouraged contact with neighbors and school friends as well as such "frivolous" pastimes as playing ball or going to school dances.
>
> In late adolescence Mr. Klein began to resent the powerful control his mother exerted. His sister was never able to break free and remained single, living with her mother for the rest of her life. Mr. Klein, however, was determined to become independent. Since he had always been told what to think, where to go, and how to behave, it was difficult to move out and be on his own. However, he was strong-willed and energetic; finally, in his mid twenties, he left home and turned his back on his mother. He moved to a distant city, started working, and eventually married.
>
> The woman he married, Liza, came from a large, closely knit, and affectionate

family. She and her four sisters were very much attached to each other and remained best friends throughout their lives. Their relationship with their parents was warm and close; none of the sisters ever questioned this model of family structure.

After she graduated from high school, Liza announced that she wanted to go to college. This was contrary to the family norm that daughters remain at home and prepare themselves to be wives and mothers. Hence a major battle ensued between Liza and her parents; they were struggling to hold on, and she was struggling to break free. Finally she left for college, but she was ever after estranged from her parents. They had forgiven, but not forgotten, her violation of the family tradition.

When Liza and Mr. Klein met, they were immediately drawn to one another. Both were lonely and cut off from their families. After a brief, passionate courtship, they married. The honeymoon didn't last long. Never having really differentiated himself from his domineering mother, Mr. Klein was exquisitely sensitive to any effort to direct him. He became furious at his wife's slightest attempt to change his habits. After years of grating against his dictatorial mother, his patience for control had long since worn thin. Mrs. Klein, on the other hand, sought to reestablish in her new marriage the closeness she had in her family. But in order to be close, she and her husband had to do things together and share interests and routines. When she moved toward him, suggesting that they do something, he was angry and resentful, feeling his individuality impinged upon. After several months of conflict, the two settled into a period of relative equilibrium. Mr. Klein put most of his energy into his work, where he felt free and autonomous, leaving his wife to adjust to the distance between them. A year later their first child, David, was born.

Both parents were delighted to have a baby, but what was for Mr. Klein a pleasant addition to the family was for Mrs. Klein the means to fulfill her desperate need for closeness. The baby meant everything to her. While he was an infant she was the perfect mother, loving him tenderly and caring for his every need. When he was hungry she fed him; when he was wet she changed him; and when he cried—whenever he cried—she held him. When Mr. Klein tried to become involved with his infant son, his wife hovered about making sure he didn't do anything "wrong" with her precious baby. Naturally this infuriated Mr. Klein, and after a few bitter arguments he gradually left David more and more in his wife's care.

As he learned to walk and talk, David got into mischief, as all children do. He grabbed things that he wasn't supposed to, refused to stay in his playpen, and fussed whenever he didn't get his way. His crying was unbearable to his mother. She found herself unable to set limits or establish control on this precious baby whose love she needed so badly. When she put him in his crib for a nap, he cried. Although she desperately needed some time by herself, and little David also needed his nap, she was so unable to stand the crying that after five minutes she went and brought him downstairs. This was the beginning of a lifelong pattern.

David grew up with a distant father and a doting mother, thinking he was the center of the universe. Whatever he wanted, he expected to get. Whenever he was frustrated, he threw a tantrum. Bad as things were at home, at least the family existed in a kind of equilibrium. Dad was cut off from his wife and son, but he had his work. Mother was cut off from her husband, but she had her baby. Although he was willful and disobedient, he gave her the affection she craved. David's difficulties began when he went off to school. Used to getting his own way, he found it impossible to share with other children or to abide by the rules. His tantrums did nothing to endear him to his schoolmates or teachers. The other children avoided him, and he grew up having few friends. With teachers he acted out his father's battle against any efforts to control him. When Mrs. Klein heard complaints about David's failure to conform to the school's demands, she sided with her son. ("These people just don't know how to deal with a creative child.") So she moved him from school to school. But everywhere the conflicts were the same.

David grew up with a terrible pattern of adjustment to school and friends, but retained his extremely close relationship with his mother. The crisis came with adolescence. Like his father before him, David tried to develop independent interests outside the home. However, he was far less capable of separating than his father had been, and his mother was equally incapable of letting him go. The result was the beginning of chronic conflicts between David and his mother. Even as they argued and fought, though, they remained centered on each other. David spent more time battling his mother than doing anything outside the family.

Although he eventually left home at twenty-five, David remained a severely limited person. He hadn't learned the knack of looking after himself, and so had to settle for a series of unrewarding and uninteresting jobs. Never having learned to compromise or adjust to other children, he found it extremely difficult to make friends. He spent the rest of his life as a lonely, isolated, and marginally adjusted person. Worst of all, he didn't even have the consolation of the warm relationship with his mother.

David's history illustrates the components of Bowen's theory of behavior disorder. Both of his parents grew up relatively undifferentiated in emotionally fused families. As dictated by their own emotional needs, Mr. and Mrs. Klein's parents held their children too close, too long. This fusion sharply limits independent thinking and acting. Smothered by parents, it's hard to do other than reflexively accept or oppose them.

As Betty Carter explains (personal communication), symptoms break out when the "vertical" problems of anxiety and toxic family issues that come down through the generations intersect with the "horizontal" stresses that come at transition points in the family life cycle. Thus David's time of greatest vulnerability came when the unresolved fusion he inherited from his mother intersected with the stress of his adolescent urge for independence.

Except in rare cases, even emotionally fused children reach a point where they try to break away. But breaking away in such instances tends to be accomplished by emotional cutoff rather than by mature resolution of family ties. In childhood we relate to our parents as children. We depend on them to take care of us, we uncritically accept many of their attitudes and beliefs, and we behave in ways that are generally effective in getting our way with them. This usually means some combination of being good, patiently waiting to be rewarded, and being upset and demanding. A good deal of this childish behavior just doesn't work in the adult world. However, most of us leave home before changing to an adult-to-adult pattern with our parents. We—and they—only begin to change before it's time to leave.

A meek, patient child may become a bit more assertive and demanding in adolescence. Predictably, parents react with disappointment and anger. But instead of weathering the storm and patiently persisting with an adult stance, most people get hurt and withdraw. This is the *emotional cutoff.* Instead of persisting long enough to transform the relationship to an adult basis, most people decide that the only way to deal with their parents is to move away. Unhappily, this only gives the illusion of independence.

The daughter who didn't get past the good little girl stage with her parents will probably adopt a similar stance outside the home. When it doesn't work, she may react with temper—which also won't work. Those who cut themselves off from their parents to minimize tension, carry their childish ways with them.

According to Bowen, people tend to choose mates with equivalent levels of undifferentiation. They may be manifest in quite different ways—perhaps extreme dependence in one, with extreme independence in the other—but, underneath, the level of immaturity is the same. Observations of sharp increases in problems after nuclear families cut off from extended families (Kerr, 1971) tend to corroborate Bowen's view. When inevitable conflict develops, each spouse will be aware of the contribution of emotional immaturity—in the other one. Each will be prepared for change—in the other one. He will discover that her treating him like a father entails not only clinging dependence, but also emotional tirades and temper tantrums. She will discover that he withdraws the closeness she found so attractive in courtship as soon as she makes any demands. He fled from his parents because he needs closeness but can't handle it. Faced with conflict, he again withdraws. Sadly, what turned them on to each other carries the switch that turns them off.

What follows is marital conflict, dysfunction in one of the spouses, debilitating overconcern with one of the children, or various combinations of all three. When families come for help, they may present with any one of these problems. Whatever the presenting problem, the dynamics are similar; undifferentiation in families of origin is transferred to marital problems, which are in turn projected onto a symptomatic spouse or child. Thus the problems of the past are visited on the future.

Goals of Therapy

Most people can accept that unresolved family problems, passed down through the generations, continue to plague us here in the present. But most people also get hopelessly confused trying to ferret out the basic pattern of those problems. They take elaborate genograms and discover that Great Uncle Fred was this and Great Grandmother Harriet did that. So?

Tracing the pattern of family problems means paying attention to two things: process and structure. These are also the keys to therapy from a Bowenian perspective. Process refers to patterns of emotional reactivity; structure refers to patterns of interlocking triangles.

The goal of Bowenian therapy is to decrease anxiety and increase differentiation of self—nothing else lasts. Genuine change in the family system requires reopening of closed family ties and detriangulation, which creates the conditions for individual autonomy and growth. Symptoms are de-emphasized in a treatment that resembles *in vivo* psychoanalysis. Problems are presumed to inhere in the system, not the person; and change in the self is sought through changing in relationship to others. In order to change the system, and enable family members to achieve higher levels of differentiation, modification must take place in the most important triangle in the family—the one that involves the marital couple. To accomplish this the therapist creates a new triangle, with himself or herself and the two primary members of the family. If the therapist stays in contact with the spouses, while remaining emotionally neutral, then the spouses can begin the process of detriangulation and differentiation that will profoundly and permanently change the family system.

Defining specific goals for therapy seems to become progressively more vague as the unit of treatment gets larger. Changes sought in individuals need to be spelled out in rather specific detail (cf., Ford & Urban, 1963); goals for nuclear families are somewhat less specific. When Bowen describes goals for the extended family (as opposed to the individual goal of differentiation) it seems enough for him to speak of developing one-to-one relationships and avoiding triangles.

Guerin's sophisticated clinical approach has led to a more differentiated set of therapeutic goals, derived from highly articulated models developed to deal with problems of children and adolescents, marital conflict, and dysfunctional adults. Guerin's general goals are: (1) placing the presenting problem in the context of the multigenerational system by doing a thorough and accurate genogram; (2) connecting with key family members and working to calm their anxiety and level of emotional arousal and, thereby, lower anxiety throughout the system; and (3) define the parameters of the central symptomatic triangle, as well as important interlocking triangles. More specific goals are determined by the presenting problem and which unit of the family (mother and child, nuclear family, marital couple, individual) is the primary clinical focus.

In working with marital conflict, Guerin and his colleagues (1987, 1996) evaluate progress by looking for specific areas of improvement. The areas evaluated correspond to the criteria used by Guerin to measure the severity of conflict. These criteria are divided into: family system criteria, which include emotional climate, cluster stress, and intensity of triangulation; marital dyad criteria, which include communication, relationship time, closeness, and pursuer–distancer synchrony; and individual criteria, which include degree of projection versus self-focus, and neutralization of resentment and bitterness. In working with individuals, using a family systems format, the goals proposed by Guerin are management of anxiety and depression, with an increase in functional attachment and operational freedom throughout the multigenerational unit.

Monica McGoldrick, speaking from a feminist perspective, argues that it isn't enough to approach marital relationships with neutrality—to help couples negotiate compromises with each other in their own terms. As long as marital relationships are based on inherent imbalances, conscientious therapists must be aware of inequality and actively work to redress it. That means introducing the subject of gender inequality, even if it isn't an active part of a couple's agenda:

> Most men have trouble with intimacy. It's part of how they were socialized. We've got to admit it to ourselves, and help men change. We need to help them see the detrimental impact of the dominant value system that makes it difficult for them to relate effectively to their families. At the same time we need to help women to become effective in the areas where they are lacking: dealing with money, anger, and effective participation in the world of paid work and success. (McGoldrick, 1990)

McGoldrick believes that economic inequality between men and women is a powerful and neglected context of marriage, making it harder for women to insist on change because it's harder for them to be financially self-sufficient. Money means options. McGoldrick therefore believes that it's important to encourage women to develop their earning power. In short, "gender-sensitive therapy" extends the goals of treatment beyond the expressed complaints of families to include the context within which those complaints develop. This means attending to the wider family context *and* to inequalities of gender and class:

> If the wife is not in an economically viable position, marital therapy may be impossible. If she does not have the power to negotiate the relationship from a position of equality, the pretense of negotiation may be a farce. Beware of urging her to leave before having some awareness of the limitations and her options.
>
> HIS therapy may involve attention to his dreams, keeping a journal, learning to be intimate with his children or his friends.
>
> HER therapy may involve focusing on her resumé, a Dale Carnegie course, or a

> consultation with a financial planner, and taking a vacation from family responsibilities. (McGoldrick, 1990)

Betty Carter puts the case for gender sensitivity in therapists this way: "Marital therapy that ignores sexism is like rearranging the deck chairs on the Titanic."

Conditions for Behavior Change

Increasing the ability to distinguish between thinking and feeling and learning to use that ability to resolve relationship problems is the guiding principle of Bowenian therapy. Lowering anxiety and increasing self-focus—the ability to see and regulate one's own role in interpersonal processes—is the primary mechanism of change.

Understanding, not action, is the vehicle of cure, and therefore two of the most important elements in Bowenian therapy may not be apparent to anyone who thinks primarily about techniques. The atmosphere of sessions and the therapist's stance are both designed to minimize emotionality. Therapists ask questions to foster self-reflection and direct them at individuals one at a time, rather than encourage family dialogues—which have an unfortunate tendency to get overheated. Because clients aren't the only ones to respond emotionally to family dramas, Bowenian therapists strive to control their own reactivity and to avoid triangulation. This is easier said than done. The keys to staying detriangled are: to never take sides, and to nudge each party toward accepting more responsibility for making things better.

Being triangled means taking sides. Whenever motives are imputed to the behavior of any one person ("the husband is domineering"), awareness of processes that transcend individuals is lost. Instead of becoming partisan (overtly or otherwise), therapists resist triangulation by urging people to work out their differences between them. And since blaming each other is what makes it hard to solve problems in the first place, individuals are encouraged to look to their own roles in the process.

Therapists must learn to tolerate the inevitable emotionality in families, *without becoming reactive themselves.* "The learning depends on having the courage to engage emotionally intense situations repeatedly and to tolerate the anxiety and internal emotional reactivity associated with that engagement. This is anxiety associated with trying to become more of a self, an anxiety of progression rather than regression" (Kerr & Bowen, 1988, pp. 130–131). Therapists must avoid automatically accommodating or rebelling, dominating, submitting, or scapegoating. In other words, just as family members must learn to overcome emotionally driven automatic reactions—appeasing, controlling, or shifting focus—so must therapists.

Guerin suggests that if a family comes in during a crisis they should be encouraged to discuss it until their agitation is relieved. Guerin calls this "cooling down the affective overload" (Guerin & Pendagast, 1976). Beginning family therapists often make the mistake of trying to divert clients too quickly from their initial concerns to those with more theoretical interest to the therapist. So, even a therapist who wants people to think about their own role in problems is well advised to first hear them out and show appreciation for what they're feeling.

Bowen differed from most systems therapists in believing that meaningful change doesn't require the presence of the entire family.[1] Instead he believed that change is initiated by individuals or couples who are capable of affecting the rest of the family. Therapy can be described as proceeding from inside to out. Differentiation of self, which begins as a personal and individ-

[1]Although willingness to see individuals has become commonplace among solution-focused and narrative therapists, these therapists don't always take a systemic perspective.

ual process, is the vehicle for transforming relationships and the entire family system. For most family therapists treating individuals doesn't make much sense; after all, their fundamental premise is that individuals are products of their social context. Although he shared this contextual perspective, Bowen came to believe that well-motivated individuals are more capable of change than are larger family groups. The therapeutic process is a cycle in which the individual differentiates a self, which transforms the family system, which in turn leads to further differentiation in the individual.

Therapy may not require the presence of the entire family, but it *does* require an awareness of the entire family. Looking at the nuclear family isn't enough. Bowen stressed the importance of a broad assessment, saying, for example, "A family therapist may treat two parents and their schizophrenic son, but not attach much importance to the fact that the parents are emotionally cut off from their families of origin. The parents' cut off from the past undermines their ability to stop focusing on their son's problems; once again, the therapy will be ineffective" (Kerr & Bowen, 1988, p. vii).

Part of the process of differentiating a self is to develop a personal relationship with everyone in the extended family. The power of these connections may seem mysterious—particularly for people who don't think of their strength or well-being as dependent on family ties. A little reflection reveals that increasing the number of important relationships will enable an individual to spread out his or her emotional energy. Instead of concentrating one's investment in one or two family relationships, it's defused into several. Freud had a similar notion on an intrapsychic level. In "The Project for a Scientific Psychology," Freud described his neurological model of the mind. The immature mind has few outlets ("cathexes") for channeling psychic energy, and hence little flexibility or capacity to delay responding. The mature mind, on the other hand, has many channels of response, which permits greater flexibility. Bowen's notion of increasing the emotional family network is like Freud's model, writ large.

Because we learn to relate to the family during childhood, we learn to relate as children. Most of us leave home before we've established adult personalities, and so we continue to react childishly to our parents, brothers, and sisters. Furthermore, we react similarly in any new relationship that restimulates our unmodified sensitivities. Returning to the family—as adults—enables us to understand and modify old habits. This in turn frees us from acting out childish reactions in future relationships. This emphasis on the extended family is one of the unique and defining features of Bowen systems theory.

Unresolved tensions in families are described as leading to a series of overlapping triangles (Andres, 1971). Conflict between two people is detoured to a third person, who is triangled in. With additional tension, a fourth person may be brought in, leaving out the third. In a family with a great deal of tension and an equivalent tendency toward emotional cutoff, the available triangles will eventually be exhausted and the family will triangle in an outsider. The outsider may be a friend, minister, colleague, or psychotherapist. If a stranger comes into contact with two parts of the triangle (e.g., a mother and father), that person will either become triangulated or withdraw (Bowen, 1976). If the stranger is a therapist, he or she can remain in contact with the twosome but avoid becoming emotionally triangulated.

Therapy with couples is based on the premise that tension in the dyad will dissipate if they remain in contact with a third person (in a stable triangle)—*if* that person remains neutral and objective rather than emotionally entangled. Thus a therapeutic triangle can reverse the insidious process of problem-maintaining triangulation. Furthermore, change in any one triangle will change the entire family system.

Family therapy with individuals is based on the premise that if one person in the family achieves a higher level of differentiation of self this will enable (or cause) other members of the family to do the same. Bowenians teach individuals about triangles and then coach them to return to their families, where they work to detriangle themselves, develop greater objectivity, and thus achieve a permanent reduction in emotional reactiveness. This in turn has a therapeutic impact on all systems of which these individuals are a part.

Techniques

Bowenian therapists believe that understanding how family systems operate is far more important that this or that technique. Bowen himself spoke of "technique" with disdain and was distressed to see anyone relying on formulaic interventions with little or no understanding of how family systems operate. While it's true that, regardless of how focused on theory they are, all therapists must *do* something, Bowenians insist that it's important not to become preoccupied with specific techniques—not to look for a magic bullet.

If there *were* a magic bullet in Bowenian therapy—one essential technique—it would be the "process question." Process questions are designed to slow people down, diminish reactive anxiety, and start them thinking—not just about how others are upsetting them, but about how they are involved as participants in interpersonal patterns.

◆

In interviewing a couple in which the husband was a recovering alcoholic with a history of abuse, the therapist asked: "Where are you with the thoughts about the damage you've done to your wife and kids with your alcoholism?"

When the man acknowledged responsibility for his abusive behavior and seemed genuinely remorseful, the therapist asked about his progress toward recovery, again using process questions to focus on rational planning and personal responsibility. For example:

"What makes that step so hard?"
"Pride."
"How does that manifest itself?"
"I get nasty."

Notice how this line of questioning explores not only the man's personal progress, but also how his problems affect others in the family. Relationships take place in a systemic web of connections, but individuals are responsible for their own behavior.

Then the therapist shifted to open a discussion of the wife's role in the couple's difficulties. "So, you're getting better at taking responsibility for the drinking and the behavior connected with it? Do you think your wife appreciates what you're doing and the progress you're making?" And then a few minutes later: "Has your wife ever been able to talk to you about the things she's contributed to the relationship going sour?"

When the therapist asked the wife about her thinking, she got upset and talked about the annoying things her husband was doing—pressuring her to forgive him and to get back together. Although he would eventually like her to think about her own role in the relationship process, the therapist began by trying to empathize with her upset. "So, he's just bugging you and annoying you by trying to get you to change your mind?" Then after a few minutes, the therapist tried to shift the wife to thinking more and feeling less. "Can you give me a summary of your thinking—how you came to that conclusion?" And when the wife again got angry and blamed her husband, the therapist just listened. A moment later he asked, "What do you do in the face of that abuse?"

"I get upset."

"Do you understand what it is about you that sets him off?"

"No."

"Has he ever been able to tell you?"

Notice how in this series of questions the therapist attempts to explore the process of the couple's relationship, asking both partners to think about what's going on between them, increase their awareness of their own contributions, and consider what they're planning to do to take responsibility to make things better.

◆

Those who followed Bowen also ask questions, but move in occasionally to challenge, confront, and explain. Betty Carter, for example, asks questions designed to help couples understand their situation, but she then tries to intensify the process and speed it up a little by explaining what works or doesn't work and by assigning tasks. Most of the tasks she assigns are calculated to move people out of triangles. She might, for example, encourage a wife to visit her mother-in-law, or a husband to begin calling his own mother on the phone. Another favorite device of Carter's is to encourage people to write letters, addressing unresolved issues in the family. One way to prevent such letter writing from degenerating into telling people off is to have clients bring in the letters and then help them edit out the anger and emotional reactivity.

Guerin, perhaps more than any other Bowenian, has worked to develop clinical models that feature specific techniques for specific situations. His categorizing marital conflict into four stages of severity with detailed suggestions for treating each stage (Guerin et al., 1987) is the most elaborate demonstration of his well worked out technique.

Bowen advocated a variety of methods all aimed at the same goals. Whether treatment involves nuclear families, couples, individuals, or multiple family groups, the effort is directed at modifying the whole family system.

Bowenian Therapy with Couples

Whenever possible, Bowenians prefer to work with both parents or partners. When a therapist joins a couple, a therapeutic triangle is formed. If the therapist avoids being triangulated, the couple will then be forced to deal with each other. The emotional tone of sessions should be lively enough to be meaningful but cool enough to be objective. This is accomplished by asking more, and less, provocative questions, and by regulating the amount of interaction between the partners. When things are calm, conflicting feelings can be dealt with more objectively and partners can talk rationally with each other. But when feeling outruns thinking, it's best to ask questions that get couples to think more and feel less, and to talk to the therapist rather than to each other. Couples who've argued for years about the same old bugaboos are often amazed to discover that the first time they ever really hear each other is when they listen as their partners talk to the therapist. It's so much easier to hear when you aren't busy planning your own response. If all else fails to cool things down, Fogarty (1976b) recommends seeing spouses in separate sessions.

Contrary to popular belief, couples don't solve problems just by talking about them. Left to their own devices they tend to argue unproductively, project responsibility onto each other, and attack instead of negotiate. Change requires talking *and* listening. Because of the universal tendency to see only others' contributions to problems, special techniques are required to help family members see the process, not just the content, of interactions; to see their part in the process, instead of just blaming others; and finally to change.

Guerin (1971) recommends the "displacement story" as a device for helping family members achieve sufficient distance to see their own roles in the family system. The displacement story is about other families with similar problems. For example, a couple too busy attacking each other to listen might be told: "It must be terribly frustrating not getting through to each other. Last year I saw a couple who just couldn't stop arguing long enough to listen to each other. Only after I split them up and they blew off steam for a few sessions individually did they seem to have any capacity to listen to what the other was saying."

Displacement can also be used to frame process questions to avoid provoking angry or defensive responses. Instead of asking someone in the throes of upset and anger when they think they might get over those feelings in order to start working to change things—which might provoke them to think that their feelings are being denied—a therapist might ask, "Do you think anyone ever gets over all that anger and upset?" Or, if asking why someone hasn't been able to accomplish something might just make him or her defensive, a therapist might ask, "What do you think makes that step so hard for people?"

Guerin also uses films as displacement materials. If the proper aesthetic distance is maintained, people can become emotionally involved with a movie so that it has an impact but at the same time they remain sufficiently removed to be objective. Underdistancing, in a therapy session or in a highly provocative movie, results in an emotional experience devoid of reflection. Overdistancing, such as may occur in a lecture or preachy film, leads to a lack of involvement and impact. Guerin selects films like *Kramer Versus Kramer, The War of the Roses, I Never Sang for My Father, Scenes from a Marriage,* and *Breaking Away* to use as displacement materials for teaching family dynamics to trainees and to families in therapy.

Armed with a knowledge of triangles, the therapist endeavors to remain neutral and objective. This requires an optimal level of emotional distance, which Bowen (1975) said is the point where a therapist can see both the tragic and comic aspects of a couple's interactions. Although other people's problems are nothing to laugh at, maybe a sense of irony is preferable to the unctuous earnestness so popular in some quarters.

Staying detriangled requires a calm tone of voice and talking about facts more than about feelings. This calm objectivity on the part of Bowen systems therapists is expressed and enhanced by the use of process questions—questions aimed to get through emotional reactivity and make contact with family members' reasonableness.

As partners talk, the therapist concentrates on the *process* of their interaction, not on the details under discussion. Concentrating on the content of a discussion is a sign that the therapist is emotionally entangled in a couple's problems. It may be hard to avoid being drawn in by hot topics like money, sex, or discipline of children, but a therapist's job isn't to settle disputes, it's to help couples do so. The aim is to get clients to express ideas, thoughts, and opinions to the therapist in the presence of their partners. Should one break down in tears, the therapist remains calm and inquires about the thoughts that touched off the tears. If a couple begins arguing, the therapist becomes more active, calmly questioning one, then the other, and focusing on their respective thoughts. Asking for detailed descriptions of events is one of the best ways to subdue overheated emotion and make room for reason.

Although strict neutrality was considered essential by Bowen, those of his followers with feminist convictions believe that it's important to address issues of inequality, even if couples don't bring them up. Betty Carter raises the issue of gender by asking questions about who does what in the family and how much time each parent spends with the kids. She asks partners how much money each makes. When the usual discrepancy emerges, she asks, "What role do you think this plays in the decision-making process?"

Metaphors of complementarity are helpful for highlighting the process underlying the content of family interactions. Fogarty (1976b), for example, described the "pursuer–distancer" dynamic among couples. The more one pursues—presses for more communication and togetherness—the more the other distances—watches TV, works late, or goes off with the kids. Frequently, partners pursue and distance in different areas. Husbands commonly distance themselves emotionally but pursue sexually. The trick, according to Fogarty, is, "Never pursue a distancer." Instead, help the pursuer explore his or her own inner emptiness. "What's in your life other than the other person?" It's also important for therapists not to pursue distancers. If no one is chasing, the distancer is more likely to move toward the family.

To underscore the need for objectivity, Bowen spoke of the therapist as a "coach" or "consultant." He didn't mean to imply coldness or indifference, but rather to emphasize the neutrality required to avoid triangulation. In traditional terms this is known as "managing transference and countertransference reactions." And just as analysts are analyzed themselves so they can recognize their own countertransference, so Bowen considered differentiating a self in one's own family the best way to avoid being emotionally triangled by couples. Guerin suggests that the best way to develop a genuine understanding of family concepts is to try them out in your own family (Guerin & Fogarty, 1972).

In order to help partners define positions as differentiated selves, it's useful for a therapist to establish an "I-position" (Guerin, 1971). The more a therapist defines an autonomous position in relation to the family, the easier it is for family members to define themselves to each other. Gradually family members learn to calmly state their own beliefs and convictions and to act on them without attacking others or becoming overly upset by their responses.

When one partner begins differentiating, the other may be thrown off balance and press for a return to the status quo (Carter & Orfanidis, 1976). If this emotional counterreaction is weathered calmly, without giving in or becoming hostile, both partners can move toward a higher level of differentiation. The process takes place in small steps, with couples alternating between separateness and togetherness. Eventually, when each has achieved a sufficiently well articulated self, they can come together in mutual caring and respect, rather than continuing to try to remake each other in their own image and likeness.

After sufficient harmony had been won with progress toward self-differentiation, Bowen taught couples how emotional systems operate and encouraged them to explore those webs of relationship in their own families (Bowen, 1971). He prepared them for this by first making occasional references to their respective families. Once couples recognized the relevance of their prior family experience to their current problems, transition to the focus on families of origin was smoother.

For example, a woman locked into the role of emotional pursuer might be asked to describe her relationship with her father and then compare it to her current relationships with men. If lessening her preoccupation with her husband and children seemed advisable, the therapist might encourage her to connect with the most emotionally distant member of her family of origin, usually her father. The idea wouldn't be to shift her attachment from one set of relationships to another, but to help her understand that the intensity of her need is due in part to unfinished business from her growing up. Understanding and beginning to address unsatisfied longings at their source can help a person achieve more balanced relationships in the present—and begin to start focusing more on herself and her own needs.

Kerr (1971) suggests that when relationship problems in the nuclear family are being discussed, therapists should occasionally ask questions about similar patterns in the family of origin. If family members can see that they're repeating earlier patterns, they are more likely to recognize their own emotional reactivity. Recently, Nichols saw a couple unable to decide what to do with their mentally ill teenage daughter. Although the daughter was seriously disturbed and virtually uncontrollable, her mother found it very difficult to consider hospitalization. When asked what her own mother would have done, without hesitating she replied that her long-suffering mother would have been too guilt-ridden even to consider placement—"no matter how much she and the rest of the family might suffer." Little more needed to be said.

More didactic teaching occurs in the transition from brief to long-term therapy. Knowledge of family systems theory enables family members to analyze their own problems and gives them a framework in which they can continue to change. Such information is useful when tensions have abated, but trying to impart it can be risky during periods of conflict and anxiety. At such times, battling couples are liable to distort any statements about how families function as support for one or the other of their opposing positions. So primed are warring mates to make the other "wrong" in order for themselves to be "right," that they "hear" much of what a therapist says as either for them or against them. But when they're calm, they get past the idea that for one to be right the other must be wrong, and they can profit from didactic sessions. As they learn about systems theory, both partners are sent home for visits, to continue the process of differentiation in their extended families. During this phase of treatment—coaching—Bowen believed that infrequent meetings aren't just possible, but desirable (1976). Having sessions less often forces people to become more responsible and resourceful. It also reduces dependency on the therapist.

Bowenian Therapy with One Person

Bowen's personal success at differentiating from his family convinced him that a single highly motivated person can be the fulcrum for changing an entire family system (Anonymous, 1972). Subsequently he made family therapy with one person a major part of his practice. He used this method with one spouse when the other refused to participate, or with single adults who lived far from their parents or whose parents wouldn't come for treatment. Aside from these cases, in which Bowen made a virtue of necessity, he used this approach extensively with mental health trainees and professionals. Extended family work with partners is also the focus of couples treatment after the presenting anxiety and symptoms subside.

The goal of working with individuals is the same as when working with larger units: differentiation. With individuals the focus is on resolving neurotic patterns in the extended family. This means developing person-to-person relationships, seeing family members as people rather than emotionally charged images, learning to observe one's self in triangles, and, finally, detriangling one's self (Bowen, 1974).

The extent of unresolved emotional attachment to parents defines the level of undifferentiation. More intense levels of undifferentiation go hand in hand with more extreme efforts to achieve emotional distance, either through defense mechanisms or physical distance. A person may handle mild anxiety with parents by remaining silent or avoiding personal discussions; but when anxiety arises he or she might find it necessary to walk out of the room or even leave town. However, the person who runs away is as emotionally attached as the one who stays home and uses psychological distancing mechanisms to control the attachment. People who shrink from contact need closeness but can't handle it. When tension mounts in intimate relationships, they will again withdraw.

Two sure signs of emotional cutoff (Bowen, 1974) are denial of the importance of the family and an exaggerated facade of independence. Cut-off people boast of their emancipation and infrequent contact with their parents. The opposite of emotional cutoff is an open relationship system, in which family members have genuine, but not confining, emotional contact. Bowen therapy is designed to increase the extent and intimacy of connections with the extended family. In fact, Bowen found the results of extended family work superior to working directly on the nuclear family (Bowen, 1974).

Two prerequisites to differentiating a self in the extended family are: some knowledge of how family systems function and strong motivation to change. It's difficult to sustain the effort to work on family relationships in the absence of distress, and many people often work only in spurts from one crisis to the next (Carter & Orfanidis, 1976). When things are calm, they relax, and when problems arise again, they renew efforts to make changes.

The actual process of change is begun by learning about one's larger family—who made up the family, where they lived, what they did, and what they were like. Most people are surprisingly ignorant of their family's history. A basic working knowledge of the family, as far back as grandparents, is an adequate beginning. A useful device for organizing this material is the *genogram.*

Genograms are schematic diagrams of families, listing family members and their relationships to one another. Included are ages, dates of marriage, deaths, and geographical locations. Men are represented by squares and women by circles, with their ages inside the figures. Horizontal lines indicate marriages, with the date of the marriage written on the line; vertical lines connect parents and children. (For more detailed suggestions, see McGoldrick & Gerson, 1985.) Let us say, in constructing a typical genogram, that I (Mike Nichols) am fifty-one (actually, I'm sixty-four, but let's say fifty-one), my wife is fifty-three, and we were married in 1968 (Figure 5.1).

The next diagram shows that we have two children, a daughter age twenty-one and a son

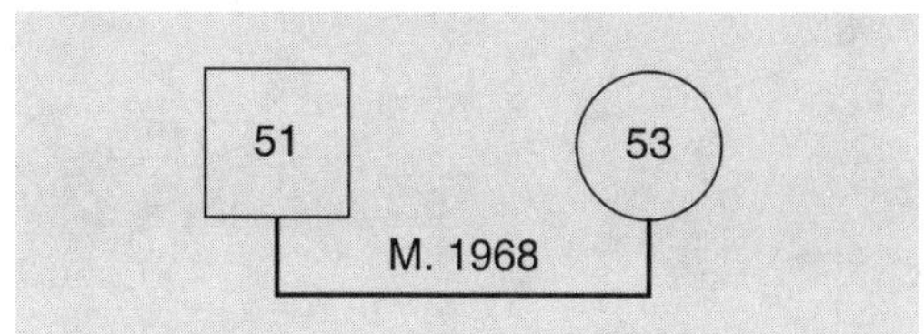

FIGURE 5.1

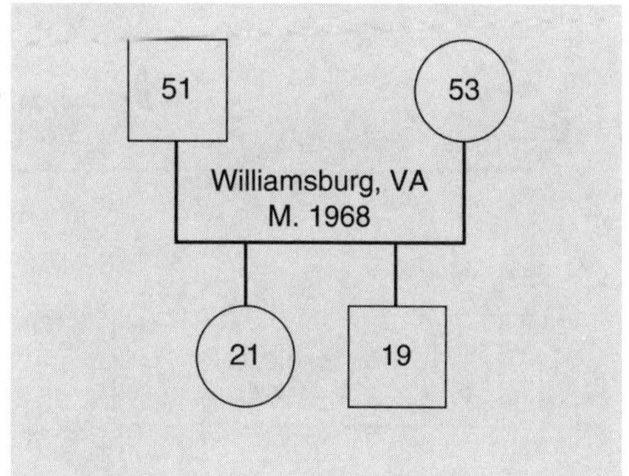

FIGURE 5.2

age nineteen, and that we live in Williamsburg, Virginia (Figure 5.2).

Next the genogram is expanded to include the extended family, beginning with my family of origin (see Figure 5.3 on page 166). My father, age eighty-one, and my mother, age seventy-eight, live in Washington, DC; my brother and his wife live in Ridgefield, Connecticut, and they have three children.

My wife's family, shown in Figure 5.4 on page 166, consists of her parents, who live in Chicago, and her brother, who lives in New Jersey. The double slash in the line joining her brother and his ex-wife indicates that they are divorced; she remarried in 1988 and is living in Philadelphia; he is living with his second wife who has a twenty-eight-year-old daughter by a previous marriage.

Dates of important events, such as deaths, marriages, and divorces, deserve careful study. These events send emotional shock waves throughout the family, which may open lines of communication and foster contact or may close off channels; in the latter case, issues may get buried and family members progressively more cut off. Divorce can bring families together or divide them. In some cases, news of the divorce reminds the family that the divorcing partners are separate individuals with emotional needs, rather than a self-sufficient unit. Sometimes

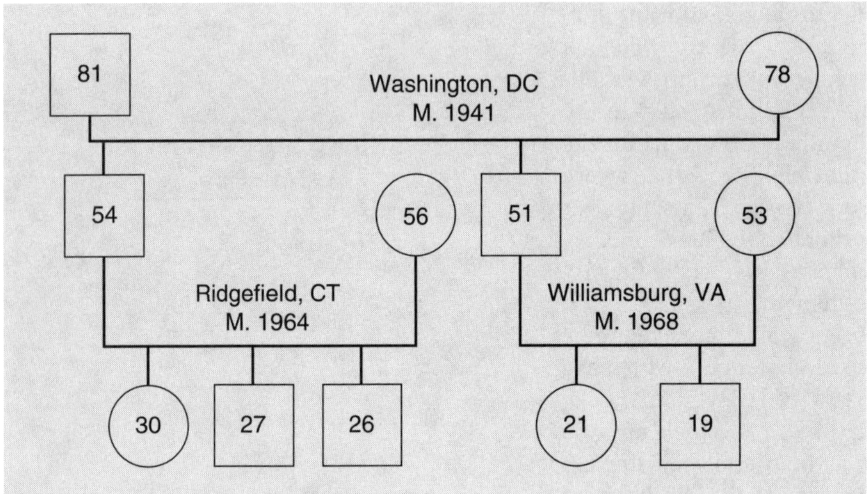

FIGURE 5.3

family members discover that it's easier to be with divorcing partners one at a time, freed from the chronic tension of being together and at odds. In other cases, families take sides after a divorce. If one side is "right" and the other is "wrong," divorce between two people can become a divorce between two segments of the family.

Another significant piece of information on the genogram is the location of various groups in the family system. Clusters of family

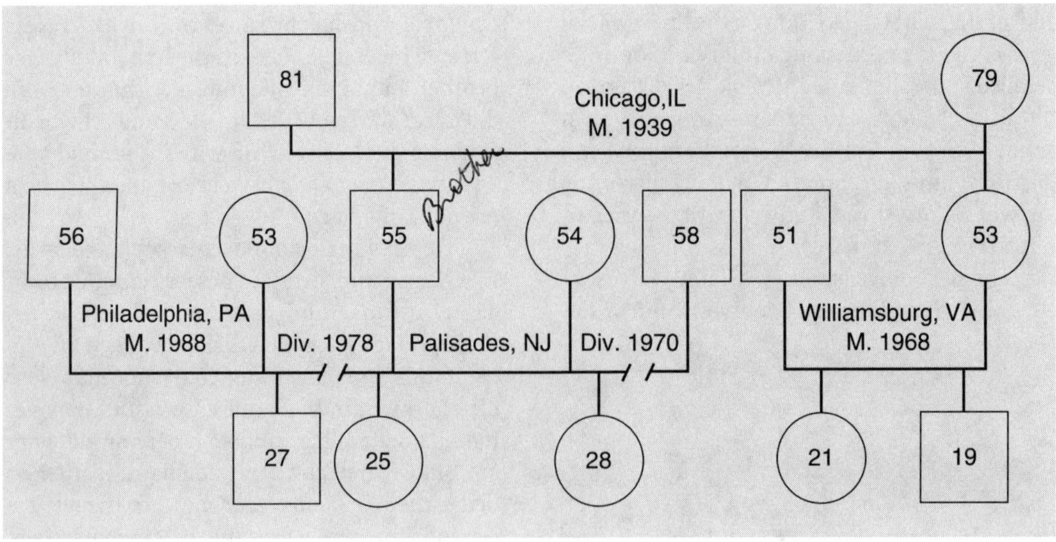

FIGURE 5.4

groups in one area suggest strong family bonds. In explosive families, emotional cutoff is illustrated by extreme geographical distances between family subunits. Of course it's possible to live in the same community and be separated by emotional distance. Also, many people choose to live where there are career opportunities, a reason that has little to do with family feeling. Nevertheless, the geographical spread of the family is a good clue to underlying emotional patterns.

Filling out the genogram isn't an end in itself, nor is it a simple matter. The genogram is only a skeleton, which must be fleshed out with pertinent information. In order to put meat on the skeleton's bones, it's necessary to know what to look for. Dates, relationships, and localities are the framework for exploring emotional boundaries, fusion, cutoffs, critical conflicts, amount of openness, and the number of current and potential relationships in the family.

If three parallel lines are used to indicate very close (or fused) relationships, a zigzag line to indicate conflict, a dotted line to indicate emotional distance, and a broken line to indicate estrangement (or cutoff), triangular patterns across three generations often become vividly clear—as shown in an abbreviated diagram of Sigmund Freud's family (Figure 5.5).

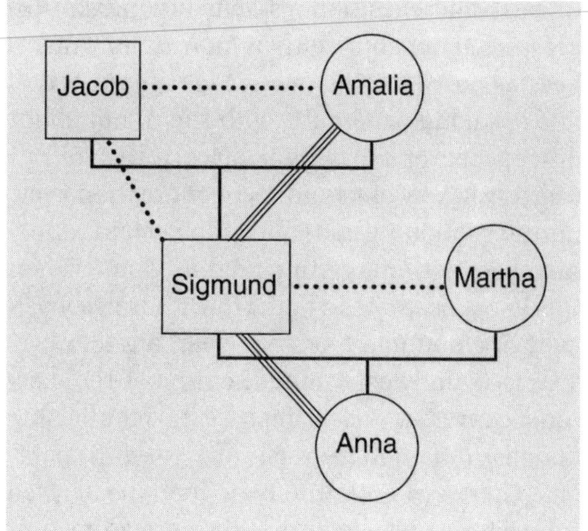

FIGURE 5.5

Family members may know some, but not all, of these things. Recent work by Nisbett and Wilson (1977) suggests people's reports about their experience often reflect their personal theories of attribution (what's *supposed to be*) rather than accurate observation (what *is*). Sometimes a "good relationship" with parents turns out to be one in which fusion and tension are managed by distancing tactics, such as infrequent contact, superficial conversation, or gossiping about other family members. Therefore it's useful to ask for descriptions rather than conclusions. Not, "Do you have a good relationship with your parents?" but, "Where do your parents live? How often do you see them, write, call? What do you and your mother talk about when you're alone together? Do you ever go out to lunch, just you and your dad?" This more detailed inquiry reveals the nature of personal relationships and the existing triangles in the system.

Other kinds of information that help explain the family include cultural, ethnic, and religious affiliations; educational and economic levels; connections to the community and social networks; and the nature of the work that family members do. Just as an individual cut off from his extended family is liable to be fused in his nuclear family, a family cut off from social and community ties is liable to be enmeshed in its own emotions, with limited outside resources for dissipating anxiety and distress.

The person who embarks on a quest of learning more about his or her family usually knows where to look. Most families have one or two members who know who's who and what's what—perhaps a maiden aunt, a patriarch, or a cousin who's very family-centered. Phone calls, letters, or, better yet, visits to these family archivists will yield much information, some of which may produce startling surprises.

Gathering information about the family is also an excellent vehicle for the second step toward differentiation, establishing person-to-person relationships with as many family members as possible. This means getting in touch and speaking personally with them, not about other people or impersonal topics. If this sounds easy, try it. Few of us can spend more than a few minutes talking personally with certain family members without getting a bit anxious. When this happens, we're tempted to withdraw, physically or emotionally, or triangle in another person. Gradually extending the time of real personal conversation will improve the relationship and help differentiate a self.

There are profound benefits to be derived from developing person-to-person relationships with members of the extended family, but they have to be experienced to be appreciated. In the process of opening and deepening personal relationships, you will learn about the emotional forces in the family. Some family triangles will immediately become apparent; others will emerge only after careful examination. Usually we notice only the most obvious triangles because we're too emotionally engaged to be rational and astute observers. Few people can be objective about their parents. They're either comfortably fused or uncomfortably reactive. Making frequent short visits helps control emotional reactiveness so that you can become a better observer.

Many of our habitual emotional responses to the family impede our ability to understand and accept others; worse, they make it impossible for us to understand and govern ourselves. It's natural to get angry and blame people when things go wrong. The differentiated person, however, is capable of stepping back, controlling emotional responsiveness, and reflecting on how to improve things. Bowen (1974) called this "getting beyond blaming and anger," and said that, once learned in the family, this ability is useful for handling emotional snarls throughout life.

Ultimately, differentiating a self requires that you identify interpersonal triangles you participate in, and detriangle from them. The goal is to relate to people without gossiping or taking sides and without counterattacking or defending yourself. Bowen suggested that the best time to do this is during a family crisis, but it can be begun at any time.

A common triangle is between one parent and a child. Suppose that every time you visit your folks your mother takes you aside and starts complaining about your father. Maybe it feels good to be confided in. If you're a mental health professional, maybe you'll have fantasies about rescuing your parents—or at least your mother. In fact, the triangling is destructive to all three relationships: you and Dad, Dad and Mom, and, yes, you and Mom. In triangles, one pair will be close and two will be distant (Figure 5.6). Sympathizing with Mom alienates Dad. It also makes it less likely that she'll do anything about working out her complaints with him.

Finally, although this triangle may give you the illusion of being close to your mother, it's at best an ersatz intimacy. Nor is defending your father a solution. That only moves you away from Mom towards Dad, and widens the gulf between them. As long as the triangulation continues, personal and open one-to-one relationships cannot develop.

Once a triangle is recognized for what it is, you can make a plan of action so you stop participating in it. The basic idea is to do something, anything, to get the other two people to work out their own relationship. The simplest and most direct approach is to suggest that they do so. In the example just given you can suggest that your mother discuss her concerns with

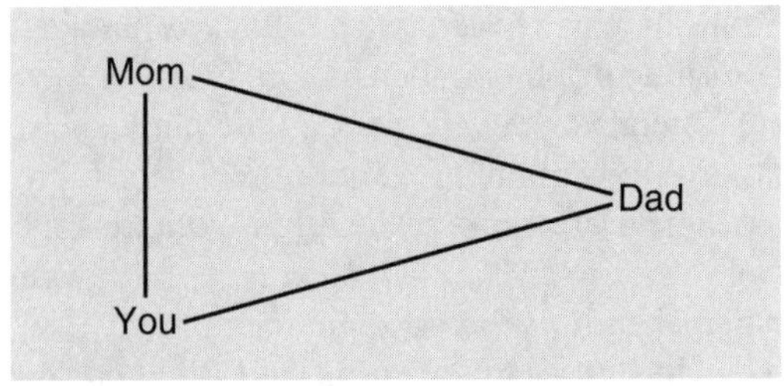

FIGURE 5.6

your father, *and* you can refuse to listen to more of her complaints. Less direct, but more powerful, is to tell Dad that his wife has been complaining about him, and you don't know why she doesn't tell him about it. She'll be annoyed, but not forever. A more devious ploy is to overagree with Mom's complaints. When she says he's messy, you says he's a complete slob; when she says he's not very thoughtful, you say he's a monster. Pretty soon she'll begin to defend him. Maybe she'll decide to work out her complaints with him, or maybe she won't. But either way you'll have removed yourself from the triangle.

Once you become aware of them, you'll find that triangles are ubiquitous. Some common examples include griping with colleagues about the boss; telling someone that your spouse doesn't understand you; undercutting your spouse with the kids; and watching television to avoid talking to your family. Breaking free of triangles may not be easy, but the rewards are great. Bowen believed that differentiating an autonomous self requires opening relationships in the extended family, and then ceasing to participate in triangles. The payoff comes not only from enriching these relationships, but also from enhancing your ability to relate to anyone—friends, fellow workers, patients, and your spouse and kids. Furthermore, if you can remain in emotional contact, but change the part you play in the family—and maintain the change in spite of family pressure to change back—the family will have to change to accommodate to your change.

Some degree of rejection is expectable when one embarks on a direction for oneself that isn't approved of by spouses, parents, colleagues, or others. The rejection, which is triggered by the threat to the relationship balance, is designed to restore the balance (Kerr & Bowen, 1988).

Some useful guidelines to resisting the family's attempts to get you to change back to unproductive but familiar patterns of the past have been enumerated by Carter and Orfanidis (1976), by Guerin and Fogarty (1972), and by Herz (1991). You can read about how to work on family tensions by resolving your own emotional sensitivities in two marvelous books by Harriet Lerner: *The Dance of Anger* (Lerner, 1985) and *The Dance of Intimacy* (Lerner, 1989).

Although differentiation in the family can be accomplished on your own, it's best to work with a coach. If you do attempt this work, an important rule of thumb is to keep your own counsel. A professional coach can give neutral and objective advice; family members and friends can't. Keep in mind that the changes you make are for yourself. Arm yourself with a plan to handle the family's counterreactions. As you move in and out of the family system, distinguish between planned and reactive distance. Distance is useful when you want to think, but interpersonal problems are never resolved at a distance.

When a problem arises in the family, examine your own behavior. Problem behavior is an expression of a family process, and you have responsibility for part of that process. The only change anyone can really make is change in oneself. If you're confused about what you're doing to maintain the status quo, try simply reversing what you were doing. Instead of pleading with your mother to visit you, try ignoring her. Instead of yelling at the kids, back off and let your spouse do it. Such reversals often have an immediate and dramatic impact on the system. But to see any real results, you may have to persist in the face of the family system's resistance to change.

Reentry into your family of origin is necessary to open the closed system. Sometimes all that's required is visiting. Other times, buried issues must be raised, activating dormant triangles by stirring up emotions in the system. If you can't move directly toward your father without his withdrawing, move toward other people with whom he is close, thus activating a triangle. If your father is tense about being alone with you, spend some time alone with your mother. This is likely to make him want to have equal time.

In reentry, it's advisable to begin by opening closed relationships before trying to change conflictual ones. Don't start by trying to resolve the warfare between yourself and your mother. Begin by looking up a sibling or cousin with whom you've been out of touch. Deal with personal issues, but avoid stalemated conflicts. If your contacts with some sections of the family are routine and regular, make them more unpredictable.

Those who continue working on their family relationships beyond the resolution of a crisis, or beyond the first flush of enthusiasm for a new academic interest, can achieve profound changes in themselves, in their family systems, and in their own clinical work. Extended family systems therapy is never finished. Coaching sessions may be spaced at more infrequent intervals, but even when these sessions are discontinued, it's usually with the understanding that the client will continue applying the principles in family, social, and work relations. If the client feels stuck or faces a new crisis, the process can always be renewed.

Evaluating Therapy Theory and Results

What makes Bowen's theory so useful and important is that it describes and explains the emotional forces within us that regulate how we relate to other people. The single greatest impediment to understanding one another is our tendency to become emotionally reactive and respond defensively instead of listening and hearing each other. Like all things about relationships, this emotionality is a two-way street: Some speakers express themselves with such emotional pressure that listeners inevitably react to that pressure rather than hearing what the speaker is trying to say. Bowenian theory describes this reactivity, explains its origins in the lack of differentiation of self, and explains how to reduce emotionalism and move toward mature self-control—by cultivating relationships widely in the family and learning to listen without becoming defensive or untrue to one's own beliefs.

In Bowenian theory, anxiety is the all-purpose explanation (for why people are dependent or avoidant and why they become emotionally reactive), reminiscent of Freudian conflict theory (which explains all symptoms as the result of anxiety stemming from conflicts over sex and aggression). The second all-purpose concept in the Bowenian system is, of course, differentiation. Since differentiation is roughly synonymous with maturity, students might ask, to what extent is the proposition that more differentiated people function better a circular argument? In respect to the Bowenian tradition of asking questions rather than imposing opinions, we'll let this stand as an open question for your consideration.

The major shortcoming of the Bowenian approach is that in concentrating on individuals and their extended family relationships, it neglects the power of working directly with the nuclear family. In many cases the most direct way to resolve family problems is to bring together everyone in the same household and encourage them to face each other and talk about their conflicts. These discussions may turn noisy and unproductive, but a skilled therapist can help family members realize what they're doing and guide them toward understanding. There are times when couples or families are so hostile and defensive that these direct dialogues must be interrupted to help individuals get beyond defensiveness to the hurt feelings underneath. At such times, it is useful, perhaps imperative, to block family members from arguing with each other. But an approach, such as Bowen's, that encourages therapists to speak to individual family members one at a time underutilizes the power of working directly with nuclear families in action.

The status of extended family systems therapy and theory rests not on empirical research but on the elegance of Murray Bowen's theory, clinical reports of successful treatment, and the personal profit experienced by those who have worked at differentiating a self in their families of origin.

Bowen's original research with schizophrenic families was more clinical observation than controlled experimentation. In fact, Bowen was decidedly cool to empirical research (Bowen, 1976), preferring instead to refine and integrate theory and practice. The little empirical work that's been done in the field is reported at the annual Georgetown Family Symposia. There, evaluations of various programs and occasional research reports have been presented. One of these, a study by Winer, was of sufficient interest to be published in *Family Process* (Winer, 1971). Winer reported on observations of four families in multiple family therapy led by Murray Bowen. Over the course of treatment, the experimenter tracked the ratio of self references to other references, and the number of differentiated-self references. Statements considered as differentiated-self references included: speaking for self without blaming, dealing with change or desired change in self rather than in others, distinguishing thoughts from feelings, and showing awareness and goal-directedness. There were two significant findings, both of which supported Bowen's position. First, in early sessions there were fewer self statements; the greatest number referred to "we" and "us," indicating that the spouses did not differentiate separate positions. Second, there was an evolution toward more differentiated I-statements over the course of treatment. Initially these occurred less than half the time, but after a few sessions differentiated statements predominated.

Although it does support the effectiveness of Bowen's therapy in increasing differentiation, the Winer study didn't test the premise that differentiation of self is synonymous with positive therapeutic outcome. In fact that is an article of faith with Bowen, and it points to a certain circularity in this theory: symptoms indicate emotional fusion, and fusion is demonstrated by the presence of symptoms (Bowen, 1966).

Bowen repeatedly stressed the importance of theory in clinical practice (Bowen, 1976), and so invites judgment on the basis of his theory. Therefore, it should be noted that although his theory is thorough, consistent, and useful, it's largely a series of constructs based on clinical observation. The basic tenets aren't supported by empirical research and, in fact, are probably not amenable to confirmation or disconfirmation in controlled experimentation. Bowen's theory, like psychoanalysis, is probably best judged not as true or false, but as useful or not useful. On balance, it seems eminently useful.

Evidence for the effectiveness of extended family systems therapy rests largely on personal experience and clinical reports. Bowenian therapists apparently do at least as well as the standard figures; that is, one-third of the patients get worse or no better; one-third of the patients get somewhat better; and one-third get significantly better.

People who develop systems of therapy are influenced by their personal and emotional experiences, and Bowen was more aware and candid than most about this (Anonymous, 1972). His family was middle-class, symptom-free, and relatively enmeshed; and his techniques seem most relevant for this sort of family. Like Bowen, most of the other therapists considered in this chapter also work in private practice with primarily middle-class patients.

Phil Guerin and Tom Fogarty have made notable contributions, not only in keeping alive and teaching Bowenian theory, but also in refining techniques of therapy. Both are master therapists. Betty Carter and Monica McGoldrick have made more of a contribution in studying how families work: the normal family life cycle, ethnic diversity, and the pervasive role of gender inequality. Because they are students of the family as well as therapists, some of their interventions have a decidedly educational flavor. In working with stepfamilies, for example, Betty Carter takes the stance of an expert and teaches the stepparent not to try to assume an equal position with the biological parent. Stepparents have to earn moral authority; meanwhile what works best is supporting the role of the biological parent. Just as Bowen's approach is influenced by his personal experience, it seems that both Carter and McGoldrick infuse their work as family therapists with their own experience as career women and their own convictions about the price of inequality.

All these therapists are fine clinicians; and they and their students have the advantage of working with theories that are sufficiently specific to provide clear strategies for treatment. Particularly now when family therapy is so fashionable, most people who see families use an eclectic hodgepodge of unrelated concepts and techniques; they're not apt to have a clear theory or a consistent strategy. The unhappy result is that most family therapists are drawn into the families' emotional processes and absorbed in content issues. The treatment that results tends to be haphazard and ineffectual.

Second-generation family therapists, like Guerin and Fogarty, are well-grounded enough in a theoretical system (for them, Bowen's) that they are able to diverge from it and add to it without losing focus. However, third-generation family therapists (students of students) are often left with no clear theoretical underpinning, and their work suffers from it. Interestingly, students of the pioneer family therapists haven't been particularly innovative. None of them has surpassed their teachers. These observations underscore the plight of graduate students who are exposed to a variety of approaches, often presented with more criticism than sympathetic understanding. Consequently they're left with no single coherent approach. Probably the best way to become an effective clinician is to begin as a disciple of one particular school. Apprentice yourself to an expert—the best you can find—and immerse yourself in one system. After you have mastered that approach and practiced it for a few years, then you can begin to modify it, without losing focus and direction.

Summary

Bowen's conceptual lens was wider than that of most family therapists, but his actual unit of treatment was smaller. His concern was always with the multigenerational family system, even though he usually met with individuals or couples. Since he first introduced the "three-generational hypothesis" of schizophrenia, he was aware of how interlocking triangles connect one generation to the next—like threads interwoven in a total family fabric. Although Bowenian therapists are unique in sending patients home to repair their relationships with parents, the idea of intergenerational connections has been very influential in the field.

According to Bowen, the major problem in families is emotional fusion; the major goal is differentiation. Emotional fusion grows out of an instinctual need for others, but is an unhealthy exaggeration of this need. Some people manifest fusion directly as a need for togetherness; others mask it with a pseudo-independent facade. The person with a differentiated self need not be isolated, but can stay in contact with others and maintain his or her own integrity. Similarly, the healthy family is one that remains in viable emotional contact from one generation to another.

In Bowenian theory the triangle is the universal unit of analysis—in principle and in practice. Like Freud, Bowen stressed the pivotal importance of early family relations. The relationship between the self and parents is described as a triangle and considered the most important in life. Bowen's understanding of triangles is one of his most important contributions and one of the seminal ideas in family therapy.

For Bowen, therapy was a logical extension of theory. Before you can make any significant inroads into family problems, you must have a thorough understanding of how family systems operate. The cure is to go backwards, to visit your own parents, grandparents, aunts, and uncles, and to learn to get along with them.

Bowen's theory espouses a balance between togetherness and independence, but the practice has a distinctly intellectual character. He saw anxiety as a threat to psychic equilibrium, consequently his approach to treatment often seems dispassionate. Bowen moved away from the heat of family confrontations in order to contemplate the history of family relationships. Like moving from the playing field into the stands, patterns become more visible, but it may be more difficult to have an immediate impact.

Bowen's model defocuses on symptoms in favor of systems dynamics. The treatment discourages therapists from trying to "fix" relationships and instead encourages clients to begin a lifelong effort at self-discovery. This isn't, however, merely a matter of introspection, but of actually making contact with the family. Clients are equipped for these journeys of self-discovery with tools for understanding their own patterns of emotional attachment and disengagement.

Seven techniques are most prominent in the practice of Bowenian family systems therapy:

1. ***Genogram.*** From his earliest NIMH days, Bowen used what he termed a "family diagram" to collect and organize important data concerning the multigenerational family system. In a 1972 publication Guerin renamed the family diagram the "genogram," a name that stuck. The main function of the genogram is to organize data during the evaluation phase and to track relationship processes and key triangles over the course of therapy. The most comprehensive guide to working with genograms is Monica McGoldrick and Randy Gerson's book, *Genograms in Family Assessment* (McGoldrick & Gerson, 1985).

2. ***The Therapy Triangle.*** This technique is based on the theoretical assumption that conflictual relationship processes within the family have activated key symptom-related triangles in an attempt to reestablish stability; and the family will automatically attempt to include the therapist in the triangling process. If they succeed, therapy will be stalemated. On the other hand, if the therapist can remain free of reactive emotional entanglements—in other words, stay detriangled—the family system and its members will calm down to the point where they can begin to work out solutions to their dilemmas.

In the treatment of couples, each spouse is asked in turn a series of process questions aimed at toning down emotion and fostering objective observation and thought. Some effort is made to slow down the overfunctioner in the dyad, while engaging and making it safe for more distant underfunctioners to open up and get involved. This same technique can be used with child-centered families by having the therapist place himself or herself at the point of a potential triangle with the symptomatic child and each parent, as well as between the parents. (Notice how similar this is to structural family therapists' attempts to get enmeshed mothers to pull back, and disengaged fathers involved. See Chapter 8.)

3. ***Relationship Experiments.*** Relationship experiments are carried out around structural alterations in key triangles. The goal is to help family members become aware of systems

processes—and learn to recognize their own role in them. Perhaps the best illustration of such experiments are those developed by Fogarty for use with emotional pursuers and distancers. Pursuers are encouraged to restrain their pursuit, stop making demands, and decrease pressure for emotional connection—and to see what happens, in themselves and in the relationship. This exercise isn't designed to be a magic cure (as some people have hoped), but to help clarify the emotional processes involved. Distancers are encouraged to move toward the other person and communicate personal thoughts and feelings—in other words to find an alternative to either avoiding or capitulating to the other's demands.

4. ***Coaching.*** Coaching allows therapists to counsel patients directly to work on their family problems. Coaching is the Bowenian alternative to a more personal and emotionally involved role common to most other forms of therapy. By acting as coach, the Bowenian therapist hopes to avoid taking over for patients or becoming embroiled in family triangles. Coaching doesn't mean telling people what to do. It means asking process questions designed to help clients figure out family emotional processes and their role in them. The goal is increased understanding, increased self-focus, and more functional attachments to key family members.

5. ***The "I-Position."*** Taking a personal stance—saying what you feel, instead of what others are "doing"—is one of the most direct ways to break cycles of emotional reactivity. It's the difference between saying "You're lazy" and "I wish you would help me more"; or between "You're always spoiling the children" and "I think we should be stricter with them." It's a big difference.

Bowenian therapists not only encourage clients to take I-positions, they also do so themselves. An example would be when after a family session the mother pulls the therapist aside and confides that her husband has terminal cancer, but she doesn't want the children to know. What to do? Take an I-position: Say to the mother: "I believe your children have a right to know about this." What she does, of course, is still up to her.

Another assumption in Bowenian therapy is that confrontation increases anxiety and decreases the ability to think clearly and see options. Therefore, displacing the focus, making it less personal and less threatening, is an excellent way to increase objectivity. This forms the basis for two related techniques, multiple family therapy and displacement stories.

6. ***Multiple Family Therapy.*** In his version of multiple family therapy, Bowen worked with couples, taking turns focusing on first one, then another, and minimizing interaction. The idea is that one couple may learn more about emotional process by observing others—others in whom they are not so invested as to have their vision clouded by feelings. James Framo uses a similar approach.

7. ***Displacement Stories.*** This is Guerin's technique, showing films and videotapes and telling stories, to teach family members about systems functioning in a way that minimizes their defensiveness.

Finally, although students of family therapy are likely to evaluate different approaches according to how much sense they make and how useful they promise to be, Bowen himself considered his most important contribution to be showing the way to make human behavior a science. Far more important than methods and techniques of family therapy, Murray Bowen made profound contributions to our understanding of how we function as individuals, how we get along with our families, and how these are related.

References

Andres, F. D. 1971. An introduction to family systems theory. In *Georgetown Family Symposium*, vol. 1, F. Andres and J. Lorio, eds. Washington, DC: Department of Psychiatry, Georgetown University Medical Center.

Anonymous. 1972. Differentiation of self in one's family. In *Family interaction*, J. Framo, ed. New York: Springer.

Boer, F. 1990. *Sibling relationships in middle childhood.* Leiden, the Netherlands: DSWO Press.

Bowen, M. 1966. The use of family theory in clinical practice. *Comprehensive Psychiatry.* 7:345–374.

Bowen, M. 1971. Family therapy and family group therapy. In *Comprehensive group psychotherapy*, H. Kaplan and B. Sadock, eds. Baltimore: Williams & Wilkins.

Bowen, M. 1972. Being and becoming a family therapist. In *The book of family therapy*, A. Ferber, M. Mendelsohn, and A. Napier, eds. New York: Science House.

Bowen, M. 1974. Toward the differentiation of self in one's family of origin. In *Georgetown Family Symposium*, vol. 1, F. Andres and J. Lorio, eds. Washington, DC: Department of Psychiatry, Georgetown University Medical Center.

Bowen, M. 1975. Family therapy after twenty years. In *American handbook of psychiatry*, vol. 5, S. Arieti, ed. New York: Basic Books.

Bowen, M. 1976. Theory in the practice of psychotherapy. In *Family therapy: Theory and practice*, P. J. Guerin, ed. New York: Gardner Press.

Carter, B., and McGoldrick, M. 1980. *The family life cycle.* New York: Gardner Press.

Carter, B., and McGoldrick, M. 1988. *The changing family life cycle: A framework for family therapy.* 2nd ed. Boston: Allyn and Bacon.

Carter, E., and Orfanidis, M. M. 1976. Family therapy with one person and the family therapist's own family. In *Family therapy: Theory and practice*, P. J. Guerin, ed. New York: Gardner Press.

Fogarty, T. F. 1976a. Systems concepts and dimensions of self. In *Family therapy: Theory and practice*, P. J. Guerin, ed. New York: Gardner Press.

Fogarty, T. F. 1976b. Marital crisis. In *Family therapy: Theory and practice*, P. J. Guerin, ed. New York: Gardner Press.

Ford, D. H., and Urban, H. B. 1963. *Systems of psychotherapy.* New York: Wiley.

Glick, P. 1984. Marriage, divorce and living arrangements. *Journal of Family Issues.* 5(1):7–26.

Guerin, P. J. 1971. A family affair. *Georgetown Family Symposium*, vol. 1, Washington, DC.

Guerin, P. J. 1972. We became family therapists. In *The book of family therapy*, A. Ferber, M. Mendelsohn, and A. Napier, eds. New York: Science House.

Guerin, P. J., ed. 1976. *Family therapy: Theory and practice.* New York: Gardner Press.

Guerin, P. G., Fay, L., Burden, S., and Kautto, J. 1987. *The evaluation and treatment of marital conflict: A four-stage approach.* New York: Basic Books.

Guerin, P. J., and Fogarty, T. F. 1972. Study your own family. In *The book of family therapy*, A. Ferber, M. Mendelsohn, and A. Napier, eds. New York: Science House.

Guerin, P. J., Fogarty, T. F., Fay, L. F., and Kautto, J. G. 1996. *Working with relationship triangles: The one-two-three of psychotherapy.* New York: Guilford Press.

Guerin, P. J., and Pendagast, E. G. 1976. Evaluation of family system and genogram. In *Family therapy: Theory and practice*, P. J. Guerin, ed. New York: Gardner Press.

Herz, F., ed. 1991. *Reweaving the family tapestry.* New York: Norton.

Hill, R. 1970. *Family development in three generations.* Cambridge, MA: Schenkman.

Kerr, M. 1971. The importance of the extended family. *Georgetown Family Symposium*, vol. 1, Washington, DC.

Kerr, M., and Bowen, M. 1988. *Family evaluation.* New York: Norton.

Lerner, H. G. 1985. *The dance of anger: A woman's guide to changing patterns of intimate relationships.* New York: Harper & Row.

Lerner, H. G. 1989. *The dance of intimacy: A woman's guide to courageous acts of change in key relationships.* New York: Harper & Row.

McGoldrick, M., 1982. Through the looking glass: Supervision of a trainee's trigger family. In *Family therapy supervision*, J. Byng-Hall and R. Whiffen, eds. London: Academic Press.

McGoldrick, M. 1990. Gender presentation. Article in progress.

McGoldrick, M., and Gerson, R. 1985. *Genograms in family assessment.* New York: Norton.

McGoldrick, M., Pearce, J., and Giordano, J. 1982. *Ethnicity in family therapy.* New York: Guilford Press.

McGoldrick, M., Preto, N., Hines, P., and Lee, E. 1990. Ethnicity in family therapy. In *The handbook of family therapy.* 2nd ed., A. E. Gurman and D. P. Kniskern, eds. New York: Brunner/Mazel.

Nichols, M. P. 1986. *Turning forty in the eighties.* New York: Norton.

Nichols, M. P., and Zax, M. 1977. *Catharsis in psychotherapy.* New York: Gardner Press.

Nisbett, R. E., and Wilson, T. D. 1977. The halo effect: Evidence for unconscious alteration of judgments. *Journal of Personality and Social Psychology. 35*:250–256.

Rodgers, R. 1960. Proposed modification of Duvall's family life cycle stages. Paper presented at the American Sociological Association Meeting, New York.

Solomon, M. 1973. A developmental conceptual premise for family therapy. *Family Process. 12*: 179–188.

Sulloway, F. 1996. *Born to rebel.* New York: Pantheon.

Toman, W. 1969. *Family constellation.* New York: Springer.

Winer, L. R. 1971. The qualified pronoun count as a measure of change in family psychotherapy. *Family Process. 10*:243–247.

6

Experiential Family Therapy

An experiential branch of family therapy emerged from the humanistic psychology of the 1960s that, like individual humanistic therapies, emphasized immediate, *here-and-now* experience. The quality of ongoing experience was both the criterion of psychological health and the focus of therapeutic interventions. Experiential family therapists consider feeling-expression to be the medium of shared experience and the means to personal and family fulfillment.

Experiential therapy was most popular when family therapy was young, when therapists talked about systems change but borrowed their techniques from individual and group therapies. Experiential family therapists drew heavily from Gestalt therapy and encounter groups. Other expressive techniques such as *sculpting* and *family drawing* bore the influence of the arts and of psychodrama. Because experiential treatment emphasizes sensitivity and feeling-expression, it wasn't as well suited to family therapy as were approaches that deal with systems and action; consequently, the experiential approach has lately been used less and some of its early exponents, such as Peggy Papp, have shifted to more systemic models. Nevertheless, the experiential emphasis on unblocking honest emotional expression in families is a valuable counterweight to the reductionistic cognitive emphasis of solution-focused and narrative approaches. The deaths of Virginia Satir and Carl Whitaker have robbed this school of its inspirational geniuses, but their influence lives on in the work of Walter Kempler, August Napier, David Keith, and Fred and Bunny Duhl. These and other experientialists are teaching and practicing expressive techniques that any family therapist may find useful. Moreover, the solid clinical and research grounding of Leslie Greenberg and Susan Johnson's emotionally focused couple therapy is currently revitalizing the experiential approach.

Sketches of Leading Figures

Two giants stand out as leaders of experiential family therapy: Carl Whitaker and Virginia Satir. Whitaker was the dean of experiential family therapy, the leading exponent of a free-wheeling, intuitive approach aimed to puncture pretense and liberate family members to be themselves. He was among the first to do psychotherapy with families, and he steadily grew in stature to become one of the most admired therapists in family therapy. Iconoclastic, even outrageous at times, Whitaker nevertheless retained the respect and admiration of the family therapy establishment. He may have been their Puck, but he was one of them.

Carl Whitaker grew up on an isolated dairy farm in Raymondville, New York. Rural isolation bred shyness and a touch of sadness but, perhaps, also conditioned Whitaker to be less hemmed in than most of us by social convention. After medical school and a residency in obstetrics and gynecology, Whitaker went into psychiatry, where he immediately became fascinated by the psychotic mind. Unfortunately—or fortunately—back in the 1940s Whitaker couldn't rely on neuroleptic drugs to blunt the hallucinatory fantasies of his patients; instead he listened and learned to understand thoughts crazy but human, thoughts that the rest of us keep buried.

After working at the University of Louisville College of Medicine and the Oakridge Hospital, Dr. Whitaker accepted the chairmanship of Emory University's Department of Psychiatry, where he remained from 1946 to 1955, building a first-rate program. In the face of mounting pressure to make the department more psychoanalytic, Whitaker and his entire faculty finally resigned to form the Atlanta Psychiatric Clinic, a productive and creative group that included Thomas Malone, John Warkentin, and Richard Felder. Experiential psychotherapy was born of this union, and the group produced a number of highly provocative and challenging papers (Whitaker & Malone, 1953). In 1965 Whitaker went to the University of Wisconsin Medical School, and also conducted a private practice in Madison. After his retirement in the late 1980s, Whitaker traveled frequently to share his wisdom, experience, and himself at conventions and workshops. His death in 1995 was a great loss. Among Whitaker's most well-known associates are August Napier, now in private practice in Atlanta, and David Keith, now at the State University of New York in Syracuse.

The other major charismatic figure among experiential family therapists was the late Virginia Satir. Satir, who was one of the well-known members of the early Mental Research Institute (MRI) group in Palo Alto, emphasized communication as well as emotional experiencing, and so her work must be considered in both the communications and experiential traditions.

Social worker Virginia Satir began seeing families in private practice in 1951. In 1955 she was invited to set up a training program for residents at the Illinois State Psychiatric Institute. (One of her students was Ivan Boszormenyi-Nagy.) In 1959 Don Jackson invited Satir to join him at MRI, where she became the first director of training and remained until she left MRI in 1966 to become the director of Esalen Institute in Big Sur, California.

Satir was the prototypical nurturing therapist in a field enamored with experience-distant concepts and tricky strategic maneuvers. Her warmth and genuineness gave her a tremendous appeal and impact as she traveled all over the country leading demonstrations and workshops. Her ability to move large audiences in experiential exercises made her a legend as family therapy's most celebrated humanist.

In the 1970s Satir's influence waned and she received less recognition than she deserved as one of the innovators of family therapy. This was very painful for her. In Venezuela, in 1974, at a *Family Process* board meeting there was a debate between Salvador Minuchin and Satir about the nature of family therapy. Minuchin argued that it was a science that required skills rather than just warmth and faith, and that the main job was to fix broken families; Satir stuck to her belief in the healing power of love, and spoke out for the salvation of humankind through family therapy. It turned out that Minuchin was speaking for the field. Satir felt out of step. After this she drifted away from the family therapy establishment and, instead, became a world traveler and spokesperson for her evangelical approach. Satir died of pancreatic cancer in 1988.

Another Californian who has written a great deal about experiential family therapy is Walter Kempler, who brings many of the ideas and techniques of Gestalt therapy to his work with families. He describes procedures commonly found in encounter groups and existential-humanistic individual therapies, which lie at the root of experiential family therapy.

Fred and Bunny Duhl, former codirectors of the Boston Family Institute, have introduced a number of expressive techniques into experiential family therapy. They use nonverbal means of communication, such as *spatialization* and *sculpting* (Duhl, Kantor, & Duhl, 1973), as well as *role playing* and *family puppets* (Duhl & Duhl, 1981). Their approach, which they call "integrative family therapy," is an amalgam of elements from numerous sources, including psychodrama, experiential psychotherapy, cognitive psychology, structural family therapy, and behavioral psychotherapy.

Cofounder of the Boston Family Institute in 1969, along with Fred Duhl, was David Kantor, who brought with him a background in psychodrama and helped emphasize the "family as theater" metaphor in family therapy (Kantor & Lehr, 1975).

Among the most recent experiential approaches to family therapy is the "emotion-focused couples therapy" of Leslie Greenberg and Susan Johnson, which draws on Perls, Satir, and the MRI group (Greenberg & Johnson, 1985, 1986, 1988).

We group such unclassifiable individualists as Virginia Satir and Carl Whitaker together in this chapter because they are united by their investment in spontaneity, creativity, and risk-taking. While they share a commitment to freedom, individuality, and personal fulfillment, experientialists are otherwise relatively atheoretical. The hallmark of this approach is the use of techniques to open individuals to their inner experience and to unfreeze family interactions. Having reached their greatest popularity in the 1960s (Nichols & Zax, 1977), experiential approaches have been largely displaced by new developments in more systems-oriented therapies. Once feeling-expression occupied center stage in psychological therapies; today that place is held by behavior and cognition. Psychotherapists have discovered that people think and act; but that doesn't mean we should ignore the immediate emotional experience that is the main concern of experiential family therapy.

Theoretical Formulations

Carl Whitaker may have best expressed the experientialists' position on theory in his "The Hindrance of Theory in Clinical Work" (Whitaker, 1976a). Whitaker described what he considered the chilling effect of theory on intuition and creativity. Theory may be useful for beginners, Whitaker says, but his advice is to give up theory as soon as possible in favor of just being yourself. He quotes Paul Tillich's existential aphorism, "being is becoming," to support his own contention that psychotherapy requires openness and spontaneity, not theory and technique; and he cites the fact that technical approaches usually don't work for second-generation therapists (as many people found out when they tried to imitate the "simple" steps of Minuchin's structural family therapy). Perhaps we hamper our own creative efforts by trying to copy our mentors.

Whitaker says that therapists who base their work on theory are likely to substitute dispassionate technology for caring, and he goes on to imply that theory is a refuge from the anxiety-provoking experience of sharing a family's emotional life. Instead of having the courage just to "be" with families and help them grapple with their problems, theoretically inclined clinicians use theory to create distance in the name of objectivity.

Whitaker says therapists don't need theories to handle stress and anxiety; what they need are supportive cotherapists and helpful supervisors. In short, it isn't technique, but personal involvement that enables therapists to do their best. By avoiding theory, Whitaker believed that he forced families to establish their own theoretical way of living. David Keith (1988) echoes this conviction, saying that he often leaves families stewing in ambiguity rather than oversimplifying life by pointing them in a particular direction. This is a therapeutic pattern modeled after benevolent parenting, which carries a deep respect for people's ability to discover their own directions in life.

No theory is, of course, itself a theory. To say that therapy shouldn't be constrained by theory is to say that it should be loose, creative, open, and spontaneous. Therapists should share feelings, fantasies, and personal stories, if that's what they feel like doing, and if that's what it takes to help families become more aware and sensitive. Despite Whitaker's disdain for theory, however, experiential family therapy is very much a child of the existential, humanistic, and phenomenological tradition.

Philosophers like Edmund Husserl and Martin Heidegger (1963) began to work out the clinical implications of existential thought. Their ideas were assimilated and developed by Ludwig Binswanger (1967), who formulated a new theory of psychotherapeutic process but remained tied to the psychoanalytic method. The same may be said of Medard Boss (1963), the developer of "Daseinanalysis," which also differed from psychoanalysis more in theory than in practice. Much of the theorizing of these existential psychologists was in reaction to perceived shortcomings of psychoanalysis and behaviorism. In place of *determinism*, existentialists emphasized *freedom* and the necessity to discover the essence of one's *individuality* in the immediacy of experience. Instead of being pushed by the past, they saw people as pulled toward the future, impelled by their *values* and *personal goals*. Where psychoanalysts posited a structuralized model of the mind, existentialists treated persons as wholes. Finally, existentialists substituted a positive model of humanity for what they believed was an unduly pessimistic psychoanalytic model. They believed that people should aim at personal fulfillment, rather than settle for partial resolution of their neuroses.

These new ideas—which Maslow (1968) called the "Third Force Psychology"—were translated into practice by Victor Frankl, Charlotte Buhler, Fritz Perls, Rollo May, Carl Rogers, Eugene Gendlin, Sidney Jourard, R. D. Laing, Carl Whitaker, and others. The most influential of these approaches were Frankl's (1963) *Logotherapy*, Perls's (1961) *Gestalt Therapy*, Rogers's (1951) *Client-Centered Therapy*, and Gendlin's (1962) *Experiencing*. Incidentally, it was probably Whitaker and Malone (1953) who first used the term "experiential psychotherapy."

The conceptual writings of experiential psychotherapists generally consist of a series of loosely connected constructs and statements of position. Most of them are melioristic, and often the language is more colorful and stagy than clear and precise. Take, for instance, the following sample from Whitaker and Keith (1981).

> Metacommunication is considered to be an experiential process, an offer of participation that implies the clear freedom to return to an established role security rather

> than be caught in the "as if" tongue-in-cheek microtheater. That trap is the context that pushes son into stealing cars or daughter into incest with father while mother plays the madame. The whimsy and creativity of the family can even be exaggerated to where family subgroups or individuals are free to be nonrational or crazy. (p. 190)

According to Virginia Satir (1972), "So many of the words professional people use to talk about human beings sound sterile and lack life-and-breath images," (p. 21) that she preferred folksy and concrete images. Consequently much of the writing done by experientialists is more evocative than elucidative.

Despite the paucity of elegant theoretical statements, there are a number of basic theoretical premises that define the experiential position on families and their treatment—a basic commitment to individual awareness, expression, and self-fulfillment. Whitaker emphasized that self-fulfillment depends on family cohesiveness, and Satir stressed the importance of good communication with other family members; but the basic commitment seems to be to individual growth. Moreover, while there was some talk about family systems (Satir, 1972), the early experiential model of families was more like a democratic group than a system with structure and hierarchy. (This is less true of more recent work by Whitaker and the highly sophisticated efforts of Gus Napier and David Keith.) Still there is great emphasis on flexibility and freedom with respect to family roles and the distribution of power. Roles are thought to be reciprocal. If one spouse is a quiet, private person, the other is apt to be sociable and outgoing. Treatment is generally designed to help individual family members find fulfilling roles for themselves, without an overriding concern for the needs of the family as a whole. This is not to say that the needs of the family system are denigrated, but they're thought to follow automatically on the heels of individual growth. At times the family was even portrayed as the enemy of individual freedom and authenticity (Laing & Esterson, 1970).

After reading the previous paragraph, David Keith (in a personal letter) helped put into perspective the experiential position about the claims of the individual versus the claims of the family, as follows:

> Our thinking is individually focused to the extent that I am very clear that I am the only one inside my skin. No one knows how I feel or how I think. Likewise I am unable to know how anyone else feels or thinks. There is a dialectical tension between the individual and the family—between dependence and independence. To overemphasize either individuality or family connectedness is to distort the human condition. This tension is transcended only by experience, not by thinking or theory. One of my basic assumptions in working with families is that, for better or worse, the family is in charge of itself. A corollary to that idea is that I am suspicious of families in that I know that families will sacrifice members in order to preserve the whole, or to shield certain members.

Theories of families as systems are translated into techniques that facilitate communication and interaction. The emphasis on altering interactions implies an acceptance of whatever level of individual experience and understanding is already present. This is where experiential theory differs (as does psychoanalytic theory) from most systems approaches. Here the emphasis is on expanding experience. The assumption is that such expansion on the individual level is prerequisite to breaking new ground for the family group, and the consequent new material and increased awareness will, almost automatically, stimulate increased communication and sharing of feelings among family members. Families will talk more when their members become more aware of what they have to say.

Underlying much of the work of experiential family therapy is the premise, seldom mentioned, that the best way to promote individual and family growth is to liberate affects and impulses. Efforts to reduce defensiveness and unlock deeper levels of experiencing rest on this basic assumption.

Normal Family Development

Experiential family therapists subscribe to the humanistic faith in the natural goodness and wisdom of unacculturated human feelings and drives. Left alone, people tend to flourish, according to this point of view. Problems arise because this innate tendency toward *self-actualization* (Rogers, 1951) runs afoul of social (Marcuse, 1955) and familial (Laing & Esterson, 1970) counterpressures. Society enforces repression in order to tame people's instincts to make them fit for productive group living. Unhappily, socially required self-control is achieved at the cost of "surplus repression" (Marcuse, 1955) and emotional devitalization. Families add their own additional controls to achieve peace and quiet, perpetuating outmoded *family myths* (Gehrke & Kirschenbaum, 1967) and using *mystification* (Laing, 1967) to alienate children from their experience.

In the ideal situation, these controls aren't excessive, and children grow up in an atmosphere of support for their feelings and creative impulses. Parents listen to their children, accept their feelings, and validate their experience, which helps the children develop healthy channels for expressing their emotions and drives. Affect is valued and nurtured; children are encouraged to experience things passionately and to express the full range of human emotions (Pierce, Nichols, & DuBrin, 1983).

Mental health is viewed as a continuous process of growth and change, not a static or homeostatic state. "The healthy family is one that continues to grow in spite of whatever troubles come its way" (Whitaker & Keith, 1981, p. 190). Furthermore, the healthy family deals with stress by pooling its resources and sharing problems, not dumping them all on one family member.

Experiential therapists describe the normal family as one that supports individual growth and experience. In so doing, clinicians may unwittingly foster a dichotomy between the individual and the family: "Bad" families repress people, "good" ones leave them alone. Neither Carl Whitaker nor Virginia Satir fell into this trap, although Whitaker seemed ambivalent about accepting the necessity for an organized family structure. At times he spoke of the need for hierarchy and generational boundaries, while at other times he emphasized creative flexibility. The following quotation (Whitaker & Keith, 1981) shows his vacillation on this point.

> The healthy family maintains a separation of the generations. Mother and father are not children and the children are not parents. The two generations function in these two separate role categories. Members of the same generation have equal rank. However, there is a massive freedom of choice in periodic role selection and each role is available to any member. Father can be a five-year-old, mother can be a three-year-old, the three-year-old can be a father, the father can be a mother, depending upon the situation, with each family member protected by an implicit "as if" clause. (p. 190)

In any case, Whitaker saw the family as an integrated whole, not a confederation of separate individuals. Other experientialists often seem to think of the whole as less than the sum of its parts. Kempler (1981), for example, emphasizes personal responsibility, which he defines as each person maximizing his or her own potential. Some call this narcissism (Lasch, 1978), but experientialists assume that enhanced personal commitment automatically leads to greater commitment to others.

Satir (1972) described the normal family as one that nurtures its members. Individual family members listen to and are considerate of each other, enabling them to feel valued and loved. Affection is freely given and received. Moreover, family members are open and candid with each other. "*Anything* can be talked about—the disappointments, fears, hurts, angers, criticisms as well as the joys and achievements" (Satir, 1972, p. 14).

Satir also considered flexibility and constructive problem-solving as characteristic of a healthy family. Nurturing parents, she says, realize that change is inevitable; they accept it and try to use it creatively. Her description of the "nurturing family" brings to mind the world portrayed by Norman Rockwell on the covers of *The Saturday Evening Post:* warm and pleasant, but not quite true to life. Perhaps Satir's (1972) idealized version of family life is better taken as a prescription for, rather than a description of, healthy family living.

In general, experiential family therapists describe the family as a place of sharing experience. The functional family supports and encourages a wide range of experiencing; the dysfunctional family resists awareness and blunts responsiveness. The vitality of each person's individual experience is the ultimate measure of sanity. Healthy people accept the truth and richness of their experience in each moment. This enables them to stand up for who they are and what they want—and to accept the same from others. Functional families are secure enough to be passionate; dysfunctional families are frightened and bloodless. Neither problem-solving skills nor particular family structures are considered to be nearly as important as expanding open, natural, and spontaneous experiencing. The healthy family offers its members the freedom to be themselves, and supports privacy as well as togetherness.

Development of Behavior Disorders

From the experiential perspective, denial of impulses and suppression of feelings are the root of family problems. Dysfunctional families are rigidly locked into self-protection and avoidance (Kaplan & Kaplan, 1978). In Sullivan's (1953) terms, they seek *security,* not *satisfaction.* They're too busy trying not to lose to ever dare to win.

Such families function automatically and mechanically, rather than through awareness and choice. Their presenting complaints are many, but the basic problem is that they smother emotion and desire. Laing (1967) described this as the *mystification* of experience, and he held parents responsible. Parents are, of course, not the villains. The process is circular. Kempler (1981) also speaks of family pressure for loyalty and cohesion as interfering with individuals' loyalty to themselves. The untested premise in these unhappy families is that assertiveness or confrontation would lead to emotional chaos. The sad result is that feelings are never acknowledged.

According to Whitaker (Whitaker & Keith, 1981), there's no such thing as a marriage—merely two scapegoats sent out by their families to perpetuate themselves. Each is programmed to recapitulate the family of origin; together they must work out the inherent conflict in this situation. Feeling helpless and frustrated, they cling even more to what is familiar, intensifying, rather than alleviating their problems. Each resists the other's way of doing things. When couples present in this struggle for control, one may appear sicker than the other. But, according to Whitaker (1958), the degree of disturbance in spouses almost always turns out to be similar, even if at first they appear different.

Couples who remain together eventually reach some kind of accommodation. Whether it's based on compromise or unilateral concession, it lessens the previous conflict. Dysfunctional families, terrified of conflict, cling rigidly to the structures and routines that they work out together. Having experienced being different—and not liking it—they now cling to togetherness. Once again alternatives are dismissed or blocked from awareness.

What distinguishes dysfunctional families is that the flow of their behavior is clogged with unexpressed emotion, robbing them of flexibility and vitality. Clinicians see fixed triangles and pathological coalitions; anyone can see their rigidity.

Avoidance of feelings is described as the cause and effect of family dysfunction. Kempler (1981) lists a number of devices commonly used to avoid feelings: asking questions, instead of stating opinions; using the editorial we ("*We* are worried about Johnny"); and changing subjects. The attention paid to these protective conversational devices used to avoid intimacy reflects the experientialists' concern with relatively minor forms of psychic difficulty.

Experiential family therapists believe that a climate of emotional deadness leads to symptoms in one or more family members. However, because they are as concerned with positive health as with clinical pathology, experientialists point to the "normal" casualties that others might overlook. Whitaker (Whitaker & Keith, 1981) spoke of "the lonely father syndrome," "the battle fatigue mother syndrome," "the infidelity syndrome," and "the parentified child syndrome." These "normal" problems concern experiential family therapists just as much as do the symptoms of the identified patient. Experiential family therapists also look for culturally invisible pathologies, such as obesity, heavy smoking, and overwork. These symptoms of family trouble are "invisible," because they're regarded as normal.

Systems-oriented family therapists generally look no deeper than interactions between family members to explain psychopathology. But experientialists, like psychoanalysts, are concerned as much with individuals as with systems, and consider intrapsychic problems when explaining psychopathology. For example, Kaplan and Kaplan (1978) speak of projection and introjection and intrapsychic defenses that lead to interpersonal problems in the family. Members of such families disown parts of themselves and fit together by adopting complementary but rigidly limiting roles. One person's "strength" is maintained by another's "weakness."

Dysfunctional families are made up of people incapable of autonomy or real intimacy. They don't know themselves and they don't know each other. The root cause is *alienation* from experience, what Kempler (1981) calls "astigmatic awareness." Their communication is restricted because their awareness is restricted. They don't say much to each other because they don't feel much. They don't really experience their own experience, much less share it with other family members.

Whitaker also spoke of family pathology as arising from an impasse in a transition in the life cycle or in the face of changing circumstances. While this is anything but novel, it's certainly consistent with the experientialists' emphasis on the need for change and flexibility. Not to change in the face of changing circumstances can be as problematic doing something actively destructive.

In her portrayal of troubled families, Satir (1972) emphasized the atmosphere of emotional deadness. Such families are cold; they seem to stay together merely out of habit or duty. The adults don't enjoy their children, and the children learn not to value themselves or care about their parents. In consequence of the lack of warmth in the family, these people avoid each other, and preoccupy themselves with work and other activities outside the family.

It's important to notice that the "dysfunction" Satir described isn't the kind of pathology found in diagnostic manuals. Satir, like others in the experiential camp, was just as concerned with "normal" people who lead lives of quiet desperation as with the more blatantly disturbed people who usually present themselves to clinics. As Satir (1972) put it,

> It is a sad experience for me to be with these families. I see the hopelessness, the helplessness, the loneliness. I see the bravery of people trying to cover up—a bravery that can still bellow or nag or whine at each other. Others no longer care. These people go on year after year, enduring misery themselves or in their desperation, inflicting it on others. (p. 12)

Satir stressed the role of destructive communication in smothering feeling and said that there were four wrong ways people communicate: *blaming, placating,* being *irrelevant,* and being *super reasonable.* What's behind these patterns of dishonest communication? Low self-esteem. If we feel bad about ourselves, it's hard to tell the truth about our feelings—and threatening to let others tell us honestly what they feel.

Goals of Therapy

Growth, not stability, is the goal of experiential family therapy. Symptom relief, social adjustment, and work are considered important, but secondary to increased personal integrity (congruence between inner experience and outer behavior), greater freedom of choice, less dependence, and expanded experiencing (Malone, Whitaker, Warkentin, & Felder, 1961). The painful symptoms families present with are regarded as tickets of admission (Whitaker & Keith, 1981); the real problem is emotional sterility. The aim is for individual family members to become sensitive to their needs and feelings, and to share these within the family. In this way, family unity is based on lively and genuine interaction, rather than on repression and self-abnegation.

Some experiential therapists have a tendency to focus on individuals and their experience more than on family organization. In Kempler's (1981) case the commitment to the individual is acknowledged: "I consider my primary responsibility to people—to each individual within the family—and only secondarily to the organization called family" (p. 27). This emphasis on the individual over the family is *not* true of the more systems-wise experiential family therapists, such as Carl Whitaker, David Keith, and Gus Napier.

In common with others in the existential–humanistic tradition, experiential therapists believe that the way to emotional health is to uncover deeper levels of experiencing—the potential for personal fulfillment locked within all of us. It's what's inside that counts. Virginia Satir (1972) stated the goals of family therapy in this way:

> We attempt to make three changes in the family system. First, each member of the family should be able to report congruently, completely, and honestly on what he sees and hears, feels and thinks, about himself and others, in the presence of others. Second, each person should be addressed and related to in terms of his uniqueness, so that decisions are made in terms of exploration and negotiation rather than in terms of power. Third, differentness must be openly acknowledged and used for growth. (p. 120)

When experiential methods are applied to treating family systems (rather than to individuals who happen to be assembled in family groups), the goal of individual growth is merged with the goal of achieving a strengthened family unit. Carl Whitaker's work nicely embodied this dual goal. According to him, personal growth requires family integration, and vice versa. A sense of belongingness and the freedom to individuate go hand in hand. In fact, it's often necessary to bring parents emotionally closer together to enable their children to leave home, since many children can't leave unless they sense that their parents can be happy without them.

Most experientialists emphasize the feeling side of human nature: creativity, spontaneity, and the ability to play. Whitaker advocated "craziness," nonrational, creative experiencing and functioning, as a proper goal of therapy. If they let themselves become a little crazy, he believed, families will reap the rewards of zest, emotionality, and spontaneity.

When writing about their treatment goals, experiential clinicians emphasize the value of experience for its own sake. Whitaker (1967), for example, saw all therapy as a process of expanding experience, which he believed leads to growth.

New experience for family members is thought to break down confluence, disrupt rigid expectancies, and unblock awareness—all of which promotes individuation (Kaplan & Kaplan, 1978). Bunny and Fred Duhl (1981) speak of their goals as a heightened sense of competence, well-being, and self-esteem. In emphasizing self-esteem, the Duhls echo Virginia Satir (1964, 1988) who believed that low self-esteem, and the destructive communication responsible for it, were the main problems in unhappy families. Expanded awareness of self and others is thought to promote flexible behavior, in place of automatic, stereotyped habits.

Most family therapists consider increased sensitivity and growth in individuals as serving the broad aim of enhanced family functioning. Some experiential family therapists keep the family-systems goal implicit and devote relatively few of their interventions to promote it; others perceive individual growth as explicitly linked to family growth, and so devote more of their attention to promoting family interactions. The Duhls (1981) espouse "new and renewed integration" within and between family members as mutually reinforcing goals of treatment. Whitaker (1976a) presumed that families come to treatment because they're unable to be close, and therefore unable to individuate. By helping family members recover their own potential for experiencing, he believed that he was also helping them recover their ability to care for one another.

Conditions for Behavior Change

Among the misconceptions of those new to family therapy is that families are fragile and therapists must be careful to avoid breaking them. A little experience teaches the opposite: Most families are so rigidly structured that it takes therapeutic dynamite to change them. Effective family therapy requires powerful interventions—and for experiential family therapists that power comes from emotional experiencing.

Experiential clinicians use evocative techniques and the force of their own personalities to create personal therapeutic encounters, regression, and intimate disclosure. The vitality of the therapist as a person is one major force in therapy; the vitality of the *encounter* is another. This powerfully personal experience is thought to help establish caring, person-to-person relationships among all family members. Gus Napier (Napier & Whitaker, 1978) wrote, in *The Family Crucible,* a nice description of what experiential therapists think causes change. Breakthroughs occur when family members risk being "more separate, divergent, even angrier" as well as "when they risk being closer and more intimate." Outbursts of anger are often followed by greater intimacy and warmth, because the unexpressed anger that keeps people apart also keeps them from loving one another.

Because feeling-expression and intimate experience within sessions are believed to be crucial, anxiety is stimulated and prized. (The opposite is true with more cerebral approaches such as Murray Bowen's.) Experiential therapists are alternately provocative and warmly supportive. In this way they help families dare to take risks. This permits them to drop protective defenses and really open up with each other.

Existential encounter is believed to be the essential force in the psychotherapeutic process (Kempler, 1973; Whitaker, 1976a). These encounters must be reciprocal; instead of hiding behind a professional role, the therapist must be a genuine person who catalyzes change using his or her personal impact on families. As Kempler (1968) said:

> In this approach the therapist becomes a family member during the interviews, participating as fully as he is able, hopefully available for appreciation and criticism as well as he is able to dispense it. He laughs, cries and rages. He feels and shares his embarrassments, confusions and helplessness. He shares his fears of revealing himself when these feelings are a part of his current total person. He sometimes cannot share himself and hopefully he is able to say at least that much. (p. 97)

Virginia Satir said it this way:

> Some therapists think people come into therapy not wanting to be changed; I don't think that's true. They don't think they *can* change. Going into some new, unfamiliar place is a scary thing. When I first begin to work with someone, I am not interested in changing them. I am interested in finding their rhythms, being able to join with them, and helping them go inside to those scary places. Resistance is mainly the fear of going somewhere you have not been. (quoted in Simon, 1989, pp. 38–39)

For Satir, caring and acceptance were the keys to helping people overcome their fear, open up to their experience, and open up to each other. It's a willingness to understand and accept people—rather than an anxious eagerness to change them—that enables experiential therapists to help people discover and acknowledge deeply held, but poorly understood fears and desires.

Therapists are advised to attend to their own responses to families. Are they anxious, angry, or bored? Once noted, these reactions are to be shared with the family. Whitaker and his colleagues at the Atlanta Psychiatric Clinic (Whitaker, Warkentin, & Malone, 1959) pioneered the technique of spontaneously communicating their feelings *fully* to patients. These therapists often seemed highly impulsive, even falling asleep and reporting their dreams. According to Kempler (1965), "By being, as nearly as possible, a total person, rather than playing the role of therapist, the atmosphere encourages all members to participate more fully as total personalities" (p. 61). He translates this into action by being extremely self-disclosing, even in his opening statements to families. At times, this seems more self-indulgent than provocative. For example, he says (Kempler, 1973), "If the therapist is hungry he should say so: 'I'm getting hungry. I hope I can make it until lunchtime'" (p. 37).

The belief is that by being a "real person," open, honest, and spontaneous, the therapist can teach family members to be the same. As Whitaker (1975) said, if the therapist gets angry, then patients can learn to deal with anger. While this is a compelling point of view, its validity rests on the assumption that the therapist is a worthwhile model—not only a healthy, mature person, but also one whose instincts are trustworthy and useful to families. Experiential therapists have great faith in themselves as barometers against which family members can measure themselves.

This is an attractive idea, and one that seems to work in the hands of experienced practitioners like Carl Whitaker. However, younger and less experienced therapists would be wise not to overestimate the salutary effects of their personal disclosures, nor to underestimate the potential for countertransference in their emotional reactions to clients.

Experiential family therapists share the humanistic faith that people are naturally healthy and if left to their own devices will be creative, zestful, loving, and productive (Rogers, 1951; Janov, 1970; Perls, Hefferline, & Goodman, 1951). The main task of therapy is therefore seen as unblocking defenses and opening up experience.

Some experiential therapists pay more attention to resistance to feeling within family members than to resistance of family systems to change. Kempler's conception of interlocking family patterns is that they're easily resolved by the therapist's pointing them out. "Often in families, merely calling attention to the pattern is sufficient for one or more members to stop their part in it, thereby eliminating the possibility of continuing that interlocking behavior" (Kempler, 1981, p. 113). Kempler believes the objective of experiential therapy is to complete interpersonal encounters. He tries to promote this objective by simply pushing family members through impasses. But, just as is true with encounter groups (Lieberman, Yalom, & Miles, 1973), these changes will probably not be sustained without being repeated and worked through.

Dysfunctional families have strong conservative (homeostatic) predilections; they opt for safety rather than satisfaction. Since passions are messy, unhappy families are content to submerge them; experiential therapists are not. Clinicians like Whitaker believe that it is important to be effective, not safe. Therefore he deliberately aimed to generate enough stress to destabilize the families he worked with.

Just as stress opens up family dialogues and makes change possible, therapeutic regression enables family members to discover and reveal hidden aspects of themselves. Once these personal needs and feelings emerge, they become the substance of progressively more intimate, interpersonal encounters within the family.

What sets experiential family therapy apart from most other family treatments is the belief that working with family interaction isn't sufficient for change. Most other approaches begin with an interpersonal focus; their aim is to help family members tell each other what's on their minds. But this means that they'll only be sharing what they're conscious of feeling. They'll have fewer secrets from each other, but they'll continue to have secrets from themselves, in the form of unconscious needs and feelings. Experiential therapists, on the other hand, believe that increasing the experience levels of individual family members will lead to more honest and intimate family interactions. The following example demonstrates this "inside out" process of change.

> After an initial, information-gathering session, the L. family was discussing ten-year-old Tommy's misbehavior. For several minutes Mrs. L. and Tommy's younger sister took turns cataloging all the "terrible things" Tommy did around the house. As the discussion continued, the therapist noticed how uninvolved Mr. L. seemed to be. Although he dutifully nodded agreement to his wife's complaints, he seemed more depressed than concerned. When asked what was on his mind, he said very little, and the therapist got the impression that, in fact, very little *was* on his mind—at least consciously. The therapist didn't know the reason for his lack of involvement, but she did know that it annoyed her, and she decided to say so.
>
> THERAPIST: (To Mr. L.) You know what, you piss me off.
>
> MR. L.: What? (He was shocked; people he knew just didn't speak that way.)
>
> THERAPIST: I said, you piss me off. Here your wife is concerned and upset about Tommy, and you just sit there like a lump on a log. You're about as much a part of this family as that lamp in the corner.

MR. L.: You have no right to talk to me that way (getting angrier by the minute). I work hard for this family. Who do you think puts bread on the table? I get up six days a week and drive a delivery truck all over town. All day long I have to listen to customers bitching about this and that. Then I come home and what do I get? More bitching. *"Tommy did this, Tommy did that."* I'm sick of it.

THERAPIST: Say that again, louder.

MR. L.: I'm sick of it! I'm sick of it!!

This interchange dramatically transformed the atmosphere in the session. Suddenly, the reason for Mr. L.'s disinterest became clear. He was furious at his wife for constantly complaining about Tommy. She, in turn, was displacing much of her feeling for her husband onto Tommy, as a result of Mr. L.'s emotional unavailability. In subsequent sessions, as Mr. and Mrs. L. spent more time talking about their relationship, less and less was heard about Tommy's misbehavior.

Following her own emotional impulse, the therapist in the example above increased the affective intensity in the session by attacking a member of the family. The anxiety generated as she did so was sufficient to expose a hidden problem. Once the problem was uncovered, it didn't take much cajoling to get the family members to fight it out.

Although the reader may be uncomfortable with the idea of a therapist attacking a family member, it's not unusual in experiential therapy. What makes this move less risky than it may seem is the presence of other family members. When the whole family is there, it seems safer for therapists to be provocative with less risk of hurting or driving patients away than is true in individual treatment. And as Carl Whitaker (1975) pointed out, families will accept a great deal from a therapist, once they're convinced that he or she genuinely cares about them.

While experiential family therapists emphasize expanded experiencing for individuals as the vehicle for therapeutic change, they are now beginning to advocate inclusion of as many family members as possible in treatment. As experientialists, they believe in immediate personal experiencing; as family therapists, they believe in the interconnectedness of the family. The family may be likened to a team in which none of the players can perform adequately without the unity and wholeness of the group.

Carl Whitaker (1976b) believed that it's important to work with three generations. He pushed for at least a couple of meetings with the larger family network, including parents, children, grandparents, and divorced spouses. Inviting these extended family members is an effective way to help them support treatment, instead of opposing and undermining it.

Whitaker believed that children should always be included, even when they aren't the focus of concern. He found it difficult to work without children, who, he believed, are invaluable for teaching parents to be spontaneous and honest. In order to overcome reluctance to attend, Whitaker invited extended family members as consultants, "to help the therapist," not as patients. In these interviews grandparents were asked for their help, for their perceptions of the family (past and present), and sometimes to talk about the problems in their own marriage (Napier & Whitaker, 1978). Parents may begin to see that the grandparents are different from the images of them they introjected twenty years before. Grandparents, in turn, may begin to see that their children are now adults.

In addition to the increased information available when the extended family is present, small changes in the large family group may have more powerful repercussions than large changes in one subsystem. Since family therapy is based on the premise that changing the system is the most effective way to change individuals, it follows that a cross-generational group holds the greatest potential for change. (In fact it may be that the real reason many family therapists don't include the extended family is that they lack the nerve or the leverage to bring them in.)

Techniques

According to Walter Kempler (1968), in experiential psychotherapy there are no techniques, only people. This epigram neatly summarizes the experientialists' emphasis on the curative power of the therapist's personality. It isn't so much what therapists do that matters, but who they are. If the therapist is rigid and uptight, then the treatment is likely to be too cool and professional to generate the intense emotional climate deemed necessary for experiential growth. If, on the other hand, the therapist is an alive, aware, and fully feeling person, then he or she will be able to awaken these potentials in families.

Carl Whitaker also endorsed this position and was himself the paradigmatic example of the spontaneous and creative therapist. The point is: therapists who would foster openness and authenticity in their patients, must themselves be open and genuine. However, this point is at least partly rhetorical. Whoever they *are*, therapists must also *do* something. Even if what they do isn't highly structured or carefully planned, it can nevertheless be described. Moreover, experiential therapists tend to do a lot; they're highly active and some (including Kempler) use quite a number of techniques.

In fact, experiential therapists can be divided into two groups with regard to therapeutic techniques. On the one hand, some employ highly structured devices such as *family sculpting* and *choreography* to stimulate affective intensity in therapy; on the other hand, therapists like Carl Whitaker rely on the spontaneity and creativity of just being themselves with patients. Whitaker hardly planned more than a few seconds in advance; and he certainly did not use structured exercises or tactics. Underlying both these strategies is a shared conviction that therapy should be an intense, moving experience in the here-and-now.

Virginia Satir had a remarkable ability to communicate clearly and perceptively. Like many great therapists, she was a vigorous and dynamic person who engaged clients authoritatively from the first session onward. Where she led, clients followed. But she didn't rely merely on spontaneity and personal disclosure. Rather, she worked actively to clarify communication, turned people away from complaining about the past toward finding solutions, supported every member of the family's self-esteem, pointed out positive intentions (long before "positive connotation" became a strategic device), and showed by example the way for family members to touch and be affectionate (Satir & Baldwin, 1983). She was a loving but forceful teacher.

Satir actively elicited emotion by asking questions about feelings and perceptions that weren't being expressed clearly, and by asking family members to shift positions and enact roles. Her shifting voice tone, tempo, and volume, and her facial and hand gestures were powerful nonverbal elements that created responsiveness in family members. Few people could be in her presence and not be moved.

One of the hallmarks of Satir's work was her use of touch. Hers was the language of tenderness. She often began by making physical contact with the children, as evidenced in her case "Of Rocks and Flowers." This was a case of a blended family with a history of severe physical abuse. Bob, a recovering alcoholic, was the father of two boys, Aaron (four) and Robbie (two), whose mother had abused them repeatedly—pushing them down stairs, burning them with cigarettes, and tying them up under the sink. At the time of the interview, she was under psychiatric care and didn't see the children. Bob's new wife, Betty, was abused by her previous husband who was also an alcoholic. She was pregnant and afraid that the boys would abuse the baby. The boys had already been expressing the anger and violence they'd been exposed to—slapping and choking other children. Bob and Betty, acting out of frustration and fear, responded to the boys roughly, which only increased their violence.

Throughout the session, Satir showed the parents how to touch the children tenderly and how to hold them firmly, yet protectively, when they wanted to stop the children from doing something. She demonstrated the difference between this gentle firmness and grabbing the boys roughly in anger.

When Bob started to tell Aaron something from a distance, Satir insisted on proximity and touch. She sat Aaron down directly in front of his father and asked Bob to take the little boy's hands and speak directly to him.

The following fragments from the session are taken from Andreas (1991).

> Those little hands know a lot of things; they need to be reeducated. OK. Now, there is a lot of energy in both these youngsters, like there is in both of you. And I am going to talk to your therapist about making some room for you to have some respite (from the children). But use every opportunity you can to get this kind of physical contact. And what I would also recommend that you do is that the two of you are clear about what you expect.
>
> And if you (Bob) could learn from Betty how to pay attention (to the kids) more quickly. I would like you to be able to get your message without a "don't" in it, without a "don't"—and that your strength of your arms when you pick them up—I don't know if I can illustrate it to you, but let me have your arm for a minute (reaching for Bob's forearm). Let me show you the difference. Pick up my arm like you were going to grab me. (Bob grabs her arm). All right. Now when you do that, my muscles all start to tighten, and I want to hit back. (Bob nods.) Now pick up my arm like you wanted to protect me. (Bob holds her arm). All right. I feel your strength now, but I don't feel like I want to pull back like this. (Bob says, "yeah.")
>
> And what I'd like you to do is to do *lots* and lots of touching of both of these children. And when things start (to get out of hand), then you go over—don't say anything—go over to them and just take them (demonstrating the protective holding on both of Robbie's forearms) but you have to know in your inside that you're not pulling them (Aaron briefly puts his hands on top of Virginia's and Robbie's arms) like this (demonstrating), but you are taking them in a strong way (stroking Bob's arm with both hands), like you saw the difference. I'll demonstrate it to you (Bob), too. First of all I am going to grab you (demonstrating) like that. (Bob says, "yeah.") You see you want to pull back. All right. Now, at this time what I am going to do is give you some strength (demonstrating holding his arm with both hands. Robbie pats Virginia's hand). But I am not going to ask you to retaliate. Now this is the most important thing for you to start with.
>
> (Virginia turns to Betty and offers her forearm.) OK. Now I'd like to do the same with you. So, take my arm really tight, just (Betty grabs Virginia's arm, and Aaron does, too.) Yeah, that's right, like you really wanted to give me "what for." OK. All right. Now give it to me like you want to give me support, but you also want to give me a boundary. (Aaron reaches toward Betty's hand and Virginia takes Aaron's free hand in her free hand.) It's a little bit tight, a little bit tight.
>
> So the next time you see anything coming, what you do is you go and make that contact (Virginia demonstrates by holding

> Aaron's upper arm) and then let it go soft. (Virginia takes Aaron's hands and begins to draw him out of Betty's lap.) Now, Aaron, I'd like you to come up here so I could demonstrate something to your mother for a minute. (Aaron says, "OK.") Now, let's suppose some moment I'm not thinking and I take you like that (grabbing Betty's arms suddenly with both hands.) You see what you want to do? (Betty nods.) All right. Now I am going to do it another way. I am giving you the same message (Virginia holds Betty's arm firmly with both hands, looking directly into her eyes, and starts to stand up), but I am doing it like this. And I am looking at you, and I'm giving you a straight message. OK. Now your body at that point is not going to respond negatively to me. It is going to feel stopped, but not negative. And then I will take you like this. (Virginia puts one arm around Betty's back and the other under her upper arm.) Just like this (Virginia puts both arms around Betty and draws her close) and now I will hold you. I will hold you like that for a little bit.

Following this session, Satir commented on her technique:

> There had been so many things happening, and the fear was so strong in relation to these children that if you thought of one image it was like they were monsters. So one of the things that I wanted to do was also to see that they had the capacity to respond with a touch, using myself in that regard by having them put their hands on my face—that was a kind of mirror for the family itself, the people in the family. And then allowing them, and encouraging them to do that with their own parents. See, touch, that comes out of the kind of ambience which was there at the time, says things no words can say.

Just as experiential therapists are theoretically eclectic, many of their techniques are also borrowed from a variety of sources. For example, the theatrical and psychodramatic origins of *family sculpting* and *choreography* are quite evident. Similarly, Whitaker's work with the extended family seems to derive from Murray Bowen's work. Experiential family therapists have also drawn on encounter groups (Kempler, 1968), Gestalt therapy techniques (Kaplan & Kaplan, 1978), psychodrama (Kantor & Lehr, 1975), and art therapy (Bing, 1970; Geddes & Medway, 1977).

Although all the therapists considered in this chapter employ evocative techniques, they differ sharply with regard to how self-consciously they do so. Some plan sessions around one or more well-practiced techniques, while others are deliberately unstructured; they emphasize *being with* the family rather than *doing* something, and say that techniques shouldn't be planned, but allowed to flow from the therapist's personal style and spontaneous impulses. Principal speaker for the latter view was Carl Whitaker. Techniques, Whitaker believed (Keith & Whitaker, 1977), are a product of the therapist's personality and of the cotherapy relationship. His own numerous published case studies reveal a playful, nonstructured approach. When children were present, Whitaker was a model parent, alternately playing with the kids in an involved, loving manner, and disciplining them with firmness and strength. Patients learned from being with Carl Whitaker to become more spontaneous and open, and to feel more worthwhile.

Since he favored a personal and intimate encounter over a theory-guided or technique-bound approach, it's not surprising that Whitaker's style was the same with individuals, couples, or groups (Whitaker, 1958). He assiduously avoided directing real-life decisions, preferring instead to open family members up to their feelings and join them in sharing their experience. This may sound trite, but it's a powerful and important point. As long as therapists (or anyone else for that matter) are anxious to change people, it's hard, very hard, to help them feel and understand their fears and desires—and it's impossible to really empathize with them.

A comparison between Whitaker's early work (Whitaker, Warkentin, & Malone, 1959; Whitaker, 1967) and his later reports (Napier & Whitaker, 1978) shows that he changed over years of seeing families. He started out as deliberately provocative and outlandish. He might fall asleep in sessions and then report his dreams; he wrestled with patients; he talked about his own sexual fantasies. In later years he was much less provocative—this seems to be what happens to therapists as they mature; they have less need to impose their own direction and more willingness to understand and sympathize. Indeed, reading some of Whitaker's early reports makes one wonder how much was genuinely spontaneous and how much a studied pose; how much was for the relationship, how much for himself, and how much for the titillation of observers.

Because Whitaker's treatment was intense and personal, he believed it essential that two therapists work together. Having a cotherapist to share the emotional burden and to interact with keeps therapists from being totally absorbed in the emotional field of the family. All family therapy tends to activate the therapist's own feelings toward types of family members. A detached, analytic stance minimizes such feelings; intense involvement maximizes them. The trouble with countertransference is that it tends to be unconscious. Therapists are more likely to become aware of such feelings after sessions are over. Easier still is to observe countertransference in others. Consider the example of Dr. Fox, a married man who specializes in individual therapy, but occasionally sees married couples in distress. In 75 percent of such cases, Dr. Fox encourages the couple to seek a divorce, and his patients have a high rate of following his advice. Perhaps if Dr. Fox were happier in his own marriage or had the courage to change it, he'd be less impelled to guide his patients where he fears to go.

Whitaker and his Atlanta Psychiatric Clinic colleagues wrote an excellent treatise on countertransference in family therapy (Whitaker, Felder, & Warkentin, 1965), suggesting that therapists should be emotionally involved—"in" the family, but not "of" the family. The therapist who's emotionally involved in the family should be able to identify with each of the family members. Thinking about experiences you've had that are similar to the family member's or asking yourself, "What would I like or need if I were that person?" facilitates the process of identification.

In order to minimize potential destructive acting out of countertransference feelings, Whitaker recommended sharing feelings openly with the family. If feelings are expressed to the family they're less likely to be lived out than if they remain hidden. At times, however, even the therapist may be unaware of such feelings. This is where a cotherapist is important. Very often the cotherapist recognizes such feelings in a colleague and can discuss them after a session or counteract them during the session. A strong investment in the cotherapy relationship (or treatment team) keeps therapists from being *inducted* (drawn into families). Therapists who see families without a cotherapist may bring in a consultant to help achieve the emotional distancing necessary to stay objective.

Young therapists are especially likely to be critical of parents and sympathetic toward the kids; the best prevention for such countertransference reactions is maturity. A mature person has the freedom to enter intense relationships, personal and professional, without becoming enmeshed or reacting as though to his or her own parents. Adequate training, experience, and supervision also immunize therapists against taking sides. In addition, having a strong and rewarding family life minimizes the likelihood of the therapist seeking ersatz gratification of personal needs with patients.

Because of their interest in current thoughts and feelings, most experientialists eschew history-taking and formal assessment. Kempler (1973) once stated his disdain for diagnosis: "Diagnoses are the tombstones of the therapist's frustration, and accusations such as defensive, resistant, and secondary gain, are the flowers placed on the grave of his buried dissatisfaction" (p. 11). The point of this flowery remark seems to be that the objective distance necessary for formal assessment removes the therapist from a close emotional interaction with families; moreover, since diagnostic terms tend to be pejorative, they may serve to discharge hostility while masquerading as scientific objectivity.

For most experientialists, assessment takes place automatically as the therapist gets to know the family. In the process of getting acquainted and developing an empathic relationship, the therapist learns what kind of people he or she is dealing with. Whitaker began by asking each family member to describe the family and how it works. "Talk about the family as a whole." "What is the family like; how is it structured?" In this way, he got a composite picture of individual family members and their perceptions of the family group. Notice also that by directing family members toward the structure of the family as a whole, he shifted attention away from the identified patient and his or her symptoms.

Kempler, who conducts family therapy much like an encounter group, often begins by sitting and saying nothing. This device generates anxiety and helps create an atmosphere of emotional intensity. There is, however, something paradoxical about opening like this; it seems nondirective and it seems to be a way of decentralizing the therapist, but it's neither. In fact, by not saying anything, the therapist calls attention to himself, and is in a very controlling position. Any pretense that this opening device signals a nondirective approach is quickly dispelled by reading the transcripts of encounter-group-style family therapists (Kempler, 1981). Whether they open with silence or by inquiring into specific content areas, they soon become extremely active and directive, asking questions, directing conversations, and actively confronting evasive or defensive family members.

Whitaker's first sessions (Napier & Whitaker, 1978) were fairly structured, and they included the taking of a family history. For him, the first contacts with families were opening salvos in "the battle for structure" (Whitaker & Keith, 1981). He labored hard to gain enough control to be able to exert maximum therapeutic leverage. He wanted the family to know that the therapists are in charge, and he wanted them to accept the idea of family therapy. This began with the first telephone call. Whitaker (1976b) insisted that the largest possible number of family members attend; he believed that three generations are necessary to ensure that grandparents will support, not oppose, therapy, and that their presence will help correct distortions. If significant family members wouldn't attend, Whitaker might refuse to see the family. Why begin with the cards stacked against you?

Experiential therapists tend to push and confront families from the outset (Kempler, 1973). Their interventions tend to be creative and spontaneous, and are described as letting the unconscious operate the therapy (Whitaker, 1967). Many seem to develop genuine and personal attachments to patients, and don't hesitate to side with first one family member, then another.

Among experiential, if not all family therapists, Carl Whitaker was the most outspoken proponent of therapists using their own personalities to effect change. For Whitaker, the therapist's personal adequacy, ability to be caring, firmness, and ability to be unpredictable were far more effective tools than any therapeutic techniques. He believed that a therapist's wisdom, experience, and creativeness will guide his or her interventions better than any preconceived plan or structure. (This probably works better for therapists who are wise, experienced, and creative than for those who are not.)

Experiential family therapists help families to become more real, direct, and alive by modeling this behavior for them. They don't just point the way, they lead the way. Most are very provocative. Whitaker (Napier & Whitaker, 1978), for example, asked a teenage daughter if she thought her parents had a good sex life. Kempler (1968) describes the therapist as a catalyst and as an active participant in family interactions. As a catalyst, he makes suggestions and gives directives. Typical directives include telling family members to look at each other, speak louder, repeat certain statements, or rephrase a remark to make it more emotional. He (Kempler, 1968) cites an example of telling a husband that he whimpers at his wife and whimpers at the therapist. Moreover, this was said in a sarcastic tone, deliberately designed to arouse the man's anger, "Tell her to get the hell off your back—and mean it!" The decision to become an active participant in family encounters depends largely on the therapist's own emotions. If he gets upset or angry, he's liable to say so. "I can't stand your wishy-washy answers!" The avowed purpose of such bluntness is to teach—by example—the use of "I-statements." As Kempler (Kempler, 1981) remarks, "The expressed experiential 'I' ness of the therapist is the epitome of experiential intervention" (p. 156). He frequently challenges and even argues with family members, while freely acknowledging that this largely has to do with his own frustration.

Although they can be blunt, these therapists also limit how far they push people. Kempler (1968) says that therapists should be spontaneous, but not impulsive; and most experientialists agree that only a very warm and supportive therapist can afford to risk being pushy and provocative. Napier and Whitaker (1978) also advised setting limits on the "let it all hang out" credo that sometimes is used to justify permitting family members to engage in destructive fights. Trying to emulate Whitaker's provocativeness without his warmth and power to restrain can lead to disaster.

Whether they are provocative or supportive, experiential family therapists are usually quite active and directive. Instead of being left to work out their own styles of interaction, family members are frequently told, "Tell him (or her) what you feel!" or asked, "What are you feeling now?" Just as the best way to get a school teacher's attention is to misbehave, the best way to get an experiential therapist's attention is to show signs of feeling, without actually expressing it.

Therapists observe nonverbal signs of feeling; they notice how interactions take place; they notice whether people are mobile or rigid; and they try to identify suppressed emotional reactions. Then they try to focus awareness (Kaplan & Kaplan, 1978). By directing attention to what a person is experiencing at the moment, the therapist may induce a breakthrough of affect or a revelation of previously withheld material. When family members appear to be blocked or disrupted, the therapist focuses on the ones who seem most energized.

THERAPIST: I see you looking over at Dad whenever you ask Mom a question, what's that about?

JOHNNY: Oh, nothing—I guess.

THERAPIST: It must mean *something.* Come on, what were you feeling?

JOHNNY: Nothing!

THERAPIST: You must have been feeling something. What was it?

JOHNNY: Well, sometimes when Mommy lets me do something, Dad gets real mad. But instead of yelling at her, he yells at me (crying softly).

THERAPIST: Tell him.

JOHNNY: (Angrily, to the therapist) Leave me alone!

THERAPIST: No, it's important. Try to tell your Dad how you feel.

JOHNNY: (Sobbing hard) You're always picking on me! You never let me do anything!

Experiential therapists use a great number of expressive techniques in their work. With some, this amounts to a kind of eclectic grab bag, as the following remark from Bunny and Fred Duhl (1981) suggests.

> For us, we feel free to choose a particular technique or methodology as one chooses a tool from a tool box—that is, the appropriate tool for the specific job—in order to achieve the goal of a changed system interaction in a manner that fits all participants, goals, and processes. (p. 511)

Among the techniques available in the experiential family therapy tool box are *family sculpture* (Duhl, Kantor, & Duhl, 1973), *family puppet interviews* (Irwin & Malloy, 1975), *family art therapy* (Geddes & Medway, 1977), *conjoint family drawings* (Bing, 1970), and *Gestalt therapy techniques* (Kempler, 1973). Included among the accoutrements of experiential therapists' offices are toys, doll houses, clay, teddy bears, drawing pens and paper, and batacca bats.

In *family sculpture*, originated by David Kantor and Fred Duhl, the therapist asks each member of the family to arrange the others in a meaningful tableau. This is a graphic means of portraying each person's perceptions of the family, in terms of space, posture, and attitude. This was also a favorite device of Virginia Satir, who frequently used ropes and blindfolds to dramatize the constricting roles family members trap each other into (Satir & Baldwin, 1983).

The following example of sculpting occurred when a therapist asked Mr. N. to arrange the other members of the family into a scene typical of the time when he comes home from work.

MR. N.: When I come home from work, eh? Okay (to his wife) honey, you'd be by the stove, wouldn't you?

THERAPIST: No, don't talk. Just move people where you want them to be.

MR. N.: Okay.

He guided his wife to stand at a spot where the kitchen stove might be, and placed his children on the kitchen floor, drawing and playing.

THERAPIST: Fine, now, still without any dialogue, put them into action.

Mr. N. then instructed his wife to pretend to cook, but to turn frequently to see what the kids were up to. He told the children to pretend to play for awhile, but then to start fighting, and complaining to Mommy.

THERAPIST: And what happens, when you come home.

MR. N.: Nothing. I try to talk to my wife, but the kids keep pestering her, and she gets mad and says to leave her alone.

THERAPIST: Okay, act it out.

As the family mimed the scene that Mr. N. had described, each of them had a powerful awareness of how he felt. Mrs. N. acted out trying to cook and referee the children's fights. The children, who thought this a great game, pretended to fight, and tried to outdo each other getting Mommy's attention. When Mr. N. "came home," he reached out for his wife, but the children came between them, until Mrs. N. finally pushed them all away.

Afterwards, Mrs. N. said that she hadn't realized her husband felt pushed away. She just thought of him as coming home, saying hello, and then withdrawing into the den with his newspaper and bottle of beer.

Family sculpture, choreography, or *spatializing* (Jefferson, 1978) is also used to illuminate scenes from the past. A typical instruction is, "Remember standing in front of your childhood home. Walk in and describe what typically happened." With this technique, the idea is to make a tableau using people and props to portray one's perceptions of family life. It's a useful device to sharpen sensitivity, and it provides useful information to the therapist. It's probably most useful if it suggests changes, which are then acted upon. "Do you like it that way? If not, change it to be the way you want it to be. And if you really care, then do something about it between sessions."

Another structured expressive exercise is *family art therapy*. Kwiatkowska (1967) instructs families to produce a series of sequentially ordered drawings, including a "joint family scribble," in which each person makes a quick scribble and then the whole family incorporates the scribble into a unified picture. Elizabeth Bing (1970) has families draw a picture of themselves as a family. Rubin and Magnussen (1974) ask for joint murals, as well as two- or three-dimensional family portraits.

Bing (1970) describes the *conjoint family drawing* as a means to warm families up and free them to express themselves. In family drawings the basic instruction is, "Draw a picture as you see yourselves as a family." The resulting pictures may disclose perceptions that haven't previously been discussed, or may stimulate the person drawing the picture to realize something that he or she had never thought of before.

> A father once drew a picture of the family that showed him off to one side, while his wife and children stood holding hands. Although he was portraying a fact well known to his wife and himself, they hadn't spoken openly of it. Once he produced his drawing and showed it to the therapist, there was no avoiding discussion. In another case, when the therapist asked each of the family members to draw the family, the teenage daughter was quite uncertain what to do. She had never thought much about the family, or her role in it. When she started to work, her drawing just seemed to emerge. After she finished, she was somewhat surprised to discover that she'd drawn herself closer to her father and sisters than to her mother. This provoked a lively discussion between her and her mother about their relationship. Although the two of them spent time together, the daughter didn't feel close, because she thought her mother treated her like a kid, never talking about her own concerns, and showing only superficial interest in the daughter's life. For her part, the mother was surprised, and not at all displeased, that her daughter felt ready to establish a relationship on a more equal, sharing basis.

Another projective technique designed to increase expressiveness is the *symbolic drawing of family life space* (Geddes & Medway, 1977). First the therapist draws a large circle. Then he or she instructs the family that everything inside the circle is to represent what is inside the family. Persons and institutions thought not to be part of the family are to be placed outside in the environment. Each person in the family is to draw a small circle, representing himself or herself, and place it inside the family circle in a position meaningfully related to the others. As the family complies with these instructions, the therapist reflects their apparent perceptions. "Oh, you feel you are on the outside, away from everyone else." "It looks like you think your sister is closer to your parents than you are."

In *family puppet interviews*, Irwin and Malloy (1975) ask one of the family members to make up a story using puppets. This technique, originally used in play therapy with small children, is supposed to be a vehicle for expression and for highlighting conflicts and alliances. In fact, its usefulness is probably limited to working with small children. Most adults resist expressing anything really personal through such a childlike medium. Even a frightened eight-year-old knows what's up when a therapist says, "Tell me a story."

Role playing is another favorite device of experimental therapists. Its use is based on the premise that experience, to be real, must be felt and exposed in the present. Recollection of past events and consideration of hoped-for or feared future events can be made more immediate by role playing them in the immediacy of the session. Kempler (1968) encourages parents to fantasize and role play scenes from childhood. A mother might be asked to role play what it was like when she was a little girl, or a father might be asked to imagine himself being a boy caught in the same dilemma as his son is.

Bunny Duhl uses lengths of rope as props to help couples enact relationship issues nonverbally, to circumvent rehearsed and defensive verbal accounts. Sometimes she has couples engage in a tug of war and then let go at a moment of their choosing, to dramatize feelings about trying and giving up. If this sounds a little hokey, like most encounter-group exercises, it can nevertheless evoke strong feeling. One partner reported, "I didn't want to let go!" Another said, "I felt like I won when I let go." A third person felt depressed because "I couldn't win; I had to let go." Duhl also finds that instructing partners to "Pull on the rope with the amount of energy you have to give to this relationship" is an evocative way to dramatize commitment.

Experiential therapists frequently break off family dialogues to work with individuals. At times this may be to explore emotional blocks, investigate memories, or even analyze dreams. "The individual intrapsychic work may require a few minutes or it may take an entire session. In some instances it has taken the better part of several sessions" (Kempler, 1981, p. 203). The reason for the individual work is the belief that an individual's unfinished business prevents him or her from authentically encountering others in the family.

When someone is mentioned who isn't present in the session, therapists may introduce Gestalt *there-and-then* techniques (Kempler, 1973). If a child talks about her grandfather, she may be asked to speak to a chair, which is supposed to personify grandfather. These techniques have proven very useful in individual therapy (Nichols & Zax, 1977) to intensify emotional experiencing by bringing memories into focus and by acting out suppressed reactions. Whether such devices are necessary in family therapy is open to question. In individual treatment patients are isolated from the significant figures in their lives, and role playing may be useful to approximate being with those people. But since family therapy is conducted with significant people present, it seems doubtful that role playing or other means of fantasy are necessary. If emotional action is wanted, plenty is available simply by opening dialogue between family members.

Whitaker (1975) used a similar role-playing technique, which he called "psychotherapy of the absurd." This consists of augmenting the unreasonable quality of a patient's response to the point of absurdity. It often amounts to calling a person's bluff, as the following example illustrates:

PATIENT: I can't stand my husband!

THERAPIST: Why don't you get rid of him, or take up a boyfriend?

At other times this takes the form of sarcastic teasing, such as mock fussing in response to a fussy child. The hope is that patients will get objective distance by participating in the therapist's distancing; the danger is that patients will feel hurt at being made fun of.

Evaluating Therapy Theory and Results

If you noticed that most of the references in this chapter were from the 1970s and inferred from this that experiential techniques were more popular in the early days of family therapy, you'd be right. Most contemporary family therapists stick closer to the family's reality, and focus less on individuals and their emotional experience than on narrative, interaction, and the organization of the family. Structured exercises (drawing, sculpting, role playing) can be evocative and compelling, and they allow therapists to control what goes on in the session. But anything more than occasional use of such devices may rob therapy of the inherent power of working directly with family dialogues, which get at how family members actually interact with each other. Emotional experiencing for its own sake may be more suited to encounter groups than to family therapy.

However, having expressed reservations about a therapy designed primarily around techniques to elicit feelings, let us add that two elements in experiential therapy are very useful and relevant. Although the extreme provocativeness of the young Carl Whitaker or Walter Kempler seem more suitable to the 1960s than to the 1990s, many family therapists would do well to be more honest and direct with the people they treat. For too many therapists, the unwritten first principle seems to be: Whatever you do, don't ever say anything that might possibly make somebody mad at you. This apprehension, sometimes rationalized as respect, holds many therapists back from honestly confronting family members about what they're doing that isn't working.

A second lesson family therapists might take from their experiential colleagues is shifting to the individual and his or her experience a way of breaking through defensive squabbling between family members. When family members argue, they usually lead with their defenses. Instead of saying, "*I'm* hurt," they say, "*You* make me mad"; instead of admitting they're afraid, they criticize the other's behavior. An effective way to interrupt the unproductive escalation of arguments that lead nowhere is to take time to explore the affect of the participants, one at a time. By talking to individuals about what they're feeling—and the roots of such feelings—family members can be helped to get past the defensiveness that keeps them apart, and to reconnect at a more genuine level.

Experiential family therapists have shown a general lack of interest in verifying their theories or their results. That emotional expression and interaction produce change is more or less taken for granted. Even Alvin Mahrer (1982), one of the most productive researchers and scholars among experiential therapists, believes that outcome studies of psychotherapy are essentially useless. His position is that studies of outcome might be of interest to insurance companies but have little impact on practitioners. Instead, he recommends studying "in-therapy outcomes": What therapeutic interventions lead to desired consequences on patients' behavior?

Although Mahrer (1982) and others (Nichols & Zax, 1977) have begun to examine such "in-therapy outcomes" in individual treatment, there are as yet no empirical studies of experiential family therapy. What's offered instead as verification consists of anecdotal reports of successful outcome (Napier & Whitaker, 1978; Duhl & Duhl, 1981) and descriptions of techniques that were observed to be effective in catalyzing emotional expression within sessions (Kempler, 1981).

Experiential family therapists aim to provide a useful experience for the families they treat, but they don't seem to believe that every family member must change overtly to validate their efforts. Moreover, change is believed to frequently come in small ways, which may be difficult to measure. If, as a result of experiential therapy, a family is able to make more direct contact with a schizophrenic son, this would be considered a success.

Whitaker (Whitaker & Keith, 1981) claimed little empirical evidence of the success of his approach, but cited the goodwill of the community, referrals from previous patients, and the satisfaction of families after treatment as evidence of success. He also mentioned his own satisfaction as a therapist, stating that when therapy is unsuccessful therapists become burned out and bitter.

Summary

Experiential family therapy is designed to change families by changing family members, reversing the direction of effect usually envisioned by family therapists. Among experientialists, families are treated as groups of individuals more than as systems. Enhanced sensitivity and expanded awareness are the essential aims of treatment.

In addition to focusing on *intra*personal change, experiential family therapy is also distinguished by a commitment to growth as opposed to problem-solving. Personal growth and self-fulfillment are seen as innate human tendencies, which naturally emerge once interference and defensiveness are reduced. Treatment is therefore aimed at reducing defenses within and between family members. Experientialists challenge and question the familiar and the automatic. In order to introduce novelty and enhance immediate experiencing, therapists use their own lively personalities as well as numerous structured, expressive techniques. Like encounter group leaders, experiential family therapists act as *agents provocateur* for intense emotional awareness and expression. Therapy is viewed as an existential encounter, conducted by therapists who participate fully and spontaneously. Interventions take the form of self-disclosure, teasing, sarcasm, humor, personal confrontation, paradoxical intention, and modeling.

These freewheeling responses may seem intimidating, but the risk is minimized by the presence of other family members (and frequently, cotherapists). Nevertheless, any therapy that features personal disclosure from the therapist has the potential to make the therapist—his or her experience, needs, values, and opinions—more important than the patients. The following is an example of "therapeutic candor" from a prominent experiential family therapist. "I'm almost ready for you people. I'm still thinking about the previous session which was quite moving" (Kempler, 1977, p. 91). Such a remark seems oblivious to the needs of the family. The rationale offered for such dumping is that it enables the therapist to be more completely focused on the present. Perhaps, but it seems equally likely to divert family members from their experience to his.

Experiential therapy derives from existential, humanistic, and phenomenological thought, from which comes the idea that individual freedom and self-expression can undo the devitalizing effects of culture. Beyond this, however, experiential family therapy tends to be relatively atheoretical. The result is an approach with little basis for systematically conceptualizing family dynamics, that instead simply borrows concepts and techniques from other approaches.

The essential vitality of this approach lies in its techniques for promoting and expanding intense experience. As they grow up, most people learn to blunt the full range of their experiencing. Indeed, defensive avoidance of anxiety may be the most prominent motivating force in most people's lives. Experiential therapy takes families who've become refractory to emotional experience and puts some of the oomph back in their lives.

At its best, experiential therapy helps people uncover their aliveness. Experience is real. Therapy conducted on the basis of putting people in touch with their own genuine experience has an undeniable validity. Moreover, when this personal discovery takes place in the context of the family, there's a good chance that family relations can be revitalized by authentic interaction among people struggling to become more real.

In order to reduce defensiveness and heighten emotional experience, experiential therapists can be highly active. Unfortunately, it's difficult to be active without also becoming directive.

Even the best of those in this tradition (Napier & Whitaker, 1978) find it difficult to resist telling people what they should be, rather than simply helping them find out who they are. Moreover, provocative directions such as, "Tell her to get the hell off your back and mean it!" (Kempler, 1968) often seem to produce compliant shows of feeling, rather than genuine emotional responses. When emotional resistance is truly reduced, feelings will emerge, without the direction of a therapist.

In experiential therapy the emphasis is on experience, not understanding. Nevertheless, experiential practitioners seem ambivalent in their attitudes about the utility of insight and understanding. Most, like Whitaker (Whitaker, Felder, & Warkentin, 1965), emphasize the nonrational forces in treatment, so that the intellectual side of human nature is subordinated to the feeling side. Whitaker's (Whitaker & Keith, 1981) statement that insight doesn't work—recognition isn't change—is typical. Elsewhere his treatment is described (Napier, 1977) as providing a complex emotional experience, not "intellectual nagging." However, case studies of experiential family therapy are filled with examples of advice-giving and interpretation. It seems that psychotherapists—of all persuasions—are as prone as the rest of humankind to offer advice and render judgment, and experiential family therapists do so no less often than members of other schools. The Duhls (Duhl & Duhl, 1981), for example, recognize the need for insight to support emotional change, and have criticized what they call "intervention without education."

Once, the idea that families are systems was both novel and controversial; today it is the new orthodoxy. Now that the pendulum has swung so far in the direction of systems thinking, individuals and their private joys and pains are rarely mentioned. Surely one of the major contributions of experiential family therapy is to remind us not to lose sight of the person in the system.

References

Andreas, S. 1991. *Virginia Satir: The patterns of her magic.* Palo Alto: Science and Behavior Books.

Bartlett, F. H. 1976. Illusion and reality in R. D. Laing. *Family Process.* 15:51–64.

Bing, E. 1970. The conjoint family drawing. *Family Process.* 9:173–194.

Binswanger, L. 1967. Being-in-the-world. In *Selected papers of Ludwig Binswanger,* J. Needleman, ed. New York: Harper Torchbooks.

Boss, M. 1963. *Psychoanalysis and daseinanalysts.* New York: Basic Books.

Duhl, B. S. 1983. *From the inside out and other metaphors.* New York: Brunner/Mazel.

Duhl, B. S., and Duhl, F. J. 1981. Integrative family therapy. In *Handbook of family therapy,* A. S. Gurman and D. P. Kniskern, eds. New York: Brunner/Mazel.

Duhl, F. J., Kantor D., and Duhl, B. S. 1973. Learning, space and action in family therapy: A primer of sculpture. In *Techniques of family psychotherapy,* D. A. Bloch, ed. New York: Grune & Stratton.

Frankl, V. E. 1963. *Man's search for meaning.* New York: Washington Square Press.

Geddes, M., and Medway, J. 1977. The symbolic drawing of family life space. *Family Process.* 16: 219–228.

Gehrke, S., and Kirschenbaum, M. 1967. Survival patterns in conjoint family therapy. *Family Process.* 6:67–80.

Gendlin, E. T. 1962. *Experiencing and the creation of meaning.* New York: Macmillan.

Greenberg, L. S., and Johnson, S. M. 1985. Emotionally focused couple therapy: An affective systemic approach. In *Handbook of family and marital therapy,* N. S. Jacobson and A. S. Gurman, eds. New York: Guilford Press.

Greenberg, L. S., and Johnson, S. M. 1986. Affect in marital therapy. *Journal of Marital and Family Therapy.* 12:1–10.

Greenberg, L. S., and Johnson, S. M. 1988. *Emotionally focused therapy for couples.* New York: Guilford Press.

Heidegger, M. 1963. *Being and time.* New York: Harper & Row.

Irwin, E., and Malloy, E. 1975. Family puppet interview. *Family Process. 14*:179–191.

Janov, A. 1970. *The primal scream.* New York: Dell.

Jefferson, C. 1978. Some notes on the use of family sculpture in therapy. *Family Process. 17*:69–76.

Kantor, D., and Lehr, W. 1975. *Inside the family.* San Francisco: Jossey-Bass.

Kaplan, M. L., and Kaplan, N. R. 1978. Individual and family growth: A Gestalt approach. *Family Process. 17*:195–205.

Keith, D. V. 1988. The family's own system: The symbolic context of health. In *Family transitions: Continuity and change over the life cycle,* C. J. Falicov, ed. New York: Guilford Press.

Keith, D. V., and Whitaker, C. A. 1977. The divorce labyrinth. In *Family therapy: Full-length case studies,* P. Papp, ed. New York: Gardner Press.

Kempler, W. 1965. Experiential family therapy. *The International Journal of Group Psychotherapy. 15*: 57–71.

Kempler, W. 1968. Experiential psychotherapy with families. *Family Process. 7*:88–89.

Kempler, W. 1973. *Principles of Gestalt family therapy.* Oslo, Norway: Nordahls.

Kempler, W. 1981. *Experiential psychotherapy with families.* New York: Brunner/Mazel.

Kwiatkowska, H. Y. 1967. Family art therapy. *Family Process.* 6:37–55.

Laing, R. D. 1967. *The politics of experience.* New York: Ballantine.

Laing, R. D., and Esterson, A. 1970. *Sanity, madness and the family.* Baltimore: Penguin Books.

Lasch, C. 1978. *The culture of narcissism: American life in an age of diminishing expectations.* New York: Norton.

Lieberman, M. A., Yalom, I. D., and Miles, M. B. 1973. *Encounter groups: First facts.* New York: Basic Books.

Mahrer, A. R. 1982. *Experiential psychotherapy: Basic practices.* New York: Brunner/ Mazel.

Malone, T. P., Whitaker, C. A., Warkentin, J., and Felder, R. E. 1961. Rational and nonrational psychotherapy. *American Journal of Psychotherapy. 15*:212–220.

Marcuse, H. 1955. *Eros and civilization.* New York: Beacon Press.

Maslow, A. H. 1968. *Toward a psychology of being.* 2nd ed. Princeton, NJ: Van Nostrand.

Napier, A. Y. 1977. Follow-up to divorce labyrinth, In *Family therapy: Full-length case studies,* P. Papp, ed. New York: Gardner Press.

Napier, A. Y., and Whitaker, C. A. 1978. *The family crucible.* New York: Harper & Row.

Neill, J. R., and Kniskern, D. P., eds. 1982. *From psyche to system: The evolving therapy of Carl Whitaker.* New York: Guilford Press.

Nichols, M. P., and Zax, M. 1977. *Catharsis in psychotherapy.* New York: Gardner Press.

Papp, P. 1976. Family choreography. In *Family therapy: Theory and practice,* P. J. Guerin, ed. New York: Gardner Press.

Perls, F. S. 1961. *Gestalt therapy verbatim.* Lafayette, CA: Real People Press.

Perls, F. S., Hefferline, R. E., and Goodman, P. 1951. *Gestalt therapy.* New York: Delta.

Pierce, R., Nichols, M. P., and DuBrin, J. 1983. *Emotional expression in psychotherapy.* New York: Gardner Press.

Rogers, C. R. 1951. *Client-centered therapy.* Boston: Houghton Mifflin.

Rubin, J., and Magnussen, M. A. 1974. A family art evaluation. *Family Process. 13*:185–200.

Satir, V. M. 1964. *Conjoint family therapy.* Palo Alto: Science and Behavior Books.

Satir, V. M. 1971. The family as a treatment unit. In *Changing families,* J. Haley, ed. New York: Grune & Stratton.

Satir, V. M. 1972. *Peoplemaking.* Palo Alto: Science and Behavior Books.

Satir, V. M. 1988. *The new peoplemaking.* Palo Alto: Science and Behavior Books.

Satir, V. M., and Baldwin, M. 1983. *Satir step by step: A guide to creating change in families.* Palo Alto: Science and Behavior Books.

Simon, R. 1989. Reaching out to life: An interview with Virginia Satir. *The Family Therapy Networker. 13*(1):36–43.

Simon, R. M. 1972. Sculpting the family. *Family Process.* 11:49–51.

Sullivan, H. S. 1953. *The interpersonal theory of psychiatry.* New York: Norton.

Whitaker, C. A. 1958. Psychotherapy with couples. *American Journal of Psychotherapy. 12*:18–23.

Whitaker, C. A. 1967. The growing edge. In *Techniques of family therapy*, J. Haley and L. Hoffman, eds. New York: Basic Books.

Whitaker, C. A. 1975. Psychotherapy of the absurd: With a special emphasis on the psychotherapy of aggression. *Family Process*. 14:1–16.

Whitaker, C. A. 1976a. The hindrance of theory in clinical work. In *Family therapy: Theory and practice*, P. J. Guerin, ed. New York: Gardner Press.

Whitaker, C. A. 1976b. A family is a four-dimensional relationship. In *Family therapy: Theory and practice*, P. J. Guerin, ed. New York: Gardner Press.

Whitaker, C. A., Felder, R. E., and Warkentin, J. 1965. Countertransference in the family treatment of schizophrenia. In *Intensive family therapy*, I. Boszormenyi-Nagy and J. L. Framo, eds. New York: Harper & Row.

Whitaker, C. A., and Keith, D. V. 1981. Symbolic-experiential family therapy. In *Handbook of family therapy*, A. S. Gurman and D. P. Kniskern, eds. New York: Brunner/Mazel.

Whitaker, C. A., and Malone, T. P. 1953. *The roots of psychotherapy*. New York: Blakiston.

Whitaker, C. A., Warkentin, J., and Malone, T. P. 1959. The involvement of the professional therapist. In *Case studies in counseling and psychotherapy*, A. Burton, ed. Englewood Cliffs, NJ: Prentice Hall.

7

Psychoanalytic Family Therapy

Many of the pioneers of family therapy were psychoanalytically trained, including Nathan Ackerman, Ian Alger, Murray Bowen, Lyman Wynne, Theodore Lidz, Israel Zwerling, Ivan Boszormenyi-Nagy, Carl Whitaker, Don Jackson, and Salvador Minuchin. But with the eager enthusiasm so essential to innovation they turned away from the old—psychodynamics—and toward the new—systems dynamics. Some, including Jackson and Minuchin, moved far indeed from their psychoanalytic roots. Others, including Bowen, Lidz, and Wynne, retained a distinctly analytic influence in their work.

In the 1960s and 1970s the burgeoning field of family therapy followed the lead of Jackson and Minuchin, not only ignoring psychoanalytic thinking but at times denigrating it. Jackson (1967) went so far as to declare the death of the individual, and Minuchin (1989) proclaimed that, "We understood that the decontexted individual was a mythical monster, an illusion created by our psychodynamic blinders." Family therapists saw themselves as forward-looking progressives, liberating the field from a fossilized view of mental disorder, namely that problems are firmly embedded inside people's heads. If at times they sounded a little self-righteous, perhaps that was due to the vehemence of the resistance they encountered from the entrenched powers of the psychiatric establishment. Understandable or not, the result was a prolonged and unfortunate rejection of all things related to depth psychology.

In the 1980s a surprising shift occurred: Family therapists took a renewed interest in the psychology of the individual. While the reemergence of psychodynamics in family therapy may not have been as significant as the crumbling of the Berlin wall, to those who remember the old antagonisms it was equally unexpected.

The revival of interest in psychoanalytic thinking reflected changes in psychoanalysis—from the individualism of Freudian theory to the more relationship-centered object relations theories and self psychology—that made it more attractive to family therapists, as well as changes in family therapy itself, especially dissatisfaction with the mechanistic elements of the cybernetic model, that made family therapists more interested in understanding personal experience. Among the books calling for a rapprochement between family therapy and psychoanalysis were: *Individual and Family Therapy: Toward an Integration* (Sander, 1979); *Object Relations: A Dynamic Bridge Between Individual and Family Treatment* (Slipp, 1984); *Object Relations Family Therapy* (Scharff & Scharff, 1987); and *The Self in the System* (Nichols, 1987).

The reason that these psychodynamic approaches found a receptive audience is that many believed that while family therapists discovered profound truths about systemic interactions, they were wrong to turn their backs on the lessons of depth psychology. There seems to be a paradox here: Psychoanalysis is a theory and therapy of individuals; family therapy is a theory of social systems and a therapy of families. How, then, can there be a psychoanalytic family therapy?

One way to answer this question, illustrated by the object relations family therapy of David and Jill Scharff, is to do psychoanalytic therapy with families. Another solution, suggested by Nichols in *The Self in the System*, is to selectively introduce psychoanalytic insights and interventions in systemic family therapy. In either case, the question—Can there be a psychoanalytic family therapy?—remains a good one.

Sketches of Leading Figures

We can distinguish four distinct groups of contributors to psychoanalytic family therapy: psychoanalytic forerunners, psychoanalytically trained pioneers, the few who pursued psychoanalytic ideas even when mainstream family therapy was vociferously anti-psychoanalytic, and those in the forefront of the contemporary resurgence of psychoanalytic family therapy.

Freud was interested in the family but viewed it as old business—the context where people learned neurotic fears, rather than the contemporary context where such fears are maintained. Presented with a phobic Little Hans, Freud (1909) was more interested in analyzing the child's Oedipus complex than trying to understand his family.

Major advances were achieved in the psychoanalytic understanding of family dynamics by child psychiatrists who began to analyze mothers and children concurrently (Burlingham, 1951). An example of the fruits of these studies is Adelaide Johnson's (Johnson & Szurek, 1952) explanation of the transmission of *superego lacunae*, gaps in personal morality passed on by parents who do things like telling their children to lie about their ages in order to save a couple of dollars at the movies.

Subsequently, the concurrent analysis of married couples revealed the family as a group of interlocking, intrapsychic systems (Oberndorf, 1938; Mittlemann, 1948; Martin & Bird, 1953). The notion of interlinked psyches remains an important feature of the psychoanalytic view of families (Sander, 1989). Most contemporary family therapists view the family as functioning in terms of a single organic unity, but psychoanalytic therapists are concerned with complex interactions among and within individual family members.

From the 1930s to the 1950s more and more psychoanalytic researchers became interested in the family. Erik Erikson explored the sociological dimensions of ego psychology. Erich Fromm's observations about cultural forces and the struggle for individuality foreshadowed later work by Bowen on the process of differentiation within the family. Harry Stack Sullivan's interpersonal theory emphasized the mother's role in transmitting anxiety to her children. Moreover, although he didn't treat families, Sullivan transformed the treatment milieu at Sheppard and Enoch Pratt Hospital into a kind of surrogate family for young schizophrenic patients.

The psychoanalysts who helped create family therapy were moving away from psychodynamics, and the analytic influence retained in their work was deliberately muted. Murray Bowen, Lyman Wynne, Theodore Lidz, and Nathan Ackerman have been discussed elsewhere. Among this group, Nathan Ackerman retained the strongest tie to psychoanalytic theory in his approach to families.

In the first two decades of family therapy, Nathan Ackerman was the leading family therapist on the East Coast. Students, among them Salvador Minuchin, flocked to the Family Institute (now Ackerman Institute) in New York to observe this master therapist at work. His book, *The Psychodynamics of Family Life*, published in 1958, was the first one devoted to diagnosis and treatment of families. Classical Freudians assumed that the individuals they treated lived in stable environments. Dreams and fantasies were the royal roads to the unconscious; consequently they didn't think it necessary to know anything about the real family. Ackerman realized that families are rarely stable, dependable, or predictable; rather than quarantine them, however, he believed they could be changed for the better (Ackerman, 1966). Since people don't live in isolation, Ackerman believed they shouldn't be treated in isolation.

Ivan Boszormenyi-Nagy, also a psychoanalyst, developed an important center of family therapy at the Eastern Pennsylvania Psychiatric Institute (EPPI) in 1957. His writings (Boszormenyi-Nagy & Framo, 1965; Boszormenyi-Nagy & Spark, 1973; Boszormenyi-Nagy & Ulrich, 1981; Boszormenyi-Nagy, 1987) merit careful study by serious students of family therapy.

In the 1940s Henry Dicks (1963) established the Family Psychiatric Unit at the prestigious Tavistock Clinic in England, where teams of psychiatric social workers attempted to reconcile couples referred by the divorce courts. By the 1960s Dicks (1967) was applying object relations theory to the understanding and treatment of marital conflict. Also at the Tavistock, John Bowlby (1949) described conjoint family interviews as an adjunct to individual psychotherapy.

In the 1950s and 1960s American psychoanalysis was dominated by ego psychology (which focuses on intrapsychic structures), while object relations theory (which lends itself to interpersonal analysis) flourished an ocean away in Britain. Edith Jacobson (1954) and Harry Stack Sullivan (1953) were the most influential thinkers who helped bring American psychiatry to an interpersonal point of view. Less well known, but more important to the development of family therapy, was the work carried out at the National Institute of Mental Health (NIMH). When NIMH opened in 1953, Irving Ryckoff jumped at the chance to move from Chestnut Lodge, where he'd been working with chronic schizophrenics isolated from their families, to develop a research project on families of schizophrenics under the leadership of Robert Cohen. He was joined by Juliana Day and Lyman Wynne and later by Roger Shapiro and John Zinner. This group produced a series of thoughtful papers introducing such concepts as *pseudomutuality* (Wynne, Ryckoff, Day, & Hirsch, 1958), *role stereotyping* (Ryckoff, Day, & Wynne, 1959), *trading of dissociations* (Wynne, 1965), and *delineations* (Shapiro, 1968). But perhaps their most important clinical contribution was the application of the concept of *projective identification* (from Melanie Klein) to the family as a group (from the work of Wilfred Bion). This group also introduced to psychoanalytic researchers the idea of seeing the family as the unit for study, and to clinicians the analytic group-interpretive approach to families (Shapiro, 1979).

In the 1960s, Ryckoff and Wynne introduced a course in family dynamics at the Washington

School of Psychiatry, which led to a family therapy training program. They were joined by Shapiro and Zinner and Robert Winer. In 1975 they recruited Jill Savege (now Scharff) and David Scharff. By the mid 1980s the Washington School of Psychiatry, under the directorship of David Scharff, had become one of the leading centers of psychoanalytic family therapy. The Scharffs left in 1994 to form their own institute. What characterizes the Scharffs's work is its object relations focus and its frank psychoanalytic approach to families.

Among others who have incorporated psychoanalytic theory into family therapy are: Helm Stierlin (1977), Robin Skynner (1976), William Meissner (1978), Arnon Bentovim and Warren Kinston (1991), Fred Sander (1979, 1989), Michael Nichols (1987), Nathan Epstein, Henry Grunebaum, and Clifford Sager. Another influential object relations approach to family therapy is that of Samuel Slipp (1984, 1988), whose work differs from the Scharffs's in attempting to be more of an integration of systems and psychoanalytic concepts and methods.

Theoretical Formulations

The practical essence of psychoanalytic theory is being able to recognize and interpret unconscious impulses and defenses against them—and, adding object relations theory, old expectations that distort current relationships.

It isn't a question of analyzing individuals instead of family interactions: it's knowing where to look to discover some of the basic wants and fears that keep those individuals from interacting in a mature way.

Psychoanalytic theory gets so complex when you get into the specifics that it's easy to get lost. Here are the basics.

Freudian Drive Psychology

At the heart of human nature are the drives—sexual and aggressive. Mental conflict arises when children learn, and mislearn, that expressing these basic impulses will lead to punishment. Conflict is signaled by unpleasant affect: anxiety or depression. Anxiety is unpleasure associated with the idea (often unconscious) that one will be punished for acting on a particular wish—for example, the anger you're tempted to express might make your partner stop loving you. Depression is unpleasure plus the idea (often unconscious) that the feared calamity *has already occurred*—for example, the anger you showed your mother long ago made her stop loving you; in fact, nobody loves you.

The balance of conflict can be shifted in one of two ways: by strengthening defenses against a conflicted wish or by relaxing defenses sufficiently to permit some gratification.

Self Psychology

The essence of *self psychology* (Kohut, 1971, 1977) is that human beings long to be appreciated. If, when we're young, our parents demonstrate their appreciation, we internalize this acceptance in the form of strong and self-confident personalities. But to the extent that our parents insufficiently demonstrate admiring acceptance, then our craving for it is retained in an archaic manner. As adults we alternately suppress the desire for attention and then allow it to emerge unmodified whenever we're in the presence of a receptive audience.

Object Relations Theory

Drive psychology and the psychology of the self describe the basic motives and fears of human nature—and the resultant conflict. Psychoanalysis is primarily the study of individuals and their elemental motives (drives and the need for attachment), and family therapy is the study of social relationships; the bridge between the two is *object relations theory*. While the details of object relations theory can be quite complicated, its essence is simple: We relate to people in the present partly on the basis of expectations formed by early experience. The residue of these early relationships leaves *internal objects*—mental images of self and other, and self in relation to others, built from experience and expectation. The unconscious remnants of those internalized objects form the core of the person—an open system developing and maintaining its identity through social relatedness, present *and* past.

Freud's original focus was on bodily appetites, particularly sex. While these appetites obviously involve other people, they are primarily biological; relationships are secondary. Sex cannot be divorced from object relations, but sexual relations can be more physical than personal. This is less true of aggression (to which Freud turned his interest in later years), because aggression isn't an organic appetite. As Guntrip (1971) put it, aggression is a personal reaction to "bad" object relations. Therefore as Freud's interest shifted from sex to aggression, the interpersonal, object-relational side of his thinking came to the fore. Eventually he ceased to regard anxiety as dammed-up sexual tension and considered it to be the ego's reaction to danger—often, loss of love or rejection.

Subsequently Melanie Klein's observations of the role of aggression in infancy led her to think about object relations. She combined Freud's psychobiological terms and concepts with her own brilliant insights into the mental life of children to develop psychodynamic object-relational thinking.

Klein's theory (Segal, 1964) stemmed from her observations of the infant's developing relationship with the first significant object, namely, the mother. According to Klein, an infant does not form impressions of mother based solely on real experience, but instead sifts experience through an already rich fantasy life. The infant's innate makeup contains forces of love and hate, which are experienced before the real objects themselves. From the start, perception of real objects is filtered through the distortions of an already formed inner world.

Klein has been criticized for failure to follow her own observations to their logical conclusion—namely, that object relations are more relevant than instincts to personality development. Ronald Fairbairn went further in the direction of object relations and away from drive psychology. His radical version of object relations theory stressed the ego as object-seeking and downplayed the role of instincts—making love more important than sex.

Because internal object relations are developed from the earliest and most primitive forms of interpersonal interaction, it's not surprising that the major advances in this field were made by people like Klein and Fairbairn who treated very young children and disturbed adults. In the late 1930s and 1940s, based on his work with schizoid patients (1952), Fairbairn elaborated the concept of *splitting*. Freud originally mentioned splitting as a defense mechanism of the ego; he defined it as a lifelong coexistence of two contradictory positions that do not influence each other.

Fairbairn's view of splitting is that the ego is divided into structures that contain (a) part of the ego; (b) part of the object; and (c) the affect associated with the relationship. The external object is experienced in one of three ways: (1) an ideal object, which leads to feelings of satisfaction; (2) a rejecting object, which leads to anger; or (3) an exciting object, which leads to longing. As a result of internalizing split objects, the resulting structure of the ego is: (1) a *central ego*, conscious, adaptable, satisfied with its ideal object; (2) a *rejecting ego*, unconscious, inflexible, frustrated by its rejecting object; or (3) an *exciting ego*, unconscious, inflexible, in a state of longing for a tempting but unsatisfying object. To the degree that splitting isn't resolved, object relations retain a kind of "all good" or "all bad" quality.

The primitive ego uses splitting to keep positive and negative images separate, at first because positive and negative experiences happen separately, and later as a way to avoid anxiety. Splitting, which prevents the anxiety associated with negative (aggressive) images from being generalized throughout the ego, usually disappears in the second year of life as positive and negative images are integrated. If it's excessive, however, splitting interferes with integration of these images and leads to the dramatic shifts from calm to upset of borderline personalities.

Internalization of object relations starts on a relatively primitive level and, as the child grows, becomes more sophisticated. *Introjection* is the earliest and most primitive form of internalization. The child reproduces and fixates its interactions with the environment by organizing memory traces which include images of the object, the self interacting with the object, and the associated affect. Included are good and bad internal objects, each with images of the object and the self. Thus, if mother yells, images of a bad mother and an unworthy self are stored. Introjection is a crude and global form of taking in, as if those fragments of self–other interaction were swallowed whole.

Identification, a higher level of internalization, involves the internalization of a role. In the earliest introjections, object- and self-images aren't clearly differentiated; in identification they are. The result of identification is that the child takes on certain roles and behaves in the same way the parents do. Notice, for example, how two-year-olds love to dress up like mommy or daddy.

Ego identity (Erikson, 1956) represents the most sophisticated level of internalization, a synthesis of identifications and introjections, which provides a sense of coherence and continuity of the self. Ego identity includes a consolidated self-concept and a consolidated world of object representations. At the highest level of development, according to Kernberg (1976),

> A harmonious world of internalized object-representations, including not only significant others from the family and immediate friends but also a social group and a cultural identity, constitute an ever growing internal world providing love, reconfirmation, support, and guidance within the object relations system of the ego. Such an internal world, in turn, gives depth to the present interaction with others. In periods of crisis, such as loss, abandonment, separation, failure, and loneliness, the individual can temporarily fall back on his internal world; in this way, the intrapsychic and the interpersonal worlds relate to and reinforce each other. (p. 73)

In their observations of infants and young children, Rene Spitz and John Bowlby emphasized the child's profound need for physical *attachment* to a single and constant object. If this primitive need is denied, the result is *anaclitic depression* (Spitz & Wolf, 1946), a turning away from the world and withdrawal into apathy. According to Bowlby (1969), attachment isn't simply a secondary phenomenon, resulting from being fed, but a basic need in all (including human) animals. We must have secure and loving attachments in infancy if we are to become secure adults. Those who don't have this experience are excessively vulnerable to even the slightest lack of support, and become chronically dependent. This, in psychoanalytic terms, explains the genesis of *enmeshed* families.

Margaret Mahler observed infants and young children and described the essential role of a process of *separation–individuation.* For the first month of life, which Mahler described as the *autistic phase,* infants are concerned primarily with their own bodily needs and sensations. The second, or *symbiotic phase,* lasts from approximately two to six months, during which the good mother relieves the baby's tension by feeding, changing, holding, and smiling. The more adequate the care given during this phase, the higher the child's self-esteem will be. After this the child begins a gradual process of separation from the mother, progressively renouncing symbiotic fusion with her. The result of successful separation and individuation is a well-differentiated and internally integrated organization of the self (Mahler, Pine, & Bergman, 1975). Failure to achieve separation and individuation undermines the development of a cohesive self and a differentiated identity, resulting in an overly intense emotional attachment to the family. Depending on the severity of the failure to separate, crises are liable to develop when a child reaches school age, enters adolescence, or prepares to leave home as an adult.

The shift in emphasis from drives to object relations can also be seen in the work of Americans Karen Horney, Erich Fromm, and Harry Stack Sullivan, whose level of analysis was more social and cultural than depth analytic. In his theory of interpersonal psychiatry, Harry Stack Sullivan (1953) emphasized that individuals interact with each other on the basis of past relations with others. Sullivan pointed out the crucial importance of early mother–child interactions on the *self-system* or *self-dynamism.* When mother is warm and nurturing, the child feels good; when mother rebuffs or frustrates the child's need for tenderness, the child feels bad; and when the child is exposed to extreme pain or frustration, he dissociates to escape anxiety which would otherwise be intolerable. These experiences create the self-dynamisms: *good me, bad me,* and *not me,* which then become part of the person's response to future interpersonal situations.

In Sullivanian theory, the child searches for *security* and *satisfaction,* and develops a self-system derived from interpersonal relations with the parents by repudiating those actions that cause the parents anxiety. Thus, the extent of the parents' anxiety sets the limits on the child's healthy growth and development.

To understand object relations theory, it's essential to bear in mind that it isn't objects that are in the psyche, but fantasies of objects. As Edith Jacobson (1964) pointed out, the object is never perceived exactly as it is; what is perceived is a representation that reflects the subjective experience of the object. Thus object relations are determined not only by how the object behaves toward the subject but also by how the subject perceives and then integrates that behavior. In *The Brothers Karamazov,* Dostoyevsky, speaking through the monk Zossima, makes exactly this point.

> From the house of my parents I have brought nothing but pleasant memories, for there are no memories more precious than those of one's early childhood in one's own home, and that is almost always so, if there is any love and harmony in the family at all. Indeed, precious memories may be retained even from a bad home so long as your heart is capable of finding anything precious.

The internal world of object relations never exactly corresponds to the actual world of real people. It's an approximation, strongly influenced by the earliest object images, introjections, and identifications. This inner world gradually matures and develops, becoming progressively synthesized and closer to reality. The individual's internal capacity for dealing with conflict and failure is intimately related to the maturity and depth of the internal world of object relations. Trust in one's self and in the goodness of others is based on the confirmation of love from internalized good objects.

Although the application of his ideas will be developed in subsequent sections, we cannot leave theory without mentioning Heinz Kohut. Not since Freud's drive psychology has there been as significant an impact on psychoanalysis as Kohut's *psychology of the self.* Kohut believed that at the heart of human desires is a longing for admiring attention. The child lucky enough to grow up with appreciative parents will be secure, able to stand alone as a center of initiative, and able to love. The unhappy child, cheated out of loving affirmation, will move through life forever craving the attention he or she was denied. As we shall see, Kohut's ideas have enormous practical application.

Normal Family Development

The psychoanalytic model of normal development contains concepts drawn from object relations theory, attachment theory, and theories of the self—all of which are modifications and additions to Freud's psychology of drives. According to Freudian models, psychological well-being depends on: (a) gratification of instincts; (b) realistic control of primitive drives; and (c) coordination of independent psychic structures. According to object relations theory, achieving and preserving psychic wholeness through good object relations is the key to psychological adjustment.

The child's innate potential doesn't mature in sublime indifference to the interpersonal world. The infant needs a facilitating environment in order to thrive. This environment doesn't have to be an unattainable ideal; an *average expectable environment* featuring *good-enough mothering* (Winnicott, 1965a) is sufficient. Tender, responsive parents first accept the infant's total dependence; but as time goes on, they support the child's growing autonomy, and eventually ratify the child's finding a life of his own through personal relations with others.

The parents' capacity to provide good-enough mothering and sufficient security for the baby's developing ego depends on whether they themselves feel secure. To begin with, the mother must be secure and selfless enough to channel most of her energy into supporting and caring for her infant. She drains interest from herself and her marriage and focuses it on the baby. As the baby comes to need less, mother gradually recovers her self-interest, which allows her to permit the child to become independent (Winnicott, 1965b). At the same time she also redevelops an interest in the marital relationship.

If the early relationship with mother is secure and loving, the infant will gradually be able to give her up, while retaining her loving support in the form of a good internal object. In the process, most little children adopt a *transitional object* (Winnicott, 1965b) to ease the loss—a soft toy or blanket that the child clings to during the period when he or she starts to realize that mother is a separate object and can go away. The toy that Mommy gives reassures her anxious baby; it's a reminder that stands for her and keeps alive the mental image of her until she returns. When Mommy says, "Good-night," the child hugs the teddy bear until morning when Mommy reappears.

The outcome of good object relations in infancy is the emergence of a secure and successfully differentiated identity. The little child who has been cared for by consistently loving and reliably supportive parents develops a sense of *libidinal object constancy* (Kernberg, 1966). The well-loved child feels worthwhile. This sense of worth endows the child with a capacity to delay gratification, tolerate frustration, and achieve competent ego functioning. The child with a backlog of good object relations matures with the ability to tolerate closeness as well as separateness.

The child's identity is continually enriched and revised, especially at nodal points of development such as the oedipal period, puberty, and adolescence. But the search for identity doesn't end with adolescence (Erikson, 1959); the sense of identity continues to be shaped by experiences in adulthood, especially social relations, career development, and family life (Levinson, 1978; Nichols, 1986).

The early attachment between mother and child has been shown to be a critical aspect of healthy development (Bowlby, 1969). Close physical proximity and *attachment* to a single maternal object are necessary preconditions for healthy object relations in childhood and adulthood. The infant needs a state of total merging and identification with the mother as a foundation for future growth of a strongly formed personal self.

After passing through the normal autistic and symbiotic phases, the child enters a long *separation–individuation period* at approximately six months (Mahler, Pine, & Bergman, 1975). First efforts at separation are tentative and brief, as symbolized playfully in the game of peekaboo. Soon the child begins to creep and then crawl, first away from and then back to mother. What enables the child to practice separating is the awareness that mother is constantly there for assurance, like a safe harbor.

The necessary and sufficient condition for successful completion of separation–individuation is reliable and loving support. "Predictable emotional involvement on the part of the mother seems to facilitate the rich unfolding of the toddler's thought processes, reality testing and coping behavior . . ." (Mahler, Pine, & Bergman, 1975, p. 79). A *good-enough mother* is physically and emotionally present; her support of separation–individuation results in the child's achieving a firm sense of identity and a lifelong capacity for developing nonsymbiotic object relations.

Recently, Otto Kernberg and Heinz Kohut have brought theories of the self to center stage in psychoanalytic circles. According to Kernberg (1966), the earliest introjections occur in the process of separating from mother. If separation is successful and securely negotiated, the child establishes himself or herself as an independent being. A mother must have the capacity to tolerate separation in order to accept her child's growing independence. If the child is excessively dependent and clings in fear of separation, or if the mother is made anxious by the loss of the symbiotic relationship, or is excessively rejecting, the process is subverted. In the normal outcome, loving parents are the objects of selective and partial identifications, in which only those features that are in harmony with the image of the self are internalized. As Kernberg (1966) says,

> Actually the enrichment of one's personal life by the internal presence of such selective, partial identifications representing people who are loved and admired in a realistic way without indiscriminate internalization, constitutes a major source of emotional depth and well-being. (p. 243)

To the very young child, parents aren't quite separate individuals; they are, in Kohut's (1971, 1977) terms, *selfobjects,* experienced as part of the self. As a selfobject, the mother transmits her love by touch, tone of voice, and gentle words, as though they were the child's own feelings. When she whispers, "Mommy loves you," the baby learns that he or she is (a) a person and (b) lovable. Steady, loving parental validation nourishes a life-long sense of security.

In self psychology, two qualities of parenting are deemed essential for the establishment of a secure and cohesive self. The first is empathy—understanding plus acceptance. Attentive parents convey a deep appreciation of how their children feel. Their implicit "I see how you feel" validates the child's inner experience. Parents also offer a model for idealization. The little child who can believe "My father (or mother) is terrific and I am part of him (or her)" has a firm base of self-esteem. In the best of circumstances, the child already basically secure in his or her self draws additional strength from identifying with the apparently infinite power and strength of the parents.

Unquestionably the most significant recent contribution to the psychoanalytic study of normal family development is the work of Daniel Stern (1985). Stern, a psychoanalyst and infant researcher, has painstakingly traced the development of the sense of self through detailed observations of infants and small children. The infant's *emergent sense of self* begins in the first two months of life as a sense of physical cohesion and continuity in time. Already at this age, the infant has a sense of himself as a person—a distinct and integrated body, an initiator of actions, an experiencer of feelings, and a communicator. From two to six months, infants consolidate the sense of a *core self* as a separate, cohesive, bounded physical unit, with confidence in their own agency and worth. At first the sense of self is a physical self; then somewhere between the seventh and ninth month infants start to develop a second organizing perspective, *intersubjective relatedness.* The most revolutionary of Stern's findings is that child development is *not* a gradual process of separation and individuation. Rather, infants differentiate themselves almost from birth, and then progress through increasingly complex modes of relatedness. From *attunement* (reading and sharing the child's affective state) to *empathy,* attachment, trust, and dependency are needs throughout life.

Michael Kahn has begun to establish a theoretical and clinical framework for understanding sibling relationships across the life span (Bank & Kahn, 1982). Since the sibling subsystem comes in so many combinations and variations, Kahn has found concepts of birth order and fixed roles characteristic of each child in the family to be insufficient and reductionistic. (Kahn & Lewis, 1988). Sibling relationships are a previously underutilized but rich resource system, particularly in light of the strain on parental resources in contemporary two-paycheck households.

From a psychoanalytic perspective the fate of family development is largely determined by the early development of the individual personalities that make up the family. If the spouses are mature and healthy adults, then the family will be happy and harmonious.

Some of the most interesting and productive psychoanalytic ideas are contained in descriptions of the psychodynamics of marriage. In the 1950s, the marital bond was described as a result of unconscious fantasy (Stein, 1956). We marry a blurry blend of real and hoped-for mates. But more recently, and more interestingly, psychoanalysts have described the overlapping and interlocking of fantasies and projections (Blum, 1987; Sander, 1989). Some authors have described this as "mutual projective identification" (Zinner, 1976; Dicks, 1967), others as "neurotic complementarity" (Ackerman, 1966), "marital collusion" (Dicks, 1967), "mutual adaptation" (Giovacchini, 1958, 1961), and "conscious and unconscious contracts" (Sager, 1981). In 1989 one of the most thoughtful contemporary psychoanalytic family therapists, Fred Sander, summed up the analytic position this way:

> Thus, we are noting explicitly what earlier authors from Freud on implicitly noted: the shared participation in neurotic conflicts. The threats of object loss, loss of love, castration, and superego disapproval—the calamities of childhood in all ages and cultures—continue to affect our relations to others, especially those with whom we live and work. The repression of such universal childhood experiences and conflicts leads to their repetition with important others who reciprocally enact similar or complementary unconscious conflicts. (pp. 165–166)

Among psychodynamic family therapists, few have made contributions as important as Ivan Boszormenyi-Nagy's "contextual therapy," which emphasizes the ethical dimension of family development. Nagy considers relational ethics—both within the family and between the family and the larger society—to be a fundamental dynamic force, holding families and communities together through reliability and trustworthiness. In a field that often seeks refuge in the illusion of clinical neutrality, Nagy reminds us of the importance of decency and fairness between people. According to Nagy, loyalty and trust provide the glue that holds families together.

For marital partners, Nagy's criterion of health is a balance between rights and responsibilities. Depending on their integrity and the complementarity of their needs, marital partners can develop a trustworthy give and take (Boszormenyi-Nagy, Grunebaum, & Ulrich, 1991). When needs clash, negotiation and compromise are necessary and must be fair.

Development of Behavior Disorders

Nonpsychoanalytic family therapists locate problems in the interactions *between* people; psychoanalytic therapists identify problems *within* the interacting people. According to classical psychoanalytic conflict theory, symptoms are attempts to cope with unconscious conflicts and the anxiety that signals the emergence of repressed impulses. As psychoanalytic thinkers shifted their emphasis from instincts to object relations, infantile dependence and incomplete ego development became the core problems in development, in place of the oedipal complex and repressed instincts. Fear-dictated flight from object relations, which begins in early childhood, is now considered the deepest root of psychological problems.

One important reason for relationship problems is that the child develops distorted perceptions by attributing qualities belonging to one person to someone else. Freud (1905) discovered this phenomenon and called it *transference* when his patient Dora displaced feelings for her father and a family friend onto him, and terminated treatment abruptly just as it was on the threshold of success. Others have observed similar phenomena and called it "scapegoating" (Vogel & Bell, 1960); "trading of dissociations" (Wynne, 1965); "merging" (Boszormenyi-Nagy, 1967); "irrational role assignments" (Framo, 1970); "delineations" (Shapiro, 1968); "symbiosis" (Mahler, 1952); and "family projective process" (Bowen, 1965). Regardless of name, all are variants of Melanie Klein's (1946) concept, *projective identification.*

Projective identification is a process whereby the subject perceives an object as if it contained elements of the subject's personality *and* evokes behavior and feelings from the object that conform to these projected perceptions. Unlike projection, projective identification is a truly interactional process. Not only do parents project anxiety-provoking aspects of themselves onto their children, the children collude and behave in a way that fulfills their parents' fears. By doing so, they may be stigmatized or scapegoated, but they also gratify aggressive impulses, as, for instance, in delinquent behavior (Jacobson, 1964); they realize their own omnipotent fantasies; they receive subtle reinforcement from their families; and they avoid the terrible fear of rejection for not conforming (Zinner & Shapiro, 1972). Meanwhile the parents are able to avoid the anxiety associated with having certain impulses; experience vicarious gratification of the projected impulses through their children; and still punish the children for expressing them. In this way, an intrapsychic, structural conflict becomes externalized, with the parent acting as the superego, punishing the child for acting on the dictates of the parental id. That's one reason parents overreact: They're afraid of their own impulses.

> The J. family sought help controlling 15-year-old Paul's delinquent behavior. Arrested several times for vandalism, Paul seemed neither ashamed of nor able to understand his compulsion to strike out against authority. As therapy progressed, it became clear that Paul's father harbored a deep but unexpressed resentment of the social conditions which made him work long hours for low wages in a factory, while the "fat cats didn't do shit, but still drove around in Cadillacs." Once the therapist became aware of Mr. J.'s strong but suppressed hatred of authority, they also began to notice that he smiled slightly whenever Mrs. J. described Paul's latest exploits.

From an object relations point of view, inadequate separation and individuation as well as introjection of pathological objects are critical determinants of poor adult adjustment. Whether premature or delayed, difficulty in separating creates lasting problems. Guntrip (1969) described how separation anxiety weakens the ego, as follows:

> However caused, the danger of separation, whether by desertion or withdrawal, is that the infant, starting life with a primitive and quite undeveloped psyche, just cannot stand the loss of his object. He cannot retain his primitive wholeness for more than a short period in the absence of mother and cannot go on to develop a strong sense of identity and selfhood without an object-relation. Separation-anxiety then is a pointer to the last and worst fear, fear of the loss of ego itself, of depersonalization and the sense of unreality. (p. 128)

Failure to develop a cohesive sense of self and a differentiated identity causes a prolonged and intensely emotional attachment to the family. This dependent attachment to parents handicaps a person's ability to develop a social and family life of his or her own. This, in object relations terms, explains the enmeshment that characterizes so many symptomatic families (Minuchin, 1974).

Parents' failure to accept the fact that their children are separate beings can take extreme forms, leading to the most severe types of psychopathology. Several investigators have remarked that anorexia nervosa is a problem that results from inadequate separation and individuation (Bruch, 1978; Masterson, 1977). Often the parents' own serious personality disorders prevent them from understanding and accepting their children's need for independence. Such parents cannot tolerate separation or deviation from their rules, and respond to independent ventures with extreme overcontrol. The result is that the children don't differentiate their own needs from those of their parents; and they become overly compliant, "perfect" children. Lidz (Lidz, Cornelison, & Fleck, 1965) described a mother of identical twins who, when she was constipated, would give her two sons an enema or laxative.

The compliant facade, or "false self" (Winnicott, 1965b), of these children is adaptive only as long as they remain at home with their parents. That's why poorly differentiated children usually face a crisis in adolescence, when developmental pressures for independence conflict with infantile family attachments. The outcome may be continued dependence or a violent adolescent rebellion. But the teenager who rebels as a reaction against unresolved dependency needs is ill-equipped for mature social relations—not to mention marriage. Behind a facade of proud self-reliance, such individuals harbor deep longings for dependence and tend to be extremely emotionally reactive. When they marry, they may seek constant approval, or automatically reject control and influence, or both.

> In their first couples therapy session, Mr. and Mrs. B.'s complaints were mirror images. He claimed she was "bossy and demanding," while she said that he "had to have everything his own way and wouldn't listen to anybody." An exploration of Mr. B's history revealed that he was the youngest child in a closely-knit family of five. He described his mother as warm and loving, but said she tried to smother him, and that she discouraged all his efforts to be independent. Subjected to these same pressures, his two older sisters conformed and still remain unmarried, living with their parents. Mr. B., however, rebelled against his mother's domination and left home to join the Marines at 17. As he related his experience in the Marine Corps and successful business ventures, it was clear that he was fiercely proud of his independence.
>
> Once the story of Mr. B.'s success in breaking away from his overcontrolling mother was brought out into the open, both

> Mr. and Mrs. B. had a clearer understanding of his tendency to overreact to anything he perceived as controlling. Deeper analysis subsequently revealed that while Mr. B. staunchly rejected what he called "bossiness," he nevertheless was terribly concerned with securing praise and approval. Apparently, he had learned to fear his deep-seated dependency needs, and he protected himself with a facade of "not needing anything from anybody." Nevertheless, the needs were still there, and had in fact been a powerful determinant of his choice of wife.

Much of the current psychoanalytic thinking about the effects of pathological object relations has come from Otto Kernberg's and Heinz Kohut's studies of borderline character disorders and narcissistic personalities. While the majority of persons seeking family therapy aren't so severely disturbed, a great many people suffer from similar dynamics.

In treating borderline personality disorders, Kernberg (1966) was struck by the fact that his patients alternately expressed complementary sides of a conflict, one minute expressing libidinal or aggressive impulses, the next minute behaving defensively in just the opposite manner. He deduced that their behavior was the result of marked compartmentalization of ego states due to a *splitting of the ego.*

The essence of Kernberg's position is that borderline pathology is an object relations disorder. Excessive rage is its cause, and splitting is the defense against it. Borderline patients are liable to sudden outbursts of anger, then equally suddenly will change to warm, friendly, and dependent behavior. When provoked to rage, their image of the hated person corresponds to an early image of mother; their self-image is as a rejected or attacked little child.

Kohut (1971, 1977) described the development of narcissistic pathology, which can take extreme forms as in narcissistic personality disorders, but in less severe forms is one of the most widespread problems in human nature. The child whose needs for *mirroring* and *idealization* aren't adequately met goes through life forever hungering to be admired. This hunger may be manifest in the showy exhibitionism most people associate with the term "narcissistic," but it's equally likely to be seen as a childlike craving for appreciation. The child who hungered in vain for praise becomes an adult who alternately suppresses the longing for attention, then lets it break through in an all-or-none form in the presence of anyone who seems responsive. If selfishness means unconcern with others, narcissistic personalities are just the opposite. They're obsessed with the opinion of others—and have an inordinate need to be loved and admired.

The more starved for appreciation the child is, the less likely the adult will ever be satisfied. The reason is that the under-responded-to child doesn't modify the *grandiose self* into realistic goals and ambitions, but represses it, where it remains as an impossible standard of unconscious ambition.

When it comes to marital choice, psychoanalysts assure us, love is blind. Freud (1921) wrote that the overvaluation of the loved object when we fall in love leads us to make false judgments based on *idealization.* The "fall" of "falling in love" reflects an overflow of narcissistic libido, so that the object of our love is elevated as a substitute for our own unattained ego ideal. Naturally our own identity glows in an ideal light. It's particularly when we have dark doubts that we seem to need this reflected radiance.

Psychoanalysts point out that marital choice is based partially on the desire to find an object who will complement and reinforce unconscious fantasies (Dicks, 1963). Depending on the nature of these fantasies, some people expect their partners always to gratify them, and others expect their partners never to gratify them. Moreover, people tend to seek mates with complementary needs (Meissner, 1978); this point is illustrated in those marriages where one partner is dominant and the other submissive.

Such relationships may be both stable and functional; beginning therapists are therefore well advised not to impose their own values, or try to "save" women from doll's-house marriages, or rescue men from being dominated by their wives—unless they ask for such help.

Further complicating marital choice is the fact that we learn early to hide some of our real needs and feelings in order to win approval. Children who are insecure tend to develop an outward appearance of being good, and to deny and repress impulses and feelings they fear may lead to rejection. Winnicott (1965a) dubbed this phenomenon the *false self*—children behave as if they were perfect angels, pretending to be what they are not. But because they're only acting, their emotional responses lack depth and genuineness.

In its most extreme form, a false self leads to schizoid behavior (Guntrip, 1969); even in less severe manifestations it affects the choice of a marital partner. During courtship both partners are eager to please and, therefore, present themselves in the best possible light. Powerful dependency needs, narcissism, and unruly impulses may be submerged before marriage; but once married, the spouses become themselves, warts and all.

Marital choice is heavily influenced by the mutual fit of the two partners' projective systems. Typically each wants the other to be an idealized parent. But since this need was frustrated in childhood, it's defended against, and neither directly felt nor revealed. The honeymoon may therefore turn out to be no honeymoon at all, as a woman realizes that the tower of strength she thought she married is in fact not her father, but a callow young man with dependency needs of his own. Likewise, a new husband may discover that he is now the target of those angry hysterics he had previously seen directed only against his wife's mother.

In addition to feeling freer to be themselves after marriage, many spouses actually regress to an earlier stage of development. While they are teenagers living with their parents, most people react to stress and frustration in immature ways, such as pouting or attacking. Such behavior isn't likely to be accepted by peers, so people tend to suppress it outside their families, while they are living on their own. However, after they marry, so that they are once again in a family situation, many people begin again to act like adolescents. Consequently the first months of marriage can be trying.

Families as well as individuals experience fixation and regression. Most families function adequately until they're overtaxed, at which time they become stuck in rigid and dysfunctional patterns (Barnhill & Longo, 1978). When faced with too much stress, families tend to decompensate to earlier levels of development. The amount of stress a family can tolerate depends on its level of development and the type of fixations its members have.

Like individuals, families may pass through one developmental stage and on to the next without having fully resolved the issues of the transition. Thus there may be partial fixations at one or more stages of the family life cycle. When stressed, the family not only reexperiences old conflicts, but also falls back on old patterns of coping. Consequently, family therapists need to identify fixation points and regressive patterns of coping, as well as current difficulties.

Psychiatrists, and especially psychoanalysts, have been criticized (Szasz, 1961) for absolving people of responsibility for their actions. To say that someone has "acted-out" "repressed" sexual urges through an extramarital affair is to suggest that he or she is not to be held accountable for infidelity. One writer, however, Ivan Boszormenyi-Nagy, stresses the idea of ethical accountability within families. Good family relationships include behaving ethically with other family members and considering each member's welfare and interests. Nagy believes that family members owe one another *loyalty*, and that they acquire *merit* by supporting each other. To the degree that parents are fair and responsible, they engender loyalty in their children; however, parents create loyalty conflicts when they ask their children to be loyal to one parent at the expense of loyalty to the other (Boszormenyi-Nagy & Ulrich, 1981).

Pathological reactions may develop from *invisible loyalties*—these are unconscious commitments that children take on to help their families, to the detriment of their own well-being. For example, a child may get sick to unite parents in concern. Invisible loyalties are problematic because they're not subject to rational awareness and scrutiny. The similarity between invisible loyalties and object relations concepts isn't surprising; many of Nagy's concepts redescribe traditional psychoanalytic concepts in the language of relational ethics. Another example is his (1967, 1972) concept of *interlocking need templates*, essentially the same as projective identification.

Nagy believes that symptoms develop when the trustworthiness of relationships breaks down because caring and accountability are absent. But while emphasizing such ethical and transactional considerations, Nagy doesn't neglect the subjective experience and unconscious dynamics of individual family members (Boszormenyi-Nagy & Ulrich, 1981).

> There is no theoretical parsimony in trying to invalidate the significance of drives, psychic development, and inner experience. On the contrary, it appears that the intensive, in-depth relational implications of psychoanalytic theory need to be explored, expanded, and integrated with the other contextual dimensions. (p. 160)

While most psychoanalytic thinkers would agree that it's appropriate and necessary to consider individual rights and responsibilities within the family, some have pointed out that individual boundaries are blurred by unconscious connections with other family members. Kernberg (1975), for example, writes that blurring of boundaries between the self and others is a result of projective identification, since part of the projected impulse is still recognized within the ego.

Marriage, on the surface, appears to be a contract between two responsible people; at a deeper level, however, marriage is a transaction between hidden internalized objects. Contracts in marital relations are usually described using the terms of behavioral or communications theories; but Sager's (1981) treatment of marital contracts also considers unconscious factors: Each contract has three levels of awareness: (1) verbalized, though not always heard; (2) conscious but not verbalized, usually because of fear of anger or disapproval; and (3) unconscious. Each partner acts as though the other ought to be aware of the terms of the contract, and is hurt and angry if the spouse doesn't live up to these terms. Spouses who behave like this don't accept each other's real personality and identity; each wants the other to conform to an internalized model, and punishes the other when these unrealistic expectations are disappointed (Dicks, 1963). Even when such behavior is overtly resisted, it may be unconsciously colluded with. It's valid and useful to emphasize individual rights and responsibilities in real relationships (Boszormenyi-Nagy, 1972), but it's also true that at an unconscious level a marital pair may represent a single personality, with each spouse playing the role of half self and half the other's projective identifications. This is why people tend to marry those with needs complementary to their own (Meissner, 1978).

A similar dynamic operates between parents and children. Even before they're born, children exist as part of their parents' fantasies (Scharff & Scharff, 1987). The anticipated child may represent, among other things, a more devoted love object than the spouse, someone to succeed where the parent has failed, or a peace offering to reestablish loving relations with grandparents.

Zinner and Shapiro (1972) coined the term *delineations* for parental acts and statements that communicate the parents' images to their children. Pathogenic delineations are based more on parents' defensive needs than on realistic perceptions of the children; moreover, parents are strongly motivated to maintain defensive delineations despite anything the children actually do. Thus it's not uncommon to see parents who insist on seeing their children as bad, helpless, and sick—or brilliant, normal, and fearless—regardless of the truth.

Any and all of the children in a family may suffer from such distortions, but usually only one is identified as "the patient" or the "sick one." He or she is chosen because of some trait that makes him or her a suitable target for the parents' projected emotions. These children shouldn't, however, be thought of as helpless victims. In fact, they collude in the projected identification in order to cement attachments, assuage unconscious guilt, or preserve their parents' shaky marriages. Often the presenting symptom is symbolic of the denied parental emotion. A misbehaving child may be acting out her father's repressed anger at his wife; an overly dependent child may be expressing his mother's fear of leading an independent life outside the home; and a bully may be counterphobically compensating for his father's projected insecurity.

Intrapsychic personality dynamics are obscured by psychological defenses, which mask the true nature of an individual's feelings, both from himself and from others. *Family myths* (Ferreira, 1963) serve the same function in families, simplifying and distorting reality. Stierlin (1977) elaborated on Ferreira's view of family myths and developed the implications for family assessment and therapy. Myths protect family members from facing certain painful truths, and also serve to keep outsiders from learning embarrassing facts. A typical myth is that of family harmony, familiar to family therapists, especially those who have worked with conflict-avoiding families. In the extreme, this myth takes the form of "pseudomutuality" (Wynne, Ryckoff, Day, & Hirsch, 1958) found in schizophrenic families. Often the myth of family harmony is maintained by the use of projective identification; one family member is delegated to be the bad one, and all the others insist they are happy and well-adjusted. This bad seed may be the identified patient or sometimes a deceased relative.

Families often view outsiders, especially family therapists, as intruders who want to stir up painful and embarrassing memories. The more they fear such inquiries, the more they cling to family myths. Therapists must neither be fooled by these myths, nor make the mistake of attacking them prematurely.

Goals of Therapy

The goal of psychoanalytic family therapy is to free family members of unconscious restrictions so that they'll be able to interact with one another as whole, healthy persons on the basis of current realities rather than unconscious images of the past. Plainly this is an ambitious task. Families in crisis are treated with understanding and support to help them through their immediate difficulty. Once the crisis is resolved, the psychoanalytic family therapist hopes to engage the family in long-term reconstructive psychotherapy. Some families accept, but many do not. When a family is motivated only for symptom relief, the therapist should support its decision to terminate, lest they drop out and feel like they failures. Some psychoanalytic family therapists deliberately plan short-term treatment. In these cases, just as in individual short-term dynamic psychotherapy (e.g., Sifneos, 1972), it's considered essential to narrow the field of exploration by selecting a specific focus for treatment. A notable exponent of short-term psychoanalytic family therapy is Christopher Dare, at the Maudsley Hospital in London. Although it's not common, some psychoanalytic family therapists also engage in explicitly crisis-oriented family therapy (Umana, Gross, & McConville, 1980).

When psychoanalytic family therapists opt for crisis resolution with symptom-reduction as the only goal, they function much like other family therapists. Hence, they focus more on supporting defenses and clarifying communication than on analyzing defenses and uncovering repressed needs and impulses. In general, however, behavioral changes that in other therapy models would be seen as goals of treatment (e.g., getting a school-phobic child to attend class) are seen by psychodynamic family therapists as byproducts of the resolution of underlying conflicts.

It's easy to say that the goal is personality change, rather more difficult to specify precisely what's meant by "change." The kind of change most commonly sought is described as separation–individuation (Katz, 1981) or differentiation (Skynner, 1981); both terms emphasize the growth and independence of individuals from their families of origin, and thus reflect the prominent influence of object relations theory. (Perhaps an additional reason for emphasizing separation–individuation is the fact that enmeshed families are more likely to seek and to remain in treatment than are isolated or disengaged families.) Individual therapists often think of individuation in terms of physical separation. Thus adolescents and young adults may be treated in isolation from their families in order to help them become more independent. Family therapists, on the other hand, believe that emotional growth and autonomy are best achieved by working through the emotional bonds within the family. Rather than remove individuals from their families, psychoanalytic family therapists convene families to help them learn how to let go of one another in a way that allows each individual to be independent as well as related. Individuation neither requires nor is achieved by severing relationship bonds. The following extended example illustrates how the goals of psychoanalytic family therapy were implemented with a particular family.

Three months after he went away to college, Barry J. had his first psychotic break. A brief hospital stay made it clear that Barry was unable to withstand separation from his family without decompensating; therefore, the hospital staff recommended that on discharge he should live apart from his parents with only minimal contact, in order to help him become an independent adult. Accordingly, he was discharged to a supportive group home for young adults and seen twice weekly in individual psychotherapy. Unfortunately, he suffered a second breakdown, and within two months was once again hospitalized.

As the time for discharge from this second hospitalization approached, the ward psychiatrist decided to convene the entire family in order to discuss plans for Barry's post-hospital adjustment. During this meeting it became painfully obvious that powerful forces within the family were binding Barry and impeding any chance for genuine separation. Barry's parents were pleasant and effective people who separately were most engaging and helpful. Toward each other, however, they displayed an icy hatred. During those few moments in the interview when they spoke to each other, rather than to Barry, their hostility was palpable. Only their concern for Barry, their youngest, prevented their relationship from becoming a battleground—a battleground on which Barry feared one or both of them might be destroyed.

At the staff conference following this interview two plans for disposition were advanced. One group, recognizing the powerful pathological influence of the family, recommended that Barry be removed as far as possible from his parents and treated in individual psychotherapy. Only by isolating Barry from the family, they argued, was there hope that he could mature into an independent person. Others on the staff disagreed, arguing that only by treating them conjointly could the collusive bond between Barry and his parents be resolved. After lengthy discussion the group reached a consensus to try the latter approach.

Most of the early family meetings were dominated by the parents' anxious concern about Barry: about the apartment complex where he lived, his job, his friends, how he was spending his leisure time, his clothes, his grooming—in short, about every detail of his life. Gradually, with the therapist's support, Barry was able to limit how much of his life was open to his parents' scrutiny. As he did so, and as they were less able to preoccupy themselves with him, they began to focus on their own relationship. As Barry became more successful at handling his own affairs, his parents became openly combative with each other.

Following a session during which the parents' marital relationship was the primary focus, the therapist recommended that the parents come for a few separate sessions in addition to the regular family meetings. Unable to divert their attention to Barry, the J.s fought viciously, leaving no doubt that theirs was a seriously destructive relationship. Rather than getting better in treatment, their relationship got worse.

After two months of internecine warfare—during which time Barry continued to improve—Mr. and Mrs. J. sought a legal separation. Once they were separated, both parents seemed to become happier, more involved with their friends and careers, and less worried about Barry. As they further released their stranglehold on their son, both parents began to develop a warmer and more genuine relationship with him. Even after the parents divorced they continued to attend family sessions with Barry.

In place of the original tensely symbiotic bond, a more balanced relationship between Barry and his parents gradually emerged. Resolution of hidden conflicts and working through of unconscious loyalties led to genuine autonomy of separate persons—enjoying but no longer needing each other—an outcome far better than isolation.

In Nagy's contextual therapy the goal is a balance of fairness in the burdens and benefits of adult life. The growth of the individual is seen to include giving and caring. Taking into account conflicts that have led to past injustices and acknowledging and redressing them is considered essential to, not in competition with, enhanced self-worth.

Nagy shares with other psychoanalytic family therapists the assumption that growth and relief of symptoms occur through facing avoided emotional conflicts. Contextual therapy considers the therapeutic implications of responsibility for imposing one's projections onto others. But the reintegration of avoided aspects of the self cannot be an isolated or selfish pursuit. Self-discovery often necessitates, and also frequently makes possible, the courageous renegotiation of avoided or inequitable relationships (Boszormenyi-Nagy, Grunebaum, & Ulrich, 1991).

The goals of contextual therapy include a balance between autonomy and mutuality. Family members are helped to face and overcome irrational, unproductive guilt and to claim their own entitlements. However, facing realistic guilt—based on actual harm done to others, deliberately or inadvertently—is seen as essential to expanding accountability within families. Thus, each person works toward self-fulfillment by asserting his or her rights and by living up to his or her obligations. Although helping people to give more generously in family relations may sound like a luxury for the well-adjusted, it isn't. The added benefits of caring about the ethical implications of relationships actually help to strengthen a weak ego.

Conditions for Behavior Change

As any student knows, psychoanalytic therapy works through insight; but the idea that insight cures is a misleading oversimplification. Insight is necessary, but not sufficient, for successful analytic treatment. In psychoanalytic family therapy, family members expand their insight by learning that their psychological lives are larger than their conscious experience, and by coming to understand and accept repressed parts of their personalities. Just as in individual therapy, interpretations, to be effective, should be limited to preconscious material—that which the patient is almost aware of; interpretations of unconscious material arouse anxiety, which means they will be rejected. Whatever insights are achieved, however, must subsequently be *worked through* (Greenson, 1967)—that is, translated into new and more productive ways of behaving and interacting.

Some (Kohut, 1977) have even suggested that psychoanalytic treatment works not as much by insight as by reducing defenses—patients simply experience and express repressed parts of themselves. From this point of view, it may be more important for family members to express their unconscious needs than to learn to understand them. Most therapists work to do both—that is, foster insight and encourage expression of repressed impulses (Ackerman, 1958).

Analytic therapists foster insight by penetrating beneath the surface of behavior to the hidden motives below. In individual therapy, dreams and free associations are considered *manifest content*, not to be taken at face value. Likewise, manifest family interactions are thought to be disguised versions of the latent agendas hidden behind them. Nonanalytic family therapists accept the meaning of the family's manifest interactions; analytic family therapists attempt to uncover other material, especially that which is hidden, unconscious, and from the past. According to Framo (1970), "The family cannot undergo deep or meaningful change if the therapist deals only with current, immediate interactions among the members" (p. 158).

Naturally, families defend against exposing their innermost feelings. After all, it's a great deal to ask of anyone to expose old wounds and embarrassing emotions. Psychoanalysts deal with this problem by creating a climate of trust and by proceeding slowly. But the risk of exposure is far greater in family therapy. Not only do family members have to acknowledge painful feelings, they are asked to do so in front of the very people they most want to hide them from. A therapist might offer as an interpretation the idea that a man hates his wife because he blames her for depriving him of the freedom of his lost youth. In individual treatment, the patient might acknowledge this fairly readily, wonder why he had suppressed his feelings, and begin to explore the roots of his reactions. But imagine how much more difficult it is to admit its truth and acknowledge his feelings in front of his wife.

Since patients in family therapy are likely to be concerned about public exposure as well as self-protection, therapists must offer them a great deal of security. Such security is necessary both for uncovering material for analysis, and also for working through this material in family interaction. Once an atmosphere of security is established, the analytic family therapist can begin to identify projective mechanisms and bring them back into the marital relationship. Then the spouses can reinternalize parts of themselves that they projected onto their mates. Once they no longer need to rely on projective identification, they can acknowledge and accept previously split-off, guilt-ridden libidinal and aggressive parts of their own egos. The therapist helps spouses resolve introjects of their parents, so they can see how their present difficulties emerged from unconscious attempts to perpetuate old conflicts from their families of origin. This work is painful and cannot proceed without the continual security offered by a competent and supportive therapist. Nichols (1987) emphasizes the need for *empathy* to create a "holding environment" for the whole family.

Guntrip (1971) wrote that analysts who emphasize instinct theory can blame treatment failures on the great strength of their patients' sexuality and aggression. But from an object-relations perspective such failures are more likely to be seen as the therapist's failure to make treatment relationships secure. For the therapist, this means listening without becoming intrusive; for family members, it means learning to hear each other's complaints as statements of feelings and requests for change, rather than as attacks that threaten their ego integrity.

To some, the idea of *transference* seems relevant only to individual therapy, where in the absence of a real relationship most of the patient's feelings toward the therapist must be inspired by fantasy. What need is there to think of transference in family therapy when the real relationships are actually present? In fact, transference is ubiquitous in all emotionally significant relationships. By reexperiencing and acting out repetitious past patterns—toward the therapist or other family members, or both—a person can begin to view these interactions objectively and, with a therapist's help, begin to break up repetitious pathological cycles. According to Nagy (1972) family therapy offers an even more fertile field of utilizing transference than does individual therapy.

> Beginning family therapists are soon struck with a different climate for therapeutic transference as they begin to see families rather than isolated individuals. The chief reason for this is the fact that family relationships themselves are embedded in a transference context and the family therapist can enter the ongoing transference relationship system rather than having to recreate it as a new relationship in the privacy of an exclusive therapist-patient work relationship. (p. 378)

Elsewhere, Nadelson (1978) wrote,

> Since marital conflict may be viewed as a result of the mutual projection, by each partner, of early internalized objects, and thus may become the battleground for past conflict, the therapist must be aware of each spouse's transference projection onto the partner as well as onto the therapist. (p. 123)

Two of the major considerations in family therapy are who should be included in the treatment and on whom should the help be focused. Some approaches, as for instance, strategic and behavioral, focus on helping the identified patient, even though the family may be seen conjointly. Most psychoanalytic family therapists seem to agree that the commitment should be to all family members; however, they're more likely to mean helping individuals grow and mature, than helping the family as an organic whole. According to Blanck (1967), "To help an individual or couple in marital conflict one must help each partner move towards a higher level of personality development" (p. 160).

The nature of this "higher level of personality development" has been defined in both structural and object-relations terms. For example, Nadelson (1978) emphasized the structural aim of bringing instinctual drives under the dominion of the ego when she wrote,

> The ultimate aim of interpretation and working through in psychoanalytically oriented marital therapy is the neutralization and integration of aggressive and libidinal needs so that behavior is motivated more in the service of the ego and less by impulse and intrapsychic conflict. (p. 146)

When aggressive and libidinal impulses are interpreted and experienced, they become conscious. Once they become aware of such impulses, family members are better able to integrate them into their lives and thus overcome their pathological, controlling power.

Techniques

For all the complexity of psychoanalytic theory, psychoanalytic technique is relatively simple—not necessarily easy, but simple. There are four basic techniques: listening, empathy, interpretation, and maintaining analytic neutrality. Two of these—listening and analytic neutrality—may not sound terribly profound or different from what other family therapists do, but they are.

Listening is a strenuous but silent activity, rare in our culture. Most of the time we're too busy waiting to get in a word edgewise to listen more than perfunctorily. This is especially true in family therapy where therapists feel a tremendous pressure to do something to help the troubled and troubling families they treat. And this is where the importance of analytic neutrality comes in. To establish an analytic atmosphere it's essential to aim for listening and understanding without worrying about making changes or solving problems. Change may come about as a byproduct of understanding, but the analytic therapist suspends anxious involvement with outcomes. It's impossible to overestimate the importance of this frame of mind in establishing a climate of analytic exploration.

The psychoanalytic therapist resists the temptation to be drawn in to reassure, advise, or confront families in favor of a sustained but silent immersion in their experience. When analytic therapists do intervene, they express empathic understanding in order to help family members open up, and they make interpretations to clarify hidden and confusing aspects of experience.

Most psychoanalytic family therapy is done with couples, where conflict between partners is taken as the starting point for exploring intrapsychic and interpersonal psychodynamics. Take, for example, a couple who reported having an argument over the breakfast table. A systemic therapist might ask them to talk with each other about what happened, hoping to observe in their interaction what they were doing to keep the argument from getting settled. The focus would be on behavior and interaction. A psychoanalytic therapist would be more interested in helping the partners explore their individual emotional reactions. Why did they get so angry? What do they want from each other? What did they expect? Where do these feelings and expectations come from? Rather than trying to resolve the argument, the analytic therapist would interrupt to ask a series of questions about the fears and longings that lay underneath it.

The signal of intrapsychic conflict is affect. Instead of focusing on who did what to whom, analytic therapists key in on strong feeling and use it as a starting point for detailed inquiry into its roots. What were you feeling? When have you felt that way before? And before that? What do you remember? Thus, rather than stay on the horizontal plane of the couple's current behavior, the therapist looks for openings into the vertical dimension of their internal experience and its history. There is also a third line of inquiry that includes the therapist and transference and countertransference reactions.

Following Sullivan, most analytic therapists see themselves less as detached observers and more as participants in the interpersonal patterns of treatment. In describing his way of engaging patients as "participant observation," Sullivan (1940) anticipated what family therapists would later call "second-order cybernetics," according to which therapists are understood as participating in the family systems they work with.

To summarize, psychoanalytic couples therapists organize their explorations along four channels: (1) internal experience, (2) the history of that experience, (3) how the partner triggers that experience, and, finally, (4) how the context of the session and therapist's input might contribute to what's going on between the partners. Here's a brief example.

◆

Having made great strides in understanding over the course of their first few couples sessions, Andrew and Gwen were all the more upset by their inability to discuss, much less settle, an angry disagreement about buying a new car. It wasn't the car but how to pay for it that set them so infuriatingly at odds. Andrew wanted to take money out of savings for the downpayment, to keep the monthly payments low. This made Gwen furious. How could Andrew even consider cutting into their savings! Didn't he understand that their mutual fund paid twice as much interest as they'd have to pay on the car loan?

Unfortunately, they were both too bent on changing the other's mind to make any real effort to understand what was going on inside it. The therapist interrupted their arguing to ask each of them what they were feeling and what they were worried about. He wasn't primarily interested in settling the disagreement—although asking about the feelings underlying an altercation is often an effective opening to understanding and compromise; rather, he felt that the intensity of their reactions indicated that this issue touched key concerns.

Inquiry into the partners' inner experience revealed that Andrew was worried about the burden of monthly expenses. *"Don't you see,"* he implored, "if we don't take out enough to make a substantial downpayment, we'll have to worry every month about making the payments?"

Gwen was ready to dispute this, but the therapist cut her off. He was more interested in the history of Andrew's worry than in the couple's trying to convince each other of anything.

It turned out that Andrew had a lifelong fear of not having enough money. Having enough money turned out to mean, not a big house or a fancy car, but enough to spend on things that might be considered indulgent—nice clothes, going out to dinner, flowers, presents. Andrew connected his urge to reward himself with modest material luxuries to memories of growing up in a Spartan household. His parents weren't poor, but they were children of the Depression who thought that things like going out to dinner and buying new clothes except when absolutely necessary were frivolous and wasteful. At a deeper level, Andrew's memories of austerity were a screen for his never having gotten the attention and affection he craved from his rather reserved mother.[1] And so he'd learned to soothe himself with a new shirt or a fancy dinner at times when he was feeling a little down. One of Gwen's chief attractions was her giving and expressive nature. She was openly affectionate and almost always happy to indulge Andrew's wish to buy something for himself.

Gwen connected her anxiety to have a cushion against the unexpected to memories of her father as an unreliable breadwinner. Unlike Andrew's parents, hers spent freely. They went out to dinner three or four times a week and took expensive vacations, and everyone in the family wore nice clothes. But, although he was a free spender, Gwen remembered her father as lacking the discipline and foresight to invest wisely or to expand his business beyond its modest success. Although it had never been part of her conscious memories, it seemed that although her father lavished attention and affection on her, he never really took her seriously as a person.[2] He treated her, in the familiar phrase, like "Daddy's little girl," as adorable—and insubstantial—as a puppy or a kitten. That's why she was so attracted to what she saw as Andrew's serious and self-disciplined nature—and his high regard for her.

[1]In Kohut's terms, Andrew's mother provided an inadequate *mirroring selfobject* function.

[2]Gwen's father was, in Fairbairn's terms, an *exciting object.*

How did these two trigger such virulent reactions in each other? Not only did Gwen's anxious need to have money in the bank conflict with Andrew's need to have discretionary money to spend, but they each felt betrayed by the other. Part of Gwen's unconscious bargain with Andrew was that she could count on him to be a secure, steady pillar, and to build for the future. Part of his unconscious expectations of her were that she would gratify and indulge him. No wonder they were so reactive to each other on this issue.

And the therapist's role in all this? On reflection he realized that he'd been a little too anxious to smooth things over with this couple. Out of his own desire to see marital happiness he'd controlled the level of conflict in the sessions, intervening actively as a peacemaker. As a result, the couple's progress had come at a price. Deep longings and resentments had been pushed aside rather than explored and resolved. Perhaps, the therapist thought, he'd picked up the couple's fears of facing their own anger.

What use should a therapist make of such countertransferential reactions? Should he disclose his feelings? To say that countertransference may contain useful information isn't to say that it's oracular. Perhaps the most useful thing to do is look to countertransference for hypotheses that need confirming evidence from the patients' side of the experience. In this case the therapist acknowledged his sense that he'd been trying too hard to smooth things over, and he asked Gwen and Andrew whether they, too, were a little afraid to open up their anger.

◆

Like many descriptions of clinical work, this one may seem a little pat. How did we get so quickly from Andrew and Gwen arguing about buying a car to a hunger for mirroring selfobject experiences on his part and someone to idealize on hers? Part of the explanation lies in the inevitably condensed account. But it's also important to recognize that one of the things that enables psychoanalysts (or anyone else) to see beneath the surface of things is knowing where to look. Here, psychoanalytic therapists are particularly well equipped because they have a comprehensive theory of personality and behavior. Moreover, as some authors (Dare, 1979) have pointed out, psychoanalytic understanding is useful for developing a comprehensive picture of family dynamics even when treatment techniques are drawn from other approaches.

What distinguishes psychoanalytic from most other diagnostic formulations of families is that, as we discussed above, they focus on the individual family members' intrapsychic dynamics; in fact, the majority of psychoanalytic concepts are about individuals or dyads. But since psychoanalytic family therapists deal with larger relationship systems, they also must consider the family's interpersonal dynamics as well as the intrapsychic lives of its members.

The following is an abbreviated sketch of an initial psychoanalytic evaluation of a family.

◆

After two sessions with the family of Sally G., who was suffering from school phobia, the therapist made a preliminary formulation of the family's dynamics. In addition to the usual descriptions of the family members, the presenting problem, and their history, the formulation included assessments of the parents' object relations and the collusive, unconscious interaction of their marital relationship.

Mr. G. had been initially attracted to his wife as a libidinal object who would fulfill his sexual fantasies, including his voyeuristic propensities. Counterbalancing his sexual feelings was a tendency to idealize his wife. Thus he was deeply conflicted and intensely ambivalent in his sexual relations with her.

At another level, Mr. G. had unconscious expectations that she would be the same long-suffering, self-sacrificing kind of person that his mother was. Thus, he longed for motherly consolation from her. However, these dependent longings were threatening to his sense of masculinity, so he behaved outwardly as though he were tough, self-sufficient, and needed no one. That he had a dependent inner object inside himself was shown by his tender solicitude towards his wife and children when they were ill. But they had to be in a position of weakness and vulnerability to enable him to overcome his defenses enough for him to gratify his own infantile dependency needs vicariously.

Mrs. G. expected marriage to provide her with an ideal father, someone who would be loving, nurturing, and supportive. Given this unconscious expectation, the very sexuality that attracted men to her was also a threat to her wish to be treated like a little girl. Like her husband, she too was highly conflicted about sexual relations. Raised as an only child, she always expected to come first. She was even jealous of her husband's warmth toward Sally, and attempted to maintain distance between father and daughter by her own intense attachment to Sally.

At the level of her early self-object images, she was a jealous, greedy, demanding little girl. Her introjection of her mother provided her with a model of how to treat a father figure. Unfortunately, what worked for her mother with her father didn't work for her with her husband.

Thus, at an object-relations level, both spouses felt themselves to be deprived little children, each wanting to be taken care of without having to ask. When these magical wishes weren't granted, both of them seethed with angry resentment. Eventually they reacted to trivial provocations with the underlying rage, and horrible quarrels erupted.

When Sally witnessed her parents' violent altercations, she became terrified that her own hostile and murderous fantasies might come true. Although her parents hated their own internalized bad parent figures, they seemed to act them out with each other. Further enmeshing Sally in their conflict was the fact that the ego boundaries between herself and her mother were blurred—almost as though mother and daughter shared one joint personality.

Dynamically, Sally's staying home from school could be seen as a desperate attempt to protect her mother-herself from her father's attacks, and to defend both her parents against her own, projected, murderous fantasies.

◆

Nonanalytic clinicians tend to focus their evaluations on overt communications and interactions, as well as on conscious hopes and expectations. From a psychoanalytic perspective, such descriptions only scratch the surface. Unconscious forces constitute the core of family life. However, this doesn't mean that psychoanalytic clinicians deal only with the psychology of individual personality defects. Family dynamics are more than the additive sum of individual dynamics. Individuals may bring impaired object relations to family life, but it's the unconscious fit between family members that determines adjustment.

Applying object relations theory to family evaluation, Dicks (1967) proposed three levels on which to assess the marital relationship: (1) cultural values and norms—race, religion, education, and values; (2) central egos—personal norms, conscious judgments and expectations, habits, and tastes; and (3) unconscious forces that are repressed or split off, including drives and object-relations needs. If a couple is in harmony on any two of these three levels, Dicks believed they will stay together, even in the face of constant conflict. However, if they are incompatible on two or more levels, the marriage will probably end in divorce.

Dicks's analysis helps to explain why many couples seem to remain together despite constant fighting, and why other couples who seem content suddenly split up. Presumably the battling couples who cleave together fit each other's unconscious needs, and their object-images dovetail. In discussing one such couple, Dicks (1967) wrote,

> At the level of social value judgment, I would have no hesitation in rating the marriage of Case Ten as more living, deeper and "truer" than the conventional whited sepulchers in which no sleeping dog is permitted to raise his head, let alone bark. (p. 119)

Analysts don't postpone treatment until they've made an exhaustive study of their cases; on the contrary, they may not even arrive at a final formulation until the end of treatment.

However, although analytic clinicians may continue to elaborate and refine their understanding of dynamics over the course of treatment, effective therapy cannot proceed without some focused dynamic formulation. Beginning therapists—who lack theory as well as experience—sometimes proceed on the assumption that if they merely sit back and listen, understanding will emerge. This is rarely true in individual therapy and almost never true in family therapy. The therapist needs a hypothesis.

An excellent model for developing a psychodynamic focus is the work of Arnon Bentovim and Warren Kinston in Great Britain (Bentovim & Kinston, 1991), who offer a five-step strategy for formulating a focal hypothesis:

1. How does the family interact around the symptom, and how does the family interaction affect the symptom?
2. What is the function of the current symptom? (In the L. family they suspected that if the parents didn't draw together and exclude their son, the result would be severe conflict between the parents.)
3. What disaster is feared in the family that keeps them from facing their conflicts more squarely? (Why, for example, in the L. family is marital conflict avoided?)
4. How is the current situation linked to past trauma?
5. How would the therapist summarize the focal conflict in a short memorable statement? (The L. family is excluding the child so as to overcome a marital breakup, which occurred in the family of origin due to a competing parent–child relationship.)

After the preliminary psychodynamic assessment, the therapist must decide who to include in treatment. Psychoanalytic family therapists today work with every possible combination of family members. Perhaps most common, however, is treatment of married couples; most psychoanalytic clinicians will prefer to emphasize the adult nucleus of the family because it is consistent with their own verbal and intellectual level.

From an object relations point of view (Dicks, 1963), marriage is a transaction between hidden, internalized objects. These internal objects, which reflect the parenting and marital relationships in the spouses' original families, are brought into awareness by interpretation of the unconscious bases for the couple's interactions. Frequently, couples are found to have dominant *shared internal objects* (Dicks, 1967), based on unconscious assimilation of parent figures. Such couples don't relate to each other as real persons, but as angry or loving parents, to be tormented or idealized. (See Sander [1989] for a recent version of this view.)

Some aspects of internalized objects are conscious, readily expressed, and easily examined. These are based on direct identification with consciously perceived parental models, or overcompensation against negative images. A bullying husband may be overcompensating for feeling weak, like his father. His behavior seems to say, "I won't be pushed around the way my father was!" Such consciously held object images will emerge regardless of therapeutic technique; however, in order to get unconscious images to emerge, psychoanalytic clinicians rely on a nondirective exploratory style.

Among the metaphors used to describe psychoanalytic treatment, "depth" and "uncovering" feature prominently. All therapies aim to uncover something. Narrative therapists begin with empathic openness to their clients' experience before switching to leading questions designed not to understand but to shift points of view. Even behaviorists make nondirective inquiries to uncover unnoticed contingencies of reinforcement before switching to a directive stance. What sets analytic therapy apart is that the process of discovery is protracted and directed not only at clients' conscious thoughts and feelings, but also at their fantasies and dreams.

◆

David Scharff (1992) related the following example of the use of dreams in couples treatment. Lila and Clive played the all-too-familiar complementary roles whereby the more she sought closeness, the more he retreated. Unlike a purely systemic therapist, however, Scharff was interested not merely in the synchronicity of their behavior but in the inner experience underlying it. Because Clive had little awareness of his internal life and few memories of his early years, the therapist was frustrated in his attempts to understand what pushed Clive into retreat. The following dream proved instructive.

Clive dreamed about a baby with a wound on its buttocks. A woman, he thought to be the sister, was supposed to take care of the baby, but because she wasn't doing much, Clive stepped in and took the baby from her. When asked for his thoughts—"Does anything come to mind in connection with the dream?"—Clive's association was to the prospect of having children and his concern that he might have to take all the responsibility if Lila didn't do enough. After acknowledging this worry, Dr. Scharff pointed out that the dream also suggested a fear of something being terribly wrong, so bad that Clive wouldn't be able to fix it. This triggered a recent memory of a time when Lila was upset and crying. Clive held her and tried to comfort her, but when her crying didn't subside, he got upset and went into the other room. It seemed that the dream could also symbolize Clive's fear of taking care of his wife. When she's upset, he may overestimate the depth of her hurt and, since he feels he's the only one who can take care of her, the responsibility feels overwhelming.

Now Lila spoke up, saying that when she gets upset and he tries to comfort her, *she* ends up in the position of having to reassure him that she's okay, that what he's doing *is* enough. Thus, even when she's in need of comfort, she has to take care of him, to prevent him from feeling overwhelmed. (As Lila's response demonstrates, dreams in couples therapy not only suggest how the dreamer experiences self and object, but also the way dreams are told and related to in the session provides additional information about the entwined identities of the partners.)

When asked if she had any other thoughts about Clive's dream, Lila hesitated, then said she wondered if Clive thinks of her as the baby. This led to the interpretation that in addition to Clive's thinking of Lila in some ways as a baby, he also thought of himself as a baby, deeply wounded by childhood hurts. This insight—that Clive's lifelong fear of female engulfment was superimposed on top of his own sense of infantile neediness and childhood losses—turned out to be pivotal. Lila began to see Clive's withdrawing less as a rejection of her than as a sign of his own vulnerability. She therefore felt less threatened by abandonment, which she now saw more as her own deep worry than any real possibility. Clive, meanwhile, began to understand his anxiety in the face of his wife's emotional needs not so much as her doing, but as something in him, his own vulnerability. As a result of this understanding he felt less urgency to withdraw from moments of intimacy and emotion.

◆

Psychoanalytic family therapy is certainly more active than classical psychoanalysis; nevertheless, it remains a nondirective uncovering technique. The discipline involved in learning to interfere minimally and to scrutinize one's responses to eliminate unessential or leading interventions is a critical part of psychoanalytic technique, with individuals or with families. Interpretations should neither reassure nor direct people; they should facilitate the emergence of new material, forgotten or repressed, and mobilize feelings previously avoided (Dicks, 1967).

In addition to limiting interpretations to specific material revealed by their patients, psychoanalytic therapists also limit the number of interpretations they make. Two or three per session is typical. Most of the rest of the activity is devoted to eliciting material without becoming overly directive. Sessions typically begin with the therapist inviting family members to discuss current experiences, thoughts, and feelings. In subsequent meetings, the therapist might begin either by saying nothing or perhaps, "Where would you like to begin today?" The therapist then leans back and lets the family talk, with minimal direction or interference with the spontaneous flow of their communication. Questions are limited to requests for amplification and clarification. "Could you tell me more about that?" "Have the two of you discussed how you feel about this?"

When the initial associations and spontaneous interactions dry up, the therapist probes gently, eliciting history, people's thoughts and feelings, and their ideas about family members' perspectives. "What does your father think about your problems? How would he explain them?" This technique underscores the analytic therapist's interest in assumptions and projections.

Although we've repeatedly emphasized the nondirective nature of psychoanalytic technique, it's far from a passive approach. While family members are speaking about whatever is on their minds, the therapist is actively analyzing what is being said for derivatives of drives, defenses, ego states, and manifestations of transference. Psychoanalytic therapists, more than most others, order the raw data of family dialogues by fitting them to their theory. The bare facts are always ambiguous; psychoanalytic theory organizes them and makes them meaningful.

In addition to fitting the raw data to theory, the psychoanalytic therapist also directs it by pursuing the past. Particular interest is paid to childhood memories and associations to interactions with parents. The following vignette shows how transitions are made from the present to the past.

◆

Among their major disappointments in each other, Mr. and Mrs. S. both complained bitterly that the other one "doesn't take care of me when I'm sick, or listen to my complaints at the end of the day." Not only did they share the perception of the other one's lack of "mothering," they both steadfastly maintained that *they* were very supportive and understanding. Mrs. S.'s complaint was typical: "Yesterday was an absolute nightmare. The baby was sick and fussy, and I had a miserable cold. Everything was twice as hard for me and I had twice as much to do. All day long I was looking forward to John's coming home. But when he finally did, he didn't seem to care about how awful I felt. He only listened to me for a minute before starting to tell me some dumb story about his office." Mr. S. responded by telling a similar account, but with the roles reversed.

At this point the therapist intervened to ask both spouses to describe their relationships with their mothers. What emerged were two very different but revealing histories.

Mr. S.'s mother was a taciturn woman, for whom self-reliance, personal sacrifice, and unremitting struggle were paramount virtues. Though she loved her children, she withheld warmth, affection, and nurturance lest they become "spoiled and soft." Nevertheless, Mr. S. craved his mother's attention and constantly sought it. Naturally, he was often rebuffed. A particularly painful memory was of a time he came home in tears after getting beaten by a bully in the schoolyard. Instead of the loving comfort he hoped for, his mother scolded him for "acting like a baby." Over the years he learned to protect himself from these rebuffs by developing a rigid facade of independence and strength.

With the second significant woman in his life, his wife, Mr. S. maintained his rigid defensiveness. He never talked about his problems, but since he continued to yearn for compassionate understanding, he resented his wife bitterly for not drawing him out. His own failure to risk rejection by asking for support served as a self-fulfilling prophecy, confirming his expectation, "She doesn't care about me."

Mrs. S.'s background was quite different from her husband's. Her parents were indulgent and demonstrative. They doted on their only child, communicating their love by expressing constant, anxious concern for her well-being. When she was a little girl, the slightest bump or bruise was the occasion for lavish expressions of solicitous concern. She came to marriage used to talking about herself and her problems. At first Mr. S. was enchanted. *Here is someone who really cares about feelings,* he thought. But when he discovered that she didn't ask him to talk about his own concerns, he became resentful and progressively less sympathetic. This convinced her, *He doesn't care about me.*

◆

After the historical roots of current family conflicts have been uncovered, interpretations are made about how family members continue to reenact past, and often distorted, images from childhood. The data for such interpretations come from transference reactions to the therapist or to other family members, as well as from actual childhood memories. Even more so than in individual therapy, psychoanalytic therapists who work with families deal less with recollections of the past than with reenactments of its influence, manifest as transference. For this reason it's considered essential to establish a milieu in which patients feel safe enough to relive unresolved conflicts and reactivate early relationship images.

The following case demonstrates how a therapist's permissive acceptance enables family members to gradually shed their outer defenses and reveal basic conflicts and object images, which provide the material for mutative interpretations.

◆

The H.'s were a wealthy, highly educated family who were worried about their oldest child's listlessness, irritability, and poor performance in school. Despite the fact that the boy showed all the signs of a depressive episode, the therapist insisted on seeing the whole family.

In the first few sessions, the family was polite and dignified, with each one playing a recognizable role. Alex, the identified patient, described his discouragement and lack of interest in school, while his parents expressed their concern, alternately supportively and critically. Alex's younger sister Susan, a lively and robust child, showed little concern for her brother, and generally spoke more about her life outside the family.

At first the family was so composed and collected that the therapist began to experience reality as they did: namely, that nothing was wrong, except for Alex. The parents voiced a few disagreements about how to respond to Alex but quickly submerged them. Gradually, however, as they felt safer in therapy—safer than they did alone together at home—Mr. and Mrs. H. began to argue more and more openly. During this process the therapist made no interpretations, but concentrated her efforts on accepting the couple's arguing, while gently blocking their efforts to detour their conflict. Because they felt protected by the therapist, the spouses allowed the full fury of their feelings to be expressed, and their arguments became increasingly vituperative.

By uncovering the hidden conflict in the marriage, and blocking the scapegoating of the identified patient, the therapist was following the same course that most nonanalytic therapists would pursue. At this point, she didn't simply stay with the couple's conflict, but instead began to explore their separate childhood histories. In short, having uncovered their conflict, she sought to trace its genetic sources.

What emerged from Mr. H.'s portrait of his childhood was a picture of a boy who had learned to appease his hypercritical mother by not openly challenging her. Moreover, since he didn't expect much positive reaction from her, he generally avoided her company as much as possible.

For her part, Mrs. H. described her close relationship with a dominant mother and a lifelong disdain for her father, a man who was very successful professionally, but played only a marginal role in her upbringing.

Only after extensive exploration of these early object relations did the therapist begin to interpret the couple's conflictual behavior. Mr. H., she pointed out, believed that he had to mollify his wife (like his mother), but didn't expect any understanding or support from her, so he withdrew from her and lavished affection on his children. In their early married years, Mrs. H. struck back in self-defense; she demanded that he spend more time with her, talk more, be more attentive. Eventually, however, she accepted his withdrawal (as she had seen her mother do with her father), and redirected her angry disappointment to her son. In short, these two apparently sophisticated adults were behaving, unconsciously, like children; he like a frightened child hiding from a harsh, critical mother, and she like a spoiled daughter hopelessly enraged at the lack of a relationship with her husband.

◆

In this case the therapist analyzed and interpreted the unconscious object representations that played a large part in the family's conflict. In addition, her acceptance of the couple's loud arguments provided them with a tolerant superego figure to be incorporated in the holding environment. Psychoanalytic family therapists are aware that their influence isn't confined to rational analysis, but also includes a kind of reparenting. Thus therapists may act in a more controlling or permissive fashion depending on their assessment of the particular needs of the family.

One psychoanalytic family therapist who was acutely aware of his personal influence on families was Nathan Ackerman. His recommendations on technique (Ackerman, 1966) were designed to penetrate family defenses in order to surface hidden conflicts over sex and aggression. To begin with, he advocated a deep personal commitment and involvement with families. His own style was intimate and provocative. Unlike the traditionally reserved and aloof analyst, Ackerman related to families in a very personal manner. In this regard he wrote (1961):

> It is very important at the outset to establish a meaningful emotional contact with all members of the family, to create a climate in which one really touches them and they feel they touch back. (p. 242)

After making contact, Ackerman encouraged honest expression of feeling by being honest himself. His spontaneous self-disclosure of his own thoughts and feelings made it hard for family members to resist doing likewise.

Ackerman certainly made full use of his charisma, but did more than simply "be himself" and "let it all hang out" in family sessions. He made conscious and deliberate use of confrontive techniques to ease family secrets and conflicts from behind their defensive facades. His own memorable phrase to describe this was "tickling the defenses."

Naturally, psychoanalytic family therapists emphasize that much of what is hidden in family dialogues is not consciously withheld, but rather repressed into unconsciousness. The approach to this material is guarded by resistance often manifest in the form of transference. In fact, it's fair to say that the goal of any form of psychoanalytic psychotherapy is to analyze resistance and to work through the past in the transferences of the present.

In families, resistance is collusive and more often manifest in overt behavior than it is in private therapy. Frank discussions of problems within the family are often painful, and most people go to great lengths to avoid them. Some of the common forms of resistance include seeking individual therapy or separate sessions to avoid facing family problems; persistently talking to the therapist instead of to other family members; avoiding conflictual topics; scapegoating; becoming depressed to avoid the danger of angry confrontations; and steadfastly refusing to consider one's own role in problematic interactions.

Most psychoanalytic family therapists deal with resistance by interpreting it early in its appearance. The family technique for interpreting resistance is different from that used in individual therapy. In individual therapy the aim is primarily to foster insight into the nature and meaning of resistance; therefore, resistances are generally not interpreted until they become obvious to the patient. Moreover, the most effective interpretations are elicited from the patient, rather than given by the therapist. For example, an individual therapist might wait for three or four recurrences before discussing a patient's lateness. Confronting lateness on its first occurrence is liable to make a patient defensive and thus impede exploration. After the lateness (or other form of resistance) has become a pattern, the therapist will ask the patient to consider its meaning.

Family therapists interpret resistance more directly and sooner. The reason for this is that resistance in family therapy is more likely to take the form of acting-out, so that family therapists have to meet resistance with confrontation very early on. The following vignette illustrates the interpretation of resistance.

◆

Mr. and Mrs. Z. had endured ten years of an unrewarding marriage, with an unhappy sexual relationship, in order to preserve the fragile security that being married offered them. Mrs. Z.'s totally unexpected and uncharacteristic affair forced the couple to acknowledge the problems in their marriage, and so they consulted a family therapist.

Although they could no longer deny the existence of conflict, both spouses exhibited major resistance to confronting their problems openly. Their resistance represented personal reluctance to acknowledge certain of their feelings, and a joint collusion to avoid frank discussions of their relational problems.

In the first session, both partners said that married life had been "more or less okay"; that Mrs. Z. had some kind of "midlife crisis"; and that it was she who needed therapy. This request for individual therapy was seen as a resistance to avoid the painful examination of the marriage, and the therapist said so. "It seems, Mr. Z., that you'd rather blame your wife than consider how the two of you may both be contributing to your difficulties. And you, Mrs. Z., seem to prefer accepting all the guilt in order to avoid confronting your husband with your dissatisfaction and anger."

Accepting the therapist's interpretation and agreeing to examine their marriage together deprived the couple of one form of resistance, as though an escape hatch had been closed to two reluctant combatants. In the next few sessions both spouses attacked each other vituperatively, but they talked only about her affair and his reactions rather than about problems in their relationship. These arguments weren't productive because whenever Mr. Z. felt anxious he attacked his wife, and whenever she felt angry she became depressed and guilty.

Sensing that their fighting was unproductive, the therapist said, "It's clear that you've put each other through a lot of unhappiness and you're both quite bitter. But unless you get down to talking about specific problems in your marriage, there's little chance that you'll get anywhere."

Thus focused, Mrs. Z. timidly ventured that she'd never enjoyed sex with her husband, and wished that he would take more time with foreplay. He snapped back, "Okay, so sex wasn't so great, is that any reason to throw away ten years of marriage and start whoring around!" At this, Mrs. Z. buried her face in her hands and sobbed uncontrollably. After she regained her composure, the therapist intervened, again confronting the couple with their resistance: "It seems, Mr. Z., that when you get upset, you attack. What makes you so anxious about discussing sex?" Following this the couple was able to talk about their feelings about sex in their marriage until near the end of the session. At this point, Mr. Z. again lashed out at his wife calling her a whore and a bitch.

Mrs. Z. began the following session by saying that she'd been depressed and upset, crying off and on all week. "I feel so guilty," she sobbed. "You *should* feel guilty!" retorted her husband. Once again, the therapist intervened. "You use your wife's affair as a club. Are you still afraid to discuss specific problems in the marriage? And you, Mrs. Z., cover your anger with depression. What is it that you're angry about? What was missing in the marriage? What did you want?"

This pattern continued for several more sessions. The spouses who had avoided discussing or even thinking about their problems for ten years used a variety of resistances to veer away from them in therapy. The therapist persisted in pointing out their resistance and urging them to talk about specific complaints.

◆

Psychoanalytic family therapists endeavor to foster insight and understanding; they also urge families to consider what they're going to do about the problems they discuss. This effort—part of the process of working through—is more prominent in family therapy than in individual therapy. Nagy, for example, considers that family members must not only be made aware of their motivations, but also held accountable for their behavior. In contextual therapy, Nagy (1987) points out that the therapist must help people face the intrinsically destructive expectations involved in invisible loyalties, and then help them find more positive ways of making loyalty payments in the family ledger. What this boils down to is developing a balance of fairness among various family members.

Ackerman too stressed an active working through of insights by encouraging families to constructively express the aggressive and libidinal impulses uncovered in therapy. In order to alleviate symptoms, impulses must become conscious; but an emotional experience must be associated with increased self-awareness in order for lives to change. To modify thinking and feeling is the essential task of psychoanalytic therapy, but family therapists are also concerned with supervising and analyzing changes in behavior.

Evaluating Therapy Theory and Results

Too many family therapists neglect psychology in general and psychoanalytic theory in specific. Regardless of what other approaches a therapist uses, the writings of psychoanalytically informed clinicians are a rich resource.

Having said this, we also wish to make a cautionary point. Doctrinaire psychoanalytic family therapies are powerful in the hands of trained psychoanalysts. However, many family therapists who get discouraged with the usual contentious family dialogues, gravitate to psychoanalytic methods as a way to break through the defensive wrangling that some families can't seem to get past. Interrupting a family's arguments to explore the feelings of individual family members is an excellent way to block arguments. But if therapists make themselves overly central (by directing all conversation through themselves) and if they overemphasize individuals and neglect family interactions, then the power of family therapy—addressing relationship problems directly at their source—may be lost. Interrupting defensive sparring to get to the authentic feelings and hopes and fears that lie beneath the usual arguments is all to the good. But unless these interrogatories are followed by extensive and free-flowing interchanges among family members themselves, these explorations may only produce the illusion of change as long as the therapist is present to act as detective and referee.

Psychoanalytic therapists have generally been opposed to attempts to evaluate their work using empirical standards. Since symptom reduction isn't the goal, it can't serve as the measure of success. And since the presence or absence of unconscious conflict isn't apparent to family members or outside observers, whether or not an analysis can be considered successful has to depend on subjective clinical judgment. Psychoanalytic clinicians, of course, consider that the therapist's observations are entirely valid as a means of evaluating theory and treatment. The following quotation from the Blancks (1972) illustrates this point. Speaking of Margaret Mahler's ideas, they wrote,

> Clinicians who employ her theories technically question neither the methodology nor the findings, for they can confirm them clinically, a form of validation that meets as closely as possible the experimentalist's insistence upon replication as criterion of the scientific method. (p. 675)

Another example of this point of view can be found in the writing of Robert Langs. "The ultimate test of a therapist's formulation," says Langs (1982), "lies in the use of the therapist's impressions as a basis for intervention" (p 186). What then determines the validity and effectiveness of these interventions? Langs doesn't hesitate; the patient's reactions, conscious and unconscious, constitute the ultimate litmus test. "True validation involves responses from the patient in both the cognitive and interpersonal spheres."

Is the ultimate test of therapy then the patient's reactions? Yes and no. First, patients' reactions are open to various interpretations—especially since validation is sought not only in direct manifest responses but also in unconsciously encoded derivatives. Moreover, this point of view doesn't take into account the changes in patients' lives that occur outside the consulting room. Occasionally therapists report on the outcome of psychoanalytic family therapy, but mostly as an uncontrolled case study. One such unsubstantiated report is Dicks's (1967) survey of the outcome of psychoanalytic couples therapy at the Tavistock Clinic, in which he rated as having been successfully treated 72.8 percent of a random sample of cases.

Summary

Psychoanalytically trained clinicians were among the first to practice family therapy, but when they began treating families most of them traded in their ideas about depth psychology for those of systems theory. Since the mid 1980s, there's been a resurgence of interest in psychodynamics among family therapists, an interest dominated by object relations theory and self psychology. In this chapter we've sketched the main points of these theories and shown how they're relevant to a psychoanalytic family therapy, which integrates depth psychology and systems theory. A few practitioners (e.g., Kirschner & Kirschner, 1986; Nichols, 1987; Slipp, 1984) have combined elements of both; some have developed more frankly psychoanalytic approaches (notably Scharff & Scharff, 1987; Sander, 1989); none has achieved a true synthesis.

References

Ackerman, N. W. 1958. *The psychodynamics of family life.* New York: Basic Books.

Ackerman, N. W. 1961. The emergence of family psychotherapy on the present scene. In *Contem-*

porary psychotherapies, M. I. Stein, ed. Glencoe, IL: The Free Press.

Ackerman, N. W. 1966. *Treating the troubled family.* New York: Basic Books.

Bank, S., and Kahn, M. D. 1982. *The sibling bond.* New York: Basic Books.

Barnhill, L. R., and Longo, D. 1978. Fixation and regression in the family life cycle. *Family Process. 17*:469–478.

Bentovim, A., and Kinston, W. 1991. Focal family therapy. In *Handbook of family therapy.* vol. II, A. S. Gurman and D. P. Kniskern, eds. New York: Brunner/Mazel.

Blanck, G., and Blanck, R. 1972. Toward a psychoanalytic developmental psychology. *Journal of the American Psychoanalytic Association. 20*:668–710.

Blanck, R. 1967. Marriage as a phase of personality development. *Social Casework. 48*:154–160.

Blum, H. P. 1987. Shared fantasy and reciprocal identification: General considerations and gender disorder. In *Unconscious fantasy: Myth and reality*, H. P. Blum et al., eds. New York: International Universities Press.

Boszormenyi-Nagy I. 1967. Relational modes and meaning. In *Family therapy and disturbed families*, G. H. Zuk and I. Boszormenyi-Nagy, eds. Palo Alto: Science and Behavior Books.

Boszormenyi-Nagy, I. 1972. Loyalty implications of the transference model in psychotherapy. *Archives of General Psychiatry. 27*:374–380.

Boszormenyi-Nagy, I. 1987. *Foundations of contextual therapy.* New York: Brunner/Mazel.

Boszormenyi-Nagy, I., and Framo, J., eds. 1965. *Intensive family therapy: Theoretical and practical aspects.* New York: Harper & Row.

Boszormenyi-Nagy, I., and Spark, G. 1973. *Invisible loyalties: Reciprocity in intergenerational family therapy.* New York: Harper & Row.

Boszormenyi-Nagy, I., and Ulrich, D. N. 1981. Contextual family therapy. In *Handbook of family therapy*, A. S. Gurman and D. P. Kniskern, eds. New York: Brunner/Mazel.

Boszormenyi-Nagy, I. Grunebaum, J., and Ulrich, D. 1991. Contextual therapy. In *Handbook of family therapy.* vol. II, A. S. Gurman and D. P. Kniskern, eds. New York: Brunner/Mazel.

Bowen, M. 1965. Family psychotherapy with schizophrenia in the hospital and in private practice. In *Intensive family therapy*, I. Boszormenyi-Nagy and J. L. Framo, eds. New York: Harper & Row.

Bowlby, J. 1949. The study and reduction of group tension in the family. *Human Relations. 2*: 123–128.

Bowlby, J. 1969. *Attachment and loss.* vol. 1: *Attachment.* New York: Basic Books.

Bruch, H. 1978. *The golden cage.* Cambridge, MA: Harvard University Press.

Burlingham, D. T. 1951. Present trends in handling the mother-child relationship during the therapeutic process. *Psychoanalytic study of the child.* New York: International Universities Press.

Dare, C. 1979. Psychoanalysis and systems in family therapy. *Journal of Family Therapy. 1*:137–151.

Dicks, H. V. 1963. Object relations theory and marital studies. *British Journal of Medical Psychology. 36*:125–129.

Dicks, H. V. 1967. *Marital tensions.* New York: Basic Books.

Dostoyevsky, F. 1958. *The Brothers Karamazov.* New York: Penguin Books.

Erikson, E. H. 1956. The problem of ego identity. *Journal of the American Psychoanalytic Association. 4*:56–121.

Erikson, E. H. 1959. Identity and the life cycle. *Psychological Issues. 1*:1–171.

Fairbairn, W. D. 1952. *An object-relations theory of the personality.* New York: Basic Books.

Fenichel, O. 1945. *The psychoanalytic theory of neurosis.* New York: Norton.

Ferreira, A. 1963. Family myths and homeostasis. *Archives of General Psychiatry. 9*:457–463.

Flugel, J. 1921. *The psychoanalytic study of the family.* London: Hogarth Press.

Framo, J. L. 1970. Symptoms from a family transactional viewpoint. In *Family therapy in transition*, N. W. Ackerman, ed. Boston: Little, Brown & Co.

Freud, S. 1905. Fragment of an analysis of a case of hysteria. *Collected papers.* New York: Basic Books, 1959.

Freud, S. 1909. Analysis of a phobia in a five-year-old boy. *Collected papers*, vol. III. New York: Basic Books, 1959.

Freud, S. 1921. Group psychology and the analysis of the ego. *Standard edition, 17*:1–22. London: Hogarth Press, 1955.

Freud, S. 1923. The ego and the id. *Standard edition. 19*:13–66. London: Hogarth Press, 1961.

Friedman, L. 1980. Integrating psychoanalytic object relations understanding with family systems interventions in couples therapy. In *Family therapy: Combining psychodynamic and family systems approaches,* J. Pearce and L. Friedman, eds. New York: Grune & Stratton.

Giovacchini, P. 1958. Mutual adaptation in various object relations. *International Journal of Psychoanalysis. 39*:547–554.

Giovacchini, P. 1961. Resistance and external object relations. *International Journal of Psychoanalysis. 42*:246–254.

Greenson, R. R. 1967. *The theory and technique of psychoanalysis.* New York: International Universities Press.

Guntrip, H. 1961. *Personality structure and human interaction.* London: Hogarth Press.

Guntrip, H. 1969. *Schizoid phenomena, object relations theory and the self.* New York: International Universities Press.

Guntrip, H. 1971. *Psychoanalytic theory, therapy, and the self.* New York: Basic Books.

Jackson, D. D. 1967. The individual and the larger context. *Family Process. 6*:139–147.

Jacobson, E. 1954. *The self and the object world.* New York: International Universities Press.

Johnson, A., and Szurek, S. 1952. The genesis of antisocial acting out in children and adults. *Psychoanalytic Quarterly. 21*:323–343.

Kahn, M. D., and Lewis, K. G., eds. 1988. *Siblings in therapy: Life span and clinical issues.* New York: Norton.

Katz, B. 1981. Separation-individuation and marital therapy. *Psychotherapy: Theory, Research and Practice. 18*:195–203.

Kernberg, O. F. 1966. Structural derivatives of object relationships. *International Journal of Psychoanalysis. 47*:236–253.

Kernberg, O. F. 1975. Countertransference. In *Borderline conditions and pathological narcissism,* O. F. Kernberg, ed. New York: Jason Aronson.

Kernberg, O. F. 1976. *Object-relations theory and clinical psychoanalysis.* New York: Jason Aronson.

Kirschner, D., and Kirschner, S. 1986. *Comprehensive family therapy: An integration of systemic and psychodynamic treatment models.* New York: Brunner/Mazel.

Klein, M. 1946. Notes on some schizoid mechanisms. *International Journal of Psycho-Analysis. 27*: 99–110.

Kohut, H. 1971. *The analysis of the self.* New York: International Universities Press.

Kohut, H. 1977. *The restoration of the self.* New York: International Universities Press.

Langs, R. 1982. *Psychotherapy: A basic text.* New York: Jason Aronson.

Levinson, D. J. 1978. *The seasons of a man's life.* New York: Ballantine Books.

Lidz, T., Cornelison, A., Fleck, S. 1965. *Schizophrenia and the family.* New York: International Universities Press.

Mahler, M. S. 1952. On child psychosis and schizophrenia: Autistic and symbiotic infantile psychoses. *Psychoanalytic Study of the Child,* vol. 7.

Mahler, M., Pine, F., and Bergman, A. 1975. *The psychological birth of the human infant.* New York: Basic Books.

Martin, P. A., and Bird, H. W. 1953. An approach to the psychotherapy of marriage partners. *Psychiatry. 16*:123–127.

Masterson, J. F. 1977. Primary anorexia nervosa in the borderline adolescent and object-relations view. In *Borderline personality disorders: The concept, the syndrome, the patient,* P. Hartocollis, ed. New York: International Universities Press.

Meissner, W. W. 1978. The conceptualization of marriage and family dynamics from a psychoanalytic perspective. In *Marriage and marital therapy,* T. J. Paolino and B. S. McCrady, eds. New York: Brunner/Mazel.

Minuchin, S. 1974. *Families and family therapy.* Cambridge, MA: Harvard University Press.

Minuchin, S. 1989. Personal communication. Quoted from *Institutionalizing madness,* J. Elizur and S. Minuchin, eds. New York: Basic Books.

Mittlemann, B. 1948. The counterpart analysis of married couples. *Psychoanalytic Quarterly. 17*: 182–197.

Nadelson, C. C. 1978. Marital therapy from a psychoanalytic perspective. In *Marriage and marital therapy,* T. J. Paolino and B. S. McCrady, eds. New York: Brunner/Mazel.

Nichols, M. P. 1986. *Turning forty in the eighties.* New York: Norton.

Nichols, M. P. 1987. *The self in the system.* New York: Brunner/Mazel.

Oberndorf, C. P. 1938. Psychoanalysis of married couples. *Psychoanalytic Review. 25*:453–475.

Ryckoff, I., Day, J., and Wynne, L. 1959. Maintenance of stereotyped roles in the families of schizophrenics. *AMA Archives of Psychiatry. 1*:93–98.

Sager, C. J. 1981. Couples therapy and marriage contracts. In *Handbook of family therapy*, A. S. Gurman and D. P. Kniskern, eds. New York: Brunner/Mazel.

Sander, F. M. 1979. *Individual and family therapy: Toward an integration.* New York: Jason Aronson.

Sander, F. M. 1989. Marital conflict and psychoanalytic therapy in the middle years. In *The middle years: New psychoanalytic perspectives*, J. Oldham and R. Liebert, eds. New Haven: Yale University Press.

Scharff, D. 1992. *Refining the object and reclaiming the self.* New York: Jason Aronson.

Scharff, D., and Scharff, J. 1987. *Object relations family therapy.* New York: Jason Aronson.

Scharff, J., ed. 1989. *The foundations of object relations family therapy.* New York: Jason Aronson.

Segal, H. 1964. *Introduction to the work of Melanie Klein.* New York: Basic Books.

Shapiro, R. L. 1968. Action and family interaction in adolescence. In *Modern psychoanalysis*, J. Marmor, ed. New York: Basic Books.

Shapiro, R. L. 1979. Family dynamics and object relations theory. In *Adolescent psychiatry*, S. C. Feinstein and P. L. Giovacchini, eds. Chicago: University of Chicago Press.

Sifneos, P. E. 1972. *Short-term psychotherapy and emotional crisis.* Cambridge, MA: Harvard University Press.

Skynner, A. C. R. 1976. *Systems of family and marital psychotherapy.* New York: Brunner/Mazel.

Skynner, A. C. R. 1981. An open-systems, group analytic approach to family therapy. In *Handbook of family therapy*, A. S. Gurman and D. P. Kniskern, eds. New York: Brunner/Mazel.

Slipp, S. 1984. *Object relations: A dynamic bridge between individual and family treatment.* New York: Jason Aronson.

Slipp, S. 1988. *Technique and practice of object relations family therapy.* New York: Jason Aronson.

Spitz, R., and Wolf, K. 1946. Anaclitic depression: An inquiry into the genesis of psychiatric conditions early in childhood. *Psychoanalytic Study of the Child.* 2:313–342.

Stein, M. 1956. The marriage bond. *Psychoanalytic Quarterly.* 25:238–259.

Stern, D. N. 1985. *The interpersonal world of the infant.* New York: Basic Books.

Stierlin, H. 1977. *Psychoanalysis and family therapy.* New York: Jason Aronson.

Sullivan, H. S. 1940. *Conceptions of modern psychiatry.* New York: Norton.

Sullivan, H. S. 1953. *The interpersonal theory of psychiatry.* New York: Norton.

Szasz, T. S. 1961. *The myth of mental illness.* New York: Hoeber-Harper.

Umana, R. F., Gross, S. J., and McConville, M. T. 1980. *Crisis in the family: Three approaches.* New York: Gardner Press.

Vogel, E. F., and Bell, N. W. 1960. The emotionally disturbed as the family scapegoat. In *The family*, N. W. Bell and E. F. Vogel, eds. Glencoe, IL: Free Press.

Winnicott, D. W. 1965a. *The maturational process and the facilitating environment.* New York: International Universities Press.

Winnicott, D. W. 1965b. *The maturational process and the facilitating environment: Studies in the theory of emotional development.* New York: International Universities Press.

Wynne, L. C. 1965. Some indications and contradictions for exploratory family therapy. In *Intensive family therapy*, I. Boszormenyi-Nagy and J. L. Framo, eds. New York: Harper & Row.

Wynne, L. C. 1971. Some guidelines for exploratory family therapy. In *Changing families*, J. Haley, ed. New York: Grune & Stratton.

Wynne, L., Ryckoff, I., Day, J., and Hirsch, S. 1958. Pseudomutuality in the family relations of schizophrenics. *Psychiatry.* 21:205–220.

Zinner, J. 1976. The implications of projective identification for marital interaction. In *Contemporary marriage: Structure, dynamics, and therapy*, H. Grunebaum and J. Christ, eds. Boston: Little, Brown & Co.

Zinner, J., and Shapiro, R. 1976. Projective identification as a mode of perception and behavior in families of adolescents. *International Journal of Psychoanalysis.* 53:523–530.

8

Structural Family Therapy

In the 1970s structural family therapy emerged as perhaps the most influential model in the field. This predominance came about, not only because of the effectiveness of the approach, but also because of the stunning virtuosity of its primary exponent, Salvador Minuchin. Known initially as a clinician rather than a theoretician, Minuchin first established his reputation in dramatic and compelling teaching demonstrations; but he also described families as having an underlying organization in terms that provided clear guidelines for diagnosis and treatment.

One of the reasons family therapy is so difficult is that families often appear as collections of individuals who affect each other in powerful but unpredictable ways. Structural family therapy offers a clear framework that brings order and meaning to those transactions. The consistent, repetitive, organized, and predictable patterns of family behavior are what allow us to consider that they have a structure, although, of course, only in a functional sense. The emotional boundaries and coalitions that make up family structure are abstractions; nevertheless, using the concept of family structure enables therapists to intervene in a systematic and organized fashion.

Salvador Minuchin began seeing families of institutionalized children in the late 1950s. Unlike other family therapists, he didn't have to make the transition from sitting in an office, listening and talking, to doing family therapy; as a child psychiatrist working with delinquents, he always had to use action and pressure. And he had to understand people in context, because even the hard-core toughs he worked with were pushed and pulled by pressures of the gang and the family. Moreover, given where he chose to start his career, it should come as no surprise that Minuchin has always been passionately concerned with social issues.

When he first burst onto the scene, Minuchin's immediate galvanizing impact was as an incomparable master of technique. But perhaps his most lasting impact will prove to be the development of a theory of family structure and a set of guidelines to organize therapeutic techniques: Families who come for treatment are seen as stuck for lack of alternatives; therapy is designed to unfreeze them from rigid habits, creating the opportunity for new structures to emerge. This approach was so successful that it captivated the field in the 1970s, and Minuchin helped build the Philadelphia Child Guidance Clinic into a world-famous complex, where thousands of family therapists have been trained in structural family therapy.

Sketches of Leading Figures

Minuchin was born and raised in Argentina. He served as a physician in the Israeli army, then came to the United States, where he trained in child psychiatry with Nathan Ackerman at the Jewish Board of Guardians in New York. After completing his studies Minuchin returned to Israel in 1952 to work with displaced children—and to become absolutely committed to the importance of families. He moved back to the United States in 1954 to begin psychoanalytic training at the William Alanson White Institute, where he was imbued with the interpersonal psychiatry of Harry Stack Sullivan. After leaving the White Institute, Minuchin took a job at the Wiltwyck School for delinquent boys, where he suggested to his colleagues that they start seeing families. Other family therapists during this period, such as Nathan Ackerman and Don Jackson, were working with middle-class families; their approaches hardly seemed suitable to multiproblem, poor families with children at Wiltwyck. Therefore Minuchin had to develop new concepts and techniques applicable to these families, one of which was of the idea of *enactment*—that is, bringing problematic sequences into the treatment room by having families act them out so that the therapist could observe and change them. Most of Minuchin's techniques were concrete and action-oriented, qualities that have continued to characterize structural family therapy ever since.

At Wiltwyck, Minuchin and his colleagues—Dick Auerswald, Charlie King, Braulio Montalvo, and Clara Rabinowitz—taught themselves to do family therapy, inventing it as they went along. To do so, they built a one-way mirror and took turns observing each other work. In 1962 Minuchin made a hajj to what was then the Mecca of family therapy, Palo Alto. Here he met Jay Haley and began a friendship that was to bear fruit in an extraordinarily fertile collaboration. A couple of years later Minuchin renewed his contact with Nathan Ackerman, who from 1950 to 1952 had guided his early development as a child psychiatrist. Minuchin credits Ackerman with demonstrating the personal power of a therapist passionately engaged with the families he treats. While most family therapists are observers, Minuchin, like Ackerman, joins the families he treats, becoming for a time an active participant in their dramas.

The clinical and conceptual success of Minuchin's work with families at Wiltwyck led to a book, *Families of the Slums*, written with Montalvo, Guerney, Rosman, and Schumer. Minuchin's reputation as a practitioner of family therapy grew, and he became the Director of the Philadelphia Child Guidance Clinic in 1965. The Clinic, located in the heart of Philadelphia's black ghetto, then consisted of less than a dozen staff members. From this modest beginning Minuchin created one of the largest and most prestigious child guidance clinics in the world. When he stepped down ten years later, there were three hundred people on the staff.

Among Minuchin's colleagues in Philadelphia were Braulio Montalvo, Jay Haley, Bernice Rosman, Harry Aponte, Carter Umbarger, Marianne Walters, Charles Fishman, Cloe Madanes, and Stephen Greenstein, all of whom had an important role in shaping structural family therapy. Many other therapists associated with the Philadelphia Child Guidance Clinic as students and staff members have also influenced structural family therapy with their own ideas and styles; these second-generation structuralists are now dispersed throughout the country. By the late 1970s, structural family therapy had become the most influential and widely practiced of all systems of family therapy.

When he was working with poor people at Wiltwyck, Minuchin says he got no flack for doing family therapy. The flack came when he turned the Philadelphia Child Guidance Clinic into a family therapy center. Both the APA and AMA raised serious questions: Was family therapy proper for the training of child psychiatrists? Could Minuchin's unorthodox notion that family therapy and child psychiatry should be synonymous be right? Accused of heresy and summoned to constant meetings to defend his point of view, Minuchin responded strategically: He didn't show up at the meetings. But even more important than his refusal to take the defensive was the fact that the influential institution he created gave him a power base from which he was able to fight and win a place for family therapy in the medical establishment.

In 1976 Minuchin stepped down as Director of the Philadelphia Child Guidance Clinic, but stayed on as head of training until 1981. After leaving Philadelphia, Minuchin started his own center in New York, where he continued to practice and teach family therapy until 1996, when he retired and moved to Boston. Long committed to addressing problems of poverty and social justice, Minuchin is now consulting with the Massachusetts Department of Mental Health on home-based therapy programs. He recently completed his ninth book, *Mastering Family Therapy: Journeys of Growth and Transformation*, co-authored with nine of his supervisees, which explains his views on the state of the art in family therapy and training.

Like good players on the same team with a superstar, some of Minuchin's colleagues are not as well known as they might be. Foremost among these is Braulio Montalvo, one of the underrated geniuses of family therapy. Born and raised in Puerto Rico, Montalvo, like Minuchin, has always been committed to treating minority families. Like Minuchin, he is also a brilliant therapist, though he favors a gentler, more supportive approach. Montalvo was instrumental in building the Philadelphia Child Guidance Clinic, but his contributions are less well known because he is a quiet man who prefers to work behind the scenes.

Following Minuchin's retirement the center in New York has been renamed the Minuchin Center for the Family in his honor, and the torch has been passed to a new generation. The staff of leading teachers at the Minuchin Center now includes Ema Genijovich, George Greenan, Richard Holm, Wai-Yung Lee, and George Simon. Their task will be to keep the leading center of structural family therapy in the forefront of the field without the charismatic leadership of its progenitor.

Among Minuchin's other prominent students are Jorge Colapinto, now at the Ackerman Institute in New York; Michael Nichols, who teaches at the College of William and Mary; and Charles Fishman, in private practice in Philadelphia.

Theoretical Formulations

The rise to prominence of structural family therapy was due in part to Minuchin's renown as a clinician and to the excellent training programs offered at the Philadelphia Child Guidance Clinic, but also to the fact that Minuchin's theory is both simple and practical.

Most therapists are impatient with theories: They see them as abstractions, which they're eager to bypass in order to learn techniques. But all the clever techniques and impressive interventions that one can pick up from books and supervisors are nothing but tactical maneuvers. Without a map you're lost—caught up in the detailed content of family discussions with no overall plan. This often occurs in individual psychotherapy, where therapists become experts at passivity: You can sit back and listen impassively, week after week, as Mr. Jones complains about his wife. As long as he gets some relief from complaining, there's no need to do much but listen and nod sympathetically. In family work it's harder to be passive. Family members aren't confirmed into the status of patienthood and they won't put up with a passive therapist. They want action! They want solutions! They want a therapist to solve their problems. Families present problem after problem, crisis after crisis, and demand that therapists *Do Something!*

Beginners tend to get bogged down in the content of family problems because they don't have a theory to help them see the process of family dynamics. Structural family therapy is a blueprint for analyzing the process of family interactions. As such, it provides a basis for consistent strategies of treatment, which obviates the need to have a specific technique—usually someone else's—for every occasion.

Three constructs are the essential components of structural family theory: *structure, subsystems,* and *boundaries.*

Family structure, the organized pattern in which family members interact, is a deterministic concept, but it doesn't prescribe or legislate behavior; it *describes* sequences that are predictable. As family transactions are repeated they foster expectations that establish enduring patterns. Once patterns are established, family members use only a small fraction of the full range of behavior available to them. The first time the baby cries, or the in-laws come to visit, or a teenager misses the school bus, it's not clear who will do what. Will the load be shared? Will there be a quarrel? Will one person get stuck with most of the work? Soon, however, patterns are set, roles assigned, and things take on a sameness and predictability. "Who's going to . . . ?" becomes "She'll probably . . ." and then "She always."

Family structure involves a set of covert rules that govern transactions in the family. For example, a rule such as "family members must always protect one another" will be manifested in various ways depending on the context and which family members are involved. If an adolescent son has to be up early for school, mother wakes him; father does all the shopping if driving makes the mother nervous; the kids intervene to diffuse conflict between the parents; and the parents' preoccupation with the kids' problems keeps the couple from spending time together. All of these sequences are isomorphic; they are structured. Changing any of them may or may not affect the underlying structure, but altering the basic structure will have ripple effects on all family transactions.

Family structure is shaped partly by universal and partly by idiosyncratic constraints. For example, all families have some kind of hierarchical structure, with adults and children having different amounts of authority. Family members also tend to have reciprocal and complementary functions. Often these become so ingrained that their origin is forgotten, and they are presumed necessary rather than optional. If a young mother, burdened by the demands of her infant, gets upset and complains to her husband, he may respond in various ways. Perhaps he'll move closer and share the demands of childrearing. This creates a united parental team. On the other hand, if he decides, and his wife concurs, that she's "depressed," she may be sent into psychotherapy to get the emotional support she needs. This creates a structure where the mother remains distant from her husband, and learns to turn outside the family for emotional support. Whatever the chosen pattern, it tends to be self-perpetuating and resistant to change. Although alternatives are available, families are unlikely to consider them until changing circumstances produce stress and dysfunction in the system.

Families don't walk in and hand you their underlying structural patterns as if they were bringing an apple to the teacher. What they bring is their own chaos and confusion. You have to discover the subtext—and you have to be careful that it's a true subtext—not imposed but discovered in the unhappy families that seek your help. Two things are necessary: a theoretical system that explains structure, and seeing the family in action. The facts aren't enough. Knowing that a family is a single-parent family with three children, or that two parents are having trouble with a middle child doesn't tell you what the family structure is. Structure becomes evident only when you observe the actual interactions among family members over time.

Consider the following example. A mother calls the clinic to complain of misbehavior in her seventeen-year-old son. She is asked to bring her husband, son, and their three other children to the first session. When they arrive, the mother begins to describe a series of minor ways in which the son is disobedient around the house. He responds angrily, saying nobody understands him, he never gets any sympathy from his mother. This spontaneous dialogue between mother and son reveals an intense involvement between them—an involvement no less real or intense simply because it's conflictual. This dyadic sequence doesn't tell the whole story, however, because it doesn't include the father or the other three children. They must be engaged in interaction to observe their role in the family structure. If the father sides with his wife but seems unconcerned, then it may be that the mother's preoccupation with her son is related to her husband's lack of involvement. If the three younger children tend to agree with their mother and describe their brother as bad, then it becomes clear that all the children are close to the mother—close and obedient up to a point, then close and disobedient.

Families are differentiated into *subsystems* of members who join together to perform various functions. Every individual is a subsystem, and dyads or larger groups make up other subsystems, determined by generation, gender, or common interests. Obvious groupings such as the parents or the teenagers are sometimes less significant than covert coalitions. A mother and her youngest child may form such a tightly bonded subsystem that others are excluded. Another family may be split into two camps, with Mom and the boys on one side, and Dad and the girls on the other. Though certain patterns are common, the possibilities for subgrouping are endless.

Every family member plays many roles in several subgroups. Mary may be a wife, a mother, a daughter, and a niece. In each of these roles she will be required to behave differently and exercise a variety of interpersonal options. If she's mature and flexible, she will be able to vary her behavior to fit the different subgroups in which she functions. Scolding may be okay from a mother, but it causes problems from a wife or a daughter.

Individuals, subsystems, and whole families are demarcated by interpersonal *boundaries*, invisible barriers that regulate the amount of contact with others. Boundaries serve to protect the autonomy of the family and its subsystems by managing *proximity* and *hierarchy*. A rule forbidding phone calls at dinner time establishes a boundary that protects the family from outside intrusion. When small children are permitted to freely interrupt their parents' conversation at dinner, the boundary separating the parents from the children is minimal. Subsystems that aren't adequately protected by boundaries limit the development of interpersonal skills achievable in these subsystems. If parents always step in to settle arguments between their children, the children won't learn to fight their own battles and will be handicapped in their dealings with peers.

Interpersonal boundaries vary from rigid to diffuse (see Figure 8.1 on page 246). Rigid boundaries are overly restrictive and permit

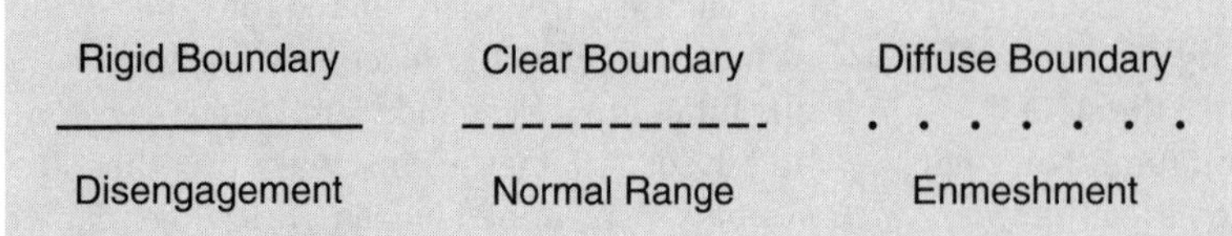

FIGURE 8.1 Boundaries

little contact with outside subsystems, resulting in *disengagement*. Disengaged individuals or subsystems are independent but isolated. On the positive side, this fosters autonomy, growth, and mastery. If parents don't hover over their children, telling them what to do and fighting their battles, then the children will be forced to develop their own resources. On the other hand, disengagement limits warmth, affection, and nurture. Disengaged families must come under extreme stress before they mobilize mutual support. If parents keep their children at a distance, affection is minimized and the parents will be slow to notice when the children need support and guidance.

Enmeshed subsystems offer a heightened sense of mutual support, but at the expense of independence and autonomy. Enmeshed parents are loving and considerate; they spend a lot of time with their kids and do a lot for them. However, children enmeshed with their parents become dependent. They're less comfortable by themselves and may have trouble relating to people outside the family.

Minuchin described some of the features of family subsystems in his most accessible work, *Families and Family Therapy* (Minuchin, 1974). Families begin when two people join together to form a spouse subsystem. Two people in love agree to share their lives and futures and expectations, but a period of often difficult adjustment is required before they can complete the transition from courtship to a functional spouse subsystem. They must learn to *accommodate* to each other's needs and preferred styles of interaction. In a normal couple, each gives and gets. He learns to accommodate to her wish to be kissed hello and goodbye. She learns to leave him alone with his paper and morning coffee. These little arrangements, multiplied a thousand times, may be accomplished easily or only after intense struggle. Whatever the case, this process of accommodation cements the couple into a unit.

The couple must also develop complementary patterns of mutual support. Some patterns are transitory and may later be reversed—perhaps, for instance, one works while the other completes school. Other patterns are more stable and lasting. Traditional sex-role stereotypes may allow couples to achieve complementarity, but at the expense of fully rounded functioning for each spouse. A traditional woman may not have to open doors, earn a living, or mow the lawn; on the other hand, she may have to deny her own intelligence, submerge her independence, and live in the shadow of her husband. A traditional husband may get to make all the decisions, not have to change dirty diapers, and be waited on hand and foot around the house; however, the price for these "masculine" prerogatives may be that he's not allowed to cry, never learns the pleasure of cooking a special meal, and doesn't share the joy of caring for his children.

Exaggerated complementary roles can detract from individual growth; moderate complementarity enables spouses to divide functions, to support and enrich each other. When one has the flu and feels lousy, the other takes over. One's permissiveness with children may be balanced by the other's strictness. One's fiery disposition may help to melt the other's icy reserve. Complementary patterns, such as pursuer–distancer, active–passive, dominant–

submissive, exist in most couples. They become pathological when they are so exaggerated that they create a dysfunctional subsystem. Therapists must learn to accept those structural patterns that work and challenge only those that do not.

The spouse subsystem must also have a boundary that separates it from parents, from children, and from the outside world. All too often, husband and wife give up the space they need for supporting each other when children are born. A rigid boundary around the couple deprives the children of the support they need; but in our child-centered culture, the boundary separating parents and children is often extremely diffuse.

The birth of a child instantly transforms the family structure; the pattern of interaction between the parental and child subsystems must be worked out and then modified to fit changing circumstances. A clear boundary enables the children to interact with their parents but excludes them from the spouse subsystem. Parents and children eat together, play together, and share much of each others' lives. But there are some spouse functions that need not be shared. Husband and wife are sustained as a loving couple, and enhanced as parents, if they have time to be alone together—alone to talk, alone to go out to dinner occasionally, alone to fight, and alone to make love. Unhappily, the demands of small children often make parents lose sight of their need to maintain a boundary around their relationship.

In addition to maintaining some privacy for the couple, a clear boundary establishes a hierarchical structure in which parents exercise a position of leadership. All too often this hierarchy is disrupted by a child-centered ethos, which influences family therapists as well as parents. Parents enmeshed with their children tend to argue with them about who's in charge, and misguidedly share—or shirk—the responsibility for making parental decisions. Offering a child the choice in picking out clothes or choosing friends is respectful and flexible. Asking children whether they want to go to school, or trying to convince a toddler to agree that it's dangerous to play in the street simply blurs the line of authority.

In a recent book, *Institutionalizing Madness* (Elizur & Minuchin, 1989), Minuchin makes a compelling case for a systems view of family problems that extends beyond the family itself to encompass the entire community. As long as they confine their attention to the nuclear family, family therapists themselves suffer from a myopia that may produce solutions that don't work. Minuchin points out, forcefully, that unless family therapists learn to look beyond the limited slice of ecology where they work to the larger social structures within which their work is embedded, their efforts may amount to little more than spinning wheels.

Normal Family Development

A common presumption is that normal family life is happy and harmonious. This is a myth. Normal families are constantly struggling with problems in living. What distinguishes a normal family isn't the absence of problems, but a functional family structure. Normal husbands and wives must learn to adjust to each other, rear their children, deal with their parents, cope with their jobs, and fit into their communities. The nature of these struggles changes with developmental stages and situational crises.

When two people marry, the structural requirements for the new union are *accommodation* and *boundary making.* The first priority is mutual accommodation to manage the myriad details of everyday living. Each spouse tries to organize the relationship along familiar lines and pressures the other to accommodate. Each must adjust to the other's expectations and wants. They must agree on major issues, such as where to live and if and when to have children; less obvious, but equally important, they must coordinate daily rituals, like what to watch on television, what to eat for supper, when to go to bed, and what to do there. Often the little things are the most irksome. Couples may argue heatedly about who will take out the garbage or wash the clothes.

In accommodating to each other, a couple must also negotiate the nature of the boundary between them, as well as the boundary separating them from the outside. A diffuse boundary exists between the couple if they call each other at work frequently, if neither has separate friends or independent activities, and if they come to view themselves only as a pair rather than as two separate personalities. On the other hand, they've established a rigid boundary if they spend little time together, have separate bedrooms, take separate vacations, have different checking accounts, and each is considerably more invested in careers or outside relationships than in the marriage. While none of these markers by itself defines enmeshment or disengagement, each of them suggests the pattern that will develop.

Typically spouses come from families with differing degrees of enmeshment or disengagement. Each spouse tends to be more comfortable with the sort of proximity that existed in the family of origin. Since these expectations differ, a struggle ensues that may be the most difficult aspect of a new marriage. He wants to go play poker with the boys; she feels deserted. She wants to hold hands and whisper in the movies; he wants to concentrate on the picture. His focus is on his career; her focus is on the marriage. Each thinks the other wrong, unreasonable, and terribly hurtful.

Couples must also define a boundary separating them from their original families. Rather suddenly the families that each grew up in must take second place to the new marriage. This, too, is a difficult adjustment, both for newlyweds and their parents. Families vary in the ease with which they accept and support these new unions.

The addition of children transforms the structure of the new family into a *parental subsystem* and a *sibling subsystem*. It's typical for spouses to have different patterns of commitment to the babies. A woman's commitment to a unit of three is likely to begin with pregnancy, since the child inside her womb is an unavoidable reality. Her husband, on the other hand, may only begin to feel like a father when the child is born. Many men don't accept the role of father until their infants are old enough to respond to them. Thus, even in normal families, children bring with them great potential for stress and conflict. A woman's life is usually more radically transformed than a man's. She sacrifices a great deal and typically needs more support from her husband. The husband, meanwhile, continues his job, and the new baby is far less of a disruption. Though he may try to support his wife, he's likely to resent some of her demands as inordinate and unreasonable.

The family takes care of the psychosocial needs of the children and transmits the culture to them. Children develop a dual identity within the family, a sense of belongingness and a sense of being separate. John Smith is both a Smith and also John, part of the family, yet a unique person.

Children require different styles of parenting at different ages. Infants primarily need nurture and support. Children need guidance and control; and adolescents need independence and responsibility. Good parenting for a two-year-old may be totally inadequate for a five-year-old or a fourteen-year-old. Normal parents adjust to these developmental challenges. The family modifies its structure to adapt to new additions, to the children's growth and development, and to changes in the external environment.

Minuchin (1974) warns family therapists not to mistake growing pains for pathology. The normal family experiences anxiety and disruption as its members adapt to growth and change. Many families seek help at transitional stages, and therapists should keep in mind that they may simply be in the process of modifying their structure to accommodate to new circumstances.

All families face situations that stress the system. Although no clear dividing line exists between normal and abnormal families, we can say that normal families modify their structure to accommodate to changed circumstances; pathological families increase the rigidity of structures that are no longer functional.

Development of Behavior Disorders

Family systems must be stable enough to ensure continuity, but flexible enough to accommodate to changing circumstances. Behavior disorders arise when inflexible family structures cannot adjust adequately to maturational or situational challenges. Adaptive changes in structure are required when the family or one of its members faces external stress and when transitional points of growth are reached.

Family dysfunction results from a combination of stress and failure to realign themselves to cope with it (Colapinto, 1991). Stressors may be environmental (a parent is laid off, the family moves) or developmental (a child reaches adolescence, parents retire). The family's failure to handle adversity may be due to inherent flaws in their structure or merely to their inability to adjust to changed circumstances.

In disengaged families, boundaries are rigid, emotional distance is excessive, and the family fails to mobilize support when it's needed. Disengaged parents may be unaware that a child is depressed or experiencing difficulties at school until the problem is far advanced. In enmeshed families, on the other hand, boundaries are diffuse and family members overreact and become intrusively involved with one another. Enmeshed parents create difficulties by hindering the development of more mature forms of behavior in their children and by interfering with their ability to solve their own problems.

In their book of case studies, *Family Healing*, Minuchin and Nichols (1993) describe a common example of enmeshment as a father jumps in to settle minor arguments between his two boys—"as though the siblings were Cain and Abel, and fraternal jealousy might lead to murder" (p. 149). The problem, of course, is that if parents always interrupt their children's quarrels, the children won't learn to fight their own battles.

Although we may speak of enmeshed and disengaged families, it is more accurate (and useful) to speak of particular subsystems as being enmeshed or disengaged. In fact, enmeshment and disengagement tend to be reciprocal, so that, for example, a father who's overly involved with his work is likely to be less involved with his family. A frequently encountered pattern is the enmeshed mother/disengaged father syndrome—"the signature arrangement of the troubled middle-class family: a mother's closeness to her children substituting for closeness in the marriage" (Minuchin & Nichols, 1993, p. 121).

Feminists have criticized the notion of an enmeshed mother/disengaged father syndrome because they reject the stereotypical division of labor (instrumental role for the father, expressive role for the mother) that they think Minuchin's belief in hierarchy implies, and because they worry about blaming mothers for an arrangement that is culturally sanctioned. Both concerns are valid. But prejudice and blaming are due to insensitive application of these ideas, not inherent in the ideas themselves. Skewed relationships, whatever the reason for them, can be problematic, though naturally no single family member should be blamed or expected to unilaterally redress imbalances. Likewise, the need for hierarchy doesn't imply any particular division of roles; it only implies that families need *some* kind of structure, *some* parental teamwork, and *some* degree of differentiation between subsystems.

Hierarchies can be weak and ineffective, or rigid and arbitrary. In the first case, younger members of the family may find themselves unprotected because of a lack of guidance; in the second, their growth as autonomous individuals may be impaired, or power struggles may ensue (Colapinto, 1991). Just as a functional hierarchy is necessary for a healthy family's stability, flexibility is necessary for them to adapt to change.

The most common expression of fear of change is *conflict-avoidance,* when family members shy away from addressing their disagreements to protect themselves from the pain of facing each other with hard truths. Disengaged families avert conflict by avoiding contact; enmeshed families avoid conflict by denying differences or by constant bickering, which allows them to vent feelings without pressing each other for change or resolution of the conflict. A common expression of conflict-avoidance between partners involves diverting conflict to the children, in which case "conflicts between the spouses are played out in the parenting battlefield—and as they pull in different directions, the confused children become casualties" (Minuchin & Nichols, 1993, p. 149).

Structural family therapists use a few simple symbols to diagram structural problems, and these diagrams usually make it clear what changes are required. Figure 8.2 shows some of the symbols used to diagram family structure.

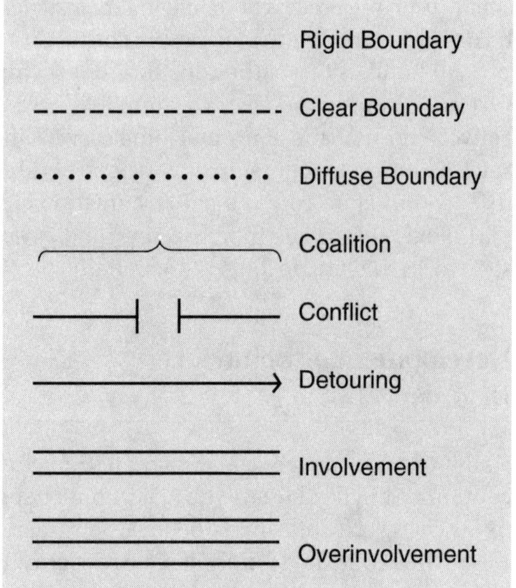

FIGURE 8.2 Symbols of Family Structure

One problem often seen by family therapists arises when parents who are unable to resolve conflicts between them divert the focus of concern onto a child. Instead of worrying about each other, they worry about the child (see Figure 8.3). Although this reduces the strain on father (F) and mother (M), it victimizes the child (C) and is therefore dysfunctional.

An alternate but equally common pattern is for the parents to continue to argue through the children. Father says mother is too permissive; she says he's too strict. He may withdraw, causing her to criticize his handling of the child, which in turn causes further withdrawal. The enmeshed mother responds to the child's needs with excessive concern and devotion. The disengaged father tends not to respond even when a response is necessary. Both may be critical of the other's way, but both perpetuate the other's behavior with their own. The result is a *cross-generational coalition* between mother and child, which excludes the father (Figure 8.4).

Some families function well when the children are small but are unable to adjust to a growing child's need for discipline and control. Parents may be particularly solicitous of children if they've had reason to worry about the

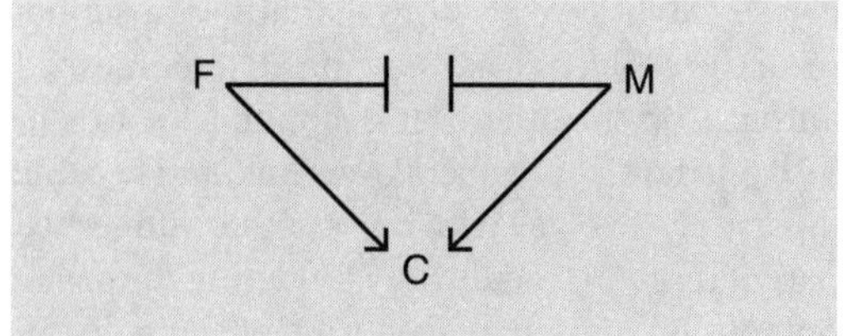

FIGURE 8.3 Scapegoating as a Means of Detouring Conflict

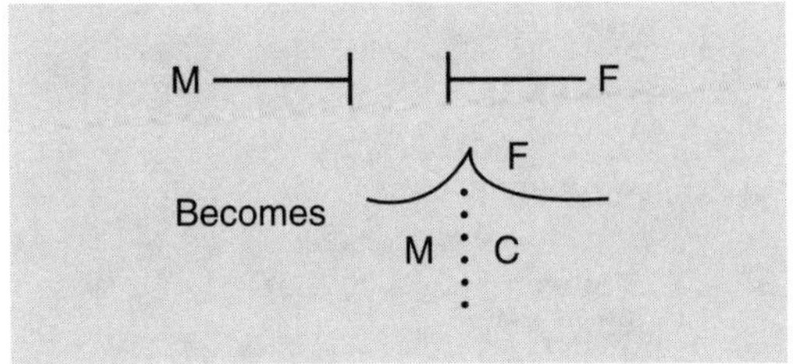

FIGURE 8.4 Mother–Child Coalition

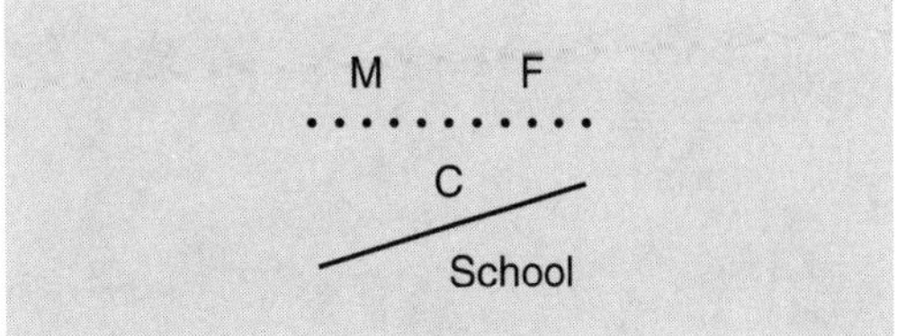

FIGURE 8.6 School Phobia

children's health, if they had to wait a long time before they had them, or if they have few interests outside the family to give meaning to their lives. Parents who are unable to have children of their own, and finally decide to adopt, may find it difficult to set appropriate limits. They're too invested and enmeshed with their children to be able to exercise appropriate control (Figure 8.5).

Infants in enmeshed families receive wonderful care: Their parents hug them, love them, and give them lots of stimulation. Although such parents may be too tired from caring for the children to have much time for each other or for outside interests, the system may be moderately successful. However, if these doting parents don't teach the children to obey rules and respect adult authority, the children may be unprepared to successfully negotiate their entrance into school. Used to getting their own way, they may be unruly and disruptive. Several possible consequences of this situation may bring the family into treatment. The children may be afraid to go to school, for instance, and their fears may be covertly reinforced by "understanding" parents who permit them to remain at home (Figure 8.6). Such a case may be labeled as school phobia, and may become entrenched if the parents permit the children to remain at home for more than a few days.

FIGURE 8.5 Parents Enmeshed with Children

The children of such a family may go to school; but since they haven't learned to accommodate to others they may be rejected by their schoolmates. These children may become depressed and withdrawn. In other cases, children enmeshed with their parents become discipline problems at school, and the school authorities may initiate counseling.

A major change in family composition that requires structural adjustment occurs when divorced or widowed spouses remarry. Such "blended families" either readjust their boundaries or soon experience transitional conflicts. When a woman divorces, she and the children must first learn to readjust to a structure that establishes a clear boundary separating the divorced spouses but still permits contact between father and children; then if she remarries, the family must readjust to functioning with a new husband and stepfather (Figure 8.7 on page 252). Sometimes it is hard for a mother and children to allow a stepfather to participate as an equal partner in the new parental subsystem. Mother and children have long since established transactional rules and learned to accommodate to each other. The new parent may be treated as an outsider who's supposed to learn the "right" (accustomed) way of doing things, rather than as a new partner who will give as well as receive ideas about childrearing (Figure 8.8 on page 252). The more mother and children insist on maintaining their familiar

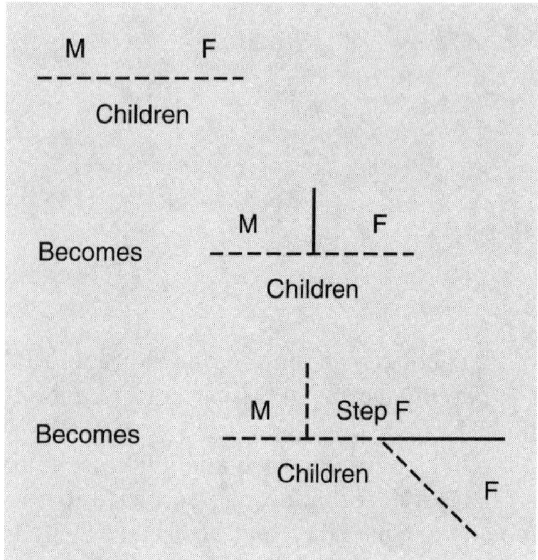

FIGURE 8.7 Divorce and Remarriage

patterns without modifications required to absorb the stepfather, the more frustrated and angry he'll become. The result may lead to child abuse or chronic arguing between the parents. The sooner such families enter treatment, the easier it is to help them adjust to the transition. The longer they wait, the more entrenched structural problems become.

An important aspect of structural family problems is that symptoms in one member reflect not only that person's relationships with others, but also the fact that those relationships are a function of still other relationships in the family. If Johnny, aged sixteen, is depressed, it's helpful to know that he's enmeshed with his mother. Discovering that she demands absolute obedience from him and refuses to let him develop his

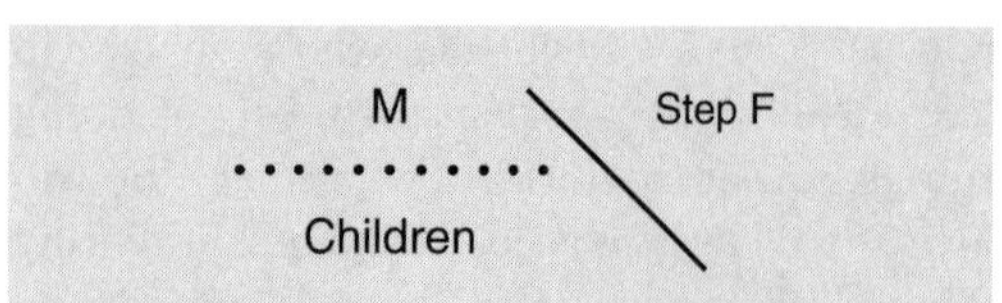

FIGURE 8.8 Failure to Accept a Stepparent

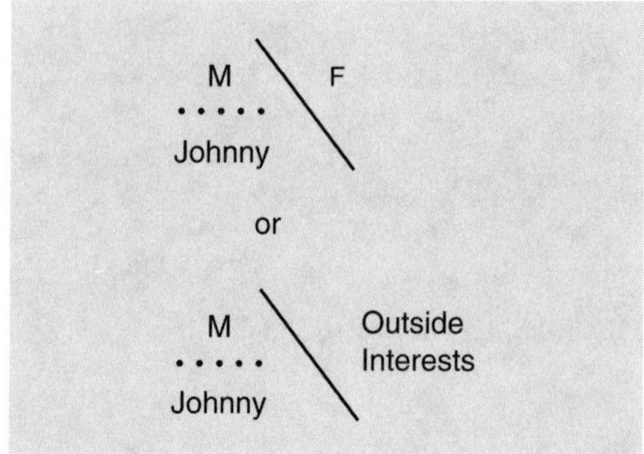

FIGURE 8.9 Johnny's Enmeshment with His Mother and Disengagement with Outside Interests

own thinking or outside relationships helps to explain his depression (Figure 8.9). But that's only a partial view of the family system, and therefore an incomplete guide to treatment.

Why is the mother enmeshed with her son? Perhaps she's disengaged from her husband; perhaps she's a widow who hasn't found new friends, a career, or any other outside interests. Helping Johnny resolve his depression may best be accomplished by helping his mother satisfy her need for closeness with her husband or friends.

Because problems are a function of the entire family structure, it's important to include the whole group for assessment. For example, if a father complains of a child's misbehavior, seeing the child alone won't help the father to state rules clearly and enforce them effectively. Nor will seeing the father and child together do anything to stop the mother from undercutting the father's authority. Only by seeing the whole family interacting is it possible to get a complete picture of their structure.

Sometimes even seeing the whole family isn't enough. Structural family therapy is based on recognition of the importance of the context of the social system. The family may not be the complete or most relevant context. If one of the parents is having an affair, that relationship is a crucial part of the family's context. It may not be advisable to invite the lover to family sessions, but it is crucial to recognize the structural implications of the extramarital relationship.

In some cases, the family may not be the context most relevant to the presenting problem. A mother's depression may be due more to her relationships at work than at home. A son's problems at school may be due more to the structural context at school than to the one in the family. In such instances, structural family therapists work with the more relevant context to alleviate the presenting problems.

Finally, some problems may be treated as problems of the individual. As Minuchin (1974) has written, "Pathology may be inside the patient, in his social context, or in the feedback between them" (p. 9). Elsewhere Minuchin (Minuchin, Rosman, & Baker, 1978) referred to the danger of "denying the individual while enthroning the system" (p. 91). Family therapists shouldn't overlook the possibility that some problems may be most appropriately dealt with on an individual basis. The therapist must not neglect the experience of individuals, although this is easy to do, especially with young children. While interviewing a family to see how the parents deal with their children, a careful clinician may notice that one child has a neurological problem or a learning disability. These problems need to be identified and appropriate referrals made. Usually when a child has trouble in school, there's a problem in the family or school context. Usually, but not always.

Goals of Therapy

Structural family therapists believe that problems are maintained by dysfunctional family structures. Therefore therapy is directed at altering family structure so that the family can solve its problems. The goal of therapy is structural change; problem-solving is a byproduct of this systemic goal.

The idea that family problems are embedded in "dysfunctional family structures" has led to the criticism of structural family therapy as a "pathologizing" approach. These critics see structural maps of dysfunctional organization as portraying a pathological core in client families. This isn't true. Structural problems are generally viewed as a simple failure to adjust to changing circumstances. Far from seeing families as inherently flawed, structural therapists see their work as activating latent adaptive structures that are already in client families' repertoires (Simon, 1995). Structural family therapy is driven by the assumption that families are competent and should be respected.

The structural family therapist joins the family system in order to help its members change their structure. By altering boundaries and realigning subsystems, the therapist changes the behavior and experience of each of the family members. The therapist doesn't solve problems; that's the family's job. The therapist helps modify the family's functioning so that family members can solve their own problems. In this way, structural family therapy is like dynamic psychotherapy—symptom-resolution is sought not as an end in itself, but as a result of lasting structural change. The analyst modifies the structure of the patient's mind; the structural family therapist modifies the structure of the patient's family.

Symptomatic change and enhanced family functioning are seen as inextricably interrelated goals. The most effective way to change symptoms is to change the family patterns that maintain them. An effectively functioning family is a system that supports its members. The goal of structural family therapy is to facilitate the growth of the system in order to resolve symptoms and encourage growth in individuals, while also preserving the mutual support of the family.

Short-range goals may be to alleviate symptoms, especially life-threatening symptoms such as anorexia nervosa (Minuchin, Rosman, & Baker, 1978). At times, behavioral techniques, suggestion, or manipulation may be used to provide temporary surcease. However, unless structural change in the family system is achieved, short-term symptom-resolution may collapse.

The goals for each family are dictated by the problems they present and by the nature of their structural dysfunction. Although every family is unique, there are common problems and typical structural goals. Most important of the general goals for families is the creation of an effective hierarchical structure. Parents are expected to be in charge, not to relate as equals to their children. A frequent goal is to help parents function together as a cohesive executive subsystem. When only one parent is present, or when there are several children, one or more of the oldest children may be encouraged to be a parental assistant. But this child's needs must not be neglected, either.

With enmeshed families the goal is to differentiate individuals and subsystems by strengthening the boundaries around them. With disengaged families the goal is to increase interaction by making boundaries more permeable.

Conditions for Behavior Change

Structural family therapy changes behavior by opening alternative patterns of family interaction that can modify family structure. It's not a matter of creating new structures, but of activating dormant ones. If, once activated, the dormant sequences are functional, they will be reinforcing; and family structure will be transformed. When new transactional patterns become regularly repeated and predictably effective, they will stabilize the new and more functional structure.

The therapist produces change by joining the family, probing for areas of flexibility, and then activating dormant structural alternatives. *Joining* gets the therapist into the family; *accommodating* to their style gives him or her leverage; and *restructuring* interventions transform the family structure. If the therapist remains an outsider or uses interventions that are too dystonic, the family will reject him or her. If the therapist becomes too much a part of the family or uses interventions that are too syntonic, the family will assimilate the interventions into previous transactional patterns. In either case there will be no structural change.

For change to occur, the family must first accept the therapist, and then respond to his or her interventions as though to a novel situation. This increases stress, which in turn unbalances family homeostasis, and thus opens the way for structural transformation.

Joining and accommodating are considered prerequisite to restructuring. To join the family the therapist must convey acceptance of family members and respect for their way of doing things. Minuchin (1974) likened the family therapist to an anthropologist who must first join a culture before being able to study it.

To join the family's culture the therapist makes accommodating overtures—the sort of thing we usually do unthinkingly, although often unsuccessfully. If parents come for help with a child's problems, the therapist shouldn't begin by asking for the child's views. This conveys a lack of respect for the parents and may lead them to reject the therapist. Only after the therapist has successfully joined with a family is it fruitful to attempt restructuring—the often dramatic confrontations that challenge families and force them to change.

Structural family therapy changes behavior by reframing the family's presentation of their problems into a systemic model. Families define problems as a function of individuals or outside forces; structural family therapists redefine these problems as a function of the family structure. The first task is to understand the family's view of their problems. The therapist does this by tracking their formulation in the content they use to explain it and in the sequences with which they demonstrate it. Then the family therapist *reframes* their formulation into one based on an understanding of family structure.

In fact, all psychotherapies use reframing. Patients, whether individuals or families, come with their own views as to the cause of their problems—views that usually haven't helped them solve the problems—and the therapist offers them a new and potentially more constructive view of these same problems. What makes structural family therapy unique is that it uses *enactments* within therapy sessions to make the reframing happen. This is the *sine qua non* of structural family therapy: observing and modifying the structure of family transactions in the immediate context of the session. Although this sounds simple, it has important implications for treatment. Structural family therapists work with what they see going on in the session, not what family members describe about what happens outside, nor with the content of family discussions. Action in the session, family dynamics in process, is what structural family therapists deal with.

There are two types of live, in-session material on which structural family therapy focuses—*enactments* and *spontaneous behavior sequences.* An enactment occurs when the therapist stimulates the family to demonstrate how they handle a particular type of problem. Enactments commonly begin when the therapist suggests that specific subgroups begin to discuss a particular problem. As they do so, the therapist observes the family process. Working with enactments requires three operations. First, the therapist defines or recognizes a sequence. For example, the therapist observes that when mother talks to her daughter they talk as peers, and little brother gets left out. Second, the therapist directs an enactment. For example, the therapist might say to the mother, "Talk this over with your kids." Third, and most important, the therapist must guide the family to modify the enactment. If mother talks to her children in such a way that she doesn't take appropriate responsibility for major decisions, the therapist must guide her to do so as the family continues the enactment. All the therapist's moves should create new options for the family, options for new behavior sequences. A common mistake made by many family therapists is to simply criticize what they see by labeling it, without offering options for change.

Once an enactment breaks down, the therapist intervenes in one of two ways: commenting on what went wrong, or simply pushing them to keep going. For example, if a father responds to the suggestion to talk with his twelve-year-old daughter about how she's feeling by berating her, the therapist could say to the father: "Congratulations." Father: "What do you mean?" Therapist: "Congratulations; you win, she loses." Or the therapist could simply nudge the transaction by saying to the father: "Good, keep talking, but help her express her feelings more. She's still a little girl; she needs your help."

In addition to working with enacted sequences, structural family therapists are alert to spontaneous sequences that are the illustrative processes of family structure. Creating enactments is like directing a play; working with spontaneous sequences is like focusing a spotlight on action that occurs without direction. In fact, by observing and modifying such sequences very early in therapy the therapist avoids getting bogged down in the family's usual nonproductive ways of doing business. Dealing with problematic behavior as soon as it occurs in the first session enables the therapist to organize the session, to underscore the process, and to modify it.

An experienced therapist develops hunches about family structure even before the first interview. For example, if a family is coming to the clinic because of a "hyperactive" child, it's possible to guess something about the family structure and something about sequences that may occur as the session begins, since "hyperactive" behavior is often a function of the child's enmeshment with the mother. Mother's relationship with the child may be a product of a lack of hierarchical differentiation within the family; that is, parents and children relate to each other as peers, not as members of different generations. Furthermore, mother's overinvolvement with the "hyperactive" child is likely to be both a result of and a cause of emotional distance from her husband. Knowing that this is a common pattern, the therapist can anticipate that early in the first session the "hyperactive" child will begin to misbehave, and that the mother will be inadequate to deal with this misbehavior. Armed with this informed guess the therapist can spotlight (rather than enact) such a sequence as soon as it occurs, and modify it. If the "hyperactive" child begins to run around the room, and the mother protests but does nothing effective, the therapist might say, "I see that your child feels free to ignore you." This challenge may push the mother to behave in a more competent manner. The therapist may have to push further, saying, "Come on now, do something about it." Once such a theme is focused on, the therapist needs to pursue it relentlessly.

Techniques

In *Families and Family Therapy*, Minuchin (1974) taught family therapists to see what they were looking at. Through the lens of structural family theory, previously puzzling family interactions suddenly swam into focus. Where others saw only chaos and cruelty, Minuchin saw structure: families organized into subsystems with boundaries. This enormously successful book (over 200,000 copies in print) not only taught us to see *enmeshment* and *disengagement*, but also let us hope that changing them was just a matter of *joining*, *enactment*, and *unbalancing*. Minuchin made changing families look simple. It isn't.

Anyone who watched Minuchin at work ten or fifteen years after the publication of *Families and Family Therapy* would see a creative therapist still evolving, not someone frozen in time back in 1974. There would still be the patented confrontations ("Who's the sheriff in this family?") but there would be fewer enactments, less stage-directed dialogue. We would also hear bits and pieces borrowed from Carl Whitaker ("When did you divorce your wife and marry your job?") and Maurizio Andolfi ("Why don't you piss on the rug, too?") and others. Minuchin combines many things in his work. To those familiar with his earlier work, all of this raises the question: Is Minuchin still a structural family therapist? The question is, of course, absurd; we raise it to make one point: Structural family therapy isn't a set of techniques; it's a way of looking at families.

In the remainder of this section, we will present the classic outlines of structural family technique, with the caveat that once therapists master the basics of structural theory, they must learn to translate the approach in a way that suits their own personal styles. Implementing specific techniques is an art; therapists must discover and create techniques that fit each family's transactional style and therapist's personality. Since every therapeutic session has idiosyncratic features, there can be no interpersonal immediacy if the specific context is ignored. Imitating someone else's technique is stifling and ineffective—stifling because it doesn't fit the therapist, ineffective because it doesn't fit the family.

In *Families and Family Therapy*, Minuchin (1974) listed three overlapping phases in the process of structural family therapy. The therapist (1) joins the family in a position of leadership; (2) maps their underlying structure; and (3) intervenes to transform this structure. This program is simple, in the sense that it follows a clear and specifiable plan, but immensely complicated because it's difficult to accomplish these tasks and because there is an endless variety of family patterns.

Observed in practice, structural family therapy is an organic whole, created out of the very real human interaction of therapist and family. If they are to be genuine and effective, the therapist's moves cannot be preplanned or rehearsed. Good therapists are more than technicians. The strategy of therapy, on the other hand, must be thoughtfully planned. In general, the strategy of structural family therapy follows these steps:

1. Joining and accommodating
2. Working with interaction
3. Diagnosing
4. Highlighting and modifying interactions
5. Boundary making
6. Unbalancing
7. Challenging the family's assumptions

The first three strategies constitute the opening phase of treatment. Without carefully planning and skillfully accomplishing the critical opening moves, therapy usually fails. When we begin, we're often too anxious or eager to consider opening wisely. Only after we get started and the jitters calm down, do we look around, assess the situation, and then act accordingly. Unfortunately this sort of catch-up strategy results in the loss of much valuable ground. The therapist who neglects the opening moves of treatment may lose all chance of having a significant impact.

Genuine preparation and an effective opening must be distinguished from obsessional rituals that do nothing but bind anxiety and use up energy. Habitually arriving ten minutes early for sessions, arranging and rearranging the furniture, and endlessly reading charts or books on technique—as many of us do—shouldn't be confused with careful planning.

Joining and Accommodating

Because families have firmly established homeostatic patterns, effective family therapy requires strong challenge and confrontation. But assaults on a family's habitual style will be dismissed unless they're made from a position of acceptance and understanding. Families, like you and me, resist efforts to change them by people they feel don't understand and accept them.

Individual patients generally enter treatment already predisposed to accept the therapist's authority. By seeking therapy, the individual tacitly acknowledges suffering, need for help, and willingness to trust the therapist. Not so with families.

The family outnumbers the therapist, and they have mutually agreed-upon and long-practiced ways of doing things. The family therapist is an unwelcome outsider. After all, why did the therapist insist on seeing the whole family rather than just the official patient? They expect to be told that they're doing things all wrong, and they're prepared to defend themselves. The family is thus a group of nonpatients who feel guilty and anxious; their set is to resist, not to cooperate.

First the family therapist must disarm defenses and ease anxiety. This is done by generously conveying understanding and acceptance to every single member of the family. The therapist greets each person by name and makes some kind of friendly contact.

These initial greetings convey respect, not only for the individuals in the family, but also for their hierarchical structure and organization. The therapist shows respect for parents by taking their authority for granted. They, not their children, are asked first to describe the problems. If a family elects one person as their speaker, the therapist notes this but does not initially challenge it.

Children also have special concerns and capacities. They should be greeted gently and asked simple, concrete questions, "Hi, I'm so-and-so; what's your name? Oh, Shelly, that's a nice name. Where do you go to school, Shelly?" Those who wish to remain silent should be "allowed" to do so. They will anyway, but the therapist who accepts their reticence will have made a valuable step toward keeping them involved. "And what's your view of the problem?" (Grim silence.) "I see, you don't feel like saying anything right now? That's fine; perhaps you'll have something to say later."

Failure to join and accommodate produces tense resistance, which is often blamed on the family. It may be comforting to blame others when things don't go well, but it doesn't improve matters. Family members can be called "negative," "rebellious," "resistant," or "defiant," and seen as "unmotivated"; but it's more useful to make an extra effort to connect with them.

It's particularly important to join powerful family members, as well as angry ones. Special pains must be taken to accept the point of view of the father who thinks therapy is hooey or of the angry teenager who feels like a hunted criminal. It's also important to reconnect with such people at frequent intervals, particularly as things begin to heat up.

A useful beginning is to greet the family and then ask for each person's view of the problems. Listen carefully and acknowledge each person's position by reflecting what you hear. "I see, Mrs. Jones, you think Sally must be depressed about something that happened at school." "So Mr. Jones, you see some of the same things your wife sees, but you're not convinced it's a serious problem. Is that right?"

Working with Interaction

Family structure is manifest in the way family members interact. It can't be inferred from their descriptions, nor from reconstructing previous discussions. Therefore, asking questions such as "Who's in charge?" "Do you two agree?" or "Can you show me what happened in yesterday's argument?" tend to be unproductive. Families generally describe themselves more as they think they should be than as they are.

Family dynamics are what happens when the family is in action, not what they *say* happens, or what the therapist *imagines* must happen. They have to talk among themselves for the dynamics to emerge. When they do, the therapist observes: Who talks to whom? when? in what way?

Getting family members to talk among themselves runs counter to their expectations, and they resist doing it. They expect to present their case to an expert and then be told what to do. If asked to discuss something in the session, they'll say: "We've talked about this many times"; or "It won't do any good, he (or she) doesn't listen"; or "But *you're* supposed to be the expert."

If the therapist begins by giving each person a chance to speak, usually one will say something about another that can be a springboard for an enactment. When, for example, one parent says that the other is too strict, the therapist can develop an enactment by saying: "She says you're too strict; can you answer her?" Picking a specific point for response is more likely to stimulate a dialogue than a vague request, such as "Why don't you two talk things over?"

Once an enactment is begun, the therapist can discover many things about the family's structure. How long can two people talk without being interrupted—that is, how clear is the boundary? Does one attack, the other defend? Who is central, who peripheral? Do parents bring children into their discussions—that is, are they enmeshed?

Families may demonstrate enmeshment by frequently interrupting each other, speaking for other family members, doing things for children that they can do for themselves, or by constantly arguing. In disengaged families one may see a husband sitting impassively while his wife cries; a total absence of conflict; a surprising ignorance of important information about the children; a lack of concern for each other's interests.

If, as soon as the first session starts, the kids begin running wildly around the room while the parents protest ineffectually, the therapist doesn't need to hear descriptions of what goes on at home to see the executive incompetence. If a mother and daughter rant and rave at each other while the father sits silently in the corner, it isn't necessary to ask how involved he is at home. In fact, asking may yield a less accurate picture than the one revealed spontaneously.

Diagnosing

Families usually conceive of problems as located in the identified patient and as determined by events from the past. They hope the therapist will change the identified patient—with as little disruption as possible to the family homeostasis. Family therapists regard the identified patient's symptoms as an expression of dysfunctional transactional patterns affecting the whole family. A structural diagnosis broadens the problem beyond individuals to family systems, and moves the focus from discrete events in the past to ongoing transactions in the present. A family diagnosis is predicated on the goal of transforming the family in a way that benefits all of its members.

Even many family therapists categorize families with constructs that apply more to individuals than to systems. "The problem in this family is that the mother is smothering the kids," or "These kids are defiant," or "He's uninvolved." Structural family therapists diagnose in such a way as to describe the interrelationship of all family members. Using the concepts of boundaries and subsystems, the structure of the whole system is described in a way that points to desired changes.

Diagnoses are based on observed interactions that take place in the first session. In later sessions the formulations are refined and revised. Although there is some danger of bending families to fit categories when they're applied early, the greater danger is waiting too long.

We see people with the greatest clarity and freshness during the initial contact. Later, as we come to know them better, we get used to their idiosyncrasies and soon no longer notice them. Families quickly *induct* therapists into their culture. A family that initially appears to be chaotic and enmeshed soon comes to be just the familiar Jones family. For this reason, it's critical to make structural formulations as quickly as possible.

In fact, it's helpful to make some guesses about family structure even before the first session. This starts a process of active thinking and sets the stage for observing the family. For example, suppose you're about to see a family consisting of a mother, a sixteen-year-old daughter, and a stepfather. The mother called to complain of her daughter's misbehavior. What do you imagine the structure might be, and how would you test your hypothesis? A good guess might be that mother and daughter are enmeshed, excluding the stepfather. This can be tested by seeing if mother and daughter tend to talk mostly about each other in the session—whether positively or negatively. The stepfather's disengagement would be confirmed if he and his wife were unable to converse without the daughter's intrusion.

Structural diagnosis takes into account both the problem the family presents and the structural dynamics they display. And it includes all family members. In this instance, knowing that the mother and daughter are enmeshed isn't enough; you also have to know what role the stepfather plays. If he's reasonably close with his wife but distant from the daughter, finding mutually enjoyable activities for stepfather and stepdaughter will help increase the girl's independence from her mother. On the other hand, if the mother's proximity to her daughter appears to be a function of her distance from her husband, then the marital pair may be the most productive focus.

Without a diagnostic formulation and a plan, a therapist is defensive and passive. Instead of knowing where to go and moving forcefully, the therapist lays back and tries to cope with the family, put out brush fires, and help them through a succession of incidents. Consistent awareness of the family's structure and focus on one or two structural changes helps the therapist see behind the various content issues that family members bring up.

Highlighting and Modifying Interactions

Once families begin to interact, problematic transactions emerge. Noticing them demands focus on process, not content. Nothing about structure is revealed by hearing who is in favor of punishment or who says nice things about others. Family structure is revealed by who says what to whom, and in what way.

Perhaps a husband complains, "We have a communication problem. My wife won't talk to me; she never expresses her feelings." The therapist then stimulates an interaction to see what actually does happen. "Your husband says it's a communication problem; can you respond to that? Talk with him." If, when they talk, the husband becomes domineering and critical while the wife grows increasingly silent and withdrawn, then the therapist sees what's wrong: The problem isn't that she doesn't talk, which is a linear explanation. Nor is the problem that he nags, also a linear explanation. The problem is that the more he nags, the more she withdraws, and the more she withdraws, the more he nags.

The trick is to highlight and modify this pattern. This requires forceful intervening. It's usually necessary to use therapeutic dynamite to break families loose from their patterns of equilibrium. Structural therapists use *intensity* to make these interventions.

Minuchin himself speaks to families with dramatic and forceful impact. He regulates the intensity of his messages to exceed the threshold family members have for not hearing challenges to the way they perceive reality. When Minuchin speaks, families listen.

Minuchin is forceful, but his intensity isn't merely a function of his personality; it reflects his clarity of purpose. Knowledge of family structure and a serious commitment to help families change makes powerful interventions possible. Families will usually respond to messages delivered with the kind of intensity that comes from being clear about the goal.

Structural therapists achieve intensity by selective regulation of affect, repetition, and duration. Tone, volume, pacing, and choice of words can be used to raise the affective intensity of statements. It helps if you know what you want to say. Here's an example of a limp statement: "People are always concerned with themselves, kind of seeing themselves as the center of attention and just looking for whatever they can get. Wouldn't it be nice, for a change, if everybody started thinking about what they could do for others? I mean, thinking about other people and the country before themselves." Compare that with, "Ask not what your country can do for you—ask what you can do for your country." John Kennedy's words had impact because they were carefully chosen and clearly put. Family therapists don't need to make speeches or be clever phrasemakers, but they do occasionally have to speak forcefully to get the point across.

Affective intensity isn't simply a matter of crisp phrasing. You have to know how and when to be provocative. For example, Mike Nichols was recently working with a family in which a twenty-nine-year-old woman with anorexia nervosa was the identified patient. Although the family maintained a facade of togetherness, it was rigidly structured; the mother and her anorexic daughter were enmeshed, while the father was excluded. In this family, the father was the only one to express anger openly, and this was part of the official rationale for why he was excluded. His daughter was afraid of his anger, which she freely admitted. What was less clear, however, was that the mother had covertly taught the daughter to avoid him, because she, the mother, couldn't deal with his anger. Consequently, the daughter grew up afraid of her father, and of men in general.

At one point the father described how isolated he felt from his daughter; he said he thought it was because she feared his anger. The daughter agreed, "It's his fault all right." The therapist asked the mother what she thought, and she replied, "It isn't his fault." The therapist said, "You're right." She went on, denying her real feelings to avoid conflict, "It's no one's fault." The therapist answered in a way that got her attention, "That's not true." Startled, she asked what he meant. "It's your fault," the therapist said.

This level of intensity was necessary to interrupt a rigid pattern of conflict-avoidance that sustained a pathogenic alliance between mother and daughter. The content—who really is afraid of anger—is less important than the structural goal: freeing the daughter from her position of overinvolvement with her mother.

Therapists too often dilute their interventions by overqualifying, apologizing, or rambling. This is less of a problem in individual therapy, where it's often best to elicit interpretations from the patient. Families are more like the farmer's proverbial mule—you sometimes have to hit them over the head to get their attention.

Intensity can also be achieved by extending the duration of a sequence beyond the point where the dysfunctional homeostasis is reinstated. A common example is the management of temper tantrums. Temper tantrums are maintained by parents who give in. Most parents *try* not to give in; they just don't try long enough. Recently a four-year-old girl began to scream bloody murder when her sister left the room. She wanted to go with her sister. Her screaming was almost unbearable, and the parents were soon ready to back down. However, the therapist urged that they not allow themselves to be defeated, and suggested that they hold her to "show her who's in charge" until she calmed down. She screamed for thirty minutes! Everyone in the room was frazzled. But the little girl finally realized that this time she was not going to get her way, and so she calmed down. Subsequently, the parents were able to use the same intensity of duration to break her of this highly destructive habit.

Sometimes intensity requires repetition of one theme in a variety of contexts. Infantilizing parents may have to be told not to hang up their child's coat, not to speak for her, not to take her to the bathroom, and not to do many other things that she's able to do for herself.

Shaping competence is another method of modifying interactions, and it's a hallmark of structural family therapy. Intensity is generally used to block the stream of interactions. Shaping competence is like altering the direction of the flow. By highlighting and shaping the positive, structural therapists help family members use functional alternatives that are already in their repertoire.

A common mistake made by beginning family therapists is to attempt to foster competent performance by pointing out mistakes. This is an example of focusing on content without regard for process. Telling parents that they're doing something wrong, or suggesting they do something different has the effect of criticizing their competence. However well-intentioned, it's still a put-down. While this kind of intervention cannot be completely avoided, a more effective approach is to point out what they're doing right.

Even when people do most things ineffectively, it's usually possible to pick out something that they're doing successfully. A sense of timing helps. For example, in a large chaotic family the parents were extremely ineffective at controlling the children. At one point the therapist turned to the mother and said, "It's too noisy in here; would you quiet the kids?" Knowing how much difficulty the woman had controlling her children, the therapist was poised to comment immediately on any step in the direction of effective management. The mother had to yell "Quiet!" a couple of times before the children momentarily stopped what they were doing. Quickly—before the children resumed their misbehavior—the therapist complimented the mother for "loving her kids enough to be firm with them." Thus the message delivered was "You're a competent person, you know how to be firm." If the therapist had waited until the chaos resumed before telling the mother she should be firm, the message would be "You're incompetent."

Wherever possible, structural therapists avoid doing things for family members that they're capable of doing themselves. Here, too, the message is "You are competent, you can do it." Some therapists justify taking over the family's functions by calling it "modeling." Whatever it's called it has the impact of telling family members that they're inadequate. Recently a young mother confessed that she hadn't known how to tell her children that they were coming to see a family therapist and so had simply said she was taking them for a ride. Thinking to be helpful, the therapist then explained to the children that "Mommy told me there were some problems in the family, so we're all here to talk things over to see if we can improve things." This lovely explanation tells the kids why they came, but confirms the mother as incompetent to do so. If instead the therapist had suggested to the mother, "Why don't you tell them now?" Then the mother, not the therapist, would have had to perform as an effective parent.

Boundary Making

Dysfunctional family dynamics are developed from and sustained by overly rigid or diffuse boundaries. Structural therapists intervene to realign boundaries, increasing either proximity or distance between family subsystems.

In highly enmeshed families the therapist's interventions are designed to strengthen boundaries between subsystems and to increase the independence of individuals. Family members are urged to speak for themselves, interruptions are blocked, and dyads are helped to finish conversations without intrusion from others. A therapist who wishes to support the sibling system and protect it from unnecessary parental intrusion may say, "Susie and Sean, talk this over, and everyone else will listen carefully." If children frequently interrupt their parents, a therapist might challenge the parents to strengthen the hierarchical boundary by saying, "Why don't you get them to butt out so that you two grownups can settle this."

Although structural family therapy is begun with the total family group, subsequent sessions may be held with individuals or subgroups to strengthen the boundaries surrounding them. A teenager who is overprotected by her mother is supported as a separate person with individual needs by participating in some separate sessions. Parents so enmeshed with their children that they never have private conversations may begin to learn how if they meet separately with a therapist.

When a forty-year-old woman called the clinic for help with depression, she was asked to come in with the rest of the family. It soon became apparent that this woman was overburdened by her four children and received little support from her husband, either as a husband or a father. The therapist's strategy was to strengthen the boundary between the mother and the children and help the parents move closer toward each other. This was done in stages. First the therapist joined the oldest child, a sixteen-year-old girl, and supported her competence as a potential helper for her mother. Once this was done, the girl was able to assume a good deal of responsibility for her younger siblings, both in sessions and at home.

Freed from some of the preoccupation with the children, the parents now had the opportunity to talk more with each other. They had very little to say to each other, however. This wasn't the result of hidden conflict or anger, but instead it reflected the marriage of a relatively nonverbal husband and wife, with different interests. After several sessions of trying to get the pair to enjoy talking with each other, the therapist realized that while talking may be fun for some people, it may not be for others. So to support the bond between the couple the therapist asked them to plan a special trip together. They chose a boat ride on a nearby lake. When they returned for the next session, the spouses were beaming. They reported having had a wonderful time, being apart from the kids and enjoying each other's company. Subsequently they decided to spend a little time out together each week.

Disengaged families tend to avoid or detour conflict, and thus minimize interaction. The structural therapist intervenes to challenge conflict avoidance, and to block detouring in order to help disengaged members increase contact with each other. The therapist creates boundaries in the session that permit family members to discuss their conflicts without being interrupted. In addition, the therapist prevents escape or avoidance, so that disagreements can be resolved.

Without acting as judge or referee, the structural therapist creates conditions in which family members can face each other squarely and struggle with the difficulties between them. When beginners see disengagement, they tend to think first of ways to increase positive interaction. In fact, disengagement is usually a way of avoiding arguments. Therefore, spouses isolated from each other typically need to fight before they can become more loving.

Most people underestimate the degree to which their own behavior influences and regulates the behavior of those around them. This is particularly true in disengaged families. Problems are usually seen as the result of what someone else is doing, and solutions are thought to require that the others change. The following complaints are typical: "We have a communication problem; he won't tell me what he's feeling." "He just doesn't care about us. All he cares about is that damn job of his." "Our sex life is lousy—my wife's frigid." "Who can talk to her? All she does is complain about the kids." Each of these statements suggests that the power to change rests solely with the other person. This is the almost universally perceived view of linear causality.

Whereas most people see things this way, family therapists see the inherent circularity in systems interaction. He doesn't tell his wife what he's feeling, because she nags and criticizes; *and* she nags and criticizes because he doesn't tell her what he's feeling.

Structural therapists move family discussions from linear to circular causality by stressing the complementarity of family relations. The mother who complains that her son is naughty is taught to consider what she's doing to stimulate or maintain his behavior. The one who asks for change must learn to change his or her way of trying to get it. The wife who nags her husband to spend more time with her must learn to make increased involvement more attractive. The husband who complains that his wife never listens to him may have to listen to *her* more, before she's willing to reciprocate.

Minuchin emphasizes complementarity by asking family members to help each other change. When positive changes are reported, he's liable to congratulate others, underscoring family interrelatedness.

Unbalancing

In boundary making the therapist aims to realign relationships between subsystems. In unbalancing, the goal is to change the relationship of members within a subsystem. What often keeps families stuck in stalemate is that members in conflict check and balance each other and, as a result, remain frozen in inaction. In unbalancing, the therapist joins and supports one individual or subsystem at the expense of others.

Taking sides—let's call it what it is—seems like a violation of therapy's sacred cannon of neutrality. However, the therapist takes sides to unbalance and realign the system, not because he or she is the judge of who's right and wrong, but in order to unfreeze and realign the system. Ultimately, balance and fairness is achieved because the therapist sides in turn with various members of the family.

For example, when the MacLean family sought help for an "unmanageable" child, a terror who'd been expelled from two schools, Dr. Minuchin uncovered a covert split between the parents, held in balance by not being talked about. The ten-year-old boy's misbehavior was dramatically visible; he resisted so strenuously that his father had to drag him, kicking and screaming, into the consulting room. Meanwhile, his seven-year-old brother sat quietly, smiling engagingly. The good boy.

To broaden the focus from an "impossible child" to the issue of parental control and cooperation, Minuchin asked about seven-year-old Kevin, who misbehaved invisibly. He peed on the floor in the bathroom. According to his father, Kevin's peeing on the floor was due to "inattentiveness." Mother laughed when Minuchin said "nobody could have such poor aim."

Minuchin talked with the boy about how wolves mark their territory, and suggested that the boy expand his territory by peeing in all four corners of the family room.

MINUCHIN: "Do you have a dog?"

KEVIN: "No."

MINUCHIN: "Oh, so you are the family dog."

In the process of discussing the boy who peed—and his parents' response—Minuchin dramatized how the parents polarized and undercut each other.

MINUCHIN: "Why would he do such a thing?"

FATHER: "I don't know if he did it on purpose."

MINUCHIN: "Maybe he was in a trance?"

FATHER: "No, I think it was carelessness."

MINUCHIN: "His aim must be terrible."

Father described the boy's behavior as accidental; mother considered it defiance. One of the reasons parents fall under the control of their young children is that they avoid confronting their differences. Differences are normal, but they become toxic when one parent undercuts the other's handling of the children. (It's a cowardly revenge for unaddressed grievances.)

Minuchin's gentle but insistent pressure on the couple to talk about how they respond, without switching to focus on how the children behave, led to their bringing up long-held but seldom-voiced resentments.

MOTHER: "Bob makes excuses for the children's behavior because he doesn't want to get in there and help me find a solution for the problem."

FATHER: "Yes, but when I did try to help, you'd always criticize me. So after a while I gave up."

Like a photographic print in a developing tray, the spouses' conflict had become visible. Minuchin protected the parents from embarrassment (and the children from being burdened) by asking the children to leave the room. Without the preoccupation of parenting, the spouses could face each other, man and woman—and talk about their hurts and grievances. It turned out to be a sad story of lonely disengagement.

MINUCHIN: "Do you two have areas of agreement?"

He said yes; she said no. He was a minimizer; she was a critic.

MINUCHIN: "When did you divorce Bob and marry the children?"

She turned quiet; he looked off into space. She said, softly: "Probably ten years ago."

What followed was a painful but familiar story of how a marriage can drown in parenting and its conflicts. The conflict was never resolved because it never surfaced. And so the rift never healed; it just expanded.

With Minuchin's help, the couple took turns talking about their pain—and learning to listen. By unbalancing, Minuchin brought enormous pressure to bear to help this couple break through their differences, open up to each other, fight for what they want, and, finally, begin to come together—as husband and wife, and as parents.

The familiar image of the therapist—kindly, benevolent, and relatively silent—is based on the analytic model of discovering meaning in a thoughtful, leisurely process.

Unbalancing is part of a struggle for change that sometimes takes on the appearance of combat. When a therapist says to a father that he's not doing enough or to a mother that she's unwittingly excluding her husband, it may seem that the combat is between the therapist and the family, that he or she is attacking them. But the real combat is between the therapist and fear—fear of change.

Challenging the Family's Assumptions

Although structural family therapy is not primarily a cognitive treatment, its practitioners sometimes challenge the way family members perceive reality. Changing the way family members relate to each other offers alternative views of reality. The converse is also true: Changing the way family members view reality enables them to change the way they relate to each other.

People have a habit of becoming the stories they tell about themselves. When memory speaks it tells a "narrative truth," which comes to have more influence than "historical truth." The "facts" presented to a therapist are partly historical truth and partly a construction. The constructions that are the shared reality of a family represent mutual understandings and shared prejudices, some of which are hopeful and helpful, some of which are not.

When six-year-old Cassie's parents complained about her behavior, they said she's "hyper," "sensitive," a "nervous child." Such labels convey how parents respond to their children and have a tremendous controlling power. Is a child's behavior "misbehavior" or is it a symptom of "nervousness?" Is it "naughty" or is it a "cry for help?" Is the child mad or bad, and who is in charge? What's in a name? Plenty.

Sometimes the structural family therapist acts as a teacher, offering information and advice based on training and experience. Information may be imparted to reassure anxious family members, to help them behave more competently, or to restructure their interactions. When family members feel embarrassed because they fight over little things, it may be helpful to tell them that most people do. Sometimes young parents will profit from a simple suggestion that they hire a baby-sitter and get out once in a while.

Minuchin occasionally teaches families about structure. Doing so is likely to be a restructuring maneuver and must be done in a way that minimizes resistance. He does this by delivering first a "stroke," then a "kick." If Minuchin were dealing with a family in which the mother speaks for her children, he might say to her, "You are very helpful" (stroke). But to the child, "Mommy takes away your voice. You can speak for yourself" (kick). Thus mother is defined as helpful but intrusive (a stroke and a kick).

Structural therapists also use constructions that are pragmatic fictions to provide family members with a different frame for experiencing. The aim isn't to educate or deceive, but to offer a pronouncement that will help the family change. For instance, telling children that they're behaving younger than they are is a very effective means of getting them to change. "How old are you?" "Seven." "Oh, I thought you were younger; most seven-year-olds don't need Mommy to take them to school anymore."

Paradoxes are cognitive constructions that frustrate or confuse family members into a search for alternatives. Minuchin himself makes little use of paradox, but sometimes it's useful to express skepticism about people changing.

Although this can have the paradoxical effect of challenging them to prove you wrong, it isn't so much a clever stratagem as it is a benign statement of the truth. Most people *don't* change—they wait for others to do so.

Evaluating Therapy Theory and Results

While he was Director of the Philadelphia Child Guidance Clinic, Minuchin developed a highly pragmatic commitment to research. As an administrator he learned that research demonstrating effective outcomes is the best argument for the legitimacy of family therapy. Both his studies of psychosomatic children and Stanton's studies of drug addicts show very clearly how effective structural family therapy can be.

In *Families of the Slums,* Minuchin and his colleagues (1967) at Wiltwyck described the structural characteristics of low socioeconomic families, and demonstrated the effectiveness of family therapy with this population. Prior to treatment, mothers in patient families were found to be either over- or undercontrolling; either way their children were more disruptive than those in control families. These observations were the basis of Minuchin's classification of families as either *enmeshed* or *disengaged.* After treatment mothers used less coercive control, yet were clearer and more firm. In this study, seven of eleven families were judged to be improved after six months to a year of family therapy. Although no control group was used, the authors compared their results favorably to the usual 50 percent rate of successful treatment at Wiltwyck. The authors also noted that none of the families rated as disengaged improved.

By far the strongest empirical support for structural family therapy comes from a series of studies with psycjosomatic children and adult drug addicts. Studies demonstrating the effectiveness of therapy with severely ill psychosomatic children are convincing because of the physiological measures employed, and dramatic because of the life-threatening nature of the problems. Minuchin, Rosman, and Baker (1978) reported one study that clearly demonstrated how family conflict can precipitate ketoacidosis crises in psychosomatic-type diabetic children. The investigators compared three groups of families—psychosomatic, behavior disorder, and normal—in terms of their response to a sequence of stress interviews. In the baseline interview parents discussed family problems with their children absent. Normal spouses showed the highest levels of confrontation, while psychosomatic spouses exhibited a wide range of conflict-avoidance maneuvers. Next, a therapist pressed the parents to increase the level of their conflict, while their children observed behind a one-way mirror. As the parents argued, only the psychosomatic children seemed really upset. Moreover, these children's manifest distress was accompanied by dramatic increases in free fatty acid levels of the blood, a measure related to ketoacidosis. In the third stage of these interviews, the patients joined their parents. Normal and behavior-disorder parents continued as before, but the psychosomatic parents detoured their conflict, either by drawing their children into their discussions or by switching the subject from themselves to the children. When this happened, the free fatty acid levels of the parents fell, while the children's levels continued to rise. This study provided strong confirmation of the clinical observations that psychosomatic children are used (and let themselves be used) to regulate the stress between their parents.

Minuchin, Rosman, and Baker (1978) summarized the results of treating fifty-three cases of anorexia nervosa with structural family therapy. After a course of treatment that included hospitalization followed by family therapy on an outpatient basis, forty-three anorexic children were "greatly improved," two were "improved," three showed "no change," two were "worse," and three had dropped out. Although ethical considerations precluded a control treatment with these seriously ill children, the 90 percent improvement rate is extremely impressive, especially compared with the usual 30 percent mortality rate for this disorder. Moreover, the positive results at termination were maintained at follow-up intervals of up to several years. Structural family therapy has also been shown to be extremely effective in treating psychosomatic asthmatics and psychosomatically complicated cases of diabetes (Minuchin, Baker, Rosman, Liebman, Milman, & Todd, 1975).

Finally, Duke Stanton has shown that structural family therapy can be an effective form of treatment for drug addicts and their families. In a well-controlled study, Stanton and Todd (1979) compared family therapy with a family placebo condition and individual therapy. Symptom reduction was significant with structural family therapy; the level of positive change was more than double that achieved in the other conditions, and these positive effects persisted at follow-up of six and twelve months.

Summary

Minuchin may be best known for the artistry of his clinical technique, yet his structural family theory has become one of the most widely used conceptual models in the field. The reason his theory is so popular is that it's simple, inclusive, and practical. The basic structural concepts—boundaries, subsystems, alignments, and complementarity—are easily grasped and applied. They take into account the individual, family, and social context, and provide a clear organizing framework for understanding and treating families.

Minuchin first created his technique while working with disorganized families from the inner-city. In order to gain entrance to these families he developed techniques of joining, and in order to change them he developed concrete and powerful restructuring maneuvers. It is a therapy of action, directed at the here and now interactions of families, but designed to alter the basic structure underlying those interactions.

The single most important tenet of this approach is that every family has a structure, and that this structure is revealed only when the family is in action. According to this view, therapists who fail to consider the entire family's structure, and intervene in only one subsystem, are unlikely to effect lasting change. If a mother's overinvolvement with her son is part of a structure that includes distance from her husband, no amount of therapy for the mother and son is likely to change the family.

Subsystems are units of the family based on function. If the leadership of a family is taken over by a father and daughter, then they are the executive subsystem, not the husband and wife. Subsystems are circumscribed and regulated by interpersonal boundaries. In healthy families boundaries are clear enough to protect the separateness and autonomy, and permeable enough to ensure mutual support and affection. Enmeshed families are characterized by diffuse boundaries; disengaged families by rigid boundaries.

Structural family therapy is designed to resolve presenting problems by reorganizing family structure. Assessment, therefore, requires the presence of the whole family, so that the therapist can observe the structure underlying the family's interactions. In the process, therapists should distinguish between dysfunctional and functional structures. Families with growing pains shouldn't be treated as pathological. Where structural problems do exist, the goal is to create an effective hierarchical structure. This means activating dormant structures, not creating new ones.

Structural family therapists work quickly to avoid being *inducted* as members of the families they work with. They begin by making concerted efforts to accommodate to the family's accustomed ways of behaving, in order to circumvent resistance. Once they've gained a family's trust, structural therapists promote family interaction, while they assume a decentralized role. From this position they can watch what goes on in the family and make a diagnosis, which includes the problem and the structure that supports it. These diagnoses are framed in terms of boundaries and subsystems, easily conceptualized as two-dimensional maps used to suggest avenues for change.

Once they have successfully joined and diagnosed a family, structural therapists proceed to activate dormant structures using techniques that alter alignments and shift power within and between subsystems. These restructuring techniques are concrete, forceful, and often highly dramatic. However, their success depends as much on the joining and assessment as on the power of the techniques themselves.

Structural family therapy's popularity is based on its theory and techniques of treatment; its central position in the field has been augmented by its research and training programs. There is now a substantial body of research that lends considerable empirical support to this school's approach. Moreover, the training programs at the Philadelphia Child Guidance Clinic have influenced an enormous number of family therapy practitioners throughout the world.

Although structural family therapy is so closely identified with Salvador Minuchin that they once were synonymous, it may be a good idea to differentiate the man from the method. When we think of structural family therapy, we tend to remember the approach as described in *Families and Family Therapy*, published in 1974. That book adequately represents structural theory, but emphasizes only the techniques Minuchin favored at the time. Minuchin, the thinker, has always thought of families in organizational terms. He read Talcott Parsons and Robert Bales and George Herbert Mead; and in Israel he saw how children from unstructured Moroccan families often became delinquents, while those from organized Yemenite families did not. Minuchin the therapist has always been an opportunist, using whatever works. In the 1990s, you can see Carl Whitaker and constructivism in Minuchin's work. From Whitaker, he took the idea of challenging families' myths and engaging with them from a position of passionate involvement. The young Minuchin followed families and watched them in action; that's why he made such use of enactments. The older Minuchin, who has seen thousands of families, now sees things faster; he uses enactment less and is likely to confront one family on the basis of what he has seen in hundreds of similar cases. Should we follow him in this? Yes, as soon as we have the same experience.

Minuchin has always been a constructivist, though he comes by it intuitively, not from reading books. He challenges families, telling them, essentially, that they are wrong; their stories are too narrow. And he helps them rewrite stories that work. Minuchin has always been interested in literature and story telling; perhaps he likes the doctrine of constructivism simply because it legitimizes his story telling. But, he cautions, when constructivism isn't grounded in structural understanding or when it neglects the emotional side of human beings, it can become arid intellectualism. Minuchin has moved toward eclecticism in technique, but not in theory. Although Minuchin the therapist has changed since 1974, his basic perspective on families, described in structural family theory, still stands, and continues to be the most widely used way of understanding what goes on in the nuclear family.

References

Colapinto, J. 1991. Structural family therapy. In *Handbook of family therapy*, vol. II. A. S. Gurman and D. P. Kniskern, eds. New York: Brunner/Mazel.

Elizur, J., and Minuchin, S. 1989. *Institutionalizing madness: Families, therapy, and society*. New York: Basic Books.

Minuchin, S. 1974. *Families and family therapy.* Cambridge, MA: Harvard University Press.

Minuchin, S., Baker, L., Rosman, B., Liebman, R., Milman, L., and Todd, T. C. 1975. A conceptual model of psychosomatic illness in children. *Archives of General Psychiatry. 32*:1031–1038.

Minuchin, S., and Fishman, H. C. 1981. *Family therapy techniques.* Cambridge, MA: Harvard University Press.

Minuchin, S., Lee, W-Y., and Simon, G. M. 1996. *Mastering family therapy: Journeys of growth and transformation.* New York: Wiley.

Minuchin, S., Montalvo, B., Guerney, B., Rosman, B., and Schumer, F. 1967. *Families of the slums.* New York: Basic Books.

Minuchin, S., and Nichols, M. P. 1993. *Family healing: Tales of hope and renewal from family therapy.* New York: The Free Press.

Minuchin, S., Rosman, B., and Baker, L. 1978. *Psychosomatic families: Anorexia nervosa in context.* Cambridge, MA: Harvard University Press.

Simon, G. M. 1995. A revisionist rendering of structural family therapy. *Journal of Marital and Family Therapy. 21*:17–26.

Stanton, M. D., and Todd, T. C. 1979. Structural family therapy with drug addicts. In *The family therapy of drug and alcohol abuse,* E. Kaufman and P. Kaufmann, eds. New York: Gardner Press.

9

Cognitive-Behavioral Family Therapy

Behavioral family therapists started out using learning theory techniques devised for treating individuals and applying them to problems encountered by families; but in the twenty years since its inception, the technology of behavioral family therapy has become increasingly sophisticated and its practitioners increasingly aware that families are more complicated than individuals. Behavior therapists have developed a variety of powerful, pragmatic techniques that they administer to a variety of family problems, but most of the emphasis remains on parent training, behavioral couples therapy, and treatment of sexual dysfunctions.

The distinctive methods of behavioral family therapy are derived from classical and operant conditioning. Target behavior is precisely specified in operational terms; operant conditioning, classical conditioning, social learning theory, and cognitive strategies are then used to produce change. As behavior therapists have built up experience treating family problems, they have begun to address such traditionally nonbehavioral concerns as the therapeutic alliance, the need for empathy, the problem of resistance, communication, and problem-solving skills. However, even when dealing with such mainstream issues, behaviorists are distinguished by their methodical and directive approach. More than by any technique, behavioral therapy is characterized by careful assessment and evaluation. Analysis of behavioral sequences prior to treatment, assessment of therapy in progress, and evaluation of final results are the hallmarks of behavioral therapy.

When behavioral therapists apply their techniques to families, they are explicit and direct; and they measure their results. This is consistent with the credo of behavior therapy, namely, that behavior is determined more by its consequences than its antecedents.

Sketches of Leading Figures

Behavior therapy is a direct descendent of the laboratory investigations of Ivan Pavlov, the Russian physiologist whose work on conditioned reflexes led to the development of *classical conditioning.* In classical conditioning, an *unconditioned stimulus* (UCS), such as food, which leads to a reflex *unconditioned response* (UCR), like salivation, is paired with a *conditioned stimulus* (CS), such as a bell. The result is that the conditioned stimulus begins to evoke the same response. Pavlov published the results of his laboratory work with animals and also reported on the application of his techniques to abnormal behavior in humans (Pavlov, 1932, 1934). Subsequently John B. Watson applied classical conditioning principles to experimentally induce a phobia in "Little Albert" (Watson & Raynor, 1920), and Mary Cover Jones successfully resolved a similar phobia in the case of "Peter" (Jones, 1924).

In the 1930s and 1940s extensions and elaborations of Pavlov's conditioning theory were applied to numerous clinical problems. Nevertheless classical conditioning was still viewed as having limited practical utility. Then, in 1948, Joseph Wolpe introduced *systematic desensitization,* with which he achieved great success in the treatment of phobias and generated enormous interest in behavioral treatment. According to Wolpe (1948) anxiety is a persistent response of the autonomic nervous system acquired through classical conditioning. Systematic desensitization deconditions the anxiety through *reciprocal inhibition,* by pairing responses that are incompatible with anxiety to the previously anxiety-arousing stimuli. For example, if Indiana Jones was frightened of snakes, Wolpe would first teach Dr. Jones how to relax deeply, and then have him imagine approaching a snake in a graded hierarchy of stages. Each time Indy became anxious, he would be told to relax. In this way the anxiety evoked by imagining snakes would be systematically extinguished by reciprocal inhibition.

Systematic desensitization has proven to be a powerful technique for reducing anxiety, and even more effective when it includes actual practice in gradually approaching the feared object or situation (*in vivo desensitization*).

The application of classical conditioning methods to family problems has been primarily in the treatment of anxiety-based disorders, including agoraphobia and sexual dysfunctions, pioneered by Wolpe (1958) and later elaborated by Masters and Johnson (1970). Effective behavioral treatments for enuresis have also been developed using classical conditioning (Lovibond, 1963).

By far the greatest influence on behavioral family therapy came from B. F. Skinner's *operant conditioning.* The term *operant* refers to voluntary behavioral responses, as opposed to involuntary or reflex behavior. The frequency of operant responses is determined by their consequences. Responses that are *positively reinforced* will occur more frequently; those that are *punished* or ignored will be *extinguished.* In 1953 Skinner published an enormously influential book, *Science and Human Behavior,* in which he presented a behaviorist approach to all human behavior.

The operant conditioner carefully observes target behavior and then quantifies its frequency and rate. Then, to complete a *functional analysis* of the behavior, the experimenter or clinician notes the consequences of the behavior to determine the *contingencies of reinforcement.* For example, someone interested in a child's temper tantrums would begin by observing when they occurred and what their consequences were. A typical finding might be that the child threw a tantrum whenever his parents denied his requests, and that the parents frequently gave in if the tantrums were prolonged. Thus the parents would be reinforcing the very behavior they least wanted. To eliminate the tantrums, they would be taught to ignore or punish them. Moreover they would be told that giving in, even occasionally, would maintain the tantrums, because behavior that is partially or *intermittently reinforced* is the most difficult to extinguish. If the child were aware of the contingencies, he might think, "They're not giving me what I want now, but if I keep fussing they'll eventually give in; if not this time, then the next."

Skinner, who first used the term "behavior therapy," argued convincingly that behavior problems can be dealt with directly, not merely as symptoms of underlying psychic conflict. The first professional journal in this field, *Behavior Research and Therapy*, started in 1963, elicited a flood of studies demonstrating dramatic and impressive behavior change. A key question that arose in those early days was, "How permanent were these changes?" Yes, therapists could shape new sequences of behavior; but would such changes last? In learning theory terms, this is a problem of *generalization*, a problem crucial to any form of therapy. Behavior therapists consider this a problem to be solved, rather than a question to be debated. Behavioral family therapists have worked to generalize their results by moving from the consultation room to natural settings (home and school), using naturalistic reinforcers, employing family members as therapists, and by *fading* (gradually decreasing) external contingencies. Generalization is now programmed rather than hoped for or lamented.

Among the first reports of effective behavior therapy for family problems was Williams's (1959) successful intervention to reduce bedtime tantrums in a young child. The parents were instructed to put the child to bed in an affectionate manner, to close his bedroom door, and ignore his subsequent protestations. The key principle here is *extinction.*

Operant conditioning is particularly effective with children, because parents have considerable control over reinforcers and punishments. Boardman (1962) trained parents in the effective use of a punishment paradigm to deal with the aggressive antisocial behavior of their five-year-old. Wolpe (1958) described how to employ spouses as cotherapists in anxiety management. Risley and Wolf (1967) trained parents in the operant reinforcement of speech in their autistic children. In technical terms, these parents and spouses were trained to eliminate the contingencies that maintained the deviant behavior and to employ different contingencies to prompt and support more desirable behavior patterns that were incompatible with the deviant behavior (Falloon, 1991). In plain English, they were taught to ignore inappropriate and to reward appropriate behavior.

Although no single figure was responsible for the development of behavior family therapy, three leaders played a dominant role: a psychologist, Gerald Patterson, a psychiatrist, Robert Liberman, and a social worker, Richard Stuart.

Gerald Patterson, at the University of Oregon, was the most influential figure in developing behavioral parent training. Patterson and his colleagues realized that observation of family interactions in a laboratory or consulting room was far removed from the behavior in the natural environment of the home. As a result, they developed methods for sampling periods of family interaction in the home, trained parents in the principles of social learning theory, developed programmed workbooks (e.g., Patterson, 1971b), and worked out careful strategies for eliminating undesirable behavior and substituting desirable behavior. Among others prominent in this field are Anthony Graziano, Rex Forehand, Daniel and Susan O'Leary, and Roger McAuley in Belfast, Ireland.

The second major figure in the development of behavioral family therapy was Robert Liberman. In his 1970 paper, "Behavioral Approaches to Family and Couple Therapy," he outlined the application of an operant learning framework to the family problems of four adult patients with depression, intractable headaches, social inadequacy, and marital discord. In addition to employing contingency management of mutual reinforcers, Liberman introduced the use of *role rehearsal* and *modeling* concepts of Bandura and Walters (1963) to family therapy.

The third major influence on behavioral family therapy was the contingency contracting approach of Richard Stuart (1969). Rather than focus on how the undesired behavior of one family member could be modified, Stuart focused on how the exchange of positive behavior could be maximized. Thus he introduced the principle of *reciprocity*.

In his first efforts, Stuart (1969) transferred operant principles, used to modify children's behavior, to couples in distress. He applied a reciprocal reinforcement paradigm in which couples learned to: (a) list the behavior they desired from each other; (b) record the frequency with which the spouse displayed the desired behavior; and (c) specify exchanges for the desired behavior. In this early work, tokens were used for reinforcers. Mutual exchanges were based on written contracts.

The early work in behavioral family therapy depended almost entirely on operant conditioning and appeared most successful where behavioral problems could be defined in terms of relatively straightforward stimulus-response exchanges.

Ed Katkin (1978) reported success with *charting* in the treatment of a paranoid and jealous wife. In charting, the patient is asked to keep an accurate record of the problem behavior. Katkin's ploy was to ask the wife to record the frequency of her irrational accusations. This approach illustrates the early attempts to approach family problems through the treatment of individuals. It also illustrates the adaptation of nonbehavioral techniques—in this case, paradoxical intention.

Other early applications of behavior therapy to couples included teaching spouses how to shape positive behavior in one another (Liberman, 1970) and having them analyze the consequences of their behavior and learn to interrupt negative interaction chains (Friedman, 1972). Mutual behavior change efforts were given even more structure by introducing behavioral contracts, written agreements to exchange desired behavior (Rappaport & Harrell, 1972).

During the 1970s behavioral family therapy was developed into three major packages: parent training, behavioral couples therapy, and sexual therapy. At present the leading figures in behavioral couples therapy include Robert Weiss, Neil Jacobson, Richard Stuart, Michael Crowe, Ian Falloon, Norman Epstein, and Gayola Margolin. Weiss took over the development of marital therapy from Gerald Patterson and was particularly influential in establishing a substantial body of research in the assessment and treatment of marital discord.

Two additional developments have further increased the popularity and influence of behavior therapy. First, many nonbehavioral family therapists selectively include behavioral interventions in their work. A good example of this was Minuchin's (Minuchin, Rosman, & Baker, 1978) use of operant conditioning in his work with anorexia nervosa. Second, there has recently been a rapprochement between stimulus-response conditioning models and cognitive theories (e.g., Mischel, 1973; Barton & Alexander, 1981; Epstein, Schlesinger, & Dryden, 1988; Dattilio, 1997b). Now many behavioral therapists are beginning to consider the role of various "internal" processes such as attitudes, thoughts, and feelings. In addition, family systems theory is having an increasing impact on behavioral family therapists. Gerald Patterson, once a pure operant behaviorist, studied systems theory with Salvador Minuchin; as first illustrated in an article published in *Family Process* by Spinks and Birchler (1982), dealing with resistance has become a major concern in behavioral family therapy; and recent books on the state of the art in behavior family therapy (e.g., Falloon, 1988; Dattilio, 1997b) are very sophisticated in their handling of family systems dynamics.

Theoretical Formulations

Those approaching behavior therapy for the first time are often confused by references to *learning theory, behavior modification, behavior therapy,* and *social learning theory.* Although sometimes used interchangeably, each of these terms has its own meaning. *Learning theory* refers to the general body of principles discovered in laboratory experiments on learning and conditioning. These laws are the scientific foundation upon which behavioral treatment rests. *Behavior modification* and *behavior therapy* have been used interchangeably, although some distinctions have been made between them. Lazarus (1971) suggested that *behavior modification* refers to strict operant procedures, while *behavior therapy* is associated with counterconditioning methods for treating anxiety. *Behavior modification* has lately been less often used and seems to conjure up an image of mindless control among the public, who sometimes confuse the ends of behavior control with the efficiency of methods used to achieve it. Because the term *behavior therapy* is now commonly used to refer to all operant and nonoperant behavioral treatments, we will follow this usage. *Social learning theory* is a broad approach to human behavior, integrating principles from social, developmental, and cognitive psychology along with those principles of learning derived from experimental psychology. In social learning theory, environmental influences are still the primary concern, but private thoughts and feelings are also used to understand behavior. This framework takes into account the pervasive effects of social influences on behavior. *Cognitive-behavior therapy* refers to those approaches inspired by the work of Aaron Beck (1976) and Albert Ellis (1962) that emphasize the need for attitude change to promote and maintain behavior change.

The central premise of behavior therapy is that *behavior is maintained by its consequences.* It follows from this that behavior resists change unless more rewarding consequences result from new behavior (Patterson, 1971b). Elaborating the consequences of behavior as well as the cues that elicit it requires an understanding of *stimuli* and *reinforcements.*

Four different stimulus functions are described by learning theorists: eliciting stimuli, discriminative stimuli, neutral stimuli, and reinforcing stimuli. *Eliciting stimuli* are aspects of a situation that reliably produce a response. These are particularly relevant to classical conditioning, where certain eliciting stimuli are known to produce reflexlike responses. *Discriminative stimuli* signal the occasions when a particular response will be followed by a certain consequence. Because they've been associated with those consequences in the past, discriminative stimuli have acquired a cuing function making particular responses more probable. Children, for example, quickly learn to detect certain discriminative stimuli that indicate their parents "really mean it" when they say something. *Neutral stimuli* have no direct relationship to behavior, but conditioning can establish a link between a previously neutral stimulus and a response. Thus Pavlov's dogs responded to a bell only after it had been paired with feeding. *Reinforcing stimuli* are consequences of behavior that affect the probability of future responses. They are cues that reinforcement will follow.

Responses are usually defined as *respondent* or *operant.* Respondents are those that are under the control of eliciting stimuli, and their consequences don't usually affect their frequency of occurrence. Operants are behaviors that aren't automatically elicited by some stimulus, but whose occurrence is affected by their consequences. From a systems point of view, the distinction between respondents and operants is problematic. Operants are causes, whereas respondents are effects. From a linear viewpoint this is a useful distinction, but when we think in terms of circular causal chains, the usefulness of this distinction breaks down. With a nagging wife and a withdrawing husband, what is cause and what is effect? Is the nagging an operant or a respondent behavior? (Both spouses can give you the answer—and both answers will be different.)

Some responses may not be recognized as operants—something done to get something—just because people aren't aware of the reinforcing payoffs. For example, whining is usually reinforced by attention, although the people providing the reinforcement may not realize it. In fact, a variety of undesired behaviors, including nagging and temper tantrums, are reinforced by attention. Even though the attention may be unpleasant—yelling—it may be the most social interaction that the nagging spouse or tantruming child receives. Thus, responses are often maintained under conditions that are counterintuitive.

Reinforcements are consequences that affect the rate of behavior, either accelerating or decelerating it. Consequences that accelerate behavior are called *reinforcers,* while those that decelerate behavior are known as *punishers.* Within the class of reinforcers there are: (a) *positive reinforcers,* positive or rewarding consequences; and (b) *negative reinforcers,* aversive consequences terminated by a response. Thus, parents can positively reinforce their child's cleaning her room by rewarding her after she does it, or negatively reinforce her by nagging until she does it.

Punishment can take the form of (a) *aversive control,* such as yelling or spanking, or (b) *withdrawal of positive consequences,* such as having to sit in the corner or being "grounded" for a week. Punishment and negative reinforcement are often confused, but do have distinctly different meanings.

Reinforcement and punishment may be either primary or secondary. *Primary reinforcers* are natural or biological outcomes, including sex and food; *primary punishments* might be physical pain or loud noises. *Secondary reinforcers* are ones that have acquired a positive meaning through social learning, like praise or eye contact, while *secondary punishers* include criticism or withdrawal of attention. Because attention has such a powerful influence on behavior, focusing attention on undesirable behavior often provides unintended social reinforcement.

Extinction occurs when no reinforcement follows a response. Inattention, as many people know, is often the best response to behavior you don't like. The reason many people fail to credit this is because withholding response rarely leads to *immediate* cessation of unwanted behavior. This is because most behavior has been partially or intermittently reinforced, and therefore takes time to extinguish.

The relationship between a response and its consequences defines the *contingencies* governing that response. *Reinforcement schedules* describe the relationship between responding and the occurrence of consequences. When reinforcement occurs at irregular intervals, the response becomes more resistant to extinction. Perhaps you can think of a reinforcement schedule with such regular contingencies of reinforcement that even a few occurrences of nonreinforcement would be sufficient to convince you that no further reinforcement is forthcoming.

While it's easy to see how simple responses can be reinforced, it may be less clear how more complicated responses, including responses not yet in someone's repertoire, can be learned. One way for this to occur is by successive approximation, or *shaping.* For example, parents can shape a child's learning to play soccer by paying attention to and praising the child's gradual development of the component skills of the game. Negative behavior can also be shaped, as in those families where children only get attention for progressively more angry and destructive behavior. (Children and recalcitrant spouses can also shape yelling by refusing to respond until the volume gets turned way up.)

In addition to shaping, *modeling* is also used to teach complex or new behavior (Bandura, 1969). People often learn by emulating others, particularly if the models are perceived as successful or prestigious, and if their behavior is seen to lead to reinforcing consequences (Bandura & Walters, 1963). Modeling can be used by a therapist or family member who exhibits a desired behavior that is then imitated by another member of the family. The amount of learning that takes place during modeling depends on the degree to which the target family member pays attention, has the capacity to understand and rehearse the new behavior, and can reproduce the behavior. Modeling has been found to be an effective way to short-cut the long and tedious process of trial-and-error learning. (Imagine trying to teach someone how to be pleasant without showing them how.)

To many people, behavior therapy seems mindless and mechanistic. With all their talk about "schedules of reinforcement" and "controlling behavior," behavior therapists seem to ignore thoughts and feelings. While this may have been true of early behaviorists, it's less true today. Behavior therapists are increasingly aware that people not only act but also think and feel. And behaviorists are becoming increasingly aware of complications with simply reeducating patients about their behavior. The most frequent form this recognition takes is in efforts to integrate pure stimulus-response behaviorism (Skinner, 1953) and cognitive theories (Mahoney, 1977). Inner events such as cognitions, verbalizations, and feelings are now recognized as events that function as stimuli in controlling behavior.

As behavior therapists shifted their attention from individuals in isolation to family relationships, they came to rely on Thibaut and Kelley's (1959) *theory of social exchange.* According to social exchange theory, people strive to maximize "rewards" and minimize "costs" in relationships. When applied to marriage, this behavioral economics provides a basis for understanding the reciprocity that develops between spouses. In a successful marriage both partners work to maximize mutual rewards, while minimizing costs. By contrast, in unsuccessful marriages the partners are too busy trying to protect themselves from being hurt to consider ways to make each other happy. Each person can trim the costs of relating by giving less value (e.g., by withdrawing) or by shifting to negative reinforcement and punishment. According to Thibaut and Kelley, behavior exchanges follow a norm of reciprocity over time, so that aversive or positive stimulation from one person tends to produce reciprocal behavior from another. Pleasantness begets pleasantness; nastiness begets nastiness.

In its early days behavior therapy tended to focus on individuals rather than relationships. This focus is reflected in the early reports of behavioral marital therapy in which therapists treated spouses separately in individual sessions (Goldiamond, 1965) or treated only one spouse. For example, in two of three marital therapy cases reported by Lazarus (1968) only the wife was treated. Typically, wives were offered desensitization and assertiveness training to help them establish a more balanced and effective relationship with their husbands. Other therapists taught wives the principles of reinforcement and extinction so that they could modify their husbands' behavior (Goldstein, 1971; Goldstein & Francis, 1969).

Asked to treat children, behaviorists initially began seeing them individually. Later, like systems theorists, they began to consider other people in the children's environments as part of the problem. But unlike systems theorists, many behaviorists continue to operate with a linear point of view. The parents' behavior is seen as *causing* the children's behavior. Moreover, despite disclaimers to the contrary (Gordon & Davidson, 1981; Liberman, 1970), the unit of behavioral analysis is *dyadic* rather than *triadic.* The focus is on changing interactions between a parent (usually the mother) and a child, or between one spouse and another. Little or no attention is paid to how these relationships are affected by others in the family. Gordon and Davidson (1981) acknowledge that deviant child behavior may be related to other problems in the family, but suggest that this is much exaggerated by systems theorists.

> Clinical experience indicates that deviant child behavior occurs in families with *and without* marital discord. The simple presence of marital discord in these families may or may not be causally related to the child's problems. (p. 522)

From a systems point of view, such a statement seems naive; the authors apparently fail to recognize that *overt* marital discord may be absent precisely *because* the spouses have triangulated their conflict onto a child.

Normal Family Development

Behaviorists deemphasize historical data in favor of analyses of current sequences of behavior. As a result, behavioral family therapists have little to say about the development of normal or abnormal behavior. Instead they focus on the current state of affairs. Moreover, most of their descriptions of healthy family relationships are extrapolated from descriptions of distressed families. However, in recent years, behavioral investigators have begun to delineate the characteristics of successful marriages directly (Jacobson, Waldron, & Moore, 1980; Markman, 1981; Wills, Weiss, & Patterson, 1974).

According to the behavior exchange model (Thibaut & Kelley, 1959), a good relationship is one in which giving and getting are balanced. Another way of stating this is that there's a high ratio of benefits relative to costs. Put as generally as this, little is added to everyday commonsense notions of family satisfaction. But behaviorists have begun to spell out, in empirical studies, some of the details of what makes for relationship satisfaction. For example, Weiss and Isaac (1978) found that affection, communication, and child care are the most important behaviors leading to marital satisfaction. Earlier, Wills, Weiss, and Patterson (1974), in a pioneering behavioral analysis of satisfaction in marriage, found that affectional and instrumental *dis*pleasures were more important than pleasures in determining marital satisfaction. They found that the exchange of displeasurable responses reduced marital satisfaction significantly more than pleasurable responses increased it. A good relationship, then, is one in which there is an exchange of pleasant behavior and, even more important, minimal unpleasant behavior. Another way of putting this is that good relationships are under positive reinforcing control.

Since satisfaction and persistence in a relationship depend on maintaining a high level of rewards relative to costs, success will depend on a couple's coping successfully with numerous obstacles to the maximization of this ratio (Holtzworth-Munroe & Jacobson, 1991). Maintaining a high ratio isn't much of a problem during the early stages of a relationship, when reinforcing value is at its peak and few of the costs inherent in a long-term commitment have yet been encountered. In time, however, spouses begin to experience each other in new roles, not all of which are rewarding; commitment requires each to accommodate to the other. Something more easily said than done.

Because behaviorists focus on overt behavior, they've tended to look at the benefits of family life in terms of manifest and tangible events. Thus they tend to overlook the fact that unconscious benefits are among the most important sources of satisfaction and stability in family life. Moreover, the behavior exchange model posits a *comparison level* or evaluation of cost/benefit reward ratio offered by the partner as compared with possible relationships outside the family. Here the behavioral bias may underestimate the importance of one's own self-evaluation of worth. Some people may be satisfied with a low benefit to cost ratio, because they feel they "don't deserve any better." Furthermore, your own evaluation of the benefits of family life is also influenced by previous models (especially parents), and by images of an ideal partner. Clinical experience demonstrates that some people are dissatisfied despite being married to partners who behave in a very rewarding fashion. Perhaps for these people internal images of what married life "should be" are more important than the overt behavior of their spouses. Put in terms of social learning theory, there's a need to consider not only the stimuli provided by other family members, but also the way these stimuli are perceived. An increasing attention to cognitive variables will allow behavior therapists to take such ideas into account.

Communication skills—the ability to talk, especially about problems—is considered by behaviorists *the* most important feature of good relationships (Gottman, Markman, & Notarius, 1977; Jacobson, Waldron, & Moore, 1980). (It's also the feature of relationships that is most obvious and easily observed.) Good communication increases the rewards and pleasures of relating by leading to effective stimulus control over behavior. Clear communication enables family members to discriminate among and between behavioral events, and enhances their ability to be understanding and to give support. Communication skills also predict later marital satisfaction levels (Markman, 1981).

In time all couples run into conflict, and therefore a critical skill in maintaining family harmony is skill in conflict resolution (Gottman & Krokoff, 1989). Families in treatment often express the desire to be free of problems, and many look to therapists to solve their problems for them. Unfortunately, problems are part of life. Healthy families aren't problem-free, but have the ability to cope with problems when they arise. Recognizing this, behavior therapists stress the need for problem-solving skills and the ability to resolve conflicts as criteria for successful marriages (Jacobson & Margolin, 1979).

In a good relationship the partners are able to speak openly and directly about conflicts. They focus on issues and keep them in perspective, and they discuss specific behaviors that are of concern to them. They describe their own feelings and request changes in the behavior of others, as opposed to just criticizing and complaining. "I've been kind of lonely and I wish you and I could go out and do things more often" is more likely to get a positive response than, "You never care what I want! All you care about is yourself!" In addition to expressing their concerns as requests rather than attacks, successful family members listen to other family members' points of view and attempt to understand what's being said.

When problems arise or when circumstances change, families need the skills to change behavior. Some behaviorists consider communications skills to be the most powerful determinant of marital success (Markman, 1979), whereas others emphasize sexual gratification (Masters & Johnson, 1970).

Many people assume that good family relationships will occur naturally if people are well matched and if they love each other. Behaviorists, on the other hand, consistently emphasize the need to develop relationship skills. Good marriages, they believe, aren't made in heaven, but are a product of learning effective coping behavior. Jacobson (1981) described a good relationship as one in which the partners maintain a high rate of rewards.

> Successful couples adapt effectively to the requirements of day-to-day intimacy. In particular, they expend their reinforcement power by frequently acquiring new domains for positive exchange. Spouses who depend on a limited quantity and variety of reinforcers are bound to suffer the ill effects of satiation. As a result, over time their interaction becomes depleted of its prior reinforcement

> value. Successful couples cope with this inevitable reinforcement erosion by varying their shared activities, developing new common interests, expanding their sexual repertoires, and developing their communication to the point where they continue to interest one another. (p. 561)

Like others, behaviorists emphasize the capacity for adaptability, flexibility, and change; they stress that these aren't personality traits but skills that can be learned, most easily in relationships that are under the stimulus control of rules and where there's a consensus about what the rules are (Weiss, 1978). Moreover, the rules should be comprehensive and flexible rather than narrow or rigid (Jacobson & Margolin, 1979). In happy relationships rewards exceed costs; social reinforcement is dispensed equitably and at a high rate. Moreover, these relationships are built upon positive control, rather than negative reinforcement, punishment, or coercion (Stuart, 1975).

Development of Behavior Disorders

Behaviorists view symptoms as learned responses, involuntarily acquired and reinforced. They don't look for underlying meaning in symptoms, nor do they posit conflict in or between spouses as leading to problems in the children. Instead they concentrate on the symptoms themselves and look for environmental responses that reinforce problem behavior.

At first glance it would seem unlikely that family members reinforce undesirable behavior. Why, for example, would parents reinforce temper tantrums? Or why would a wife reinforce her husband's withdrawal, when it appears to cause her so much pain? The answer isn't to be found in some kind of convoluted motive for suffering, but in the simple fact that people often inadvertently reinforce precisely those responses that cause them the most distress.

Naturally it's easier to see how *other* people cause their own problems. How many times have you seen parents threaten their children with punishments they don't carry out? And most of us still remember how our own parents failed to reward us for certain skills and achievements. The local shopping mall, American family life's public stage, is a good place to observe how harried parents fail to punish misbehavior and reward good behavior in their children. And while it's a little harder, it's also possible to begin observing yourself and discovering how often you use reinforcement to shape the behavior of people in your own social context.

It's also possible to notice that "punishments" may have the opposite effect from what's intended. Consider the following scenario.

> Five-year-old Sandy is playing quietly while her father reads the newspaper. After a few minutes, she knocks the Tinker Toys off the table and onto the floor. Her father puts down the paper and tells her to be quiet. A little later she starts singing; again her father tells her to quiet down. Finally, she begins making so much noise that her father slams down the paper, storms into the room where she's playing, and gives her a long lecture on the virtues of playing quietly and not disturbing her parents.

What is Sandy apt to learn from this episode? That if she makes enough noise she'll get her father's attention.

Parents usually respond to problem behavior in their children by scolding and lecturing. These reactions may seem like punishment, but they may in fact be reinforcing, because attention—even from an angry parent—is an extremely powerful *social reinforcer* (Skinner, 1953). The truth of this is reflected in the sound advice to "Ignore it and it will go away." The problem is that most parents have trouble ignoring undesirable behavior in their children. Notice, for example, how quickly children learn that certain words get a big reaction. Moreover, even when parents do resolve to ignore some misbehavior, they usually don't do so consistently. This can make things even worse, because *intermittent reinforcement* is the most resistant to extinction (Ferster, 1963).

In addition to behavior problems unwittingly maintained by parental attention, others persist because many parents are unaware of how to make effective use of punishment. Parents make threats that they don't follow through on; they punish so long after the fact that the child doesn't associate the punishment with the bad behavior; they use punishments so mild as to have no effect; or they use punishments so severe as to cause fear and anxiety instead of discriminative learning.

Systems thinkers would find the previous discussion wanting, because it's based on a linear view of causality: Children continue to misbehave *because* their parents use ineffective contingencies of reinforcement. While it's true that most behavioral family therapists do operate with a linear model, some have attempted to offer a more complex model. For example, Liberman (1972) has described the family as a system of *interlocking reciprocal behaviors;* Gerald Patterson has described patterns of *reciprocal reinforcement* in families. Consider the behavior of a mother and daughter in the supermarket.

> The little girl asks her mother for a candy bar; the mother says, "No." The child begins crying and complaining, and the mother says, "If you think I'm going to buy you candy when you make such a fuss you have another think coming, young lady!" But the child escalates her tantrum, getting louder and louder. Finally, the exasperated and embarrassed mother gives in, saying, "All right, if you'll quiet down first, I'll buy you some cookies."

Obviously, the child has been reinforced for throwing a temper tantrum. Not so obviously, but also true, the mother has been reinforced for giving in—by the child's quieting down after being promised cookies. Thus a spiral of undesirable behavior is maintained by reciprocal reinforcement.

Behavioral family therapists have described a number of defective patterns of reinforcement in cases of marital discord. Azrin, Naster, and Jones (1973) listed the following causes of marital discord:

1. Receiving too little reinforcement from the marriage.
2. Too few needs given marital reinforcement.
3. Marital reinforcement no longer provides satisfaction.
4. New behaviors are not reinforced.
5. One spouse gives more reinforcement than he or she receives.
6. Marriage interferes with extramarital sources of satisfaction.
7. Communication about potential sources of satisfaction is not adequate.
8. Aversive control predominates over positive reinforcement.

The use of *aversive control* is often cited as the major determinant of marital unhappiness. In dysfunctional marriages, spouses react to problems with attempts at aversive control—nagging, crying, withdrawing, or threatening. Rarely do these couples think to shape positive alternatives. So, as a result, the spouses feel more and more negatively about each other. If someone yells at you to stop doing something, you will probably feel upset and anxious; you may understand what the person wants you to do, but you certainly won't feel like going out of your way to please that person. You may not even understand; you may be too anxious or bitter.

In distressed marriages there are fewer rewarding exchanges and more punishing exchanges, verbal and instrumental (Stuart, 1975). Spouses typically reciprocate their partners' use of punishment, and a vicious circle develops (Patterson & Reid, 1970). Partners enter marriage expecting that the rewards of being married will exceed the rewards of remaining single.

Marriage provides countless opportunities for rewarding exchanges, and well-functioning couples exchange many benefits. However, when there's a failure to exchange benefits, the reward system shifts from positive to aversive control. The wife whose generosity toward her husband is neither acknowledged nor reciprocated begins to demand her share of exchanged rewards. Unfortunately, as Weiss (1978) observed, "Forced rewards, like solicited compliments, lose their value" (p. 189).

People in distressed family relationships also have poor problem-solving skills (Vincent, Weiss, & Birchler, 1975; Weiss, Hops, & Patterson, 1973). When they discuss a problem, they frequently change the subject; they phrase wishes and complaints in vague and critical ways; and they respond to complaints with countercomplaints. The following exchange demonstrates sidetracking, cross-complaining, and name-calling, all typical of distressed marriages.

> "I'd like to talk about all the sweets you've been giving the kids lately." "What sweets! Talk about me, you're always stuffing your face. And what do you ever do for the kids? You just come home and complain. Why don't you just stay at the office! The kids and I get along better without you."

According to Patterson and Reid (1970), reciprocity also exists between parents and children: Parents who behave aversively toward their children get the same in return. This also holds true for negative reinforcement. Children as well as parents develop patterns of reinforcement that exert a powerful controlling effect. If the children are consciously aware of these contingencies, they may be called "manipulative," but often they are as oblivious to the consequences of their responses as are their parents.

Most behavioral analyses point to the lack of reinforcement for adaptive strivings in distressed families. The old adage, "The squeaky wheel gets the grease," seems to apply in such families. Depressions, headaches, and temper tantrums tend to elicit concern and therefore more attention than prosocial behavior. Because this process is unwitting, family members are often mystified about their role in maintaining maladaptive behavior. Behavior therapists believe that since abnormal behavior is learned and maintained by the same processes as normal behavior, it can therefore be treated directly, without reference to underlying causes.

Goals of Therapy

The goals of behavioral therapy are unambiguous and limited: modifying specific behavior patterns to alleviate the presenting symptoms. There is little concern with systems change or growth and development. Symptom change isn't thought to lead to symptom substitution, but to inaugurate a positive spiral of behavior, and is dealt with by techniques designed to substitute desirable alternative behaviors.

The behavioral family therapist tailors treatment to fit each family; the goal is to eliminate undesirable behavior or increase positive behavior as defined by the family (Azrin, Naster, & Jones, 1973). Sometimes it may be necessary to redefine a family's goal of decreasing negative behavior in terms of increasing positive and incompatible behavior (Umana, Gross, & McConville, 1980), or to one that is interpersonal rather than centered on one individual. But these are essentially strategies to solve the presenting problem, not broader goals.

Couples often state goals of reducing aversive behavior, but this pain-avoidance strategy only reduces dissatisfaction without increasing positive feelings (Weiss, 1978). Therefore behavioral couples therapists also help spouses increase their satisfaction by accelerating positive behavior. "The goal of behavioral marital counseling is to provide couples with behavior change operations based upon positive control procedures" (Weiss, 1978, p. 206).

The general goals of behavioral therapy are to increase the rate of rewarding interactions by fostering positive behavior change; to decrease the rate of coercion and adversive control; and to teach more effective communication and problem-solving skills (Gurman & Knudson, 1978).

Some of the goals of behavioral family therapy may be shaped by the clientele and setting in which it is practiced. Behavior marital therapy, for example, is most frequently practiced in university teaching clinics. The therapists are often graduate students, and much of the treatment is conducted on an experimental basis. Clients in these settings tend to be relatively young and advantaged; and clients and therapists are often close to each other in age, outlook, and values. Not surprisingly, therapy in such a context often becomes a collaborative effort between people who feel each other to be peers, and a fair amount of teaching goes on. In case studies of behavioral family therapy, many of the interventions take the form of interpretations designed to foster conscious insight. For example, Liberman (1972) reported on his treatment of a couple in which the wife got her husband's attention only when she had headaches. Liberman explained the dynamics of this to the couple; thereafter the husband started paying attention to the appropriate wifely and motherly behavior, while ignoring the headaches. Sounds simple, doesn't it?

What this demonstrates is that behavioral family therapists aim not only to alleviate symptoms, but also to teach skills and foster understanding so that families will be able to solve their own problems in the future. This point is supported by Robert Weiss (1978) who suggests that many forms of behavioral family therapy are more concerned with prevention than with cure.

Conditions for Behavior Change

The basic premise of behavior therapy is that behavior will change when the contingencies of reinforcement are altered. Behavioral family therapy aims to change specific targeted family problems through the identification of behavioral goals, social learning theory techniques for achieving these goals, and the use of natural or contrived social reinforcers to facilitate this process. Significant others are trained to use contingency management techniques to influence behavior of other family members and to provide appropriate consequences for desired behavior.

The hallmarks of behavioral family therapy are: (1) careful and detailed assessment, to determine the baseline frequency of problem behavior, to guide therapy, and to provide accurate feedback about the success of treatment; and (2) specific strategies designed to modify the contingencies of reinforcement in each unique client family.

To begin with, a *functional analysis of behavior* is required to identify the antecedents and consequences of the target behavior. Once this is complete, a specific approach is designed for specific problems. First, behavioral family therapists specify family problems in concrete, observable—and measurable—terms. Second, they plan specific strategies based on an empirical theory of behavior change. And third, their efforts are subjected to empirical analysis of their effects in achieving specified behavioral goals. Thus, each family is treated as a unique case, whose therapy program is conceived of as a single-subject experiment.

Careful observation is considered a prerequisite to attempts to control behavior. The first task of the therapist is to observe and record the frequency and duration of problem behavior, as well as the stimulus conditions that precede it and the reinforcement that follows it. This enables the therapist to design an individually tailored treatment program.

Moving out of the playroom and the office into the natural world of the home and classroom enabled behavior therapists to discover that some of their previous notions about child aggression were fundamentally erroneous. Contrary to Skinner's assumptions, punishment *does* have long-term effects. The data show that reinforcement of positive behavior, such as cooperation and compliance, doesn't lead to reductions in antisocial behavior. Introducing punishment (time out, point loss) produces long-term reductions in antisocial behavior (Patterson, 1988).

Furthermore, behavioral family therapists now realize that the manner in which problems are reinforced in families is often a complex process (Falloon, 1991). In addition to the reinforcing responses that immediately follow a specific problem behavior, more remote reinforcers may play a part in creating support for problem behavior. These may include tacit approval of aggressive behavior, particularly by men in the family, often accompanied by modeling of this behavior. Spanking children for fighting demonstrates by example the violence that a parent may wish to discourage. In addition, behavior that is approved of by peers or other groups outside the family may be extremely difficult to modify at home—especially if the therapist fails to take this wider context into account.

The primary approach in behavioral family therapy is operant rather than classical conditioning (with the exception of treating sexual dysfunctions), and the focus is on changing dyadic interactions (parent–child or spouse–spouse). This dyadic focus differs from the triadic approach of systems-oriented family therapists. Although behavioral family therapists (Liberman, 1970; Falloon & Lillie, 1988) have disputed this distinction, we believe this is a major difference between behavioral and nonbehavioral family therapists.

Although behavior change remains the primary focus, more and more behavioral family therapists are recognizing the critical role of cognitive factors in developing and resolving relationship problems. In a classic study Margolin and Weiss (1978) first demonstrated the effectiveness of a cognitive component to behavioral marital therapy by comparing couples treatment using a strictly behavioral approach with a group that also received a cognitive component. The treatment that included cognitive restructuring techniques proved significantly more effective than behavioral marital therapy alone on several outcome measures.

During the 1980s, cognitive techniques became increasingly prominent as behavior therapists realized that the straight behavioral approach failed to address the complicating dynamics of couple and family interactions. Gradually it became clear that behavior therapy's strength was dealing with specific behavioral problems, such as poor communication or acting-out behavior, as opposed to handling the more comprehensive problems posed by dysfunctional family dynamics (Sanders & Dadds, 1993; Goldenberg & Goldenberg, 1991).

The cognitive approach first gained attention as a supplement to behavioral-oriented couples and family therapy (Margolin, Christensen, & Weiss, 1975). In addition to the work of Ellis (1977), the Margolin and Weiss study (1978) sparked intense interest in cognitive techniques with dysfunctional couples (Baucom & Epstein, 1990; Baucom & Lester, 1986; Beck, 1988; Dattilio, 1990; Dattilio & Padesky, 1990; Doherty, 1981; Ellis et al., 1989; Epstein, 1992; Finchman, Bradbury, & Beach, 1990; Schindler & Vollmer, 1984; Weiss, 1984). This interest in cognitive-behavioral approaches to couples therapy eventually led to the recognition by behavioral family therapists that cognition plays a significant role in the events that mediate family interactions (Alexander & Parsons, 1982). The important role of cognitive factors, not only in determining relationship distress but also in mediating behavioral change, has become a topic of increasing interest (Epstein, Schlesinger, & Dryden, 1988; Alexander, 1988; Dattilio, 1993).

Although marital and family therapists began to realize decades ago that cognitive factors were important in the alleviation of relationship dysfunction (Dicks, 1953), it took some time before cognition was formally included as a primary component of treatment (Munson, 1993).

Barton and Alexander, who call their approach *functional family therapy* (Barton & Alexander, 1981; Morris, Alexander, & Waldron, 1988), point out that members of unhappy families tend to attribute their problems to negative traits (laziness, irresponsibility, poor impulse control) in other members. Such views block therapeutic change by projecting blame in a way that makes it impossible for anyone to change. Such negative and incomplete views of what's going on leave family members with a limited sense of control over their lives. After all, what can one person do to change another person's "laziness," "irresponsibility," or "poor impulse control"?

Cognitive behavior therapists believe that attributional shifts are necessary to make behavior change possible, but that, in turn, behavior change is necessary to reinforce new and more productive attributions.

In general, behaviorists deemphasize the "art" of therapy, treating it instead as a technical procedure dependent largely on the application of learning theory. Some behavioral writers have argued that change will occur if current behavioral principles are applied regardless of the individual personality or style of the therapist (Stuart, 1969; Hawkins, Peterson, Schweid, & Bijou, 1966). But contemporary behavior therapists now realize that successful treatment requires complex skills and great tact. According to Ian Falloon (1991), the supportive therapeutic alliance essential for effective treatment is maintained by displaying respect for the family, reliably adhering to the agreed-on time and place and focus of therapy (this means not shifting from parenting to marital problems without the explicit agreement of the couple), and appreciating that family members are doing the best they can. "The role of the therapist is not to confront the inadequacies of these best efforts, but to facilitate efforts to overcome manifest deficits and to improve the efficiency of the family members' responses" (Falloon, 1991, p. 85). Falloon advises that confrontation, coercion, and criticism be minimized and that therapists concentrate instead on validating the efforts family members are making.

Traditionally, behaviorists have been little concerned with resistance, despite the fact that systems theorists have established that any ongoing social system resists change, either from within or without. Although behavior therapists have lately recognized the importance of resistance (Birchler, 1988), most have tended to assume that people seeking psychotherapy are capable of rational, collaborative effort to change. As Spinks and Birchler (1982) put it:

> Most behaviorists view so-called resistance phenomena as the results of ineffective case management. That is, resistance is a sign that the treatment model or the therapist have been unsuccessful, not that the clients inherently resist change, or will not change. (p. 172)

Cognitive behavior therapists have become more concerned with resistance (Birchler, 1988), but their view of it differs from systemic family therapists in two ways. First, they see resistance as primarily a property of individuals, rather than a homeostatic tendency in systems. Second, they assume that although family members may have beliefs or expectancies that interfere with change, these beliefs are relatively straightforward—easily reexamined and reevaluated. Once an individual's concerns are addressed, therapy can continue. While this happy optimism seems preferable to those systemic therapists who assume family members are blindly driven by mechanical forces they're powerless to resist, it also seems a little naive.

As their experience with families increased in the 1970s and 1980s, behavioral family therapists began to incorporate more principles and techniques from systems theory into their work. Gerald Patterson, for example, studied Minuchin's structural family therapy, and Gary Birchler integrated systems theory and behavioral marital therapy (Birchler & Spinks, 1980; Spinks & Birchler, 1982). According to Birchler, straight behavioral family therapy is overly structured and fails to deal with underlying relationship dynamics.

A major tenet of behavioral family treatment is that behavior change is better achieved by accelerating positive behavior than by decelerating negative behavior. Although, as we've seen, there may be a need to introduce punishment to eliminate antisocial behavior in aggressive children, behavior therapists generally try to minimize coercion by aversive control or extinction. It's believed that most distressed families already use these approaches to excess. Therefore only positive reinforcement is consistently and widely used in behavioral family therapy.

Behavioral family therapists directly manipulate contingencies of reinforcement in the families they treat, and may provide reinforcement themselves when family members comply with their instructions. Once new behaviors are established, therapists counsel family members to use intermittent positive reinforcement and then to fade out material reinforcements in favor of social ones. Following this direct control, therapists teach family members how to observe and modify their own contingencies of reinforcement to maintain their initial gains using self-control procedures.

Learning theory may have been developed by observing white rats in laboratory mazes, but applying learning theory to families is quite a different matter. In behavioral family therapy it's important not to make simplistic assumptions about what may be rewarding and what may be punishing. Instead, it's critical to examine the interpersonal consequences of behavior. The therapist must find out what is reinforcing for each person and each family, rather than assume that certain things are universally rewarding. Moreover, a variety of different behaviors may be aimed at the same payoff. For example, a child might throw tantrums, whine, or drop things at various times, but all of these may be reinforced by parental attention. Therefore, in order to understand how to help families change, the therapist must shift attention from the behavior *(R)* to the consequences *(KC)*.

Techniques

Since behavioral family therapy is usually practiced as either parent training, couples therapy, or treatment of sexual dysfunction, we shall describe each of these approaches separately.

Behavioral Parent Training

Most family therapists begin with the assumption that the family, not the individual, is the problem, so that the whole family should be convened to solve it. Behavioral therapists, on the other hand, accept the parents' view that the child is the problem, and generally meet with only one parent (guess which one) and the child, although some behaviorists (Gordon & Davidson, 1981) recommend that both parents and even older siblings be included.

Clients also expect therapy to be a kind of education, and behavior therapists tend to operate as educators (Liberman, 1972). Thus, from the outset, behavioral family therapists employ a model that accords with the typical parents' view of the nature of their problems and the sort of solutions that would be helpful.

The early work of Patterson, Risely, Wolf, and others working with disturbed children was packaged in a diverse array of educationally oriented programs to train parents in behavioral skills. With the aid of instruction and programmed workbooks, parents were taught the application of social learning principles to temper tantrums, bed-wetting, autistic behavior, homework, hyperactivity, toilet training, disobedience, phobias, and aggressive behavior. The advantage of these educational efforts was bringing a knowledge of how behavior is reinforced to bear on a large number of problems. The disadvantage is that when therapy is reduced to teaching, therapists fail to uncover and resolve conflicts responsible for maintaining problems and bringing them about in the first place. Moreover, as Falloon and Lillie (1988) observed:

> Many of these training programs were conducted in workshops attended by large numbers of parents and presented by professionals with limited therapeutic skills and understanding of behavior therapy principles. As a result, the cornerstone of behavior therapy, the behavioral analysis and evaluation of specific goals, was frequently overlooked. (p. 10)

Thus the advantage of behavior therapy—being a straightforward approach with simple strategies—became a disadvantage in the hands of therapists who wrongly assumed that if the principles of reinforcement were simple then therapy, too, could be simple. It isn't.

Behaviorists say that what distinguishes them isn't so much a set of techniques, but the fact that they apply experimental principles to clinical problems, and that they carefully verify the results of their procedures. Liberman (1972) expressed this by referring to therapeutic tactics as "behavioral change experiments," and the literature is replete with a variety of behavioral techniques, together with empirical demonstrations of their utility. In fact behavioral parent training has been successfully applied to almost every type of behavioral problem in children (Graziano, 1977; O'Dell, 1974; McCauley, 1988). Graziano (1977) classified these problems in six categories: (1) somatic symptoms (seizures, eating problems, toilet training); (2) complex syndromes (brain damage, retardation, psychosis); (3) negativistic and aggressive behavior (hyperactivity, fighting, physical and verbal abuse); (4) fears and phobias (school phobia, fear of loud noises); (5) language and speech disorders (elective mutism); and (6) common behavior problems in the home (bedroom cleaning, persistent whining, getting dressed).

The many techniques developed to address these various problems can be grouped in three major categories: operant conditioning, respondent conditioning, and cognitive/affective techniques. By far the most commonly used approach is operant conditioning, where the reinforcers employed may be tangible or social. In fact, smiling, praise, and attention have been found to be as effective as money or candy (Bandura, 1969). Operant techniques may be further divided into *shaping, token economies, contingency contracting, contingency management,* and *time out. Shaping* (Schwitzgebel & Kolb, 1964) consists of reinforcing change in small steps that gradually approximate the desired goals. *Token economies* (Baer & Sherman, 1969) use a system of points or stars to reward children for successful behavior. In this very popular approach, children collect a reward once they have accumulated a sufficient number of tokens. *Contingency contracting* (Stuart, 1971) involves agreements by the parents to make certain changes following changes made by their children. *Contingency management* (Schwitzgebel, 1967) consists of giving and taking away rewards and punishments based upon the children's behavior. *Time out* (Rimm & Masters, 1974) is a punishment where children are made to sit in the corner or sent to their rooms.

Respondent conditioning techniques involve modification of physiological responses. Most common of these are systematic desensitization (Wolpe, 1969), assertiveness training (Lazarus, 1971), aversion therapies (Risley, 1968), and sex therapies (Masters & Johnson, 1970). Most of these (particularly the last) are used primarily with adults but have also been applied to training parents to use with their children.

Some commonly used cognitive/affective techniques include thought-stopping (McGuire & Vallance, 1964), rational emotional therapy (Ellis, 1962), modeling (Bandura, 1969), reattribution (Kanfer & Phillips, 1970), and self-monitoring (Rimm & Masters, 1974).

In common with other forms of behavioral family therapy, parent training begins with an extensive assessment procedure. While the exact procedure varies from clinic to clinic, most assessments are based upon Kanfer and Phillips's (1970) *SORKC* model of behavior: *S* for stimulus, *O* for the state of the organism, *R* for the target response, and *KC* for the nature and contingency of the consequences. The following example illustrates how this assessment model is applied.

> In the case of parents who complain that their son pesters them for cookies between meals and throws tantrums if they don't give him any, the tantrums would be considered the target behavior, *R*. *O*, the state of the organism, might turn out to be mild hunger or, even more likely, boredom. The stimulus, *S*, might be the sight of cookies in the cookie jar; and the nature and contingency of the consequences, *KC*, might be that the parents give in by feeding the boy cookies occasionally, especially if he makes enough of a fuss.

Like any useful diagnostic scheme, the *SORKC* model begins to suggest solutions as soon as it is applied.

In simple cases, such as the one above, applying the *SORKC* model is straightforward, but it quickly becomes more complex with families, where there are long chains of interrelated behavior, and therapists must examine the mutual impact of behavior on each family member. Consider the following.

> Mr. and Mrs. J. complain that their two small children whine and fuss at the dinner table. A home observation reveals that when Mr. J. yells at the children for misbehaving they start to whine and stand by their mother's chair.

Given this sequence it's not difficult to apply the *SORKC* model. Imagine, however, that the above sequence is only part of a more complex picture.

> In the morning, Mr. J. makes a sexual overture to his wife, but she, tired from taking care of the children, rolls over and goes back to sleep. Mr. J. is hurt and leaves for work after making some unkind remarks to his wife. She, feeling rejected by her husband, spends the entire day playing with the children for solace. By the time she has to cook dinner, Mrs. J. is exhausted and exasperated with the children. Mr. J. comes home after a difficult day at the office and tries to make up with his wife by hugging her. She responds but only perfunctorily because she's busily trying to cook. While she's at the stove, the children and Mr. J. vie for her attention, each one wanting to tell her something. Finally, she blows up—at her husband—"Can't you see I'm busy!" He goes into the den and sulks until dinner is ready. Just as his wife finds it difficult to express her anger at the children and takes it out on him, Mr. J. has trouble directing anger at his wife and so tends to divert it onto the children. At the dinner table he yells at them for the slightest infraction, at which they whine and turn to their mother. She lets one sit on her lap while she strokes the other's hair.

In this longer, but not atypical sequence, what is stimulus and what response? Obviously these definitions become circular, and their application depends on the perspective of the observer.

Assessment in behavioral parent training entails defining, observing, and recording the frequency of the behavior that is to be changed, as well as the events that precede it and those that follow. Interviews, usually with the mother, are designed to provide basic information, such as a definition of the problem and a list of potential reinforcers. Observations may be conducted behind a one-way mirror or during a home visit. Baseline data, collected prior to the initiation of therapy, may be recorded by therapists or family members. Typically, parents are trained to pinpoint problem behavior, to observe and record its occurrence, and to note the occurrence and frequency of various events which might serve as stimuli and reinforcers.

Parents generally find it difficult to pinpoint specific problem behavior; instead their complaints are phrased by attributing the cause and effect of problems to personality traits. "The problem with Johnny is that he's lazy—shy, hostile, hyperactive, or disrespectful." Therapists respond by probing for descriptions with concrete behavioral referents, and by developing a picture of the interactions between the parents and child. The question, "What does Johnny *do* that indicates his laziness?" helps pinpoint the problem. When this is followed by an inquiry such as, "And what do you do when he does that?" a picture of the interaction emerges. Asking for detailed descriptions elicits information about the frequency, intensity, duration, and social consequences of the problem behavior. Behaviorally oriented checklists and questionnaires are also administered. These provide information that may have been omitted or overlooked in interviews. The final product of this stage of the assessment is the selection of target behaviors for modification.

The measurement and functional analysis stage consists of actually observing and recording the target behavior, as well as its antecedents and consequences. This may be done by the parents at home or by therapists in the clinic—and, now, more and more, by therapists in the natural setting (Arrington, Sullaway, & Christensen, 1988).

In the next stage the therapist designs a specific treatment package to match the particular needs of the family. Among the factors considered are the degree to which environmental control is possible; whether or not serious interpersonal problems between the parents may preclude their working together collaboratively; possible psychological problems in either parent that might interfere with parent training; and whether or not other forms of treatment might be more effective or economical.

The second consideration, possible conflict between the parents, is usually assumed to be of critical importance by nonbehavioral therapists. Behavioral therapists vary considerably in the degree to which they consider parental conflict to be a problem. Most minimize the role of conflict between the parents, as the following quotation (Gordon & Davidson, 1981) illustrates.

> On several occasions we have observed parents whose marriage is characterized by extreme dislike for each other who have, nevertheless, been able to put aside their differences in order that they may work together in a constructive fashion to help their child. (p. 526)

Once the assessment is complete, the therapist decides which behaviors should be increased and which decreased. To accelerate behavior, the *Premack principle* (Premack, 1965) is applied; that is, high probability behavior (particularly pleasant activities) is chosen to serve as a reinforcer for behavior with a low probability of occurrence. Where once it was thought that reinforcers must satisfy some basic drive, such as hunger or thirst, it's now known that behaviors chosen more frequently (given a wide variety of choices) can serve as reinforcers for those chosen less frequently. The following example shows how the Premack principle can be applied in parent training.

> Mrs. G. stated that she couldn't get her five-year-old son Adam to clean up his room in the morning. She went on to say that she had already tried rewarding him with candy, money, and toys, but "Nothing works!" A

> functional analysis of Adam's behavior revealed that, given his choice of things to do, the most probable behaviors were watching television, riding his bicycle, and playing in the mud behind his house. Once these activities were made contingent on tidying his room he quickly learned to do so.

A variety of material and social reinforcers have been employed to accelerate desired behaviors, but as the Premack principle demonstrates, to be effective, reinforcers must be popular with the particular child in question. While money and candy seem like powerful rewards, they may not be as effective for some children as a chance to play in the mud.

Once effective rewards are chosen, parents are taught to shape the desired behavior by reinforcing successive approximation to the therapeutic goal. They are also taught to raise the criteria for reinforcement gradually, and to present reinforcement immediately contingent on the desired behavior.[1] Once the child is regularly performing the desired response, reinforcement becomes intermittent in order to increase the durability of the new behavior.

Interestingly, although parents are taught to apply operant conditioning principles to their children, behavioral therapists generally don't apply these same principles to the parents. Instead they rely on the assumption that the process of training is inherently reinforcing. There are exceptions to this, however, as the following (Rinn, 1978) illustrates.

> It is advisable that the clinician be as reinforcing as possible (e.g., praise, smiles, excited voice) whenever the family carries out homework assignments and procedures. Therapists who are not particularly enthusiastic about the importance of data collection have a tendency to reinforce low rates of data presentation from families. (p. 378)

Deceleration techniques apply contingent punishment and extinction. The most common technique for decelerating behavior is *time-out* from positive reinforcement. This means ignoring or isolating the child after he or she misbehaves. This procedure has been shown to be effective with a wide variety of child problems (Forehand & MacDonough, 1975). Studies have shown that a duration of about five minutes is most effective (Pendergrass, 1971). Children are first warned, to give them a chance to control their own behavior, before they are put into time-out. Other techniques used to decelerate behavior include verbal reprimand, ignoring, and isolation. Simply repeating commands to children has been shown to be a most ineffective way to change their behavior (Forehand, Roberts, Doleys, Hobbs, & Resnick, 1976). Response-contingent aversive stimulation (LeBow, 1972) is little used with families, although it has been used effectively working directly with children (Jacobson & Martin, 1976).

Because of the inconvenience of reinforcing behavior immediately after it occurs, token systems have been very popular with parent trainers. Points are earned for desirable behavior and lost for undesirable behavior (Christophersen, Arnold, Hill, & Quilitch, 1972). The principles of behavioral parent training described above are exemplified and more clearly delineated in the following case study.

◆

Mrs. F. is a twenty-five-year-old housewife and mother of two small children who came to the clinic complaining of headaches and crying spells. The intake interviewer found her to be mildly depressed and, although she had symptoms of a passive dependent personality disorder, concluded that the depression was primarily a reaction to her difficulty coping with her chil-

[1]The importance of immediate proximity is what makes time-out such an effective punishment and grounding second only to lecturing as an ineffective one.

dren. Suzie, age five, was a shy child who rarely played with other children and had frequent temper tantrums. Robert, who was eight, was more outgoing and sociable, but did very poorly in school. Between them the children were a handful, and Mrs. F. felt helpless and resentful in her dealings with them.

A functional analysis of behavior revealed that Suzie's shyness resulted in her getting extra attention from her anxious mother. Whenever Suzie declined an invitation to play with other children, her mother spent a great deal of time talking with her and doing special things to make her feel better. The therapist selected social behavior (not shyness) as the first target response, and instructed Mrs. F. to reinforce all efforts at socializing and to ignore Suzie when she avoided social contact. Thereafter, whenever Suzie made any attempt to socialize with other children, Mrs. F. would immediately reinforce her with attention and praise. When Suzie chose to stay home rather than play with other children, her mother ignored her, instead busying herself with her own activities. In three weeks, Mrs. F. reported that Suzie had made remarkable changes and "seemed to have gotten over her shyness."

Following this initial successful experience the therapist felt it was time to help Mrs. F. tackle the more difficult problem of Suzie's temper tantrums. Since the temper tantrums were unlikely to occur while the family was at the clinic or during a home visit, the therapist instructed Mrs. F. to make observational notes for a week. These notes revealed that Suzie generally had her tantrums when either of her parents denied her requests for a treat or some special indulgence, such as staying up an extra half an hour to watch television. Moreover, tantrums were especially likely to occur at the end of the day when Suzie (and her parents) were tired. As for how the parents responded to these maddening temper tantrums, Mrs. F. reported that "We've tried everything. Sometimes we try to ignore her, but that's impossible; she just screams and shrieks until we can't stand it anymore. Then we sometimes spank her, or sometimes give her what she wants—just to shut her up. Sometimes after we spank her she cries so much that we let her stay up and watch television until she calms down. That usually works to quiet her down."

After listening to this description, the therapist explained as gently and carefully as she could how Mr. and Mrs. F. had inadvertently been reinforcing the tantrums, and told them what they would have to do to stop them. For the next week, the F.'s were instructed to ignore temper tantrums whenever they occurred. If they occurred at bedtime, Suzie was to be put in her bed; if she continued to cry and scream, she was to be left alone until she stopped. Only when she stopped were her parents to talk with her about what was on her mind. The following week Mrs. F. reported that the temper tantrums had indeed decreased, except for one night when they took on a new and more troubling form. When Suzie was told that she wouldn't be able to stay up late to watch television she began to yell and cry as usual. Instead of relenting, Mrs. F. put Suzie in her room and told her to get ready for bed. However, realizing that her parents were going to ignore her, as they had earlier in the week, Suzie began to scream and smash things in her room. "It was awful, she was completely out of control. She kicked and struck out at everything in sight, even smashing the little dog-shaped lamp I bought her. We didn't know what to do, so just that once we let her stay up." Again the therapist described the consequences of such behavior, and explained to Mrs. F. how, should Suzie again become destructive, both parents should hold her until the tantrum subsided.

At the next session, Mrs. F. described how Suzie did "get out of control again." This time, instead of giving in, the parents held her as they had been told. Mrs. F. was amazed at the fury and duration of the resulting tantrum. "But we remembered what you said—there was no way we were going to give in!" It took twenty minutes, but Suzie finally calmed down. This, it turned out, was the last time Suzie ever became so violent during a temper tantrum. Nevertheless she did continue to have an occasional tantrum during the next few weeks of therapy. According to Mrs. F., the few tantrums that did occur seemed to take place in different settings or under different conditions than the usual episodes at home (which Suzie had now learned would not be reinforced). For example, one episode took place in a supermarket, when Suzie was told she couldn't have a candy bar. By this time, however, Mrs. F. was thoroughly convinced of the necessity of not reinforcing the tantrums, and so she didn't. Because she was embarrassed at all the noise her daughter was making in public, she did find it necessary to take her out of the store. But she made Suzie sit in the car and took pains not to let it be a pleasant experience for her. Very few tantrums followed this one.

Next the therapist turned her attention to the problem of Robert's poor performance at school. A careful assessment revealed that Robert rarely brought assignments home from school and when asked usually denied that he had any homework. After checking with Robert's teacher the therapist discovered that the children generally did have homework, and that they were expected to work between thirty minutes and an hour a night. Mrs. F. selected a high probability behavior, watching television, and made it contingent upon Robert's having first completed his homework. For the first two weeks of this regimen, Mrs. F. found it necessary to call the teacher every night to verify the assignments. But soon this was no longer necessary. Doing homework fairly quickly became a habit for Robert, and his grades increased from Ds and Cs to Bs and As by the end of the school year. At this point, everyone was happier, and Mrs. F. felt the family no longer needed help.

A follow-up session in the fall found things continuing to go well. Suzie was now much more sociable and had not had any temper tantrums in months. Robert was doing well in school, although he had begun to neglect some of his more difficult assignments. To address this, the therapist explained to Mrs. F. how to institute a token system, and she was able to use it with excellent results in a short space of time.

◆

The preceding example illustrates a form of behavioral parent training in which the therapist meets with the mother and instructs her in the use of operant conditioning principles. Another format is to observe parent and child interacting behind a one-way mirror in the clinic. In this way, the therapist can get a first-hand look at what actually transpires. With this approach, parents can be taught how to play with their children, as well as how to discipline them, and how to negotiate with them. Sometimes the observing therapist may communicate to the parents through a remote microphone, called a "bug in the ear."

The techniques that have been described are particularly effective with small children and preadolescents. With teenagers the use of *contingency contracting* (Alexander & Parsons, 1973; Rinn, 1978) is more widely used. Contracting is introduced by the therapist as a way for everybody in the family to get something by compromising. Both parent and teenager are asked to specify what behavior they'd like the other to change. These requests form the nucleus of the initial contract. In order to help family members arrive at contracts, the therapist models, prompts, and reinforces: (a) clear communication of content and feelings; (b) clear presentation of demands; leading to (c) negotiation, with each person receiving something in exchange for some concession.

Alexander and Parsons (1973) recommend starting with easy issues while the family is learning the principles of contingency contracting. Success in dealing with minor issues will increase the family's willingness to deal with more difficult problems. Some parents are reluctant to negotiate with their children to do things "that they *should do anyway*, without being bribed." In fact, these parents have a legitimate point, and they should be helped to understand the difference between rules (which are nonnegotiable) and privileges (which can be negotiated).

Behavioral parent training is also conducted in general child training programs, which are designed for preventive education. The content of these programs varies from general principles of operant behavior to specific techniques for dealing with specific problems. They usually begin with an introduction to social learning theory. Following this, parents are instructed how to pinpoint behaviors and to select one or two for modification. After being taught to analyze the antecedents and consequences of the target behavior, parents learn to monitor the frequency and duration of the responses. Many of these programs include instruction in charting, or graphing, the target behavior. Parents are also taught how to state and enforce rules, and the necessity for being consistent. Usually, techniques for accelerating desired behavior are used concomitantly. Training in the use of positive reinforcement includes helping the parents to increase the frequency and range of reinforcers that they apply. In addition to increasing behavior that their children are already engaging in, the parents are taught to develop new behaviors through shaping, modeling, instructing, and prompting.

Behavioral Couples Therapy

Most forms of psychotherapy begin as art and move toward science; behavioral couples therapy did the reverse. Early reports in the literature (Goldiamond, 1965; Lazarus, 1968) consisted of relatively straightforward application of learning theory principles to problems of married couples. A strictly operant conditioning approach was common (Goldstein, 1971), and therapists were relatively naive about the interpersonal dynamics of families. Since that time behavioral couples therapy has become increasingly popular and increasingly sophisticated.

As in other forms of behavioral therapy, couples therapy begins with an elaborate, structured assessment process. This process usually includes clinical interviews, ratings of specific target behaviors, and standard marital assessment questionnaires. Most widely used of the latter is the Locke-Wallace Marital Adjustment Scale (Locke & Wallace, 1959), a twenty-three-item questionnaire covering various aspects of marital satisfaction, including communication, sex, affection, social activities, and values. Rating scales are used to describe and quantify couples' most troublesome problems. Weiss and his colleagues at the Oregon Marital Studies Program ask couples to record their spouse's "pleasing" and "displeasing" behavior during the week.

Assessments are designed to reveal the strengths and weaknesses of the couple's relationship and the manner in which rewards and punishments are exchanged. Several relationship skills are evaluated, including the ability to discuss problems; current reinforcement value for one another; skill in pinpointing relevant reinforcers; competencies in sex, childrearing, financial management, distribution of roles; and decision-making.

Interviews are used to specify and elaborate target behaviors first revealed on the structured assessment devices. Some attempt is also made during interviews to understand the etiology of the problems that couples describe as well as to discover problems other than those noted by the spouses themselves. In general, however, behavioral marital therapists deemphasize interviews (Jacobson & Margolin, 1979) in favor of written questionnaires and direct observation of couples' interactions. Jacobson (1981) offers an outline for pretreatment assessment (see Table 9.1 on pages 294–295).

After completing the assessment, the behavioral clinician presents the couple with an analysis of their relationship in social learning terms. In doing so, therapists take pains to accentuate the positive, striving to maintain positive expectancies and a collaborative set (Jacobson, 1981). Married partners tend to state their

TABLE 9.1 Jacobson's Pretreatment Assessment for Marital Therapy

A. Strengths and skills of the relationship

What are the major strengths of this relationship?
Specifically, what resources do these spouses have to explain their current level of commitment to the relationship?
What is each spouse's current capacity to reinforce the other?
What behaviors on the part of each spouse are highly valued by the other?
What shared activities does the couple currently engage in?
What common interests do they share?
What are the couple's competencies and skills in meeting the essential tasks of a relationship: problem-solving, provision of support and understanding, ability to provide social reinforcement effectively, sexual capabilities, childrearing and parenting skills, ability to manage finances, household responsibilities, interpersonal skills regarding interaction with people outside the relationship?

B. Presenting problems

What are the major complaints, and how do these complaints translate into explicit behavioral terms?
What behaviors occur too frequently or at inappropriate times from the standpoint of each spouse?
Under what conditions do these behaviors occur?
What are the reinforcers that are maintaining these behaviors?
What behaviors occur at less than the desired frequency or fail to occur at appropriate times from the standpoint of each spouse?
Under what conditions would each spouse like to see these behaviors occur?
What are the consequences of these behaviors currently, when they occur?
How did the current problems develop over time?
How are current lines of decision-making authority drawn?
Is there a consensus on who makes important decisions in regard to various areas of the relationship?
What kinds of decisions are made collectively as opposed to unilaterally?

C. Sex and affection

Are the spouses physically attracted to one another?
Is either currently dissatisfied with rate, quality, or diversity of sex life together?
If sex is currently a problem, was there a time when it was mutually satisfying?
What are the sexual behaviors that seem to be associated with current dissatisfaction?
Are either or both partners dissatisfied with the amount or quality of nonsexual physical affection?
Are either or both partners currently engaged in an extramarital sexual relationship?
If so, is the uninvolved partner aware of the affair?
What is the couple's history regarding extramarital affairs?

TABLE 9.1 *Continued*

D. Future prospects
Are the partners seeking therapy to improve their relationship, to separate, or to decide whether the relationship is worth working on?
What are each spouse's reasons for continuing the relationship despite current problems?
What steps has each spouse taken in the direction of divorce?
E. Assessment of social environment
What are each person's alternatives to the present relationship?
How attractive are these alternatives to each person?
Is the environment (parents, relatives, friends, work associates, children) supportive of either continuance or dissolution of present relationship?
Are any of the children suffering from psychological problems of their own?
What would the probable consequences of relationship dissolution be for the children?
F. Individual functioning of each spouse
Does either spouse exhibit any severe emotional or behavioral problems?
Does either spouse represent a psychiatric history of his/her own? Specify.
Have they been in therapy before, either alone or together? What kind of therapy? Outcome?
What is each spouse's past experience with intimate relationships?
How is the present relationship different?

Adapted from: Jacobson, N. S. 1981. Behavioral marital therapy. In *Handbook of Family Therapy*, A. S. Gurman and D. P. Kniskern, eds. (pp. 565–566) New York: Brunner/Mazel.

goals negatively, in terms of decelerating aversive behavior: "I want less arguing from him"; or "She nags too much." Most have difficulty describing behavior that they want their spouses to accelerate. To help them do so, some therapists (Azrin, Naster, & Jones, 1973) assign a homework task asking the spouses to make a list of pleasing things their partners do during the week. Reviewing these lists in the following session provides the opportunity to emphasize the importance of giving positive feedback.

Since disturbed marital interaction is viewed as resulting from low rates of positive reinforcement (Stuart, 1969; Patterson & Hops, 1972), a major treatment strategy is to increase positive control while decreasing the rate of aversive control. This strategy is promoted both while the couple is interacting in the clinic, and by assigning them homework to alter their pattern of interaction at home. A second major strategy is to improve communication, which in turn facilitates couples' abilities to solve problems. Stuart (1975) lists five intervention strategies that summarize the behavioral approach to treating troubled marriages. First, couples are taught to express themselves in clear, behavioral descriptions, rather than in vague and critical complaints. Second, couples are taught new behavior exchange procedures, emphasizing positive in place of aversive control. Third, couples are helped to improve their communication. Fourth, couples are encouraged to establish clear and effective means of sharing power and making decisions. Fifth, couples are taught strategies for solving future problems, as a means of maintaining and extending gains initiated in therapy.

In his initial efforts Stuart (1969) employed the operant method of exchanging tokens as rewards for targeted desired behaviors. In this way one person could build up a "credit balance" by performing a high frequency of behaviors desired by other family members, which could later be exchanged when he or she was the recipient of rewarding behavior from others. Refinements of this approach dispensed with tokens. Mutual exchanges were based on written contracts. Although much of Stewart's work has been devoted to marital discord, his contingency contracting and principles of enhancing the mutual positive reinforcement potential of family members has been used widely by behavioral family therapists (Patterson, 1971b).

Behavior exchange procedures are taught to help couples increase the frequency of desired behaviors. Couples are advised to express their wishes and annoyances specifically and behaviorally. A typical device is to ask each spouse to list three things that he or she would like the other to do more often. These can provide the basis for a trade, or *quid pro quo.* While explicitly exchanging "strokes" in this way, spouses are implicitly learning ways of influencing each other through positive reinforcement. An alternative tactic is to ask each partner to think of things the other might want, do them, and see what happens. Weiss and his associates direct couples to have "love days," where one spouse doubles his or her pleasing behaviors toward the other (Weiss & Birchler, 1978). Stuart (1976) has couples alternate "caring days," where one spouse demonstrates caring in as many ways as possible.

The major intent of these procedures is to help couples establish *reinforcement reciprocity,* based on rewarding behavior, in place of coercion. Positive control is doubtless more pleasant and effective than aversive control. However, the concept of reinforcement reciprocity implies a symmetrical relationship. While this pattern may characterize some couples seen in university clinics, it surely does not apply to all; and it certainly does not apply to the majority of couples seen in other settings. Unfairness and inequality in marriage are among the knottiest problems in American families. Assuming that husbands and wives can nicely negotiate agreements about who does what seems a little like assuming that rich nations will bargain in good faith with poor ones.

Behavioral couples therapists try to help partners learn to ask for what they want, rather than expect the other to intuit it. In fact, the whole field has moved from stressing patterns of reinforcement to working on communication and problem-solving (Weiss, 1978). Unlike some other couples therapists, however, behavior therapists emphasize communication that is agreement-oriented rather than expression-oriented. The stress is always more on negotiating agreements than on expressing feelings. Because of this, some critics (Gurman & Kniskern, 1978) have suggested that behavioral couples therapists try to eliminate arguing and expressions of anger in the pursuit of dispassionate problem-solving. Indeed, Jacobson (1981) recommends that couples not try to solve a problem while they're fighting about it, but postpone the discussion to a prearranged problem-solving session. "Couples report that if they postpone the discussion to the next scheduled problem-solving session, by the time the session occurs the problem seems trivial" (Jacobson, 1981, p. 579). Perhaps, but it also seems likely that the postponement allows for the reconstitution of defensiveness and, further, that the feelings involved are suppressed, not resolved. Angry feelings are part of being alive; to suppress them is to deaden oneself—and stultify one's relationships.

In a carefully designed longitudinal study Gottman and Krokoff (1989) found that disagreement and angry exchanges, which have often been considered destructive to relationships, may not be harmful in the long run. These patterns were correlated with immediate dissatisfaction, but they were predictive of improved marital satisfaction after three years. Defensiveness, stubbornness, and withdrawal from conflict, on the other hand, *did* lead to long-term deterioration in marriages. Passive compliance may create a facade of harmony, but it doesn't work in the long run—as many dominating partners with compliant mates discover when their partners, who "used to be so agreeable," suddenly become "so critical."

Conflict engagement may make couples uneasy, but it's often an essential prelude to facing and solving problems. The anger that accompanies direct expression of dissatisfaction may be painful but it may also be healthy. Gottman and Krokoff conclude (1989): "If the wife must introduce and elaborate disagreements in marriages, our data suggest that, for the sake of long-term improvement in marital satisfaction, she may need to do this by getting her husband to confront areas of disagreement and to openly vent disagreement and anger" (p. 51). In other words, confrontation is effective only if it doesn't make the partner defensive. It isn't just honesty that counts, but honesty expressed in a way the partner can tolerate.

Training in communications skills may be done in a group format (Ely, Guerney, & Stover, 1973; Hickman & Baldwin, 1971; Pierce, 1973) or with individual couples. The training includes instruction, modeling, role playing, structured exercises, behavior rehearsal, and feedback (Jacobson, 1977; Patterson, Hops, & Weiss, 1973; Stuart, 1976). Couples are taught to be specific, phrase requests in positive terms, respond directly to criticism instead of cross-complaining, talk about the present and future rather than the past, listen without interruption, minimize punitive statements, and eliminate questions that sound like declarations (O'Leary & Turkewitz, 1978).

After explaining these principles, therapists invite couples to incorporate them in their discussions, during which the therapists provide feedback. Many therapists recommend that couples replay previous arguments during therapy, and ask spouses to paraphrase each other's remarks before replying.

Once a couple has been taught to communicate in ways that are conducive to problem-solving, they are introduced to the principles of *contingency contracting.* Contingency contracting means changing something contingent on the partner making changes. There are two forms of contract negotiation used in behavioral family therapy. The first is the *quid pro quo* contract (Knox, 1971; Lederer & Jackson, 1968), where one spouse agrees to make a change after a prior change by the other. Contracting is highly structured and the agreements are usually written down. Each spouse specifies desired behavior changes, and with the therapist's help they negotiate agreements. At the end of the session a written list is made and each spouse signs it. According to Rappaport and Harrell (1972) written agreements act as references, obviating the need to rely on memory; they can be easily modified, they act as cues (discriminative stimuli) reminding spouses of their agreements, and they symbolize the couple's commitment to change. Such a contract might take the following form:

Date ________

This week I agree to:

(1) Come home from work by 6 P.M.
(2) Play with the children for half an hour after supper.

____
Husband's signature

Contingent on the above changes, I agree to:

(1) Go bowling once a week with my husband.
(2) Not serve leftovers for supper on weeknights.

____
Wife's signature

This form of contracting substitutes positive for aversive control and ensures that changes in one spouse are immediately reinforced by the other (Eisler & Hersen, 1973). Therapists guide the couple's choices of reinforcement so that the rewards desired by one spouse aren't aversive to the other, and contracts for sexual behavior are avoided (O'Leary & Turkewitz, 1978).

Jacobson and Martin (1976) have argued that *quid pro quo* contracts are more efficient and less time-consuming than other forms. However, the *quid pro quo* arrangement requires one spouse to be the first to change. In an atmosphere of mistrust and animosity neither may be willing to do so. An alternative form of contracting is the *good faith* contract, in which both spouses agree to make changes that aren't contingent on what the other does (Weiss, Hops, & Patterson, 1973). Each spouse's independent changes are independently reinforced. In the example above, the husband who comes home each night by 6 P.M. and plays with the children after supper might reward himself by buying a new shirt at the end of the week, or be rewarded by his wife with a back rub. Stuart (1980) emphasizes training couples to negotiate exchanges in a "two-winner" context, rather than the "win–lose" orientation that typifies many distressed relationships. Knox (1973) has suggested a combined form of contracting, using *good faith* contracts until appropriate changes are initiated and then switching to *quid pro quo* contracts once an atmosphere of trust and confidence is established.

Problem-solving training is used to deal with problems that are too conflictual or complicated for simple exchange agreements. The key to successful problem-solving is developing a collaborative set. Negotiations are preceded by a careful and specific definition of problems. Only when spouses agree on the definition of a problem can they effectively begin to discuss a solution. Discussions are limited to one problem at a time. Each spouse begins by paraphrasing what the other has said, and they are taught to avoid inferences about motivation—especially inferences of malevolent intent. They're also encouraged to avoid verbal abuse and other aversive responses. When defining a problem it's most effective to begin with a positive statement; instead of saying, "You never . . . ," spouses are taught to say, "I appreciate the way you . . . and, in addition I wish. . . . "

Behavior therapists are very active in these discussions, teaching structured procedures for problem-solving and giving feedback. The discussions are frequently punctuated by such therapist comments as "You just interrupted him"; "As soon as she makes a request, you change the subject"; or "When you blamed her for the problem, the two of you started arguing instead of discussing the issue at hand."

The trouble with the activity and directiveness of behavioral couples therapists is that couples may learn what they're doing wrong, but without having sufficient independent practice to correct it. There is a real danger that such a directive approach will tie couples into becoming dependent on the therapist to referee their fights. To avoid fostering such dependent relationships most nonbehavioral family therapists remain sufficiently decentralized to promote independent self-sufficiency on the part of their clients (Minuchin, 1974; Ables & Brandsma, 1977; Guerin, Fay, Burden, & Kautto, 1987). Behavioral therapists emphasize the need to resolve dependency by gradually tapering off treatment, so that the therapist's influence can be faded out.

As we move into the late 1990s the methods employed by most behavioral couples therapists differ little from those described by Stuart (1969) and Liberman (1970). The contingency contract remains the mainstay of treatment, both in enhancing the quality and quantity of mutually pleasing transactions and diminishing the frequency of negative communication sequences and arguments. The most significant advance in behavioral treatment is the increasing use and sophistication of cognitive-behavioral methods (Epstein, Schlesinger, & Dryden, 1988; Dattilio, 1997b).

The cognitive mediation model (Beck, 1976) posits that emotions and actions are mediated by specific cognitions. Understanding these cognitions (*beliefs, attributions,* and *expectancies*) makes it possible to identify factors that trigger and maintain the dysfunctional emotional and behavioral patterns that families bring to treatment. In Barton and Alexander's (1981) "functional family therapy," it's assumed that members of disturbed families tend to attribute their problems to negative traits; and therefore the therapist's goal is to provide family members with new information that will impel them to new emotional and behavioral reactions in order to maintain cognitive consistency. In practice this boils down to repeatedly ferreting out and confronting negative assumptions that keep people stuck.

A Cognitive-Behavioral Approach to Family Therapy

As mentioned earlier, cognitive couples therapy developed from the behavioral approach, first as a supplemental component and then as a more comprehensive system of intervention. The same progression occurred for cognitive family therapy. Munson (1993) noted that there were at least eighteen different types of cognitive therapy used by various practitioners. Consequently, the focus of this discussion will be limited to those approaches proposed by the rational-emotive (Ellis, 1978, 1982; DiGiuseppe & Zeeve, 1985) and cognitive-behavioral theories (Beck, 1988; Wright & Beck, 1993; Epstein, Schlesinger, & Dryden, 1988; Dattilio, 1993, 1994, 1997b; Teichman, 1984, 1992).

The rational-emotive approach to family therapy, as proposed by Albert Ellis (1978), concentrated on individuals' perceptions and interpretations of events that occur in the family. The underlying theory assumes that "family members largely create their own world by the phenomenological view they take of what happens to them" (p. 310). The focus of therapy is on how particular problems of family members affect their well-being as a unit. During the process of treatment, family members are treated as individuals, each of whom subscribes to a particular set of beliefs and expectations (Huber & Baruth, 1989; Russell & Marrill, 1989).

The rational-emotive therapist helps family members come to the realization that illogical beliefs and distortions serve as the foundation for their emotional distress. The use of the "*A-B-C* theory" is introduced, according to which family members blame their problems (*C*) on certain activating events in the family (*A*) and are taught to look for irrational beliefs (*B*), which are then to be logically reexamined by each family member and finally debated and disputed. The goal is to modify beliefs and expectations by putting them on a more rational basis (Ellis, 1978). The therapist's role is to teach the family in an active and directive manner that emotional problems are caused by irrational beliefs and that by changing these self-defeating ideas, they may improve the overall quality of the family relationship.

With rational-emotive therapy it's a little hard to separate the approach from the personality of its creator. Ellis didn't merely challenge people's assumptions, he punctured them with fierce and gleeful sarcasm. It isn't necessary to imitate Ellis's acerbic style to take advantage of his insights. However, it seems fair to say that rational-emotive therapists generally content themselves with lecturing people about generic assumptions rather than probing for more personal and closely held beliefs. There's little or no emphasis on uncovering "core schemata" (deeper assumptions) or much awareness of family systems dynamics.

The cognitive-behavioral approach, which balances the emphasis on cognition and behavior, takes a more expansive and inclusive approach by focusing in greater depth on patterns of family interaction and by remaining consistent with elements derived from a systems perspective (Epstein, Schlesinger, & Dryden, 1988; Leslie, 1988). Within this framework, family relationships, cognitions, emotions, and behavior are viewed as exerting a mutual influence on one another, so that a cognitive inference can evoke emotion and behavior, and emotion and behavior can likewise influence cognition. Teichman (1992) describes in detail the reciprocal model of family interaction, proposing that cognitions, feelings, behavior, and environmental feedback are in constant reciprocal interaction among themselves and sometimes serve to maintain the dysfunction of the family unit.

The cognitive-behavioral approach to families is consistent and compatible with systems theory, and includes the premise that members of a family simultaneously influence and are influenced by each other. Consequently, the behavior of one family member triggers behavior, cognitions, and emotions in other members, which, in turn, elicit reactive cognitions, behavior, and emotions in the original member (Epstein & Schlesinger, 1996). As this process plays out, the volatility of family dynamics escalates, rendering the family vulnerable to negative spirals of conflict. As the number of family members involved increases, so does the complexity of the dynamics, adding momentum to the escalation process. Epstein and Schlesinger (1991, 1996) cite four means by which family members' cognitions, behavior, and emotions may interact and build to a volatile climax:

1. The individual's own cognitions, behavior, and emotion regarding family interaction (e.g., the person who notices himself or herself withdrawing from the rest of the family)
2. The actions of individual family members toward him or her
3. The combined (and not always consistent) reactions several family members have toward him or her
4. The characteristics of the relationships among other family members (e.g., noticing that two other family members usually are supportive of each other's opinions)

The above serve as stimuli or combinations of stimuli during family interactions and often become ingrained in family patterns and permanent styles of interaction.

Cognitive therapy, as set forth by Aaron Beck (1976), places a heavy emphasis on *schema* or what has otherwise been defined as "core beliefs" (Beck, Rush, Shaw, & Emery, 1979; DeRubeis & Beck, 1988). Therapeutic intervention is aimed at the assumptions whereby family members interpret and evaluate one another and the emotions and behavior generated in response to these assumptions. While cognitive-behavioral theory doesn't suggest that cognitive processes cause *all* family behavior, it does stress that cognitive appraisal plays a significant part in the interrelationships existing among events, cognitions, emotions, and behaviors (Epstein et al., 1988). In the cognitive therapy process, restructuring distorted beliefs has a pivotal impact on changing dysfunctional behaviors.

The notion of schema is also very important in the application of cognitive-behavior therapy with families. Just as individuals maintain their own basic schema about themselves, their world, and their future, they maintain a schema about their family. Some cognitive-behavior therapists place a heavier emphasis on examining cognitions among individual family members as well as on what may be termed the "family schemata" (Dattilio, 1993, 1997b). These are jointly held beliefs about the family, formed as a result of years of integrated interaction among members of the family unit. Frank Dattilio suggests that individuals maintain two separate sets of schemata about families: schemata related to the parents' family of origin and schemata related to families in general. Both types of schemata have a major impact on how individuals think, feel, and behave within the family setting. Epstein, Schlesinger, and Dryden (1988) propose that these schemata are "the longstanding and relatively stable basic assumption that he or she holds about how the world works and his or her place in it" (p. 13). Schwebel and Fine (1992) elaborated on the term *family schemata* as used in the family model by describing it as follows:

> All of the cognitions that individuals hold about their own family life and about family life in general. Included in this set of cognitions are an individual's schema about family life, attributions about why events occur in the family, and beliefs about why events occur in the family, and beliefs about what should exist within the family unit (Baucom & Epstein, 1990). The family schema also contains ideas about how spousal relationships should work, what different types of problems should be expected in marriage and how they should be handled, what is involved in building and maintaining a healthy family, what responsibilities each family member should have, what consequences should be associated with failure to meet responsibilities or to fulfill roles, and what costs and benefits each individual should expect to have as a consequence of being in a marriage. (p. 50)

Dattilio contends that the family of origin of each partner in a relationship plays a crucial role in the shaping of immediate family schema. Beliefs, conscious and unconscious, passed down from the family of origin contribute to a joint or blended schema that leads to the development of the current family schema. This family schema is conveyed and applied in the rearing of children and, when mixed with their own individual thoughts and perceptions of their environment and life experiences, contributes to the further development of the family schema. The family schema is subject to change as major events occur during the course of family life (e.g., death, divorce, etc.), and it also continues to evolve over the course of ordinary day-to-day experience.

Later theorists such as Baucom (1981) and Epstein (1982) expanded the cognitive approach as applied to couples and the treatment of marital discord. These authors culminated their works in a major text entitled *Cognitive-Behavioral Marital Therapy* (Baucom & Epstein, 1990). Around the same time, Dattilio (1989) and Dattilio and Padesky (1990) presented a more purely cognitive approach with couples. This was paralleled by works by Ellis and coworkers (1989), who applied the rational-emotive approach to couples therapy. Beck (1988) also introduced his cognitive therapy approach with couples in the popular book *Love Is Never Enough*, which introduced the cognitive approach to the general public.

The late 1980s and early 1990s saw the cognitive-behavioral approach being applied more widely in family therapy. Edited works by Epstein, Schlessinger, and Dryden (1988) and a short text produced by Huber and Baruth (1989) were among the first works to address the family therapy approach. This was elaborated in subsequent articles by Schwebel and Fine (1992), Dattilio (1993, 1994, 1997a), and Teichman (1992). Most recently, Dattilio (1997b) has produced a major casebook that discusses the integration of cognitive-behavioral strategies with various modalities of couples and family therapy. This important work allows practitioners and theorists of couples and family therapy to appreciate the compatibility that cognitive-behavior therapy has with a wide array of modalities.

Cognitive-behavior couples and family therapy is still in its infancy and in need of additional outcome studies to support its effectiveness as a treatment modality. It does show promise, however, as a major theoretical approach.

Treatment of Sexual Dysfunction

It's often difficult to decide whether to focus directly on sexual problems or to treat them as a symptom of underlying problems in the relationship. At times it may be possible to resolve sexual problems indirectly, by working on the interpersonal relationship (Gill & Temperley, 1974). On the other hand, what appear to be intractable interpersonal problems can sometimes be resolved with improvement in a couple's sexual relationship (Kaplan, 1974). After all, sex and affection provide a bond that helps couples endure the inevitable hurts and slights that come into every relationship. In all cases, the decision to treat sexual dysfunction directly should be based on informed clinical judgment, not ignorance of the techniques available.

Prior to the 1970 publication of Masters and Johnson's *Human Sexual Inadequacy*, the prevailing treatment for sexual dysfunction was a combination of analytic discussion and commonsense suggestions. Men suffering from premature ejaculation were often advised to think distracting thoughts during intercourse. For women who failed to reach orgasm the most common advice was to fake it.

Wolpe's (1958) introduction of *systematic desensitization* led to major advances in the treatment of sexual dysfunction. According to Wolpe most sexual problems are the result of conditioned anxiety. His therapy consists of instructing couples to engage in a graded series of progressively more intimate encounters, avoiding thoughts about erection or orgasm. A second behavioral approach that frequently proved effective was *assertive training* (Lazarus, 1965; Wolpe, 1958). In assertive training, socially and sexually inhibited persons are encouraged to accept and express their needs and feelings.

While these behavioral remedies were often helpful, the real breakthrough came with the publication of Masters and Johnson's (1970) approach. This was followed by a number of others who applied and extended Masters and Johnson's basic procedure (Lobitz & LoPiccolo, 1972; Kaplan, 1974, 1979).

Although the specific details vary, there is a general approach to treatment followed by most sex therapists. As with other behavioral methods, the first step is a careful and thorough assessment. Included in the assessment is a complete medical examination to rule out organic problems, and extensive interviews to determine the nature of the dysfunction as well as to establish goals for treatment. In the absence of organic problems, cases involving lack of information, poor technique, and poor communication in the sexual area are most amenable to sexual therapy. Moreover, those people suffering from premature ejaculation, vaginismus, or orgasmic dysfunction generally respond well to brief treatment (five to twenty sessions); cases of ejaculatory incompetence, erectile failure, and longstanding lack of sexual desire are generally more difficult to resolve (Heiman, LoPiccolo, & LoPiccolo, 1981).

Therapists following Masters and Johnson tended to lump sexual problems into one category—anxiety that interfered with couples' ability to relax into arousal and orgasm. Helen Singer Kaplan (1979) pointed out that there are three stages of the sexual response and, hence, three types of problems: disorders of desire, arousal disorders, and orgasm disorders. Disorders of desire range from "low sex drive" to sexual aversion. Treatment of these problems is often successful, with motivated clients. Treatment focuses on (a) deconditioning anxiety, and (b) helping clients identify and stop negative thoughts that interfere with sexual desire. Arousal disorders include decreased emotional arousal and difficulty achieving and maintaining an erection or dilating and lubricating. These problems are often helped with a combination of relaxation techniques and teaching couples to focus on physical sensations involved in touching and caressing, rather than worrying about what comes next. Orgasm disorders include the timing of orgasm (e.g., premature or delayed), the quality of the orgasm, or the requirements for orgasm (e.g., some people only have orgasm during masturbation). Problems with orgasm can be either chronic or situational. Premature ejaculation usually responds well to sex therapy; lack of orgasm in women may respond to sex therapy, usually involving teaching the woman to practice on her own and learning to fantasize.

Following the assessment, clients are presented with an explanation of the role of conditioned anxiety in problems with sex, and they are told how anxiety developed and is being maintained in their sexual relationship. Insight and attitude change are thus a fundamental part of this "behavioral" therapy. Not only may a couple's ignorance be creating problems, but they may also harbor attitudes about sex that are incompatible with the aims of treatment. John Bancroft, who uses a behavioral approach to treat sexual problems, noted (1975) that, "Changing attitudes is an essential part of treatment which has been sadly neglected by behavior therapists" (p. 149). Kaplan (1974) makes extensive use of psychodynamic theory and technique to deal with attitudinal resistance. Attitudes may be changed by confronting clients with discrepancies between their attitudes and reality; by subtly fostering behavior change (sometimes, where the body goes the heart follows); and by facilitating the cathartic expression of feelings.

Although sex therapy must be tailored to specific problems, most treatments are initiated with *sensate focus.* In this phase of treatment couples are taught how to relax and enjoy touching and being touched. They're told to go home and find a time when they're both reasonably relaxed and free from distraction, and then get in bed together naked. Then they take turns gently caressing each other. The person being touched is told to simply relax and concentrate on the feeling of being touched. Later the one being touched will let the partner know which touch is most pleasing and which is less so. At first couples are told not to touch each other in the sensitive breast or genital areas, in order to avoid undue anxiety.

After they learn to relax and exchange gentle, pleasant caressing, couples are encouraged to gradually become more intimate—but to slow down if either should feel anxious. Thus sensate focus is a form of *in vivo desensitization.* Couples who are highly anxious and fearful of "having sex" (which many people reducc to a hectic few minutes of poking and panting) learn to overcome their fears through a gradual and progressively more intimate experience of mutual caressing. As anxiety drops and desire mounts, they're encouraged to engage in progressively more intimate exchanges. In the process, couples are also taught to communicate what they like and don't like. So, for example, instead of enduring something unpleasant until she finally gets so upset that she snaps at her partner or avoids sex altogether, a woman might be taught how to gently show him, "No, not like that, like this." Sex therapists also emphasize the need to become comfortable with initiating and refusing sexual contact. Couples are taught how to initiate sex without the ambiguity or poor timing that leads to a history of tension, anxiety, and, eventually, dread.

Once sensate focus exercises have gone smoothly, the therapist introduces specific techniques to deal with specific problems. Among women the most common sexual dysfunctions are difficulties with orgasm (Kaplan, 1979). Frequently these problems are rooted in lack of information. The woman and her partner may be expecting her to have orgasms reliably during intercourse without additional clitoral stimulation. In men, the most common problem is premature ejaculation, for which part of the treatment is the *squeeze technique* (Semans, 1956), in which the woman stimulates the man's penis until he feels the urge to ejaculate. At that point, she squeezes the frenulum (at the base of the head) firmly between her thumb and first two fingers until the urge to ejaculate subsides. Stimulation begins again until another squeeze is necessary.

Techniques to deal with erectile failure are designed to reduce performance anxiety and increase sexual arousal. These include desensitization of the man's anxiety; discussions in which the partners describe their expectations; increasing the variety and duration of foreplay; the *teasing technique* (Masters & Johnson, 1970), in which the woman alternately starts and stops stimulating the man; and beginning intercourse with the woman guiding the man's flaccid penis into her vagina.

Successful sex therapy usually ends with the couple's sex life much improved, but not as fantastic as frustrated expectations had led them to imagine—expectations that were part of the problem in the first place. As in any form of directive therapy, it's important for sex therapists to gradually fade out their involvement and control. Therapeutic gains are consolidated and extended by reviewing the changes that have occurred; by anticipating future trouble spots; and by planning in advance to deal with problems according to principles learned in treatment.

Evaluating Therapy Theory and Results

Behavior therapy was born and bred in a tradition of research, and so it's not surprising that behavioral family therapy is the most carefully studied form of family treatment. Almost all reports of behavioral family therapy are accompanied by some assessment of outcome, and there are hundreds of reports of successful parent training, couples' treatment, and sex therapy. However, the majority of these are single case studies, both anecdotal and experimental. They do help substantiate the efficacy of the behavioral approach to problems in family living, but such case reports are probably better considered demonstrations than investigations. In addition, there are also a host of controlled experimental studies of behavior family therapy. Gordon and Davidson (1981) summarized studies of the effectiveness of behavioral parent training, and found that the majority of measures yielded positive results in the majority of cases. They reported hundreds of documented successes with a wide variety of problem children. The outcome criteria in studies of parent training are usually based on parents' and observers' frequency counts of prosocial and deviant behavior. Researchers have found that more advantaged families show distinctly better results from behavior parent training (O'Dell, 1974). This isn't surprising considering the heavy emphasis on education in this approach.

A typical finding is that targeted behavior improves; only marginal changes, however, can be seen for nontargeted problem behavior. Apparently the specific focus on presenting problems lends leverage to resolving focal complaints, but only minimally generalizes to overall family functioning. Moreover, improvements don't generalize from home to other settings, such as school (Gurman & Kniskern, 1978). Finally, there is a tendency for therapeutic gains to decrease sharply between termination and follow-up.

The behavioral literature also contains a large number of empirical studies of couples therapy. These studies are usually done on brief treatment (approximately nine sessions) and the most common criteria of success are observers' ratings and couples' self-reports. In 1978 Gurman and Kniskern (1978) reported on eight controlled analogue studies; two showed behavioral couples therapy to be significantly better than no treatment; in five controlled analogue studies behavioral couples therapy was found to be more effective than alternative forms of treatment in only one case. In the same survey, Gurman and Kniskern found that six of seven naturalistic comparative studies favored behavioral couples therapy. These findings provide support for the efficacy of this approach; however, as the authors noted, behavioral therapy is still relatively untested on couples with severe marital problems. When they updated their survey in 1981, Gurman and Kniskern (1981) found similar results and concluded that behavioral marriage therapy appears to be about as effective for mild to moderate marital problems as are nonbehavioral approaches.

Several studies have shown that the most effective ingredient in any form of couples therapy is increasing communication skills (Jacobson, 1978; Jacobson & Margolin, 1979). Jacobson's studies strongly support his approach, based on observational measures of communication and self-reported marital satisfaction. Liberman and his colleagues (Liberman, Levine, Wheeler, Sanders, & Wallace, 1976) found that on objective measures of marital communication, behavioral couples therapy in a group setting was more effective than insight-oriented couples groups. However, the two approaches didn't differ in effecting increased marital satisfaction. O'Leary and Turkewitz (1978) have shown that behavior exchange procedures are effective, especially with young couples; older couples tend to respond more favorably to communications training.

Despite the tremendous growth of public and professional interest in sex therapy, there are still few well-controlled studies of its effectiveness. In a careful review, Hogan (1978) found that most of the literature consists of uncontrolled, clinical case studies. These reports are little more than box scores of successes and failures. Absent are pre- and post-measures, detailed specification of techniques, points of reference other than the therapists, and follow-up data. Moreover, since most of these reports come from the same handful of therapists, it's impossible to discern what's being evaluated—the techniques of sex therapy or the skill of these particular therapists. This state of the research hadn't changed much by 1990, according to more recent summary reports (Crowe, 1988; Falloon & Lillie, 1988).

The greatest success rates with sexual therapy have been found in treating vaginismus, orgasmic dysfunction, and premature ejaculation. Vaginismus, the spastic contraction of vagina muscles, has been successfully treated in 90 to 95 percent of cases (Fuchs, Hoch, Paldi, Abramovici, Brandes, Timor-Tritsch, & Kleinhaus, 1973). Eighty-five to 95 percent of the women who had never previously achieved orgasm did so after treatment. Success rates are lower, 30 to 50 percent, when limited to those who had previously reached orgasm during coitus (Heiman, LoPiccolo, & LoPiccolo, 1981). The reported success rates for treatment of premature ejaculation using the squeeze technique (Masters & Johnson, 1970) are uniformly high, 90 to 95 percent.

For men who had never had erectile functioning, the success rates are between 40 and 60 percent—though, as Michael Crowe (1988) has noted, this problem turns out to be medically related more often than we used to think. For those who once had adequate erectile functioning and then developed difficulty, success rates average 60 to 80 percent (Heiman, LoPiccolo, & LoPiccolo, 1981). Retarded ejaculation or failure to ejaculate is relatively uncommon; consequently there are fewer reported treatment cases. Among this small sample, reported success rates range from 50 to 82 percent (Heiman, LoPiccolo, & LoPiccolo, 1981). Treatment of individuals with very low levels of interest in sex is relatively new (Kaplan, 1979) and there are as yet few statistics, but apparently such cases respond well to treatment (LoPiccolo & LoPiccolo, 1978).

The fact that there are relatively few published studies shouldn't obscure the fact that sex therapy appears to be an effective procedure for some very vexing problems. Most observers (Gurman & Kniskern, 1981) agree that it should be considered the treatment of choice when there is an explicit complaint about a couple's sex life.

Currently there are three areas of research in family intervention that seem to be ready to move to a more advanced stage of development. These areas are: conduct disorders in children (Patterson, 1986; Morris, Alexander, & Waldron, 1988), marital conflict (Follette & Jacobson, 1988), and schizophrenic adults (Falloon, 1985).

Summary

Although behavior therapists have begun to apply their techniques to family problems, they have done so for the most part within a linear frame of reference. Behavioral problems are regarded as *caused* by dysfunctional patterns of reinforcement between parents and children, or between spouses. Therefore, behavioral family therapy is used to teach parents how to apply learning theory to control their children; to help couples substitute positive for aversive control; and to decondition anxiety in partners with sexual problems. Behavioral family therapists give little consideration to complex and circular family interactions.

Family symptoms are treated as learned responses, involuntarily acquired and reinforced. Treatment is generally time-limited and symptom-focused. The behavioral approach to families is based on social learning theory, which is a complex and sophisticated model, according to which behavior is learned and maintained by its consequences, and can be modified by altering those consequences.

Behaviorists' systematic analysis of behavior and their insistence on technically sound interventions make it clear that a therapist's personality isn't all that's needed to help people change. Behaviorists don't believe that therapists have to *be* something—warm, self-disclosing, forceful—rather, they have to *do* something. Personal skills are required, not personal style.

An essential adjunct to social learning theory is Thibaut and Kelley's exchange theory, according to which people strive to maximize interpersonal "rewards" while minimizing "costs." Social behavior in a relationship is maintained by a high ratio of rewards to costs, and by the perception that alternative relationships offer fewer rewards and more costs (comparison level of alternatives). In this view, marital and family conflicts occur when optimal behavior-maintaining contingencies don't exist, or when dysfunctional behavior change methods are applied. In unhappy families, coercion replaces reciprocity.

The general goals of behavioral family therapy are to increase the rate of rewarding exchanges; to decrease aversive exchanges; and to teach communication and problem-solving skills. Specific techniques are applied to target behaviors; in the process, families are also taught general principles of behavior management.

The behaviorists' focus on modifying the consequences of problem behavior accounts for the strengths and weaknesses of behavioral family therapy. By concentrating on presenting problems, behaviorists have been able to develop an impressive array of effective techniques. Even such relatively intractable problems as delinquent behavior in children and severe sexual dysfunctions have yielded to behavioral technology. On the other hand, behavior is only part of the person, and the problem person is only part of the family. Any form of therapy must deal with the whole person, who not only acts but also thinks and feels. Different therapies may concentrate on only one of these three human functions—psychoanalysts concentrate on thinking, just as behaviorists concentrate on action—but to be successful a therapy must affect all three. You can't simply teach people to change if unrecognized conflict is keeping them stuck.

Unhappiness may center around a behavioral complaint, but resolution of the behavior may not resolve the unhappiness. Treatment may succeed with the symptom but fail the family. Attitudes and feelings may change along with changes in behavior, but not necessarily. And teaching communication skills may not be sufficient to resolve real conflict. Mere behavior change may not be enough for family members whose ultimate goal is to feel better. "Yes, he's doing his chores now," a parent may agree. "But I don't think he *feels* like helping out. He still isn't really part of our family." Behavior isn't all that family members in distress are concerned about, and to be responsive to all their needs therapists need to deal with cognitive and affective issues, as well as behavioral.

Although behavioral family clinicians recognize the need to modify interpersonal interactions, they generally limit their attention to units of two, and they tend to accept the family's definition of one person (or couple) as *the* problem. Virtually no consideration is given to the role of marital problems in behavioral treatment of children, and behavioral couples therapists rarely discuss the role that children or extended family members play in marital distress.

Behaviorists hardly ever treat whole families. Instead they bring in only those subsystems they consider central to the targeted behaviors. Unfortunately, failure to include—or even consider—whole families in treatment may be disastrous. A therapeutic program to reduce a son's aggressiveness toward his mother can hardly succeed if the father wants an aggressive son, or if the father's anger toward his wife isn't addressed. Moreover, if the whole family isn't involved in change, new behavior may not be reinforced and maintained.

Despite these shortcomings, behavioral family therapy offers impressive techniques for treating problems with children and troubled marriages. Furthermore, its weaknesses can be corrected by broadening the focus of conceptualization and the scope of treatment to include whole families as systems. Although some behavior therapists may be naive about circular interactions and systemic structure, there's nothing inherently limiting in the usefulness of their technology.

Perhaps the greatest strength of behavior therapy is its insistence on observing what happens and then measuring change. Behaviorists have developed a wealth of reliable and valid assessment methods and applied them to initial evaluation, treatment planning, and monitoring progress and outcome. A second important advance has been the gradual movement from eliminating or reinforcing discrete "marker" behaviors to the teaching of general problem-solving, cognitive, and communicational skills. A third major advance in current behavioral family therapy is modular treatment interventions organized to meet the specific and changing needs of the individual and the family.

References

Ables, B. S., and Brandsma, S. J. 1977. *Therapy for couples.* San Francisco: Jossey-Bass.

Alexander, J. F., and Barton, C. 1976. Behavioral systems therapy with families. In *Treating relationships,* D. H. Olson, ed. Lake Mills, IA: Graphic Publishing.

Alexander, J. F., and Parsons, B. V. 1973. Short-term behavioral intervention with delinquent families: Impact on family process and recidivism. *Journal of Abnormal Psychology. 51*:219–225.

Alexander, J., and Parsons, B. V. 1982. *Functional family therapy.* Pacific Grove, CA: Brooks/Cole.

Alexander, P. 1988. The therapeutic implications of family cognitions and constructs. *Journal of Cognitive Psychotherapy. 2*:219–236.

Anderson, C. M., and Stewart, S. 1983. *Mastering resistance.* New York: Guilford Press.

Arrington, A., Sullaway, M., and Christensen, A. 1988. Behavioral family assessment. In *Handbook of behavioral family therapy,* I. R. H. Falloon, ed. New York: Guilford Press.

Azrin, N. H., Naster, J. B., and Jones, R. 1973. Reciprocity counseling: A rapid learning-based procedure for marital counseling. *Behavior Research and Therapy. 11*:365–383.

Baer, D. M., and Sherman, J. A. 1969. Reinforcement control of generalized imitation in young children. *Journal of Experimental Child Psychology. 1*:37–49.

Bancroft, J. 1975. The behavioral approach to marital problems. *British Journal of Medical Psychology. 48*:147–152.

Bandura, A. 1969. *Principles of behavior modification.* New York: Holt, Rinehart & Winston.

Bandura, A., and Walters, R. 1963. *Social learning and personality development.* New York: Holt, Rinehart & Winston.

Barton, C., and Alexander, J. F. 1975. Therapist skills in systems-behavioral family intervention: How the hell do you get them to do it? Paper presented at the annual meeting of the Orthopsychiatric Association, Atlanta.

Barton, C., and Alexander, J. F. 1981. Functional family therapy. In *Handbook of family therapy,* A. S. Gurman and D. P. Kniskern, eds. New York: Brunner/Mazel.

Baucom, D. H. 1981. Cognitive-behavioral strategies in the treatment of marital discord. Paper presented at the annual meeting of the Association of the Advancement of Behavior Therapy, Toronto, Canada.

Baucom, D. H., and Epstein, N. 1990. *Cognitive-behavioral marital therapy.* New York: Brunner/Mazel.

Baucom, D. H., and Lester, G. W. 1986. The usefulness of cognitive restructuring as an adjunct to behavioral marital therapy. *Behavior Therapy. 17*:385–403.

Beck, A. T. 1976. *Cognitive therapy and the emotional disorders.* New York: International Universities Press.

Beck, A. T. 1988. *Love is never enough.* New York: Harper & Row.

Beck, A. T., Rush, J. A., Shaw, B. F., and Emery, G. 1979. *Cognitive therapy of depression.* New York: Guilford Press.

Birchler, G. R. 1988. Handling resistance to change. In *Handbook of behavioral family therapy,* I. R. H. Falloon, ed. New York: Guilford Press.

Birchler, G. R., and Spinks, S. H. 1980. Behavioral-systems marital therapy: Integration and clinical application. *American Journal of Family Therapy. 8*:6–29.

Boardman, W. K. 1962. Rusty: A brief behavior disorder. *Journal of Consulting Psychology. 26*:293–297.

Christophersen, E. R., Arnold, C. M., Hill, D. W., and Quilitch, H. R. 1972. The home point system: Token reinforcement procedures for application by parents of children with behavioral problems. *Journal of Applied Behavioral Analysis. 5*: 485–497.

Crowe, M. 1988. Indications for family, marital, and sexual therapy. In *Handbook of behavioral family therapy,* I. R. H. Falloon, ed. New York: Guilford Press.

Dattilio, F. M. 1989. A guide to cognitive marital therapy. In *Innovations in clinical practice: A source book,* vol. 8, P. A. Keller and S. R. Heyman, eds. Sarasota, FL: Professional Resource Exchange.

Dattilio, F. M. 1990. Cognitive marital therapy: A case study. *Journal of Family Psychotherapy. 1*:15–31.

Dattilio, F. M. 1993. Cognitive techniques with couples and families. *The Family Journal. 1*: 51–65.

Dattilio, F. M. 1994. Families in crisis. In *Cognitive-behavioral strategies in crisis interventions,* F. M. Dattilio and A. Freeman, eds. New York: Guilford Press.

Dattilio, F. M. 1997a. Family therapy. In *Casebook of cognitive therapy,* R. Leahy, ed. Northvale, NJ: Jason Aronson.

Dattilio, F. M. 1997b. *Integrative cases in couples and family therapy: A cognitive-behavioral perspective.* New York: Guilford Press.

Dattilio, F. M., and Padesky, C. A. 1990. *Cognitive therapy with couples.* Sarasota, FL: Professional Resource Exchange.

DeRubeis, R. J., and Beck, A. T. 1988. Cognitive therapy. In *Handbook of cognitive-behavioral therapies,* K. S. Dobson, ed. New York: Guilford Press.

Dicks, H. 1953. Experiences with marital tensions seen in the psychological clinic. In Clinical Studies in Marriage and the Family: A symposium on methods. *British Journal of Medical Psychology. 26*:181–196.

DiGiuseppe, R. 1988. A cognitive-behavioral approach to the treatment of conduct disorder in children and adolescents. In *Cognitive-behavioral therapy with families,* N. Epstein, S. E. Schlesinger, and W. Dryden, eds. New York: Brunner/Mazel.

DiGiuseppe, R., and Zeeve, C. 1985. Marriage: Rational-emotive couples counseling. In *Clinical applications of rational-emotive therapy,* A. Ellis and M. Bernard, eds. New York: Springer.

Doherty, W. J. (1981). Cognitive processes in intimate conflict: 1. Extending attribution theory. *American Journal of Family Therapy. 9*:5–13.

Eisler, R. M., and Hersen, M. 1973. Behavior techniques in family-oriented crisis intervention. *Archives of General Psychiatry. 28*:111–116.

Ellis, A. 1962. *Reason and emotion in psychotherapy.* New York: Lyle Stuart.

Ellis, A. 1977. The nature of disturbed marital interactions. In *Handbook of rational-emotive therapy,* A. Ellis and R. Greiger, eds. New York: Springer.

Ellis, A. 1978. Family therapy: A phenomenological and active-directive approach. *Journal of Marriage and Family Counseling.* 4:43–50.

Ellis, A. 1982. Rational-emotive family therapy. In *Family counseling and therapy,* A. M. Horne and M. M. Ohlsen, eds. Itasca, IL: Peacock.

Ellis, A., Sichel, J. L., Yeager, R. J., DiMattia, D. J., and DiGiuseppe, R. 1989. *Rational emotive couples therapy.* Needham Heights, MA: Allyn and Bacon.

Ely, A. L., Guerney, B. G., and Stover, L. 1973. Efficacy of the training phase of conjugal therapy. *Psycho-*

therapy: Theory, Research and Practice. *10*:201–207.

Epstein, N. 1992. Marital Therapy. In *Comprehensive casebook of cognitive therapy,* A. Freeman and F. M. Dattilio, eds. New York: Plenum.

Epstein, N. 1982. Cognitive therapy with couples. *American Journal of Family Therapy.* *10*:5–16.

Epstein, N., Schlesinger, S. E., and Dryden, W., eds. 1988. *Cognitive-behavioral therapy with families.* New York: Brunner/Mazel.

Epstein, N., and Schlesinger, S. E. 1991. Marital and family problems. In *Adult clinical problems: A cognitive-behavioral approach,* W. Dryden and R. Rentoul, eds. London: Routledge.

Epstein, N., and Schlesinger, S. E. 1996. Cognitive-behavioral treatment of family problems. In *Casebook of cognitive-behavior therapy with children and adolescents,* M. Reinecke, F. M. Dattilio, and A. Freeman, eds. New York: Guilford Press.

Falloon, I. R. H. 1985. *Family management of schizophrenia: A study of the clinical, social, family and economic benefits.* Baltimore: Johns Hopkins University Press.

Falloon, I. R. H., ed. 1988. *Handbook of behavioral family therapy.* New York: Guilford Press.

Falloon, I. R. H. 1991. Behavioral family therapy. In *Handbook of family therapy,* vol. II, A. S. Gurman and D. P. Kniskern, eds. New York: Brunner/Mazel.

Falloon, I. R. H., and Liberman, R. P. 1983. Behavioral therapy for families with child management problems. In *Helping families with special problems,* M. R. Textor, ed. New York: Jason Aronson.

Falloon, I. R. H., and Lillie, F. J. 1988. Behavioral family therapy: An overview. In *Handbook of behavioral family therapy,* I. R. H. Falloon, ed. New York: Guilford Press.

Ferster, C. B. 1963. Essentials of a science of behavior. In *An introduction to the science of human behavior,* J. I. Nurnberger, C. B. Ferster, and J. P. Brady, eds. New York: Appleton-Century-Crofts.

Fincham, F. D., Bradbury, T. N., and Beach, S. R. H. 1990. To arrive where we began: A reappraisal of cognition in marriage and in marital therapy. *Journal of Family Psychology.* 4:167–184.

Follette, W. C., and Jacobson, N. S. 1988. Behavioral marital therapy in the treatment of depressive disorders. In *Handbook of behavioral family therapy,* I. R. H. Falloon, ed. New York: Guilford Press.

Forehand, R., and McDonough, T. S. 1975. Response-contingent time out: An examination of outcome data. *European Journal of Behavioral Analysis and Modification.* *1*:109–115.

Forehand, R., Roberts, M. W., Doleys, D. M., Hobbs, S. A., and Resnick, P. A. 1976. An examination of disciplinary procedures with children. *Journal of Experimental Child Psychology.* *21*:109–120.

Friedman, P. H. 1972. Personalistic family and marital therapy. In *Clinical behavior therapy,* A. A. Lazarus, ed. New York: Brunner/Mazel.

Fuchs, K., Hoch, Z., Paldi, E., Abramovici, H., Brandes, J. M., Timor-Tritsch, I., and Kleinhaus, M. 1973. Hypnodesensitization therapy of vaginismus: Part 1. "In vitro" method. Part 11. "In vivo" method. *International Journal of Clinical and Experimental Hypnosis.* *21*:144–156.

Gill, H., and Temperly, J. 1974. Time-limited marital treatment in a foursome. *British Journal of Medical Psychology.* *47*:153–161.

Goldenberg, I., and Goldenberg, H. 1991. *Family therapy: An overview.* Pacific Grove, CA: Brooks/Cole.

Goldiamond, I. 1965. Self-control procedures in personal behavior problems. *Psychological Reports.* *17*:851–868.

Goldstein, M. K. 1971. Behavior rate change in marriages: Training wives to modify husbands' behavior. *Dissertation Abstracts International.* *32* (18):559.

Goldstein, M. K., and Francis, B. 1969. Behavior modification of husbands by wives. Paper presented at the National Council on Family Relations, Washington, DC.

Gordon, S. B., and Davidson, N. 1981. Behavioral parent training. In *Handbook of family therapy,* A. S. Gurman and D. P. Kniskern, eds. New York: Brunner/Mazel.

Gottman, J., and Krokoff, L. 1989. Marital interaction and satisfaction: A longitudinal view. *Journal of Consulting and Clinical Psychology.* *57*:47–52.

Gottman, J., Markman, H., and Notarius, C. 1977. The topography of marital conflict: A sequential analysis of verbal and nonverbal behavior. *Journal of Marriage and the Family.* *39*:461–477.

Graziano, A. M. 1977. Parents as behavior therapists. In *Progress in behavior modification,* M. Hersen, R. M. Eisler, and P. M. Miller, eds. New York: Academic Press.

Guerin, P. J., Fay, L., Burden, S. L., and Kautto, J. B. 1987. *The evaluation and treatment of marital conflict: A four-stage approach.* New York: Basic Books.

Gurman, A. S., and Kniskern, D. P. 1978. Research on marital and family therapy: Progress, perspective and prospect. In *Handbook of psychotherapy and behavior change: An empirical analysis,* S. L. Garfield and A. E. Bergin, eds. New York: Wiley.

Gurman, A. S., and Kniskern, D. P. 1981. Family therapy outcome research: Knowns and unknowns. In *Handbook of family therapy,* A. S. Gurman and D. P. Kniskern, eds. New York: Brunner/Mazel.

Gurman, A. S., and Knudson, R. M. 1978. Behavioral marriage therapy: A psychodynamic-systems analysis and critique. *Family Process. 17:*121–138.

Hawkins, R. P., Peterson, R. F., Schweid, E., and Bijou, S. W. 1966. Behavior therapy in the home: Amelioration of problem parent-child relations with a parent in the therapeutic role. *Journal of Experimental Child Psychology. 4:*99–107.

Heiman, J. R., LoPiccolo, L., and LoPiccolo, J. 1981. The treatment of sexual dysfunction. In *Handbook of family therapy,* A. S. Gurman and D. P. Kniskern, eds. New York: Brunner/Mazel.

Hickman, M. E., and Baldwin, B. A. 1971. Use of programmed instruction to improve communication in marriage. *The Family Coordinator. 20:* 121–125.

Hogan, D. R. 1978. The effectiveness of sex therapy: A review of the literature. In *Handbook of sex therapy,* J. LoPiccolo and L. LoPiccolo, eds. New York: Plenum Press.

Holtzworth-Munroe, A., and Jacobson, N. S. 1991. Behavioral marital therapy. In *Handbook of family therapy,* vol. II, A. S. Gurman and D. P. Kniskern, eds. New York: Brunner/Mazel.

Huber, C. H., and Baruth, L. G. 1989. *Rational-emotive family therapy: A systems perspective.* New York: Springer.

Jacobson, N. S. 1977. Problem solving and contingency contracting in the treatment of marital discord. *Journal of Consulting and Clinical Psychology. 45:*92–100.

Jacobson, N. S. 1978. Specific and nonspecific factors in the effectiveness of a behavioral approach to the treatment of marital discord. *Journal of Consulting and Clinical Psychology. 46:*442–452.

Jacobson, N. S. 1981. Behavioral marital therapy. In *Handbook of family therapy,* A. S. Gurman and D. P. Kniskern, eds. New York: Brunner/Mazel.

Jacobson, N. S., and Margolin, G. 1979. *Marital therapy: Strategies based on social learning and behavior exchange principles.* New York: Brunner/Mazel.

Jacobson, N. S., and Martin, B. 1976. Behavioral marriage therapy: Current status. *Psychological Bulletin. 83:*540–556.

Jacobson, N. S., Waldron, H., and Moore, D. 1980. Toward a behavioral profile of marital distress. *Journal of Consulting and Clinical Psychology. 48:* 696–703.

Jones, M. C. 1924. A laboratory study of fear: The case of Peter. *Journal of Geriatric Psychology. 31:* 308–315.

Kanfer, F. H., and Phillips, J. S. 1970. *Learning foundations of behavior therapy.* New York: Wiley.

Kaplan, H. S. 1974. *The new sex therapy: Active treatment of sexual dysfunctions.* New York: Brunner/Mazel.

Kaplan, H. S. 1979. *Disorders of sexual desire and other new concepts and techniques in sex therapy.* New York: Brunner/Mazel.

Katkin, E. S. 1978. Charting as a multipurpose treatment intervention in family therapy. *Family Process. 17:*465–468.

Keefe, F. J., Kopel, S. A., and Gordon, S. B. 1978. *A practical guide to behavior assessment.* New York: Springer.

Kimmel, C., and Van der Veen, F. 1974. Factors of marital adjustment in Locke's Marital Adjustment Test. *Journal of Marriage and the Family. 36:*57–63.

Knox, D. 1971. *Marriage happiness: A behavioral approach to counseling.* Champaign, IL: Research Press.

Knox, D. 1973. Behavior contracts in marriage counseling. *Journal of Family Counseling. 1:*22–28.

Lazarus, A. A. 1965. The treatment of a sexually inadequate male. In *Case studies in behavior modification,* L. P. Ullmann and L. Krasner, eds. New York: Holt, Rinehart & Winston.

Lazarus, A. A. 1968. Behavior therapy and group marriage counseling. *Journal of the American Society of Medicine and Dentistry. 15:*49–56.

Lazarus, A. A. 1971. *Behavior therapy and beyond.* New York: McGraw-Hill.

LeBow, M. D. 1972. Behavior modification for the family. In *Family therapy: An introduction to theory and technique,* G. D. Erickson and T. P. Hogan, eds. Monterey, CA: Brooks/Cole.

Lederer, W. J., and Jackson, D. D. 1968. *The mirages of marriage.* New York: Norton.

Leslie, L. A. 1988. Cognitive-behavioral and systems models of family therapy: How compatible are they? In *Cognitive-behavioral therapy with families*, N. Epstein, S. E. Schlesinger, and W. Dryden, eds. New York: Brunner/Mazel.

Liberman, R. P. 1970. Behavioral approaches to family and couple therapy. *American Journal of Orthopsychiatry. 40:*106–118.

Liberman, R. P. 1972. Behavioral approaches to family and couple therapy. In *Progress in group and family therapy*, C. J. Sager and H. S. Kaplan, eds. New York: Brunner/Mazel.

Liberman, R. P., Levine, J., Wheeler, E., Sanders, N., and Wallace, C. 1976. Experimental evaluation of marital group therapy: Behavioral vs. interaction-insight formats. *Acta Psychiatrica Scandinavia* Supplement.

Lobitz, N. C., and LoPiccolo, J. 1972. New methods in the behavioral treatment of sexual dysfunction. *Journal of Behavior Therapy and Experimental Psychiatry. 3:*265–271.

Locke, H. J., and Wallace, K. M. 1959. Short-term marital adjustment and prediction tests: Their reliability and validity. *Journal of Marriage and Family Living. 21:*251–255.

LoPiccolo, J., and LoPiccolo, L. 1978. *Handbook of sex therapy.* New York: Plenum.

Lovibond, S. H. 1963. The mechanism of conditioning treatment of enuresis. *Behavior Research and Therapy. 1:*17–21.

Madanes, C. 1981. *Strategic family therapy.* San Francisco: Jossey-Bass.

Mahoney, M. J. 1977. Reflections on the cognitive learning trend in psychotherapy. *American Psychologist. 32:*5–13.

Margolin, G., Christensen, A., and Weiss, R. L. 1975. Contracts, cognition and change: A behavioral approach to marriage therapy. *Counseling Psychologist.* 5:15–25.

Margolin, G., and Weiss, R. L. 1978. Comparative evaluation of therapeutic components associated with behavioral marital treatments. *Journal of Consulting and Clinical Psychology. 46:*1476–1486.

Markman, H. J. 1979. Application of a behavioral model of marriage in predicting relationship satisfaction of couples planning marriage. *Journal of Consulting and Clinical Psychology. 47:*743–749.

Markman, H. J. 1981. Prediction of marital distress: A 5-year follow up. *Journal of Consulting and Clinical Psychology. 49:*760–762.

Masters, W. H., and Johnson, V. E. 1970. *Human sexual inadequacy.* Boston: Little, Brown & Co.

McCauley, R. 1988. Parent training: Clinical application. In *Handbook of behavioral family therapy*, I. R. H. Falloon, ed. New York: Guilford Press.

McGuire, R. J., and Vallance, M. 1964. Aversion therapy by electric shock: A simple technique. *British Medical Journal. 1:*151–153.

Meichenbaum, D. 1977. *Cognitive behavior modification.* New York: Plenum.

Minuchin, S. 1974. *Families and family therapy.* Cambridge, MA: Harvard University Press.

Minuchin, S., Rosman, B. L., and Baker, L. 1978. *Psychosomatic families.* Cambridge, MA: Harvard University Press.

Mischel, W. 1973. On the empirical dilemmas of psychodynamic approaches: Issues and alternatives. *Journal of Abnormal Psychology. 82:*335.

Morris, S. B., Alexander, J. F., and Waldron, H. 1988. Functional family therapy. In *Handbook of behavioral family therapy*, I. R. H. Falloon, ed. New York: Guilford Press.

Morton, T. L., Twentyman, C. T., and Azar, S. T. 1988. Cognitive-behavioral assessment and treatment of child abuse. In *Cognitive-behavioral therapy with families*, N. Epstein, S. E. Schlesinger, and W. Dryden, eds. New York: Brunner/Mazel.

Munson, C. E. 1993. Cognitive family therapy. In *Cognitive and behavioral treatment: Methods and applictions*, D. K. Granvold, ed. Pacific Grove, CA: Brooks/Cole.

O'Dell, S. 1974. Training parents in behavior modification: A review. *Psychological Bulletin. 81:*418–433.

O'Leary, K. D., O'Leary, S., and Becher, W. C. 1967. Modification of a deviant sibling interaction pattern in the home. *Behavior Research and Therapy.* 5:113–120.

O'Leary, K. D., and Turkewitz, H. 1978. Marital therapy from a behavioral perspective. In *Marriage and marital therapy*, T. J. Paolino and B. S. McCrady, eds. New York: Brunner/Mazel.

O'Leary, K. D., and Wilson, G. T. 1975. *Behavior therapy: Application and outcome.* Englewood Cliffs, NJ: Prentice-Hall.

Patterson, G. R. 1971a. Behavioral intervention procedures in the classroom and in the home. In *Handbook of psychotherapy and behavior change: An empirical analysis*, A. E. Bergin and S. L. Garfield, eds. New York: Wiley.

Patterson, G. R. 1971b. *Families: Application of social learning theory to family life.* Champaign, IL: Research Press.

Patterson, G. R. 1986. The contribution of siblings to training for fighting; A microsocial analysis. In *Development of antisocial and prosocial behavior: Research, theories, and issues,* D. Olweus, J. Block, and M. Radke-Yarrow, eds. Orlando, FL: Academic Press.

Patterson, G. R. 1988. Foreword. In *Handbook of behavioral family therapy,* I. R. H. Falloon, ed. New York: Guilford Press.

Patterson, G. R., and Hops, H. 1972. Coercion, a game for two. In *The experimental analysis of social behavior,* R. E. Ulrich and P. Mountjoy, eds. New York: Appleton-Century-Crofts.

Patterson, G. R., Hops, H., and Weiss, R. L. 1973. A social learning approach to reducing rates of marital conflict. In *Advances in behavior therapy,* R. Stuart, R. Liberman, and S. Wilder, eds. New York: Academic Press.

Patterson, G. R., and Reid, J. 1970. Reciprocity and coercion; two facets of social systems. In *Behavior modification in clinical psychology,* C. Neuringer and J. Michael, eds. New York: Appleton-Century-Crofts.

Patterson, G. R., Weiss, R. L., and Hops, H. 1976. Training in marital skills: Some problems and concepts. In *Handbook of behavior modification and behavior therapy,* H. Leitenberg, ed. Englewood Cliffs, NJ: Prentice-Hall.

Pavlov, I. P. 1932. Neuroses in man and animals. *Journal of the American Medical Association. 99:* 1012–1013.

Pavlov, I. P. 1934. An attempt at a physiological interpretation of obsessional neurosis and paranoia. *Journal of Mental Science. 80:*187–197.

Pendergrass, V. E. 1971. Effects of length of timeout from positive reinforcement and schedule of application in suppression of aggressive behavior. *Psychological Record. 21:*75–80.

Pierce, R. M. 1973. Training in interpersonal communication skills with the partners of deteriorated marriages. *The Family Coordinator. 22:*223–227.

Premack, D. 1965. Reinforcement theory. In *Nebraska symposium on motivation,* D. Levine, ed. Lincoln, NB: University of Nebraska Press.

Rappaport, A. F., and Harrell, J. A. 1972. A behavior-exchange model for marital counseling. *Family Coordinator. 21:*203–213.

Rimm, D. C., and Masters, J. C. 1974. *Behavior therapy: Techniques and empirical findings.* New York: Wiley.

Rinn, R. C. 1978. Children with behavior disorders. In *Behavior therapy in the psychiatric setting,* M. Hersen and A. S. Bellack, eds. Baltimore: Williams & Wilkins.

Risley, T. R. 1968. The effects and side effects of punishing the autistic behaviors of a deviant child. *Journal of Applied Behavior Analysis. 1:*21–34.

Risley, T. R., and Wolf, M. M. 1967. Experimental manipulation of autistic behaviors and generalization into the home. In *Child development: Readings in experimental analysis,* S. W. Bijou and D. M. Baer, eds. New York: Appleton.

Romanczyk, R. G., and Kistner, J. J. 1977. The current state of the art in behavior modification. *The Psychotherapy Bulletin. 11:*16–30.

Russell, T., and Marrill, C. M. 1989. Adding a systematic touch to rational-emotive therapy for families. *Journal of Mental Health Counseling. 11:* 184–192.

Sanders, M. R., and Dadds, M. R. 1993. *Behavioral family intervention.* Boston, MA: Allyn and Bacon.

Satir, V. 1967. *Conjoint family therapy.* Palo Alto, CA: Science and Behavioral Books.

Schindler, L., and Vollmer, M. 1984. Cognitive perspectives in behavioral marital therapy: Some proposals for bridging theory, research and practice. In *Marital interaction: Analysis and modification,* K. Hahlwag and N. S. Jacobson, eds. New York: Guilford Press.

Schwebel, A. I., and Fine, M. A. 1992. Cognitive-behavioral family therapy. *Journal of Family Psychotherapy. 3:*73–91.

Schwitzgebel, R. 1967. Short-term operant conditioning of adolescent offenders on socially relevant variables. *Journal of Abnormal Psychology. 72:*134–142.

Schwitzgebel, R., and Kolb, D. A. 1964. Inducing behavior change in adolescent delinquents. *Behaviour Research and Therapy. 9:*233-238.

Semans, J. H. 1956. Premature ejaculation: A new approach. *Southern Medical Journal. 49:* 353–357.

Skinner, B. F. 1953. *Science and human behavior.* New York: Macmillan.

Spinks, S. H., and Birchler, G. R. 1982. Behavior systems marital therapy: Dealing with resistance. *Family Process. 21:*169–186.

Stuart, R. B. 1969. An operant-interpersonal treatment for marital discord. *Journal of Consulting and Clinical Psychology. 33*:675–682.

Stuart, R. B. 1971. Behavioral contracting within the families of delinquents. *Journal of Behavior Therapy and Experimental Psychiatry. 2*:1–11.

Stuart, R. B. 1975. Behavioral remedies for marital ills: A guide to the use of operant-interpersonal techniques. In *International symposium on behavior modification,* T. Thompson and W. Docken, eds. New York: Appleton.

Stuart, R. B. 1976. An operant interpersonal program for couples. In *Treating relationships,* D. H. Olson, ed. Lake Mills, IA: Graphic Publishing.

Stuart, R. B. 1980. *Helping couples change: A social learning approach to marital therapy.* New York: Guilford Press.

Teichman, Y. 1984. Cognitive family therapy. *British Journal of Cognitive Psychotherapy. 2*:1–10.

Teichman, Y. 1992. Family treatment with an acting-out adolescent. In *Comprehensive casebook of cognitive therapy,* A. Freeman and F. M. Dattilio, eds. New York: Plenum.

Thibaut, J., and Kelley, H. H. 1959. *The social psychology of groups.* New York: Wiley.

Umana, R. F., Gross, S. J., and McConville, M. T. 1980. *Crisis in the family: Three approaches.* New York: Gardner Press.

Vincent, J. P., Weiss, R. L., and Birchler, G. R. 1975. A behavioral analysis of problem solving in distressed and nondistressed married and stranger dyads. *Behavior Therapy. 6*:475–487.

Watson, J. B., and Raynor, R. 1920. Conditioned emotional reactions. *Journal of Experimental Psychology. 3*:1–14.

Weiss, R. L. 1978. The conceptualization of marriage from a behavioral perspective. In *Marriage and marital therapy,* T. J. Paolino and B. S. McCrady, eds. New York: Brunner/Mazel.

Weiss, R. L. 1984. Cognitive and strategic interventions in behavioral marital therapy. In *Marital interaction: Analysis and modification,* K. Hahlwag and N. S. Jacobson, eds. New York: Guilford Press.

Weiss, R. L., and Birchler, G. R. 1978. Adults with marital dysfunction. In *Behavior therapy in the psychiatric setting,* M. Hersen and A. S. Bellack, eds. Baltimore: Williams & Wilkins.

Weiss, R. L., Hops, H., and Patterson, G. R. 1973. A framework for conceptualizing marital conflict, a technology for altering it, some data for evaluating it. In *Behavior change: Methodology, concepts and practice,* L. A. Hamerlynch, L. C. Handy, and E. J. Marsh, eds. Champaign, IL: Research Press.

Weiss, R. L., and Isaac, J. 1978. Behavior vs. cognitive measures as predictors of marital satisfaction. Paper presented at the Western Psychological Association meeting, Los Angeles.

Williams, C. D. 1959. The elimination of tantrum behavior by extinction procedures. *Journal of Abnormal and Social Psychology. 59*:269.

Wills, T. A., Weiss, R. L., and Patterson, G. R. 1974. A behavioral analysis of the determinants of marital satisfaction. *Journal of Consulting and Clinical Psychology. 42*:802–811.

Wodarski, J., and Thyer, B. 1989. Behavioral perspectives on the family: An overview. In *Behavioral family therapy,* B. Thyer, ed. Springfield, IL: Charles C. Thomas.

Wolpe, J. 1948. An approach to the problem of neurosis based on the conditioned response. Unpublished M.D. thesis. University of Witwatersrand, Johannesberg, South Africa.

Wolpe, J. 1958. *Psychotherapy by reciprocal inhibition.* Stanford, CA: Stanford University Press.

Wolpe, J. 1969. *The practice of behavior therapy.* New York: Pergamon Press.

Wright, J. H., and Beck, A. T. 1993. Family cognitive therapy with inpatients: Part II. In *Cognitive therapy with inpatients: Developing a cognitive milieu,* J. H. Wright, M. E. Thase, A. T. Beck, and J. W. Ludgate, eds. New York: Guilford Press.

10

Family Therapy Enters the Twenty-First Century

In the 1960s and 1970s family therapy grew from a radical new experiment to an established force, complete with its own journals, conferences, and thousands of adherents. Unlike other fields that were relatively homogeneously organized around one theory or approach (behavior therapy, psychoanalysis, hypnotherapy) or by professional degree (psychology, psychiatry, social work), family therapy had a wide variety of leaders and theories and drew followers from many backgrounds.

The systems-oriented family therapy models had differentiated from each other in large pendulum swings and were equally polarized from the psychoanalytic and behavioral establishments (though both behaviorism and analysis had their own representative models of family therapy). Boundaries around each model were rigid. If, for example, you were a structuralist and met someone at a conference who was interested in Bowen or Satir, the conversation wasn't likely to last long.

In the early 1970s family therapy was like the American automobile industry in its heyday. Just as the big three automakers competed among themselves but otherwise dominated the booming market, the big four or five models of family therapy competed with each other, also in a booming market. As a result, both automakers and schools of family therapy evinced the chauvinism and complacency that typify organizations on the rise—organizations that, because of their prosperity, have little incentive to question their own beliefs or practices.

The "family" that each of these models was trying to understand was not well differentiated. Most descriptions related to two-parent nuclear family systems, with scant attention paid to differences in ethnicity, class, race, or sexual orientation, or to family variations (single-parent families, foster families, or stepfamilies), and even less attention given to the power differential between men and women within families. The pioneers rarely considered the possibility that their observations might not be objective and unbiased. They assessed families as if they were dissecting a specimen that was unaffected by their behavior or assumptions, by the strange context in which they observed it, or, possibly, by the crisis state it was in.

In these early days family therapists saw themselves as experts who would overcome families' homeostatic tendencies and reorganize their structure or convert them to a better way to view their problems. In their enthusiasm for patterns of interaction, family therapists often lost sight of the personal experience of individual family members and viewed their expression of feelings as distractions from the real—systemic—issues. Just as individual therapists had ignored the family system, the fascination with the family blinded family therapists to the impact of larger systems like schools, social agencies and institutions, peer groups, work settings, and the general problems of our culture.

Erosion of Boundaries

The 1980s and 1990s saw family therapy undergo a gradual but dramatic transformation, similar to a cocky adolescent who thought he didn't need anybody and could do anything, but who matured to a humbler adult aware of his limits and unafraid to ask others for help.[1] Now it's uncommon to encounter a therapist who describes himself or herself as a purely structural or behavioral or strategic family therapist. The boundaries between the discrete schools within the field have largely melted, such that many therapists borrow liberally from a variety of approaches, not all of which could be classified as family therapy. Conference presentations are less likely to be organized around particular techniques than around general topic areas that transcend schools. General topics such as multiculturalism, dealing with managed care, or dealing with violent families help therapists negotiate the real world they face every day in their caseloads.

As Philadelphia family therapist Charles Fishman said, "Years ago we used to think that if we just figured out the right intervention, we could transform most families; we had the hubris to say that we would 'provide the context' that families needed to get better. But now I think we're too frail, too weary to do it all" (quoted in Wylie, 1992). That therapists can't do it all is particularly clear to those working with inner-city multiproblem families in which violence and despair have almost outrun hope. When between five to ten public agencies are involved in a family's life, and when the family is up against the crushing weight of poverty and racism, family therapy can seem quite puny. Recognizing limits has made therapists rethink their roles.

Now therapists approach families less as experts confident of fixing them and more as partners hoping to shore up their inherent resources. These resources are constrained not only by the family's structure but also by the social forces mentioned earlier. Family therapists increasingly realize that while they may not be able to change social conditions or even the family's structure, they can help family members reexamine the beliefs they live by. Thus beliefs have replaced behavior as the target of change. With this shift, family therapists are less focused on family dynamics and more interested in the belief system each family member carries. Therapists feel less compelled to convene whole families and more free to focus on

[1] There are exceptions to this characterization. Two of the new schools to emerge during this period—solution-focused and narrative—show some of the same signs of adolescent fervor (disdain for what preceded them, thick boundaries, grand claims) that once characterized the pioneering schools.

individuals. Ironically, the field has come full circle, first viewing individual issues as distracting from family dynamics to now seeing them as the key to change.

What caused this momentous shift? Some of the change is attributable to the death or retirement of many of the pioneers of the systems approach and the absence of dominating figures to replace them. Certainly the transformation was also due to the growing recognition among clinicians that following doctrinaire models was limiting, left them feeling distanced from clients, and wasn't always relevant to the difficulties their clients faced. In addition, family therapy was one of many social sciences turned upside down by the postmodern revolution.

Postmodernism

The 1980s ushered in an unsettling stage in the field's development, during which family therapy's biases and blindspots were challenged. The resulting changes, described in this chapter, parallel changes occurring in many other fields during this period in which established truths were challenged. This era of skepticism and reexamination has been called postmodernism.

To understand postmodernism, you need to know something about modernism. Modernism began around the turn of the century as an optimistic, pragmatic replacement for romanticism, which held that there were unseen, unknowable forces at work in the world. The advances in science at the beginning of the twentieth century gave people a sense that, rather than being unknowable, the truth of things could be uncovered through objective scientific observation and measurement. In addition, the universe was conceived of as a machine whose laws of operation were awaiting discovery. Thus, modernists were interested in large-scale theories (grand narratives) that could explain human behavior. Once these universal laws were discovered, humanity could control its environment—problems could be solved because anything and everything could be understood and overhauled. This modernist perspective influenced the way family therapy's pioneers approached their clients—as cybernetic machines to be decoded and then reprogrammed. The therapist was the technical expert who could diagram and diagnose functional from dysfunctional family systems. Structural and strategic blueprints were used to search out flaws and glitches that needed repair, regardless of whether families saw things that way themselves. Facts that didn't fit theories were ignored, and, all too often, therapists put more faith in their technologies than in their clients' experience.

Postmodernism was a reaction to the hubris of modernism. To get a feel for the impact of postmodernism, you might recall the first time you realized your parents didn't know everything. It suddenly seemed that they often presented opinion as fact and sometimes just made things up. In all likelihood, that realization was both disturbing and liberating. You gave up the security of a world where there is a truth and your parents knew what it was, for the exhilaration of a world where there is no absolute truth—where your truth may be as good as theirs.

This questioning of authority is what's been happening in our culture for the past couple of decades. Not only are we losing faith in the absolute validity of scientific, political, and religious truths, we're also coming to doubt whether absolute truth can be known. This is a big shift from the modern era, during which we assumed that truth existed and we fought fiercely over who possessed it. As Walter Truett Anderson (1990) writes in his thoughtful book *Reality Isn't What It Used to Be*, "Most of the conflicts that tore the now-ending modern era were between different belief systems, each of which professed to have the truth: this faith against that one, capitalism against communism, science against religion. On all sides the assumption was that somebody possessed the real item, a truth fixed and beyond mere human conjecture" (p. 2). In family therapy it was structural truth versus psychodynamics; Bowen versus Satir.

Modernists not only believed that truth could be known, but that universal principles could be discovered to explain all human behavior. In this, modernists are essentialists—they look inside a phenomenon for its essence. The effort to identify these universal factors, these essences, governed most fields of science, from medicine and genetics to physics and mathematics. This search for the essence of things contributed to the reductionism of the times, where history and context were ignored because it was assumed that the essence resided in the structure of the thing itself (Doherty, 1991).

Even during the modern period, many people wrote of the difficulty of knowing reality objectively (for example, Bertalanffy's perspectivism, discussed in Chapter 4). As Minuchin (1991) points out, ". . . the idea that all truth is relative, that there is no way of escaping the closed perceptual limitations of the individual mind, has haunted thinkers throughout recorded history" (p. 48). Thus, the conviction that all belief systems are social constructions is not entirely new. What is new is how pervasive this skepticism has become and how willing people are to challenge accepted truths in every human endeavor.

Skepticism has been building in our culture this century. Einstein's relativity undermined our faith in the solid certainties of Newtonian physics. Marx challenged the right of one class to dominate another. In the 1960s we lost trust in the establishment and, from drug experiences and Eastern religion, gained a sense that there were other realities besides those of ordinary consciousness. The feminist movement challenged patriarchal assumptions about gender that had been considered laws of nature. As the world shrank and we were increasingly exposed to people of different cultures, we had to reexamine our assumptions regarding their "primitive" or "exotic" beliefs. Instead we had to look at our reality as only one of many ways people see the world.

This accumulating skepticism became a major force in the 1980s and shook the pillars of many fields. In literature, law, education, architecture, religion, political science, art, and psychology, accepted practices and knowledges were "deconstructed." That is, they were shown to be social conventions developed by people with their own biased perspectives and motives. French philosopher Michel Foucault interpreted the accepted knowledges in many fields, presented as objective reality, as stories perpetuated to maintain power structures and marginalize alternative stories.

Constructivism

With this postmodern assumption—that there are no realities, only points of view—came an interest in how the narratives that organize people's lives are generated. Postmodern psychologies concern themselves with how people make meaning in their lives, how they construct reality. One of these psychologies, called *constructivism*, took hold of family therapy in the early 1980s and has exerted a powerful impact on the field.

Constructivism was the crowbar that pried family therapy away from its belief in objectivity—the belief that what one *sees* in families is what *is* in families. Constructivism is a philosophy that arose from certain concepts in neurobiology, for example, Maturana and Varela's (1980) belief that living systems are self-contained neural units that can have no direct experience of their environments; von Foerster's (1981) reminder that observers have an effect on the systems they interpret; and von Glasserfeld's (1984) "radical constructivism," which says that we can never know the real world because we can only know our internal images of it. These ideas were imported into and adapted for family therapy by Paul Watzlawick (1984), Paul Dell (1985), and Lynn Hoffman (1985, 1988).

Constructivism asserts that reality doesn't exist as a "world out there" but, instead, is a mental construction of the observer. The implications for therapy of the constructivist position are that therapists should not consider what they're seeing in families as existing in the family. Instead they should understand that what they're seeing is the product of their particular set of assumptions about people, families, and problems, and their interactions with the family. In other words, we should be less certain about the validity of our observations and should examine carefully the assumptions that we bring to our encounters.

This concern about the influence of therapists' preconceptions on their observations expanded to become an increased interest in belief systems in general. Through Bateson's influence, family therapy adopted the term *epistemology* as a synonym for belief system, perspective, or world view (even though the term properly refers to the branch of philosophy concerned with the development of knowledge). Family therapy has always shown some interest in changing meanings, as evidenced by the early popularity of reframing techniques and the value put on "creating a workable reality." But these meaning changes were primarily devices in the service of behavioral change, which remained the primary target.

Instead of focusing on patterns of family interaction, constructivism shifted the focus toward exploring and reevaluating the assumptions that people involved with a problem have about it. Meaning itself became the primary target. Extending this thinking, some writers proposed that we jettison our arbitrary focus on family systems and instead examine the total meaning systems in which problems are embedded, which might include family members but also all the other helpers, including the therapist (Anderson, Goolishian, & Winderman, 1986).

The idea that our belief systems influence what we see may not come as a great revelation to students of philosophy, and it had been a cliché within family therapy from the beginning—Bateson frequently cited Alfred Korzybski's (1942) saying, "the map isn't the territory." But until this philosophical mid-life crisis, many structural and strategic family therapists were acting as if their maps *were* the territory. For this reason, constructivism had a profound impact on clinical theory and practice in the 1980s.

One consequence of constructivism has been to make therapists humbler in their dealings with families. For example, many structural family therapy maneuvers, such as unbalancing or creating intensity require a high level of confidence in the correctness of one's assumptions. If the therapist waivers, intensity will be lost and, theoretically, the family's homeostasis will not be perturbed. But if therapists believe that their assessment is just one of many stories about the family, it's hard to avoid wavering. Lynn Hoffman (1988) describes her initial reaction to constructivism this way: "One suddenly doesn't know how to 'teach' therapy, much less how to 'do' it. One loses one's status, one loses one's expert position" (p. 124).

Taking constructivism seriously means that we can no longer judge theories by how well they match an objective reality. Instead, we can only assess how well theories help us fit with our environment; that is, how useful, ethical, and ecologically sensitive the theories are. An additional implication is that there isn't necessarily only one most useful theory; there may be many.

These ideas inject a note of humility into the clinical discourse. Rather than believing that our favorite therapy approach most accurately reflects reality, we can see it as only one of many potentially useful stories about people. We also lose our status as experts. Our client families are no longer "homeostatic systems of enmeshed relationships;" the individuals in them are no longer "borderline personalities" or "adult children of alcoholics." Instead, these labels are part of the stories we bring to the consulting room. Our clients bring their own stories, which may be more or less useful than ours—but no more or less true.

Collaborative, Conversational Approaches

In the 1980s and 1990s several theorists translated constructivist philosophy into a collaborative approach that democratized the traditional therapist–client hierarchy. Harlene Anderson and the late Harry Goolishian, Lynn Hoffman, and Tom Andersen were united in their opposition to the cybernetic model and its mechanistic implications. These postmodernists focused more on caring than curing, as Thomas Moore (1992) urged in *Care of the Soul.*

They eschewed established techniques that try to manipulate language and, instead, held empathic conversations from which emerged new meanings. As Harlene Anderson (1992) wrote:

> In this concept of therapy, the therapist is not a narrative editor of the client's story, someone who uses language as a rhetoric-like editing tool. Rather, the therapist is in language with the client . . . [which implies] a therapy that is less hierarchical, more egalitarian, mutual, respectful, and human, a therapy which allows a therapist to be aware of the depth, existence, and experiences of the individual. . . . (p. 21)

The major commitment of these theorists was to move the therapist out of the expert-in-charge position to form a more egalitarian partnership with clients. In so doing they hoped to empower families and turn therapy into a mutual search for new options and understanding.

Because these theorists downplayed technique, their approach was difficult to describe. It was more of an attitude or philosophy than a particular method. Consequently, the leaders of this movement have written far more about their point of view than about what they actually do in therapy. These leaders include: *Harlene Anderson* (director of the Galveston Family Institute), who collaborated with *Harry Goolishian* for many years until his death in 1991. Together they were on the vanguard of the movement away from the cybernetic metaphors and toward the postmodern focus on language and interaction.

Lynn Hoffman, who works with a team in Northampton, Massachusetts, has a long career of championing new developments in family therapy. Beginning as a strategic therapist, she was smitten by the Milan model and has followed Anderson and Goolishian into this collaborative territory with equal enthusiasm. *Tom Andersen,* a Norwegian psychiatrist, is another veteran of the Milan movement who grew tired of the hierarchical, interventive emphasis of that and other family therapy models. In what he calls "reflecting processes," he levels the therapy playing field by hiding nothing from his clients, so that he and his team discuss openly their reactions to what the family says. This *reflecting team* (Andersen, 1991) approach has become a widely used aspect of the collaborative model's therapy-by-consensus. In this method, observers come from behind the one-way mirror to discuss their impressions of the family while the family and therapist watch and listen. The family is then invited to react while the team watches. This process produces a supportive, open environment in which the family feels a part of a larger team and the team feels more empathy for the family from interacting directly with them.

What these theorists shared was the conviction that too often clients aren't heard because therapists are doing therapy *to* them rather than *with* them. As Tom Andersen (1993) admitted, ". . . what I myself found important, but extremely difficult, to do was to try to listen to what clients say instead of making up meanings about what they say. Just listen to what they say" (p. 321). Harlene Anderson (1993) recommends that therapists take a position of "not knowing," which leads to genuine conversations with clients in which "the therapist's pre-experiences and pre-knowledges do not lead. In this process both the therapist's and the client's expertise are engaged to dissolve the problem" (p. 325).

Collaborative therapists distinguish these conversations from the nondirective, empathic Rogerian style because they don't just reflect but also offer ideas and opinions, though always tentatively. As in the other postmodern approaches, questions are primary. As Harlene Anderson (1993) explained,

> Conversational questions come from a position of not knowing and are the therapist's primary tool. They involve responsive or active listening, which requires attending to the clients' stories in a distinct way, immersing oneself in clients' conversations, talking with them about their concerns, and trying to grasp their current story and what gives it shape . . . the questions are not formed by the therapist's preconceived theories of what the story should be. . . . Conversational questions are, therefore, not generated by technique, method, or a preset template of questions. . . . Each question . . . comes from an honest, continuous therapeutic posture of not understanding too quickly, of not knowing. (pp. 330–331)

This paragraph contains elements that demonstrate the conversational approach's fidelity to postmodernism. It reflects the disdain for grand theories (Hoffman, for example, advances the idea that there are no patterns intrinsic to human affairs) and the reluctance to claim expertise or value one perspective over another, which are hallmarks of that philosophical tradition. As Anderson remarked, this approach "suggests that the therapist's knowledge, experience, and values are no truer than the client's—nor more final" (Hoffman-Hennessay, & Davis, 1993, p. 343).

Describing this language-based, collaborative approach is difficult because there is no formula and published descriptions are rare (de Shazer, 1991). Harlene Anderson (1993) reported a case that we will summarize, bearing in mind that it only illustrates what she did on that particular day. She consulted to a therapist whose thirteen-year-old client Anna was repeatedly running away from home and having physical confrontations with her mother and older sister. Initially Anderson talked with Anna, her mother, and the therapist together, asking what they were concerned about. By asking clients to discuss their concerns or problems, Anderson tries to "make room for the familiar," that is, show curiosity and excitement about the clients' experience and perspective, which then brings forth the client's curiosity.

Both Anna and her mother gave their views on Anna's running away and other problems while Anderson followed along, asking for clarification and elaboration, occasionally broadening the focus. Predictably, Anna and her mother interrupted and argued with each other, to the point where Anna began to cry. Anderson then suggested that she speak with mother while Anna and the therapist watched from behind the mirror. Mother told her story of personal struggle: getting into drugs, being a single-parent with two children, losing her job, having a "breakdown," and losing custody of her kids for nine months. She reported that during much of this Anna was on the streets and that since gaining such independence, Anna won't give it up.

Throughout this conversation, Anderson made supportive, empathic comments and asked questions. She told the mother, "So you're kind of three gutsy ladies. Is that hereditary?" She then asked what Anna might be like if many of those difficult things hadn't happened and what it would take to have more peaceful encounters with Anna. After the mother responded that she wanted to enjoy the girls more and that she and Anna were both adventurous, Anderson said "So in a way, it's how to maintain this spirit of adventure, this spirit of independence, while at the same time not being self-destructive or dangerous."

Anderson then talked to Anna while her mother watched from behind the mirror. Anna described her reasons for running away, and Anderson asked her to put herself in her mother's place and imagine what she would do. Anna was able to do this and also talked of her many worries and issues. Anderson ended the interview without giving any advice and thanked them for coming. The therapist reported months later that this consultation had a variety of positive effects.

In reviewing this session, it's apparent that what Anderson did isn't radically different from what many good therapists might do: reflect, empathize, offer a positive reframe here and there—in other words, give clients the feeling that their story has been heard and help them hear each other's stories. What's different is that many therapists wouldn't think this was enough. At some point when they thought they had the information they needed, they would intervene more forcefully, they would drop the not-knowing stance and become the expert. Perhaps the most difficult aspect of this approach is the discipline it takes to care, not cure.

There are, of course, questions and concerns that can be raised about this approach. Its relativism regarding the kinds of stories that emerge from these conversations raises concerns that one can inadvertently collude with families to deny or minimize their problems. For example, Anna repeatedly voiced concern about an episode in which she "blacked out," that is dissociated, during a fight with her mother, and feared that in the middle of a future episode she might kill someone. Anderson didn't explore this episode, which would raise red flags for therapists familiar with the effects of abuse. For constructionists, a focus on these red flags might lead to the kinds of pathologizing conversations that these therapists were trying to avoid.

On the other hand, these theorists were trying to bring family therapy in from the cold. For too many years the field's infatuation with technology hardened its heart. Anderson, Goolishian, Hoffman, and Andersen gave us permission to be human again, which means to be compassionate, humble, and straightforward. The fact that this represented a big shift isn't something the field should be proud of.

The Hermeneutic Tradition

The collaborative approaches didn't constitute a new school of family therapy. Rather, they were a manifestation of a new way of thinking about how to understand people. This new perspective has been heavily influenced by an approach to knowledge that emerged from Biblical studies called *hermeneutics,* which originates from the Greek word for interpretation.

Before it surfaced in family therapy, hermeneutics had already shaken up psychoanalysis. In the 1980s theorists like Donald Spence, Roy Schafer, and Paul Ricoeur led analysts away from the Freudian notion that there was one correct and comprehensive interpretation of a patient's symptoms, dreams, and fantasies. The analytic method isn't, they argued, archaeological or reconstructive; it's constructive and synthetic; it organizes whatever is there into patterns it imposes (Mitchell, 1993).

From a hermeneutic perspective, whatever it is that a therapist knows, it's not simply discovered or revealed through a process of free association and analysis—or enactment and assessment—it's organized, constructed, fitted together by the therapist alone, or collaboratively with the patient or family. Understanding experience, including one's own, is never simply a process of seeing it, grasping it, or decoding it. Human experience is fundamentally ambiguous. Fragments of experience without determinate meaning are understood only through a process that organizes them, selects what's salient, and assigns meaning and significance.

Although there's nothing inherently democratic about hermeneutic exegesis, it's perspectivist challenge to modern essentialism went hand in hand with a similar challenge to therapeutic authoritarianism. And so in family therapy the hermeneutic tradition seemed a perfect partner to efforts to make therapy a more collaborative enterprise.

It's hard to give up certainty. Harder still for many therapists is giving up the role of one who constructs the official storyline in favor of a role that respects the right of clients to arrive at their own useful version of events. A lot is asked of a listener who, in order to be genuinely open to the speaker's story, must put aside his or her own deepest beliefs and, at least temporarily, enter the other's world. In so doing, the listener may find those deepest beliefs challenged and changed. This is more than many therapists are willing to risk because they have strong values regarding such issues as childrearing, abuse, addictions, and religious practices that trigger reflexive judgments and the impulse to intervene rather than to understand.

This problem is clearly illustrated when cultures collide. Take, for example, the forced virginity tests of females in Turkey (Fowers & Richardson, 1996). From the perspective of the American middle class, this seems like a barbaric and immoral subjugation of women. To understand this ritual contextually, however, you would have to set aside your repugnance and your assumptions about the motives behind it (e.g., the patriarchal domination of women), and instead try to comprehend the network of meanings in which the ritual is embedded.

In conversing with a Turk, you might learn of his belief in the sacredness of the body, the importance of sexual intercourse being confined to marriage, and the responsibility of men to honor and protect the female's body as the bearer of life. It's unlikely that these understandings would convince you to sanction or adopt this practice, but you might convey a new respect for the Turk's point of view that could make him more open to hearing yours. As he listened to you stress the importance of gender equality and a person's right to privacy, however, he would likely point out the many social ills (teenage pregnancy, the domination of sex in our lives, the lack of connectedness in our culture, etc.) that could be attributed to our emphasis on freedom and equal rights. The point is that in this kind of conversation, whether you or the Turk altered your fundamental beliefs, you might both walk away feeling understood and with some new perspectives on your own and the other's beliefs.

Translated into clinical practice, the collaborative therapist is forever setting aside presumptions and assessments in order to sincerely understand the client's world. A single mother from the inner city who severely scolds and spanks her ten-year-old son will be more likely to consider her therapist's opinions about corporal punishment if the therapist has shown a genuine appreciation of the realities of her world.

Social Constructionism

Constructivism focuses on how individuals create their own realities, but family therapy has always emphasized the power of interaction. As a result, another postmodern psychology called social constructionism now influences many family therapists. Its main proponent, social psychologist Kenneth Gergen (1985, 1991a, 1991b), emphasizes the power of social interaction in generating meaning for people. From the social constructionist perspective, not only are we unable to perceive an objective reality, the realities we do construct are anchored in the language systems in which we exist. Gergen challenges the notion that we are autonomous individuals, holding independent beliefs, and implies instead that our beliefs are highly plastic, changing radically with changes in our social context. Gergen (1991b) asks, "Are not all the fragments of identity the residues of relationships, and aren't we undergoing continuous transformation as we move from one relationship to another? Indeed, in postmodern times, the reality of the single individual, possessing his/her own values, emotions, reasoning capacities, intentions and the like, becomes implausible. . . . The sense of what is real and what is good emerges from relationships" (pp. 28, 32).

Gergen challenges previous views of the self that had informed family therapy theory. People don't have innate resources that therapists can draw out; instead, like sponges, people internalize the conversations around them. Nor are people overly affected by early childhood experiences. Their personalities can be reconstituted rapidly once situated in a new conversational environment.

From Gergen's (1991a) perspective, because we have a sponge-like self, we can become easily overwhelmed by the many messages with which we are bombarded on a daily basis. "Emerging technologies saturate us with the voices of humankind—both harmonious and alien. As we absorb their varied rhythms and reasons, they become part of us and we of them" (p. 6). As a result, we lack a sense of coherence and feel torn in many directions, a condition that Gergen suggests produces incoherent and disconnected relationships. In addition, we come to use criteria developed by our culture's experts to define ourselves. For example, Gergen (1991a) asserts that "As psychiatrists and psychologists try to explain undesirable behavior, they generate a technical vocabulary of deficit. . . . As people acquire the vocabulary, they also come to see self and others in these terms" (p. 15).

There are several clinical implications of this view. The first is in line with postmodern skepticism, suggesting that since everyone's thinking is governed by their social environment, no one has a corner on the truth; all truths are merely social constructions. This idea invites therapists to help clients understand the cultural roots of their beliefs, even those they had previously assumed were givens of nature. The second implication is that therapy is a linguistic exercise such that if therapists can lead clients to new constructions about their problems, the problems open up. "The individual is viewed as a participant in multiple relationships, with 'the problem' only a problem because of the way it is constructed in certain of these relations" (Gergen, 1991a, p. 51). Third, therapy should be collaborative. Since neither therapist nor client brings truth to the table, new realities emerge through conversations where both sides share opinions and respect the other's perspective. Fourth, because people are so thoroughly influenced by their current relationships, once the therapist succeeds in becoming significant to the client and in co-creating new, more useful constructions about the problem, therapy is basically complete. Consequently, it can be quite brief.

The Narrative Revolution

Social constructionism was welcomed with open arms by those family therapists who were trying to shift the field's focus toward changing meaning rather than changing action. It fortified their position with an academic theory that suggested the therapist's job was to co-create new realities with families, not to direct or advise them. It became the basis for an intriguing approach that took family therapy's center stage in the 1990s, *narrative therapy*, which is described in depth in Chapter 12.

The narrative metaphor focuses on how experience creates expectations and how expectations shape experience through the creation of organizing stories. Narrative therapists follow Gergen in considering the "self" a socially constructed phenomenon. A person's sense of self is thought to emerge when interpersonal conversations are internalized as inner conversations.

These conversations are then organized into stories by which we understand our experience.

In a postmodern world, what we have are points of view and their effects. The question for the narrative therapist isn't one of truth but of which points of view are useful and which lead to preferred effects for clients. Problems aren't in persons (as psychoanalysis had it) or in relationships (as family systems theory had it); rather, problems are embedded in points of view about individuals and their situations. Narrative therapy then becomes a process of helping people reexamine the stories they live by.

In a similar way, social constructionism has provided a rationale for therapists who want to bring issues of social justice into their clinical work. If, as the theory implies, people are sponges for the messages that surround them, it follows that the self-hate, pessimism, and passivity that disempower many clients would be related to having internalized toxic cultural narratives regarding their worth. Narrative therapy's popularity in the 1990s is related in part to its using social constructionism to highlight the impact of patriarchy, heterosexism, racism, social class, and materialism (all cutting-edge themes for family therapy that are explored later in this chapter) on family members' self-concepts. The goal of narrative therapists is to expose these internalized narratives so they can be replaced with more empowering life stories.

Family Therapy's Answer to Managed Care: Solution-Focused Therapy

Solution-focused therapy is the other new model to rise to prominence in family therapy this decade. Steve de Shazer and his colleagues (see Chapter 11) took the ideas of social constructionism and constructivism in a different, more pragmatic, direction. If a person's reality is merely a social construct—a product of language—then the goal of therapy is simply to change the way he or she "languages" the problem. Once described differently, the problem disappears, since it only existed in the way the person talked about it. "Language is reality" (Berg and de Shazer, 1993 p. 7).

Solution-focused therapists aren't interested in identifying and debunking internalized cultural narratives. All they want to do is get people to shift from dwelling on their problems to identifying solutions—and often seeing that they already had solutions but weren't using them. Whatever solution the family comes up with is fine as long as they are satisfied with it. Ironically, though solution-focused and narrative both claim to be rooted in similar philosophies, de Shazer's model is as relativistic as White's is political.

The goal of this approach is to get clients to shift from "problem talk"—trying to understand or analyze their problems—to "solution talk"—focusing on what's working or could work in the future—as quickly as possible. The idea is that the act of focusing on solutions, in and of itself, eliminates problems. Solution-focused therapists have designed a number of clear-cut techniques for getting clients into this future-oriented, productive mindset.

While they do lead clients toward solution talk, therapists try to remain collaborative in the sense of not imposing particular kinds of solutions and trusting clients to find their own way. They also embrace a view of people that is strengths-oriented, concentrating on client resources and successes. They aren't interested in assessing problems, believing that such explorations encourage paralyzing problem talk and that solutions are often unrelated to the way that problems are formed.

The solution-focused model is of interest in this chapter for one more reason. In the 1980s its popularity grew rapidly during a period in which mental health agency budgets were slashed and managed care began to erode the number of sessions for which private practitioners could be reimbursed. This produced a tremendous demand for a brief, formulaic, commonsensical approach, and solution-focused is all of those. Without managed care, the solution-focused approach might still be what it started as, an interesting offshoot of strategic therapy. Instead, because everyone has to deal with managed care, it has become hugely popular, not only with family therapists but with clinicians of all orientations.

Feminism and Family Therapy

Feminists initiated family therapy's interest in the pernicious effects of cultural attitudes on families and on our theories about families. In an eye-opening critique that began with an article by Rachel Hare-Mustin in 1978, feminist family therapists not only exposed the gender bias inherent in the existing models, they also advocated a style of therapy that, like Anderson and Goolishian's, is collaborative and interested in meaning. Feminism and postmodernism are not, however, entirely compatible (Rosenau, 1992). Feminist family therapists don't advocate relativistic neutrality and have trouble with the idea of trusting the family, steeped as it is in patriarchal values, to find its own solutions. For feminists, all realities are not created equal.

The feminist critique was family therapy's rudest awakening. The field's increasing popularity through the 1970s left it with a feeling of smugness. Family therapists were the progressive avant garde whose theories and techniques were going to revolutionize psychotherapy. It didn't occur to them that they could have been blind to sexism along the way. As Lois Braverman (1988) confessed,

> As long as we thought systemically and did not buy into a traditional linear long-term psychotherapy approach to treatment, we considered ourselves to be far ahead of other helping professionals. So while other therapeutic frameworks and treatment modalities of the 1970's were marked by feminist critiques . . . which questioned traditional psychodynamic theory and practice, we, as family therapists, had our heads buried in the sand. (p. 6)

The Apolitical Machine

Heads came out of the sand in the early 1980s and began to look around at our model of the functional family and at our precious systems theory. It became increasingly and painfully clear that cybernetics and functionalism had led us astray. Cybernetics encouraged us to view a family system as a flawed machine. Judith Myers Avis (1988) described this family machine as one that

> . . . functions according to special systemic rules and is divorced from its historical, social, economic, and political contexts. By viewing the family out of context, family therapists locate family dysfunction entirely within interpersonal relationships in the family, ignore broader patterns of dysfunction occurring across families, and fail to notice the relationship between social context and family dysfunction. (p. 17)

Thus the mechanistic philosophy of cybernetics narrowed our vision and made us oblivious to the parallels between disharmonies in our culture and in our families.

Additionally, the Batesonian version of cybernetics was strongly opposed to the use of power metaphors. Bateson claimed that unilateral control in systems was impossible because all elements are continually and circularly influencing one another in repetitious feedback loops. If all parts of a system are equally involved in its problems, no one is to blame. This idea had great appeal for family therapists because family members often enter therapy pointing fingers at each other and failing to see their own steps in their circular dances.

To feminists, however, this idea of equal responsibility for problems looked "suspiciously like a hypersophisticated version of blaming the victim and rationalizing the status quo" (Goldner, 1985, p. 33). This critique was particularly evident in crimes against women, such as battering, incest, and rape, for which psychological theories have long been used to imply that the woman either provoked or consented to the crime (James & MacKinnon, 1990).

But those crimes are only the most obvious instances in which the systemic doctrine of equal responsibility is troublesome. The larger issue is that if one accepts the feminist premise that in our patriarchal society, marriage and family life inherently subjugate women, then to suggest that husbands and wives have contributed equally to and have equal responsibility for changing their problems is to collude with the rules of these patriarchal microcosms of society.

Mother Blaming

The dysfunctional family constellation most commonly cited by family therapists as contributing to problems is the peripheral (but dominant) father, the mother who is overinvolved with her children, and the symptomatic child who is caught up in the parents' relationship. For years, psychodynamic therapists blamed the mother's attachment to the child for the symptoms. Family therapy's apparent advance was to show how the father's lack of involvement contributed to mother's overinvolvement, and so therapists tried to pry the mother loose by inserting the father in her place. This, however, wasn't the advance for women that it might seem because, in too many cases, mothers were viewed no less negatively. Mothers were still enmeshed and incompetent, but now there appeared a new solution—to bring good old competent, rational dad to the children's rescue.

What feminists contend therapists failed to see, and to help their client families see, is that "the archetypal 'family case' of the overinvolved mother and peripheral father is best understood not as a clinical problem, but as the product of an historical process two hundred years in the making" (Goldner, 1985, p. 31). Women are overinvolved, insecure, controlling, ineffectual, and overemotional—not because of psychopathology but because they are put in, and encouraged by society to desire, emotionally isolated, economically dependent, overresponsible positions in families, positions that are crazy-making.

Feminist family therapists help families reorganize so that no one, male or female, remains stuck in such positions. Thus, instead of further diminishing an insecure mother's self-esteem by replacing her with a peripheral father (who's likely to have been critical of her parenting all along), a feminist family therapist might help the family examine and change the rules and roles that kept mother down and father out. During this process, fathers may be encouraged to become more involved with parenting—not because mothers are incompetent, but because it's a father's responsibility as a parent and because it will allow the mother to begin to move out of that crazy-making position (Ault-Riche, 1986; Goodrich, Rampage, Ellman, & Halstead, 1988; Walters, Carter, Papp, & Silverstein, 1988; McGoldrick, Anderson, & Walsh, 1989).

Looking through the Lens of Gender

Feminist family therapists are not simply asking therapists to be more sensitive to gender issues in working with families. Rather, they assert that issues of gender or, more specifically, patriarchy, permeate therapists' work, even though they have been conditioned not to notice them. They therefore believe that gender should be a primary organizing concept for family therapists, on a par with the concept of generation (Goldner, 1988, 1993; Luepnitz, 1988).

Only when therapists look through this lens of gender can they effectively stop blaming mothers or stop looking to them to do most of the changing simply because they are the most invested in change or the most cooperative. Only then will they be able to fully counter the unconscious biases toward seeing women as primarily responsible for childrearing or housekeeping; as needing to support their husbands' careers by neglecting their own; as needing to be married or at least to have a man in their lives (Anderson, 1995). Only then can they stop relying on traditional male traits, such as rationality, independence, competitiveness, as their standards of health and stop denigrating or ignoring traits traditionally encouraged in women, like emotionality, nurturance, and relationship focus.

In essence, the feminist revolution in family therapy isn't just asking that family therapists try on some new concepts or techniques. It's also asking them to get personal. It forces therapists to look in the mirror at their own attitudes and their lives outside of the professional safety of their offices. It forces them to reexamine the values and structure of our society and evaluate how they are helping to perpetuate or change those values and that structure. It tarnishes the halos of many of family therapy's pioneers, and it challenges the field's fundamental framework, systems theory.

As one might anticipate, the feminist critique wasn't immediately welcomed or accepted by the established models in the field. The early to mid 1980s was a period of polarization and tension between male and female therapists at conferences, as feminists tried to exceed the establishment's "threshold of deafness." By the 1990s, that threshold has been exceeded, in the sense that many of the major feminist points are no longer debated and the field is evolving toward a more collaborative, but socially enlightened, form of therapy.

Family Violence

In the early 1990s family therapy took its first real look at the dark side of family life. Perhaps it wasn't until the other aspects of the feminist critique had been accepted that the field was ready to take this step, because other fields had been exploring the problems of wife-battering and sexual abuse for years. In the late 1980s and early 1990s books and articles on these topics began appearing in the mainstream family therapy literature (e.g., Controneo, 1987; Trepper & Barrett, 1989; Dell, 1989; Goldner, Penn, Sheinberg, & Walker, 1990; Friedrich, 1990; Markowitz, 1992; Schwartz, 1992, 1993; Barrett & Trepper, 1992; Scheinberg, 1992; Canavan, Higgs, & Meyer, 1992; Serra, 1993; Calof, 1992; Gorman-Smith & Tolan, 1992; Goulding & Schwartz, 1995). But it wasn't until 1991 that the field of family therapy was shaken out of its collective denial regarding the horrifying extent of male-to-female abuse in families. This rude awakening took the form of three plenary addresses at the annual meeting of the American Family Therapy Academy (AFTA), which were later published in the *Journal of Marital and Family Therapy* (Avis, 1992; Kaufman, 1992; Bograd, 1992).

Judith Myers Avis (1992) delivered a barrage of staggering statistics regarding such things as the proportion of women who have experienced sexual abuse before the age of 18 (37 percent), percent of abusers who are male (95 percent), number of women abused each year by the man they live with (1 in 6), percent of male college students who had coerced sex from an unwilling partner (25 percent), and those who said they would commit rape if guaranteed immunity from detection or punishment (20 percent). After reiterating the indictment of family therapy theories that strive for therapist neutrality and that view the abused as partially responsible for their abuse, she concluded that:

> As long as we train therapists in systemic theories without balancing that training with an understanding of the non-neutrality of power dynamics, we will continue pro-

> ducing family therapists who collude in the maintenance of male power and are dangerous to the women and children with whom they work. Taking a feminist position in relation to male power means taking a non-neutral position, challenging male control and domination, naming the abuse, and naming the abuser. (p. 231)

Gus Kaufman (1992) heated up the rhetorical intensity:

> Constructivists and systems theorists . . . should know this: violence follows the old Newtonian physics of mass, velocity, momentum and inertia—as in a fist hitting a face and breaking bones. . . . We don't hear [about violence in the families we treat] because we never ask the right questions in the right context of the right people. We are like Red Cross workers visiting the P.O.W. camp asking "How are they treating you?" as the guards stand by. She is a prisoner; he is a guard; and we—the well-meaning helper—won't be there to insure her safety after the visit. (pp. 236, 237)

Michele Bograd (1992) concluded with a series of questions that summarize some of the central predicaments for family therapy in this decade.

> In working with family violence, how do we balance a relativistic world view with values about human safety and the rights of men and women to self-determination and protection? When is the clinical utility of neutrality limited or counterproductive? When is conviction essential to the change process? How do we confront the batterer about the destructive nature of his behavior without condemning him? How strongly and passionately do we employ our values to therapeutic advantage while maintaining a caring and respectful connection with family members struggling with the trauma of violence? (pp. 248, 249)

Part of what made these presentations so controversial was their rejection of family therapy's traditional point of view, according to which family violence, like many other problems that occur in families, involves the interacting influences of all members of the family. The traditional systemic view, now under attack, was that such violence was the outcome of cycles of mutual provocation, an escalation, albeit unacceptable, of the emotionally destructive behavior that characterizes many marriages. Moreover, the audience of therapists was told that they themselves might be part of the problem by excusing or minimizing wife-beating. Violent men, from this perspective, don't lose control, they *take* control, and will stop only when they are held accountable.

While these presentations generated complaints that they were unnecessarily inflammatory and unfairly stereotyping of men (Meth, 1992; Erickson, 1992; Combrinck-Graham, 1991), they also provided a wake-up call. Domestic violence—let's call it what it is, wife-battering and child-beating—is a major public health problem, right up there with alcoholism and depression.

As family therapists become more sensitive to family violence, they will encounter it more often; more client families will reveal these dirty secrets, ongoing or former abuses that had formerly passed unnoted through therapist caseloads. As family therapists listen to stories of beating and molestation, they will become more aware of the devastating effects of trauma and terror on people. They will be less satisfied with approaches that solve all problems in ten sessions and claim that historic traumas or abuses are irrelevant to present problems or solutions. They will become less tolerant of approaches that accept whatever new story a family wants to create, or co-create stories that paper over the impact of violence. They will become more aware of the social and political climate of violence in our culture.

Multiculturalism

The postmodern movement was triggered, in part, by recent developments in the United States. First came the gradual recognition, beginning in the 1960s with a growing awareness of mounting problems in our culture, that our own worldview may not be all that healthy. This eroded our ethnocentrism and made us more open to other points of view. Second, due to increased immigration and contact with the global media, we were exposed to cultures with entirely different perspectives and life styles. This has led to a shift in the goal for our country from a melting pot, where ethnic differences were assimilated, to a stew pot, where different groups coexist but all lend flavor to the whole dish. We now strive to be a pluralistic society that values diversity.

This postmodern pluralism launched another assault on our comfortable image of how families should look. The map of the "healthy family" we inherited from family therapy's pioneers contained not only patriarchal but also ethnocentric biases. What American middle-class therapists had been seeing as pathological family structures may simply have been different. Those differences aren't necessarily problematic just because they don't match the American middle-class norm.

Monica McGoldrick and her colleagues (McGoldrick, Pearce, & Giordano, 1982)[1] dealt one of the first blows to our ethnocentricity with an edited book, each chapter of which described the characteristic values and structure of a different ethnic group. Following this and a spate of related books (e.g., Falicov, 1983, and in press; Boyd-Franklin, 1989; Szapocznik & Kurtines, 1989; Saba, Karrer, & Hardy, 1989; Mirkin, 1990; Breunlin, Schwartz, & Mac Kune-Karrer, 1992; Ingoldsby & Smith, 1995; Okun, 1996), we are now more sensitive to the importance of knowing some of the characteristics of the ethnic group from which a family descends, so we don't assume they're sick just because they're different. For example, many non-American middle-class families have a strong rule that each family member should think of the good of the family before what might be good for himself or herself. While navigating by the early maps, family therapists were likely to view this selfless loyalty to the family as pathological—demonstrating a lack of differentiation, evidence of enmeshment or overprotectiveness—and would challenge it. Now, when encountering such a family value, therapists are more likely to consider, or even explore with the family, the ethnic heritage of the family's belief while evaluating its functionality.

In trying to overcome family therapists' ethnocentrism, they had to look again at many of the things they previously considered pathological. For example, Celia Falicov (Falicov & Brudner-White, 1983) drew from the work of anthropologist Francis Hsu to point out that in many cultures the dominant or governing dyad in a family isn't the husband and wife. Instead, the primary dyad is often intergenerational—husband–son in some cultures and wife–son in others. Thus, the very cross-generational coalitions therapists had been trained to seize upon as the root of a family's problem, may well be normative in that family's culture. This same kind of critique can apply to many other ideas about family life, such as the importance of democratic versus autocratic parenting styles, of open, expressive communication, and of encouraging autonomy versus loyalty in children.

As Monica McGoldrick (1993) writes,

> Ethnicity patterns our thinking, feeling, and behavior in both obvious and subtle ways, although generally operating outside our awareness. It plays a major role in determining what we eat, how we work, how we relate, how we celebrate holidays and

[1]The new edition of this book (McGoldrick, Giordano, & Pearce, 1996) more than doubles the number of ethnic groups covered.

rituals, and how we feel about life, death, and illness. (p. 335)

In other words, ethnicity is a powerful meaning generator. Given family therapy's current obsession with belief systems, this interest in ethnicity makes sense, although the new schools like the narrative and solution-focused ones, with their focus on the family's language in the session and their reluctance to generalize, have had little to say about ethnicity.

It's one thing for therapists to be respectful of the ethnic legacy on a client family's beliefs and structure, but it's also important to help families assess how well that legacy fits with their current context (Breunlin, Schwartz, & Mac Kune-Karrer, 1992; Schwartz, 1995). For example, if a family structured to fit best within a stable, homogenous ethnic network finds itself isolated in a middle-class American suburb, they may be in for trouble. Simply helping families understand their problems in terms of lack of fit can help them find new solutions.

In the 1990s, multiculturalism has become a dominant theme in family therapy, as reflected in the agendas for conferences of the major organizations in the field with such recent titles as "Social, Cultural and Economic Diversity" and "Culture, Power and the Family." The popularity of these issues represents a welcome sensitizing to issues of ethnicity. Yet there are some problems with this focus that remain to be resolved in the coming years.

First, ethnicity is just one of many factors that influence a family's belief system. Other factors such as geographic location, religion, race, economic class, stage of acculturation, and level of education can be obscured by an overemphasis on ethnicity (Breunlin, Schwartz, & Mac Kune-Karrer, 1992; Falicov, 1995). For example, a poor family in Guatemala may have more in common with a poor family in Chicago than with a wealthy Guatemalan family. To see such a family exclusively through the Guatemalan lens is to stereotype them and to miss other windows to their beliefs. Therapists may also miss opportunities to connect with them because, for example, while not many therapists in the United States are Guatemalan, many are from poor backgrounds.

Second, an overemphasis on ethnicity can lead therapists to exaggerate the differences between themselves and their clients, which can constrain the therapeutic connection. Despite the vast diversity of our socialization, we are all more human than otherwise. While we should honor our differences, there are commonalities among us that transcend our backgrounds and can provide crucial empathy and rapport. These commonalities can be obscured when any source of difference becomes foreground.

In addition, the ethnic-focused approach to understanding families is very taxing for therapists because they are expected to learn generalizations about all the possible ethnic groups that they might conceivably work with. Celia Falicov (1995) simplifies the therapist's task with a comparative approach. Rather than memorize details about scores of different ethnic groups, therapists select a key family dimension, family life cycle, for example, and explore how the different contexts in which a family developed (e.g., the family's social class, religion, ethnicity, location [rural, suburban, urban], etc.) affected its values regarding life cycle transitions.

For example, a Protestant, Anglo-American, middle-class family's attitudes regarding the time when children should leave home are fairly predictable based on the family's membership in the three contexts mentioned. That family's leaving home values will differ from a rural, working-class, Roman-Catholic, Mexican-American family who are likely to expect children to stay in the parents' home until they marry. This is because for families whose values developed in contexts with little geographic or economic mobility (working-class, Mexico), and where children are needed to help the family survive (rural), there is no incentive for children to leave the nest and many reasons to keep them home.

If therapists learn how various contexts typically shape family structure and values, then many aspects of a family's life can be predicted by understanding those contexts, of which ethnicity is only one.

With all this talk about predicting, however, it's important to remember that most families will gladly educate the therapist who shows genuine curiosity and interest in their values and customs. An ability to be curious and empathic will get therapists further than an encyclopedic knowledge of what to expect from different kinds of families.

Multiculturalism is certainly an advance over American ethnocentrism. Yet in highlighting differences, the danger exists of creating a new ethnocentrism around the highlighted group. Segregation, even in the name of ethnic pride, isolates people within their own group, which can foster prejudice. Perhaps pluralism is a better term than multiculturalism because it implies more balance between ethnic identity and connection to the larger group.

In addition, there is a constant tension between the relativistic position that we should not impose our values on the practices of other cultures and the ethical position that certain practices are universally destructive and should be discouraged. For example, just because a belief or behavior pattern is normative in another culture, does that mean that it's healthy and shouldn't be challenged? Many cultures are at least as patriarchal as our own. Should we respect a husband's domination over his wife simply because it's customary in their native country? If a family's culture condones using a belt to discipline the children, should we not intervene? In other words, can we become so afraid of imposing our cultural values that we condone inequity and violence? McGoldrick (1993) takes a decidedly nonrelativistic position on this issue.

> Even as we learn to appreciate cultural differences and the limitations of any one perspective, it makes no sense to say that just because a culture proclaims a certain value or belief that it is sacrosanct. We must not move away from responsibility for the complex ethical stance required of us in our clinical work. All cultural practices are not equally ethical. Every intervention we make is political. We must not use notions of neutrality or deconstruction to shy away from committing ourselves to the values we believe in. (p. 357)

These issues are complex and difficult. While we cannot dictate where therapists should draw the line of tolerance, we can encourage them to draw the line somewhere. The key is to find respectful ways to convey alternative perspectives to clients or help them find those perspectives within themselves. The collaborative approach described earlier in this chapter provides a way for therapists and ethnic clients to explore their differences with mutual respect.

Race and Class

Where awareness of ethnicity shattered family therapy's homogenized image of families in the early 1980s, the issues of racism and poverty are just beginning to break through. In the early days of family therapy poor African-American families received some attention (e.g., Minuchin et al., 1967), but for many years it seemed that the field, like the rest of the country, tried to forget about this group and the racism they endure. Recently, African-American family therapists such as Nancy Boyd-Franklin (1993) and Ken Hardy (1993), through lectures and writing, have brought these issues out of the shadows and forced them on our consciousness.

One thrust of this work is to help therapists understand African-American families and break through stereotypes, fears, and pessimism. As Boyd-Franklin (1993) laments,

> ". . . for poor, inner-city, African-American families, the day-to-day realities of racism,

> discrimination, classism, poverty, homelessness, violence, crime, and drugs create forces that continually threaten the family's survival. Many clinicians who have no framework with which to view these complicated interrelationships become overwhelmed. (p. 361)

To help overwhelmed clinicians refocus away from family deficits and cultural obstacles, Boyd-Franklin (1989) describes the strengths of African-American families, including a large and strongly bonded kinship network, an adaptability of family roles, a strong religiosity and connection to the church, and an ability to adapt to economic hardship.

Boyd-Franklin (1993) also describes the predicaments that face African-American families. For example, what messages do parents give their children regarding the racism they will encounter? "Parents must walk a fine line between giving children the tools with which to understand racism so they do not internalize the process and instilling in their children a belief that they can achieve despite the odds and overcome racism without becoming consumed with rage and bitterness" (p. 363). African-American families not only have to overcome barriers to opportunity and achievement but also the anxiety, frustration, and despair that such obstacles create. In addition, it is impossible to survive the war zone in which many inner-city families dwell without some symptoms of post-traumatic stress syndrome, symptoms that are often misunderstood by clinicians, but that in this context are anything but abnormal.

Thus, the task of therapists working with poor, black families is to avoid being overwhelmed by the obstacles they face and to understand their symptoms, reluctance to engage in treatment, and distance or hostility (particularly if the therapist is white), in the context of their environment and their history of negative or unhelpful interaction with white people, including the many agents of social control they encounter. In addition, the therapist must focus on the family's many strengths and draw from their networks or, if the family is isolated, help create networks of support.

Finally, the therapist must look inside and face his or her own attitudes about race, class, and poverty. Toward this end, several authors recommend curricula that go beyond didactic lectures to personal, experiential encounters—that is, confronting our own demons of racism (Pinderhughes, 1989; Boyd-Franklin, 1989).

A therapist's ignoring his or her own racial attitudes can harm clients. As an example, Laura Markowitz (1993) quotes a black woman's therapy experience:

> I remember being in therapy years ago with a nice white woman who kept focusing me on why I was such an angry person and on my parents as inadequate individuals. . . . We never looked at my father as a poor black man, my mother as a poor black woman and the context in which they survived and raised us. . . . Years later, I saw a therapist of color and the first thing out of her mouth was, "Let's look at what was going on for your parents." It was a joyous moment to be able to see my dad not as a terrible person who hated us but as a survivor living under amazingly difficult conditions. I could embrace him, and I could understand my anger instead of blaming myself for feeling that way. (p. 29)

Racism has also become an issue within the family therapy field. As Markowitz (1993) points out,

> the largest of the professional associations, the AAMFT, has never had a person of color as board president, executive director, nor included more than one or two as board members in its 51-year history, despite having a reported 10 percent of members identify as minorities. (p. 29)

In contrast, the National Organization for Social Workers (NASW), which has the same percentage of minorities, is structured so that at least every third term a minority person is elected president.

In an issue of the *Family Therapy Networker,* African-American family therapists spoke about their experiences in the predominantly white field. Ken Hardy (1993), for example, describes the masquerade that many black professionals live and the bonds they feel:

> To avoid being seen by whites as troublemakers, we suppress the part of ourselves that feels hurt and outraged by the racism around us, instead developing an "institutional self"—an accommodating facade of calm professionalism calculated to be nonthreatening to whites. . . . Familiar only with our institutional selves, white people don't appreciate the sense of immediate connection and unspoken loyalty that binds black people together. . . . We are united by being raised with the same messages most black families pass on to their children: "You were born into one of the most despised groups in the world. You can't trust white people. You are somebody. Be proud, and never for one minute think that white people are better than you." (pp. 52–53)

These voices have initiated an important discussion that we hope will make family therapy a more hospitable place for African- American therapists and clients alike.

Gay and Lesbian Issues

Family therapy's consciousness was raised about gay and lesbian issues in the same way it was for race. After a long period of neglect and denial (we could find only one article: Krestan & Bepko, 1980), in the late 1980s, family therapy began to face these issues with which a sizable percentage of the population struggles (Crawford, 1988; Goodrich et al., 1988; Krestan, 1988; Roth & Murphy, 1986; Roth, 1989; Carl, 1990; Hersch, 1991; Dahlheimer & Feigal, 1991; Laird, 1993; Sanders, 1993). The recent releases of a major book (Laird & Green, 1996) and magazine (*In the Family*, edited by Laura Markowitz) indicate that these issues are finally out of family therapy's closet.

The early signs of sensitization in family therapy to gay and lesbian issues have included a special issue of the *Family Therapy Networker* (January, 1991) and a powerful AFTA conference plenary (1992) titled "The Love that Dares to Speak Its Name." Perhaps the biggest sign of change in the field's attitude, however, is that the second edition of *Normal Family Processes,* an influential text, includes a chapter on gay and lesbian families, whereas the first edition, ten years earlier, did not. That gay and lesbian families are now considered one of many normal family types is quite a change for our field and our culture.

Yet many straight family therapists ignore this literature and receive little if any exposure to gay and lesbian issues in graduate school, despite the fact that, even if they don't work with many openly gay or lesbian clients, many of their client families struggle with polarizations from having a gay or lesbian child. To avoid doing harm to these families or to other gay and lesbian clients, therapists must examine their attitudes about sexuality and understand what such clients face in a homophobic world.

Harmonious relationships are more difficult to achieve for gay and lesbian couples, not because they are inherently more pathological than straight couples, but because our society presents them with far more obstacles. After a childhood of confusion, shame, and fear of discovery, many gays and lesbians are disowned by their families once they come out. Where heterosexual couples are often supported and encouraged to remain together by their families, gay and lesbian couples often have the opposite experience. Despite gains in tolerance in some segments of our society, they continue to face humiliation, discrimination, and even violence because of their sexuality. Due to the lack of social support, the bonds in gay and lesbian relationships can be strained, generating stress, jealousy, and the pressures of isolation.

Rather than explore the impact of these pressures and constraints, many therapists (even those who consider themselves tolerant) continue to push gay and lesbian clients to look into their pasts to find the "cause" of their homosexuality or to try to resolve their "sexual confusion." Relatedly, many therapists harbor unexamined prejudices regarding these couples having children through adoption or alternative insemination.

We hope the day will arrive soon when gay and lesbian families, African Americans, and other marginalized groups are studied by family therapists to learn not only about the problems they face but also about how they survive and thrive against such great odds. As Joan Laird (1993) suggested, these families have much to teach us, "about gender relationships, about parenting, about adaptation to tensions in this society, and especially about strength and resilience" (p. 284). The question is whether we are ready to learn.

Specialized Treatments and Knowledges

Another trend, begun in the 1980s and related to the recognition of ethnicity as an important consideration, was the increased specialization of treatment models. Books emerged that focused on how to provide family therapy for a host of specific types of problems and family constellations. In fact, this trend predated the 1980s (for example, Minuchin and his colleagues had written books about treating "families of the slums" and "psychosomatic families"), but the number of recent specialized texts and articles reflects a maturing of the field.

There are books on working with families of people who abuse drugs (Stanton, Todd, & Associates, 1982; Kaufman, 1985; Barth, Pietrzak, & Ramier, 1993), alcohol (Steinglass, Bennett, Wolin, & Reiss, 1987; Bepko & Krestan, 1985; Wegscheider-Cruse, 1985; Treadway, 1989; Elkin, 1990; Berg & Miller, 1992), food (Root, Fallon, & Friedrich, 1986; Schwartz, 1995), and each other (Trepper & Barrett, 1989; Friedrich, 1990; Madanes, 1990; Combrinck-Graham, 1995).

In addition there are books for treating single-parent families (Morawetz & Walker, 1984), step-parent families (Visher & Visher, 1979, 1988), divorcing families (Sprenkle, 1985; Wallerstein & Kelley, 1980; Ahrons & Rogers, 1989), blended families (Hansen, 1982; Sager et al., 1983), families in transition among these states (Pittman, 1987; Falicov, 1988), and for all combinations of relationships within families (Walters, Carter, Papp, & Silverstein, 1988).

There are also books for families with young children (Zilbach, 1986; Combrinck-Graham, 1989; Wachtel, 1994; Gil, 1994), with troubled adolescents (Mirkin & Koman, 1985; Price, 1996) and young adults (Haley, 1980), with problems among siblings (Bank & Kahn, 1982; Kahn & Lewis, 1988), as well as a book about "normal families" (Walsh, 1982, 1993) and another about "successful families" (Beavers & Hampson, 1990).

There are books for working with schizophrenic families (Anderson, Reiss, & Hogarty, 1986); families with AIDS (Walker, 1991; Boyd-Franklin, Steiner, & Boland, 1995); families who have suffered trauma (Figley, 1985), chronic illness or disability (Rolland, 1994; McDaniel, Hepworth, & Doherty, 1992); and those who are grieving a death (Walsh & McGoldrick, 1991), have a child with a disability (Seligman & Darling, 1996), or have an adopted child (Reitz & Watson, 1992).

In addition to these specialized books, the field has broadened its scope and extended systems thinking beyond the family to include the impact on families of larger systems like other helping agents or social agencies and schools (Schwartzman, 1985; Berger, Jurkovic, & Associates, 1984; Imber-Black, 1988; Minuchin,

1984; Elizur & Minuchin, 1989), the impact of the absence of family rituals and the use of family rituals in therapy (Imber-Black, Roberts, & Whiting, 1988), and the socio-political context in which families exist (Mirkin, 1990; Berger Gould & DeMuth, 1994).

One point to be made about this trend is that many of these books transcend individual models of family therapy. The author may have a particular orientation but that orientation takes enough of a backseat to the specific content that the book can be read by therapists from other orientations without engendering rivalry. Thus, as opposed to the 1960s and 1970s, during which the followers of a particular model read little but what came out of that school and eagerly awaited the next offering from the school's leadership, this recent trend toward specialization by content area rather than by model has made the field more pluralistic.

Few themes are more important in contemporary family therapy than the current emphasis on designing specific treatment approaches for specific problems and populations. Where therapists used to make families fit into their models, now one-size-fits-all therapies are less viable. Family therapists have come down from the towers of their training institutes to grapple with the messy problems of the real world. Currently a number of innovative groups are designing specific approaches for specific problems. For example, the Ackerman Institute is home to projects for treating incest and family violence; the Minuchin Center has a program for treating pregnant addicted women and their families; and the Family Institute in Chicago has a project for treating wife-battering.

Research Groups

While much of family therapy in the 1990s has been guided by postmodernism's distrust of traditional science, groups of serious, full-time clinician/researchers have been conducting unabashedly modernist studies of families and family therapy. Several of these groups have been struggling for years to develop family therapy approaches that are effective with multiproblem families and violent, antisocial behavior. Funded by large federal grants, they strive to carefully test the results of their interventions and use this knowledge to refine their approach. In doing rigorous, quantitative research, they are swimming against the postmodern current of research skepticism. Since skeptical postmodernists believe there's no such thing as objectivity, they contend that research is used to bolster established knowledges and marginalize alternatives. They believe that since each theory or model is just another story about families or therapy, none better than any other, there's no point in trying to compare or test them. In addition, the approaches these researchers are testing generally involve aspects of behavioral and/or structural family therapies that have been deemed modernist and passé by the new wave in the field.

As a result, many of these projects operate in relative obscurity as far as most family therapists are concerned. This is unfortunate because, despite what the postmodernists say, this research movement is vital to the future of the field. Family therapists have an ethical obligation to evaluate the effectiveness of their approaches and to address society's most difficult problems. In addition, their economic future depends on their ability to demonstrate to third-party payers that family therapy is effective. We hope and trust that the obscurity of these projects is temporary, and that once their results are completed and published they will have the influence they deserve.

The best known of these research projects is led by Gerald Patterson, who has been refining his behavioral methods for two decades at the Oregon Social Learning Center in Eugene. Other prominent leaders in this movement include Jose Szapocznik and Howard Liddle at the University of Miami, Jim Alexander at the

University of Utah, Scott Henggeler at the Medical College of South Carolina in Charleston, and Pat Tolan and Deborah Gorman-Smith at the University of Illinois at Chicago.

Ironically, these groups are well known and highly regarded outside family therapy. Because of the urgent need for ways to work with the problems these projects target, national policymakers are well aware of them and look to them for direction. These researchers provide credibility for family therapy within the larger mental health field, credibility that has been strained by the eccentric practices and unsubstantiated outcome claims of some of the other models described in this book.

Medical and Psychoeducational Family Therapy

Traditionally, family therapy has been oriented toward curing symptoms and solving problems. Over the past decade a new conception of family therapy has emerged. Rather than curing medical or psychiatric syndromes, the goal of this group is to maximize the functioning and coping abilities of ill or disabled patients and their families. This represents a shift from the idea that families cause problems to the idea that problems, like natural disasters, sometimes happen to families.

This movement has two related sources. One, called *psychoeducational family therapy*, came from working with schizophrenic patients and their families. The other, *medical family therapy*, developed from helping families struggle with chronic illnesses such as cancer, diabetes, and heart disease.

The medical and psychoeducational approaches don't subscribe to the idea that families cause these syndromes, so the family members they work with don't feel blamed. These approaches share the belief, however, that families can have a powerful effect on the course of these syndromes and try to collaborate with them to maximize adjustment and minimize disruption to the family.

Psychoeducation and Schizophrenia

The search to find a cause and cure for schizophrenia within families launched the field of family therapy in the 1950s. Ironically, forty years later, the psychoeducational model, which doesn't attempt to find a cause or cure, may help schizophrenics the most.

The psychoeducational model was born of dissatisfaction with both traditional family therapy and psychiatric approaches to schizophrenia. As Carol Anderson, Douglas Reiss, and Gerald Hogarty (1986) lamented,

> We have blamed each other, the patients themselves, their parents and grandparents, public authorities, and society for the cause and for the too often terrible course of these disorders. When hope and money become exhausted, we frequently tear schizophrenic patients from their families, consigning them to the existential terror of human warehouses, single room occupancy hotels, and more recently to the streets and alleys of American cities. (p. vii)

Family therapists, in their attempts to get at the putative function of the schizophrenic's symptoms or to get family members to express bottled-up feelings, created sessions full of highly charged emotion, which often generated blame and defensiveness. After noticing the frequent decline in functioning of patients and increased anxiety in their families after such sessions, Anderson and her colleagues (1986) "began to wonder if most 'real' family therapy was in fact antitherapeutic" (p. 2).

Psychiatry, on the other hand, had put all its eggs in the medication basket and hardly bothered with the patient's family. Psychiatrists believed that the high relapse rate for schizophrenics was due mainly to patients discontinuing their medication. As studies of relapse rates emerged, demonstrating that compliance with medication regimens didn't necessarily prevent relapse, the patient's environment was reconsidered. Several studies concluded that the schizophrenic patients who fared best after being hospitalized were those who returned to the least stressful households. A British group, including George Brown, John Wing, Julian Leff, and Christine Vaughn, had focused on what they called "expressed emotion" (EE) in the families of schizophrenics—particularly criticism, hostility, and emotional overinvolvement (Brown et al., 1962; 1972). Studies suggested that patients returning to high EE households had much higher rates of relapse than those returning to low EE homes (Brown et al., 1972; Vaughn & Leff, 1976; Vaughn et al., 1984).

These observations indicated that schizophrenia was a thought disorder involving a biological vulnerability of unknown origin that makes people highly reactive to and easily overwhelmed by stress. Apparently when family members are hypercritical or intrusive, the schizophrenic patient cannot process these communications adequately and becomes overloaded, which leads to decompensation.

With this view in mind, three different groups in the late 1970s and early 1980s began experimenting with ways to reduce stress in the most common environments for schizophrenic patients, their parents' homes. Michael Goldstein led a group at UCLA (Goldstein et al., 1978) who designed a brief, structured model focused on anticipating the stresses the family was likely to face and reducing conflict around the patient. The Goldstein group demonstrated that this family program, in combination with medication, could achieve an impressive decrease in relapse rates. Following the Goldstein study, groups headed by Ian Falloon at the University of Southern California (whose model is primarily behavioral) and Carol Anderson at the Western Psychiatric Institute in Pittsburgh experimented with psychoeducational models. Rather than trying to describe all these models, we will focus on Anderson's because it is clearly articulated and, despite the psychoeducational antipathy for what family therapists have done to schizophrenics and their families, it contains many concepts and methods derived from family therapy.

Anderson and her colleagues (1986) focus on the devastating impact of schizophrenia on family systems, rather than on the possible effects of preexisting family characteristics on either the onset or maintenance of the syndrome. They see the isolation and enmeshment of many families of schizophrenics as an inevitable consequence of the embarrassment, frustration, and concern that family members feel.

> During an acute illness in any family member, of course, it is necessary for the rest of the family to focus their attentions and their energies on the patient. However, in any long-term illness (like diabetes, heart disease, *or* schizophrenia), patients must learn to live with their limitations and life must go on for those around them. If this does not happen, the impact of illness can become debilitating to families. (p. 125)

Thus, while family members may be contributing to a less than optimal course of their child's schizophrenia, it isn't because their system needs symptoms; it's because the illness has drained the family's resources and generated dysfunctional patterns both within the families and with those whose attempts to help are making things worse.

Thus, psychoeducators try not only to help families change their ideas about and interactions with patients but also to reverse the damage that may have been done to families by insensitive professionals. Instead of providing the information, support, structure, and sense of control that these families need when in crisis, many mental health professionals ignore family members except to gather information about the patient and the family—information about what went wrong. The implications of this line of questioning add to the sense of guilt, shame, and confusion that family members already feel. It's no wonder that many families either give up and hand their patients over to these authoritarian professionals, or get into antagonistic battles with them.

Instead, psychoeducators seek to establish a collaborative partnership in which family members feel empathized with, supported, and empowered to deal with the patient. Following any contact with a professional, families should leave with a sense of their importance in the treatment process and also with a sense that they aren't alone—that caring helpers are involved with them. To achieve this kind of partnership, Anderson and colleagues find that they must reeducate professionals to give up ideas that the family caused or wants the schizophrenia, to scan for and emphasize family strengths, and to share with the family what information exists about schizophrenia.

It is this information-sharing that constitutes the educational element of psycho*education.* Anderson and her colleagues believe that information about the nature and course of schizophrenia helps family members develop a sense of mastery—a way to understand and anticipate the often chaotic and apparently uncontrollable process. Too often in the past, this information was withheld out of neglect or antagonism toward families, or because schizophrenia's less than rosy prognosis might discourage them. Since families are usually the principle caretakers, however, it makes sense that they should be the most, rather than the least, informed members of the team.

In a one-day "survival-skills workshop," Anderson and her colleagues teach groups of family members the history and epidemiology of schizophrenia and current information about its etiology, prognosis, psychobiology, and treatment. They discuss in some depth the EE findings regarding the impact of the social environment on patients, and they suggest how families can reorganize to deal with these special needs. Research demonstrating the importance of medication in preventing relapse is also presented.

The goal of these workshops is to translate what's known about schizophrenia into a framework that allows family members to understand and not feel bad about their behavior, the patient's behavior, and the behavior of professionals. Family members are also given the sense that they are part of a turning point in psychiatric history when schizophrenics and their families are treated with compassion and understanding. They are given hope that life can be better, although psychoeducators are careful not to give what they consider to be the false hope of a complete cure.

Families are encouraged to provide an atmosphere of low stimulation and expectation, but not without structure or limit-setting. While patients are to be given a lot of latitude regarding their desire to withdraw from stimulation or other idiosyncrasies, they aren't to be allowed to engage in strange or irritating behavior that upsets others in the household. Family members are to minimize conflict and criticism among themselves and toward the patient, so that when parents set limits they are to do so in a matter-of-fact, rather than angry, manner. If necessary, they are to set up chores and rules around the house as they might for a much younger child so that the patient has the structure he or she might need.

One of psychoeducation's key interventions is to lower expectations, to reduce pressure on the patient to perform normally. For example, the goals for the first year following an acute episode are primarily the avoidance of a relapse and the gradual taking on of some responsibilities in the home. Family members are to view the patient as someone who's had a serious physical illness and needs a long recuperation. Patients may need an excessive amount of sleep, solitude, and limited activity for some time following an episode, and may seem restless and have trouble concentrating. By predicting these developments, psychoeducators try to prevent conflict between the patient and family members due to impatience or frustration with lack of movement toward unrealistic goals.

These recommendations are in sharp contrast to the traditional family therapy attitude of "treat people as if they are normal and they will behave normally." Haley's (1980) *Leaving Home* model encouraged parents to expect normal behavior from schizophrenics and to work together to get the patient to pursue a normal life as soon as possible. The Milan Associates (Selvini Palazzoli et al., 1978) implied that schizophrenics could be cured after a few sessions. As we shall see, Michael White (1989) gets families and patients to fight against, rather than to expect, the schizophrenic person's "in-the-corner-lifestyle." The psychoeducational shift in goals away from cure and toward coping is a radical and difficult one for family therapists, and represents one of the biggest and most controversial departures from the family therapy mainstream.

Anderson and her group (1986) point to the results of these workshops in responding to criticism of their methods:

> Whether it is the information itself, the decreased sense of blame and guilt that is communicated by the absence of an emphasis on family etiology, the conveying of respect and equality, or the increase in hope generated by a new approach, the response to these workshops has been dramatic. The climate between staff and families seems to become less polarized, less tense and resistant family members become more cooperative. Family and professionals both become less isolated, and less subject to burnout. (p. 131)

This workshop and the initial meetings with the family that may have preceded it are only part of the psychoeducational regimen. Regularly scheduled outpatient family sessions and crisis support are likely to last for a year or more after an acute episode. These sessions include assigning small tasks to the patient and monitoring their performance. But it's in these later sessions that the Anderson group allows the focus to shift from the patient and on to problems in the family's structure, which may have arisen as a result of the schizophrenia, or even to problems that family members are facing that aren't directly related to the patient.

From this point on, Anderson's psychoeducational approach looks very much like structural family therapy, except that the family's structural flaws are construed as the *result* of rather than the *cause* of the presenting problem.

> During the chronic course of a schizophrenic illness, generational and interpersonal boundaries within families often become blurred. When the patient is an adolescent or young adult, one or both parents may become involved with the patient to the detriment of their relationship with one or another of the children. Wives or husbands come to treat their ill spouses as children, and children come to perform parental roles to fill in for ill parents. Often, the patient's illness dominates the household, so that all decisions and plans are made on the basis of what the patient needs, wants, or will tolerate. This, in effect, puts the patient in control of the rest of the family. These confused generational boundaries are a problem for everyone, as is the central position the patient occupies within the family. The familial structure becomes skewed in such a way that the normal needs of its members cannot be satisfied or attended to properly. (p. 173)

Thus, much of the therapy follows the familiar themes of reinforcing generational boundaries by encouraging parents to work together on discipline and moving children out of parental roles, opening up the family's boundary to the outside world and developing support networks, urging parents to reinvest in their marriage, and getting family members to not speak for or do for the patient.

In addition, the Anderson model doesn't shy away from dealing with problems in family members' lives that aren't obviously related to the schizophrenia. They find that marital conflict, problems with the patient's siblings, and depression are common and can interfere with the family's ability to reorganize to help the patient. They are careful, however, to address these problems only when the family asks for help with them or when such problems are clearly impeding the patient's progress. The danger in going after problems without an invitation from the family is that they may feel blamed and defensive—as if the therapist suspected that those problems were behind the schizophrenia. Anderson and coworkers (1986) report that frequently these other problems improve without direct attention as the family reorganizes to help the patient.

Is the psychoeducational model effective? The answer to that question depends on one's definition of success. By psychoeducational standards, all psychoeducational studies show comparably dramatic success. For example, in the study by Anderson and colleagues (1986),

> Among treatment takers (n = 90), 19% of those receiving family therapy alone experienced a psychotic relapse in the year following hospital discharge. Of those receiving the individual behavioral therapy, 20% relapsed, but *no* patient in the treatment cell that received both family therapy and social skills training experienced a relapse. These relapse rates constitute significant effects for both treatments when contrasted to a 41% relapse rate for those receiving only chemotherapy and support. (p. 24)

Other studies have shown equally impressive results (Falloon et al., 1982; Leff et al., 1982). There seems to be little question that psychoeducation can delay relapse and readmission to a hospital better than other approaches to schizophrenia. The question for family therapists is whether they are willing to settle for that kind of limited goal.

Anderson's version of psychoeducation can be seen as a nonantagonistic, less intense form of structural family therapy. The consistent message to families that they are in no way responsible for the patient's illness and the consistent empathy and support for the family's struggle with that illness create a nondefensive, collaborative therapeutic atmosphere in which the therapist can help families address structural problems without having to attack or blame them. Whether the structural problems predate the schizophrenia or were caused by it seems irrelevant as long as the problems are addressed.

Anderson and her colleagues (1986) suggested that this model need not be limited to the treatment of schizophrenia, but may be applied to any chronic problem, and Anderson (1988) also described its application to depression. Much of the work with addictions, based on Alcoholics Anonymous and the Adult Children of Alcoholics models, can be seen as fitting this psychoeducational mold. Alcoholism is viewed as a disease, and families are educated, empathized with, and supported regarding its effects on them (Steinglass, Bennett, Wolin, & Reiss, 1987).

Medical Family Therapy

If one considers schizophrenia a chronic disease, then psychoeducational family therapy can be seen as a specialized form of medical family therapy. Medical family therapists work with families struggling with any chronic illness or disability in much the same way as described above for families of schizophrenics. This work is less controversial within family therapy than is psychoeducation, however, because fewer people would assert that illnesses like multiple sclerosis, diabetes, and stroke are caused by family patterns, should not be medicated, or might be cured by family therapy. Thus, the families that medical family therapists work with are less ashamed and defensive to begin with, and less polarized with helping professionals than families of schizophrenics.

Medical family therapy was pioneered by Don Bloch, who started the journal *Family Systems Medicine* in 1982 with the goal of connecting the psychosocial and the biomedical aspects of health care. The journal is now called *Families, Systems and Health* (Dept. CC-7, P.O. Box 20838, Rochester, NY 14602-0838) to reflect the expanding scope of the enterprise to encompass all aspects of health care. In the early 1990s, the field came of age, with three books setting the pace (McDaniel, Hepworth, & Doherty, 1992; Ramsey, 1989; Rolland, 1994). Now, in the late 1990s it has mushroomed into a whole new paradigm called *collaborative family health care,* with a large annual conference that began in 1996 and now offers 14 plenaries and more than 50 workshops. There, well-known medical family therapists, such as John Rolland, Bill Doherty, Lorraine Wright, Susan McDaniel, and Thomas Campbell, present their work alongside experts in medicine, nursing, social work, and hospital administration. The hope and promise of this movement are to provide new careers for family therapists but also to become a new model for cost-effective and humane health care nationally.

Medical family therapists work in close collaboration with pediatricians, family practitioners, rehabilitation specialists, and nurses. They advocate that near the time of diagnosis, families should receive a routine consultation to explore their resources relative to the demands of the illness or disability. They cite the growing body of research suggesting a strong relationship between family dynamics and the clinical course of many medical conditions (Campbell, 1986) as evidence that such consultation and collaboration may be highly productive.

Just as family therapy was taken to task for not recognizing the impact of issues like gender, ethnicity, and race, medical family therapists say that the field has ignored the impact of chronic illness. For example:

> A woman with multiple sclerosis, hospitalized for depression, was seen by a family therapist in sessions with her husband and their three daughters. The family therapist slid by the issue of the woman's multiple sclerosis and focused on the true underlying problem, which she decreed was the overinvolvement of the patient's daughters with their mother. (McDaniel, Hepworth, & Doherty, 1992, p. 23)

As a result, two of the daughters withdrew support, leaving the youngest, who was already consumed by her own family obligations, as the sole support of her struggling parents.

Chronic illness often has a devastating impact. It can take over the patient's and the family's lives, ravaging health, hope, and peace of mind. As Peter Steinglass says, "it can be like a terrorist, who has appeared on the doorstep, barged inside the home and demanded everything the family has" (quoted in McDaniel et al., 1992, p. 21).

How can we help families cope with this terrible impact? John Rolland (1994) has constructed a helpful framework that clarifies how qualities of an illness or disability will interact with qualities of a family. He points out that illness can vary according to several qualities: *onset* (sudden or gradual), *course* (stable, progressive deterioration, or unpredictable relapsing), *degree of incapacitation* (from none to severe), and *outcome* (whether it will affect longevity or possibly result in sudden death). Different illnesses have different combinations of these qualities and, depending on the combination, place varying demands on a family. For example, if, because of an accident, a family member goes blind, there is a sudden crisis followed by a stable course but the condition doesn't shorten life expectancy and isn't totally incapacitating. On the other hand, if a person is found to be HIV positive, the family faces a gradual onset of illness in the person and a progressive, highly incapacitating course resulting in death.

These demands of the illness interact with qualities of the family, such as the family's life cycle stage and the role the stricken family member plays; the family's leadership resources and degree of isolation; and their beliefs about serious illness and who should help, derived from their ethnicity and history with illness. With an awareness of these factors, therapists can help families prepare to deal with an illness or, if the illness has been with them for years, gain perspective on their resulting polarizations and enmeshments. The therapist helps families reorganize their beliefs and resources to keep the illness from dominating them.

In conclusion, psychoeducational and medical family therapy approaches share many elements with the other models in this chapter which together represent a significant trend: a strong move away from an antagonistic relationship with families, toward a collaborative partnership. Therapists are now encouraged to look for a family's strengths rather than deficits and find ways to lift families out of the guilt and blame that accompany their problems. Medical family therapy represents a natural and important collaboration among therapists, physicians, and families that is likely to shape family therapy's future.

The Self in the System

The postmodern swing away from intrapsychic speculation and grand theories is reversed by another trend in family therapy. The pendulum that swung the field away from intrapsychic, individual models of psychotherapy began to swing back in the 1980s, despite the postmodern disdain for the idea that we have a separate self that can be explored and mapped. The reasons for this are many.

The first of these reasons is developmental. Family therapy has become sufficiently accepted as a valid discipline so that it no longer has to maintain the us-versus-them attitude of its early days. Like an adolescent taking a second look at parents she once rejected, the field has grown strong and confident enough to admit that it may not have all the answers after all and that psychological considerations may also be important.

A second factor has to do with the immigration of increasing numbers of psychodynamically trained clinicians into the family therapy field as family therapy became more popular and less polarized from the psychotherapy establishment. This influx has created an increasing demand for models that can bridge the gap between the self and the system.

Finally, several offshoots of psychoanalysis have evolved to the point that they seem more compatible with family therapy. Classic Freudian drive theory gives people's environment little credit for their problems and, consequently, gives little justification for working with their families. Freud taught us that human nature is propelled by unconscious forces buried deep within the psyche. Both object relations theory and self psychology put more emphasis on a person's interactions with family.

The essence of object relations theory is quite simple: We relate to people in the present partly on the basis of expectations formed by early experience. For the more interpersonally oriented object relations theorists like Ronald Fairbairn and Donald Winnicott, interpersonal relatedness replaces drives, aggression, and the pleasure principle as the driving force in human personality.

Object relations theory says that the past is alive—in memory—and it runs people's lives more than they know. From our early relationships with caretakers, we formed mental images, called *internal objects*, that structure the way we experience the world. As adults, we react to other people based in large part on how much those people resemble these internal objects, rather than on the real characteristics of the people.

As applied to family therapy, the idea is that the dysfunctional patterns that family therapists have identified are often maintained by the internal object relations of key family members. Through a process called *projective identification*, the images of certain internal objects are projected onto other family members, who are then induced to act out these projections. Object relations family therapists interpret these projections to families so that their members can be more aware of the unseen forces behind their unhappy interactions and more able to change them.

In the 1980s a number of books were written on object relations and family therapy (Nichols, 1987; Luepnitz, 1988; Wachtel & Wachtel, 1986; Kirshner & Kirshner, 1986; Slipp, 1984; Scharff & Scharff, 1987). In addition, the self psychology of Heinz Kohut (1971, 1977) has had a revolutionizing impact on the psychoanalytic world and, indirectly, on family therapy. Kohut replaced Freud's raging id with an insecure self at the core of human nature and taught us that our lives are organized around a striving for fulfillment and longing for acceptance, more than around sex and aggression. Recently, Bill Pinsof (1996) has attempted to integrate self psychology with systems-based family therapy.

These ideas have strong implications for the nature of the relationship between therapist and client. Therapists are to be more nurturant and empathic—to provide a safe, warm envelope known as a *holding environment*—rather than remaining distant, passive, and neutral. This is a large and controversial step for psychoanalysis and also for family therapy.

The attempted marriage of even these more interpersonally oriented psychoanalytic theories with family therapy is a delicate matter. These models still contain concepts and assumptions that do not blend well with systems thinking, and various writers have handled this problem in different ways. Some advocate giving up on systems theory and replacing it with object relations as a basis for family therapy. Others try to use both but keep them separated and use them sequentially or to complement each other. Still others have tried to integrate the concepts and methods of the two paradigms, a process very much like trying to mate animals across species.

One model has taken a different tack. Instead of trying to work with the incompatibilities between object relations and systems thinking, Richard Schwartz (1987, 1995) extended systems principles and techniques to intrapsychic process, applying them to the interaction of internal subpersonalities. In the process, he stumbled onto a new method of working intrapsychicly and a useful language for therapy, as well as a way to move fluidly from family to internal considerations (see Chapter 13).

Many family therapists continue to maintain the systemic position of the pioneers and view this return to the individual as regressive. For them, the discovery of systemic concepts and techniques was as clarifying as turning on a light in a dark room. Where once there was only chaos and confusion, they could now see triangles, boundary violations, and circular interaction sequences. The idea of diving back into the murky, speculative, and emotional intrapsychic realm, from which they were rescued by family therapy, is quite unsavory.

We agree that there are dangers in this reversion. It's easy to get lost in the fascinating inner life of individuals and, once again, to minimize the importance of their external context. It's easy to become daunted by stories of pathological interactions in a person's early life and underestimate their ability to change in the present. It's easy to become overwhelmed by the complexity of trying to understand the many psyches that comprise a family system.

We mustn't forget, however, that even though families act like systems, individuals still do the acting, and they, as you may have noticed, can sometimes be pretty courageous.

If the field proceeds carefully toward a systemic appreciation of individuals, then these dangers can be addressed. When this is achieved, our models will be enriched and blindspots will be filled as we will be able to appreciate both internal and external levels of system and shift between them as needed. We will respect the power of family systems without losing sight of the abilities of individuals to control their own lives. We will be able to identify problematic interaction patterns in the family while also knowing each family member as a flesh-and-blood person rather than as a cog in the machine. That is an exciting prospect.

The Influence of Managed Care

It seems ironic that with all the exciting developments in family therapy, the most powerful shaper of the field as we enter the twenty-first century has nothing to do with clinical theory or technique. Managed care, the attempt by insurance corporations and other regulating bodies to control the cost of mental health services, has had a profound and controversial impact on every aspect of family therapy practice. This is because increasingly throughout the United States and other countries, managed care companies are controlling not only access to clients but also what kinds of therapy they receive, how long they can be treated, and how much therapists can be paid.

Since the goal of managed care companies is to reduce costs, they are interested in efficient treatment and encourage therapists to work as rapidly as possible. As a result, brief therapy models like solution-focused therapy have flourished while longer-term models like psychoanalytic or Bowenian therapies haven't fared as well. On the brighter side, some of the more enlightened managed care companies actually favor family therapists because they recognize that clinicians who view and treat people in their social context are more likely to keep them out of the hospital.

In the first wave of managed care, therapists applied to be on panels so as to receive referrals. Once they received a referral, they had to ask permission from a case manager for more sessions and had to justify their treatment approach. Increasingly managed care companies are finding this micromanagement approach too expensive and antagonistic, so the second wave involves incentives for therapists themselves to reduce their costs. This involves giving "capitated" contracts in which a group of therapists agrees to provide, for a preset annual fee, all mental health services for a specific group of people. This system eliminates the need for case managers, because therapists know that to make money they have to limit their services as much as possible. While the capitated system may discourage therapists from offering some needed services, at least therapists will be wrestling with their own consciences rather than with faceless strangers. And therapists will have more latitude in selecting treatment and less concerns about violations of confidentiality inherent in the micromanaged system.

Before managed care, family therapists were either in private practice or worked in social service agencies, subsidized by federal, state, or local governments. Referrals were based primarily on reputation and were relatively abundant. Therapists weren't limited in their treatment approach or number of sessions, and they could ensure client confidentiality. Therapists made a good income and felt like professionals. All that seems like a distant dream in many parts of the country.

If the capitation system becomes widespread, it will spell the demise of the solo practitioner, because clients will be treated only by therapists connected to groups that can provide a comprehensive range of services. That change alone represents a revolution in family therapy as it moves from being a cottage industry, in which quality of treatment was the paramount concern and therapist–client collaboration around treatment decisions was possible, to becoming corporate, where profit is paramount and collaboration difficult. As managed care companies realized huge profits this way, the fees or salaries they paid therapists shrank.

Contracts are given to groups that offer availability, accessibility, affordability, and acceptability (Heath, 1995), rather than those known to do innovative or high-quality therapy. Therapists have large case loads and little supervision. Perhaps the worst aspect of this revolution is the elimination of the creative groups that generated new views of people and how to help them. Therapists no longer have time to think or room to experiment. Not only will psychotherapy suffer as a result, but so too will the larger culture because so much of how society understands and relates to its members has been influenced by innovations in psychotherapy.

Therapists have reacted in a variety of ways. Some see managed care as a positive, or at least inevitable, correction to a situation that was out of control. They suggest that before managed care, psychotherapy was unaccountable and exploitative, with no incentive to contain runaway costs. These therapists learn how to please managed care companies and have plenty of business, even though they make less per hour than before. Others are trying to survive by increasing their marketing for clients who can pay out of pocket and by finding other ways to use their skills, such as divorce mediation; consulting to businesses, schools, and courts; teaching and leading workshops; and working in human resource departments for businesses. Still others are actively fighting the managed care tidal wave by organizing in groups that offer alternatives to managed care, by feeding the media a constant stream of managed care horror stories, and by pursuing antitrust suits.[2] The fighters believe that ultimately consumers and politicians will get fed up with the lack of choice and quality and will regain control.

It seems clear to us that the final verdict on the shape of the field for the twenty-first century isn't in yet. While there are huge profits to be made by those who want to restrict services, there is rapidly growing dissatisfaction with those restrictions, and some recognition that in many cases unrestricted outpatient family therapy saves money that otherwise would be spent on hospitalizations or other more expensive treatments that result from family crises. It's unlikely that we will ever return to the totally unrestricted golden days that some long for, and perhaps that's as it should be. It is likely, however, that as consumers realize they aren't getting the help they need, new alternatives will emerge to fill the demand, and these new alternatives will be more palatable to both clients and therapists.

Conclusion

During the past two decades, the family therapy juggernaut, which had been steadily picking up converts and rolling over opposition from the psychotherapy establishment, hit the wall and is now groping for direction. The wall came in the form of a series of hard-hitting critiques from within the field—from feminists, postmodernists, constructivists, social constructionists, multiculturalists, those who work with violence and abuse, gays and lesbians, the poor, and the chronically ill.

While these critics differed in the details of their complaints, the basic message was the same. The original models were too narrow,

[2]One such group is the National Coalition of Mental Health Professionals and Consumers (telephone: 516-424-5232).

hierarchical, patriarchal, behavioral, and pathologizing. Therapists were challenged to become more respectful; collaborative; sensitive to differences in ethnicity, race, class, gender, and sexual orientation; and interested in beliefs and values rather than behavior and structure. The confident, charismatic, master therapist who could quickly assess and actively reorganize dysfunctional family patterns was dethroned by the compassionate, curious, conversationalist, who carried few presumptions and mainly asked questions. Goodbye Rambo, hello Mr. Rogers.

Also, the juggernaut has become a welcome wagon. We're much friendlier with groups we originally rebelled against and felt superior to, such as the psychoanalysts, the psychiatric establishment, the medical and twelve-step communities. More surprisingly, now we also get along with each other. The fortresses built up around the original models have dropped their drawbridges. Therapists now sample concepts and methods from all of the different schools and from outside the field. The fervor and chauvinism of some followers of the newer models, like narrative and solution-focused, seems anachronistic in this postmodern era. It seems we can no longer take ourselves so seriously.

This new interest in collaborating with rather than confronting or directing families is no accident—it reflects a maturing of the field. The pioneers first encountered the family as a powerful adversary—"homeostatic," "resistant"—in part because they approached with a built-in prejudice. Bent on rescuing "family scapegoats," they saw mothers as enemies to be overcome and fathers as peripheral figures to be ignored. Human systems do fear and resist change, particularly when the system's members feel pushed or judged. Family therapists provoked resistance and then viewed that as evidence that families were highly resistant.

Every advance contains the seeds of its own excess. Family therapists taught us to see past individual personalities to the patterns that make them a family—an organization of interconnected lives governed by strict but unspoken rules. But in the process they also created a nonhuman, mechanistic entity—the family system—and then set out to do battle with it. Most of the challenges that have rocked and reshaped family therapy in recent years have been in reaction to this mechanist approach.

The best part of the postmodern revolution has been that by giving up our expert status and grand theories, we've been able to find our hearts. Family therapy is becoming humanized, with more attention given to qualities of the therapist–client relationship than ever before. The field is discovering what theorists like Carl Rogers, Donald Winnicott, and, in our own field, Virginia Satir were saying years ago: that in order to change, people need to feel accepted, appreciated, and respected. This therapeutic attitude, once seen as too "touchy–feely," is now called being collaborative.

Family therapy's bridge to the twenty-first century is collaborative social constructionism. Much as was the case when the pioneers shifted their focus from individuals to families, this recent shift from action to narrative, and from challenging to collaborating, is opening up a new world of possibilities. The next few chapters will demonstrate how exciting some of those possibilities are. As with many revolutionary movements, however, this shift was not only toward the new but also away from the old—away from systems thinking and attention to family dynamics. Rejecting past metaphors may be necessary to fully explore the limits of new ones. Perhaps the pendulum will swing back.

In the meantime it is important to remember that while the postmodern, constructionist revolution has been the headline story for the past decade, family therapists practicing less trendy approaches (behavioral, psychoanalytic, structural, strategic, Bowenian, experiential, and integrative) have continued their work. As we hope is made clear in their chapters, these models haven't remained static. Exciting developments coming from those traditions receive less attention because they're not in step with the hot new movements, but they are no less significant. While it's important for the field to keep exploring virgin territories, it's also important to build on a set of ideas or practices for more than just a few years. Every field needs explorers and gardeners. Family therapy has had plenty of the former and not enough of the latter.

The collaborative movement has raised new questions about the therapist's style of leadership. Some advocates of the nonexpert position have reversed the old hierarchy by privileging a family's opinions over that of therapists. There is a danger that in the effort to avoid imposing their viewpoint on families, therapists will abdicate leadership (Atkinson, 1992; Nichols, 1993). The authoritarian stances of old came from the belief that therapists needed to make families change. The great advance of the past decades has been the realization that when we don't try to make families change but instead create a climate in which problems or solutions can be explored in less defensive or polarized ways, families are able to change themselves.

Because therapists are no longer the technocrats of change doesn't mean that they shouldn't be experts. Being collaborative requires leadership and expertise, but of a different kind than when we used to make families see things our way. Leadership doesn't mean pushing, confronting, or controlling, but it does mean creating a context in which difficult issues can be addressed safely. Being a collaborative partner for families doesn't mean being passive and going along with whatever clients say, or allowing their conflicts to escalate or remain underground.

We also worry that postmodernist therapists can become too accepting or upbeat to the point of denial. Many troubled families tend to deny their problems or their pain. If, for example, one has a nondirective "conversation" with an alcoholic or abusive family, it's possible to co-create with them a reality that their problems aren't as bad as they think and everyone will walk away, at least temporarily, feeling much better. This isn't to imply that constructionist therapists routinely co-create problem-denying realities with families, but rather to suggest that too strong an emphasis on respecting a family's reality can be blinding.

Finally, it should be said that, just as the family therapy field hasn't stood still in recent years, neither has the family. Today's family is evolving and stressed. We've gone from the complementary model of the family in the 1950s to a symmetrical version—but we haven't come to terms with it yet. Perhaps it's time to ask and begin to answer the question: As the American family struggles through this stressful time of transition, what concepts does family therapy offer to help us understand and deal with the protean family forms of the twenty-first century?

Family therapy is a fascinating and challenging field to cover in part because it's constantly evolving. It's like the weather in Chicago—if you don't like it, all you have to do is wait five minutes and it'll change. We hope this chapter has provided some previews of what's to come in the twenty-first century, but who knows when the next philosophical front will roll in and completely alter the climate once again.

References

Ahrons, C., and Rogers, R. 1989. *Divorced families: Meeting the challenges of divorce and remarriage.* New York: Norton.

Andersen, T. 1987. The reflecting team: Dialogue and meta-dialogue in clinical work. *Family Process. 26:*415–428.

Andersen, T. 1991. *The reflecting team.* New York: Norton.

Andersen, T. 1993. See and hear, and be seen and heard. In *The new language of change,* S. Friedman, ed. New York: Guilford Press.

Anderson, C. M. 1986. The all-too-short trip from positive to negative connotation. *Journal of Marital and Family Therapy. 12:*351–354.

Anderson, C. M. 1988. Psychoeducational model different than paradigm. *Family Therapy News. 19:*3.

Anderson, H. 1993. On a roller coaster: A collaborative language systems approach to therapy. In *The new language of change,* S. Friedman, ed. New York: Guilford Press.

Anderson, C. M. 1995. *Flying solo.* New York: Norton.

Anderson, C. M., Reiss, D., and Hogarty, G. E. 1986. *Schizophrenia and the family: A practitioners guide to psychoeducation and management.* New York: Guilford Press.

Anderson, H., and Goolishian, H. 1988. Human systems as linguistic systems: Preliminary and evolving ideas about the implications for clinical theory. *Family Process. 27:*371–394.

Anderson, H., Goolishian, H., and Winderman, L. 1986. Problem determined systems: Toward transformation in family therapy. *Journal of Strategic and Systemic Therapies. 5:*14–19.

Anderson, H. T. 1990. *Reality isn't what it used to be.* San Francisco: Harper & Row.

Atkinson, B. 1992. Aesthetics and pragmatics of therapy revisited. *Journal of Marital and Family Therapy. 18:*389–393.

Ault-Riche, M., ed. 1986.*Women and family therapy.* Rockville, MD: Aspen Systems.

Avis, J. M. 1988. Deepening awareness: A private study guide to feminism and family therapy. In *Women, feminism, and family therapy,* L. Braverman, ed. New York: Haworth Press.

Avis, J. M. 1992. Where are all the family therapists? Abuse and violence within families and family therapy's response. *Journal of Marital and Family Therapy. 18:*223–230.

Bank, S., and Kahn, M. 1982. *The sibling bond.* New York: Basic Books.

Barrett, M. J., and Trepper, T. 1992. Unmasking the incestuous family. *Family Therapy Networker. 16:* 39–46.

Barth, R., Pietrzak, J., and Ramier, M. 1993. *Families living with drugs and HIV.* New York: Guilford Press.

Beavers, W., and Hampson, R. 1990. *Successful families: Assessment and intervention.* New York: Norton.

Bepko, C., and Krestan, J. 1985. *The responsibility trap.* New York: Free Press.

Berg, I. K., and Miller, S. 1992. *Working with the problem drinker.* New York: Norton.

Berg, I. K., and de Shazer, S. 1993. Making numbers talk: Language in therapy. In *The new language of change,* S. Friedman, ed. New York: Guilford Press.

Berger, M., Jurkovic, G., and Associates, eds. 1984. *Practicing family therapy in diverse settings.* San Francisco: Jossey-Bass.

Berger Gould, B., and DeMuth, D. 1994. *The global family therapist.* Boston, MA: Allyn and Bacon.

Berkowitz, R., Kuipers, L., Eberlain-Vries, R., and Leff, J. 1981. Lowering expressed emotion in relatives. In *New developments in interventions with families of schizophrenics.* M. J. Goldstein, ed. San Francisco: Jossey-Bass.

Bograd, M. 1992. Values in conflict: Challenges to family therapists' thinking. *Journal of Marital and Family Therapy. 18:*243–253.

Boyd-Franklin, N. 1989. *Black families in therapy: A multisystems approach.* New York: Guilford Press.

Boyd-Franklin, N. 1993. Race, class, and poverty. In *Normal family processes,* F. Walsh, ed. New York: Guilford Press.

Boyd-Franklin, N., Steiner, G., and Boland, M. 1995. *Children, families, and HIV/AIDS.* New York: Guilford Press.

Braverman, L., ed. 1988. *Women, feminism, and family therapy.* New York: Haworth Press.

Breunlin, D., Schwartz, R., and Mac Kune-Karrer, B. 1992. *Metaframeworks: Transcending the models of family therapy.* San Francisco: Jossey-Bass.

Brown, G. W., Birley, J. L. T., and Wing, J. K. 1972. The influence of family life on the course of schizophrenic disorders: A replication. *British Journal of Psychology. 121,* 241–258.

Calof, D. 1992. Adult children of incest and child abuse: Holograms of the trance generational family. *AFTA Newsletter,* Winter, 35–40.

Campbell, T. 1986. Family's impact on health: A critical review and annotated bibliography. *Family Systems Medicine,* 4:135–148.

Canavan, M., Higgs, D., and Meyer, W. 1992. The female experience of sibling incest. *Journal of Marital and Family Therapy. 18:*129–142.

Carl, D. 1990. *Counseling same-sex couples.* New York: Norton.

Chamberlain, P., Patterson, G., Reid, J., Kavanaugh, K., and Forgatch, M. 1984. Observation of client resistance. *Behavior Therapy. 15:*144–155.

Coleman, S. 1987. Milan in Bucks County. *Family Therapy Networker. 11:*42–47.

Combrinck-Graham, L. 1989. *Children in family contexts.* New York: Guilford Press.

Combrinck-Graham, L. 1991. Review of the Plenary, "Violence: The dark side of the family," *AFTA Newsletter. 45:*12–14.

Combrinck-Graham, L. 1995. *Children in families at risk.* New York: Guilford Press.

Contróneo, M. 1987. Women and abuse in the context of the family. *Journal of Psychotherapy and the Family. 3:*81–96.

Crawford, S. 1988. Cultural context as a factor in the expansion of therapeutic conversation with lesbian families. *Journal of Strategic and Systemic Therapies. 7:*2–10.

Dahlheimer, D., and Feigal, J. 1991. Bridging the gap. *Family Therapy Networker. 15:*44–53.

Dell, P. 1985. Understanding Bateson and Maturana. *Journal of Marital and Family Therapy. 11:*1–20.

Dell, P. 1989. Violence and the systemic view: The problem of power. *Family Process. 23:*1–14.

de Shazer, S. 1991. Putting difference to work. New York: Norton.

DeWitt, K. N. 1978. The effectiveness of family therapy: A review of outcome research. *Archives of General Psychiatry. 35:*549–561.

Doherty, W. 1991. Family therapy goes postmodern. *Family Therapy Networker. 15:*36–42.

Duncan, B. L., and Solevey, D. 1989. Strategic-brief therapy: An insight-oriented approach. *Journal of Marital and Family Therapy. 15:*1–10.

Elizur, J., and Minuchin, S. 1989. *Institutionalizing madness: Families, therapy and society.* New York: Basic Books.

Elkin, M. 1990. *Families under the influence.* New York: Norton.

Erickson, B. 1992. Feminist fundamentalism: Reactions to Avis, Kaufman and Bograd. *Journal of Marital and Family Therapy. 18:* 263–267.

Everett, C. A. 1987. *The divorce process: A handbook for clinicians.* New York: Haworth Press.

Falicov, C. 1983. *Cultural perspectives in family therapy.* Rockville, MD: Aspen Systems.

Falicov, C. 1988. *Family transitions: Continuity and change over the life cycle.* New York: Guilford Press.

Falicov, C. (in press). *Latino families in therapy.* New York: Guilford Press.

Falicov, C. 1995. Training to think culturally: A multidimensional comparative framework. *Family Process. 34:*373–388.

Falicov, C., and Brudner-White, L. 1983. The shifting family triangle: The issue of cultural and contextual relativity. In *Cultural perspectives in family therapy,* C. Falicov, ed. Rockville, MD: Aspen Systems.

Falloon, I., Boyd, J. L., and McGill, C. W. 1985. *Family care of schizophrenia.* New York: Guilford Press.

Falloon, I. R. H., Boyd, J. L., McGill, C. W., Razani, J., Moss, H. B., and Gilderman, A. M. 1982. Family management in the prevention of exacerbations of schizophrenia. *New England Journal of Medicine. 306:*1437–1440.

Figley, C. 1985. *Trauma and its wake: The study and treatment of post-traumatic stress disorder.* New York: Brunner/Mazel.

Fish, V. 1993. Poststructuralism in family therapy: Interrogating the narrative/conversational mode. *Journal of Marital and Family Therapy. 19:* 223–232.

Foucault, M. 1980. *Power/knowledge: Selected interviews and other writings.* New York: Pantheon Books.

Foucault, M. 1984. *The history of sexuality.* Middlesex, Great Britain: Peregrine Books.

Fowers, B., & Richardson, F. 1996. Why is multiculturalism good? *American Psychologist. 51:*609–621.

Freedman, S. 1995. *The reflecting team in action.* New York: Guilford Press.

Friedman, S. ed. 1993. *The new language of change.* New York: Guilford Press.

Friedrich, W. 1990. *Psychotherapy of sexually abused children and their families.* New York: Norton.

Gergen, K. 1985. The social constructionist movement in modern psychology. *American Psychologist. 40:*266–275.

Gergen, K. 1991a. *The saturated self.* New York: Basic Books.

Gergen, K. 1991b. The saturated family. *Family Therapy Networker. 15:*26–35.

Gil, E. 1994. *Play in family therapy.* New York, Guilford Press.

Goldner, V. 1985. Feminism and family therapy. *Family Process. 24*:31–47.

Goldner, V. 1988. Generation and gender: Normative and covert hierarchies. *Family Process. 27*: 17–33.

Goldner, V. 1993. Power and hierarchy: Let's talk about it. *Family Process. 32*:157–162.

Goldner, V., Penn, P., Sheinberg, M., and Walker, G. 1990. Love and violence: Gender paradoxes in volatile attachments. *Family Process. 29*:343–364.

Goldstein, M. 1988. Correction on views offered by awardee. *Family Therapy News. 19*:7–9.

Goldstein, M. J., Rodnick, E. H., Evans, J. R., May, P. R., and Steinberg, M. 1978. Drug and family therapy in the aftercare treatment of acute schizophrenia. *Archives of General Psychiatry. 35*:1169–1177.

Goodrich, T. J., Rampage, C., Ellman B., and Halstead K., 1988. *Feminist family therapy: A casebook.* New York: Norton.

Gorman-Smith, D., and Tolan, P. 1992. Ethics and empirical basis of treatment of adult survivors of childhood sexual abuse. *AFTA Newsletter.* Winter, 41–44.

Goulding, R., and Schwartz, R. 1995. *Mosaic Mind: Empowering the tormented selves of child sexual abuse survivors.* New York: Norton.

Haley, J. 1980. *Leaving home.* New York: McGraw-Hill.

Hansen, J. C. 1982. *Therapy with remarriage families.* Rockville, MD: Aspen Systems.

Hardy, K. 1993. War of the worlds. *Family Therapy Networker. 17*:50–57.

Hare-Mustin, R. T. 1978. A feminist approach to family therapy. *Family Process. 17*:181–194.

Hare-Mustin, R. T. 1986. The problem of gender in family therapy theory. *Family Process. 26*:15–27.

Heath, A. 1995. The future of family therapy in Illinois. *The Illinois Family Therapist. 16*:7–10.

Held, B., and Pols, E. 1987. Dell on Maturana: A real foundation for family therapy. *Psychotherapy. 24*:455–461.

Held, B. S. 1990. What's in a name? Some confusions and concerns about constructivism. *Journal of Marital and Family Therapy. 16*:179–186.

Hersch, P. 1991. Secret lives. *Family Therapy Networker. 15*:36–43.

Hoffman, L. 1985. Beyond power and control: Toward a second-order family systems therapy. *Family Systems Medicine. 3*:381–396.

Hoffman, L. 1988. A constructivist position for family therapy. *The Irish Journal of Psychology. 9*: 110–129.

Hoffman-Hennessay, L., and Davis, J. 1993. Tekka with feathers: Talking about talking. In *The new language of change,* S. Friedman, ed. New York: Guilford Press.

Imber-Black, E. 1988. *Families and larger systems: A family therapist's guide through the labyrinth.* New York: Guilford Press.

Imber-Black, E., Roberts, J., and Whiting, R. 1989. *Rituals in families and family therapy.* New York: Norton.

Ingoldsby, B., and Smith, S. 1995. *Families in multicultural perspective.* New York: Guilford Press.

James, K., and MacKinnon, L. 1990. The "incestuous family" revisited: A critical analysis of family therapy myths. *Journal of Marital and Family Therapy. 16*:71–88.

Kahn, M., and Lewis, K. G. 1988. *Siblings in therapy.* New York: Norton.

Kaufman, E. 1985. *The power to change.* New York: Gardner Press.

Kaufman, G. 1992. The mysterious disappearance of battered women from family therapists' offices. *Journal of Marital and Family Therapy. 18*:231–241.

Kirshner, D. A., and Krishner, S. 1986. *Comprehensive family therapy: An integration of systemic & psychodynamic models.* New York: Brunner/Mazel.

Kohut, H. 1971. *The analysis of the self.* New York: International University Press.

Kohut, H. 1977. *The Restoration of the self.* New York: International University Press.

Korzybski, A. 1942. *Science and sanity: An introduction to non-Aristotelian systems and general semantics,* 2nd ed. Lancaster, PA: Science Books.

Krestan, J. 1988. Lesbian daughters and lesbian mothers: The crisis of disclosure from a family systems perspective. *Journal of Psychotherapy and the Family. 3*:113–130.

Krestan, J., and Bepko, C. 1980. The problem of fusion in the lesbian relationship. *Family Process. 19*:277–289.

Laird, J. 1993. Lesbian and gay families. In *Normal family processes,* 2nd ed., F. Walsh, ed. New York: Guilford Press.

Laird, J., and Green, R. J. 1996. *Lesbians and gays in couples and families: A handbook for therapists.* San Francisco: Jossey-Bass.

Leff, J., Kuipers, L., Berkowitz, R., Eberlein-Vries, R., and Sturgeon, D. 1982. A controlled trial of social intervention in the families of schizophrenic patients. *British Journal of Psychiatry. 141*:121–134.

Luepnitz, D. 1988. *The family interpreted: Feminist theory in clinical practice.* New York: Basic Books.

Madanes, C. 1990. *Sex, love and violence.* New York: Norton.

Markowitz, L. 1992. Reclaiming the light. *Family Therapy Networker. 16*:17–24.

Markowitz, L. 1993. Walking the walk. *Family Therapy Networker. 17*:18–24, 27–31.

Mashal, M., Feldman, R., and Sigal, J. 1989. The unraveling of a treatment paradigm: A follow up study of the Milan approach to family therapy. *Family Process. 28*:457–470.

Maturana, H., and Varela, F. 1980. *Autopoiesis and cognition: The realization of living.* Boston: D. Reidel.

McDaniel, S., Hepworth, J., and Doherty, W. 1992. *Medical family therapy.* New York: Basic Books.

McGoldrick, M., Anderson, C., and Walsh, F., eds. 1989. *Women in families: A framework for family therapy.* New York: Norton.

McGoldrick, M. 1993. Ethnicity, cultural diversity, and normality. In *Normal family process,* F. Walsh, ed. New York: Guilford Press.

McGoldrick, M., Giordano, J., and Pearce, J. 1996. *Ethnicity and family therapy,* 2nd ed. New York: Guilford Press.

McGoldrick, M., Pearce, J., and Giordano, J. 1982. *Ethnicity and family therapy.* New York: Guilford Press.

Meth, R. 1992. Marriage and family therapists working with violence: Strained bedfellows or compatible partners? A commentary on Avis, Kaufman, and Bograd. *Journal of Marital and Family Therapy. 18*:257–261.

Minuchin, S. 1984. *Family kaleidoscope.* Cambridge, MA: Harvard University Press.

Minuchin, S., Baker, L., Rosman, B., Liebman, R., Milman, L., and Todd, T. 1975. A conceptual model of psychosomatic illness in children. *Archives of General Psychiatry. 32*:1031–1038.

Minuchin, S., and Fishman, H. C. 1981. *Techniques of family therapy.* Cambridge, MA: Harvard University Press.

Minuchin, S., Montalvo, B., Guerney, B., Rosman, B., and Schumer, F. 1967. *Families of the slums.* New York: Basic Books.

Minuchin, S., Rosman, B., and Baker, L. 1978. *Psychosomatic families.* Cambridge, MA: Harvard University Press.

Minuchin, S. 1991. The seductions of constructivism. *Family Therapy Networker. 15*:47–50

Mirkin, M. P., and Koman, S. L., eds. 1985. *Handbook of adolescents and family therapy.* New York: Gardner Press.

Mirkin, M. P. 1990. *The social and political contexts of family therapy.* Boston: Allyn and Bacon.

Mitchell, S. 1993. *Hope and dread in psychoanalysis.* New York: Basic Books.

Moore, T. 1992. *Care of the Soul.* New York: Harper Collins.

Morawetz, A., and Walker, G. 1984. *Brief therapy with single-parent families.* New York: Bruner/Mazel.

Nichols, M. P. 1987. *Self in the system.* New York: Brunner/Mazel.

Nichols, M. P. 1993. The therapist as authority figure. *Family Process. 32*:163–165.

O'Hanlon, W., and Weiner-Davis, M. 1989. *In search of solutions.* New York: Norton.

O'Hanlon, W., and Wilk, J. 1987. *Shifting contexts: The generation of effective psychotherapy.* New York: Guilford Press.

Okun, B. 1996. *Understanding diverse families.* New York: Guilford Press.

Pinderhughes, E. 1989. *Understanding race, ethnicity and power: The key to efficacy in clinical practice.* New York: The Free Press.

Pinsof, W. M. 1982. Integrative problem-centered therapy: Toward the synthesis of family and individual psychotherapies. *Journal of Marital and Family Therapy. 9*:19–36.

Pinsof, W. M. 1996. *Integrative problem-centered therapy: A synthesis of family, individual, and biological therapies.* New York: Basic Books.

Pittman, F. 1987. *Turning points: Treating families in transition and crisis.* New York: Norton.

Price, J. 1996. *Power and compassion: Working with difficult adolescents and abused parents.* New York: Guilford Press.

Ramsey, R. N. ed. 1989. *Family systems in medicine.* New York: Guilford Press.

Reitz, M., and Watson, K. 1992. *Adoption and the family system.* New York: Guilford Press.

Rolland, J. 1994. *Helping families with chronic and life-threatening disorders.* New York: Basic.

Rosenau, P. M., 1992. *Post-modernism and the social sciences.* Princeton, NJ: Princeton University Press.

Root, M., Fallon, P., and Friedrich, W. 1986. *Bulimia: A systems approach to treatment.* New York: Norton.

Roth, S. 1989. Psychotherapy with lesbian couples: Individual issues, female socialization, and the social context. In *Women in families,* M. McGoldrick, C. Anderson, and F. Walsh, eds. New York: Norton.

Roth, S., and Murphy, B. 1986. Therapeutic work with lesbian clients: A systemic therapy view. In *Women and family therapy,* M. Ault-Riche and J. Hansen, eds. Rockville, MD: Aspen Systems.

Saba, G., Karrer, B., and Hardy, K. 1989. *Minorities and family therapy.* New York: Haworth.

Sager, C., Brown, H. S., Crohn, H., Engel, T., Rodstein, E., and Walker, L. 1983. *Treating the remarried family.* New York: Brunner/Mazel.

Sanders, G. 1993. The love that dares not speak its name: From secrecy to openness in gay and lesbian affiliations. In *Secrets in families and family therapy,* E. Imber-Black, ed. New York: Norton.

Satir, V. 1972. *Peoplemaking.* Palo Alto, CA: Science and Behavior Books.

Scharff, D., and Scharff, J. 1987. *Object relations family therapy.* New York: Jason Aronson.

Schwartz, R. C. 1987. Our multiple selves. *Family Therapy Networker. 11:*23–31, 80–83.

Schwartz, R. C. 1992. Rescuing the exiles. *Family Therapy Networker. 16:*33–37, 75.

Schwartz, R. C. 1993. Constructionism, sex abuse, and the self. *American Family Therapy Academy Newsletter.* Winter, 6–10.

Schwartz, R. C. 1995. *Internal family systems therapy.* New York: Guilford Press.

Schwartz, R. C., Barrett, M. J., and Saba, G. 1985. Family therapy for bulimia. In *Handbook for the psychotherapy of anorexia nervosa and bulimia,* D. Garner and P. Garfinkel, eds. New York: Guilford Press.

Schwartz, R. C., and Breunlin, D. C. 1983. Research: Why clinicians should bother with it. *Family Therapy Networker. 7:*22–27, 57–59.

Schwartz, R. C., and Perrotta, P. 1985. Let us sell no intervention before its time. *Family Therapy Networker.* July–August, 18–25.

Schwartzman, J. 1985. *Families and other systems: The macrosystemic context of family therapy.* New York: Guilford Press.

Seligman, M., and Darling, R. B. 1996. *Ordinary families, special children: A systems approach to childhood disability, 2nd ed.* New York: Guilford Press.

Selvini Palazzoli, M., Boscolo, L., Cecchin, G., and Prata, G. 1978. *Paradox and counterparadox.* New York: Jason Aronson.

Serra, P. 1993. Physical violence in the couple relationship: A contribution toward the analysis of the context. *Family Process. 32:*21–34.

Sheinberg, M. 1992. Navigating treatment impasses at the disclosure of incest: Combining ideas from feminism and social constructionism. *Family Process. 31:*201–216.

Simon, R. 1986. An interview with Cloe Madanes. *The Family Therapy Networker. 10*(5):64–65.

Simon, R. 1987. Good-bye paradox, hello invariant prescription: An interview with Mara Selvini Palazzoli. *Family Therapy Networker. 11*(5):16–33.

Slipp, S. 1984. *Object relations: A dynamic bridge between individual and family treatment.* New York: Jason Aronson.

Smith, H. 1989. *Beyond the post-modern mind.* Wheaton, IL: Theosophical Publishing House.

Sprenkle, D. 1985. *Divorce therapy.* New York: Haworth Press.

Stanton, M. D. 1981. Strategic approaches to family therapy. In *Handbook of Family Therapy,* A. Gurman and D. Kniskern, eds. New York: Bruner/Mazel.

Stanton, M. D., Todd, T., and Associates. 1982. *The family therapy of drug abuse and addiction.* New York: Guilford Press.

Steinglass, P., Bennett, L., Wolin, S. J., and Reiss, D. 1987. *The alcoholic family.* New York: Basic Books.

Szapocznik, J., and Kurtines, W. M. 1989. *Breakthroughs in family therapy with drug abusing and problem youth.* New York: Springer.

Taggert, M. 1989. Epistemological equality as the fulfillment of family therapy. In *Women in families: A framework for family therapy,* M. McGoldrick, C. Anderson, and F. Walsh, eds. New York: Norton.

Tolan, P. H., Cromwell, R. E., and Brasswell, M. 1986. Family therapy with delinquents: A critical review of the literature. *Family Process. 25:*619–649.

Treadway, D. 1989. *Before it's too late: Working with substance abuse in the family.* New York: Norton.

Trepper, T. S., and Barrett, M. J. 1989. *Systemic treatment of incest: A therapeutic handbook.* New York: Brunner/Mazel.

Vaughn, C., and Leff, J. 1976. The measurement of expressed emotion in the families of psychiatric patients. *British Journal of Psychology.* 15:157–165.

Vaughn, C. E., Snyder, K. S., Jones, S., Freeman, W. B., & Falloon, I. R. H. 1984. Family factors in schizophrenic relapse: Replication in California of British research on expressed emotion. *Archives of General Psychiatry.* 41:1169–1177.

Visher, E., and Visher, J. 1979. *Stepfamilies: A guide to working with stepparents and stepchildren.* New York: Brunner/Mazel.

Visher, E., and Visher, J. 1988. *Old loyalties, new ties: Therapeutic strategies with stepfamilies.* New York: Brunner/Mazel.

von Foerster, H. 1981. *Observing systems.* Seaside, CA: Intersystems Publications.

von Glaserfeld, H. 1984. An introduction to radical constructivism. In *The invented reality,* P. Watzlawick, ed. New York: Norton.

Wachtel, E. 1994. *Treating troubled children and their families.* New York: Guilford Press.

Wachtel, E. F., and Wachtel, P. L. 1986. *Family dynamics in individual psychotherapy: A guide to clinical strategies.* New York: Guilford Press.

Walker, G. 1991. *In the midst of winter: Systemic therapy with families, couples, and individuals with AIDS infection.* New York: Norton.

Wallerstein, J., and Kelly J. 1980. *Surviving the breakup: How children and parents cope with divorce.* New York: Basic Books.

Walsh, F. 1982. *Normal family processes.* New York: Guilford Press.

Walsh, F. 1993. *Normal family processes,* 2nd ed. New York: Guilford Press.

Walsh, F., and McGoldrick, M. eds. 1991. *Living beyond loss: Death in the family.* New York: Norton.

Walters, M., Carter, B., Papp, P., and Silverstein, O. 1988. *The invisible web: Gender patterns in family relationships.* New York: Guilford Press.

Watzlawick, P., ed. 1984. *The invented reality.* New York: Norton.

Wegscheider-Cruse, S. 1985. *Choicemaking: For codependents, adult children and spirituality seekers.* Pompano Beach, FL: Health Communications.

White, M. 1989. *Selected papers.* Adelaide, Australia: Dulwich Center Publications.

Winderman, L. 1989. Generation of human meaning key to Galveston Paradigm: An interview with Harlene Anderson and Harold Goolishian. *Family Therapy News. 20*(6):11–12.

Wylie, M. S. 1992. The evolution of a revolution. *Family Therapy Networker.* 16:16–29, 98–99.

Zilbach, J. 1986. *Young children in family therapy.* New York: Brunner/Mazel.

11

From Strategic to Solution-Focused: The Evolution of Brief Therapy

In this chapter we trace the lineage of strategic to solution-focused therapy. While the models that emerged during this evolution differ substantially in concepts and methods, they share a belief that (1) therapy should be brief, (2) people are not pathological, and (3) clients can change rapidly. We will describe three of these models—the approach of the *Mental Research Institute* (MRI model), the *strategic therapy* of Jay Haley and Cloe Madanes, and the *Milan systemic school*—in the first section of this chapter and reserve the second section for the currently popular *solution-focused approach.*

The MRI, Strategic, and Milan Systemic Models

The strategic and systemic schools applied Gregory Bateson's ideas directly to family treatment, resulting in a set of creative ways to generate change and outwit resistance in families seen as cybernetic systems. The power and cleverness of these methods captured the imagination of the field during the 1970s and early 1980s. But in the 1990s, as family therapy rejected the model of therapist-as-expert-manipulator in favor of therapist-as-collaborator, these models fell out of favor. As we shall see, however, these approaches contain elements of sophisticated understanding of family complexities and powerful techniques that may be getting lost in our rush to embrace a kinder, gentler version of family therapy.

Sketches of Leading Figures

Among the leading strategic family therapists are Jay Haley, currently living in La Jolla, California; Cloe Madanes, in Washington, DC; and members of the MRI in Palo Alto, including Paul Watzlawick, Richard Fisch, and the late John Weakland.

Haley's development is unique among family therapists in that he studied with the three people who had the greatest influence on the evolution of family therapy: Gregory Bateson, Milton Erickson, and Salvador Minuchin. The impact of each of these pioneers is apparent in Haley's model, which, more than any other in this chapter, integrated divergent trends as family therapy developed.

In 1967 Haley left MRI to join Minuchin and Braulio Montalvo at the Philadelphia Child Guidance Clinic. For approximately ten years he was director of family therapy research there, as well as a clinical member of the University of Pennsylvania's Department of Psychiatry. His association with Minuchin was productive for both men. Minuchin credits Haley with helping him articulate many of the principles elaborated in *Families and Family Therapy* (Minuchin, 1974), and Haley gives Minuchin credit for helping him understand the structure of families. Since Haley's first description of his approach in *Problem-Solving Therapy* (Haley, 1976), he has used the structural view of family organization as the context within which to apply his strategic techniques. Haley's example may serve to help bridge the gap between other competing approaches in the field.

In the early 1970s Haley left Philadelphia for Washington, DC, to establish his own family therapy clinic with Cloe Madanes. Madanes, known as one of the most creative therapists in the field, started at MRI in 1966 as a research assistant. In 1971 she was hired as a supervisor at the Philadelphia Child Guidance Clinic, where she worked with Haley, Minuchin, and Montalvo. In 1974, Haley and Madanes opened the Family Therapy Institute of Washington, DC, which is now one of the major training institutes in the country, although Haley has recently retired.

Haley and Madanes are such towering figures in family therapy that their names often overshadow those who follow in their footsteps. At the Washington School, James Keim is ably carrying on the Haley–Madanes tradition. Other prominent students of this model include Jerome Price in Michigan, who specializes in working with difficult adolescents, and Pat Dorgan, who combines strategic therapy with a community mental health model in Gloucester, Virginia.

The MRI led the way in research and training in family therapy's first decade. MRI was established in 1959 when its founding director, Don Jackson, who was a consultant to the Bateson project, assembled an energetic and creative staff interested in communication, therapy, families, and schizophrenia. Among them were Jules Riskin, Virginia Satir, Jay Haley, John Weakland, Paul Watzlawick, Arthur Bodin, and Janet Beavin. Haley and Weakland brought to MRI both the exciting cybernetic ideas of Bateson and the revolutionary clinical ideas of Milton Erickson.

This group started one of the first formal training programs in family therapy, conducted some of the first family interaction research, and made several of the most important early contributions to the family therapy literature, including Satir's (1964) *Conjoint Family Therapy*, Watzlawick, Beavin, and Jackson's (1967) *Pragmatics of Human Communication*, and Haley's (1963) *Strategies of Psychotherapy*.

Later, MRI was also home to several other influential strategic writers, including Carlos Sluzki, its director for several years and editor of *Family Process* through much of the 1980s; James Coyne, who used the model to understand and treat depression; and Steve de Shazer, who expanded on the original MRI model to create his solution-focused approach, described in the second section of this chapter.

In 1967 the Brief Therapy Center of MRI opened under the directorship of Richard Fisch. The staff included John Weakland, Paul Watzlawick, and Arthur Bodin. Their mission was to develop the briefest possible treatment for psychiatric disorders. What emerged was an active approach, focused on the presenting symptoms, and limited to ten sessions. This approach, known as the MRI model, was described in Watzlawick, Weakland, and Fisch's (1974) book, *Change: Principles of Problem Formation and Problem Resolution*, which popularized strategic therapy, and later in a follow-up volume, *The Tactics of Change: Doing Therapy Briefly* (Fisch, Weakland, & Segal, 1982).

The MRI group and the whole field suffered a painful loss in 1995 when John Weakland died of Lou Gehrig's disease. He was a quiet man, never pushy, always thoughtful, always inventive; and he never gave up. He will be missed.

The MRI model and Haley's work had a major impact on the Milan Associates, Mara Selvini Palazzoli, Luigi Boscolo, Gianfranco Cecchin, and Guiliana Prata.

Selvini Palazzoli was a prominent Italian psychoanalyst, specializing in eating disorders, when, out of frustration with the results of her individual orientation (Selvini Palazzoli, 1981) she discovered the writings of many of the theorists mentioned above and began to develop her own approach to families. In 1967 she led a group of eight psychiatrists who originally tried to apply psychoanalytic ideas to working with families. Later they turned to the ideas of Bateson, Haley, and Watzlawick, which, in 1971, led the systemic faction of the group (Selvini Palazzoli, Boscolo, Cecchin, and Prata) to form the Center for the Study of the Family in Milan, where they developed the "Milan model."

In 1980 the Milan Associates underwent another split, with Boscolo and Cecchin moving in the direction of training and Selvini Palazzoli and Prata more interested in research. Each group formed separate centers with new staffs, and their approaches also diverged, the women pursuing their interest in understanding and interrupting the destructive games they believe severely disturbed families are caught up in, and the men becoming increasingly less strategic and more interested in changing family belief systems through a process of asking questions. This shift away from interaction patterns and toward belief systems paved the way for the solution-focused and narrative approaches that have dominated the 1990s.

In addition to these primary developers of the MRI, strategic, and Milan models, other people have also contributed. Lynn Hoffman's evolution as a therapist parallels that of the strategic-systemic branch of family therapy. In the 1960s she collaborated with Haley and, in 1977, joined the Ackerman Institute in New York, where she experimented with strategic approaches and later became a major proponent of the Milan model in the United States (Hoffman, 1981). Subsequently, she left Ackerman for Amherst, Massachusetts, and left the Milan model for a "second-order" approach based on social constructionist, narrative principles (see Chapter 12).

The Ackerman Institute has been an incubator for both the strategic and Milan models. Prominent contributors from the Ackerman faculty include Peggy Papp (1980, 1983), who has been a creative force in the strategic school; Joel Bergman (1985), who developed many original strategies for dealing with difficult families; Peggy Penn (1982, 1985), who elaborated on the Milan innovation of circular questioning; and Olga Siverstein, who is known for her clinical artistry.

Karl Tomm (1984a, 1984b, 1987a, 1987b), a psychiatrist in Calgary, Canada, had been the most prominent interpreter and elaborator of the Milan model in North America, but recently, with the influence of Michael White's work (see Chapter 12), has been developing his own ideas about the impact of the therapist on families.

Joseph Eron and Thomas Lund (1993, 1996), in Kingston, New York, have tried to bring strategic therapy up to date by integrating it with narrative approaches, based on constructionist principles.

Finally, Richard Rabkin (1977), a literate and eclectic social psychiatrist practicing in New York City, was influenced by and influenced all the developers of strategic therapy.

Theoretical Formulations

Strategic therapists are more interested in changing behavior than in understanding; consequently, they write more about technique than theory. The hallmark of strategic therapy is designing novel strategies for solving problems. Like most clinicians, their theories are simpler and more pragmatic than those of scholars and academicians. Haley has often remarked that clinicians need simple maps to guide their action, while researchers can entertain complex ones because they have the luxury of not having to change things.

Because Milton Erickson's work had such an impact on the strategic theorists, we will present first the aspects of Ericksonian theory that were incorporated into their formulations. Erickson boldly broke with the prevailing psychiatric traditions of his time. Unlike psychoanalysts, who held that symptoms shouldn't be attacked directly because they were only the tip of the intrapsychic iceberg, Erickson was highly symptom- or problem-focused. He sought to discover details regarding the impact and context of symptoms in order to find leverage for changing them (Haley, 1981).

Rather than viewing the unconscious mind as a seething caldron of dangerous and aggressive impulses, Erickson saw it as a source of wisdom and creativity that, if unfettered by conscious inhibition, could solve problems and heal symptoms. Thus he found little value in traditional attempts to foster insight through interpretation, or in historical fishing expeditions, because the conscious minds of therapist and client were doing the interpreting and the fishing. He assumed that deep down clients knew what to do; they just didn't have access to that wisdom. One way to get access was to break out of habitual patterns of behavior and thinking, so Erickson developed a host of clever ways of getting people to simply do something different in the context of the old behavior, or to do the old behavior in a new context.

At a time when therapy was considered a laborious, multiyear proposition, Erickson's experience as a hypnotherapist convinced him that people could change quickly, and he tried to make therapy as brief as possible. He also took responsibility for the outcome. Failures weren't explained away as being due to "resistance"; Erickson saw his job as finding ways to bypass or use resistance. Many of what have been called paradoxical techniques came out of Erickson's application of hypnotic principles to turn resistance to advantage (Haley, 1981). For example, to induce trance, a hypnotherapist learns not to point out that a client is fighting going under but, instead, might tell the client to keep his or her eyes open until they become unbearably heavy.

Through Haley and Weakland's translations of Erickson's work, these assumptions about rapid change and utilization of resistance became cornerstones of strategic family therapy. These radical ideas about the nature of therapy and change were combined with the cybernetic concepts that Bateson introduced to the remarkable group of theorist–clinicians who were in Palo Alto during the late 1950s and 1960s.

From cybernetics, strategic theorists borrowed the concept of the *positive feedback loop* and applied it to problematic family interaction. For the MRI group, that translated into a simple yet powerful principle of problem formation:

Families encounter many difficulties over the course of their lives, but whether a difficulty becomes a "problem" (that needs intervention) depends on how family members respond to it (Watzlawick, Weakland, & Fisch, 1974). That is, families often make commonsensical but misguided attempts to solve their difficulties and, on finding that the problem persists or gets worse, apply more-of-the-same attempted solutions. This only produces an escalation of the problem, which provokes more of the same, and so on—in a vicious cycle.

For example, Johnny feels threatened by the arrival of his baby sister and so he becomes temperamental. His father thinks he is being defiant and self-centered and tries to get him to act his age by punishing and criticizing him. Father's harshness confirms Johnny's belief that his parents love his sister more than him, so he acts even younger. Father, in turn, becomes more critical and punitive, and Johnny becomes increasingly sullen and alienated from the family. This is an escalating positive feedback loop: The family system is reacting to a deviation in the behavior of one of its members with feedback designed to dampen that deviation (*negative feedback*), but it actually has the effect of amplifying the deviation (*positive feedback*).

What's needed is to get father to reverse his attempted solution. If he could comfort rather than criticize Johnny and help him see that he isn't being displaced, then Johnny would calm down. The system is governed, however, by unspoken rules that allow for only one interpretation of Johnny's behavior—as being disrespectful. For father to reverse his attempted solution, this rule would have to change.

Thus, MRI theorists, Don Jackson in particular, also borrowed from cybernetics an interest in *family rules*—underlying premises that govern the operation of systems. A thermostat, as an example of a cybernetic system, has settings (rules) that govern the range of deviation the system will tolerate before negative feedback in the form of heating or air conditioning is activated. In most families, there are unspoken rules governing all sorts of behavior, most of which serve them well. Where a rule promotes the kind of rigid attempted solutions described above, it isn't just the behavior (father's critical discipline), but the rule governing that behavior (father's *interpretation* of Johnny's behavior) that must change. When only behavior or interactions within a system change, this is *first-order change*, as opposed to *second-order change*, which occurs when the rules of the system that govern those interactions change (Watzlawick et al., 1974). How does one change the rules? One way that the MRI group emphasized is the technique of *reframing*—that is, changing father's interpretation of Johnny's behavior from disrespect to fear of displacement, from bad to sad.

Thus, the MRI approach to problems is quite simple: first, identify the more-of-the-same, positive feedback loops that maintain problems; second, determine the rules (or frames) that support those interactions; and third, find a way to change those rules. Their interest, then, is limited to problem-centered, short-term sequences of interaction; they don't look beyond these sequences at other potential problems in a family, unless the family identifies them as problems. With this minimalistic ethic, the MRI group, unlike Haley or the Milan team, doesn't speculate about the function a family member's symptoms may be serving for the family or about problematic family boundaries or coalitions.

Haley, on the other hand, added a functionalist emphasis to the Ericksonian and cybernetic influences, with his interest in the interpersonal and system-wide payoff of behavior. Later, he added many structural concepts picked up in the years he spent working with Minuchin in Philadelphia. Haley lengthened the duration of sequences he considered important in understanding problems from those immediately surrounding a problem, often involving only two people, to sequences involving at least three people and lasting longer periods of time. For example, Haley might notice that whenever

Johnny and his father fight, mother protects Johnny by criticizing father for being so harsh. He might also see Johnny becoming more agitated when mother criticizes father, trying to get his parents' attention off their conflicts and onto him.

From this interest in larger and longer sequences, Haley also considers a different level of rules that govern them. He believes that the rules around the *hierarchy* in the family are crucial and finds a malfunctioning family hierarchy lurking behind most problems. Indeed, Haley (1976) suggests that, "an individual is more disturbed in direct proportion to the number of malfunctioning hierarchies in which he is embedded" (p. 117). It may be obvious that Johnny's parents don't work together effectively to discipline and nurture Johnny, and so Johnny is embedded in one malfunctioning hierarchy, but it might also be the case that Johnny's grandparents undermine his father too. In this case, two generational boundaries would be violated.

Haley (1980) also identifies long-term sequences within families of troubled young adults. In these sequences, which might take place over months or years, the parents start to argue, which distresses the young adult to the point that he or she becomes symptomatic; the parents unite to try to deal with the strange symptoms and, perhaps, hospitalize the now identified patient; the patient gets better in the hospital and begins to take steps toward autonomy; without being able to focus on the patient, the parents are distressed and begin to argue; so the patient's symptoms return; and so on and on. The rule governing this disabling sequence is that the parents' marriage can't survive if they are left alone to face each other. Haley tried to change this rule by showing parents that if they work together they can control and help their troubled child. The good feeling produced by successfully improving the family hierarchy sets the stage for challenging their belief that they can't face the differences between them.

Thus, Haley's assessment and his goals are structural: to improve the family's hierarchy and boundary problems that support dysfunctional sequences. It's his calculated approach and step-by-step tactics that are strategic.

Along these lines, the book *Problem-Solving Therapy* contains one of Haley's (1976) unique contributions: the idea that families change in stages, some of which may be less than ideal, before reaching a healthy structure—much as a broken arm must remain in a cast for a period of time and then be exercised before it can heal. For example, Haley might suggest that before Johnny's parents feel good about each other and work together to deal with him, the family may have to go through a stage in which father and son get closer and exclude mother from their relationship. Or the parents may need to go through a stage in which they work only on cooperating on discipline, putting aside their marital resentments, before reaching a stage in which they can address those issues.

Haley's approach could be called "plan-ahead therapy." He helped therapists consider the importance of developing strategies for the overall course of therapy, as well as anticipating a family's reaction to events in their lives, and in therapy. He also encouraged the planning of each session and developed a how-to model of a first session with families that consisted of several stages (Haley, 1976).

Finally, Haley differed from his MRI colleagues, who tried to avoid imputing motives to the behavior they observed, because he viewed human interactions as interpersonal struggles for control and power. He kept a functionalist eye on family patterns, looking for the purpose problems might serve for the individual or for the family. To counter the problem's payoff, he often borrowed Erickson's technique of prescribing ordeals so that the price for keeping a problem outweighed that of giving it up. To illustrate this technique, consider Erickson's famous maneuver of prescribing that an insomniac set his alarm every night to wake up and wax his kitchen floor for several hours. Haley tried to explain all therapy as based on ordeals, suggesting people will change to avoid the many ordeals inherent in being a client (Haley, 1984).

Cloe Madanes (1981, 1984) also emphasized this function-of-the-symptom aspect of problems, particularly the *incongruous hierarchy* created when children use their symptoms to try to change their parents. For example, when a daughter sees her mother looking depressed, the daughter can provoke a fight which prods the mother from being sad and helpless to acting strong and competent. Much of Madanes's approach involved finding creative ways for symptomatic children to help their parents openly and directly so that they wouldn't have to resort to symptoms as the only way to help their parents.

Madanes's (1990) later formulations became more elaborate. As an overview, she stated, "All problems brought to therapy can be thought of as stemming from the dilemma between love and violence" (p. 5), and she described strategies for transforming violence into love. She categorized family problems according to four basic intentions of the family members involved. First is the desire to *dominate and control*, and Madanes sees symptoms like delinquency and behavioral problems as related to this kind of motivation. The second intention is *to be loved*, and she associates psychosomatic symptoms, depression, anxiety, and eating disorders with this motive. The third desire is *to love and protect others;* related symptoms include suicide threats, abuse and neglect, obsessions, and thought disorders. The final category of intention is *to repent and forgive*, and she finds that these families have problems like incest, sexual abuse, and sadistic acts.

For each of these categories of families, Madanes recommends certain strategies for helping them change. For example, for the first category of domination and control, she suggests that therapists get parents to work together to take charge of their problem children, whereas if the problem were more related to the third category, love and protection, the children might be asked to find a different way to protect or care for their parents. In generating these guidelines, Madanes offered a more comprehensive framework for using strategic interventions than was previously available.

Mara Selvini Palazzoli and her associates in Milan (1978b) had read the work of Bateson, the MRI group, and Haley, and were working with families of schizophrenic and anorexic patients. Like Haley, they focused on the power-game aspect of family interaction and, similarly, on the protective function symptoms served for the whole family. The Milan Associates (Selvini Palazzoli, Gianfranco Cecchin, Luigi Boscolo, and Guiliana Prata) extended the length of family sequences considered in their assessments beyond the months-long sequences that Haley (1980) described in *Leaving Home.* They interviewed families about their history, sometimes over several generations, searching for evidence to confirm their hypotheses about how the children's symptoms came to be necessary. These hypotheses often involved elaborate networks of covert family alliances and coalitions, including extended family. They usually concluded that the patient developed symptoms to protect one or more other family members so as to maintain the delicate network of family alliances.

While the various strategic models had some theoretical elements in common, each model covered a different range of family phenomena and focused on a different length of family sequence (Breunlin & Schwartz, 1986). The MRI model focused exclusively on the brief, more-of-the-same, interactions surrounding the problem and had little concern for structural formulations. Haley included those short sequences but was also interested in longer ones that lasted months or years and reflected chronic structural problems. The Milan Associates were interested in some of those longer sequences but also in the way that families evolved over generations, which led to the network of alliances that necessitated symptoms.

Normal Family Development

The MRI group was vehemently opposed to setting up standards of normality and instead adopted what they called a "non-normative" stance. "By non-normative, we mean that we use no criteria to judge the health or normality of an individual or family. As therapists, we do not regard any particular way of functioning, relating, or living as a problem if the client is not expressing discontent with it" (Fisch, 1978). Thus, by limiting their task to eliminating problems presented to them, the MRI group avoided taking any position regarding how families *should* behave. This relativism has deep roots. As early as 1967, Don Jackson wrote an essay called "The Myth of Normality" in which he argued that because there is no one model of health or normality, it's a mistake to impose one on clients.

Despite their rejection of normative goals, it's clear that MRI therapists believe that healthy families are flexible enough to modify attempted solutions that don't work. This flexibility is needed not only with everyday difficulties but also to navigate transitional points in the family's development (Weakland et al., 1974). In addition, it's implied that successful families don't overreact or underreact to difficulties, and avoid the kind of utopian thinking that makes people try to fix things that don't need fixing—like the "generation gap."

The Milan Associates also adopted a non-normative stance (Selvini Palazzoli et al., 1978). Their hypotheses about systems of relationships that maintained problems usually involved any number of covert, cross-generational alliances, so one could infer that they believed families should have clear generational boundaries. (Normality isn't the converse of abnormality, however, so one can't always make that extrapolation.)

They also strove to maintain an attitude of "neutrality" (Selvini Palazzoli et al., 1980), later known as "curiosity" (Cecchin, 1987) regarding families. Therapists who adopt this attitude don't apply preconceived goals or normative models for their client families. Instead, by raising questions that help a family examine itself and that expose hidden power games, they trust that the family will reorganize on its own in a better way, even if that way doesn't conform to some normative map.

In contrast to the relativism of these other two approaches, Haley's thinking about families *was* based on assumptions about normal (or at least functional) family functioning. His therapy was designed to help families reorganize dysfunctional structures into what he considered to be functional ones (Haley, 1976). The normative map that he used in this endeavor is similar to the one that Minuchin and the structuralists used, with its clear generational boundaries and hierarchy (see Chapter 8). But while Haley emphasized the vertical elements of structure—who was up and who was down in the family's power hierarchy—Minuchin highlighted the horizontal aspects. Minuchin's concepts of enmeshment and disengagement emphasized how close or distant family members were from each other, and how their relative proximity affected the course of problems. Therapists trained by Haley and Madanes focused on confusions or incongruities in authority and were taught to notice times when a parent or grandparent sided with a child after another parent attempted to enforce discipline. Haley (1973) also emphasized the impact of life cycle stages on a family's structure, most famously, of course, the leaving home stage.

Development of Behavior Disorders

In strategic and systemic models there are three basic explanations for the way problems develop. The first is cybernetic: Difficulties are turned into chronic problems by the persistence of misguided attempted solutions, forming positive feedback escalations (Watzlawick et al., 1974). The second is structural: Problems are the result of flaws in a family's hierarchy or boundaries. The third is functional: Problems result when people try to protect or control one another indirectly, such that their problems come to serve a function for the system. The MRI group limited itself to the first explanation, while the other strategic and systemic models embraced all three, although each model emphasized one explanation over the others.

To clarify these differences, consider the following example: sixteen-year-old Tommy recently began refusing to leave the house. An MRI therapist might ask his parents about how they had been trying to get him to venture out. This therapist would focus on the parents' attempted solutions, believing that these were maintaining Tommy's refusal, and on the parents' explanation or "frame" for Tommy's behavior, believing that the parents' frame for Tommy's problem may be maintaining their attempted solutions.

A Haley-style strategic therapist might be interested in the parents' attempted solutions but would also search for information about the parents' marriage, the ways in which Tommy was involved in struggles between his parents or other family members, or the protective nature of Tommy's problem. This therapist would be acting on the assumption that Tommy's behavior was part of a sequence in a dysfunctional triangle consisting of mother, father, and Tommy, that was maintaining Tommy's symptoms. This therapist might further assume that this triangular sequence was fueled by unresolved conflicts between the parents. A Madanes-style strategic therapist might also be interested in this triangle but, in addition, would be curious about how Tommy's behavior might be protecting one or the other parent from having to face some threatening issue. This protecting would be seen as the problem-maintaining dynamic.

A Milan-style, systemic therapist wouldn't focus so much on attempted solutions but, instead, would ask questions about a variety of past and present relationships in the family. In so doing, the Milan therapist would be trying to uncover an elaborate network of power alliances, often running across generations, that constituted the family's "game." Such a game left Tommy in the position of having to use his symptoms to protect another family member or to help that member win. Through this process the family might disclose, for example, that if Tommy were to grow up and leave home, mother would be sucked back into a power struggle between her parents, which she had avoided only by having a child on whom to focus. Also, by not succeeding in life, Tommy might be protecting his father from the shame of having a child who exceeded him in accomplishment, just as he had done with his father.

From the above discussion we can see that, while all of these approaches view problems as embedded in interactional sequences among family members, they differ in terms of the number of family members included and the duration of the sequences in which they are interested, beginning with the MRI model, in which the focus is on short, present-day sequences involving only a few family members, and ending with the Milan model, which examines long-term, historical sequences involving many family members. Haley and Madanes fall between these two positions, taking into account both short and longer sequences, and involving at least three family members.

Goals of Therapy

For all strategic and systemic therapies, the primary goal is the resolution of the presenting problem. They differ considerably, however, on how best to achieve this goal, how much must happen for improvement in the problem to last, and how much responsibility the therapist should take for creating these changes.

The MRI group is proudly minimalistic. Once the presenting problem is resolved, therapy is concluded. Even where other problems are apparent to the therapist, if the family doesn't ask for help with those problems, they aren't targeted. MRI therapists justify this minimalist position by asserting that, because they view people who have problems as stuck rather than sick, their job is simply to help people get unstuck and moving again, not to overhaul their personalities or family structures.

They disdain more open-ended forms of family therapy in which the goals are less clear. Fisch and colleagues (1973) wrote sarcastically of such therapies: "By no means should the therapist encourage any discussion about concrete goals of treatment, since the family would then know when to stop treatment" (p. 601). MRI therapists pride themselves on helping families define clear and reachable goals so that everyone knows when and how successfully treatment has concluded. They often find that much of the therapy takes place simply in the process of pushing clients to set such clear, behavioral goals, because in doing so clients are forced to clarify vague ambitions and dissatisfactions. Also, in getting clients to define achievable goals, MRI therapists help people let go of the utopian goals with which they often enter therapy and thereby diminish frustration and hopelessness.

Like behaviorism, which dominated psychology at the time the MRI approach was developed, the MRI model is behavioral in both its goals and its primary assessment of observable patterns of interaction, preferring not to speculate about intrapsychic states or intentions. In trying to achieve the larger goal of problem-resolution, the immediate goal is to change people's behavioral responses to their problems. More specifically, as described earlier, MRI therapists try to interrupt (often to reverse) more-of-the-same vicious feedback loops. To achieve this behavioral change they may try to "reframe the problem," and, in that sense, aren't strictly behavioral. But any cognitive change still is in the service of the primary goal of behavior change.

In response to the perception that strategic therapists ignore emotions, Trudy Kleckner and her colleagues (1992) suggested that,

> It's not that strategic therapist's don't deal with feelings—it's just that they don't talk about it with each other, write about it in the literature, or teach it to trainees . . . strategic therapists do not spend significant amounts of time merely talking about feelings or getting clients to recognize and own feelings; they concentrate instead on getting clients to express their feelings in ways that are more likely to lead to client satisfaction in daily life. (p. 49)

Again, the emphasis is on using the expression of emotion pragmatically, in the service of changing behavioral interactions.

Haley's approach is also quite behavioral and, even more than the MRI group, minimizes the importance of insight or awareness. He has always been scornful of therapies that helped clients understand why they did things but did little to get them to do something different.

Haley's ultimate goal often is a structural reorganization of the family, particularly its hierarchy and generational boundaries, but since he approaches therapy in stages, he has intermediate goals along the way. Unlike structural family therapy, however, all of these structural goals are directly connected to the presenting problem. For example, to improve the relationship between the polarized parents of a rebellious teenager, a structural family therapist might get the parents to talk to each other about their marital issues, whereas Haley would have them talk about their difficulty working together to deal with their rebellious son. Only after the problems with their son had improved would Haley allow their discussion to shift to the marriage.

Unlike the MRI group, who focused exclusively on the presenting problem because that was all they wanted to change, Haley's problem-focus was a strategy. He shared the strategic therapists' commitment to avoid dealing directly with client resistance. He found that if therapists make the presenting problem the center of their interventions, a family's motivation to change the problem will keep them engaged even while they change their structure.

To continue contrasting structural and strategic, structural therapists don't shy from and sometimes deliberately provoke conflict in sessions, and they rely on their personal relationship with each family member to keep them engaged. Strategic therapists rely on strategies rather than on their personalities to minimize resistance or conflict while people change. One of these strategies is to focus on the problem until it's resolved and then explore other, often more threatening, family issues, after the family has more trust in the therapist and in each other because of their previous success. Unlike the MRI group, Haley doesn't necessarily believe that therapy should end with the resolution of the presenting problem, but instead should continue until the structural problems that produced it are resolved.

Haley's inclination to divide therapy into stages extended to specific sessions. Haley (1976) recommended that therapists follow a clear first session format that included several stages: a social stage in which the goal is to make the family feel comfortable, a stage in which the problem is defined and family members' opinions about it are solicited, and a stage in which family members interact about the problem.

Haley's interest in stages and his systematic approach reflect the strategic therapist's ethic that responsibility for change rests with the therapist rather than with the client. Strategic therapists believe that therapists shouldn't blame treatment failures on their clients' lack of readiness but rather should find ways to motivate them. With this conviction comes the responsibility on strategic theorists like Haley to develop and clearly describe specialized techniques for all kinds of problems or resistances, as well as the steps and stages of therapy. Thus, the writing of strategic therapists tends to be short on theory and long on technique.

Madanes (1990) expanded the goals of strategic therapy well beyond the problem-focused or even the structural goals to include growth-oriented objectives like balance, harmony, and love. She stated that, "A goal of therapy is to bring harmony and balance into people's lives. To love and to be loved, to find fulfillment in work, to play and enjoy: All are part of a necessary balance" (p. 13). Despite the fact that her practice of therapy is still strategic, this is a big departure from the standard goals of strategic therapy and brings Madanes closer to people like Satir and other experientalists. Indeed, the name of her therapy has shifted to "strategic humanism" to emphasize its softer aspects.

It's in this area of goals of and responsibility for therapy that strategic and systemic therapies eventually diverged. The early work of the Milan group (Selvini Palazzoli, Boscolo, Cecchin, & Prata, 1978b) was heavily influenced by the MRI and Haley models. The Milan Associates, as described above, expanded the network of people involved in maintaining the problem, but were still primarily interested in finding powerful techniques to interrupt family games. The techniques they developed differed from those of the strategic schools in that they were less behavioral and instead were designed to expose games and reframe motives for strange behavior. Thus, while being less problem-focused and more interested in changing a family's awareness or beliefs than strategic therapists, the original Milan approach was no less manipulative: The responsibility for change rested on the therapist whose job it was to outwit resistance.

When the Milan Associates split into two groups in the early 1980s, this strategic emphasis remained with Selvini Palazzoli and the group she subsequently formed. However, she took a low profile during the 1980s while she researched her hypotheses and developed a new strategic approach (Selvini Palazzoli, 1986). The goal of that therapy was to disrupt and expose the "dirty games" that severely disturbed family members play with each other. Later, she abandoned brief, strategic models altogether and now does long-term therapy with more focus on insight for the individual patient (Selvini, 1993).

After the breakup, Luigi Boscolo and Gianfranco Cecchin moved in a different direction, away from strategically manipulating families and toward collaborating with them to form systemic hypotheses about their problems. For this branch of the Milan group, therapy became more of a research expedition that the therapist entered without specific goals or strategies, trusting that this process of self-examination would allow families to better choose to change rather than unconsciously continuing their patterns. The therapist was released from responsibility for any certain outcome and took an attitude of curiosity (Cecchin, 1987) toward families, rather than the interventive attitude of strategic therapists.

In moving in this direction, Boscolo and Cecchin took a position relative to therapist goals and attitudes directly opposite to that of their strategic predecessors. This collaborative philosophy became the bridge over which many other strategic and Milan therapists crossed into the narrative approaches of the 1990s.

Conditions for Behavior Change

As we've discussed, for the MRI strategic school the primary condition for resolving problems is to change the behavior associated with them. It's believed that through seeing the results of altering rigid behavioral responses, clients will become more flexible in their problem-solving strategies. When this happens, clients will achieve second-order change—a change in the rules governing their response to problems.

For example, Jill argues with her father about her curfew and her father grounds her. She then runs away and stays with a friend. A first-order intervention at this point might be to help Jill's father find a more effective punishment to tame this out-of-control child. A second-order strategic intervention might be to direct her father to act distracted and sad around his daughter and to imply to her that he has given up trying to control her. This shifts Jill from feeling trapped by father to feeling concerned about him, and she becomes more reasonable. Her father learns that when attempted solutions aren't working, try something different. This change is second-order in that it is a change in the rules governing the way father and daughter interact.

Clients may not need to be educated about their problems or require insight into why they have them or how they arose. Families may not need to reorganize their relationships—especially those not directly involved in the presenting problem. They may simply need to do something different, even if it goes against common sense, as did the strange advice given Jill's father. Second-order change often seems to arise out of apparently illogical solutions. This is because many logical or commonsense solutions have been tried by families before they come to treatment. What families don't need is more of the same. What they do need is flexibility.

Effective therapists must sometimes be able to convince clients to try something completely different. To achieve this, strategic therapists give directives that clients are to follow between sessions. To get clients to comply, since these directives often require behavior that is counterintuitive, therapists must be able to maximize motivation and minimize resistance.

Along these lines, MRI therapists try to find out who is the "customer" in the family, that is, who has the most motivation for things to change.[1] Often the customer isn't the person with the problem, and sometimes isn't even in the family. Frequently the therapist will work primarily, or even exclusively, with the customer, believing that it is most efficient to work with the most motivated person in the system, and that frequently the problem will clear up even if only one person in the system changes.

On many of these points, Haley would agree. Haley (1976) believed that telling people what they're doing wrong doesn't help them

[1]The concept of the "customer" for change was introduced by Steve de Shazer (1988).

change, it only mobilizes resistance. The same is true, Haley believed, of cathartic expression of feeling. He believed that changes in behavior alter feelings and perceptions, rather than the other way around. Madanes (1980) said "if a problem can be solved without the family's knowing how or why, that is satisfactory" (p. 79). It may seem curious, then, that Madanes, Haley, and the MRI group have relied heavily on the technique of reframing, in which the therapist tries to change the way clients perceive or understand their problems. The strategic theorist's response to this inconsistency is likely to be that reframing is in the service of behavior change, which is what really changes client perception or feeling. According to Haley, until people have a different experience with a problem, they won't be able to see it differently.

Over time, the Milan group turned this behaviorism on its head. From the beginning they were more interested in getting a family to *see* things differently (through a reframing technique called "positive connotation," to be discussed later) than in getting family members to *behave* differently. Increasingly, they (Boscolo and Cecchin, in particular) moved toward a meaning-changes-behavior position as they found that helping people examine the systemic evolution of their problems allowed them to relate differently. This led to a style of therapy that contained few directives and mostly involved asking questions designed to help family members reexamine their predicaments. This shift from behavior to meaning set the stage for the constructivist and narrative movements (See Chapter 12).

Techniques

Strategic therapy is the most technique-driven of all family therapies. Strategic therapists maintained Erickson's tradition of tailoring interventions to the particularities of person and problem. As a result, rather than presenting a general method that is to be adapted to different contexts, the strategic literature is full of unique interventions, customized to fit specific problems. For example, in surveying the strategic literature up to 1980, Duncan Stanton (1981) found references that describe interventions for over forty different syndromes or types of problems, covering everything imaginable, from adolescent problems to schizophrenia to thumb-sucking. The flow of problem-specific strategic interventions still hasn't slowed, even though fewer of these articles appear in mainstream family therapy journals. With the emergence of their own journal, the *Journal of Strategic and Systemic Therapies* (now called the *Journal of Systemic Therapies*), strategic and systemic writers, while no less productive, have become more insular and reach a smaller audience.

While this parade of articles and books describing customized techniques has continued since the basic strategic theory and techniques were described in the mid 1970s (most notable among these: Fisch, Weakland, & Segal, 1982; Papp, 1983; Coyne, 1987; Coyne, Kahn, & Gotlib, 1987; Haley, 1984; Madanes, 1984; Stanton, Todd, and Associates, 1982), there haven't been major (second-order) shifts in strategic concepts or methods since then. We will describe the basic methods of the MRI, Haley, and Milan models.

The MRI Approach. Members of the MRI's Brief Therapy Center follow a six-step treatment procedure:

1. Introduction to the treatment set-up
2. Inquiry and definition of the problem
3. Estimation of the behavior maintaining the problem
4. Setting goals for treatment
5. Selecting and making behavioral interventions
6. Termination

On arrival, clients fill out a form covering basic demographic data. Next, the therapist explains that sessions are recorded and observed, and points out the advantages of having several professionals involved in the case. The therapist also explains that treatment is conducted within a maximum of ten sessions, thereby setting up a powerful expectation of change.

Once the preliminaries are concluded, the therapist asks for a clear definition of the major problem. The MRI group believes that clients must be able to define a specific concrete problem for therapy to succeed. When the problem is stated in vague terms, such as "We just don't seem to get along," or in terms of presumptive causes, such as "Dad's job is making him depressed," the therapist helps translate it into a clear and concrete goal, asking questions like "What will be the first small sign that things are getting better?"

When the problem and goals are defined clearly and behaviorally, MRI therapists begin to ask about attempted solutions that may be maintaining the problem. For example, the husband who nags at his wife to spend more time with him may succeed only in driving her further away; the parents who criticize their son in an attempt to get him to quit fighting with his sister may perpetuate his sense that they like her better; or the husband who does everything his wife asks to reassure her of his love may feel so resentful that he begins to hate her.

In general, the solutions that tend to perpetuate problems fall into one of three categories:

1. The solution is simply to deny that a problem exists; action is necessary, but not taken. For instance, parents do nothing despite growing evidence that their teenage son is heavily involved with drugs.
2. The solution is an effort to solve something that isn't really a problem; action is taken when it shouldn't be. For example, parents punish a child for masturbating.
3. The solution is an effort to solve a problem within a framework that makes a solution impossible; action is taken, but at the wrong level. A husband, for instance, buys increasingly expensive gifts for his unhappy wife, when what she wants is affection (Watzlawick, Weakland, & Fisch, 1974).

These three classes of problem-maintaining attempted solutions imply therapeutic strategies. In the first, clients need to act; in the second, to stop acting; and in the third, to act in a different way. Once the therapist conceives of a strategy for changing the problem-maintaining sequences, clients must be convinced of the value of following this strategy. To sell their directives to clients, MRI therapists will reframe the problem (provide a new meaning for problem behaviors) to increase the likelihood of compliance. Thus, MRI reframes are different from psychodynamic interpretations in that the goal of a reframe isn't to produce insight or to educate, but simply to induce compliance. Traditionally, the MRI therapist wasn't constrained only to use reframes he or she believes to be true. These pragmatists felt free to use any plausible rationale that might bolster their directives. Thus a therapist might tell an angry, disengaged teen that when his father calls him worthless and locks him out of the house, it's the only way his father knows how to show love to him. This cavalier "anything goes" kind of reframing has been criticized as callous trickery (Flaskas, 1992). Many strategic therapists now pay closer attention to their clients' beliefs and try to be more sensitive in the way they construct and present their reframes.

> Believing in the absence of any absolute "truth" is not synonymous with ignoring or riding roughshod over the "subjective truths" of others. The usefulness of any "truths" used in the proposing of different frames for a client's or family's consideration rests primarily on how these frames are viewed from the subjective perspectives of those involved. . . . To do this helpfully and respectfully clearly means listening at all times with foreground levels of care and attention to what the family members are saying. (Cade & O'Hanlon, 1993, p. 116)

As we described earlier, in order to change problem-maintaining sequences, strategic therapists often try to get family members to do or believe things that run counter to common sense. Such counterintuitive techniques have been called *paradoxical interventions* because it seems paradoxical that people must sometimes do things that are in apparent opposition to their goals in order to reach those goals (Frankl, 1960; Haley, 1973, 1976; Hare-Mustin, 1975; Watzlawick, Weakland, & Fisch, 1974).

For example, Watzlawick and his colleagues (1974) described a young couple who were bothered by their parents' tendency to treat them like children by doing everything for them. Despite the husband's adequate salary, the parents continued to send money and to lavish gifts on them, refused to let them pay even part of a restaurant check, and so on. The strategic team helped the couple solve their difficulty with their doting parents by having them become less rather than more competent. Instead of trying to show the parents that they didn't need help, the couple was told to act helpless and dependent, so much so that the parents got disgusted and finally backed off. This form of paradox is an *outpositioning* strategy (Rohrbaugh et al., 1981) in the sense that the couple forced the sequence to change by taking their parents' position—that they were dependent—and exaggerated it to an absurd extreme.

The techniques most commonly thought of as paradoxical are symptom prescriptions in which the family is told to continue or expand the behavior they complain about. In some contexts, such a prescription might be made with the hope that the family will try to comply with it, and thereby be forced to reverse their attempted solutions. If sad Johnny is told to try to become depressed several times a day and his family is asked to encourage him to be sad, then they will no longer try ineffectively to cheer him up and he won't feel guilty for not being happy. Michael Rohrbaugh and his colleagues (1981), in their useful taxonomy of paradoxical techniques, called this a *compliance-based* paradox because the therapist wants the family to comply with the directive.

At other times, a therapist may prescribe the symptom while secretly hoping that the clients will rebel against this directive. The therapist may encourage Johnny to continue to be depressed because, in doing so, he's helping his brother (with whom Johnny is competitive) feel superior. This is called a *defiance-based* intervention because the therapist wants the client to defy the directive and reframes the reason for the directive in terms that will maximize Johnny's defiance.

At still other times, the therapist may *prescribe the symptom* with the hope that in doing so the network of family relationships that maintain the problem will be exposed. The therapist says that Johnny should remain depressed because that way he can continue to keep his mother's attention, which will keep her from looking to father for affection, since father is still emotionally involved with his own mother, and so on. Since Rohrbaugh didn't include this category, we will call it an *exposure-based* paradox, which is most frequently associated with the Milan model rather than the MRI model.

From this, we can see that the reframe or rationale that accompanies a paradoxical directive is quite important. It will include different content and use different language, depending on whether the therapist wants to maximize compliance, defiance, or exposure.

Rohrbaugh described another class of paradoxical directives also designed to manipulate resistance. Most families enter therapy with a certain amount of ambivalence regarding the problem and the changes required to improve it. When the therapist encourages the family to make these changes, family members are likely to respond with the fearful side of their ambivalence and increase their resistance. If the therapist were instead to preempt these fears by warning the family of the dangers of change and restraining them from trying to change too fast, the family may react with the side of their ambivalence that wants the changes. Thus, MRI therapists will frequently use such *restraining techniques* as asking about the negative consequences of change and warning family members to go slowly, or to worry about the relapse when improvements occur.

To increase cooperation and sidestep power struggles, MRI therapists avoid assuming an authoritarian position. Their "one-down" stance implies equality and invites clients to reduce anxiety and resistance. Although some strategists adopt a one-down position disingenuously, this modest stance was consistent with the late John Weakland's own shy and unassuming character. While sitting clouded in the smoke of his pipe, Weakland used restraint from change, suggesting that change would be difficult. This intervention also reinforced the therapist's one-down position.

While paradoxical techniques are still used by some strategic therapists, others, because of the deception involved in their use, have abandoned them or present them humorously and are honest about their intent. As Cade and O'Hanlon (1993) comment,

> We now find ourselves rarely, if ever, using covert and deceptive interventions. However, we here intend no sanctimonious, "holier-than-thou" comments on erstwhile paradoxical therapists. After all, we have been numbered among their ranks. It is just that our ideas about therapy have evolved over time. Along with the majority of our colleagues, we no longer see therapy in the same adversarial way that we used to. (p. 157)

Haley and Madanes Approach. Jay Haley's approach is harder to describe because it's specifically tailored to address the unique requirements of each case. If "strategic" implies systematic, as in the MRI approach, it also implies artful, which is true of Haley's strategies. As with other strategic approaches, the definitive technique is the use of directives. But Haley's directives aren't ploys simply to outwit families or reverse what they're doing. Rather, they are thoughtful suggestions derived from long experience.

Haley (1976) believes that if therapy is to end well, it must begin properly. Therefore, he devotes a good deal of time and attention to the opening moves of treatment. Regardless of who is presented as the official patient, Haley begins by interviewing the entire family, or as much of it as can be assembled. His approach to this initial interview is highly structured and regularly follows four stages: a social stage, a problem stage, an interaction stage, and finally a goal-setting stage. These stages, with clear-cut instructions for each, provided a secure structure for a generation of novice family therapists who wanted to know just what to do in their first session.

Families are often uncomfortable and defensive when they come to therapy for the first time. Family members may not know why they're there or what to expect, and fear that the therapist will blame them for the problem. Therefore, Haley has therapists use the initial minutes of a first session to help everyone relax. He makes a point of greeting each family member and trying to make sure they're comfortable. He acts as though he were a host, making sure that his guests feel welcome. While making small talk, Haley observes how each family member behaves and how they all interact.

After this brief *social stage*, Haley gets down to business in the *problem stage*. Before asking for the family's position, he introduces himself, repeats what he knows about the family, and explains why he asked the entire family to come—because he wants everyone's ideas and opinions. Haley then asks each person to give his or her perspective on the problem. His clear and practical suggestions even address such specific issues as whom to speak to first. Since mothers are usually more central than fathers, Haley recommends that the therapist speak first to the father in order to increase his involvement. This suggestion nicely illustrates Haley's strategic maneuvering, which begins with the first contact and characterizes the course of all subsequent meetings.

Haley listens carefully to the way each family member defines the problem and his or her involvement in it, making sure that no one interrupts until each has had a turn. During this phase, Haley observes the reactions of each family member for clues to the family's triangles and hierarchy, but he discourages therapists from making any interpretations or comments regarding these observations because this might make the family defensive. Instead, these observations are filed away to await further confirmation, and to provide the basis for future interventions. He does "interactionalize" problems presented as belonging to only one member. For example, mother says that Johnny is just a depressed person. In listening to everyone's report, Haley noticed that the parents disagreed regarding the best way to help Johnny, so he can list this disagreement, which certainly doesn't help Johnny, as another aspect of the problem.

Once everyone has had a chance to talk, Haley encourages them to discuss their various points of view among themselves. In this, the *interactional stage*, the therapist can observe, rather than just hear about, the sequences that surround the problem. As they talk, Haley looks for coalitions between family members against others. How functional is the hierarchy? Do the parents work well together or do they undercut each other? How does the client respond to conflict between others? During this stage, the therapist is like an anthropologist, watching for patterns in the family action.

Sometimes Haley ends the first session by directing the family to carry out a task. In subsequent sessions, directives play a central role in his problem-solving therapy. Effective directives don't take the form of simple advice. Advice is rarely helpful, unless clients happen to be ignorant of some piece of information or the problems are minor. As Haley says, advice generally doesn't help because people don't always have control over what they do.

The purpose of a directive isn't necessarily to have it carried out, but to have a process of negotiation with clients. Accordingly, there are two kinds of directives: straightforward and indirect. Which to use depends on the therapist's power and authority with a particular case. Indirect directives are often paradoxical—having the client enact the symptomatic behavior or the family enact the problematic sequence.

To design an effective directive, the therapist has to learn what solutions have already been tried. To persuade family members to do a task, they must be convinced that each will gain something by cooperating with the therapist. They also need to see themselves as competent to try something new, so therapists are well advised to find ways to boost their self-concepts (Madanes, 1990).

The following two tasks are taken from Haley's *Problem-Solving Therapy*. A couple who were out of the habit of being affectionate with each other were told to behave affectionately in order to teach their child how to show affection. In another case, a mother who was unable to control her twelve-year-old son had decided to send him away to military school. Haley suggested that since the boy had no idea how tough his life would be at military school, it would be a good idea for the mother to help prepare him. They both agreed. Haley directed her to teach the boy how to stand at attention, be polite, and wake up early every morning to make his bed. The two of them followed these instructions as if playing a game, with mother as sergeant and son as private. After two weeks the son was behaving so well that his mother no longer felt it necessary to send him away.

Madanes (1981) used the observation, illustrated by the second case, that people will often do something they wouldn't ordinarily do if it is framed as play or pretend, to develop a whole range of *pretend techniques*. One such strategy is to ask a symptomatic child to pretend to have the symptom and encourage the parents to pretend to help. The child can give up the actual symptom now that pretending to have it is serving the same family function. The following two case studies summarized from Madanes (1981) illustrate the pretend technique.

In the first case, a mother sought therapy because her ten-year-old son had night terrors. Two older daughters and a baby brother were also in the family. Madanes suspected that the boy was concerned about his mother, who was poor, spoke little English, and had lost two husbands. Since the boy had night terrors the therapist asked all the members of the family to describe their dreams. Only the mother and the son had nightmares. In the mother's nightmare someone was breaking into the house. In the boy's, he was being attacked by a witch. When Madanes asked what the mother did when the boy had nightmares, she said that she took him into her bed and told him to pray to God. She explained that she thought his nightmares were the work of the devil.

The treatment team's conjecture was that the boy's night terrors were both a metaphorical expression of the mother's fears and an attempt to help her. As long as the boy was afraid, his mother had to be strong. Unfortunately, while she tried to protect him, she frightened him further by talking about God and the devil. Thus, both mother and child were helping each other in unproductive ways.

The family members were told to pretend that they were home and mother was afraid that someone might break in. The son was asked to protect his mother. In this way the mother had to pretend to need the child's help instead of really needing it. At first the family had difficulty playing the scene because the mother would attack the make-believe thief before the son could help. Thus she communicated that she was capable of taking care of herself and didn't need the son's protection. After the scene was performed correctly, with the son attacking the thief, they all discussed the performance. The mother explained that it was difficult for her to play her part because she was a competent person who could defend herself. Madanes sent the family home with the task of repeating this dramatization every evening for a week. If the son started screaming during his sleep, his mother was to wake him up and replay the scene. They were told that this was important to do no matter how late it was or how tired they were. The son's night terrors completely disappeared.

In the second case, a mother sought psychiatric treatment for her five-year-old son because he had uncontrollable temper tantrums. After talking with the family for a few minutes Madanes asked the son to show her what his tantrums were like by pretending to have one. The boy said, "Okay, I'm the Incredible Hulk!" He puffed out his chest, flexed his muscles, made a monstrous face, and started screaming and kicking the furniture. Madanes then asked the mother to do what she usually did in such circumstances. The mother responded by telling her son, in a weak and ineffective way, to calm down. She pretended to send him to another room as she tried to do at home. Next, Madanes asked the mother if the boy was doing a good job of pretending. She said that he was.

Madanes asked the boy to repeat the scene. This time he was Frankenstein and his tantrum was performed with a more rigid body posture and a face more appropriate to Frankenstein's monster. Then Madanes talked with the boy about the Incredible Hulk and Frankenstein and congratulated the mother for rearing such an imaginative child.

Following this discussion, mother and son were told to pretend that he was having a tantrum while she was walking him to his room. The boy was told to act like the Incredible Hulk and to make lots of noise. Then they were told to pretend to close the door and hug and kiss. Next Madanes instructed the mother to pretend that she was having a tantrum, and the boy was to hug and kiss her. Madanes instructed mother and son to perform both scenes every morning before school and every afternoon when the boy came home. After every performance the mother was to give the boy milk and cookies if he did a good job. Thus the mother was moved from a helpless position to one of authority in which she was in charge of rewarding his make-believe performance. The next week the mother called to say that they didn't need to come for therapy because the boy was behaving very well and his tantrums had ceased.

Both of these cases contain the hallmarks of strategic therapy: tracking the sequences around the problem and giving directives that alter those sequences. Like Haley, Madanes is primarily interested in the sequences that relate to the family's hierarchy. Unlike Haley, however, her directives are usually aimed less at getting parents back in control through power plays and more through structuring new, enjoyable opportunities for parents and children to care for and protect each other.

Haley's preference is often to get parents to work together to control their out-of-control children. This preference is clearly illustrated in the strategies he recommends for dealing with severely disturbed young adults in the book *Leaving Home*. Parents are to put aside their personal resentments and collaborate in planning and implementing a highly structured, rather authoritarian, regimen of discipline for their young adult, treating him or her as younger-than-age until the child is back on track toward normality. Haley speculates that by forcing the parents to cooperate for the good of their child, he is interrupting the sequence in which the tension from their marital conflicts precipitates their child's crazy behavior as a way to distract them.

While Haley believed that a problematic marriage often lurks behind a child's problem, he also warned therapists not to target these marital issues too soon or, in some cases, at all. He believed that families were often protective of and threatened by disturbances in that relationship. Instead, by getting parents to work together to help their child, the couple may make simultaneous changes in their relationship without it ever being overtly addressed. If marital issues do come up, the parents will feel less fear of dealing with them if they have had success in cooperating to help their child. All of this reinforces Haley's commitment to remain focused on the presenting problem until it improves.

Later, Haley (1984) returned to his strategic, Ericksonian roots in a book called *Ordeal Therapy*, a collection of case studies in which ordeals were prescribed that made the clients' symptoms more trouble than they were worth. Haley's general approach is based on this premise: "If one makes it more difficult for a person to have a symptom than to give it up, the person will give up the symptom" (p. 5). For example, a standard ordeal is for a client to have to get up in the middle of the night and exercise strenuously whenever he or she had symptoms during that day. Another example might be for the client to have to give a present to someone with whom he or she has a poor relationship—for example, a mother-in-law or ex-spouse—each time the symptoms occur. As these examples illustrate, the ordeal should be something that clients don't want to do, but might be good for them and would improve their health or relationships. In constructing ordeals, clients should feel they are making a deal with themselves rather than with the therapist.

Since Haley also subscribed to structural goals in therapy, he used ordeals to restructure families. For example, a sixteen-year-old boy put a variety of items up his behind and then expelled them, leaving his stepmother to clean up the mess while his father remained peripheral. Haley (1984) arranged that, after each such episode, the father had to take his son to their backyard and have the boy dig a hole three feet deep and three feet wide, in which he was to bury all the things he was putting up his rear end. After a few weeks of this, Haley reported that the symptom stopped, the father became more involved with his son, and the stepmother became closer to the father.

The current form of Haley/Madanes therapy, called strategic humanism, still involves giving directives based on hypotheses the therapist generates. In this, strategic humanism isn't in step with the contemporary trend in family therapy toward collaborative approaches. The directives they deliver, however, are more oriented toward increasing family members' abilities to soothe and love than to gain control over one another. This represents a major shift and *is* in sync with family therapy's shift away from the power elements of hierarchy and toward finding ways to increase harmony. The expression of emotions like repentance, sorrow, love, and empathy is a larger part of this new form of strategic therapy than existed in former versions. The strategic therapist, too, has been humanized. The expression of empathy for clients is given as much weight as the ability to design effective directives.

An excellent example of strategic humanism's combination of compassion and technology is James Keim's work with families of oppositional children. Keim begins by reassuring anxious parents that they aren't to blame for their children's oppositionalism. Next he explains that there are two sides of parental authority—discipline and nurture. To reinforce the parents' authority while avoiding power struggles, Keim encourages them to concentrate on being sympathetic and supportive for a while. The parent who soothes a child with the forgotten language of understanding is every bit as much in charge as one who tries to tell the child what to do. Then, after progress has been made in calming the child down—especially in breaking the pattern by which oppositional children control the mood in the family by arguing with anything you say—Keim coaches the parents to post rules and enforce consequences. This strategy puts parents back in charge of unruly children without the kind of high-intensity melodrama that usually attends work with that population.

The Milan Model. The original Milan model was ultrastrategic and formulaic. Families were treated by male-female cotherapists while being observed by other members of a therapy team. Sessions were held, on the average, once a month and initially were limited to ten, in emulation of the MRI model. The monthly sessions were an artifact of the long distances many families had to travel to the center in Milan; however, the team came to believe that the long interval between sessions was beneficial. If families were seen weekly, the effects of the previous session's paradoxical prescription might be diminished because families seemed to take longer to react fully.

The standard session format had five parts: the presession, the session, the intersession, the intervention, and the postsession discussion. As Boscolo, Cecchin, Hoffman, and Penn (1987) describe:

> During the presession the team came up with an initial hypothesis about the family's presenting problem. . . . During the session itself, the team members would validate, modify, or change the hypothesis. After about forty minutes, the entire team would meet alone to discuss the hypothesis and arrive at an intervention. The treating therapists would then go back to deliver the intervention to the family, either by positively connoting the problem situation or by a ritual to be done by the family that commented on the problem situation and was designed to introduce change. . . . Finally, the team would meet for a postsession discussion to analyze the family's reactions and to plan for the next session. (p. 4)

As indicated in that description, the main intervention was either a ritual or a positive connotation.

The *positive connotation* was the most distinctive innovation to emerge from this original Milan model. Derived from the MRI technique of reframing the symptom as serving a protective function for the family—for example, Johnny needs to continue to be depressed to distract his parents from their marital issues—the positive connotation eliminated the implication inherent in such reframes that some family members wanted or benefited from the patient's symptoms. This implication made for resistance that the Milan team found could be circumvented if the patient's behavior was construed not as protecting specific people or relationships but as preserving the family's homeostasis or rigid rules. Indeed, every family member's behavior was often connoted in this system-serving way.

The treatment team would hypothesize about the way the patient's symptom fit into the family system, and after the mid-session break the therapists would turn this hypothesis into a statement and deliver it to the family, along with the injunction that the situation should not change. Johnny should continue to sacrifice himself by remaining depressed as a way to reassure the family that he will not become an abusive man like his grandfather. Mother should also maintain her overinvolvement with Johnny as a way to make him feel valued while he sacrifices himself. Father should continue to criticize mother and Johnny's relationship so that mother will not be tempted to abandon Johnny and become a wife to her husband.

Rituals were used to engage the whole family in a series of actions that run counter to, or exaggerate, rigid family rules and myths. For example, one family of four was highly enmeshed with their large extended family. They were told to hold family discussions behind locked doors every other night after dinner during which each family member was to speak for fifteen minutes about the family. Meanwhile they were to redouble their allegiance and courtesy to the other members of the clan. By exaggerating the family's loyalty to the extended family while simultaneously breaking that loyalty's rule by meeting apart from the clan and talking about it, the family could examine and break the rule that perpetuated their dysfunctional system.

Rituals were also used to dramatize the positive connotation. For example, each family member might have to express his or her gratitude each night to the patient for having the problem (Boscolo et al., 1987). The Milan group also devised a set of rituals based on an "odd and even days" format (Selvini Palazzoli et al., 1978b). For example, a family in which the parents were deadlocked over parental functions might be told that on even days of the week father should be in charge of the patient's behavior and mother should act as if she wasn't there. On odd days, mother's in charge and father's to stay out of the way. Here, again, the family's rigid sequences are interrupted and they must react differently to each other.

These positive connotations and rituals are powerful and provocative interventions. To keep families engaged while using such methods, the therapist–family relationship becomes crucial. Unfortunately, the Milan team originally portrayed therapy as a struggle for power between therapists and families. Their main advice to therapists was to remain neutral in the sense of avoiding the appearance of taking sides with one or another family member. This *neutrality* was often interpreted by practitioners as distance, so that therapists often delivered these dramatic interventions while seeming aloof; not surprisingly, families often became angry and didn't return.

In the late 1970s and early 1980s, the original Milan team began to split around the nature of therapy. Selvini Palazzoli maintained the model's strategic and adversarial bent, although she stopped using paradoxical interventions. Instead she and Guiliana Prata experimented with a specific kind of ritual called the *invariant prescription*, which they assigned to every family they treated.

Selvini Palazzoli (1986) believed that psychotic or anorexic patients are caught up in a "dirty game," a power struggle originally between their parents that these patients are pulled into and, ultimately, wind up using their symptoms in an attempt to defeat one parent for the sake of the other. In the invariant prescription parents were directed to tell their children they had a secret. They were to go out together for varying periods of time and to do so mysteriously, without warning other family members. Therapy continued this way until the patient's symptoms abated.

In the early 1990s Selvini Palazzoli reinvented her therapy once more, this time abandoning any form of strategic, short-term therapy (invariant prescription included) for long-term therapy with patients and their families (Selvini, 1993). Thus, she came full circle, beginning with psychodynamic roots, then abandoning any concerns with the individual to focus on family patterns, and now returning to a long-term therapy that emphasizes insight and focuses again on the individual. This new therapy revolves around understanding the denial of family secrets and suffering over generations. In this way it is linked conceptually, if not technically, to her former models.

Boscolo and Cecchin also have moved away from strategic intervening, but they moved toward a collaborative style of therapy. This therapy grew from their increasing impression that the value in the Milan model wasn't so much in the directives (positive connotations or rituals), which had been the model's centerpiece, but in the interview process itself. Their therapy came to center around *circular questioning,* a clinical translation of Bateson's notion of double description. Circular questions are designed to decenter clients by orienting them toward seeing themselves in a relational context and toward seeing that context from the perspectives of other family members. For example, a therapist might ask, "How would your father have characterized your mother's relationship with your sister, if he had felt free to speak with you about it?" Such a question is structured so that one has to give a relational description in answer.

By asking about relationship patterns, the circular nature of problems becomes apparent as family members are lifted out of their limited and linear perspectives. Circular questions have been further refined and cataloged by Peggy Penn (1982, 1985) and Karl Tomm (1987a, 1987b). Boscolo (Boscolo & Bertrando, 1992) remains intrigued with their potential. As an example, let's return to Johnny's family and imagine the following conversation (adapted from Hoffman, 1983):

Q: Who is most upset by Johnny's depression?

A: Mother.

Q: How does mother try to help Johnny?

A: She talks to him for hours and tries to do things for him.

Q: Who agrees most with mother's way of trying to help Johnny?

A: The psychiatrist who prescribes his medication.

Q: Who disagrees?

A: Father. He thinks Johnny shouldn't be allowed to do what he wants.

Q: Who agrees with father?

A: We all think Johnny is babied too much. And grandma too. Grandpa would probably agree with mother but he died.

Q: Did Johnny start to get depressed before or after grandfather's death?

A: Not long after, I guess.

Q: If grandfather hadn't died, how would the family be different now?

A: Well, mother and grandma probably wouldn't fight so much because grandma wouldn't be living with us. And mother wouldn't be so sad all the time.

Q: If mother and grandma didn't fight so much and mother wasn't so sad, how do you think Johnny would be?

A: Well, I guess he might be happier too. But then he'd probably be fighting with father again.

Just by asking questions, the frame for Johnny's problem gradually shifts from a psychiatric one to being symptomatic of difficult changes in the family structure.

Boscolo and Cecchin became aware that the spirit in which these questions are asked determined the usefulness of this technique. If a therapist maintains a strategic mindset—uses the questioning process to strive for a particular outcome—the responses of family members will be constrained by their sense that the therapist is after something. If, on the other hand, the therapist asks circular questions out of genuine curiosity (Cecchin, 1987), as if joining the family in a research expedition regarding their problem, an atmosphere can be created in which the family can arrive at new understandings of their predicament.

More recently, Cecchin (Cecchin, Lane, & Ray, 1993) has suggested that, in addition to remaining curious, the therapist should maintain an attitude of "irreverence." By irreverence is meant not becoming too attached to any model or belief and helping families become more irreverent toward the beliefs that constrain them. In this, Cecchin joins the postmodernist narrative movement in their efforts to deconstruct clients' assumptions, described in Chapter 12.

Other Contributions. Up to this point we have described the techniques developed by the major schools of strategic or systemic therapy: the MRI group, Haley and Madanes, and the Milan Associates. There are many other people who have added innovations.

Strategic therapists pioneered the *team approach* to therapy. Originally, the MRI group used teams behind one-way mirrors to help brainstorm strategies, as did the Milan group. Peggy Papp (1980) and her colleagues at the Ackerman Institute brought the team more directly into the therapy process by turning the observers into a kind of "Greek chorus" that reacted to events in the therapy session. For example, the team might, for strategic purposes, disagree with the therapist. In witnessing the staged debates between the team and their therapist over whether a family should change, family members might feel that both sides of their ambivalence were appreciated and represented in the therapy session. Having the team interact openly with the therapist or even with the family during sessions paved the way for later approaches in which the team might enter the treatment room and discuss the family while the family watched (Andersen, 1987).

Jim Alexander was a behaviorist who, out of frustration with the limits of his exclusively behavioral orientation, incorporated strategic ideas. The result was *functional family therapy* (Alexander & Parsons, 1982), which, as the name implies, is concerned with the function that family behavior is designed to achieve (see also Chapter 9). Functional family therapists assume that most family behaviors are attempts to become more or less intimate and, through "relabeling" (another word for reframing), help family members see each other's behavior in that benign light. They also help family members set up contingency management programs to help them get the kind of intimacy they want more directly. Functional family therapy represents an interesting blend of strategic and behavioral therapies and, unlike many strategic schools, retains the behaviorist ethic of basing interventions on sound research.

Carlos Sluzki has made a number of contributions to strategic theory and technique, including an innovative approach to marital therapy, a topic rarely addressed by strategic writers (Sluzki, 1978). Some authors have combined strategic and structural approaches. Duncan Stanton (1981) begins with straightforward structural techniques and resorts to strategic interventions only when a family strongly resists his restructuring attempts. After the often paradoxical strategic interventions have reduced resistance, he returns to the structural approach. Maurizio Andolfi (1979; Andolfi & Zwerling,1980; Andolfi, Angelo, & di Nichilo, 1989) does it the other way, starting strategically and ending structurally. He restrains severely dysfunctional families from changing until the identified patient improves and the family members are more accessible to him, at which point he becomes more structural. Unlike other strategic therapists, however, Andolfi gets personally and actively involved. His freewheeling and provocative interventions are reminiscent of his mentor, Carl Whitaker, and it's this high-intensity style that has drawn many American family therapists to study with him in Rome.

Evaluating Therapy Theory and Results

The strategic therapies reached the height of their popularity in the early 1980s. They were clever, prescriptive, and systematic—qualities appreciated by therapists who often felt overwhelmed by the chaos and emotionality of families in treatment. Then in the mid 1980s a reaction set in, and people began criticizing the manipulative and calculating aspects of strategic therapy. What the field came to reject was a mechanistic view of families, as though they were puppets of a system they were too blind to see, and a hierarchical view of therapy, as though only an oh-so-clever therapist could pull the strings.

In the 1990s, the strategic and systemic approaches described in this chapter were replaced on family therapy's center stage by more collaborative approaches. As the field moves away from an overreliance on technique and manipulation, and toward therapy done *with*, not *to*, families, we shouldn't lose sight of valuable aspects of strategic therapy. These include having a clear therapeutic goal, anticipating ways that families will react to interventions, understanding and tracking sequences of interaction, and using directives creatively. We should also remember that strategic therapists have been evolving toward warmer relations with clients.

Most of the meager research on the effectiveness of strategic therapy isn't rigorous. More than any other model in this book, information about strategic therapy is exchanged through the case report format. Nearly all of the hundreds of articles and books on strategic therapy include at least one description of a successful technique or therapy outcome. Thus, strategic therapy appears to have a great deal of anecdotal support for its efficacy (although people tend not to write about their failed cases).

Some strategic groups have tracked their outcome a little more systematically. In the book *Change*, which launched the MRI model, Watzlawick and colleagues (1974) conducted follow-up phone interviews with 97 consecutive cases three months after treatment was terminated. Interviewers asked clients whether their complaints were relieved, if they had sought additional treatment elsewhere, and if any new problems had developed. To minimize the possibility that patients might exaggerate the benefits of treatment to please their therapists, all interviews were conducted by team members who were not involved in treatment. With an average length of treatment of seven sessions, 40 percent reported complete relief, 32 percent considerable but not complete relief, and 28 percent reported no change. In none of the complete relief cases were there any signs of symptom substitution.

When Haley (1980) reported on the outcome of his "leaving home" model with schizophrenic young adults, he used rehospitalization as his only criterion. Fourteen such patients, each of whom had been hospitalized for the first time, were treated by different therapists for an average of fourteen sessions. The therapists of these patients followed up on their treatment between two and four years after terminating. In that time, three of the fourteen had been rehospitalized and one patient had committed suicide.

Some studies of the outcome of family therapies are based on, or are similar to, the methods of strategic therapy. In their classic study, Langsley, Machotka, and Flomenhaft (1971) studied the effectiveness of their family crisis therapy, which has some similarities with both the MRI and Haley models. Patients who were seen as needing hospitalization were randomly assigned to either a psychiatric hospital or to crisis family therapy on an outpatient basis. Eighteen months later, the group who received family therapy had spent less than half the number of days in the hospital than the group who had been hospitalized previously. Furthermore, the cost of treatment during this period was six times as high for the hospitalized group.

In another carefully controlled study, Parsons and Alexander found their functional family therapy (described earlier in this chapter) to be more effective in treating a group of delinquents than a client-centered family approach, an eclectic–dynamic approach, or a no-treatment control group (Parsons & Alexander, 1973). Recidivism was cut in half by the functional approach, in contrast to the other three groups, which did not differ significantly from each other. Furthermore, a three-year follow-up showed that the incidence of problems in the siblings was significantly lower for the functional treatment.

Stanton, Todd and associates (1982) demonstrated the effectiveness of an approach combining structural and Haley's strategic family therapies for treating heroin addicts. The results of this study were impressive because family therapy resulted in twice as many days of abstinence from heroin than a methadone maintenance program.

The Milan group's early work was filled with anecdotal case reports of amazing outcomes with anorexia nervosa, schizophrenia, and delinquency (Selvini Palazzoli, Boscolo, Cecchin, & Prata, 1978b, 1980). Later, however, members of the original team expressed reservations about the model and implied that it wasn't as effective as they originally suggested (Selvini Palazzoli, 1986; Selvini Palazzoli & Viaro, 1988; Boscolo, 1983).

Some who have studied the Milan model more systematically concur with these less enthusiastic impressions (Machal, Feldman, & Sigal, 1989). In discussing their disappointing results with the Milan model, the authors cited clients' negative reactions to the therapist or team. Families frequently felt that the therapists were cold and distant and the team was impersonal. It seems that the attitude of adversarial strategizing recommended in *Paradox and Counterparadox* showed through the therapists' attempts to positively connote family members. We seem to have to learn the same lesson over and over: People have trouble changing if they don't feel cared about.

These questions regarding the effectiveness of the original Milan model and the fact that none of its founders continues to practice it indicate that, despite its initial appeal and popularity, it had problems. There is a lesson in family therapy's initial infatuation and later disillusionment with the Milan model. We need to study outcome carefully and thoroughly before declaring our therapies successful.

Summary

Strategic therapy, which was derived from a combination of Ericksonian hypnotherapy and Batesonian cybernetics, developed a body of powerful procedures for treating psychological problems. Strategic approaches vary in the specifics of theory and technique, but share a problem-centered, pragmatic focus on changing behavioral sequences, in which therapists take responsibility for the outcome of therapy. Insight and understanding are eschewed in favor of directives designed to change the way family members relate to each other.

While the original Milan model seems to have gone the way of the dinosaurs, there currently exist two main strategic camps: the MRI group on the West Coast, and the Washington School started by Haley and Madanes on the East Coast. The MRI model tries to remain strictly interactional—observing and intervening into sequences of interaction surrounding a problem rather than speculating about the feelings or intentions of the interactants. Haley and Madanes are interested in motives, Haley mainly in the desire to control others and Madanes in the desire to love and be loved. In addition, unlike the MRI group, Haley and Madanes incorporate structural goals in their model and don't limit their efforts to simple problem resolution. They believe successful treatment often requires structural change, with an emphasis on improving family hierarchy.

Like Haley, the Milan Associates originally saw power in the motives of family members and tried to understand the elaborate multigenerational games that surrounded symptoms. They designed powerful interventions—positive connotation and rituals—to expose or disrupt these games and to change the meaning of the problem. Later the original group split, with Selvini Palazzoli and new colleagues going through several transformations until their current long-term approach based on family secrets. Cecchin and Boscolo moved away from the power of single interventions, became more interested in the questioning process as a way to help families to new understandings, and in so doing paved the way for family therapy's current interest in conversation and narrative.

What people came to rebel against was the gimmickry of formulaic techniques. But gimmickry was never inherent in the strategic models. For example, the MRI's emphasis on reversing attempted solutions that don't work is a sound idea. People *do* stay stuck in ruts as long as they pursue self-defeating strategies. If, in some hands, blocking more-of-the-same solutions resulted in a rote application of reverse psychology, that's not the fault of the cybernetic metaphor, but of the way it was applied.

Currently strategic therapists are trying to keep their approach vital by learning from past mistakes. As Cade and O'Hanlon (1993) report,

> Beginners will often overconcentrate on technique, on devising "clever" interventions, paying insufficient attention to respect, understanding and validation. This may be, to some extent, the fault of writers on brief/strategic approaches, including ourselves, who may at times have overconcentrated on techniques and interventions and underplayed the importance of basic attitudes and values, and of wisdom, integrity, and restraint. . . . Brief/strategic therapists have also not been very good at demonstrating the patient, painstaking, and sometimes exhaustive groundwork that often precedes the "brilliant" interventions, nor the many cases in which steady, competent work rather than dramatic "fireworks" has brought about significant changes. (p. 18)

Strategic therapists are also integrating other ideas and keeping up with the postmodern spirit of the 1990s. For example, in 1993 Haley and Madanes met in a large conference with Minuchin to discuss the integration of structural and strategic approaches. Haley also published a book of conversations about therapy between himself and an associate in which the evolution of his thinking is apparent (Grove & Haley, 1993), and a book of new case examples and transcripts (Haley, 1996). A new book on the influence of the MRI on the field has been released (Weakland & Ray, 1995). In addition, some authors have integrated MRI strategic concepts with narrative approaches (Eron & Lund, 1993, 1996). They incorporate strategic's emphasis on clear therapeutic goals and strategies with the collaborative therapist's stance and the breadth of scope of narrative therapy. It's good to see that strategic thinking is evolving because even in this era of the nonexpert therapist, there is still room for thoughtful problem-solving strategies and therapeutic direction.

Solution-Focused Therapy

Judging by its immense popularity, solution-focused therapy must be the treatment for our times. Its pragmatic minimalism, cognitive emphasis, and easily teachable techniques have combined to make it the hottest thing on the workshop circuit. Its seductive promise of quick and easy solutions has endeared it to the managed care industry. Indeed, when asked to indicate their therapeutic orientation, many applicants for provider status call themselves "solution-focused" regardless of whether or not they have any training in this approach. And it seems that including the term *solution-focused* in a book or journal article hasn't hurt anyone's sales. There are now a spate of books on the model itself (de Shazer, 1988, 1991b, 1994; O'Hanlon & Weiner-Davis, 1989; Walter & Peller, 1992; Furman & Ahola, 1992; Cade & O'Hanlon, 1993: O'Hanlon & Martin, 1992; Miller, Hubble, & Duncan, 1996), on the model applied to couples (Weiner-Davis, 1992; Hudson & O'Hanlon, 1992), and on the model applied to alcoholism (Berg & Miller, 1992).

What is it—besides its remarkably appealing name—that has made the solution-focused approach so popular? Its model sprang from the soil of strategic therapy (particularly the MRI model) and yet it also represents a departure from that tradition. It maintains the strategic school's deemphasis on history and underlying pathology, and its commitment to brevity, but it moves away from the focus on problems. Where strategic family therapists talk with clients about the interactions that surround problems, with an eye toward discovering attempted solutions that aren't working, solution-focused therapists get clients to concentrate on solutions that *have* worked. At first glance, this shift may seem trivial, but it isn't.

Sketches of Leading Figures

Most of the leading figures in this movement worked together at one time or another at the Brief Family Therapy Center (BFTC) in Milwaukee. This private training and treatment institute was started in the late 1970s when a group within a Milwaukee community agency who were drawn to the MRI model became dissatisfied with the agency's constraints and broke out on their own to form the BFTC. The initial group included married partners Steve de Shazer and Insoo Berg. De Shazer is considered the primary developer of solution-focused theory and no longer does much clinical work, preferring to devote his time to researching, theorizing, and writing. De Shazer had worked earlier in Palo Alto with the MRI group, and was strongly influenced by their brief approach.

Berg is known primarily as a clinician but has also contributed substantially to theory. She has trained most of the leaders in this movement and has applied the model to alcoholism (Berg & Miller, 1992).

Other notable clinician/theorists associated with the BFTC include Eve Lipchik, who was there for eight years. She has pioneered in applying the solution-focused model to wife-battering (Lipchik & Kubicki, 1996). After training with de Shazer, Michele Weiner-Davis converted an agency in Woodstock, Illinois, to the solution-focused model. Weiner-Davis (1992) applied the model to marital problems in her popular book, *Divorce-Busting.* Scott Miller, now based in Chicago, was with the BFTC for three years, directing the alcohol and drug treatment services, and has written widely about the model. All three of these therapists are currently in private practice and no longer associated with the center, and present the solution-focused approach in workshops around the country.

The married couple John Walter and Jane Peller are in private practice together in Chicago. They trained at the BFTC and, after writing a book laying out the steps of the approach (Walter & Peller, 1992), are also popular presenters on the solution-focused workshop circuit.

Bill O'Hanlon, who has recently moved his practice from Omaha to Santa Fe, was never formally associated with the BFTC but, having been trained by Milton Erickson and become a prominent translator of Erickson's ideas, the step toward the solution-focused approach was an easy one. He and Weiner-Davis (O'Hanlon & Weiner-Davis, 1989) have collaborated to expand on the groundwork laid by de Shazer.

Every year since 1993, many of these leaders and others from all over the world present at the movement's primary gathering, the East Coast Conference on Solution-Focused Therapy, in Virginia.

Theoretical Formulations

With their roots in the MRI tradition, it's no surprise that the assumptions that form the basis of solution-focused therapy are straightforward and uncomplicated. As Insoo Berg said, "We are very proud of our simplicity. It took a great deal of discipline to become so simple" (Wylie, 1990, p. 27). By that she means that it's always tempting for therapists to overexplain their clients' problems or get caught up in intricate descriptions of family dynamics. It takes discipline to ignore all that and focus only on solutions. One benefit of streamlining the theory so much is that it is easily understandable and translates readily into schematic techniques.

Because solution-focused therapists set their sights on solutions rather than on problems, they have little to say about how problems arise. One of the defining characteristics of family therapy has always been its focus on the present, where problems are maintained, rather than on the past that "caused" them. Solution-focused therapists prefer to focus on the future, where problems can be solved, rather than on either the past or the present. They contend that therapists don't need to know a great deal about the nature of the problems that bring people to therapy. Indeed, a problem's solution may be totally unrelated to how it developed.

Like the MRI model, they believe that people are constrained by narrow, pessimistic views of their problems and generate rigid sequences of more-of-the-same attempted solutions. As O'Hanlon and Weiner-Davis (1989) put it:

> So, the meanings people attribute to behavior limit the range of alternatives they will use to deal with a situation. If the methods used do not produce a satisfactory outcome, the original assumption about the meaning of the behavior is generally not questioned. If it were, new meanings might be considered, which in turn might prompt a different, perhaps more effective, approach. Instead, people often redouble their efforts to solve the problem in an ineffective way, thinking that by doing it more, harder or better (e.g., more punishments, more heart-to-heart talks, and so on) they will finally solve it. (p. 48)

Solution-oriented therapists also take a strong position against the idea that problems serve ulterior motives or that people are ambivalent about their problems. They assume that clients *really do* want to change. De Shazer (1984), in fact, has declared the death of resistance as a concept, suggesting that when clients don't follow directives, it's their way of "cooperating" by teaching the therapist the best way to help them.

Solution-focused therapists also believe that people are quite suggestible, and that therapists may unwittingly create or maintain problems that, to solution-focused therapists, don't exist (O'Hanlon & Weiner-Davis, 1989):

> If the client walks into a behaviorist's office, he or she will leave with a behavioral problem. If clients choose psychoanalysts' offices, they will leave with unresolved issues from childhood as the focus of the problem. If a client seeks help from a Jungian analyst, he or she is likely to get a problem that can be treated most effectively by examining symbolism in the client's dreams. (p. 54)

Thus, much of the work for solution-focused therapists lies in the negotiation of an achievable goal, and isn't related to the therapist's preconceptions about what lies behind the problem.

The MRI model was strongly influenced by Milton Erickson's view of people as containing untapped and often unconscious resources. According to this view, people are basically competent and only need slight shifts of thinking or behavior to release that competence. Early solution-focused theory showed more evidence of this Ericksonian view of people as containing resources. Since the postmodern revolution, the theorizing has moved increasingly from releasing resources to changing language.

Many constructivist therapists have espoused the idea that language creates reality. Through the influence of the philosopher Ludwig Wittgenstein, de Shazer's theorizing has gradually moved toward a more radical position—that language *is* reality. "Language constitutes 'the human world and the human world constitutes the whole world' " (de Shazer & Berg, 1992, p. 73). Nothing exists outside of language. Thus, de Shazer (1993) asserts that "There are no wet beds, no voices without people, no depressions. There is only *talk* about wet beds, *talk* about voices without people, *talk* about depression" (p. 89). If one accepts that language is reality, therapy becomes a relatively simple procedure. All that's needed is to change the talk about the wet beds or the depressions. From this idea flows the solution-focused emphasis on therapists using techniques to steer clients from "problem-talk" to "solution-talk."

Recently, however, a number of authors have shifted their attention from the idea that the "words are magic" (to paraphrase the title of de Shazer's [1994] last book), to look at the power of the therapist–client relationship (Tuyn, 1992; Metcalf, Thomas, Duncan, Miller, & Hubble, 1996; Butler & Powers, 1996; Simon, 1996). As William Butler and Keith Powers (1996) assert, "[Solution-focused therapy] works. . . . But it is not the model or the techniques that really matter. It is the attitude of the therapist and the interchange between the client and the therapist that is the real key" (p. 245).

If this line of thinking among solution-focused therapists continues, it will represent a radical shift because most previous theorizing had pointed to the techniques as the model's centerpiece and led to the model's formulaic application. If "it's the relationship, stupid," then what is it about the relationship? Dvorah Simon (1996) suggests that the ability of the therapist to bring clients a sense of hope "seems to me to be at the spiritual heart of this work—placing longing, desire, and the belief that a better life is not only possible but available in a central position around which everything else can flow" (p. 46). Others suggest that solution-focused therapy works by making clients feel good about themselves by highlighting their strengths and successes—the cheerleader effect (Metcalf et al, 1996).

Butler and Powers (1996) even make the blasphemous suggestion that solution-focused therapists reread Carl Rogers. They point out that Rogers (1961) did what solution-focused therapists preach. He not only tried to accept and understand the client's frame of reference, but also helped him or her imagine a desired future. Butler and Powers conclude that, "It seems that we keep reinventing the wheel, or at least renaming it. . . . Perhaps we should do more looking back toward what has worked in the past and *do more of that*" (p. 245). Now there's an idea.

Thus, there seems to be a growing tension among solution-focused theorists as to whether the heart of the model is its ability to alter clients' language, the uplifting, you-are-competent message, or the Rogerian, empathic aspects of the relationship that release client resources. This is an important debate because each of the three positions dictates different practices.

Normal Family Development

Solution-focused therapists borrow from constructivists the idea that there is no absolute reality, so therapists shouldn't impose what they think is normal on clients. The search for structural flaws that characterizes most other forms of psychotherapy is rejected. As de Shazer (1991b) writes, "Structuralist thought points to the idea that symptoms are the result of some underlying problem, a psychic or structural problem such as incongruent hierarchies, covert parental conflicts, low self-esteem, deviant communication, repressed feelings, 'dirty games', etc." The solution-focused therapist dispenses with such speculations and instead is interested only in language—the way people describe themselves and their problems.

Therapy, then, is highly relativistic. The therapist should be concerned only with the complaints that clients present and shouldn't impose values by suggesting that clients address other, unpresented, problems.

> Solution-oriented therapists don't believe that there is any single "correct" or "valid" way to live one's life. We have come to understand that what is unacceptable behavior in one family or for one person is desirable behavior in another. Therefore, clients, not therapists, identify the goals to be accomplished in treatment. (O'Hanlon & Weiner-Davis, 1989, p. 44)

Development of Behavior Disorders

In the solution-focused world, this category is obsolete. Just as they steer clients away from speculating about problem formation, they also dissuade therapists from such conjecture. Their conviction is that a solution to a problem is often unrelated to the way the problem developed, and that tracking etiological factors is engaging in "problem talk"—exactly what they seek to avoid.

Problem talk and the related preoccupation with the problem is the furthest solution-focused therapists go in identifying etiological factors. They believe that problem-focused thinking keeps people from recognizing the effective solutions they've already used or could come up with in the future.

Goals of Therapy

As with MRI therapists, the goal of solution-focused therapy is to resolve the presenting complaints by helping a client do or think something different so as to become more satisfied with his or her life. More than MRI therapists, however, solution-focused therapists trust and use the resources of clients to help them reach their goals. They believe that people already have the skills to solve their problems but have lost sight of these abilities because the problems loom so large to them that their strengths are crowded out of the picture. Sometimes a simple shift in focus from what's not going well to what they're already doing that works can remind clients of, and expand their use of, these resources. Other times, people may have to search for abilities that they aren't currently using and bring those dormant skills to bear on their problems.

At another level, the goal is simply to help clients begin to shift their language from talking about their problems to talking about solutions. Once people begin speaking about what they can do differently, what resources they have, what they've done in the past that worked, solution-focused therapists have achieved their primary aim. From that point on the work is to build on the solutions that emerge from those more hopeful conversations.

Because solution-focused therapists aren't out to reorganize personalities or family structures, they're willing to settle for modest goals. A homeless woman may simply want to find a place to live, a single man may want the courage to ask someone for a date. If a client's goal is vague—"I'd like to feel happier"—or utopian—"I never want to be sad again"—they ask questions designed to reduce the goal to something clear and specific. Helping clients set reachable and clear goals is a major intervention in itself, and the process of thinking about the future and what one wants to be different is a large part of what some solution-focused therapists do (Walter & Peller, 1996).

Conditions for Behavior Change

The task of solution-focused therapy is to help clients amplify exceptions to their problems—effective solutions of which they are already in possession. The therapist strives to work from the client's understanding of the problem and seeks behavioral change. But, although the model is consistent with the brevity and pragmatism of strategic approaches, the current trend among solution-focused therapists is to emphasize the collaborative construction of solution-oriented narratives.

From Berg and de Shazer's (1993) current point of view, what's needed for change is that therapist and client engage in a discussion that shifts the way the problem is "languaged."

> Rather than looking behind and beneath the language that clients and therapists use, we think that the language they use is all that we have to go on. . . . What we talk about and how we talk about it makes a difference, and it is these differences that can be used to make a difference (to the client) . . . we have come to see that the meanings arrived at in a therapeutic conversation are developed through a process more like negotiation than the development of understanding or an uncovering of what it is that is "really" going on. (p. 7)

Thus, changing the way people talk about their problems is all one needs to accomplish because "as the client and therapist talk more and more about the solution they want to construct together, they come to believe in the truth or reality of what they are talking about. This is the way language works, naturally" (Berg & de Shazer, 1993, p. 9). This is why solution-focused therapy can be so brief—it's a lot easier to get clients to use different language about their problems than it is to produce significant changes in behavior patterns or intrapsychic structure.

From the Ericksonian resources perspective that used to inform de Shazer's thinking, the therapist is to create an atmosphere in therapy in which people's strengths can move out of the shadows and into the foreground. De Shazer (1985, 1986) found these strengths lurking in the spaces between problems—in the "behaviors, perceptions, thoughts, feelings, and expectations that are outside the complaint's constraints. These exceptions . . . can be used as building blocks in the construction of a solution . . . solutions involve determining what 'works' so that the client can do more of it" (de Shazer, 1986, p. 48).

To illustrate this process, de Shazer (1986) uses the metaphor of a man whose problem is that he wants to leave Chicago. To solve this problem much of the following information has little relevance: how he got to Chicago, how long he's been there, what's kept him from leaving earlier, or the nature of Chicago. Instead, the traveler need only focus on where he wants to go and on the resources at his disposal for getting there.

It may be, however, that in discussing his desires, he remembers some good days in Chicago, and that while these exceptions had seemed insignificant, in thinking about what made them exceptional he realizes that those were days when he was having fun with other people. He decides that he doesn't really have to leave Chicago after all, and instead directs his energy toward spending more time with people he enjoys. It's this focus on goals, resources, and exceptions to the problem that characterizes solution-focused models. With that focus people will either find a solution to their original problem (leaving Chicago) or decide that their problem is something else (not enough time with friends) and find a solution to it.

Because solution-focused therapists aren't interested in observing family dynamics, they don't feel the need to convene any particular grouping of people, like a whole family. Instead, they say that anyone who's concerned about the problem should come. They also need very little intake information because they want to hear the clients' constructions of the problem first-hand and without preconceptions.

Following de Shazer (1988), solution-focused therapists distinguish between "customers" and "complainants." A complainant is someone who describes a complaint but isn't willing to work on solving it. A customer is someone motivated to change. These categories aren't qualities of character but qualities of the therapeutic relationship, and therefore are fluid. With a complainant the therapist's job is to engage in a solution-focused conversation, compliment the client, and possibly give an assignment to observe exceptions to the problem. By not pushing for change but shifting attention away from problems and toward solutions, the relationship may evolve into one in which the client becomes a customer.

Techniques

In the early 1980s, de Shazer's team began experimenting with this orientation toward solutions by giving all clients the same assignments, which they called "formula tasks." Some of these assignments seemed to be universally effective regardless of the problem. One of these tasks, given in the first session, was to ask clients to observe what happens in their life or relationships that they want to continue (de Shazer, 1985). They found that this assignment helped reorient clients from focusing on the bad things in their lives to thinking about and expecting the good. They also found that this shift in perspective seemed to build on itself—to create a more positive outlook that led to better interactions, which in turn reinforced and expanded that positive outlook.

This has become known as the *formula first session task* and is the standard assignment given clients at the end of the first session. "Between now and the next time we meet, I would like you to observe, so you can describe to me next time, what happens in your (family, life, marriage, relationship) that you want to continue to have happen" (de Shazer, 1985, p. 137).

With the success of these formula tasks, it began to dawn on the team that the process of change could be initiated without much knowledge of the problem or the personalities of those suffering from it. They began to focus on ways to initiate and maintain this problem-solving faculty in people, which they believed was inhibited by a focus on problems and deficits. This thinking led to the development of the "miracle question" and the "exception question," two mainstays of the solution-focused approach (de Shazer, 1985, 1988).

The *miracle question* is: "Suppose one night, while you were asleep, there was a miracle and this problem was solved. How would you know? What would be different?" This question activates a problem-solving mindset by giving people a clear vision of their goal, perhaps in the same way that visualization of the perfect serve helps a tennis player. It also helps clients look beyond the problem to see that what they really want may not be the eradication of the problem per se, but instead to be able to do the things that the problem has been obstructing. If the therapist can encourage them to begin doing those things despite the problem, suddenly the problem doesn't loom as large. For example, Mary, who suffers from bulimia, says that if not for her symptoms she'd get closer to people and have more fun. If, with her therapist's encouragement, Mary begins to take interpersonal risks and has more fun, then her bulimia may become less of a problem, less of an obstacle in her life, which might also increase her ability to control it.

The *exception question* ignores the picture the problem clients hold up and, instead, directs their attention to the negative of that image—to times in the past or present when they didn't have the problem when ordinarily they would. By exploring these times and what was different about them, clients find clues to what they can do to expand those exceptions. In addition, clients may find that in light of the fact that they were able to change or eliminate the problem, their outlook towards it may change. It seems less oppressive and omnipresent, more controllable.

Mary remembers several times the previous week when she had the urge to binge and purge but didn't. She discovers that at those times she was away from her parents and didn't feel like she was disappointing them. She decides that it's time to become more independent. "Thus, a solution is a joint product of therapist and client talking together about whatever it is that the problem/complaint is not" (Berg & de Shazer, 1993, p. 21).

More recently, *scaling questions* have become prominent in the solution-focused literature. Scaling questions were first developed to help therapists and clients talk about vague topics such as depression and communication, where it's difficult to identify concrete behavioral changes and goals (Berg & de Shazer, 1993). The therapist asks the depressed client, for example, "On a scale of zero to ten, with zero being how depressed you felt when you called me and ten being how you feel the day after the miracle, how do you feel right now?" The client might say two and the therapist might say, "So you feel a little better than when you called. How did you achieve this improvement?" Or the therapist might ask, "What do you think you need to do to achieve a three?" In this way, the therapist and client can recognize and nurture small changes toward the goal rather than being stuck in the "I'm either depressed or I'm not" kind of thinking that typifies such problems.

Scaling questions are often used to ask clients to quantify their confidence that they can stick to their resolve. "On a scale of one to ten, how confident are you that you will be able to avoid losing your temper this week?" In practice this device has a kind of "prove it" implication. The response is followed up by asking clients what they might do to increase the odds of success. "What do you have to do to stick to your guns this time?" Scaling questions are a clever way of anticipating and disarming resistance and backsliding, and of encouraging commitment to change.

A Woman Who Was Stronger Than She Thought. To illustrate the process of solution-focused therapy we will summarize a session reported by Insoo Berg and Peter De Jong (1996). The client, Lucinda, is a nineteen-year-old African-American mother of two children, ages three and four, who had been removed from Lucinda and placed with foster parents eighteen months earlier. Lucinda had also been physically abused by a former partner. This is all the information the therapist chose to know before seeing Lucinda.

◆

The therapist begins the session by asking "What can I do that would be helpful to you?" rather than asking her what her problems are. Lucinda says she's depressed and stressed out and wants someone to talk to because her kids aren't with her. She also alludes to the abusive relationship with a man she no longer sees.

Without any further discussion of Lucinda's feelings or predicament, the therapist asks a series of questions about how Lucinda was able to break off from the abusive relationship. Lucinda says it was hard because the man, Marvin, didn't want to leave and was threatening to kill her and that he beat her when he saw her. The therapist said "So that's when most women sort of become weak and they take him back. How come you didn't?" Lucinda said "A couple of times I did because I was scared. And the more I kept getting back with him, it got worse and worse. And then he ended up hurting my son." She goes on to describe how Marvin broke the child's leg, which is why she lost custody of her children, and that's when she drew the line and wouldn't take him back. The therapist punctuates her story with comments highlighting Lucinda's competence in protecting her kids like, "But some women . . . would either get scared of him or, you know, somehow think that he's gonna change and take him back," and "Wow, I'm amazed by this. How did you do this?"

After letting Lucinda know she's impressed with her competence, the therapist turns to goal-setting questions. Lucinda says she wants her kids back and doesn't want to be afraid of Marvin anymore. She wants advice on how to be strong with Marvin. The therapist says, "Sounds like you already are, though."

To clarify Lucinda's goal, the therapist asks her the "miracle question." She asks Lucinda to imagine that after she goes to bed that night a miracle will happen and her problems—that she wants her kids back and wants to be stronger—will be solved. How would Lucinda be able to tell that the miracle has happened? Lucinda responds that her kids would be home and she would be very excited. The therapist asks her to elaborate on that miracle picture and Lucinda spends much of the session happily describing what she'd do with her children and how she and they would feel, with the therapist interjecting questions like, "Where did you learn to be such a good, loving mother?"

The therapist asks a scaling question, ". . . on a scale of one to ten, ten stands for how you will be when you finally get your kids back and one is what you were like when your children were taken away from you . . . where would you say things are today?" Lucinda says between eight and nine. The therapist asks how she was able to climb that high. Lucinda says it's because she's sure her kids are coming back soon. After giving more compliments, the therapist takes a break and returns to summarize her feedback. She says that it makes sense that Lucinda would be depressed given what she's lost and what she's experienced in her life, but the therapist is amazed at how Lucinda's used what she's learned. "And that's really absolutely amazing to me. For someone as young as you are . . . you are very wise already." The therapist also compliments her again on breaking up with Marvin. Lucinda is agreeing with all this, so the therapist says, " . . . at this point I'm not sure if we need to get together again even. What do you think?" Lucinda agrees that she doesn't need any more help and they end the session. She never called for another appointment and her children were returned to her.

◆

Berg and De Jong (1996) believe that during the solution-focused conversation Lucinda's perceptions of herself as depressed and her passive demeanor shifted. They think she left with a clearer sense of what she wanted and how to make it happen.

Solution-focused therapists hold that if both client and therapist can reorient themselves in the direction of strengths—exceptions to the problem, clarified goals, and strategies to achieve them—then therapy can be quite brief. Two assumptions justify this belief. The first draws again from constructivism and the power of suggestion. As O'Hanlon and Weiner-Davis (1989) explain,

> Since what you expect influences what you get, solution-oriented therapists maintain those presuppositions that enhance client–therapist cooperation, empower clients, and make our work more effective and enjoyable. We hold assumptions which focus on strengths and possibilities; fortunately, these assumptions also help create self-fulfilling prophecies. (p. 34)

If one perspective is as valid as the next, why not assume that solutions can be found easily and quickly?

The second assumption is borrowed from the MRI model—that a small change is usually all that's needed because it can snowball into bigger changes. As O'Hanlon and Weiner-Davis (1989) put it, "Once a small positive change is made, people feel optimistic and a bit more confident about tackling further changes" (p. 42).

With these two assumptions about change, the solution-focused theorists have fashioned a set of questions and tasks designed to create an optimistic perspective and start the snowball rolling. In Lucinda's case, the therapist used the miracle question, exception questions, coping questions ("How did you do that?"), in-session compliments, and end-of-session feedback that emphasized and summarized her competencies. Lucinda left with the sense that the therapist thought she could achieve her goals.

Evaluating Therapy Theory and Results

One would think that because solution-focused therapy has spread so widely, it would have been thoroughly evaluated by now. There are plenty of subjects and therapists using it, and it's an ideal model to be tested in outcome studies—brief and easily standardized. With managed care's emphasis on accountability, there's plenty of motivation to try to prove effectiveness. But despite all that, there is virtually no empirical evidence of solution-focused therapy's effectiveness.

The solution-focused camp cites two studies of outcome, both from the Brief Family Therapy Center in Milwaukee (Kiser, 1988; De Jong & Hopwood, 1996). In both studies, clients at the center were asked to rate their satisfaction with the treatment at termination and again, by phone, some months after termination. A high percentage of these former clients said they had made at least some progress toward their goals. Unfortunately, this kind of testimonial is about as substantial as the usual response to the waiter's question, "How was everything?" "Fine" may just mean you don't want to make a fuss. When clients tell interviewers that they were "satisfied" with therapy, it may mean they achieved their goals—or that they don't wish to return for more treatment, or merely that they don't want to hurt the therapist's feelings by complaining.

One study of the process of solution-focused therapy stirred things up a bit. Linda Metcalf (1993; Metcalf et al., 1996) interviewed six couples who were considered to have achieved good outcome at the BFTC. She also interviewed their therapists. She found that in several ways what the therapists said happened (and what solution-focused theory says should happen) didn't match the clients' experiences.

For example, in discussing what was helpful, therapists focused primarily on the techniques they used, whereas clients were far more likely to point to qualities of their relationship with the therapist. In addition, while all the therapists believed that the decision to terminate therapy had been reached collaboratively, four of the six couples thought that their therapist had made the decision unilaterally, and some of them felt pushed out prematurely. The study also found that the therapists generally took a more directive role than is suggested by the solution-focused literature.

In reviewing Lucinda's experience, described earlier, a case could be made that the therapist steered the interview in a certain upbeat direction and that the decision to stop after one session was less than mutual. After the therapist said ". . . at this point I'm not sure if we need to get together again even. What do you think?" It would have taken an assertive client to say"No, I need more sessions," even if she did want more.

The issue of whether solution-focused therapy is genuinely collaborative or directive has been raised frequently (Wylie, 1990; Storm, 1991; Lipchik, 1992, 1993, 1996; Efron & Veendendaal, 1993; Efran & Schenker, 1993; Miller, 1994; Nylund & Corsiglia, 1994; O'Hanlon, 1996). It has even been called "solution-forced" therapy by some people because of the perceived tendency for therapists to pressure clients into discussing only the positive and aggressively disregarding anything negative. As Efran and Schenker (1993) ask, "what assurance is there that clients of solution-focused therapists haven't simply learned to keep their complaints to themselves in the presence of the therapist?"

Lucinda came in saying she just needed someone to talk to about feeling stressed out and depressed. By immediately shifting to Lucinda's strengths in breaking up with her abusive boyfriend, the therapist certainly wasn't collaborating with her request and was giving the message that if an empathic listener was what she wanted, she wouldn't get one there. When Lucinda agreed to not return it might have been more related to that message than to no longer feeling the need for help.

Recently solution-focused therapists themselves have begun expressing reservations about the model's injunction to remain constantly upbeat (Storm, 1991; Lipchik, 1992, 1993; Efron & Veenendaal, 1993). As Cheryl Storm (1991) reported, "I have found that being relentlessly solution-focused is a mismatch for some clients. These individuals insist on talking about the problem in detail and, if ignored, fire the therapist. I thought I was misapplying the approach but now believe I . . . overemphasized change." Others (e.g., Efron & Veenendaal, 1993) echo these sentiments: "When we attempt to use these models and stances exclusively, we build up a sense of wrongness and futility, as if we were somehow pulling the wool over the eyes of clients and ourselves" (p. 17).

Eve Lipchik (1993, p. 27) even reported including discussions of client feelings in therapy (a major breech of solution-focused orthodoxy) because "I sense within all my clients . . . the desire to be loved and affirmed by a significant other or others." Yet, in a recent case report she still was impatient with a client's refusal to follow her lead away from feeling depressed. Each time she tried to shift "Lyle" away from his efforts to tell her how bad he felt by focusing on how well he'd coped with his adversity, he disagreed with her and returned to talking about his depression. At a certain point Lipchik (1996) thought,

> Ventilation—or problem talk—is certainly not a solution-focused technique. But I realized that if I did not allow Lyle to set the tone and pace of our conversations, he would probably not come back. At one point, I said, "I know this is very hard for you and you want me to understand how much pain you felt in the past. I don't mean to discount it, but the past is gone, and you came here to talk about happier feelings. Is this helpful or do you want to talk about how you can feel differently in the future?" Lyle kept right on ventilating. (p. 85)

It's this kind of strict adherence to the model's formula and disdain for "ventilating" feelings that bring solution-focused so much criticism.

To their credit, however, some solution-focused therapists are reading the feedback. As mentioned earlier, the name Carl Rogers is popping up frequently. Bill O'Hanlon (1996) said, "Carl Rogers taught us years ago that listening repectfully to clients and letting them know we can hear their perceptions and feelings and that we accept them as they currently are is a prerequisite for most people to cooperate in the change process" (p. 85).

Similarly, William Butler and Keith Powers (1996) stress the importance of validating the client's experience of the problem, and note the absence of such validating in the solution-focused literature. The reader might contrast their case description with Lipchik's, above.

> During the first interview the client complained about feeling increasingly depressed due to recent losses. . . . The therapist listened intently, reflected her feelings, and made many empathic comments. The most important thing the therapist did, however,

was to *not ask* a series of future-oriented questions. . . . In the second interview, one week later, the client again told details of her long history of depression and loss. The therapist picked up on the theme of multiple losses and the many years of struggle. (p. 230)

It was only after going over in detail and empathizing with the large number of losses over the past ten years that the therapist introduced a solution-focused question: "But when I look over this long list [of losses] and consider what you've been through, I can't help but wonder—how do you keep it from getting worse?" (p. 230). The authors conclude that it was crucial to allow the client to fully express her struggles and have her experience validated before shifting the conversation to her strengths.

The problem some solution-focused therapists may have with this line of thinking is that the model could lose its claim to being distinctively brief. It may take several sessions before some clients feel fully understood and acknowledged. If they added an acknowledgement stage to the current model, wouldn't solution-focused therapy begin to resemble the usual supportive therapy, both in duration and in practice?

In other words, the refusal to talk about problems, which is what makes solution-focused therapy unique, turns out to be problematic. Reassuring someone who's worried that there's nothing to worry about isn't very reassuring. It can cause you to believe that your feelings aren't valid, because you wouldn't have them if you would only look at the bright side of things. Unfortunately, most people aren't very eager to be changed by someone they feel doesn't understand them.

We hope that this debate helps solution-focused therapists continue to move away from the formulaic way the model was originally packaged. Many of the techniques are no doubt valuable to clients if properly timed and flexibly applied. But techniques can obscure therapists' intuitive humanity. We hope students will remember Michele Weiner-Davis's (1993) candid confession that she doesn't always practice what she preaches: ". . . my clients cry and express pain, anger, disappointment and fears just as they might in any other therapist's office. And I respond with compassion . . . my therapy story [what she presents in workshops] is not the total picture of how I do therapy" (p. 157).

Summary

Solution-focused therapy descends directly from the MRI approach described in the first section of this chapter, with its emphasis on brevity, minimal intervention, a nonpathological view of people, and formulaic technique. Yet it turns a major MRI emphasis on problems on its head. Where the MRI approach was totally focused on problems, solution-focused therapy is totally focused on solutions.

The idea is that clients have problems largely because they become attached to trying to get to the bottom of their problems and obsessing about their problems' enormity, a process that obscures solutions that are sometimes right under their noses.

This idea has led to the development of a set of techniques for changing "problem talk" into "solution talk." These techniques include: *exception questions* (e.g., "Can you think of a time when you didn't have the problem? What were you doing then?"); the *miracle question* (e.g., "Suppose you went to sleep and a miracle happened such that when you awoke, your problem was solved. What would be different?); *scaling questions* (e.g., "On a scale from zero to ten, how do you feel now compared to when you called?"); *coping questions* (e.g., "Given how bad that was, how were you able to cope?"); *the formula first interview* (e.g., "After you leave today, observe what happens that you want to continue during the next week."); and *giving compliments* ("Wow, you must be very smart to have thought of that!"). These techniques are put into practice as soon as possible to keep the work brief and to discourage clients from dwelling on the negative side of their experience.

More recently, therapists have questioned the model's emphasis on technique and speculated that qualities of the therapist–client relationship may be at the heart of the model's effectiveness. This has led to a call for greater collaboration with clients such that their feelings are acknowledged and validated before introducing solution-focused techniques.

Solution-focused therapy continues to have great appeal in the world of psychotherapy. Some of its popularity relates to the number of therapists who are struggling to find ways to feel effective while living with managed care's limited number of sessions. Because of its reputation for brevity, solution-focused treatment is favored by managed care companies, so therapists can get approval to use it. In addition, its formula version is easy to learn—it can be picked up in a few workshops—and its upbeat nature makes it more enjoyable for many therapists.

Among the questions asked by critics are: Is the therapist really having a respectful conversation with a client when the therapist only praises, searches for exceptions, and coaxes optimism? Do such insistently upbeat dialogues have the effect of silencing people's doubts and their pain? Can the solution-focused therapist find a way to honor client perceptions that don't fit into the formula? Can clients trust the feedback of someone who constantly strives to find things to praise and never challenges or questions them? Can clients be honest regarding the outcome of their therapy with someone who seems to want so much for them to feel better about things?

Other questions highlight the model's strengths. For example: Isn't it important for therapists to have clear, concrete guidelines so therapy doesn't become vague and directionless? Isn't it more empowering to help people envision their future goals and focus on their strengths than on their problems and deficits? If people's experience of pain is tied to the way they think or talk about it, then isn't it better to use language to lead people out of pain than to dwell on it?

Solution-focused therapy is struggling to answer all these questions and thereby find a coherent identity as we enter the twenty-first century. We hope that this evolution won't be dictated entirely by the constraints of managed care or dogmatic adherence to doctrine. Instead, we imagine that the maturing of solution-focused therapy will reflect a growing appreciation that, while a focus on solutions can be helpful, people need acknowledgement for their lived experience, which isn't always upbeat.

References

Alexander, J., and Parsons, B. 1973. Short-term behavioral intervention with delinquent families: Impact on family process and recidivism. *Journal of Abnormal Psychology. 81*:219–225.

Alexander, J., and Parsons, B. 1982. *Functional family therapy.* Monterey, CA: Brooks Cole.

Andersen, T. 1987. The reflecting team: Dialogue and meta-dialogue in clinical work. *Family Process. 26*:415–417.

Andolfi, M. 1979. *Family therapy: An international approach.* New York: Plenum Press.

Andolfi, M., Angelo, C., and di Nichilo, M. 1989. *The myth of Atlas.* New York: Brunner/Mazel.

Andolfi, M., and Zwerling, I., eds. 1980. *Dimensions of family therapy.* New York: Guilford Press.

Berg, I. K., and De Jong, P. 1996. Solution-building conversations: Co-constructing a sense of competence with clients. *Families in Society: The Journal of Contemporary Human Services.* June, 376–391.

Berg, I. K., and de Shazer, S. 1993. Making numbers talk: Language in therapy. In *The new language of change,* S. Friedman, ed. New York: Guilford Press.

Berg, I., and Miller, S. 1992. *Working with the problem drinker: A solution-focused approach.* New York: Norton.

Bergman, J. 1985. *Fishing for barracuda: Pragmatics of brief systemic therapy.* New York: Norton.

Boscolo, L. 1983. Final discussion. In *Psychosocial intervention in schizophrenia: An international view,* H. Stierlin, L. Wynne, and M. Wirsching, eds. Berlin: Springer-Verlag.

Boscolo, L., and Bertrando, P. 1992. The reflexive loop of past, present, and future in systemic therapy and consultation. *Family Process. 31:* 119–133.

Boscolo, L., Cecchin, G., Hoffman, L., and Penn, P. 1987. *Milan systemic family therapy.* New York: Basic Books.

Breunlin, D., and Schwartz, R. 1986. Sequences: Toward a common denominator of family therapy. *Family Process. 25:*67–87.

Butler, W., and Powers, K. 1996. Solution-focused grief therapy. In *Handbook of solution-focused brief therapy,* S. Miller, M. Hubble, and B. Duncan, eds. San Francisco: Jossey-Bass.

Cade, B., and O'Hanlon, W. 1993. *A brief guide to brief therapy.* New York: Norton.

Cecchin, G. 1987. Hypothesizing, circularity and neutrality revisited: An invitation to curiosity. *Family Process. 26:*405–413.

Cecchin, G., Lane, G., and Ray, W. 1993. From strategizing to nonintervention: Toward irreverence in systemic practice. *Journal of Marital and Family Therapy. 19:*125–136.

Coleman, S. 1987. Milan in Bucks County. *Family Therapy Networker. 11:*42–47.

Coyne, J. 1987. Depression, biology, marriage and marital therapy. *Journal of Marital and Family Therapy. 13:*393–408.

Coyne, J., Kahn, J., and Gotlib, I. 1987. Depression. In *Family interaction and psychopathology,* T. Jacob, ed. New York: Plenum Press.

De Jong, P., and Hopwood, L. 1996. Outcome research on treatment conducted at the Brief Family Therapy Center, 1992–1993. In *Handbook of solution-focused brief therapy,* S. Miller, M. Hubble, and B. Duncan, eds. San Francisco: Jossey-Bass.

de Shazer, S. 1984. The death of resistance. *Family Process. 23:*11–21.

de Shazer, S. 1985. *Keys to solutions in brief therapy.* New York: Norton.

de Shazer, S. 1986. An indirect approach to brief therapy. In *Indirect approaches in therapy,* S. de Shazer and R. Kral, eds. Rockville, MD: Aspen Systems.

de Shazer, S. 1987. Minimal elegance. *Family Therapy Networker.* September/October, 59.

de Shazer, S. 1988. *Clues: Investigating solutions in brief therapy.* New York: Norton.

de Shazer, S. 1991a. Muddles, bewilderment, and practice theory. *Family Process. 30:*453–458.

de Shazer, S. 1991b. *Putting difference to work.* New York: Norton.

de Shazer, S. 1993. Creative misunderstanding: There is no escape from language. In *Therapeautic Conversations,* S. Gilligan and R. Price, eds. New York: Norton.

de Shazer, S. 1994. *Words were originally magic.* New York: Norton.

de Shazer, S., and Berg, I. K. 1993. Constructing solutions. *Family Therapy Networker. 12:*42–43.

de Shazer, S., Berg, I. K., Lipchik, E., Nunnally, E., Molnar, A., Gingerich, W., and Weiner-Davis, M. 1986. Brief therapy: Focused solution development. *Family Process. 25:*207–222.

Efran, J., and Schenker, M. 1993. A potpourri of solutions: How new and different is solution-focused therapy? *Family Therapy Networker. 17*(3): 71–74.

Efron, D., and Veenendaal, K. 1993. Suppose a miracle doesn't happen: The non-miracle option. *Journal of Systemic Therapies. 12:*11–18.

Eron, J., and Lund, T. 1993. An approach to how problems evolve and dissolve: Integrating narrative and strategic concepts. *Family Process. 32:* 291–309.

Eron, J., and Lund, T. 1996. *Narrative solutions in brief therapy.* New York: Guilford Press.

Fisch, R. 1978. Review of problem-solving therapy, by Jay Haley. *Family Process. 17:*107–110.

Fisch, R., Watzlawick, P., Weakland, J., and Bodin, A. 1973. On unbecoming family therapists. In *The book of family therapy,* A. Ferber, M. Mendelsohn, & A. Napier, eds. Boston: Houghton Mifflin.

Fisch, R., Weakland, J., and Segal, L. 1982. *The tactics of change.* San Francisco: Jossey-Bass.

Flaskas, C. 1992. A reframe by any other name: On the process of reframing in strategic, Milan and analytic therapy. *Journal of Family Therapy. 14:* 145–161.

Frankl, V. 1960. Paradoxical intention: A logotherapeutic technique. *American Journal of Psychotherapy. 14*:520–535.

Furman, B., and Ahola, T. 1992. *Solution talk: Hosting therapeutic conversations.* New York: Norton.

Gelcer, E., and Schwartzbein, D. 1989. A piagetian view of family therapy: Selvini-Palazzoli and the invariant approach. *Family Process. 28*:439–456.

Grove, D., and Haley, J. 1993. *Conversations on therapy.* New York: Norton.

Haley, J. 1963. *Strategies of psychotherapy.* New York: Grune & Stratton.

Haley, J. 1973. *Uncommon therapy.* New York: Norton.

Haley, J. 1976. *Problem-solving therapy.* San Francisco: Jossey-Bass.

Haley, J. 1980. *Leaving home: The therapy of disturbed young people.* New York: McGraw-Hill.

Haley, J. 1981. *Reflections on therapy.* Chevy Chase, MD: The Family Therapy Institute of Washington, DC.

Haley, J. 1984. *Ordeal therapy.* San Francisco: Jossey-Bass.

Haley, J. 1996. *Learning and teaching therapy.* New York: Guilford Press.

Hare-Mustin, R. 1975. Treatment of temper tantrums by a paradoxical intervention. *Family Process. 14*:481–485.

Held, B. 1996. Solution-focused therapy and the postmodern: A critical analysis. In *Handbook of solution-focused brief therapy,* S. Miller, M. Hubble, and B. Duncan, eds. San Francisco: Jossey-Bass.

Hoffman, L. 1981. *Foundations of family therapy.* New York: Basic Books.

Hoffman, L. 1983. A co-evolutionary framework for systemic family therapy. In *Diagnosis and assessment in family therapy,* J. Hansen and B. Keeney, eds. Rockville, MD: Aspen Systems.

Hudson, P., and O'Hanlon, W. H. 1992. *Rewriting love stories: Brief marital therapy.* New York: Norton.

Jackson, D. D. 1967. The myth of normality. *Medical Opinion and Review. 3*:28–33.

Keim, J. 1997. Working with oppositional children. In *Integrative cases in couples and family therapy,* F. Dattilio, ed. New York: Guilford Press.

Kiser, D. 1988. A follow-up study conducted at the Brief Family Therapy Center. Unpublished manuscript.

Kleckner, T., Frank, L., Bland, C., Amendt, J. and duRee Bryant, R. 1992. The myth of the unfeeling strategic therapist. *Journal of Marital and Family Therapy. 18*:41–51.

Langsley, D., Machotka, P., and Flomenhaft, K. 1971. Avoiding mental hospital admission: A follow-up study. *American Journal of Psychiatry. 127*: 1391–1394.

Lipchik, E. 1986. Purposeful interview. *Journal of Strategic and Systemic Therapies. 5*:88–99.

Lipchik, E. 1992. Interview. *Journal of Strategic and Systemic Therapies. 11*(4).

Lipchik, E. 1993. "Both/and" solutions. In *The new language of change,* S. Friedman, ed. New York: Guilford Press.

Lipchik, E. 1996. Mr. Spock goes to therapy. *Family Therapy Networker.* Jan/Feb, 79–84.

Lipchik, E., and Kubicki, A. 1996. Solution-focused domestic violence views: Bridges toward a new reality in couples therapy. In *Handbook of solution-focused brief therapy,* S. Miller, M. Hubble, and B. Duncan, eds. San Francisco: Jossey-Bass.

Machal, M., Feldman, R., and Sigal, J., 1989. The unraveling of a treatment program: A follow-up study of the Milan approach to family therapy. *Family Process. 28*:457–470.

Madanes, C. 1980. Protection, paradox and pretending. *Family Process. 19*:73–85.

Madanes, C. 1981. *Strategic family therapy.* San Francisco: Jossey-Bass.

Madanes, C. 1984. *Behind the one-way mirror.* San Francisco: Jossey-Bass.

Madanes, C. 1990. *Sex, love, and violence: Strategies for transformation.* New York: Norton.

Metcalf, L. 1993. The pragmatics of change in solution-focused brief therapy. Unpublished doctoral dissertation, Texas Women's University, Denton, Texas.

Metcalf, L., Thomas, F., Duncan, B., Miller, S., and Hubble, M. 1996. What works in solution-focused brief therapy: A qualitative analysis of client and therapist's perceptions. In *Handbook of solution-focused brief therapy,* S. Miller, M. Hubble, and B. Duncan, eds. San Francisco: Jossey-Bass.

Miller, S. 1994. The solution-conspiracy: A mystery in three installments. *Journal of Systemic Therapies. 13*:18–37.

Miller, S., Hubble, M., and Duncan, B. 1996. *Handbook of solution-focused brief therapy.* San Francisco: Jossey-Bass.

Minuchin, S. 1974. *Families and family therapy.* Cambridge, MA: Harvard University Press.

Nylund, D., and Corsiglia, V. 1994. Becoming solution-focused in brief therapy: Remembering something important we already knew. *Journal of Systemic Therapies. 13*:5–12.

O'Hanlon, W. 1996. Case commentary. *Family Therapy Networker.* Jan/Feb: 84–85.

O'Hanlon, W., and Martin, M. 1992. *Solution oriented hypnosis: An Ericksonian approach.* New York: Norton.

O'Hanlon, W. H., and Weiner-Davis, M. 1989. *In search of solutions: A new direction in psychotherapy.* New York: Norton.

Papp, P. 1980. The Greek chorus and other techniques of paradoxical therapy. *Family Process. 19*:45–57.

Papp, P. 1983. *The process of change.* New York: Guilford Press.

Parsons, B., and Alexander, J. 1973. Short term family intervention: A therapy outcome study. *Journal of Consulting and Clinical Psychology. 41*:195–201.

Penn, P. 1982. Circular questioning. *Family Process. 21*:267–280.

Penn, P. 1985. Feed-forward: Further questioning, future maps. *Family Process. 24*:299–310.

Price, J. 1996. *Power and compassion: Working with difficult adolescents and abused parents.* New York: Guilford Press.

Rabkin, R. 1977. *Strategic psychotherapy.* New York: Basic Books.

Rogers, C. 1961. *On becoming a person.* Boston: Houghton Mifflin.

Rohrbaugh, M., Tennen, H., Press, S., and White, L. 1981. Compliance, defiance, and therapeutic paradox: Guidelines for strategic use of paradoxical interventions. *American Journal of Orthopsychiatry. 51*:454–466.

Satir, V. 1964. *Conjoint family therapy.* Palo Alto, CA: Science and Behavior Books.

Selvini, M., ed. 1988. *The work of Mara Selvini Palazzoli.* Northvale, NJ: Jason Aronson.

Selvini, M. 1993. Major mental disorders, distorted reality and family secrets. Unpublished manuscript.

Selvini Palazzoli, M. 1981. *Self-starvation: From the intrapsychic to the transpersonal approach to anorexia nervosa.* New York: Jason Aronson.

Selvini Palazzoli, M. 1986. Towards a general model of psychotic games. *Journal of Marital and Family Therapy. 12*:339–349.

Selvini Palazzoli, M., Boscolo, L., Cecchin, G., and Prata, G. 1978a. A ritualized prescription in family therapy: Odd days and even days. *Journal of Marriage and Family Counseling. 4*:3–9.

Selvini Palazzoli, M., Boscolo, L., Cecchin, G., and Prata, G. 1978b. *Paradox and counterparadox.* New York: Jason Aronson.

Selvini Palazzoli, M., Boscolo, L., Cecchin, G., and Prata, G. 1980. Hypothesizing—circularity—neutrality: Three guidelines for the conductor of the session. *Family Process. 19*:3–12.

Selvini Palazzoli, M., and Prata, G. 1983. A new method for therapy and research in the treatment of schizophrenic families. In *Psychosocial intervention in schizophrenia: An international view,* H. Stierlin, L. Wynne, and M. Wirsching, eds. Berlin: Springer-Verlag.

Selvini Palazzoli, M., and Viaro, M. 1988. The anorectic process in the family: A six-stage model as a guide for individual therapy. *Family Process. 27*: 129–148.

Simon, D. 1996. Crafting consciousness through form: Solution-focused therapy as a spiritual path. In *Handbook of solution-focused brief therapy,* S. Miller, M. Hubble, and B. Duncan, eds. San Francisco: Jossey-Bass.

Sluzki, C. 1978. Marital therapy from a systems theory perspective. In *Marriage and marital therapy: Psychoanalytic, behavioral and systems therapy perspectives,* T. J. Paolino and B. S. Mc Crady, eds. New York: Brunner/Mazel.

Stanton, D. 1981. Strategic approaches to family therapy. In *Handbook of family therapy,* A. Gurman and D. Kniskern, eds. New York: Brunner/Mazel.

Stanton, D., Todd, T., and Associates. 1982. *The family therapy of drug abuse and addiction.* New York: Guilford Press.

Storm, C. 1991. The remaining thread: Matching change and stability signals. *Journal of Strategic and Systemic Therapies. 10*:114–117.

Tomm, K. 1984a. One perspective on the Milan systemic approach: Part I. Overview of development, theory and practice. *Journal of Marital and Family Therapy. 10*:113–125.

Tomm, K. 1984b. One perspective on the Milan systemic approach: Part II. Description of session format, interviewing style and interventions. *Journal of Marital and Family Therapy. 10*:253–271.

Tomm, K. 1987a. Interventive interviewing: Part I. Strategizing as a fourth guideline for the therapist. *Family Process. 26:*3–13.

Tomm, K. 1987b. Interventive interviewing: Part II. Reflexive questioning as a means to enable self-healing. *Family Process. 26:* 167–184.

Tuyn, L. K. 1992. Solution-focused therapy and Rogerian nursing science: An integrated approach. *Archives of Psychiatric Nursing. 6:*83–89.

Walter, J., and Peller, J. 1992. *Becoming solution-focused in brief therapy.* New York: Brunner/Mazel.

Walter, J., and Peller, J. 1996. Rethinking our assumptions: Assuming anew in a postmodern world. In *Handbook of solution-focused brief therapy,* S. Miller, M. Hubble, and B. Duncan, eds. San Francisco: Jossey-Bass.

Watzlawick, P., Beavin, J., and Jackson, D. 1967. *Pragmatics of human communication.* New York: Norton.

Watzlawick, P., Weakland, J., and Fisch, R. 1974. *Change: Principles of problem formation and problem resolution.* New York: Norton.

Weakland, J., Fisch, R., Watzlawick, P., and Bodin, A. 1974. Brief therapy: Focused problem resolution. *Family Process. 13:*141–168.

Weakland, J., and Ray, W., eds. 1995. *Propagations: Thirty years of influence from the Mental Research Institute.* Binghamton, NY: Haworth Press.

Weiner-Davis, M. 1992. *Divorce-busting.* New York: Summit Books.

Weiner-Davis, M. 1993. Pro-constructed realities. In *Therapeutic conversations,* S. Gilligan and R. Price, eds. New York: Norton.

Wylie, M. S. 1990. Brief therapy on the couch. *Family Therapy Networker. 14:*26–34, 66.

12

Narrative Therapy

The narrative approach that now dominates the landscape of family therapy is a perfect expression of the postmodern revolution. When all knowledge is regarded as constructed rather than discovered, it's fitting that the leading approach to family therapy is concerned with the ways people construct meanings rather than the ways they behave. Narrative therapy focuses on understanding how experience creates expectations and how expectations then shape experience through the creation of organizing stories.

The central assumption of the narrative approach is that personal experience is fundamentally ambiguous. This is an easily misunderstood concept. It doesn't mean that experience isn't real or that it's necessarily mysterious or opaque, but rather that understanding human experience, including one's own, is never simply a process of seeing it or analyzing it. The elements of human experience are understood only through a process that organizes those elements, puts them together, assigns them meaning, and prioritizes them. To say that experience is fundamentally ambiguous is to say that its meaning isn't inherent or apparent but that it lends itself to multiple understandings and interpretations.

To illustrate how experience is shaped by the language we use to describe it, consider the difference between calling the heart-racing tension most people feel before speaking in public "stage fright" or "excitement." The former description makes this familiar palpitating agitation a problem, something to overcome. The latter description suggests that it's natural, an almost inevitable and not necessarily problematic response to standing up in front of people whose approval you hope to win.

Whether people experience stage fright or excitement depends on how they interpret their physiological arousal. Strategic therapists gave clients reframes—new interpretations—for their experiences. "The next time you're speaking, just think of yourself as excited rather than frightened." Narrative therapists recognized that such new interpretations don't survive long unless they fit into the story people construct about themselves. A man whose life narrative is that he's boring and unappealing will have trouble consistently interpreting his trembling hands as due to excitement no matter how hard he tries to sell that frame to himself. If the same man were helped to construct a new, more positive, story about himself, the reframe becomes unnecessary. He automatically interprets his reactions as excitement because, since he thinks he's interesting, he expects people to like what he has to say.

The stories we tell ourselves are powerful because they determine what we notice and remember, and, therefore, how we face the future. Imagine, for example, what a woman who thought of herself as "reasonably successful" would remember from high school and how this version of events would affect her approach to college. Then picture what the same past and future would look like if that woman thought of herself as "never quite good enough."

Life is complicated so we find ways to explain it. These explanations, the stories we tell ourselves, organize our experience and shape our behavior. Unfortunately, the narratives clients bring to treatment are often discouraging and negative. Their stories selectively highlight past events that confirm them and minimize contradictory events. Stories function as inner screens and spin doctors. They let in experiences that fit and keep out experiences that don't. They put a spin on all experiences, reinterpreting events until they confirm the overarching life picture.

Family therapy was founded by revolutionaries and still attracts them. We seem compelled to reinvent our field every few years, and the departure represented by narrative therapy is in this revolutionary tradition. Unlike the cybernetic metaphor, which focused the field on self-defeating patterns of *behavior*, the narrative metaphor focuses on self-defeating *cognitions*—the stories people tell themselves about their problems. With the cybernetic metaphor, therapy meant blocking maladaptive patterns of interaction, with or without the client's understanding of the process. The narrative metaphor, on the other hand, focuses on clients' understanding and experience, expanding their attention to allow them to consider alternative ways of looking at themselves and their problems.

Systems thinking was once the inspiration for the field, but narrative therapists criticize systems thinking and replace it with the narrative metaphor. Family therapists used to work mainly with whole families and rarely addressed the issues of individuals; narrative therapists spend far more time helping individuals reexamine themselves than discussing family issues. Family therapists were interested in the family's impact on the problem; narrative therapists are interested in the problem's impact on the family. Where family therapists once gave directives and prescribed rituals, narrative therapists mainly ask questions. Family therapists once ignored a family's history, believing that present interactions were the important targets. Narrative therapists spend a great deal of time going over clients' pasts, listening to their life stories and looking for events that can open up alternative stories.

Thus, narrative therapy isn't just another school of family therapy; it's something entirely different. It brings fresh ideas, excitement, and controversy to a field that's struggled to find its identity and passion in the era following the first wave of original schools.

Sketches of Leading Figures

Michael White is a family therapist living in Adelaide, South Australia. He and his wife, Cheryl White, are based at the Dulwich Centre in Adelaide, out of which comes training, clinical work, and publications related to White's approach. The *Dulwich Centre Newsletter,* a quarterly journal, is the major vehicle through which White's ideas are disseminated. In addition, the Dulwich Centre has published several collections of his writing and interviews, available by writing Dulwich Centre Publications, Hutt Street, PO Box 7192, Adelaide, South Australia 5000.

Now in his late 40s, White initially worked as an electrical and mechanical draftsman before realizing that he wasn't an engineer at heart. He preferred working with people to working with machines. Not surprisingly, White is staunchly anti-mechanistic and rejects systems thinking and cybernetics because of their mechanistic qualities. In 1967 he trained to be a social worker and for over thirty years now has been struggling to find ways to help people. Some of his early experiences on inpatient units soured him on traditional approaches to therapy and piqued his interest in the writings of Michel Foucault and Erving Goffman, who criticized the dehumanizing processes of institutions and expert discourses.

After learning about some of the original schools of family therapy, in the late 1970s White became interested in examining the ideas from which those schools emerged. "I decided to go back and make my own interpretation of those ideas, rather than just accept the interpretations of the originators of these schools" (White, 1995, p. 11). Initially he was drawn to the work of Gregory Bateson and found himself more interested in what Bateson said about information and how people map the world than in the behavioral patterns and functionalist ideas that had informed other systems-based models. Under the influence of Bateson and Foucault, White crystallized his original ideas about externalizing problems (regarding them as something operating on persons, rather than as something they're doing). In the late 1980s White was introduced to the narrative metaphor by his friend and colleague, David Epston, and by Cheryl White, who had discovered it in her readings on feminism. White found that the narrative metaphor fit well with the map-making aspects of Bateson's thinking and with Foucault's interest in releasing people from the grip of dominant discourses.

David Epston, a family therapist from Auckland, New Zealand, is the second most influential shaper of the narrative landscape. Through his interest in anthropology, Epston encountered the narrative metaphor and convinced White that it was more useful for clients than cybernetics. He always had an interest in literature and for years was known as a storyteller, writing the "Story Corner" for the *Australian and New Zealand Journal of Family Therapy* (Freedman & Combs, 1996).

Epston has contributed to most aspects of narrative theory and practice, but in particular has developed and categorized a variety of questions and emphasized that to maintain their new narratives, clients need supportive communities. He fostered the development of "leagues"—groups of clients battling the same problem, such as the Anti-Anorexia/Anti-Bulimia League of New Zealand. He serves as archivist for a number of such leagues, collecting tapes and letters that provide ideas to others about the resourceful ways that people are escaping from their problems.

He also pioneered the use of letter-writing to clients, pointing out that long after the influence of the therapist's presence has faded, clients can read letters that bolster their new stories and resolve. Epston and White coauthored two collections of writings that have served as bibles for the narrative model (Epston & White, 1992; White & Epston, 1990).

While White and Epston are the principle leaders of the narrative movement, a number of clinicians have applied narrative in creative ways and taken it in new directions.

Jill Freedman and Gene Combs direct a small narrative therapy training center in Evanston,

Illinois. Before joining the narrative camp, they were strategic therapists and well-known interpreters of Milton Erickson's work. They were also political activists and were drawn to White's approach in large part by its political emphasis. This combination of former strategic therapist and political activist characterizes the backgrounds of many prominent narrative therapists. Their book, *Narrative Therapy* (Freedman & Combs, 1996), is an excellent, practical guide to narrative therapy.

Jeffrey Zimmerman and Vicki Dickerson are codirectors of the Bay Area Family Therapy Training Associates and together with John Neal conduct training in narrative therapy for the Mental Research Institute in Palo Alto. These two creative therapists pioneered the use of narrative therapy with difficult adolescents and with couples (Dickerson & Zimmerman, 1992; Zimmerman & Dickerson, 1993). Their most recent book, *If Problems Talked: Adventures in Narrative Therapy* (Zimmerman & Dickerson, 1996), is a very useful explication of narrative practice, animated by the novel device of personifying problems and having them speak about how "they" conspire to take over peoples' lives.

Stephan Madigan (1994; Madigan & Epston, 1995) is a therapist in Vancouver, Canada, who has contributed to narrative theory and founded the Vancouver Anti-Anorexia/Anti-Bulimia League, a grass-roots activist organization that provides support for members and has become politically active, educating public and professional groups and protesting images in the media that promote "body-guilt" (Freedman & Combs, 1996). This group represents a logical extension of the narrative movement's therapy of liberation, helping people organize not only to create a supportive subculture but also to take an active role in trying to change the dominant culture.

While Karl Tomm has made original contributions of his own, he has also played the role in the history of family therapy of introducing innovators and translating their work. Originally a strategic therapist, he was a strong promoter and translator of the Milan model and then of the philosophy of Chilean biologist, Humberto Maturana. While he doesn't totally embrace the narrative metaphor, his admiration and support of White's work (Tomm, 1993) has hastened the spread of narrative therapy throughout North America. Other prominent narrative therapists include Kathy Weingarten in Newton Centre, Massachusetts; Sallyann Roth with the Family Institute of Cambridge; and Janet Adams-Wescott in Tulsa, Oklahoma.

Harlene Anderson and the late Harry Goolishian, who developed a linguistic, conversational approach to family therapy (described in Chapter 10), can be seen as forerunners of the narrative model. Their work was based on the premise that problems are maintained in language and are subsequently dissolved through conversation. By taking a stance of determined unknowingness, Goolishian and Anderson subsumed their own expertise to allow clients to become the experts on their own lives. The link between this work and the narrative school was the belief that conversation generates meaning and that therapy should be a collaborative enterprise. The difference is that Anderson and Goolishian were less active in co-creating new stories with clients, preferring to keep their agendas out of their questions.

Theoretical Formulations

The notion that people's lives are organized by their life narratives isn't original to family therapy. Indeed, well before family therapy adopted this idea, the fields of anthropology and sociology had shifted from studying the structure of cultures and societies to studying their belief systems, a shift that parallels recent developments in family therapy. Jerome Bruner, a sociologist who pioneered the narrative metaphor in his field and strongly influenced family therapy's conception of narrative, describes this evolution:

> By the mid 1970s the social sciences had moved . . . toward a more interpretive posture: meaning became the central focus—how the world was interpreted, by what codes meaning was regulated, in what sense culture itself could be treated as "text" that participants "read" for their own guidance. (Bruner, 1986, p. 8)

What became clear to social scientists was that the way people interpreted their experience had a powerful influence on their lives, and that people interpreted their experience in the form of coherent stories that helped them make sense of the diverse events that constituted their lives. As Bruner (1991, p. 4) put it, "we organize our experience and our memory of human happening mainly in the form of narrative—stories, excuses, myths, reasons for doing and not doing, and so on." Of particular interest was the way people construct personal narratives, highlighting events that fit the plot and ignoring those that don't fit.

The narrative approach first found its way into psychotherapy in the hermeneutic tradition in psychoanalysis. Following Freud, classical analysts believed that there was one correct and comprehensive way to interpret experience. Patients might not understand their dreams or symptoms because their motives were unconscious, but an analyst possessed of the truth of psychoanalytic theory could discover unconscious meaning much like an archaeologist uncovers the buried remains of the past. Then in the 1980s, revisionists such as Donald Spence, Roy Schafer, and Paul Ricoeur began to argue against this positivistic conception of psychoanalytic reality.

The truth of experience, they said, isn't discovered or uncovered, it's created. Therapists deal only with versions of reality, and these are mediated by narration. The goal of therapy shifted from historical truth to narrative intelligibility. The challenge was to construct truths in the service of self-coherence—not a true picture of the past. The therapist was now more of a poet or novelist than an archaeologist.

Family therapists who tried on this narrative metaphor for understanding human interactions found it extremely useful. As they began to ask clients about their stories, therapists came to recognize how much stories affected clients' perceptions and their interpretations of those perceptions. That is, life stories function as filters that screen out experiences that don't fit the plot line or, if they can't be screened out, distort events until they somehow fit. In keeping with the expression "to a man with a hammer, everything looks like a nail," a man whose narrative says that he's incompetent chalks up successes to dumb luck or to having fooled people once again. From this perspective, trying to get such a man to change his behavior without addressing his overarching life story is futile, because no matter how many successes he has, he'll still find a way to dismiss them and continue to emphasize his failures.

These therapists also found they preferred the humane implications of the narrative metaphor to the mechanism of cybernetics, the metaphor that had previously dominated the field. Michael White, for example, had originally drawn heavily on the cybernetic thinking of Gregory Bateson, but he renounced systems thinking after being encouraged to pursue narrative ideas by Cheryl White and David Epston.

> It is very often assumed that the narrative metaphor can be tacked on to these other metaphors [of system and pattern], and the narrative metaphor is often conflated with them . . . this tacking on and conflation of disparate metaphors simply does not work, and, in my view, suggests a lack of awareness of the basic premises and very different political consequences that are associated with these different metaphors. (White, 1995, p. 214)

What's wrong with the systems metaphor? Narrative therapists assert that systems thinking encourages therapists to view families from the position of objective, outside observer as one might study a dysfunctional machine, without reference to its history, point of view, or environment. This objectification has several consequences that narrative therapists don't like. The systems-oriented therapist: (1) is positioned as the expert relative to the family, (2) searches for flaws in the system and intervenes to repair those flaws, (3) views his or her own assessment as objective and more accurate than the family's, (4) treats people as objects to be manipulated, and (5) doesn't consider the larger historical/political/cultural context in which the family is embedded.

In contrast, narrative theory is viewed as encouraging therapists to: (1) take a collaborative, listening position with strong interest in the client's story; (2) search for times in a client's history when he or she was strong or resourceful; (3) use questions to take a nonimposing, respectful approach to any new story put forth; (4) never label people and instead treat them as human beings with unique personal histories; and (5) help people separate from the dominant cultural narratives they have internalized so as to open space for alternative life stories (White, 1995; Freedman & Combs, 1996).

Narrative therapists also take a strong stand against the functionalist elements of both family systems and psychoanalytic models that led therapists to believe that problems are inherent in individuals (as psychoanalysis would have it) or in families (as family systems would have it). Instead, they believe that problems arise because people are induced by our culture into subscribing to narrow and self-defeating views of themselves and the world. In a sense, narrative therapies complete the process of widening the circle of culpability for problems. That is, psychoanalysis blamed individuals, family systems rescued individuals and blamed families, and now narrative rescues families and blames society.

To keep the family and individual family members blameless, and to counter the way our culture convinces people that people are their problems, narrative therapists *externalize* problems. They speak of the problem as if it were a separate entity that is oppressing everyone in the family, including the client. Neither the client nor the family is the problem—the problem is the problem. In keeping with this philosophy, and unlike many family therapists, narrative therapists don't explore family dynamics or structure to locate flaws that might be maintaining problems. They aren't interested in the family's impact on the problem, but rather are interested in the problem's impact on the family—and on the socially constructed points of view that support that impact.

The idea that families and individuals are not the culprits in creating problems requires a particular view of people and how easily influenced they are by what narrative therapists call dominant discourses (prevalent, and often toxic, cultural themes) in society. Social constructionism, a philosophy that has become popular in psychology, fills this bill nicely because it portrays people as almost hypnotically susceptible to the narratives of the culture.

For decades family therapists adopted Milton Erickson's view of people as wellsprings of untapped resources. By altering a person's interpersonal context, we released these inner resources. This position is repudiated by social constructionists who reject the idea of the self as a source of anything. Theirs is a fluid or plastic version of the self, powerfully and constantly affected by interaction with others (Gergen, 1991; Weingarten, 1991). Such a self is not essentially good or bad, but is continually reconstituted through interaction, which is why White calls it a "constitutionalist self" (White, 1991, 1993). With this emphasis on the internalization of external phenomena, this constitutionalist self has more in common with the neoanalytic object relations view (see Chapter 7) than with the Ericksonian self.

Because in the constitutionalist view we are so easily influenced by dominant cultural narratives, we have to constantly reexamine our beliefs to ensure that we constitute ourselves in the way we want to be, rather than the way we are induced to be by society. This is a key shift in theory that has profound implications for personal and professional relations. When Jill Freedman moved from seeing herself as containing resources to having to constantly choose how to think and act, she became motion-sick.

> I had always believed that "deep down" I was a good person no matter what I did. If we were really to adopt these new ways of thinking and perceiving . . . we would become responsible for continually constituting ourselves as the people we wanted to be. We would have to examine our taken-for-granted stories in our local culture, the contexts we moved in, the relationships we cultivated, and the like, so as to constantly re-author and update our own stories. (Freedman & Combs, 1996, p. 17)

This conception of a fluid, plastic self as constituted by whatever narratives are currently believed, and not consisting of essential or enduring qualities, is a pillar in the foundation of narrative therapy. It allows therapists to believe that in coauthoring new narratives with clients they are doing all that's necessary to produce profound and lasting change in their clients' self-concepts and lives. The new narrative becomes the reconstituted self.

As narrative therapists shifted their attention from individuals and families as the source of problems to cultural beliefs and practices, they looked to philosophers who could provide some perspective on society. If our constitutionalist selves are polluted by the narrative environments we inhabit, perhaps we should know more about those environments.

Michel Foucault (1965, 1975, 1980, 1984), the French social philosopher, devoted his life to studying and exposing how various discourses within a society (the large-scale narratives that shape the distribution of power) dehumanized, objectified, and marginalized various social groups and maintained the power of other groups. Foucault had a tremendous impact on Michael White and, through White, the whole narrative movement. Foucault considered himself a historian of systems of thought and exposed the arbitrary process throughout history by which certain people or practices have been labeled abnormal around madness, illness, criminality, and sexuality, and then oppressed based on that labeling.

Foucault not only believed that those constructing the dominant narratives in a society (those deemed to have expert knowledge in various fields) had the power to exclude groups, but that the narratives themselves become internalized truths within all citizens of the society, such that all people come to judge their bodies, achievements, and personalities on the basis of standards set by society's judges (doctors, educators, clergy, psychotherapists, politicians, celebrities). Just as the dominant discourses within a culture suppress marginalized voices, the same process occurs within individuals whose conceptions of themselves aren't given credence because they differ from cultural norms.

Thus, Foucault influenced White to take the social constructionist axiom that there are no absolute truths in the world in a political direction, toward deconstructing (reexamining with an eye toward their origins and their effects) the established truths that oppress peoples lives. Narrative therapists may not always bring up cultural themes in sessions, but they always view problems through a political lens. They aren't just interested in the effects of obviously toxic social narratives such as misogyny, racism, class bias, and heterosexism; they're also interested in more subtle pressures regarding such day-to-day issues as how much money people believe they need to make, how perfect their children need to be, and how many cars they need to have.

Narrative therapists are also expected to explore the influence of these cultural themes on their own narratives. For many therapists, then, the narrative approach is more than simply another school of therapy, it's an orientation to life. Many therapists came to the field with strong political predilections and desires to help society's oppressed. It's this political element that made narrative therapy so attractive to them. As prominent narrative therapists Jill Freedman and Gene Combs (1996, p. 14) reported on their first encounter with White,

> . . . he was citing Michel Foucault who wrote about the objectification and subjugation of persons, and talking about helping people stand up to "the gaze" of the dominant culture. Now middle-aged 60s activists, we had no idea what these ideas would look like when applied to therapy, but we sure wanted to find out!

For many narrative therapists doing therapy is just one aspect of a life committed to the pursuit of social justice.

Given narrative therapists' readiness to reexamine received truths, it was almost inevitable that many of the established doctrines of family therapy would also come under their scrutiny. Starting with the feminist critique, the deconstruction of the field's fundamental tenets was already underway. Feminist family therapists had exposed the impact of patriarchy on families, and feminist theory had a strong impact on narrative thinking. The narrative movement not only deconstructed but also rejected much of the family therapy theory that preceded it.

To summarize: narrative therapists applied Foucault's political analysis of societies to an understanding of individuals and families as dominated by oppressive, internalized narratives from which they need liberation. They drew from the work of Jerome Bruner and other social scientists studying narratives to understand how personal narratives are constructed and can be deconstructed.[1] The narrative approach demands a new conception of the self, and White's notion of a constitutionalist self is derived from the social constructionists' view of the self as a socially constructed phenomenon. These new theoretical positions weren't added to existing family therapy theory but rather were proposed to replace the systems view of families and the view of individuals as containing untapped resources.

Normal Family Development

Narrative therapists avoid judgments of what's normal and abnormal. The reader may recall that Foucault criticized the ways that theories of what's normal have been used to maintain unjust power divisions and oppress certain groups. Too often in human history the judgments made by people in power regarding normal and abnormal thinking and behavior have been imposed in ways that harmed those who had no voice in the matter. People or families were held up to the normative ideal and deemed healthy or unhealthy depending on their fit. With their bias hidden behind the cloak of science or religion, these conceptions become reified and internalized. One-size-fits-all standards have pathologized differences due to gender, cultural and ethnic background, sexual orientation, and socioeconomic status. Postmodernists strive to avoid grand narratives full of sweeping generalizations, as Barbara Held (1995, p. 21) summarizes:

> . . . postmodern narrative therapy is the first to argue explicitly for the elimination of all general categories of problems (e.g.,

[1]The term *deconstructionism* is most closely associated with Jaques Derrida (1992), who analyzed literary texts to show that they had no one true meaning. Narrative therapists use the term in a political way, as subverting dominant discourses, whereas Derrida's intent was more relativistic.

> diagnoses) embedded within general laws of problem causation and problem resolution. These categories and laws are themselves denounced by postmodern therapists as misleading, misguided, and irrelevant to the therapeutic process precisely because of their generality and because they lay claim to objectivity, which postmodern therapists take to be unobtainable.

While many family therapists can see the dangers of reducing people to DSM-IV diagnoses, they may have trouble seeing their favorite concepts, such as rigid boundaries, cross-generational coalitions, or differentiation of self, as dehumanizing or marginalizing. But becoming a postmodern narrative therapist means giving up all such categorizing. In fact, narrative therapists are so concerned about inadvertently imposing their own cultural biases on families that they continually reexamine their assumptions and solicit input from the marginalized groups that they treat. For example, the Just Therapy team from New Zealand formed gender and cultural caucuses composed of people from dominated groups with which they regularly consult regarding matters of therapy or policy (Waldegrave, 1990; Tamasese & Waldegrave, 1993). In addition, narrative therapists endeavor to "situate" themselves with clients—that is, disclose the narratives and beliefs that inform their therapy so that clients know what they're getting into and can critically examine the therapy's direction. Clients are also encouraged to educate therapists regarding their cultural predicaments and correct therapists when they make assumptions that don't fit their experience (White, 1993; Freedman & Combs, 1996). As White (1993, p. 57) suggests,

> Therapists can undermine the idea that they have privileged access to the truth by consistently encouraging persons to assist them in the quest for understanding. . . . Therapists can challenge the idea that they [the therapists] have an expert view . . . [or] an objective and unbiased account of reality.

Narrative therapists try not to make assumptions about people so as to honor each client's unique story and cultural heritage. But maybe it's impossible to be a therapist and not have some basic presuppositions about people and how they change.

From the narrative theory described in the previous section we can distill basic assumptions. People: (1) have good intentions—they don't want or need problems; (2) are profoundly influenced by the discourses around them; (3) are not their problems; and (4) can develop alternative, empowering stories once separated from their problems and from the cultural common wisdom they have internalized. From these basic beliefs springs most of narrative therapy practice.

Development of Behavior Disorders

When the stories people tell themselves lead them to construe their experience in unhelpful ways, they may get bogged down with problems. Such problems are likely to persist as long as these unhelpful stories remain fixed in place, obscuring more optimistic stories that could be developed just as easily from a person's history.

Thus, for example, a single mother whose life narrative is that she can't trust that anyone loves her reacts severely to her teenage daughter whenever the daughter breaks curfew. This narrative makes the mother notice all the times her daughter stays out late or leaves cigarette butts on the porch and not notice the times when she gets her homework done or volunteers to wash the dishes. Each of the daughter's transgressions confirms the mother's story line that, like all the other people in her life, her daughter really doesn't love her. The daughter, in turn, is keenly aware of how often her mother criticizes her friends and/or explodes over small mistakes, but doesn't remember the times her mother showed respect for her opinion or praised her achievements. The daughter gradually develops a narrative around never being able to satisfy people and becomes increasingly controlled by "rebelliousness," which makes her not care what mother thinks, and instead indulges in whatever makes her feel better, like partying late into the night. In short, both sides remain stuck not simply in a pattern of control and rebellion but, more specifically, in a pattern of noticing only incidents of control or rebellion.

So far, this may not sound all that different from the description many other schools of family therapy might give of an escalating vicious cycle between mother and daughter. The difference, however, is that the narrative approach doesn't focus on the sequences of behavior between mother and daughter. They reject the cybernetic metaphor according to which mother and daughter would be seen as stuck in a dysfunctional feedback loop—acting and reacting to each other in unhelpful ways. Instead, they concentrate on the way mother and daughter story their exchanges. It's their stories (being unloved, being picked on) that affect not only what they notice (lateness, scolding) but also how they interpret what they notice.

Narrative therapists refer to these patterns of tunnel vision as "problem-saturated" stories, which, once they take hold, encourage each party to respond to the other in ways that fit—and maintain—the problem story. As long as they focus on their children's misbehavior, parents will be concerned mainly with criticizing and controlling them. As long as they think of their parents primarily as hassling them, youngsters are likely to remain reactive and rebellious. Their responses to each other become invitations to more of the same and support further hardening of problem stories.

Such closed and rigid narratives make people vulnerable to being overtaken by destructive emotional states or beliefs that narrative therapists like to portray as external invaders rather than as inherent in persons. Narrative therapists don't really see problematic feelings or beliefs as separate, devilish beings, but they do believe that such feelings and beliefs *are* external to people in the sense that they are cultural constructs and are not really inside people. Narrative therapists find that externalizing problems this way frees people from thinking of themselves as pathological. Externalizing problems cuts down on guilt and blame. The daughter *isn't* the problem, "rebelliousness" is. Mother *isn't* the problem, "oversensitivity" is. Mother and daughter can unite to combat rebelliousness and oversensitivity rather than each other.

Where do family members get the disempowering narratives that ultimately lead to behavior disorders? In part, of course, from interactions with each other. But narrative therapists believe that searching within persons or families for the determinants of problems is a way of colluding with problem-saturated stories. To avoid such collusion, from early in his career, Michael White has taken the position that the person or the family is not the problem, the problem is the problem (White, 1987, 1989). People often enter therapy dominated by the story of how they are the problem or are embattled over who is. They dwell on how they've failed in life because of the existence of the problem and their inability to resolve it. This leads people to bring the negative events in their lives and the negative aspects of their personalities into the foreground, making them feel powerless, and, consequently, they become easy prey to more problems. In White's (1989) words,

> Although the problem was usually defined as internal to the child, all family members were affected by it, and often felt overwhelmed, dispirited and defeated. In various ways they took the ongoing existence of the problem, and their failed attempts to solve it, as a reflection on themselves, each other and/or on their relationships. (p. 5)

If problems aren't caused by family interaction or by psychodynamics, then how do they arise? To answer this question, narrative therapists ask that we shift our attention away from a search for pathology within people or families and toward an appreciation of the toxic effects the cultural narratives that govern our lives can have.

> The discourses of pathology make it possible for us to ignore the extent to which the problems for which people seek therapy are the outcome of certain practices of relationship and practices of the self, many of which are actually informed by modern notions of "individualism" . . . [and] are so often mired in the structures of inequality of our culture, including those pertaining to gender, race, ethnicity, class, economics, age, and so on. (White, 1995, p. 115)

Anorexia nervosa, for example, can be viewed as an internalization of our culture's obsession with thinness and beauty, and the worship of self-discipline and competitiveness. By seeing women who starve themselves as having a disease or by looking within their families for structural problems, we not only ignore the bigger picture but also avoid having to confront our own participation in these cultural stereotypes.

For example, White believes that thinking of men who abuse women as batterers or perpetrators, or as the products of violent families, allows male therapists to avoid considering the link between their clients' violence and our culture's glamorizing of domination, conquest, and aggression. White (1995) says this would allow him, as a man, to "avoid confronting the ways that I might be complicit in the reproduction of these dominant ways of being and thinking" (p. 218). He sees therapists as having the responsibility not only to be aware of their own attitudes and actions, but also to actively challenge cultural injustices that subjugate and marginalize people.

This is another break from clinical tradition that has long warned therapists of the dangers of imposing their own values on clients, in favor of strict neutrality. Yet, White's political stance is a logical extension of his position on the development of disorders. If problems are products of the internalization of our culture's dominant discourses, there's no reason to assume that therapists are immune to this internalization process. We swim in the same cultural soup as our clients.

Goals of Therapy

The goals of narrative therapy aren't modest. Narrative therapists aren't problem-solvers. They're interested in awakening people from the trances they've been lulled into by powerful forces of culture, so they can have a full range of choices. Or, as narrative therapists prefer to put it: coauthoring with clients new stories about themselves that emphasize their preferred ways of relating to themselves and to the larger culture.

Narrative therapy is designed to transform clients' identities, from flawed to heroic. This isn't accomplished by getting family members to confront their conflicts or be more honest with one another but rather by separating the person from the problem and then uniting the family to fight a common enemy. It's also done by combing the family's history to find "unique outcomes" or "sparkling events"—times when they resisted the problem or behaved in ways that contradicted the problem story.

For example, if Alice sees herself as "codependent" because of the ways she relates to men, White wouldn't explore the reasons for this condition nor would he give Alice directives for altering this pattern. Instead, he would ask questions about the effect of "Self-blame" on her life, ask family members to help her beat Self-blame, and highlight times in her life when she behaved or felt toward men the way she would prefer. He might also invite her to explore how our society's view of women contributed to Self-blame's grip on her life, and how seeing herself as codependent contributed, and whether she agrees with those views.

This, then, is a therapy of liberation. Alice is liberated from the self-blame that accompanies her view of herself as a codependent; from the disdain of her family for being codependent; from the cultural view of women that made her think of herself as codependent; and, as she expands her ability to stand up to Self-blame, from her previous patterns with men. Once liberated from these old stories, there is room for preferred self-narratives that had been marginalized or covered over by the old ones. Alice and her therapist can construct a new version of herself (for example, as a heroine fighting an uphill battle against the subjugation of women) that will need maintenance to withstand the influence of the dominant culture and the people around her who are steeped in it.

Narrative therapy is more than a problem-solving approach. It's a commitment to helping people rewrite the stories of their lives—re-envisioning their pasts and rewriting their futures. Rather than objectifying people in terms of syndromes to be cured or problems to be solved, narrative therapists help clients develop life stories as people with dignity and competence. Narrative therapists see their work as a political enterprise—freeing clients from oppressive cultural assumptions and empowering them to become active agents in charge of their own lives.

Conditions for Behavior Change

Because narrative therapists see people's actions as being derived from the stories they use to explain themselves, a change in narrative is required to produce a change in behavior. People need to be helped to identify and separate themselves from the problem-saturated stories and disempowering cultural themes they've internalized. Once separated from these unproductive narratives, space is opened for new, alternative, and more constructive views of themselves. Armed with new stories, family members unite with one another and with communities of support to deal with their problems with more agency, optimism, and persistence.

Narrative therapy works by helping clients *deconstruct* unproductive stories and reconstruct (reauthor) new and more productive ones. Deconstruction, a term borrowed from literary criticism, means for narrative therapists questioning or challenging assumptions. They *externalize* problems from persons as one way to deconstruct the pathologizing assumptions that often surround problems. Rather than talk of "Sally's laziness," for example, they'll inquire about times when "Procrastination takes hold of Sally." Once the problem is externalized and redefined in more experience-near terms, the person can begin to resist it. By viewing the problem as an external entity, narrative therapists free families to challenge its influence on their lives.

After externalizing the problem, narrative therapists ask about "unique outcomes"—times when clients resisted the problem's influence. Unique outcomes open room for counterplots, new and more empowering ways of constructing events. A man who identifies himself as depressed sees his life through a glass darkly. Depression becomes a life style, a career. But if that person begins to think of, say, "Self-doubt getting the best of him," then he may be able to remember times when he didn't let Self-doubt get him down. These newly attended to times of effectiveness provide openings around which to weave a new and more optimistic story.

Just as externalization is used to shift clients' perceptions of themselves, narrative therapists also endeavor to shift family members' perceptions of each other from "totalizing views" (reducing them to one set of frustrating responses) that lead to antagonism and polarization. Thus parents who see their teenagers as "irresponsible"—as though that were the sum total of their being—are likely to be seen in return as "not really caring." Likewise, parents who totalize their children as "lazy" may be seen as "pushy and demanding." As long as both sides remain fixed in such polarized negative perspectives, they may be too busy to think about their own desires and preferences. In unhappy families, people may be so busy *not* being what others want or expect, that they have no time to figure out how they want to be themselves.

In addition to the obvious cognitive emphasis in the narrative approach, narrative therapists point to an affective component by emphasizing how much they must be interested in and willing to appreciate their clients' experience. Attempting to reduce any form of treatment to a set of techniques would obscure the essential human qualities of the good therapist and of the therapeutic relationship.

Michael White sets an inspiring example of seeing the best in people even when they've lost faith in themselves. He's famous for his persistence in questioning people's negative stories about themselves. He just won't allow people who consult with him to slip away into their misery. This relentless optimism seems to be as vital to the success of narrative therapy as any of the specifics of the approach. As Bill O'Hanlon (1994) pointed out,

> . . . if you don't believe, to the bottom of your soul, that people are not their problems and that their difficulties are social and personal constructions, then you won't be seeing these transformations. When Epston or White are in action, you can tell they are absolutely convinced that people are not their problems. Their voices, their postures, their whole beings radiate possibility and hope. (p. 28)

The tenacious confidence in people that narrative therapists convey with genuine respect and caring is contagious. As clients come to trust the therapist, they can borrow that confidence and use it in dealing with their externalized problem. Without that kind of conviction, therapists will have difficulty breaking the grip of pessimistic life stories.

Because they believe that the self is constituted in social interaction and, consequently, that people are susceptible to having their new stories undermined by the same contexts that bred the old ones, narrative therapists use a variety of methods to fortify clients. One way is to help clients create an audience to notice and support their progress in constructing new stories for themselves.

Clients might be asked to contact people from their past who can authenticate their new story—who can confirm and add to examples of the person's acting competently or heroically. Clients are also encouraged to recruit people in their lives who can serve as a supportive audience to their new story. Friends, relatives, co-workers, or anyone who might bear witness to the changes the client is shaping can be asked to serve in this role. In some cases these people might be organized into a "nurturing team" (White, 1995), with scheduled meetings in which the group discusses how they can facilitate the client's work in countering the effects of the problem story. Sometimes "leagues" are formed that are ongoing groups of people who have similar problems and support one another's efforts to resist the problem. For example, the Vancouver Anti-Anorexia/Anti-Bulimia League (Madigan, 1994) has a newsletter and monitors the media, writing letters to company presidents, newspapers, and magazines that portray an emaciated ideal for women and encourage them to diet.

David Epston has pioneered the use of letters in therapy to extend the conversation of therapy beyond the session. These letters often convey a deep appreciation of what the client endured, the outline of the new story, and the therapist's confidence in the client's ability to continue to progress. The advantage to this technique is that the words in a letter don't vanish the way words do after a conversation. Letters endure well beyond the boundaries of a session or even a course of therapy, with a client being able to read and reread them days, months, and even years later. Clients have reported to Epston that they regularly reread letters he sent them years earlier to remind themselves what they went through and how far they had come (Epston, 1994).

All of these efforts—recruiting authenticators and audiences, forming teams and leagues, writing letters and making certificates—are in keeping with the importance that social constructionists place on interaction in creating and maintaining change. For people to maintain their new identities, they need communities or documents that confirm and reinforce emerging new narratives and counter the ubiquitous cultural or familial messages to the contrary. What is done in a session is just a beginning step in this kind of therapy because the goal is not just to solve a problem; it is to change a whole way of thinking and living.

Techniques

The techniques of narrative therapy are all designed to help people feel understood and empowered. The techniques initiate a process by which clients reauthor stories about themselves, their problems, and their relationships.

Almost all narrative techniques are delivered in the form of questions. In making questions its centerpiece, White's approach is similar to a number of other models (Bowen, the Milan Associates, solution-focused, Anderson and Goolishian), yet none of those relies on questions as exclusively or has categorized questions as thoroughly. When he's working, Michael White almost never asserts anything or makes any interpretations. He just asks question after question, often repeating back the answers and writing them down.

Learning all these different types of questions would be overwhelmingly complex if each of them weren't informed by a certain goal at each step of the process of coauthoring new narratives. In the following discussion we present the typical steps in the narrative therapy process and include samples of the kinds of questions associated with each step.

Beginning Therapy

Some narrative therapists, such as Jeff Zimmerman and Vicki Dickerson, try to include everyone in the family who is affected by the problem. Others, such as Jill Freedman and Gene Combs, often work with individuals.

In the first session, narrative therapists will spend a few minutes finding out how people spend their time. This gives the therapist a chance to appreciate how clients see themselves, without getting into a lengthy history, and the likelihood of attributions of blame so frequently a part of such histories. They pay special attention to people's talents and competencies. As a further means of establishing a collaborative atmosphere, Zimmerman and Dickerson (1996) invite clients to ask any questions they might care to about the therapists. They also invite clients to look at their notes if they wish. And they often take notes as each person talks, which not only helps them retain important points in the client's story, but also gives clients a sense that their point of view is respected.

Externalizing: The Person Is Not the Problem

Narrative therapists begin by asking clients to tell their problem-saturated story, and they listen long enough to convey the sense that they have an appreciation for what the family has been going through. During that telling or later, after a sense of trust has been established between therapist and family, the therapist begins asking questions that externalize the problem and make apparent the effects of the problem on their lives and relationships.

From the outset, the problem is seen as separate from people and as influencing them—"*it* brought them there"—and each person is asked for his or her own perspective on *it*. Externalizing language is used from the beginning. One major way of doing this is to ask about the problem's effects rather than its causes (causative questions usually lead to attributions of fault and blame). This is called "mapping the influence of the problem." "How does *Guilt* affect you?" "What other effects does it have?" "What does *Guilt* 'tell' you?"

The therapist's questions about the identified problem immediately imply that it isn't possessed by anyone, but instead is trying to possess them. For example, in a case where parents described the problem as a lack of trust in their daughter because of her sneakiness, the therapist doesn't reflect back, "so your daughter's sneakiness bothers you." Instead the therapist might say "so *Sneakiness* made your daughter act in ways that caused a rift between you, is that right?"

Sometimes whole patterns of interaction, rather than just a feeling or belief, are externalized, especially with people who tend to blame each other and rarely discuss their relationship. For example, in the case in which a teenager's parents were responding to her sneakiness with increasing control, Vicki Dickerson chose to highlight the rift that was encouraging this pattern—because one thing they could all agree on was that they didn't like the breach that was splitting them apart. Thus, instead of identifying the daughter's sneakiness or the parent's distrust as the problem, the *Rift* became the enemy that encouraged the sneakiness and controlling. The *Rift* told the parents their daughter couldn't be trusted and it made the daughter more secretive and told her to pull away from her parents. So, the *Rift* was something they could join forces against (Zimmerman & Dickerson, 1996).

Whether it's an internal experience (guilt, self-hate), a syndrome (anorexia, schizophrenia), or a relationship pattern (a rift), the externalized problem is always personified—portrayed as an unwelcome invader that tries to dominate family members' lives. For example, while discussing her eating problems, a woman is asked how *Anorexia* convinces her to starve herself. A phobic child is asked how often *Fear* is able to make him do what it wants and how often he is able to stand up to it. A guilt-ridden mother is asked how *Self-hate* is making her feel bad about her parenting.

It's also possible to externalize unquestioned cultural assumptions and standards ("oppressive cultural discourses"). For example, the woman who was asked about *Anorexia's* impact might also be asked how she thinks the expectations of women in our society collaborate with or fuel *Anorexia. Expectations of women* then becomes another externalized entity to be named and fought.

This line of questioning is often an odd shift for families, unaccustomed as they are to talking about imaginary entities living in their households. Consequently, therapists who view externalization merely as a technique will probably lack the conviction necessary to overcome their own and the family's discomfort in thinking this way. On the other hand, therapists will find that externalizing questions flow freely if they actually learn to think of problems as demons that feed on families' polarizations and misunderstandings. White suggests that problems are dependent on their effects for their survival, so by standing up to the problem and not allowing it to affect them, clients cut off the problem's "life-support system."

Sallyann Roth and David Epston (1996) developed an exercise to help therapists grasp what it's like to think of problems as external. They have a group of trainees take turns being a problem—such as Self-hatred—while others interview him or her. The interviewers might ask the person playing Self-hatred such questions as: "Under what circumstances do you manage to get into X's world?" "How are you intervening in the lives of X's family and friends?"

If such an entity really exists in a family's life, it would be natural to ask family members about how it affects their lives and how it makes them feel about themselves and one another. It would also be natural to ask how it tricks them into complying with it and how they want to work together to starve or defeat it. If these questions flow smoothly, confidently, and persistently, most clients will enter into the spirit of this idea that problems are external to people. Externalizing, by itself, can have a powerful impact. Over time, people become identified with their problems. They believe that their problem's existence is symbolic of their flawed character. This way of thinking poisons confidence. When the problem is externalized, it's as if the person can peek out from behind it; and family members can see that there is a healthier person that the problem has been hiding from them.

Bill no longer *is* a depressed person, instead he is overcome at times by *Depression*, an antagonist he dislikes as much as his family does. As the therapist queries him about *Depression's* tactics and effects, Bill becomes motivated to fight back. And now he has allies in the battle, including the therapist, his family, and other friends he might recruit. In addition, without depression as the central feature of his identity, he can take another look at who he is and what he wants—there is space for new, preferred narratives.

Other examples of externalizing questions include: "So *Jealousy* has been getting the better of you. How does *Jealousy* do that?" "When *Tantrums* convince Joey to yell and scream, do you think your response gives *Tantrums* more or less fuel?" "What tricks does *Self-doubt* use to keep you from taking any risks?"

Who's in Charge, the Person or the Problem?

Sometimes externalizing conversations are effective right away. In more entrenched cases, however, the questioning needs to be more extensive. The therapist can ask a multitude of questions over many sessions that map how the problem has managed to disrupt or dominate the family, versus how much they have been able to control it. These are called "relative influence questions," and by including all family members in the discussion it becomes clear that everyone has had a relationship with the problem and, in many cases, the problem has succeeded in disturbing their relationships with each other—dividing and conquering them. This implies that it's imperative that everyone, not just the one identified with the problem, needs to change his or her relationship to it and needs to unite in that effort.

It helps to demonstrate how much the problem has made people think and act in ways they would prefer not to with questions like, "To what degree has *Bulimia* convinced you to think about and act toward your friends in ways you regret?" "How much has the *Bulimia* that's taken over Jenny kept you from being the way you want to be with her?" "How much has *Pessimism* kept you from achieving the goals you want to achieve at work?" "When *Depression* gets the better of Dad, how does that affect family life?" "When *Paranoia* tricks you into believing everyone wants to hurt you, how much do you believe it and how much are you just going along with it, while knowing what it's saying is wrong?"

Reading Between the Lines of the Problem Story

While asking these relative influence questions, the therapist listens for and highlights "sparkling events" or "unique outcomes" when the person was able to avoid the problem's effects and asks for elaboration on how that was done. When families are dominated by problem-saturated stories, these successes and victories are often obscured by totalizing narratives of failure and pessimism. Other therapies may collude with problem-saturated stories by dwelling on their influence and giving them more power by labeling them with pessimistic and intimidating diagnoses. Fortunately, however, people have always resisted complete domination, so, if the therapist is persistent, aspects of a client's "lived experience" (as opposed to their experience as dictated by the dominant discourse) that contradict the problem-saturated story will emerge from the questioning. These unique outcomes and sparkling events become the building blocks of new, more heroic stories.

It is this aspect of narratives that gives them their power—the way they bring events that fit the story into the foreground and marginalize events that don't fit. By turning the spotlight on heroic episodes, no matter how small, and linking them together over the person's or family's history, a new narrative emerges that reverses the figure and ground. People who formerly viewed themselves as powerless because of the way they had been dominated by the problem suddenly see themselves as courageous protagonists involved in a struggle for their souls.

Examples of questions designed to elicit unique outcomes or sparkling events include: "Can you remember a time when *Anger* tried to take you over, but you didn't let it? How did you do that?" "Have there been times when your daughter didn't believe the lies that *Anorexia* tells her about her body?" "When Jenny has withstood the tremendous pressure she feels from *Alcoholism*, have you appreciated the magnitude of that accomplishment?"

While unique outcomes are the central ingredients of the recipes for new narratives, it's unwise to pursue them prematurely. If the therapist is constantly underlining and cheering small victories while the client feels totally oppressed by the problem, the client is apt to believe the therapist doesn't understand how bad things are and may exaggerate difficulties until he or she feels the therapist appreciates the severity of the predicament. Or, because the therapist seems so invested in the client's performance, the client may feel pressure to change too quickly or may begin fabricating victories just to please the therapist. It's recommended, therefore, that therapists might try to identify one unique outcome in the first session but not make a big deal out of it. In subsequent sessions, they can further expand and explore the implications of unique outcomes, always trying to go at the client's pace and being careful not to minimize the difficulties involved with the problem (Zimmerman & Dickerson, 1996).

Reauthoring the Whole Story

Up to this point, the person's identity *as it relates to the problem* has been profoundly affected. Narrative therapists, however, are interested in a revision of the client's whole identity, not just the part connected to the problem. Evidence of a client's competence relative to the problem, gathered from sifting through his or her history, can be used as the beginning of new narratives regarding who the client is in general. To make this connection, the therapist begins by asking about what the series of past and present victories over the problem say about the client. For example: "What does it say about you as a person that you were able to defeat *Depression* on those occasions?" "What qualities of personality must your son possess to be able to do that?" The therapist can also expand the historical purview beyond episodes relating to the problem to find more evidence to bolster the new self-narrative. "What else can you tell me about your past that helps me understand how you were able to handle *Anger* so well?" "Who knew you as a child who wouldn't be surprised that you have been able to stand up to *Fear* on these occasions?"

As the new self-narrative begins to take shape, the therapist can shift the focus to the future, inviting the client or family to envision the upcoming changes that will fit the new story. "Now that you've discovered these things about yourself, how do you think these discoveries will affect your relationship with *Self-hate*." "How do you think your daughter's friendships will look now that she no longer lets *Anorexia* make her decisions?" These questions hold up a hopeful picture of the future that family members can rally around. There is nothing as healing as hope. The self-story now has a past, present, and future—it's a complete narrative.

Reinforcing the New Story

Remember, however, that the narrative approach is based in social constructionism. A new story may be constructed in therapy, but its maintenance is dependent on its becoming embedded in communities supportive of it. As described in the previous section, narrative therapists are always helping clients find an audience or create groups to nurture and strengthen the budding identity and write letters to reinforce the new story.

In addition, there are regular practices designed to nurture new stories. For example, narrative therapists often begin the second and subsequent sessions by asking about any small victories. For example, "How much did the problem control you last week and how much were you in control?" As people gradually recognize that they have some agency over the problem, they can get more distance from their pessimistic, problem-saturated story about it. The less they're burdened by that story, the more agency they notice they have, and so on. So such questioning can trigger a virtuous cycle in which problems quickly lose influence. If, as may happen, clients remain pessimistic and reply that nothing has improved, narrative therapists might ask whether the clients have noticed any "slightly new responses" or if they at least were able to "imagine what they might do differently?"

At the end of each session, narrative therapists often summarize what happened, being sure to use externalizing language and emphasizing any unique outcomes that were mentioned. These summaries are what Epston often puts into his letters to clients. The effect of these summaries is to convey to clients that the therapist was with them during the session and celebrates their blossoming new identity. This sense of being cheered on by the therapist can be extremely encouraging.

Deconstructing Dominant Cultural Discourses

In the theory section of this chapter we devoted a lot of attention to the political aspects of the narrative approach—to the importance placed on deconstructing insidious cultural discourses by which people come to judge themselves. Although externalizing a problem allows a person to get enough distance to see it in a new light, which is a form of deconstruction, it is not overtly political. There are times when narrative therapists will make the connection to dominant cultural narratives more explicit. For example, an anorexic woman might be asked how she was recruited into the belief that her only value was her appearance. This would lead to other questions regarding the position of women in our society. Similarly, a violent man might be asked how he came to believe that men in our culture should never be weak or soft, and a deconstructing of the messages men receive would ensue.

To clarify what this deconstructing of cultural discourses might look like, we will present one of White's cases as described by Mary Sikes Wylie (1994):

> John . . . came to see White because, says White, "he was a man who never cried"—he had never been able to express his emotions—and he felt isolated and cut off from his own family. As a child, John had been taught, both at home and at his Australian grammar school, that any show of gentleness or "softness" was unmanly and would be met with harsh punishment and brutal public humiliation. White asks John a series of questions that are at once political and personal, eliciting information about the man's "private" psychological suffering and linking it to the "public" cultural practices, rigidly sexist and aggressively macho,

> that dominated his youth. "How were you recruited into these thoughts and habits [of feeling inadequate, not sufficiently masculine, etc.]? What was the training ground for these feelings? Do you think the rituals of humiliation [public caning by school authorities, ridicule by teachers and students for not being good at sports or sufficiently hard and tough] alienated you from your own life? Were they disqualifications of you? Did these practices help or hinder you in recognizing a different way of being a male?" (p. 43)

After deconstructing the cultural male image in this way, White helped John remember times when he resisted it and to recognize the nobility of his efforts to remain gentle and loving in spite of his socialization.

While we have presented narrative techniques in a sequential fashion, it's important to remember that the goal of coauthoring a new story with clients isn't achieved in a formulaic way. Selecting the precise question to use at the proper time is far less important than maintaining the spirit of deconstruction and liberation. It's the therapist's conviction that the client is a competent person, not the ability to memorize and deliver a set of questions, that opens the door to new self-narratives.

A Case of Sneaky Poo

◆

The concepts and methods of White's therapy come to life in his case descriptions, as in the following excerpts from his description of a family with an encopretic child (White, 1989):

> When mapping the influence of family members in the life of what we came to call "Sneaky Poo," we discovered that:
>
> 1. Although Sneaky Poo always tried to trick Nick into being his playmate, Nick could recall a number of occasions during which he had not allowed Sneaky Poo to "outsmart" him. These were occasions during which Nick could have co-operated by "smearing," "streaking" or "plastering," but he declined to do so. He had not allowed himself to be tricked into this.
> 2. There was a recent occasion during which Sneaky Poo could have driven Sue into a heightened sense of misery, but she resisted and turned on the stereo instead. Also, on this occasion, she refused to question her competence as a parent and as a person.
> 3. Ron could not recall an occasion during which he had not allowed the embarrassment caused by Sneaky Poo to isolate him from others. However, after Sneaky Poo's requirements of him were identified, he did seem interested in the idea of defying these requirements. . . .
> 4. . . . it was established that there was an aspect to Sue's relationship with Nick that she thought she could still enjoy, that Ron was still making some attempts to persevere in his relationship with Nick, and that Nick had an idea that Sneaky Poo had not destroyed all of the love in his relationship with his parents.
>
> After identifying Nick's, Sue's, and Ron's influence in the life of Sneaky Poo, I introduced questions that encouraged them to perform meaning in relation to these examples, so that they might "re-author" their lives and relationships.
>
> How had they managed to be effective against the problem in this way? How did this reflect on them as people and on their relationships? . . . Did this success give them any ideas about further steps that they might take to reclaim their lives from the problem? . . . In response to these questions, Nick thought that he was ready to stop Sneaky Poo from outsmarting him so much,

> and decided that he would not be tricked into being its playmate anymore. . . . (pp. 10–11)

White met with the family two weeks later and found that Nick had fought Sneaky Poo valiantly, having only one minor episode, and he seemed happier and stronger. Sue and Ron had also done their parts in the battle. In her effort to not cooperate with Sneaky Poo's requirements for her to feel guilty, Sue had begun to "treat herself" when Sneaky Poo was getting her down, and Ron had fought Sneaky Poo's attempts to keep him isolated by talking to friends about the problem.

> I encouraged the family to reflect on and to speculate about what this success said about the qualities that they possessed as people and about the attributes of their relationships. I also encouraged them to review what these facts suggested about their current relationship with Sneaky Poo. In this discussion, family members identified further measures that they could take to decline Sneaky Poo's invitations to them to support it. (p. 11)

White reports that the family expanded these efforts in the interim, and by the third session they felt confident that Sneaky Poo had been defeated. At a six-month follow-up they were still doing well.

◆

Evaluating Therapy Theory and Results

Stories don't mirror life, they shape it. That's why people have the interesting habit of becoming the stories they tell about their experience. It's also why therapists in too much of a hurry to impose their own perspectives on clients often fail—and why, by delving deeply into people's stories, narrative therapists are able to understand and influence what makes them act as they do.

The two most powerful ingredients in narrative therapy are the narrative metaphor itself and the technique of externalizing problems. Both ideas represent a radical departure from traditional family therapy, and both have pluses and minuses.

The strength and weakness of the narrative approach is its cognitive focus. In rejecting the cybernetic model—families stuck in dysfunctional feedback loops—narrative therapists repudiated the idea that families with problems have something wrong with them. Unfortunately, they also turned their backs on the three defining characteristics of family therapy: (1) that psychological symptoms are often related to family conflict; (2) thinking about human problems as interactional, which means thinking in terms of twos (complementarity, reciprocity) and threes (triangles); and (3) treating the family as a unit.

By focusing on cognitions, narrative therapists neglect family conflict and relationship dynamics. Treating problems as stories to be deconstructed overlooks the fact that some families have real and long-standing conflicts that don't disappear because they join together temporarily to fight an externalized problem. For example, parents whose lives are empty may have trouble letting their children grow up. Does that emptiness evaporate while they help their children battle Rebelliousness?

In the process of helping people restory their experience, narrative therapists often subscribe to a view of unhappy emotions—anger, fear, anxiety, depression—much like that of cognitive-behaviorists or solution-focused therapists: as annoyances to move away from rather than explore. They ask, How does anger or fear "defeat" clients, but rarely do they ask, Why are you angry? What are you afraid of?

Early versions of family therapy *did* cast families in a pathological light and blamed them for maintaining problems. The narrative movement has helped shift the field toward more respect for and collaboration with families. In the process of rejecting the patronizing consciousness of that earlier age, however, narrative therapists have rejected systems thinking, emphasizing the mechanistic side of systems thinking called cybernetics while ignoring more humanistic forms derived from theorists like Ludwig von Bertalanffy (see Chapter 4). One of family therapy's greatest contributions was to bring a contextual understanding of people and their problems to psychotherapy. Nonsystemic therapists, influenced by the disease model, had encouraged people to fight problems (with medication, support groups, education) rather than to explore the network of relationships in which their problems were embedded. While strongly opposed to the disease model, narrative therapists advocate returning to a similarly acontextual view of problems as things to be fought, and eschew efforts to understand their ecological contexts.

As much as narrative therapists prefer to see themselves as nonmanipulative and collaborative, they are more directive than they purport to be. They point to their frequent use of questions rather than interpretations, statements, or directives as evidence of a collaborative, nonimpositional stance. As Freedman and Combs (1996) assert,

> People can choose how to respond to a question, and when we genuinely listen to and value people's responses, *their* ideas, not ours, stay at the center of therapy. . . . (p. 277) We endeavor not to ask questions that we think we know "the" answers to, or ones that we want *particular* answers to. (p. 118)

Regardless of how many questions they use, they *are* looking for a certain class of answers and, consequently, are leading clients to particular conclusions. The famous hypnotherapist Milton Erickson often appeared to be collaborative and nondirective, but he was still trying to influence people in certain directions. As Bill O'Hanlon (1994, p. 28) says, "Narrative therapists would generally bristle at the suggestion that they use hypnosis, but they can take my word for it, they do." That narrative therapists gently induct clients away from problem-saturated stories and into empowering ones isn't necessarily a bad thing. We just wish that they would deconstruct the story that they don't impose their perspectives on clients.

There may be times, however, when prodding people toward heroic narratives can be a bad thing. As postmodernists, narrative therapists claim to carry no general assumptions about people so as to honor each client's unique story and cultural heritage. But is it really possible to have no metatheory or grand narrative and still go about helping people change in a systematic way. As Barbara Held (1995) points out, one can avoid prejudging people to some extent by emptying one's mind of diagnostic categories and normative developmental schemes, but to practice therapy, one cannot avoid presumptions about the nature of people and how they change.

While we don't doubt that many people have been helped by having their problems externalized, when one becomes as active a coauthor as narrative therapists do, there is a danger of subtly selling a story that itself becomes a dominant discourse and marginalizes inner voices that don't fit the new story. This may be one reason why the narrative approach has come to rely so extensively on adjunctive supports (creating client "leagues" or writing letters). Perhaps in some cases clients need constant reinforcement to maintain the new story and suppress the old.

Fortunately, some narrative therapists seem to have recognized the danger of reifying the narrative paradigm. Lowe (1991) foresees how, armed with the narrative metatheory,

> therapists would be cast as Experts on postmodernism, and Master deconstructionists,

> editors, conversationalists and story-tellers. All kinds and levels of human experience would be reduced to abstract conceptions of "conversation" and "discourse" which would become "natural" foundational terms for a new form of universal knowledge. (p. 51)

Narrative therapists are quick to point out the negative consequences of the grand narratives of most other models. The narrative approach would benefit from more self-assessment of what's gained and lost by adopting or reifying its metatheory.

A Therapy of Social Justice

In looking beyond families to the cultural assumptions and practices in which they're embedded, narrative therapists have given a distinctly political cast to their work. Family therapy's political consciousness raising began with the feminist critique in the 1980s and expanded in the 1990s to include interest in multicultural, racial, sexual orientation, and social class issues. Therapists were studying the effects of these cultural forces but weren't clear on how to incorporate their political beliefs into their practices. Much of the excitement around the narrative movement is because it's the first school of family therapy to not only advocate but also present a clear and systematic method for deconstructing cultural narratives.

Most narrative therapists would agree with Vicki Dickerson's statement that narrative therapy is "primarily about situating problems in their cultural context" (Freedman, 1996). That is, it's about helping clients identify and challenge the ubiquitous, but commonly unexamined, prescriptions that permeate society and make self-worth and harmonious relating difficult at best. But how does one do that without imposing one's own political biases?

In 1996, three narrative therapists presented their answers to that question during what proved to be one of the most controversial plenary presentations in the history of the American Family Therapy Academy. Jill Freedman, Jeffrey Zimmerman, and Stephen Madigan showed videotaped excerpts of their attempts to introduce cultural themes into their therapy. These themes included the traditional gender arrangements of a married couple (Freedman), what it means to be a "real man" for an adult male client (Zimmerman), and the impact of heterosexism on a lesbian couple (Madigan). In each case, the therapists asked clients to tell their stories regarding the impact of those themes on their lives and either led or followed an ensuing conversation about that impact.

It is reflective of how politically oriented the American Family Therapy Academy has become that the appropriateness of bringing these issues into therapy wasn't questioned by the audience. Instead, criticism was aimed at the fact that all the presenters were white and that racial issues weren't addressed, that the language used by the presenters and a reflecting team afterward was stilted and artificial, and that there was an air of political correctness permeating the whole experience.

Although some therapists still make a case for strict therapeutic neutrality, many now agree that often it is important to question invidious cultural assumptions. It's true that our culture imbues us with unhelpful beliefs and values. The question is what is the best way to help people free themselves from those without imposing, subtly or overtly, one's own values. This is a complex question, and narrative therapy answers it one way. We hope that their example provokes all family therapy models to struggle further with this question.

Summary

The narrative approach is built around two organizing metaphors: personal narrative and social construction. When memory speaks it tells a "narrative truth," which comes to have more influence than "historical truth." The "facts" presented to a therapist are partly historical truth and partly constructions. The constructions that make up the shared reality of a family represent mutual understandings and shared prejudices, some of which are hopeful and helpful, some of which are not.

Narrative therapists break the grip of unhelpful stories by *externalizing* problems. By challenging fixed and pessimistic versions of events, therapists make room for flexibility and hope. Uncovering *unique outcomes* provides an opening through which new and more optimistic stories can be envisioned. Finally, clients are encouraged to create audiences of support to witness and promote their progress in restoring their lives along preferred lines.

The strategies of narrative therapy fall into three stages. First comes the problem narrative stage: recasting the problem as an affliction by focusing on its effects, rather than on its causes. Second, finding exceptions: partial triumphs over the affliction and instances of effective action. Third, the recruitment of support. Encouraging a "performance of meaning"—some kind of public ritual to reinforce new and preferred interpretations—moves cognitive constructions past private insight and reflection into not just action but socially supported action.

The tactics by which these strategies are put into practice involve an elaborate series of questions:

Deconstruction Questions—Externalizing the problem. "What does Depression whisper in your ear?" "What conclusions about your relationship have you drawn because of this problem?"

Opening Space Questions—Uncovering unique outcomes. "Has there ever been a time when Arguing could have taken control of your relationship but didn't?"

Preference Questions—Making sure unique outcomes represent preferred experiences. "Was this way of handling things better or worse?" "Was that a positive or negative development?"

Story Development Questions—To develop a new story from the seeds of (preferred) unique outcomes. "How is this different from what you would have done before?" "Who played a part in this way of doing things?" "Who will be the first to notice these positive changes in you?"

Meaning Questions—Designed to challenge negative images of self and to emphasize positive agency. "What does it say about you that you were able to do that?"

Questions to Extend the Story into the Future—To support changes and reinforce positive developments. "What do you predict for the coming year?"

The social constructionist foundation of narrative therapy gives the approach its political cast and deemphasizes family dynamics and conflict. Instead of looking within families for dysfunctional interactions, narrative therapists look outside families for destructive influences of certain cultural values and institutions. They invite family members to pull together to oppose these values and practices. Instead of neutrality, they offer advocacy.

Narrative therapists suggest that the narrative metaphor is incompatible with systems thinking and have distanced themselves from the concepts and methods of traditional family therapists. It's typical of revolutionary movements to differentiate by highlighting incompatibilities and minimizing commonalities. But to dismiss narrative therapy as merely a rebellion against an imaginary family therapy establishment would be a great injustice. The narrative approach takes family therapy several steps further in the direction of being a nonpathologizing, uplifting, and empowering alternative to traditional psychiatric approaches. It brings fresh new metaphors for the self (socially constructed or constituted), for the process of therapy (coauthoring new stories), and for the source of problems (dominant cultural discourses). It offers therapists who are interested in issues of social oppression and injustice a way to translate their convictions into clinical practice. It extends therapy beyond the walls of the therapist's office to the fostering of communities of support and empowerment for clients.

The narrative approach also has introduced a host of exciting new techniques designed to enhance clients' sense of agency relative to their problems and connection to those around them and those with similar struggles. By externalizing problems; deconstructing rigid, culturally derived beliefs; and exhibiting an abiding, tenacious confidence in clients' abilities and goodness, narrative therapists have created a powerful recipe for change. Packaging their influence in the form of questions makes their input easier for clients to swallow and digest and fosters a collaborative therapy relationship.

Finally, narrative therapy has energized (as well as polarized) family therapy. Their concepts and methods, not to mention the style in which they are presented, are provocative. As the discussion above indicates, we too have been provoked and have enjoyed the process of teasing out our reactions and concerns. It's important to periodically question taken-for-granted assumptions and practices, and narrative therapy has not only helped clients but all of family therapy to do that. The field has been invigorated by the narrative critique and contribution. Family therapy's story will never be the same.

References

Anderson, C. M., Reiss, D., and Hogarty, B. 1986. *Schizophrenia and the family.* New York: Guilford Press.

Bruner, J. S. 1986. *Actual minds, possible worlds.* Cambridge, MA: Harvard University Press.

Bruner, J. S. 1987. Life as narrative. *Social Research. 54:*12–32.

Bruner, J. S. 1991. The narrative construction of reality. *Critical Inquiry. 18:*1–21.

Derrida, J. 1992. In *Derrida: A critical reader,* D. Wood, ed. Oxford: Blackwell.

Dickerson, V., and Zimmerman, J. 1992. Families with adolescents: Escaping problem lifestyles. *Family Process. 31:*341–353.

Epston, D. 1994. Extending the conversation. *Family Therapy Networker. 18:*30–37, 62.

Epston, D., and White, M. 1992. *Experience, contradiction, narrative, and imagination: Selected papers of David Epston and Michael White, 1989–1991.* Adelaide, South Australia: Dulwich Centre Publications.

Foucault, M. 1965. *Madness and civilization: A history of insanity in the age of reason.* New York: Random House.

Foucault, M. 1975. *The birth of the clinic: An archeology of medical perception.* London: Tavistock.

Foucault, M. 1980. *Power/knowledge: Selected interviews and other writings.* New York: Pantheon.

Foucault, M. 1984. *The history of sexuality.* Middlesex, Great Britain: Peregrine Books.

Freedman, J. 1996. AFTA voices on the annual meeting. *AFTA Newsletter.* Fall, 30–32.

Freedman, J., and Combs, G. 1996. *Narrative therapy: The social construction of preferred realities.* New York: Norton.

Geertz, C. 1973. *The interpretation of cultures: Selected essays.* New York: Basic Books.

Geertz, C. 1983. *Local knowledge: Further essays in interpretive anthropology.* New York: Basic Books.

Gergen, K. 1991. *The saturated self.* New York: Basic Books.

Goffman, E. 1961. *Asylums: Essays in the social situation of mental patients and other inmates.* New York: Doubleday.

Goffman, E. 1986. *Frame analysis.* Boston: Northeastern University Press.

Goulding, R., and Schwartz, R. 1995. *Mosaic mind: Empowering the tormented selves of child abuse survivors.* New York: Norton.

Held, B. 1995. *Back to reality: A critique of postmodern theory in psychotherapy.* New York: Norton.

Lowe, R. 1991. Postmodern themes and therapeutic practices: Notes towards the definition of "family therapy": Part 2. *Dulwich Centre Newsletter. 3:* 41–52.

Madigan, S. 1994. Body politics. *Family Therapy Networker. 18:*27.

Madigan, S., and Epston, D. 1995. From "spy-chiatric gaze" to communities of concern: From professional monologue to dialogue. In *The reflecting team in action,* S. Friedman, ed. New York: Guilford Press.

O'Hanlon, W. 1994. The third wave. *Family Therapy Networker. 18:*18–26, 28–29.

Parry, A., and Doan, R., 1994. *Story re-visions: Narrative therapy in the postmodern world.* New York: Guilford Press.

Roth, S. A., and Epston, D. 1996. Developing externalizing conversations: An introductory exercise. *Journal of Systemic Therapies. 15:*5–12.

Selvini Palazzoli, M., Boscolo, L., Cecchin, G., and Prata, G. 1978. *Paradox and counterparadox.* New York: Jason Aronson.

Tamasese, K., and Waldegrave, C. 1993. Cultural and gender accountability in the "Just Therapy" approach. *Journal of Feminist Family Therapy. 5:* 29–45.

Tomm, K. 1987a. Interventive interviewing: Part I. Strategizing as a fourth guideline for the therapist. *Family Process. 26:*3–14.

Tomm, K. 1987b. Interventive interviewing: Part II. Reflexive questioning as a means to enable self-healing. *Family Process. 25:*167–184.

Tomm, K. 1993. The courage to protest: A commentary on Michael White's work. In *Therapeutic conversations,* S. Gilligan and R. Price, eds. New York: Norton.

Waldegrave, C. T. 1990. Just therapy. *Dulwich Centre Newsletter. 1:*5–46.

Waters, D. 1994. Prisoners of our metaphors. *Family Therapy Networker. 18:*73–75.

Weingarten, K. 1991. The discourses of intimacy: Adding a social constructionist and feminist view. *Family Process. 30:*285–305.

White, M. 1987. Family therapy and schizophrenia: Addressing the "in-the-corner" lifestyle. *Dulwich Centre Newsletter.* Spring:14–21.

White, M. 1989. *Selected papers.* Adelaide, South Australia: Dulwich Centre Publications.

White, M. 1991. Deconstruction and therapy. *Dulwich Centre Newsletter.* 3:21–40.

White, M. 1993. Deconstruction and therapy. In *Therapeutic conversations,* S. Gilligan and R. Price, eds. New York: Norton.

White, M. 1995. *Re-authoring lives: Interviews and essays.* Adelaide, South Australia: Dulwich Centre Publications.

White, M., and Epston, D. 1990. *Narrative means to a therapeutic end.* New York: Norton.

Wylie, M. S. 1994. Panning for gold. *Family Therapy Networker. 18:*40–48.

Zimmerman, J., and Dickerson, V. 1993. Bringing forth the restraining influence of pattern in couples therapy. In *Therapeutic conversations,* S. Gilligan and R. Price, eds. New York: Norton.

Zimmerman, J., and Dickerson, V. 1996. *If problems talked: Adventures in narrative therapy.* New York: Guilford Press.

13

Integrative Models

In any human endeavor it seems that integration is only possible after a period of differentiation. It's no surprise then, that in the early years of family therapy the energies of the emerging schools were devoted to differentiating themselves from one another as well as from individual therapy. In those days, the term *integration* had a negative connotation—it was seen as a watering-down of the hard-won insights of the pure models.

In its first four decades, the field of family therapy evolved into a complex network of competing and often contradictory models and techniques. During those years many practitioners concluded that integration of family therapy models, let alone integration of family and individual therapy, was impossible. In the past decade, however, postmodern developments have blurred the artificial boundaries of these approaches and made possible a spirit of integration. When you think about it, there's a certain hubris to thinking that your approach works and all the others don't.

The obvious argument in favor of integrating elements from different approaches is that human beings are complicated, thinking, feeling, and acting creatures, who exist in a complex system of biological, psychological, and social influences. No therapy can succeed without having an impact on all of these domains. There is, however, an equally valid argument that eclecticism can rob therapy of the intensity made possible by strategic concentration on certain elements of experience. There may be many ways to skin a cat, but it might not be advisable to try all of them at once.

Effective integration involves more than borrowing a little of this and a little of that from various models of therapy. The important thing is to increase complexity without losing coherence.

A productive integration draws on existing models in such a way that they can be synthesized with a clear and consistent direction.

Creating a workable integration of disparate practices isn't easy. If done haphazardly it produces the kind of incoherent eclecticism in which therapists shift back and forth between this idea and that technique, without consistency or conviction. When done well, however, a synthetic approach builds on the best of two or more worlds of experience. As we enter the twenty-first century, integrative models appear to be the future of family therapy.

There are several ways to go about trying to produce an integration. You can apply principles or techniques from one field to the phenomena of another (e.g., using psychodynamic concepts to understand family processes). You can blend concepts and methods from separate schools together (e.g., creating a synthesis of structural and strategic therapies). You can create something new by selecting valuable ideas and techniques from a variety of sources and connecting them with common presuppositions (e.g., sampling from the various schools of family therapy). Or, you can juxtapose different models sequentially, using one for one stage of therapy and a second for another stage (e.g., starting out with solution-focused and switching to Bowenian if necessary).

In this chapter we present a sample of integrative models representing these various ap proaches to integration. The *internal family systems* model imports family systems thinking and techniques into the world of intrapsychic process. The *narrative solutions* approach is a synthesis of strategic and narrative models, and *integrative couple therapy* synthesizes behavioral techniques with emotional acceptance and strategic change. *Metaframeworks* selects key ideas that run through the different schools of family therapy and connects them with a set of presuppositions. *Problem-centered brief therapy* brings together structural family therapy with self psychology in a sequential fashion.

Internal Family Systems Therapy

The internal family systems (IFS) model extends systems thinking beyond the boundaries of the family, initially to people's inner lives and, later, to larger cultural issues. In a sense, then, rather than an integration, the IFS model can be seen as an expansion. Out of this expansion has come a new approach to therapy that embodies many of the attractive elements of the postmodern approaches—it's collaborative, empowering, and co-creates changes in life stories—but also retains features that can be traced to the structural, strategic, Satir, and Bowen schools. In addition, with its belief that everyone at the core has a healing and compassionate self, the IFS model offers a way for therapists to integrate aspects of spirituality into their clinical work and their lives.

Over the past several years, particularly following the release of two books on the model in 1995 (Schwartz, 1995; Goulding & Schwartz, 1995), internal family systems therapy has developed into a substantial movement with training programs around the United States and in Europe, an annual conference in Chicago, and an association, the Internal Family Systems Association (IFSA).

The IFS model was developed in the early 1980s by Richard Schwartz (1987, 1995, 1997; Goulding & Schwartz, 1995) and his colleagues at the Institute for Juvenile Research (IJR) in the Department of Psychiatry of the University of Illinois at Chicago. In 1996, after 17 years, Schwartz left IJR to join the faculty of the Family Institute at Northwestern University, a place that, as we shall see later in this chapter, has become a Mecca for integrative thinkers. His doctorate is in marital and family therapy and consequently he had little indoctrination in intrapsychic dynamics. As a result, when his clients began describing their inner worlds he had few preconceptions and was forced to listen because he had no theoretical dogma to fall back on. For this reason, the IFS model is client-driven and often feels intuitively accurate to people.

The IFS model is based on a synthesis of two already existing paradigms: systems thinking and the multiplicity of the mind. It brings concepts and methods from the structural, strategic, narrative, and Bowen systems models of family therapy to the world of subpersonalities.

In the early 1980s, while conducting an outcome study of structural-strategic family therapy with bulimia that, overall, achieved good results (Schwartz, Barrett, & Saba, 1985), Schwartz worked with some clients for whom family therapy alone didn't seem to be enough. Frustrated with the limits imposed by the exclusion of internal process, he broke this tradition by asking clients about what went on inside them before, during, and after a binge.

Subpersonalities or "Parts"

He discovered that each client described a similar sequence of interaction among what they called their internal "voices" or "parts." "A part of me attacks me for being so fat, then another part feels hurt and lonely, and then still another takes over and makes me binge. . . ." Their descriptions made it seem as if these parts or voices were more than just habitual thought patterns or feeling states—as if they were autonomous internal personalities. Schwartz wondered if the same systemic principles and techniques that had been so effective in working with families might also apply to his clients' internal systems. He continued to interview clients, tracking the interaction patterns among their competing voices, trying to understand the relationships among them, and experimenting with ways to intervene systemically in this inner ecology.

Schwartz found that not only did systemic principles and methods apply to internal processes, but that when they were applied, family members began to understand themselves and each other in ways that allowed them to change more easily than other intrapsychic models predicted. With these techniques clients could tap into previously obscured inner resources and change their relationship with the various parts of themselves.

Schwartz also found that the language of parts itself was a powerful tool for helping family members understand one another and their problems. It's easier to consider changing a small part of yourself than to have to change your whole personality.

The observation that the personality is subdivided isn't new. Many other theorists have described a similar inner phenomenon, beginning with Freud's id, ego, and superego, and more recently the object relations conceptions of internal objects. Multiplicity is also at the core of less traditional approaches, such as transactional analysis (ego states), psychosynthesis (subpersonalities), and lately in cognitive-behavioral approaches under the term *schemata.*

After Schwartz was able to set aside his preconceived notions about therapy and the mind, and began really listening to what his clients were saying, he learned that the parts not only had autonomy, but each had unique talents and intentions and a full range of emotion and expression. The parts also organized into alliances, vied for control, and, at times went to war against each other.

To understand how this process of subterranean interaction works, consider a time in your life when you were facing a difficult decision. You probably experienced internal debates among conflicted thoughts or feelings regarding the right move to make. If you had focused exclusively on one of those thoughts or feelings and asked it questions, you might have found that it was more than just a transient thought or feeling. You might have discovered that it had a lot to say, that it had been saying similar things to you all of your life, and that it commonly fought with the same parts it was fighting with at that point.

Steeped in systems thinking, it was natural for Schwartz to begin tracking the sequences of interaction among these parts of his clients. He found that they often protected or distracted one another much as happens in distressed families. He also found that most people habitually favor and listen to some parts while disliking and shutting out others. From these observations, he became interested in the parallels between clients' internal systems and their external family systems.

Take the example of Jane, who grew up in a family that strongly feared overt expressions of anger and taught girls to take care of others and to neglect themselves. Jane, like most of us, had a part of her that wanted to help her stand up and assert herself, but because of her family background, she was cut off from that assertive part. Instead, she listened to her fearful and selfless parts' warnings that bad things would happen if she spoke up for herself. Since Jane's assertive part was forced to watch helplessly while people continually exploited her, it became extremely angry. On the rare occasions when Jane couldn't contain this angry part, it seized control and made her fly into a rage, surprising and scaring people around her who were used to her passivity. These outbursts only confirmed to her fearful and selfless parts how dangerous the assertive part was, increasing their conviction to keep it silent, which, of course, made it angrier, and so on. Thus, Schwartz found that the same positive feedback loops that characterize escalations among family members occurred in the polarizations within "internal families" as well.

He also found that often when these internal positive feedback sequences were reversed, the formerly polarized parts quickly returned to their natural state, which was always valuable, just as happens when polarizations among family members are reversed. To achieve this kind of depolarization among a person's parts, Schwartz gained access to the person's inner system with Gestalt therapy's "open-chair" technique or through guided imagery, and then he began experimenting with a variety of family therapy techniques. He found that by using a simple boundary-making technique from structural family therapy he could help people get their polarized parts to deal with each other while blocking the interference of other parts.

The IFS model, then, sees people as containing an ecology of relatively discrete minds, each of which has valuable qualities and is designed to play a valuable role within. These parts are forced out of their useful roles by life experiences that can disorganize the system in unhealthy ways. A good analogy is an alcoholic family, in which the children are forced into protective and stereotypic roles by the rigid dynamics of their family. While one finds similar sibling roles across alcoholic families (e.g., scapegoat, mascot, lost child, etc.), one doesn't conclude that the roles represent the essence of the children. Instead, each child is unique and, once released from his or her role by intervention, can find interests and talents separate from the demands of the chaotic family. The same process seems to hold for internal families—parts are forced into rigid roles by external circumstances and, once it seems safe, they gladly transform into valuable members (Schwartz, 1995).

After studying inner systems for years, Schwartz (1995) grouped into three categories the roles that parts commonly adopt when a person has been hurt. One group, called the *exiles*, are those parts that contain the pain, fear, and sadness from past hurtful experiences. Because these exiles make us vulnerable to being hurt again, another group of parts, the *managers*, try to keep them locked away, out of our consciousness. These managers organize our lives in ways that minimize the activation of the exiles, for example, by making us withdraw from relationships or strive for perfection or power so we feel in control. Despite these managerial efforts, exiles sometimes become upset and threaten to take over. When that happens, a third group of parts called *firefighters* take action to put out the fires of feeling emerging from the exiles by dousing them with something—food, drugs, alcohol, and so on—or by distracting us from them through activities like sex, self-mutilation, or work. Understanding this three-group system has allowed IFS therapists to work safely with clients who have been extremely abused and, as a result, seem severely disturbed (Goulding & Schwartz, 1995).

This ecological view of a person's inner world leads to a different understanding of resistance. An IFS therapist who encounters "resistance" assumes that he or she has inadvertently activated protective manager or firefighter parts of family members. Since the therapist expects parts of a person, family, or any other ecology to react protectively when threatened, he or she views this as a natural reaction.

Rather than trying to overpower or outwit resistance, the therapist respects the protective parts as holding important information regarding the therapy's impact on this delicate ecology and may suggest that clients ask their parts what they're upset about. Once protective parts disclose their fears, both therapist and client can look for ways to accommodate or reassure those parts.

The Self

Is the personality simply a collection of parts, or is there something more at our core? Initially Schwartz believed the former because he was relying on his clients' descriptions and all they described were the parts. As Schwartz began asking clients to interact with their parts, at first through the Gestalt therapy open-chair technique and later through imagery, he found that the conversation would be going well until a certain point at which the client would become upset with the part and change his or her view of it entirely. Or the person might have extreme feelings or beliefs about that part from the outset. When an interaction between two family members isn't going well, it's often because a third family member is interfering—interjecting comments, making faces, taking sides, and in general violating the boundary around the other two family members. Maybe when a client is having difficulty relating to a part, it might be because of the interference of another part. In those situations Schwartz began asking clients to see if they could find another part that was influencing them to see the original part in an extreme way. As Schwartz (1995) describes,

> For example, Sally initially saw her angry part as a monster and was afraid of it. But when I asked her to find and separate from any parts that were making her feel afraid of it, she found a scared little girl. After Sally moved the little girl to a safe place in her mind and convinced it to separate its fear from her, she immediately felt sorry for this angry monster. In addition, the monster changed. It looked less fierce. After that, the conversation with the angry part was more productive. . . . I consistently found that if I asked a client to separate from extreme and polarized parts in this way, most clients could shift quickly into a compassionate or curious state of mind. In that state, they often knew just what to do to help their parts. It seemed that at their core, everyone contained a state of mind that was well suited to leadership. It was through this boundary-making, differentiating process that I encountered what people called their true or core Self. This Self felt different to them than their parts. (pp. 36–37)

After working with hundreds of clients Schwartz concluded that everyone has a Self, no matter how dysfunctional he or she seems or how polarized his or her internal system. The Self has the clarity of perspective and other qualities needed to lead effectively. When one's Self is fully differentiated, for example through an imagery exercise in which the person is asked to climb a mountain and leave the parts in the valley, people universally report similar experiences. They describe feeling "centered," a state of calm well-being and lightheartedness. They feel confident, free, and open-hearted. They describe "being in the present," just experiencing with no thinking. This state is similar to what people describe when they meditate.

Schwartz (1995) likens this state of Self-leadership to what psychologist Mihalyi Csikszentmihalyi (1990) calls "flow," an experience reported by participants in a variety of human activities, from sports to creative endeavors. Flow is characterized by a deep concentration and absence of distracting thoughts; a lack of concern for reward other than the activity itself; a sense of confidence, mastery, and well-being; a loss of the sense of time or of self-consciousness; and a feeling of transcendence. People also can be actively engaged in the mundane aspects of their lives or interacting with others while in this mindset, a state the Buddhists call *mindfulness.* The Self, then, isn't only a passive witness to one's life, but it also can be an active and effective leader internally and externally.

This concept, that we have at out core a Self, a state of compassion and calm from which emanates wise, healing energy, is the key assumption in the IFS model and is very difficult for most therapists to accept fully. Virtually all the world's spiritual practices are designed to help people get in touch with their soul, a state similar to what Schwartz calls the Self, yet many popular psychotherapies view clients as lacking anything resembling this healthy inner state and, consequently, try to add ego strength where it's believed that little previously existed.

IFS therapists' belief in the existence of the Self and their ability to access it in people is what allows them to be truly collaborative. If one doesn't believe people have innate competence or wisdom regarding what's best for themselves, it's difficult to trust them enough to truly collaborate. Instead, one will always lead clients to certain conclusions even when asking questions in the name of collaboration.

The goal of IFS therapy is to help people differentiate their Selves, and then to heal their parts and relationships with the people around them. When working with a family, the goal is similar—to elicit the Selves of each family member in the room and bring them together to deal with the extreme parts of each that are involved in the problem. This, in turn, releases each family member from his or her rigid role in the family.

Schwartz (1995) makes the point that the IFS model is a conceptual framework for understanding people, not a particular set of techniques. Since there are various ways to access and work with parts, therapists have used the model with a wide range of methods, including psychodrama, dance therapy, art therapy, and play therapy with children. In this chapter, however, we will focus on the techniques related to working with families.

The belief in the existence of a Self in every family member provides the basis for a collaborative, nonpathologizing family therapy. The role of the therapist is to create a context in which it's safe for clients' Selves to emerge and to interact with one another. Thus the therapist doesn't have to create competence within family members by, for example, becoming an internalized good object or by teaching them skills of communicating. Instead, in addition to creating a safe, empathic atmosphere, the main roles of the therapist are to (1) help family members notice when their parts have taken over and help them return to Self-leadership; (2) help family members create a vision of how they want to relate; (3) lead discussions of the constraints that exist in the family's environment, in the family's structure, or within each family member that keep the family from achieving that vision and maintaining Self-leadership; and (4) collaborate with the family to find ways to release those constraints. This isn't to say that there are never times when the therapist makes interpretations or educates. It's just that even during those interventions, the therapist's attitude is imbued with respect for the abilities of the clients.

Identifying Parts and Using Parts Language

When someone in a family has a problem that frustrates others, usually parts of one family member struggle to change parts of another, leading to positive feedback escalations between family members and also within each family member.

For example, Tony has been fighting at school and rebelling at home. The therapist asks about the parts that make him do that, and Tony describes a conflict between a rebellious part of him and a part that worries about displeasing his parents and criticizes him for rebelling. He thinks that things might go better for him if he could resolve this internal conflict, but he does not know how. The therapist asks Father what parts of him are activated by Tony's rebellion. Father describes a frustrated and furious part, and agrees that things don't get better when this part of him takes over; he feels ashamed afterward, but he can't seem to control this "temper." Mother says that Father's temper triggers scared parts of her that try to protect Johnny from Father's temper.

Thus, the therapist asks each family member to describe the parts of them that are involved in the problem and may ask questions such as: How difficult is it for them to control their parts? How might the problem be affected if they could stay their Selves rather than letting their parts take over? And how do they want to change their relationship with these parts that interfere in their life? People respond naturally and nondefensively to this language. (Admitting that a little part of yourself contributes to the problem feels less shameful and overwhelming than implicating your whole personality.)

In addition, the model's language alters people's views of themselves and each other. Instead of having a rebellious, disrespectful child, the parents find they have a son who has some trouble with a few of his parts, but also has a Self that wants to work on those parts. Father is transformed from a raging tyrant to being a good man struggling with his angry part. The view of Mother is likewise changed by this multiplicity perspective of personality, which is more benevolent and holds more potential for change than the idea that people have unitary and fixed personalities.

Maintaining Self-Leadership

During discussions of issues in the family, it's expected that parts of family members will overtake them as they talk. When the therapist detects this, he or she can stop the action, ask the family member to see if a part has taken over, and ask that part to step back and trust his or her Self to lead. Thus, the therapist develops a "parts detector"—a sense of when people are and are not leading with their Selves—and uses it to help family members maintain Self-leadership as they interact. In this way, each person gains trust in the Self because they see that things go better when they lead from that awareness. In addition, the issues between them often are resolved quickly because it was the rigidity of their parts that was driving the conflict. Now they feel heard, even empathized with, and suddenly solutions are more available.

Using the IFS Model with the Family of an Anorexic Child

To illustrate these and other techniques, we will present a summary of a family case that's described in detail elsewhere (Schwartz, 1997). Schwartz first met Rebecca and her family in the hospital. Rebecca was a fifteen-year-old who had been hospitalized four times during the past year for severe anorexia and bulimia, and was being discharged once again. By now her parents, Bob and Faye, were exasperated, scared, and reluctant to try yet another course of therapy.

◆

At the initial contact Schwartz mainly listened to the parents' story of frustration, while also offering hope that his approach might be different, in an effort to calm the protective manager parts of the parents so as to have more access to their Selves. He did that by empathizing with their skepticism and frustration, giving them total control over the decision about continuing, while conveying confidence that their predicament could change and that he was competent to help them change it. This reassurance often begins the process of gaining the trust of manager parts. Bob and Faye reluctantly agreed to continue, and the ensuing sessions took place after Rebecca, their only child, came home.

In the first session they told the following story. Bob had divorced his first wife, Rebecca's mother, when Rebecca was nine and married Faye shortly afterward. Rebecca felt abandoned by her mother and looked to Faye as a savior, but now she and Faye fought frequently and Bob tried to be peacemaker. Both parents were confused and frustrated by Rebecca's eating problems. Rebecca herself said she knew she should gain weight but couldn't control her urges to purge whatever she ate. She also admitted that she didn't like herself very much.

In the second session, both parents were angry that Rebecca had already resumed her bulimic behavior. Faye complained that "a lot of her bulimic behavior is very irritating to me—I find it sort of slovenly, and it really bothers me. I have a very short fuse when it comes to messiness. I'm a little quirky in that way. I find it remarkable, extremely irritating."

Schwartz said "So you've been having to struggle with yourself this week. Would you like some help in that area?"

"No!" Faye snapped, "I don't think it's dysfunctional!"

Schwartz said, "I'm not saying there's anything wrong with it, but I mean the part of you that gets so activated by Rebecca's behavior. Do you think that if that part wasn't so upset, it would be easier for you to help her?"

"Yes," said Faye tentatively, "If I could get help but not have to discombobulate my life any more than it already is, I guess it would be helpful."

As soon as possible in therapy, Schwartz tries to identify the parts of each family member connected to the problems they present. Thus, when Faye talked about her strong reactions, he asked her about whether that part of her got in the way of her relationship with Rebecca. It's usually fairly easy to introduce the parts language in this way—feeding back what clients say about their thoughts or feelings but construing that as coming from a part of them. This parts language, in and of itself, is usually very helpful. In this case, for example, it was easier for Faye to acknowledge that her "quirkiness" got in the way when it was framed as just a part of her than when Schwartz initially asked if she wanted to change her (as in all of her) thoughts or behavior.

Schwartz finds that clients are more able to disclose feelings and beliefs they are ashamed of when they can speak about a part of them feeling or thinking it. Also, the language helps people feel better about themselves and one another because if their extremes are contained in small parts of them, there's hope that those parts can change. The implication is that, beyond those parts, they have many other resources or feelings. Finally, this language encourages family members to remember that behind the protective parts they often show each other are the parts that love them. Thus, simply using parts language can change the way family members see themselves, each other, and their problems. They aren't asked to minimize or deny the seriousness of problems or damage done by one another, only to recognize that there is much more to each other than those extremes.

Schwartz then turned to Rebecca. "That angry part of Faye seems to trigger a sad, hurt part in you, is that right?" She nodded. "Are you interested in finding ways to help those hurt parts of you feel better so you won't be so vulnerable to that part of Faye and maybe won't have such urges to binge and purge?" Rebecca nodded again.

In asking that question, Schwartz implied that it's possible for Rebecca to handle her feelings herself and that he knows how to help her get there. The idea that she no longer has to be so vulnerable to her parents is attractive to any teenager. It was also important for her to hear that her mother was willing to try to get more control over her own angry part. This willingness to change can begin a kind of depolarization process in which, as each person sees their adversary begin to back down, they think it may be safe to do the same. Depolarizing is a big part of the early stages of IFS therapy.

Schwartz then asked Bob what parts of him get in the way, and he replied "I don't know—maybe being passive, but I don't think of that as a part of me—just what I do, and I don't necessarily see it as a part of the problem." It was obvious that Bob's managers weren't buying into this process. Schwartz accommodated to that resistance until the family trusted him more.

After Faye had elaborated on her feelings, Schwartz said, "So the part of you that gets upset about the food and the one that's so outraged by what you call Rebecca's deceptiveness . . . those parts interfere with the affection you have for her?"

Faye's tone softened considerably. "Yeah, its down there some place, but it's buried under a lot of resentment."

Schwartz turned to Rebecca and asked gently, "Is there a part of you that agrees with Faye when she gets so upset with you?" Rebecca nodded and alluded to getting angry inside too. She tried to push away that angry part, however, "because if I get angry at Faye, she'll get more angry at me, and it will make me feel more sad."

At this point Schwartz described a sequence of parts he saw taking place between stepmother and daughter and asked if this description seemed to fit. When Faye became irritated and disgusted with Rebecca, it triggered Rebecca's own inner critic, which then set off her hurt parts, which in turn released her binge and purge parts, which only further frustrated and infuriated Faye, and the sequence escalated. He also made it clear that this was, no doubt, only a small piece of a larger picture, but it was a place where they could start. Both Faye and Rebecca agreed with this depiction of their interactions as a vicious circle they felt powerless to change. They also agreed that they both wanted to find a way back to the closeness they used to have and were willing to work on the parts that kept them from it.

Gradually it was becoming evident to Schwartz that the Selves of each of them were peeking out from behind their protectors. Faye's voice was very different—less harsh, more caring; Rebecca had stopped crying, she was taking risks. This is largely the goal of IFS family therapy—to create an atmosphere in which it's safe for the Selves of family members to emerge and interact rather than the polarizing parts that had been dominating their interactions. When people are able to have Self-to-Self contact, they often find that the problems they thought were intractable begin to crumble as the veils of fixed belief and angry emotion are lifted.

Once it's clear that the amount of Self-leadership in the room is increased and stable, Schwartz asks family members to speak with one another directly about their issues. Until then, however, he remains fairly central, providing the system Self-leadership until family members are more able to provide their own.

Since it was feeling safer, Schwartz asked whether Faye or Rebecca wanted to work with him on their parts. Faye agreed to work on her angry part because exposing it in the presence of Bob and Rebecca wouldn't make her feel too vulnerable. When one family member does internal work in front of others it can generate hope and empathy in the observers and a feeling of being accepted by the one doing it. On the other hand, this exposure can make a person quite vulnerable in front of people who have hurt him or her in the past.

Schwartz had Faye focus on her anger and see if, in her mind, she could separate it from her into a room. She said she could and saw it as a dragon, waving its arms menacingly and "doing dragon things." Schwartz asked how she felt toward it, and she said, "Kind of amazed. It looks so angry and vicious, with teeth, but it's kind of like watching something in the zoo, so I'm not frightened of it." He asked Faye to see if she could find a way to help calm it down. She found that when she approached it carefully and put her hand out and then stroked it like a dog, the dragon stopped raging and sat down. Faye said, "It's really friendly, actually. I'm calm, I stand there. I can reassure him." After some time with her dragon, Faye felt more confident that she could help it calm down in that way when it got upset in the future.

When Faye came back out of her imagery, both Bob and Rebecca seemed in a lighter mood. They each said they knew that dragon. Bob said he was glad to see that Faye could calm it down. Schwartz warned them not to get their hopes too high, because there were probably hurt parts of Faye that the dragon protected that they hadn't helped yet, so she may remain fairly explosive for a while yet. This shifting of focus back and forth between external and internal family interactions is characteristic of Schwartz's approach.

The family entered the next session seeming upbeat. Faye's dragon had little occasion to get upset. She said, however, that at mealtimes, when Rebecca got edgy and seemed anxious to go upstairs, Faye always assumes she is rushing away to vomit. At that, Rebecca became defensive and an argument ensued over how often she was still vomiting.

Schwartz asked the parents to let him try to help Rebecca with the parts of her involved in her eating problems and to give up trying to coerce her. They reluctantly agreed, and Schwartz had them go to the waiting room so that he and Rebecca could do work with her parts privately.

Rebecca was upset and wanted help with the part of her that felt hurt. As Rebecca focused on her sadness, she saw a Raggedy Ann doll slumped in the corner of a room. Schwartz asked her to be outside the room looking at it, and she said she wanted to go in and help it. Ultimately in that session, Rebecca was able to hold and comfort that doll. She also found and calmed the part that made her binge, which appeared to her as a frenzied ogre.

Afterward, Schwartz asked Rebecca what she felt comfortable telling her parents about the session and he asked them to return. Rebecca described in a lively way what she did with her doll and ogre. Her parents listened politely and asked a few questions. Their demeanor was supportive.

At the next session, Bob was angry because of an incident in which Rebecca "went crazy" when he refused to help her with her homework. Rebecca responded calmly, saying that she didn't go crazy, but she did get angry because Bob rarely does anything with her or shows her much affection. Faye jumped in at that point saying "That's right, he's not demonstrative in any shape or form, for wonderful things or bad things. That's just the way he is. We need to learn to accept it." Bob and Faye both pushed the focus back on Rebecca's being oversensitive, but she stood her ground.

In this session, Rebecca was different. Previously she'd been dominated by her sad Raggedy Ann part, so she sounded very young and was crying frequently. Now she stood up for herself and, in so doing, shifted the spotlight onto her father's behavior. This seemed threatening to both parents and they repeatedly returned to Rebecca's deficits. Faye, in particular, came to Bob's defense, as if fearing that something bad would happen if he were challenged.

Schwartz had to work hard with his own parts to avoid becoming angry with the parents for their apparent denial and scapegoating. It's the position of the IFS model that people deny or distract from problems because their parts fear facing those problems. The goal of therapy isn't to force them to confront those issues while they're still terrified, but instead to help them feel safe enough to take them on. Therefore, rather than confronting Faye or Bob at that point, Schwartz chose to remind them that he had predicted it would be a difficult week and asked to meet privately with Rebecca again.

When Rebecca's parents left, Schwartz asked her how she had kept her hurt part, the doll, from taking over during those painful exchanges. She said that she had moved it, in her mind, to a safe, protected, back room and the ogre was holding it. She said the doll believed that her parents didn't care about her and, while she was feeling that now, she wasn't overwhelmed by the feeling. Schwartz said that her parents seemed to have parts that reacted negatively to neediness in her—and in each other—and that while he hoped to be able to help them change at some point, it wasn't going to be soon. In the meantime, he and Rebecca would continue to help her feel less vulnerable to those parts of them.

The next session Schwartz asked to meet with only Bob and Rebecca to give Rebecca the opportunity to deal with her father without Faye protecting him. Clearly Rebecca felt neglected and rejected by him, and Schwartz hoped to set up a Self-to-Self interaction between them around those issues. Schwartz also wanted a chance to connect with Bob's Self.

Bob said coldly that Rebecca expected too much; he was very busy with his job and didn't have time. Schwartz asked Bob what he said to himself when Rebecca asked him for something, and he replied that he felt angry because she never understood how busy he was. Rebecca interrupted in a hurt voice, saying that she rarely asked him for anything anymore. Schwartz asked her to find the part that interrupted and ask it to step back and not interfere while he and her father talked. She paused for a moment and, in a stronger voice, said it had stepped back.

Schwartz then asked Bob to ask the same of the part of him that gets impatient with Rebecca. He said he didn't understand what Schwartz wanted from him. Schwartz replied that this was just a way to help them talk less emotionally so they could avoid the painful patterns of the past.

Schwartz asked Bob what he felt in his body when he got angry at Rebecca. He felt a burning in his gut. Schwartz had him focus on his gut and simply ask his anger to step back. Bob tried it and his voice softened somewhat.

This process, in which as clients get upset the therapist asks them to find the parts that are interfering and ask those parts to step back, is a common practice in IFS family therapy. There are many variations on that technique, but the basic goal is to maintain Self-to-Self interaction, trusting that when Selves are connected, healing can occur.

By this point in the case description, we have illustrated most of the basic IFS techniques for working with families, so we'll provide a brief summary of the rest of the sessions and refer the reader elsewhere for more details (Schwartz, 1997). After the session with her father, Rebecca felt great, but was quickly deflated the next time her father snubbed her. In a subsequent individual session Schwartz helped Rebecca find a hopeless part that protected her doll from being disappointed and a perfectionistic woman who criticized everything about her, calling her a loser.

In other sessions, Rebecca was able to heal several of her parts. For example, she found that her rag doll had turned into a five-year-old girl who wanted Rebecca to know what life had been like for her at that age. Rebecca was able to compassionately witness scenes from her parents' fights during her childhood that were very frightening. After sensing that Rebecca finally understood her story, the little girl part's demeanor transformed and she was able to be playful. As Rebecca became stronger the tension in the house increased and her parents ultimately refused to continue. Rebecca moved out of the house and in with her birth mother. Schwartz had a series of sessions with Rebecca and her mother. Rebecca was able to tell her mother how scared and hurt she was during those past times, and her mother was able to listen compassionately.

Rebecca's bulimia gradually abated over the one and one-half years of therapy, and her weight improved throughout. Schwartz remained in periodic phone contact with her for four years after therapy, during which she went off to college and did quite well.

◆

The following summarizes the IFS techniques for helping families illustrated in this case in the order that they were used. The therapist:

1. tried to deactivate the parents' managers by giving them compassion and control, but also by giving hope that their situation could change and that he was competent to help them do it;
2. used the parts language to facilitate more open communication; to bring a new, nonpathological view of themselves, one another, and the problem; and to offer hope and outline clear steps toward change;
3. helped them track the pattern of parts interaction across people, uncovering vicious cycles, and then invited each to focus on his or her own parts rather than trying to coerce change in the others;
4. elicited the Selves of family members by detecting parts of each of them as they were manifest, and having them ask their parts to step back and allow their Selves to lead;
5. worked with one member's parts privately (Rebecca) or while the others observed (Faye);
6. warned family members, as things began to change, to prepare for parts' reactions to a relapse;
7. explored and resolved past traumas both in private sessions with Rebecca and in family sessions with her and her mother.

Aspects of these methods will seem familiar to family therapists from different schools, but they also each have novel qualities that are shaped by the different view of people offered by the IFS model. Indeed, most family therapy techniques can be adapted to fit with this approach because the IFS model is not a set of techniques, but rather a conceptual package or philosophy.

In family therapy the impact of the IFS model has been limited by the field's long-standing reluctance to consider intrapsychic process. For example, structural family therapist Jorge Colapinto (1993) complained that the IFS model's notion that we all have a core Self was turning family therapy back toward a contextual, individual psychotherapy.

> Under Schwartz's proposal, the main role of the therapist is to help the client take distance from his or her family and turn towards his or her Self. . . . As in traditional psychotherapy, the strength of the client must grow in isolation from significant others. . . . From an ethics of interdependency, one can challenge Schwartz's emphasis on the Self as a denial of connectivity. (pp. 53, 55)

It's true that therapists can become so preoccupied with a client's fascinating inner world, particularly as they are just learning the model, that they ignore or underestimate the resources of the client's family. Therapists using the IFS model need to be aware of this tendency and consciously maintain focus at the family level.

Colapinto's reaction can also be seen in light of the challenge the IFS model presents to a fundamental premise of family therapy: that people are dependent on their context to the point that for them to change, their families must change. The IFS model's assertion that people have inner resources that, if necessary, can help them transcend the influence of their families takes issue with this premise. This question of how individually resourceful or context-dependent people are is one with which every clinician grapples. The way it's answered determines much of how therapy is practiced.

In many ways, the IFS model also runs counter to the postmodern movement in family therapy. It emphasizes releasing inner resources, whereas social constructionists co-create new narratives and stay away from beliefs about internal qualities. It tries to understand the structures of both internal and external systems, whereas solution-focused and narrative therapists are poststructural in their aversion to exploring dynamics surrounding problems. It proposes a grand narrative regarding human nature, whereas postmodernists try to avoid large-scale theorizing. In doing IFS work, clients often move toward their pain in order to heal it, whereas postmodern therapists often actively lead clients away from pain.

On the other hand, IFS therapists trust the wisdom of the Selves of their clients and, consequently, are able to be truly collaborative partners once Self-leadership emerges. In addition, the model is empowering in that clients often can do the inner work on their own and leave therapy believing they healed themselves. Finally, by helping people become compassionate witnesses to their own painful stories, IFS allows them to let go of the grip of their history and the extreme beliefs and emotions that come with it. Then, as they construct new, preferred narratives, they don't constantly struggle to hold past stories at bay.

The Metaframeworks Model

Metaframeworks was the product of a collaboration among three family therapy teachers who worked together in the Family Systems Program at the Institute for Juvenile Research in Chicago: Douglas Breunlin, Richard Schwartz, and Betty Mac Kune-Karrer. (Breunlin and Schwartz are now on the faculty of the Family Institute at Northwestern University.) Before metaframeworks, they had fashioned a hybrid of structural and strategic family therapies to teach their students. In the 1980s they, along with the rest of the field, grappled with the disconcertion brought on by the feminist and postmodern critiques described in Chapter 10, which made them question their cherished beliefs.

The developers of the metaframeworks model weren't trying to create a new school of family therapy when they put it together. They believed the field was already struggling with too many competing schools. Instead, they developed a unifying theoretical framework, operationalized around six core domains of human experience they called metaframeworks: organization, sequences, development, culture, gender, and internal process (Breunlin, Schwartz, & Mac Kune-Karrer, 1992). These domains bridge structural (organization), strategic (sequences), and incorporate intrapsychic (internal process), as well as addressing newer concerns in the field like gender and multiculturalism.

Previous schools of family therapy had treated these topics more narrowly. For example, structural family therapy's perspective on family organization was limited pretty much to boundaries and subsystems. The strategic therapy of Jay Haley focused almost exclusively on hierarchical control in families. Bowen concentrated on triangles. The point is, each school included ideas about family organization but each emphasized a different aspect of it. Similarly, they noticed that each school used the concept of sequences of interaction, but each was concerned with sequences of different length. Structural family therapy focused on short, in-session sequences; Haley scanned the day-to-day patterns in a family's life and the circular patterns around a child's symptoms that might play out over months or years; and Bowen was interested in transgenerational patterns.

The metaframeworks perspective freed topics like family organization, sequences, and development from the narrow view of a particular model, so they became frameworks that transcended the individual schools of family therapy. For example, a therapist using metaframeworks will attend to sequences of all the different lengths (what they call S1, S2, S3, and S4; with S1 being the short, in-session kind and S4 the transgenerational kind). When this wider view of sequences is interwoven with the other five metaframeworks, a therapist's perspective on families expands, and the knowledge base of family therapy is brought together in a new way.

To connect all six metaframeworks they identified a set of presuppositions about people and the world that runs through each. The metaframeworks then becomes six different lenses through which to view a family or problem. Each lens examines the problem from a different angle or has a different focal point, but they are all ground from the same glass, so they're highly compatible and can be used simultaneously.

The clinical application of metaframeworks is centered around the practice of releasing constraints rather than finding deficits. Because one of the model's presuppositions is that people have the resources they need to relate harmoniously, then, when they aren't, the assumption is that something is constraining them from using those resources. Because constraints may exist at one or more levels, therapy helps families identify and release constraints at whatever level they exist. In other words, therapist and family collaboratively explore the different metaframeworks, and they can shift from one to another fluidly as constraints at different levels are released.

For example, a depressed woman may be constrained at many levels. At the level of internal process, she may be burdened by guilt over wanting to have some time for herself or because her children complain that they have no friends. (If children are unhappy, it must be their mother's fault, right?) At the level of family organization, she may be stuck in a stale marriage to a man who's obsessed with his career and friends, while she's running the house and raising the kids. In addition, she may be highly involved with her hyperactive son and polarized with her own mother over how to deal with him. This pattern may be part of a sequence in which her son's behavior gets worse after bimonthly visits with her ex-husband. Finally, her life situation may be part of a transgenerational sequence maintained by the family and cultural belief that women should be devoted to their families and never be "selfish."

As the therapist discusses this network of constraints that are impeding her and her husband, one metaframework often emerges as a point of departure, but the therapist is always considering the others and can shift to another at any point. Thus, therapy may start in the gender metaframework by reexamining the value of her beliefs about selfishness and her husband's imbalanced expectations about what he deserves. At some point the focus might shift to the internal metaframework when the therapist asks about the parts of each that hold these beliefs and what they are related to from their pasts. This exploration might make her want to reorganize the family responsibilities, and the shift is to the organizational metaframework. At another point the couple may discuss their son's oscillating between acting younger and older than his age, and they're in the developmental metaframework, and so on.

The multicultural metaframework expanded the way that cultural issues have been understood in family therapy—which had been to equate culture with ethnicity. Instead, ethnicity becomes only one of many cultural contexts that influence a family's belief and values, and it may not be the primary influence. Thus, for example, although the family of our depressed mother may be a less obvious place to look for cultural influences than, say, a poor immigrant family from Guatemala, the impact of their middle-class culture and values of striving materialism may be just as important in understanding her dilemma. The multicultural metaframework encourages therapists to have conversations with families regarding the impact of their ethnicity, but also their socioeconomic class, education, religion, race, minority/majority status, and regional background. Additional important considerations are the degree to which the family fits with its community and how recently it has immigrated.

The gender metaframework applies the concept of balance of influence, resources, and responsibilities to a feminist understanding of families. Breunlin and associates (1992) noticed that families evolved through stages of gender consciousness. They identified five phases that families pass through as they evolve from being highly patriarchal to egalitarian: traditional, gender-aware, polarized, in transition, and balanced. In each phase families have predictable organizations and issues. Thus, this couple is affected not only by global assumptions about gender, but also by their particular stage of gender evolution.

Breunlin, Schwartz, and Mac Kune-Karrer emphasize that while the six metaframeworks are presented as discrete perspectives, in practice they are all interrelated. With practice therapists are able to shift from trying each lens on with a family, one at a time, to moving fluidly among them. In some cases, key constraints can be quickly found and released using only one or two metaframeworks; in other cases, the therapist and family collaborate to deal with constraints in each of the six.

The following dialogue between two fictional colleagues about a family with an anorexic daughter clarifies how metaframeworks can be used.

> A: You mean you can put on the lens of sequences as you look at the family, and then the lens of gender or structure or parts, and all these views would be tied together somehow? That's an attractive idea because I always felt that if I wanted to think about sequences I would use strategic models of therapy, and then if I wanted to think about organizations, I'd have to shift to the structural model, with all its different assumptions. And to think about intrapsychic process, I'd have to shift again, to object relation or self-psychology, and so on.
>
> B: Exactly. That's one big advantage of this metaframework perspective. . . . For example, you can work one session with Nancy on the extreme parts of her that are constraining her from eating the way she wants to, and in the next session you can explore with her and her family how our culture's gender values affect those parts of Nancy. All the while, you can ask questions about sequences among Nancy's parts or among these three family members. Or you can help them look at structural or developmental issues that might be creating these sequences. If one of these metaframeworks seems more relevant to or useful with a particular case, I will stay with it, but the others are still in the back of my mind. (Breunlin, Schwartz, & Mac Kune-Karrer, 1992, p. 7)

In their book, Breunlin and colleagues (1992) offer a blueprint for using metaframeworks that involves a circular process of having conversations with families about potential constraints, collaborating with them to form hypotheses, planning ways to address the constraints, and then reading the feedback regarding the plan's impact.

Metaframeworks isn't for therapists looking for simple, formulaic concepts and techniques. It challenges clinicians to consider a wide range of phenomena and to learn a host of new concepts in an age when therapy is increasingly circumscribed and therapists are pressured to keep it simple.

Yet, for many therapists who've felt boxed in by the narrow scope and rigidity of the original models of family therapy, metaframeworks knocks down the walls and lets them breathe. Breunlin and colleagues present metaframeworks as an ongoing project rather than a finished product. Whether or not therapists agree with all the concepts, they can use the format as a model for expanding their perspectives.

Integrative Problem-Centered Therapy

Where metaframeworks distilled key elements from family therapy models and combined them to form a new synthesis, integrative problem-centered therapy (IPCT) uses a variety of family and individual approaches in sequence, without trying to synthesize them.

IPCT has been developed over the past twenty years by William Pinsof and his colleagues at the Family Institute at Northwestern University. In addition to developing IPCT, Pinsof is a highly regarded family therapy researcher who has worked in the area of process research. Like metaframeworks, IPCT provides a multilevel model for understanding how family problems are maintained, but IPCT emphasizes some different domains (like the biological, the level of object relations, and the self system) than metaframeworks.

One unique aspect of the IPCT is that rather than combining models, it leaves each intact and encourages therapists to shift from one to another according to a set of guidelines for deciding at what point to use which approach. The approaches used range from those focused on here-and-now interactions and cognitions (structural, strategic, cognitive-behavioral, solution-focused, and psychopharmacological therapies), to those targeting historical factors (Bowenian, object relations, and self psychology).

To illustrate this approach, let's return to the depressed woman described in the metaframeworks section earlier. In addition to the family organizational problems she experienced, Pinsof would be interested in biological factors that constrained the family—whether she suffered from an imbalance in serotonin levels or was run-down from being the one responsible for dealing with her hyperactive son. Pinsof might also wind up exploring aspects of her and her husband's families of origin and the narcissistic injuries each suffered in those families.

But you may not need to go that far. IPCT takes the position that the simplest and least expensive intervention should be tried before more complex and expensive methods. Thus, the therapist begins by exploring here-and-now organizational and cognitive constraints, and only shifts to biological, family of origin, or psychodynamic constraints when the initial interventions aren't effective.

For example, a couple in their sixties has been caught up in picky but intense fights for the past year. They relate the fighting to the husband's increasing impotence, which began about the same time as the fighting. In exploring the meaning each attaches to these events, the therapist finds that the wife sees her husband's lack of sexual response as a reflection of her diminished attractiveness, while he thinks it reflects his waning sexuality. These conceptions are painful to each of them, and so they avoid discussing, much less having, sex.

The therapist forms an alliance with each of them so they feel safe enough to disclose their private pain and clear up their misconceptions regarding the other's feelings. If at that point they respond well—fewer fights and more satisfactory sex—therapy can stop. If not, the therapist would explore possible physiological causes of and solutions to the impotence—fatigue, depression, incipient diabetes. If improvements don't follow the exploration at that level, the therapist might discuss with each the unexamined beliefs and emotions that they have about the aging process. If the problem still remains unsolved, the focus would shift to intrapsychic blocks, and each of them might be engaged in individual therapy based on the self psychology of Heinz Kohut.

Pinsof doesn't expect therapists to be competent in all these approaches. IPCT often involves teamwork among a number of therapists, particularly when key family members are quite vulnerable and need their own therapists. While assemblages of therapists with such differing orientations can be a nightmare, the IPCT framework provides common ground for collaboration where therapists respect and learn from one another.

The Narrative Solutions Approach

One of the things that troubles some senior practitioners of family therapy is the tendency for adherents of the newer solution-focused and narrative approaches to turn their backs on valuable elements of the traditional models. If it's true that a new broom sweeps clean, they're worried that some of what's being swept out is worth keeping. That's why Eron and Lund's narrative solutions approach (Eron & Lund, 1993, 1996), which combines the insights of the MRI model with narrative technique, is a welcome addition.

Among the reasons the strategic model fell into disfavor were it's mechanistic assumptions and manipulative techniques. The way some strategists applied the cybernetic model, families were seen as stubborn and couldn't be reasoned with. You don't talk sense to a cybernetic machine. Family histories were dismissed as irrelevant to their current dilemmas. Therapy was ideological and therefore to a certain extent impersonal. The meretriciousness of this kind of thinking, however, wasn't essential to the insight that families get stuck applying more of the same solutions that don't work. Eron and Lund have resuscitated that insight and incorporated it into a blend of strategic and narrative therapy.

Joseph Eron and Thomas Lund of the Catskill Family Institute in New York began collaborating in the early 1980s as brief, strategic therapists. Although they were attracted to the narrative movement, there were aspects of the strategic approach they didn't want to give up. So they put the two together and added some key elements of solution-focused therapy. The resulting narrative solutions approach revolves around a concept called the *preferred view.* Eron and Lund (1996) assume that people have strong preferences for how they would like to see themselves and be viewed by others. They believe problems arise when people aren't living their preferred views. To address this discrepancy, Eron and Lund use a combination of reframing technique from the MRI model and restorying from the narrative approach.

They subscribe to the fundamental premise of the MRI model that problems develop innocently from the mishandling of life transitions. However, Eron and Lund are more specific. They propose that people begin to think and act in problematic ways when they experience a discrepancy between their preferred view of themselves, their perception of their own actions, and their impression of how others regard them. It's often during life transitions that these shifts in meaning and action occur.

Note that while Eron and Lund follow the MRI model in looking for more-of-the-same cycles, they differ in focusing not just on behavior, but also on what people think about their problems. Conflict, according to this model, is driven by disjunctions between individuals' preferred views of themselves and how they perceive others as seeing them.

They also incorporate questions regarding how people prefer and hope to be and what the future will look like once the problem is solved. These questions are similar to solution-focused techniques. Thus, they have created a flexible approach that isn't tied to any particular school, and instead therapists try a variety of methods, as long as the techniques are in the service of empowering clients.

In *Narrative Solutions in Brief Therapy*, Eron and Lund (1996) offer an example of Al, who became depressed in the wake of two life transitions: retirement and the onset of emphysema. Al preferred to think of himself as productive and useful. He was accustomed to being a person that family members relied on. Yet Al worried that he might not be able to remain as active as in the past and that his family would no longer view him as productive and useful. The disjunction between Al's preferences and his current perceptions was linked to feeling sad and listless. As Al seemed more depressed, family members began to do more for him, finishing projects he started and trying to cheer him up, which only deepened his despondency. The negative *frame* through which Al viewed his current circumstances affected the *stories* he recalled from the past. For example, he pictured himself following in the footsteps of his own father, who deteriorated rapidly after retiring. According to Eron and Lund, negative frames of the present shape the stories people recall from the past, which in turn influence their perspectives on the present and future.

Eron and Lund (1996) offer the following guidelines for managing helpful conversations. The therapist:

1. maintains a position of interest in clients' preferences and hopes, paying attention to stories that reflect how clients prefer to see themselves, to act, and to be seen by significant others;
2. explores how the problem keeps people from acting in line with their preferences;
3. finds past and present stories that are in line with their preferences and contradict problem-maintaining views;
4. discusses what the future will look like when the problem is resolved;
5. asks *mystery questions*—for example, how did a person with *X* preferred attributes (hard working, productive) wind up in *Y* situation (acting listless and feeling depressed)?
6. co-creates with clients alternative explanations for the evolution of the problem that fit with how they prefer to be seen and inspires new actions;
7. encourages clients to talk to significant others about their preferences, hopes, and intentions.

As these guidelines are followed, clients become aware that the therapist is seeing them in their preferred ways and they begin to notice their own strengths. They begin seeing the problem as a mystery to be explained rather than as a truth that speaks to who they really are. They begin to restory how the problem evolved (a narrative practice) and to reframe (a strategic technique) their immediate situation. For example, Al felt empowered to talk to his doctor about his illness after he was able to recall preferred experiences indicating that he was a take-charge kind of guy. He also began reframing the motives of family members away from the belief that they saw him as useless to viewing them as bewildered, not knowing how to help him. His depression lifted after he met with his family and told them what was and wasn't helpful.

Within the framework provided by their guidelines for helpful conversations, Eron and

Lund suggest that therapists can use methods from a wide variety of approaches if they might be helpful to clients. Thus, they don't hesitate to ask "miracle questions" like solution-focused therapists, engage in "externalizing conversations" like Michael White, link thinking and behavior like cognitive-behavioral therapists, reframe meanings like MRI therapists, or discuss transference like a psychodynamic therapist.

This shifting of methods works only if therapists maintain a deep respect for their clients. It's clear from reading Eron and Lund's book that with them, empathy and understanding aren't just feel-good bromides; these qualities are deeply ingrained in their approach.

Integrative Couple Therapy

Neil Jacobson of the University of Washington, one of the preeminent behavioral family therapists, teamed with Andrew Christensen of UCLA to figure out how to improve the limited success rates they were finding with traditional behavioral couples therapy. They discovered that their results improved when they added elements of other therapies—strategic, experiential, and ego analytic—to the standard mix of communication training, conflict resolution, and problem-solving. The approach they developed is described in a new book called *Integrative Couple Therapy* (Jacobson & Christensen, 1996).

When a respected pioneer of behavior therapy like Neil Jacobson decides that it's time to overhaul the approach he's been promoting for twenty years, it's reasonable to assume two things: first, that something was missing in the original model; and second, that what was added is important.

Traditional behavioral couples therapy is based on the behavior exchange model. After a "functional analysis" showing how partners in a relationship influence one another, they're taught how to reinforce changes they wish to bring about in each other. Anyone who's been married for a long time could tell you what's missing from this approach to relationships. Therapy may be about change, but a successful relationship also involves a certain amount of acceptance of differences and disappointments. Some things in an unhappy marriage may need to change for the relationship to survive; but some things about our partners are part of the package, and couples who survive the break-in period learn to accept these things. It's this element, acceptance, that Jacobson has added in his new approach to couples therapy.

According to Jacobson, what led to his dissatisfaction was an accumulation of research data showing that only about 50 percent of couples treated with traditional behavioral couples therapy improve and maintain their improvement over the long term (Jacobson et al., 1984; Jacobson, Schmaling, & Holtzworth-Monroe, 1987). So, together with Christensen, a researcher/clinician who had studied conflicted marriages, Jacobson added procedures for promoting acceptance to his standard protocol.

In contrast to the teaching and preaching characterizing traditional behavioral therapy, integrative couple therapy emphasizes support and empathy, the same qualities that therapists want couples to learn to show each other. To create a conducive atmosphere, this approach begins with a phase called the *formulation*, which is aimed at helping couples let go of blaming and open themselves to acceptance and change. The formulation consists of three components: a *theme* that defines the primary conflict; a *polarization process* that describes their destructive pattern of interaction; and the mutual trap that is the impasse that prevents the couple from breaking the polarization cycle once it's triggered.

Common themes in couples' problems include conflicts around closeness and distance, a desire for control but unwillingness to take responsibility, and disagreements about sex. Whereas partners view these differences as indicating deficiencies in the other person and as problems to be solved, Jacobson and Christensen encourage couples to see differences as inevitable, in order to become more accepting of one another. This can break the cycles that build up when each is constantly trying to change the other. Also, as this formulation phase continues, each partner begins to see that he or she is not a victim of the other, but of the pattern they've both been trapped in. As with Michael White's externalizing, the couple can unite to fight a mutual enemy, the pattern.

For example, Jacobson recently asked a couple to describe their pattern.

> The husband replied, "We fight over whether or not to be close. When she is not as close to me as she wants to be, she pressures me into being close, and I withdraw, which leads to more pressure. Of course, sometimes I withdraw before she has a chance to pressure me. In fact, that's how it usually starts." (Jacobson & Christensen, 1996, p. 100)

Notice how the formulation process helps this couple describe their fight as a pattern they both contribute to, rather than in the accusatory language more typical of distressed couples.

To further foster acceptance, partners are encouraged to talk about their own experience rather than attack their mates. Shifting from statements such as, "She never shows me any affection!" to disclosure of vulnerability—"I'm not always sure she cares about me"—is more likely to promote understanding. The listening partner is encouraged to convey empathy for such disclosures.

Strategies to produce change include the two basic ingredients of behavior couples therapy: behavior exchange and communication skills training. Behavior exchange interventions (described more fully in Chapter 9) involve "quid pro quo" and "good faith" contracts, by which couples learn to exchange favors or to initiate pleasing behavior in the hopes of getting the same in return. For example, each partner might be asked to generate a list of things he or she could do that would lead to greater satisfaction for the other. (Ask not what your partner can do for you; ask what you can do for your partner.) After each compiles a list, they're instructed to start doing some of the things they think will please their partners—and to observe the effect of this benevolence on the relationship.

The second ingredient—communication training—involves teaching couples to listen and to express themselves in direct but nonblaming ways. Learning to use "active listening" and to make "I-statements" is taught by assigned reading, instruction, and practice. As they learn to communicate nondefensively, couples not only are better able to resolve conflicts, but they also become more accepting of each other.

It's too early to evaluate the effectiveness of integrative couple therapy, but it seems to be an improvement over traditional behavioral couples therapy. Its significance isn't only in improving a model, but in the shift it represents toward the humanizing of behavioral therapies. In emphasizing empathy, acceptance, and compassion, integrative couple therapy joins many other family therapies of the 1990s—from solution-focused to strategic to narrative—in recognizing the importance of nurturing relationships. Carl Rogers would be proud.

Given Jacobson and Christensen's commitment to empirical research, we can look forward to careful studies of the outcome of this new approach. Meanwhile, we salute them for having the courage to reevaluate the model they pioneered.

Other Integrative Models

Although we've singled out five of what we consider the most innovative examples, there are in fact so many integrative approaches to family therapy that it's impossible to list them all.

While many of the models described as integrative are new, some of them have been around so long they don't always get the attention they deserve. Just to cite one example, Carol Anderson and Susan Stewart wrote one of the most useful integrative guides to family therapy back in 1983. That tradition of offering practical advice that transcends schools of family therapy is upheld in a recent book by Robert Taibbi (1996) called *Doing Family Therapy.*

There are other integrative approaches that haven't received as much attention in mainstream family therapy as they have in federal funding agencies. These include Scott Henggeler's multisystemic model and Howard Liddle's multidimensional family therapy. These approaches both evolved out of research projects with difficult adolescents, a population that challenges theorists to expand their purviews beyond the limits of one school of therapy or one level of system. As Richard Schwartz found during his research with bulimic clients and their families, whenever one treats difficult adolescents and carefully studies the outcome, one is forced to expand and innovate.

Liddle, of the University of Miami, developed his integrative approach while working with drug-abusing, inner-city adolescents in federally funded projects. His multidimensional family therapy brought together the risk factor models of drug and problem behavior, developmental psychopathology, family systems theory, social support theory, peer cluster theory, and social learning theory. In practice, the model applies a combination of structural family therapy, parent training, skills training for adolescents, and cognitive-behavioral techniques.

One of the most useful aspects of Liddle's approach is the way he integrates individual and systems interventions. While he makes liberal use of the structural technique of enactment, he frequently meets with individual family members to coach and prepare them to participate more effectively in these family dialogues. Liddle also uses these individual sessions to focus on teenagers' experiences outside the home. Here, sensitive subjects like drug use and sexual behavior can be explored more safely than when the whole family is present. The need to meet with teenagers to focus on their lives outside the family reflects the growing recognition among therapists working with adolescents of the limited influence families have in comparison to peers and culture.

Scott Henggeler of the University of South Carolina and a number of colleagues who are research oriented and work with "difficult-to-treat" populations of children tried to improve on their systems-oriented family therapy by (1) more actively considering and intervening into the extrafamilial systems in which families are embedded, in particular their school and peer contexts; (2) including individual developmental issues in assessments; and (3) incorporating cognitive-behavioral interventions (Henggeler & Borduin, 1990).

The multisystemic model has shown promising results in several well-designed outcome studies of juvenile offenders and families referred for abuse or neglect. For that reason, it is highly regarded among governmental funding agencies, and Henggeler has received a number of large grants.

Summary

In the founding decades of family therapy, a number of clearly articulated models were developed, and most family therapists became disciples of one of these models. Each of the major schools concentrated on a particular aspect of family life. Experientalists opened people up to feeling, behaviorists helped them reinforce more desirable behavior, and Bowenians taught them to think for themselves. By concentrating their attention this way, practitioners of the classic models focused their power for change. If in the process they got a little parochial and competitive, what was the harm?

The harm is that by ignoring valuable insights of other approaches, orthodox disciples of the various schools may have unnecessarily limited their impact and applicability. But maybe this parochialism is better understood from a developmental perspective, as a necessary stage in the consolidation of the original insights of the various models. Perhaps it was useful for the schools to pursue the truth as they knew it in order to mine the full potential of their essential ideas. If so, that time has passed.

Most of the schools of family therapy have been around long enough to have solidified their approach and proven their worth. That's why the time is ripe for integration.

Valuable as integrative efforts are, however, there remains a serious pitfall in mixing ingredients from different approaches. You don't want to end up with what happens when you blend three or more colors from a set of poster paints. The trick is to find unifying conceptual threads that can tie together disparate ideas, and to add techniques from various models without subtracting the power that focusing offers. A successful integrative approach draws on existing therapies in such a way that they can be practiced coherently, under one umbrella. Adding techniques willy-nilly from here or there doesn't work.

To succeed, a synthesizing effort must strike a balance between breadth and focus. Breadth may be particularly important when it comes to conceptualization. Contemporary family therapists are wisely adopting a broad, biopsychosocial perspective in which biological, psychological, relational, community, and even societal processes are viewed as relevant to understanding people's problems. When it comes to techniques, on the other hand, the most effective approaches don't overload clinicians with scores of interventions.

Finally, an effective integrative approach must have clear direction. The trouble with being too flexible is that families have strong and subtle ways of inducting therapists into their habits of avoidance. Good family therapy creates an environment where conversations that should happen at home, but don't can take place. These dialogues won't happen, however, if therapists are abruptly shifting from one type of intervention to another in the face of resistance.

Family therapy is ultimately a clinical enterprise, its worth measured in results. The real reason to combine elements from various approaches is to maximize their usefulness, not merely their theoretical inclusiveness. To contradict Billy Crystal, it's better to be effective than to look marvelous.

References

Anderson, C., and Stewart, S. 1983. *Mastering resistance: A practical guide to family therapy.* New York: Guilford Press.

Breunlin, D., Schwartz, R., and Mac Kune-Karrer, B. 1992. *Metaframeworks: Transcending the models of family therapy.* San Francisco: Jossey-Bass.

Christensen, A., Jacobson, N. S., and Babcock, J. C. 1995. Integrative behavioral couple therapy. In *Clinical handbook of couples therapy,* N. S. Jacobson and A. S. Gurman, eds. New York: Guilford Press.

Csikszentmihalyi, M. 1990. *Flow: The psychology of optimal experience.* New York: Harper & Row.

Colapinto, J. 1993. Superman and the Self. *American Family Therapy Academy Newsletter,* Spring, 52–56.

Eron, J., and Lund, T. 1993. An approach to how problems evolve and dissolve: Integrating narrative and strategic concepts. *Family Process. 32:* 291–309.

Eron, J., and Lund, T. 1996. *Narrative solutions in brief therapy.* New York: Guilford Press.

Goulding, R., and Schwartz, R. 1995. *Mosaic mind: Empowering the tormented selves of child abuse survivors.* New York: Norton.

Henggeler, S., and Borduin, C. 1990. *Family therapy and beyond: A multisystemic approach to treating the behavior problems of children and adolescents.* Pacific Grove, CA: Brooks/Cole.

Jacobson, N., and Christensen, A. 1996. *Integrative couple therapy.* New York: Norton.

Jacobson, N. S., Follette, W. C., Revenstorf, D., Baucom, D. H., Halweg, K., and Margolin, G. 1984. Variability in outcome and clinical significance of behavioral marital therapy: A reanalysis of outcome data. *Journal of Consulting and Clinical Psychology. 52:*497–504.

Jacobson, N. S., Schmaling, K. B., and Holtzworth-Munroe, A. 1987. Component analysis of behavioral marital therapy: A two year follow-up and prediction of relapse. *Journal of Marital and Family Therapy. 13:*187–195.

Pinsof, W. 1995. *Integrative problem-centered therapy.* New York: Basic Books.

Schwartz, R. 1987. Our multiple selves. *Family Therapy Networker. 11:*25–31, 80–83.

Schwartz, R. 1988. Know thy selves. *Family Therapy Networker. 12:*21–29.

Schwartz, R. 1995. *Internal family systems therapy.* New York: Guilford Press.

Schwartz, R. 1997. Internal family systems family therapy. In *Integrative cases in couples and family therapy: A cognitive-behavioral perspective,* F. M. Dattilio, ed. New York: Guilford Press.

Schwartz, R., Barrett, M. J., and Saba, G. 1985. Family therapy for bulimia. In *The handbook of psychotherapy for anorexia nervosa and bulimia,* D. Garner and P. Garfinkel, eds. New York: Guilford Press.

Taibbi, R. 1996. *Doing family therapy.* New York: Guilford Press.

14

Comparative Analysis

The exponential growth of family therapy has crowded the field with competing schools, every one of which has made important contributions. This diversification has produced a rich and varied literature, bearing witness to the vitality of the profession while at the same time presenting a confusing array of options. With the bewildering variety of family therapies, how is one to choose among them?

A therapist's orientation is no accident. The choice is overdetermined and rooted in personal experience. For some the choice of which approach to follow is dictated by what's available from teachers and supervisors. Others pick and choose ideas from here and there, hoping to mold their own eclectic approach. Unfortunately, with no framework to ensure coherence, this strategy may be intellectually satisfying but clinically ineffective. Finally, there are those who pledge allegiance to a single approach, which provides them with a consistent but often incomplete model.

In this chapter we offer a comparative analysis of models of family therapy to sharpen the reader's appreciation of the separate approaches and to serve as a guide to their similarities and differences. Each model proclaims a set of truths, yet despite some overlap there are notable conflicts among these "truths." This chapter highlights the conflicts and examines the competing positions.

Theoretical Purity and Technical Eclecticism

Systems of family therapy are most clearly distinguished by their conceptual positions. Whether they claim to be based on theory (behavioral, Bowenian, psychoanalytic) or to be primarily pragmatic (experiential, solution-focused), each system is supported by a set of beliefs about families and how to change them. These theories relate to practice in a circular and mutually reinforcing manner. Practice generally precedes theory; thereafter progress in theory and practice proceeds in leapfrog fashion: Developments in one lead to modifications in the other, in a continuing process.

Because theories offer a preconceived way of looking at clinical data, they have a biasing effect on observation. Students tend to see what the theories they've studied prepare them to see. This is easily demonstrated by showing a videotape of the opening minutes of a family therapy session to a group of students. Even if the family conducts itself in a perfectly unremarkable fashion, students will see evidence of pathology, phrased in terms of whatever concepts they've learned.

Theories can bias observation, but they also bring order out of chaos. They organize our awareness and help us make sense of what families are doing. Instead of seeing a "blooming, buzzing confusion," we begin to see patterns of pursuit and distance, enmeshment and disengagement, or problem-saturated stories. The minute you begin to see ineffective parental attempts to settle arguments between children as a manifestation of enmeshment, your goal for the parents will shift from intervening more effectively to backing off and letting the children learn to settle their own disputes.

Theories also serve a political purpose. They demarcate one system from the others and announce its unique point of view. For this reason, theoretical positions tend to be stated in doctrinaire terms that maximize their differences. While this makes interesting reading, it's somewhat misleading. The truth is that the various systems of family therapy are more alike in practice than their theories suggest.

Practice is the expected consequence of theory, but it doesn't always work out that way. Theory is molded by the requirements of logical consistency and elegance, and often reflects a desire to be seen as original and clever. Practice is molded in the pragmatic arena of clinical treatment; it's shaped by encounters with real people, who usually turn out to be more complicated than the abstract models.

In everyday practice the schools of family therapy tend to become synthetic and integrative. Therapists from technique-oriented schools, which focus on small sequences of interaction (behavioral, strategic, solution-focused), have begun to adopt the organizing frameworks of schools with more comprehensive models of family dynamics (Bowenian, structural). At the same time, certain techniques with proven potency have been adopted almost universally. Family therapists of all persuasions are now likely to clarify communication, direct enactments, and express skepticism about clients' ability to change, no matter what their approach.

Family Therapist—Artist or Scientist?

Expertise requires training and experience, but training and experience aren't synonymous with expertness. Accomplished therapists begin with a grounding in theory; beyond that they must learn to extemporize. The therapist isn't the model. Just because Minuchin cures anorexia nervosa doesn't mean that anyone can do it simply by following his technique of joining, unbalancing, and boundary-making.

The phrase "the art and science of psychotherapy" (Jasnow, 1978) calls attention to the therapist's dual nature, creative and systematic. On the surface, this formula seems innocuous, even banal. We can all agree that a practitioner should first master general principles and proven techniques. Later, these ideas must be applied creatively in a way that's appropriate to each case and congruent with the therapist's personality. There is, however, much room for disagreement about how much latitude is desirable.

On the other hand, nearly everyone agrees that techniques alone don't make a family therapist. Personal qualities, like respect for people and reverence for life, are also important. Techniques are the tools, but human qualities are the supreme qualification of the good psychotherapist. Thus, Michael White's tenacious optimism and Phil Guerin's unflappable calm are probably more responsible for their success than their choice to use externalizing or process questions. Compassion—a deeply felt understanding of other people's sufferings—and sensitivity—an appreciation of other people's inner worlds—can be lost in preoccupation with theoretical concepts. Without understanding and respect for individuals, family therapy remains a technical operation, instead of a living human experience.

In the wake of constructivism and postmodernism, as the field struggles to avoid what is perceived as the authoritarian stance of earlier approaches, the art-or-science question is very much with us. If, as some constructivists maintain, therapy should be a nonhierarchical conversation, where is the place for professionalism and expertise? Is the good therapist just an artist of relationships, warm and respectful, but not uniquely privileged by training? Is the science of therapy too often practiced with inadequate respect for clients' own wisdom and cultural traditions? Does an overemphasis on the scientific aspect of therapy mask judgmental intrusiveness? Or is the real danger not the science of therapy—learning to be an expert at understanding and intervening—but intervening in bossy and controlling ways? Is the current emphasis on the art of conversation a repudiation of the science of family therapy or merely a corrective attempt to rebalance the two?

Theoretical Formulations

All schools of family therapy have theories. Some are elaborate (Bowenian, psychoanalytic), some less complex (experiential, solution-focused, narrative); some are borrowed from other disciplines (behavioral, narrative), others are developed directly from family work (structural, strategic). Theories are ideas abstracted from experience and observation. Their purpose is to simplify and order the raw data of family life as an aid to understanding. Here we will evaluate theories in terms of their pragmatic function: understanding families in order to better treat them. The schools of family therapy will be compared on the basis of their theoretical positions on a sample of key conceptual dimensions: families as systems; stability and change; past or present; communication; content/process; monadic, dyadic, or triadic points of view; the nuclear family in context; the personal as political; and boundaries.

Families as Systems

Communications family therapists introduced the idea that families are systems. More than the sum of their parts, systems are the parts and the way they function together. Family group therapists also treated families as more than collections of individuals, but their idea of a superordinate group process is a limited concept that refers to something that happens when a group of people interact rather than to an organizing principle that governs a family's entire life.

In family work, not believing in systems theory is like not believing in apple pie and motherhood. Schools of family therapy vary, however, in the degree to which they actually incorporate systems thinking in their practice. Behavioral family therapists say very little about systems and treat individuals as separate entities who influence each other only as stimuli and reinforcers. Most of the traditional family therapy models—Bowenian, communications, strategic, Milan, and structural—base their approach to families on some version of systems thinking. Some of the newer approaches, including solution-focused and narrative models, concentrate their attention on individuals, so much so that many of their practitioners don't even consider themselves family therapists.

Systems theory once seemed intrinsic to family therapy because it was part and parcel of treating families as organized groups. Now, however, the postmodern movement has challenged systems thinking as just another modernist framework, a metaphor taken literally, and has shifted emphasis from action to meaning and from the organization of the family to the thinking of its members.

Stability and Change

Communications theorists describe families as rule-governed systems with a tendency toward stability or homeostasis (Jackson, 1965). If a family member deviates from the family's rules, this constitutes feedback, and if the family reacts to it as *negative feedback,* they'll try to force that person to change back. Families, like other living systems, maintain their interactions within a relatively fixed range in order to remain stable in the face of environmental stresses. In structural family theory the same point is made by saying that families have a relatively stable structure that enables them to function effectively as a system, with various subsystems, each fulfilling part of the family's overall task.

Families must also change to adapt to changing circumstances. To do so they must be capable of revising their rules and modifying their structure. Dysfunctional families are distinguished by their rigidity and inflexibility; when circumstances change, they don't.

The dual nature of families—homeostatic and changing—is best appreciated by family therapists from the communications, structural, and strategic schools; they expect clients to come to treatment because they failed to adapt to changing circumstances. They don't presume that the families they see are inherently pathological.

Anyone who ignores this principle runs the risk of placing undue emphasis on pathology. If a therapist sees a family that's having trouble, but fails to consider that they may be stuck at a transitional impasse, then he or she is apt to think that they need an overhaul, when a tune-up might do. The therapies that emphasize long-range goals are all susceptible to this therapeutic overkill. Although they emphasize growth rather than pathology, psychoanalytic, experiential, and extended family therapists are inclined to assume that the families they see are basically flawed and need fundamental reorganization. Since they have the equipment for major surgery—long-term therapy—they tend to see the patient as needing it. Sometimes the patient doesn't.

The pioneers of family therapy (with the notable exception of Virginia Satir) tended to overestimate homeostatic forces in families and underestimate family flexibility and resourcefulness. This viewpoint encouraged therapists to act as provokers, controllers, and strategizers. The corollary of the family held fast by systemic forces they can't understand was the oh-so-clever therapist who would do the understanding for them. Many of the newer approaches to family therapy are designed to elicit families' resources, rather than struggle with their fears. These models encourage therapists to collaborate with families to help them work out solutions, rather than to assume they won't change unless provoked.

Past or Present

Family therapy was heralded at its outset as a treatment that emphasized the present, in contrast to individual therapies that emphasized the past. Psychoanalysis was the chief whipping boy of family therapists eager to define themselves as different in every way. Psychoanalysis was portrayed as a monadic theory that focused on early traumas as the cause of problems and tried to cure people by helping them resurrect the past. While this picture accurately describes Freud's treatment in 1895, modern psychoanalysis is quite a bit more complicated.

That people are influenced by past experiences is an unarguable fact. The question is, how necessary is it to think about the past to understand the present? All family therapists work in the here-and-now; some emphasize residues of the past, others don't.

Emphasis on the past is correlated with concern for individuals. Psychoanalytic practitioners view the determinants of behavior as resting with individuals. Theirs is a personality-trait model, in which family life is seen as a product of enduring dispositions, internalized from early object relations. This viewpoint affects practice, but not in the obvious way. Psychoanalytic therapists use their knowledge of past influences to inform their understanding of the present. They don't concentrate on helping people remember the past; instead they use psychoanalytic theory to help them understand what's going on in the present. The present may be understood in terms of transference and projection from the past, but it's still the present.

Surprisingly, the therapists who spend the most time talking with their patients about the past are the very ones who emphasize the here-and-now in their writings. Experiential therapists believe that unfinished business from the past interferes with full experiencing in the present. For this reason, they spend a lot of time talking with patients about old preoccupations in order to help them let go of the past (Pierce, Nichols, & DuBrin, 1983). An example of this approach is Norman Paul's (1967) *operational mourning*.

The past also plays a prominent role in Bowen systems theory. Present family relationships are assumed to be products of relationships within the original family. Problems with a child, for example, are presumed to result from the parents' unresolved conflicts with their own parents. Unlike psychoanalytic therapists, who deal with the residuals of those relationships by pointing out their influence in the current family, Bowen systems therapists send patients back to their families. Is this a return to the past? In practice, that's impossible; conceptually it is a return to the past.

The schools of family therapy that view the determinants of behavior as being outside—that is, between—individuals stress the present, in theory and practice. Family group therapists, communication therapists, strategists, and structuralists have little to say about the past. They're less interested in how or why problems got started than in what maintains them.

Behavior therapists once explained all behavior as a result of past learning history. Pavlov's dogs salivated at the sound of a bell because they'd been conditioned to do so; children misbehaved because their parents trained them improperly. Today, behavior therapists rely on operant conditioning as the model to explain behavior. According to this model, behavior is maintained by its consequences in the present. Parents have trouble with their children because of the way they respond to them now. Therapy derived from this model deals with how people currently reinforce maladaptive behavior. The classical conditioning model is still used to explain certain anxiety disorders, especially sexual dysfunction, but treatment is designed to relax anxiety in the present.

Most of the newer models try to strike a balance between past and present. Michael White helps families explore the historical evolution of how the problem got the upper hand over them, but then tries to empower family members to deal with the problem in the present. Narrative therapists also explore the past in order to convince clients that their life stories contain elements of competence and courage. To keep this from being merely a glib reframing, the narrative therapist asks for stories and evidence from the past to show that the person was indeed courageous, even though he or she may not have realized it.

Richard Schwartz finds people carry elements of outmoded or irrational beliefs and feelings from the past, but he helps clients change their relationship with these parts in the present, so they learn about the past but stop living there. Not only is Steve de Shazer not interested in the past, he is also not interested in present conditions maintaining problems. Instead, he's interested in future solutions. Taking a page from their solution-focused colleagues, narrative therapists also invite clients to project a future in which they continue to make strides in overcoming their problems. ("As you continue to stand up to Self-Doubt, what do you think will be different about your future than the future Self-Doubt planned for you?") Harlene Anderson is interested in anything, past, present, or future, that seems important to the family.

Communication

Working with communication no longer distinguishes one school of family therapy from the others. All behavior is communicative, and all family therapists deal with verbal and nonverbal behavior. But although they all think about communication, they do so in very different ways.

Virginia Satir and the early communications family therapists had the most straightforward and simple view of communication. For them, communication is the medium of exchange through which family members interact. Their treatment was to help transform blocked, incomplete, and covert communication into clear and open expression. They'd take what's conscious but unexpressed (except perhaps nonverbally) and bring it out into the open.

Behaviorists also think of communication in simple terms, as a skill that can be taught. In addition, they understand something less obvious about communication, namely that the message received may not be the one intended. They distinguish reinforcement from aversive control and have, for example, pointed out that yelling at a child may be reinforcing (by giving attention), even though it's intended to be punishing. On the other hand, berating your partner for not spending more time with you may be aversive, driving him further away, rather than drawing him closer.

In psychoanalytic work, manifest communication is taken as metaphor, with the manifest content conveying derivatives of hidden needs and feelings. The therapist's job is to decode these latent meanings in order to help patients better understand themselves. In family therapy the psychoanalytic therapist not only brings these hidden meanings to light but also helps family members express their latent emotions to each other. The therapist uses a knowledge of defenses, especially displacement and symbolization, to understand the unconscious content of family members' communications, and a knowledge of family dynamics to help complete these communications in the family.

According to structural family theory, patterns of communications are what create family structure. Family organization develops from repeated sequences of interaction, or communication; therapists detect the family's underlying structure by observing who speaks to whom and in what way. If a mother complains that she "can't communicate" with her teenage daughter, the structural therapist will enact a sequence where mother and daughter talk to each other in the session. If they talk only briefly before breaking off, the therapist will conclude that they're disengaged; if they argue back and forth like squabbling sisters, the therapist may conclude that there is no hierarchical distinction and that they're enmeshed. If their conversation is repeatedly interrupted by the father, the therapist may conclude that interpersonal boundaries are blurred, and that the communication problem between the mother and daughter is a product of the father's enmeshment.

In Madanes and Haley's version of strategic therapy the main purpose of communication is to gain power in interpersonal relationships. Symptoms are seen as communications designed to manipulate other people. More recently, Haley and Madanes have emphasized love and protection as motives for communication.

But, as we all know, much that is controlling can be done in the name of love.

A child's phobic fear of going to school may be a covert way to communicate that he's afraid his parents might separate; the symptom serves to keep them together to take care of him. Family members' responses to problems are thought to create symptoms. In this case the parents' decision to stay home to take care of the child only makes matters worse. A strategic therapist wouldn't try to help the family understand the meaning of these symptoms, but would instead try to provoke them to relate—communicate—in a way that makes the symptoms unnecessary. If the parents, together, took the child to school and, together, helped him with his homework, the improvement of the child could be divorced from whether or not the parents stay together.

The experientialists' interest in communication is also two-layered; what they consider important are unexpressed feelings lying beneath the surface content of family members' communications. Like psychoanalytic therapists, they consider it important to reduce defenses so that people can communicate what's really on their minds. Unlike psychoanalysts, they look in the present for conscious but unexpressed feelings. Instead of interpreting defenses, they confront them to help people break out of their inhibitions. Because they work with families, they're concerned not only with uncovering feelings but also with helping family members communicate their feelings honestly and openly within the family. Satir, in particular, focused on communication style as reflective of a person's level of self-esteem. She encouraged straight talk as a way to straighten out relationships—and to make people feel better about themselves for being honest.

Bowen family systems therapists foster communication as a vehicle for opening up relationships with the wider kinship group. In emotional cutoffs there's a breakdown in communication; in emotional reactivity communication comes from an undifferentiated stance in which people lose sight of their own thoughts and feelings; and in triangulated relationships communication is diverted. Therapy is designed to help people reestablish communication with extended family members, teach them to communicate "I-positions," and redirect communication from a triangulated third party to the person for whom it was originally intended.

The conversation-based models of the 1990s try to open channels of communication so that family members can tell their stories and be heard by others in the family. There's less interest in teaching communication styles than in creating a communicative environment in which people can reauthor their personal and family narratives. Because narrative therapists focus on individuals and their cognitions, it's not surprising that they pay less attention to communication in the family than therapists who practice more traditional approaches to family treatment.

To Steve de Shazer of the solution-focused school, communication is everything. Problems are created and dissolved through the ways people communicate about them. In other words, problems don't exist in reality. If you can get clients to focus on their mastery over their submission to their problems, their communications about them will reflect a new perspective in which problems don't loom so large.

Content/Process

Focusing on the process of communication, or how people talk, rather than on its content, or what they talk about, may be the single most important conceptual shift a family therapist can make. Imagine, for example, that a therapist encourages a recalcitrant teenager to talk to his mother. Imagine further that the boy rarely expresses himself in words but rather in dangerous and risky behavior, and that his worried mother is, in contrast, all too good at putting her opinions into words. Suppose that with prodding the boy finally begins to express his opinion that high school is a waste of time, and his mother counters with a forceful argument about the importance of staying in school. A therapist made anxious by the idea that the boy might actually drop out of school and so intervenes to support the content of the mother's position will miss an important opportunity to support the process whereby the boy learns to put his feelings into words rather than into dangerous actions.

A system is the parts of a whole plus the way they function together; *process* is the way families and groups function. Family and group therapists learn to attend to process and attempt to change it. When a mother and her teenaged daughter discuss the daughter's curfew, the mother and daughter are interested in *what* the other one says; the mother listens to when the daughter wants to come home and the daughter listens to her mother's response. A systemic family therapist, listening to the same conversation, will be more interested in *how* the mother and daughter talk to each other. Does each state her point of view directly? Do they listen to each other? Is the mother clearly in charge? These questions have to do with the process of the conversation; they may not determine when the daughter comes home, but they reveal how the dyad functions.

Families who come for treatment are usually focused on a content issue; a husband wants a divorce, a child refuses to go to school, a wife is depressed, and so on. The family therapist talks with the family about the content of the problem but thinks about the process by which they try to solve it. While the family discusses what to do about a child's refusal to go to school, the therapist notices whether the parents seem to be in charge and whether they support each other. A therapist who tells the parents to solve the problem by making the child go to school is working with content, not process. The child may go to school, but the parents won't have improved their decision-making process.

All schools of family therapy have a theoretical commitment to working with the process of family interaction. Psychoanalytic and experiential clinicians try to reduce defensiveness and foster open expression of thoughts and feelings; family group and communications therapists increase the flow of interactions and help family members reduce the incongruence between different levels of communication; Bowen systems therapists block triangulation and encourage family members to take differentiated, "I-position" stances; strategic therapists ferret out and interdict problem-maintaining sequences of interaction; behaviorists teach parents to use positive control and couples to eliminate coercive communication; structural therapists realign emotional boundaries and strengthen hierarchical organization.

Despite their theoretical commitment to process, family therapists often get distracted by content issues. Sometimes content is important. If a wife is drinking to drown her worries or a husband is molesting his daughter, a therapist needs to know and do something about it. But to the extent that therapists focus exclusively on content, they're unlikely to help families become better functioning systems. Psychoanalytic therapists sometimes lose sight of process when they concentrate on individual family members and their memories of the past. Similarly, experientialists are prone to becoming overly central while working with individual family members to help them overcome emotional defensiveness. The danger is that by so doing the therapist will neglect interactional processes in the family that affect individual expression.

Behavioral family therapists neglect process in favor of content when they isolate a particular behavioral sequence from its context in the family and ignore the pattern that maintains it. They also interfere with the process of family interaction by assuming a directive, teaching role. As long as a teacher stands in front of the class and lectures, there's little opportunity to observe what the students do on their own.

Process concepts are so central to extended family systems therapy that there's little danger of therapists in this school forgetting them. Only naive misunderstanding of Bowen systems therapy would lead someone to think merely of reestablishing family ties, without also being aware of processes of triangulation, fusion, and differentiation. The same is true of structural family therapy, family group therapy, and communications therapy; process issues are always at center stage.

Strategic therapists have a dual focus—their goals are content-oriented, but their interventions are directed at process. As in behavioral therapy, the goal in terms of content is to solve the presenting problem. To understand what maintains the problem, however, strategic therapists shift their attention to process. Usually this involves discrete sequences of interaction, which they try to block by using directives. The goal, however, isn't to improve the process of family functioning, but merely to interdict a particular sequence in order to resolve the content of the presenting problem.

The difference between structural and strategic interest in process is reflected in supervision styles. Structuralists rely on direct observation of family sessions through one-way mirrors and videotapes because they believe that nonverbal interactions (who sits where, who makes faces while someone talks, who looks to whom for permission to answer) are crucial. Strategic and solution-focused therapists are more concerned with verbal interaction and, consequently, more apt to use audiotapes or therapist reports when supervising.

The newer models of family therapy, with their deemphasis on systems thinking, have moved away from a focus on process. Narrative constructivists are less interested in changing family interaction patterns than in changing the ways family members understand their problems and themselves—they are less interested in changing behavior than in expanding stories. Similarly, because solution-focused therapists have no interest in how problems were created, they too ignore the family processes that surround problems. The only processes they do attend to are the interaction sequences that constitute "exceptions" to problems—times when the problem wasn't a problem.

Monadic, Dyadic, or Triadic Model

Family therapy came into being when clinicians recognized that the identified patient's behavior is a function of the whole family. Almost all family practitioners now subscribe to this systems viewpoint. In practice, however, family therapists sometimes think in terms of units of one, two, or three persons. Some clinicians (e.g., psychoeducational therapists) continue to think of a single individual as the patient and include the rest of the family only as an adjunct to that person's treatment. Keep in mind that psychoeducational therapists work primarily with cases of serious mental illness (schizophrenia, bipolar disorder), where the family's influence is almost certainly less than in the majority of cases treated by more systemic family therapists.

The same cannot, however, be said for narrative therapists, whose focus on cognition leads them to concentrate on individuals and largely ignore the three defining characteristics of family therapy: (1) that psychological symptoms are often the result of family conflict; (2) thinking about human problems as interactional, which means thinking in twos and threes (complementarity, triangles); and (3) treating the family as a unit. But although narrative therapists disregard family conflict in their formulations, their efforts to redefine problems as malevolent invaders have the effect of uniting families to work together to defeat the problem's influence. It would be interesting to speculate on whether ignoring family conflict but rallying family members to unite in concern would be more effective in some cases, for example where problems like anorexia take on a life of their own, than in others, like school refusal or misbehavior, where the problem is more likely a direct result of family conflicts.

Psychoanalytic therapists tend to think about intrapsychic dynamics, whether they meet with people alone or with their families. They see current family relations as a product of internalized relationships from the family of origin, and they're often more concerned with these mental ghosts than with flesh-and-blood families. Child behavior therapists use a monadic model when they accept a family's definition that their symptomatic child is the problem and set about teaching the parents to change their child's behavior. Experiential therapists focus on individuals to help them uncover and express their feelings.

Actually, no living thing can adequately be understood in monadic terms. A bird's egg may be the closest thing in nature to a self-contained monad. The fetus is locked away inside its shell with all the nutrients it needs to survive. Even this view is incomplete, however, for there is an exchange of heat between the egg and the surrounding environment. Without the mother's warmth, the baby bird will die.

A dyadic model is necessary to understand the fact that people act in relationship to one another. In the space of a relationship one person's behavior is always at least partly a function of the other's. Even the psychoanalytic patient, free-associating on the couch, filters memories and dreams through reactions to the analyst. Most of the time family therapists operate with a dyadic model, working on relationships between two people at a time. Even with a large family in treatment, the focus is usually on various pairs of family members, considered in succession.

Helping two people learn to relate better doesn't always mean that the therapist thinks in dyadic terms. Behavioral couples therapists work with two spouses but treat them as separate individuals, each deficient in the art of communicating. A true dyadic model is based on the understanding that two people in a relationship aren't separate monads interacting with each other; they each define the other. Using this model, a wife's agoraphobia would be understood as a reaction to her husband and as a means of influencing him. Likewise, his decision to send her for behavior modification reflects his refusal to accept his role in her life.

Family therapists of all schools use some dyadic concepts; unconscious need complementarity, expressive/instrumental, projective identification, symbiosis, intimacy, quid pro quo, double bind, symmetrical, complementary, pursuer/distancer, and behavioral contract. Some terms are based on dyadic thinking even though they may involve more than two people: compliant (referring to a family's relationship to a therapist) or defiant. Some seem to involve only one: countertransference, dominant, and supercompetent. Still other concepts are capable of encompassing units of three or more, but are often used to refer to units of two: boundary, coalition, fusion, and disengagement.

Too often family therapists think in dyadic terms and neglect triadic complications. Murray Bowen, who introduced the concept of emotional triangles into the family therapy literature, did more than anyone to point out that human behavior is always a function of triadic relationships. Structural family therapists have also consistently been aware that enmeshment or disengagement between two people is always a function of reciprocal relationships with a third. Communications therapists wrote about triadic relationships but tended to think in terms of units of two. The same is true of most strategic therapists, although Haley, Selvini Palazzoli, and Lynn Hoffman are consistently aware of triadic relationships.

The advantage of triadic thinking is that it permits a more complete understanding of behavior in context. If a boy misbehaves when his mother doesn't use firm discipline, teaching her to be more strict won't work if her behavior is a function of her relationship with her husband. Perhaps she subtly encourages her child to misbehave as a way of undermining her husband's authority, or she and her husband may have worked out a relationship where her incompetence reassures him that he's the strong one.

The fact that triadic thinking permits a more complete understanding doesn't mean that family therapists must always include all parties in treatment. The issue isn't how many people are in the consulting room, but whether the therapist considers problems in their full context.

The Nuclear Family in Context

Just as most family therapists espouse the ideas of systems theory, most also regard families as open systems. The family is open in that its members interact not only with each other, but also with extrafamilial systems in a constant exchange of information, energy, and material.

Indeed a major emphasis in family therapy in the 1990s has been to expand the focus of attention to include how families are affected by race, gender, ethnicity, class, and sexual orientation. For today's family therapists, talking about the social context of families is no longer just an idle abstraction.

Members of the Palo Alto group introduced the concept of open systems to family therapy but actually treated families as closed systems. They paid little attention to sources of stress outside the family and rarely considered the impact of friends or extended family on the nuclear unit. The first clinicians to take the extrafamilial into account (and into treatment) were Murray Bowen and Ross Speck. Bowen always stressed the critical role of extended family relationships, and Speck mobilized the patient's network of family and friends to aid in treatment.

Bowen systems therapists and network therapists virtually always include people outside the nuclear family in treatment; psychoanalytic, solution-focused, behavioral, and narrative therapists almost never do. Among experientialists, Whitaker routinely included members of the extended family in treatment for one or two sessions. Including extended family members or friends in treatment is often useful, sometimes essential. It is not, however, the same thing as thinking of the family as an open system. An open system isn't a larger system; it's a system that interacts with its environment.

Nowhere is the idea of families as open systems better articulated than in Minuchin's (1974) *Families and Family Therapy.* Writing about "Man in His Context," Minuchin contrasts family therapy with psychodynamic theory. The latter, he says, draws on the concept of man as a hero, remaining himself in spite of the circumstances.[1] On the other hand, "The theory of family therapy is predicated on the fact that man is not an isolate. He is an acting and reacting member of social groups" (p. 2). Minuchin credits Gregory Bateson with erasing the boundary between inner and outer space, and goes on to say that just as the boundary separating the individual from the family is artificial, so is the boundary separating the family from the social environment.

Structural family therapists recognize that families are embedded in a social context, and they often include teachers, school administrators, and other social agents in family assessment and treatment. If a single mother is enmeshed with her children, a structural therapist might help her get more involved with friends and community activities as a way of helping her loosen her grip on the children.

Strategic therapists may not treat families as open systems, but they don't confine their search for problem-maintaining sequences to the nuclear family. Selvini Palazzoli's work illustrates that in close-knit Italian families

[1]While we recognize that it was until recently the rule, use of the masculine pronoun here may be particularly apt. The model of the hero is of a man who keeps his moral integrity hard and intact. He is an isolate, stoic and enduring, cut off from family, community, and faith—that is, the trivial, suffocating world of women.

grandparents are often directly involved in interactions that support symptoms, and members of the Mental Reseach Institute (MRI) group often work with problem-maintaining sequences that involve someone outside the family, such as a supervisor at work or a neighbor. Routinely including grandparents or friends in family therapy is useful but not essential; however, to gain a full understanding of families you must consider the forces outside the family acting and interacting with them.

One of the things that anyone who works with agency families quickly learns is that attempts to help them often get caught in a sticky web of competing influences from courts, probation departments, child protective agencies, family services, housing programs, group homes, domestic violence agencies, and so on. If middle-class families can be at times treated as organizationally closed units, with poor families it's impossible. Poor families live in homes without walls.

As services proliferate, fiefdoms multiply. The most obvious problem is lack of coordination. Take for example a recent case involving a fifteen-year-old boy who had sexually abused his two adolescent sisters and younger brother. There were agencies working with the female victims, one with the older girl and another with the younger one. One agency worked with the young boy, one worked with the perpetrator, and one worked with the mother of the victims. There was an art therapist in the public school working with the sexually abused children, and the fifteen-year-old was in a residential school where he had individual and group therapy. Is it any wonder that these helpers were pulling in different directions? A second, more invidious, problem is that most agencies are mandated to serve individuals—victims or victimizers, adults or children. By addressing themselves to the rights of specific persons in need of protection or correction, these agencies support individuals, not the family unit.

The usual reaction of therapists who run into these networks of highly unorganized altruism is to first make an effort to coordinate the various inputs, and then, when they discover their own lack of leverage with all these agencies and helpers, to give up and do the best they can with the family in the office. Among those who aren't willing to give up, Evan Imber-Black (1988) and Richard Kagan and Shirley Schlosberg (1989) have written moving and practical books about working with families in "perpetual crisis."

Under the influence of social constructionism, narrative therapists are particularly sensitive to social and political influences on the nuclear family. They point to the destructive impact of messages we're bombarded with from television and newspapers, telling us how to think and who to be. Indeed, one of the most powerful ways they motivate people to become more active in their own destinies is to help them think of themselves as not flawed but oppressed. Once they start to make progress, the narrative therapist seeks to recruit other people as witnesses and a cheering squad to support the client's new and more positive sense of self.

Despite apparent similarities to narrative-therapy, the solution-focused approach is remarkably acontextual. Solution-focused therapists concern themselves only with the way problems are talked about. They aren't interested in any factors, whether in the family or its context, that might create problems.

Internal family systems therapists often examine the impact of cultural themes in shaping family members' subpersonalities, which in turn shape family dynamics. For example, Richard Schwartz described the way society's materialism, striving ambition, and appearance consciousness are absorbed in toxic doses in some families, which then polarize the inner worlds of anorexic and bulimic young women within those families.

The Personal as Political

Another issue in treating the nuclear family in context about which there are varying positions concerns political and moral influences from the surrounding culture. Once it was axiomatic that therapists should maintain therapeutic neutrality: They shouldn't make judgments, take sides, or tell people what to do. They should remain steadfastly objective, encouraging communication or making interpretations, but refrain from imposing their personal values and opinions on the people they worked with. Today, however, many practitioners believe that therapists should stand for some things and against others. These therapists prefer advocacy to neutrality.

Since feminist family therapists first challenged us to face the pervasive consequences of gender inequality in our culture (e.g., Hare-Mustin, 1978; Goldner, 1985), a growing number of practitioners in the narrative tradition have begun to work with family members to identify the destructive influence of certain cultural values and practices on their lives and relationships (e.g., White & Epston, 1990; Freedman & Combs, 1996).

There is certainly a case to be made for helping people question internalized standards and expectations that may be contributing to their problems. Who says that women should be as rail-thin as runway models? That adolescence is always a time of turmoil? That a mans's first obligation is to his career? Moreover, by defining certain destructive attitudes as culturally imposed, narrative therapists invite family members to pull together in opposing those values, institutions, and practices. Questions can be raised, however, about how this sense of political awareness is put into practice, both inside the consulting room and in family therapy organizations.

Sometimes a readiness to identify oppressive cultural attitudes can lead to ignoring a client's role in his or her own problems in favor of projecting blame outward. Take, for example, a case of a woman who starts to wonder if something about what she's doing might be responsible for her lack of success with men. What happens if the therapist redefines the woman's problem as "the voice of insecurity" and urges her to consider this doubt as part of a cultural pattern whereby women learn to conform their lives to accommodate men? It is no doubt true that women generally do more accommodating than men. But what about *this* woman? If her wondering about how she might be contributing to the pattern of unsuccessful relationships in her life is blamed on a patriarchal society, does this empower her? Even more important, whether a therapist assumes that the client might be doing something wrong or is a victim of patriarchal conditioning, what is the effect of selling the therapist's attitude to the client? It's fine to be sympathetic, even to be the client's champion, but when therapists start assuming that their patients are victims of patriarchy, men, racism, or heterosexism, they may fall into the kind of linear and blaming mentality that family therapy was created to combat in the first place.

At times the readiness to identify cultural influences as villains in the lives of clients seems like romantic adolescent posturing, with the therapist as knight in shining armor against the forces of evil. On the other hand, ignoring racism, sexism, ethnocentrism, poverty, crime, and alienation—thinking of families as though they were self-contained units—makes about as much sense as hiding your head in the sand. What is the proper professional role of individual family therapists and of national family therapy associations with respect to larger issues of social injustice?

Given the powerful impact of social conditions on families, do family therapists have a unique role to play in politics and society, or are they, at least in their professional capacity, primarily clinicians, trained to treat families for psychological problems but having no special authority or expertise to right social wrongs? These are important questions without easy answers.

Boundaries

Family practitioners study and treat people in context—individuals in the context of their families and families in the context of their extended families and communities. One of the most useful concepts in family therapy is that of boundaries, a concept that applies to the relationships of all systems within systems in terms of the nature of their interface. The individuality and autonomy of each subsystem (individual, siblings, parents, nuclear family) is regulated by a semipermeable boundary between it and the suprasystem.

The clearest and most useful concepts of interpersonal boundaries are in the works of Murray Bowen and Salvador Minuchin. Bowen is best at describing the boundary between the self and the family; Minuchin is best at describing boundaries between various subsystems within the family. In Bowen's terms, individuals vary on a continuum from fusion to differentiation, and Minuchin describes boundaries as ranging from diffuse to rigid, with resultant enmeshment or disengagement.

Bowen's thinking reflects the psychoanalytic emphasis on separation and individuation (Mahler, Pine, & Bergman, 1975), with special attention to resolution of oedipal attachments and leaving home. In this model, we become ourselves by learning to stand alone. Bowen's treatment continued the somewhat one-sided emphasis on strengthening the boundary between self and other. He paid little attention to the problems of emotional isolation stemming from too rigid boundaries, treating this as an artifact—a defense against—a basic lack of psychological separateness. Bowen used a variety of terms—togetherness, fusion, undifferentiation, emotional reactivity—all of which refer to the danger he was most concerned with, that people will lose themselves in relationships.

Minuchin offers a more balanced view, describing the problems that result when boundaries are either too rigid or too diffuse. Diffuse boundaries allow too much outside interference into the functioning of a subsystem; rigid boundaries allow too little communication, support, and affection between different segments of the family. Bowen described only one boundary problem—fusion—and only one goal—differentiation. Minuchin speaks of two possibilities—enmeshment or disengagement—and his therapy is designed to fit the specific case.

Minuchin (1974) explains the function of boundaries, their reciprocal relationship, and how a knowledge of boundaries can be used to plan therapy. Boundaries protect individuals and subsystems from intrusion so that they can function autonomously. Newlyweds, for instance, need to establish a clear boundary between themselves and their parents in order to work out their own independent relationship. A diffuse boundary will leave them overly reliant on their parents, preventing them from developing their own autonomy and intimacy. If a wife calls her mother whenever she's upset, she won't learn to work things out with her husband; if she borrows money from her father whenever she wants to make a large purchase, she won't learn to be financially responsible for herself.

In Bowen systems theory, people tend to be either emotionally fused or differentiated. Fusion is like a disease—you can have a bad case or a mild one. In structural family theory the enmeshment–disengagement distinction plays two roles. Families can be described as either enmeshed or disengaged; but more accurately families are described as made up of different subsystems, with enmeshment in one relationship supporting disengagement in another. For example, a mother and child may be described as enmeshed (Bowen would say fused); this will be seen not in isolation but as a product of the woman's disengaged relationship with her husband. Using this understanding of the interlocking nature of subsystem boundaries, it's possible to design therapy to fit a specific family and to coordinate change among its subsystems.

Bowen's "fusion" and Minuchin's "enmeshment" both deal with blurred boundaries, but they aren't synonymous. Fusion is a quality of individuals; it's the opposite of individuation. Both are intrapsychic concepts for a person's *psychological* embeddedness—undifferentiation—within a relationship context. The dynamics of fusion have an impact on other relationships (especially in the form of triangulation), but fusion is *within* the person. Enmeshment is a social systems concept; enmeshment is *between* people. These conceptual differences also lead to differences in treatment. Bowen systems therapists coach individuals to stay in contact and maintain an "I-position"; success is measured by individual differentiation. Structuralists join the system and realign coalitions by strengthening *or* weakening boundaries; success is measured by change in the whole system. Bowen's conceptualization aims at individual personality change, which hopefully will affect the whole family system; Minuchin's conceptualization permits greater leverage and quicker change. The difference is between working with individuals to change the system and working with the system to change individuals.

Normal Family Development

Family therapists as a rule have little to say about developmental issues. One of the distinguishing characteristics of family therapy is its focus on here-and-now interactions around family problems. Normal family development, which involves the past and what's healthy, has therefore been underemphasized.

Most therapists do have ideas about what's normal, and these assumptions influence their work. The problem is that these implicit models are based largely on personal experience; as long as they remain unarticulated and unexamined they may reflect personal bias instead of systematic study. It's tempting to assume that healthy families are just like our own (or just the opposite). However, the fact that a therapist comes from a relatively disengaged, upwardly striving, intact nuclear family doesn't make this the only, or the best, model of family life. When it comes to setting goals for family treatment, the choice isn't between having or not having a model of normality, but between using a model that's been spelled out and examined or operating on the basis of ill-defined and personal standards.

Family therapists concerned with the past, especially members of Bowenian and psychoanalytic schools, have had the most to say about normal development. These two schools share an evolutionary, developmental perspective. Whereas most family therapists explain problems in terms of ongoing interactional difficulties, Bowenians and psychoanalysts are interested in the developmental history of problems. Although their main interest in development is to understand how problems arise, their analyses also describe normal development.

Although most schools of family therapy aren't concerned with how families get started, the Bowenian and psychoanalytic schools have a great deal to say about marital choice. Bowen talked about differentiation, fusion, and triangles, while psychoanalytic writers speak of unconscious need complementarity, projective identification, and idealization; but they seem to be using different terms to describe similar phenomena. Psychodynamic therapists speak of marital choice as an object of transference from the family of origin and of people choosing partners to match their level of maturity; Bowen said that people pick partners who replicate familiar patterns of family interaction and select mates at the same level of differentiation.

These are descriptions of significant ways in which people marry partners with similar underlying personality dynamics. Both the Bowenian and psychoanalytic schools also discuss how people choose mates who appear to be different, at least on the surface, in ways that are exciting and that seem to make up for deficiencies in the self. Obsessives tend to marry hysterics, and, according to Bowen, togetherness-oriented people often marry distancers. This brings up another way in which the Bowenian and psychodynamic schools are similar to each other and different from others. Both have an appreciation of depth psychology; both recognize that personalities have different strata. Both think that the success of a relationship depends not only on the partners' shared interests and values but also on the nature of their internal, introjected object images.

Psychoanalysts emphasize the importance of good object relations in early childhood. The infant's ability to develop a cohesive self-image and good internal objects depends on "good-enough mothering" in an "average expectable environment." With a cohesive sense of self a child will grow up able to be with others and to be independent; without a coherent self, being with others may feel like being engulfed and being alone may feel like being abandoned. Early object relations aren't just memories, they actually form psychic structures of the mind, preserving early experiences in the form of self-images and object-images. These internalized images determine how people in the environment will later be experienced. Thus, the child's future—and the future of his or her family development—is laid down at an early age.

Bowen's description of normal family development was highly deterministic. Parents transmit their immaturity and lack of differentiation to their children; emotional fusion is passed on in a multigenerational transmission process. A family's fate is a product of relationships worked out in preceding generations.

Bowenian and psychoanalytic therapists also describe the triangular relationship between mother and father and child as crucial to all later development. Psychoanalytic writers describe the oedipal drama in terms of conflicting drives and believe that their resolution affects all future relationships. Bowen systems therapists describe this triangle in terms of stabilizing unresolved emotional tension in the marital dyad and see it as the prototype of all subsequent relationships.

Clinicians are most likely to see people from families in which the triangular family romance wasn't resolved, but these theories include the possibility of successful resolution. Both theories, Bowenian and psychoanalytic, hold up visions of ideal functioning toward which people can strive but which they can never fully achieve. The result can be either a utopian model that condemns patients to dissatisfaction with their lives or a standard used to guide people toward an enriched but not perfect life.

The clearest statement of such a standard is Bowen's (1966) description of families with "moderate to good differentiation." In these families the marriage is a functioning partnership in which spouses can be intimate without losing their autonomy. They permit their children to develop autonomous selves without becoming unduly anxious or trying to mold the children to their own images. Everyone in these families is responsible for himself or herself and no one credits others for personal success nor blames them for failure. They are able to function well with other people or to be alone, as the situation requires. Their intellectual functioning isn't infused with emotionality at times of stress; they're adaptable, flexible, and independent, able to cope with good times and bad.

While they don't emphasize the past, most of the other schools of family therapy have a few isolated concepts for describing processes of normal family development. For example, communications therapists speak of the *quid pro quos* (Jackson, 1965) exchanged in normal marriages. The behaviorists describe the same phenomenon in terms of social exchange theory (Thibaut & Kelley, 1959).

Virginia Satir described normal families as those in which communication is direct and honest, where differences are faced rather than hidden, and were emotions are openly expressed. Under these conditions, she believed, people develop healthy self-esteem, which enables them to take the risks necessary for authentic relationships.

Minuchin is one of the few (other than Bowen and the psychodynamic therapists) to say that it's important to know what's normal in order to recognize what's abnormal. According to Minuchin (1974), clinicians need to have both an intellectual and emotional appreciation of the facts of ordinary family life to become effective family therapists. First, it's important to recognize that normal family life isn't a bed of roses. When two people marry they must learn to accommodate to each other; each succeeding transition in the life cycle requires further modifications of the family structure. Clinicians need to be aware of this and to be able to distinguish functional from dysfunctional structures, as well as pathological structures from structures that are simply transitional. Moreover, Minuchin adds, it's hard to be truly effective as a therapist without having personally experienced some of the problems that your client families are struggling with. (This is a point that older and more experienced therapists are more apt to make than young ones.)

Because structural family therapy begins by assessing the adequacy of the client family's structure, it sometimes appears to have an ideal standard. In fact, however, normality is defined in terms of functionality, and structural family therapists recognize that diverse patterns may be equally functional. The clarity of subsystem boundaries is far more important than the composition of the subsystem. For example, a parental subsystem made up of a father and oldest child can function effectively if the lines of responsibility and authority are clearly drawn. Patterns of enmeshment and disengagement are viewed as preferred styles, not necessarily as indications of abnormality.

Other schools of family therapy imply standards of normality in their descriptions of what's missing in dysfunctional families. Strategic therapists, for example, portray dysfunctional families as creating symptoms out of normal problems by failing to adjust to meet the demands of changing circumstances, then trying to solve problems by doggedly doing more of what they've always done.

Most family therapists don't think in terms of remaking families and therefore believe they have little need for models of what a family should be like. Instead, they intervene around specific problems—problem-maintaining interactions, problem-saturated stories, forgotten solutions—conceptualized in terms of function, not structure. The patterns they observe are dysfunctional; therefore, by implication, what's functional must be just the opposite.

While it may not be necessary to have a way of understanding a family's past in order to help them, it is useful to have a way of understanding the family's organization of the present, using a model of normal behavior to set goals for treatment. Such a model should include a design for the present and for change over time. Among the ideas presented in this book the most useful for a basic model of normal family functioning include structural hierarchy, effective communication, and family life cycle development.

The issues involved in whether to hold up normative maps as goals are thorny. If therapists adhere too strongly to a normative model, they may impose it on families for whom it does not fit—families from other cultures, for example—and they're more likely to take an authoritarian stance regarding the proper ends of treatment. On the other hand, therapy without a model of healthy family functioning can degenerate into a directionless exercise. Any normative model must be taken as a rough guideline and used flexibly rather than taken as a Procrustean bed onto which families are forced to fit.

Ironically, at the same time that integration is breaking down the distinctions between models of family therapy, an opposite trend is taking place in American society at large. Multiculturalism has replaced the ideal of the melting pot. Surely ethnic pride and a renewed respect for the culture and traditions of various groups make for a richer and more diverse society than the white-bread WASPy standard once aspired to by anxious immigrants. Most of us are learning that differences aren't problems; intolerance and oppression are—not just the overt and ugly kind, like the police assault on Rodney King, but also everyday subtle acts of prejudice and disrespect. But is there a danger in the multicultural ideal of setting up an insulating pride, fostering an us-against-them attitude on behalf of America's ethnic groups? Maybe "pluralism" is a better term for celebrating the uniqueness of one's own heritage without promoting factionalism and separatism. Perhaps minority cultures can find common cause while accepting the equality of other cultures without at the same time striving for undifferentiated likeness.

Another recently questioned assumption about normal families concerns the role of the nuclear family. Almost 30 percent of American families are headed by one parent, up from about 20 percent in 1980. Although the percentage is still higher in African-American families, the rate of increase in both single parenthood and illegitimacy is now higher among whites than blacks. Not only have family therapists learned to see the single-parent family as a workable alternative to the two-parent model, many have questioned the normality and importance of the nuclear arrangement.

Anyone who works extensively with African-American families learns to recognize that these families often have more fluid boundaries and that "fictive kin" (enduring relationships with people not actually related by blood) may be important connections in these families. Yet the idea that the American nuclear family is in danger of disappearing, or of becoming unrecognizable, may, like a lot of other millennial prophesies, turn out to be premature. After nearly two decades of studious neutrality about different family arrangements, the two-parent model has once again become the rallying cry of family commissions, policy analysts, and social scientists. They hail it not only as the best hedge against poverty for children, but also as the most reliable prescription for their success and happiness. Maybe God invented the idea of two parents for more than merely biological reasons. What do you think? Meanwhile family therapists who are more clinicians than social critics will continue to work with a variety of families and family forms, endeavoring not to fit them to any abstract model, but to help them realize their own unique potential.

Development of Behavior Disorders

In the early days of family therapy patients were seen as innocents—"scapegoats"—on whom families projected their conflicts and whose deviance maintained family stability. Much of the literature was about dysfunctional ways of keeping the peace: scapegoating, pseudomutuality, rubber fence, family projection process, double bind, disqualification, mystification, and so on. The notion was that these malignant mechanisms may have driven young people crazy but they helped keep families together. It was a simple and satisfying tale of malevolent influence. No one exactly blamed the parents—their concealed coercions weren't really deliberate—but such explanations did rest on parental faults and failings, and as such had mythic force. The idea that schizophrenia was a sacrifice children made for their families was absolutely riveting—and absolutely untrue.

Initially, the patterns of disturbed communication observed in schizophrenic families were thought to cause schizophrenia. Eventually, etiological models gave way to transactional ones. Instead of causing schizophrenia, these impaired family interactions came to be seen as patterns of relationship in which schizophrenia was embedded. Neither the family nor the symptomatic member was the locus of the problem—the problem isn't *within* people, it's *between* them.

Today, family therapists think less about what causes problems than about how families unwittingly maintain the problems that come their way. Each of the systems of family therapy has unique ideas about how pathological families fit together, but the following themes are useful to define some of the important differences of opinion in the field; inflexible systems, the function of symptoms, underlying dynamics, and pathological triangles.

Inflexible Systems

Families, like other groups, have rich possibilities for relationship and satisfaction. (Don't we marry and later bring children into the world with clear and simple hopes for happiness?) Walt Whitman said, "I contain multitudes." The same could be said of family relationships, though, sadly, many soon congeal into limited and limiting molds.

Chronic inflexibility is a striking feature of families with disturbed members; it's virtually impossible to grow up healthy in these families because they are so rigid. Acute inflexibility explains why other families become dysfunctional at transitions in the life cycle; disorder breaks out when they fail to modify their organization in response to developmental or environmental stresses.

Early observers of schizophrenic families emphasized their rigid inflexibility. Wynne coined the term *rubber fence* to dramatize how psychotic families resist outside influence, and the term *pseudomutuality* to describe their rigid facade of harmony. R. D. Laing showed how parents, unable to tolerate their children's healthy strivings, used *mystification* to deny and distort their experience. Communication theorists thought that the most striking disturbance in schizophrenic families was the extreme inflexibility of their rules. According to this analysis, these families were unable to adapt to the environment because they lacked mechanisms for changing their rules; they were rigidly programmed to negative feedback, treating novelty and change as deviations to be resisted. Forces of homeostasis overpowered forces of change, leaving these families stable but chronically disturbed.

This tradition of viewing families of mentally ill patients as rigidly homeostatic was taken into the 1980s by Selvini Palazzoli in the form of her concept of "dirty games." Carol Anderson and Michael White countered this negative way of looking at families with disturbed members by suggesting that their rigidity may be the result of living with serious problems—and being blamed by mental health professionals.

Explaining family problems in terms of rigid homeostatic functioning became one of the cornerstones of the strategic school. Strategists describe dysfunctional families as responding to problems with a limited range of solutions. Even when the attempted solutions don't work, these families stubbornly keep trying; thus the attempted solutions, rather than the symptoms, are the problem. Behaviorists use a similar idea when they explain symptomatic behavior as resulting from faulty efforts to modify behavior. According to behaviorists, often when parents think they're punishing misbehavior, they're actually reinforcing it with attention.

Psychoanalytic and experiential clinicians have identified pathological inflexibility in individuals and couples, as well as in whole families. According to these two schools, intrapsychic rigidity, in the forms of conflict, developmental arrest, and emotional suppression, is the individual's contribution to family pathology. Psychoanalysts consider pathological families as closed systems that resist change. According to this line of thought, symptomatic families treat the present as though it were the past. When faced with a need to change, dysfunctional families regress to earlier levels of development, where unresolved conflicts left them fixated.

Experientialists describe pathological families as stagnant and inflexible. If it's true that sometimes you have to try something different just to know you're alive, families too afraid of rocking the boat become moribund. The symptom-bearer is seen to be signaling a family pattern of opposition to the life force. Unfortunately this model perpetuates the tradition of making families villains and individuals victims.

Structural family therapists locate the inflexibility of dysfunctional families in the boundaries between subsystems. Disturbed families tend to be either markedly enmeshed or markedly disengaged. Young therapists who have trouble diagnosing family structure are at first happily surprised when confronted with a profoundly disturbed family. The structure is so easy to see. Unfortunately, when structural problems are conspicuously clear, they are also conspicuously entrenched.

Structural family therapy also identifies acute inflexibility in symptomatic families. Rigidity, for example, was one of the most prominent characteristics found in psychosomatic families. Minuchin (1974) stresses that otherwise normal families will develop problems if they are unable to modify a previously functional structure to cope with an environmental or developmental crisis. Family therapists should be very clear on this point: symptomatic families are often basically sound; they simply need help adjusting to a change in circumstances.

Solution-focused and narrative therapists avoid conceptions about family systems that implicate family members in the development of problems. Both camps prefer to focus on the strengths of individuals in the family and on times when they used their resources to triumph over their problems. What both models do identify as maintaining problems are rigid habits of thought that lead people to consider themselves hopeless and defeated.

Solution-focused therapists leave it at that; they don't speculate about the origins of defeatist thinking. They believe that you don't need to know how problems developed in order to find solutions. In fact, they argue that dwelling on problems keeps the focus on the negative—what to stop doing—while focusing on solutions shifts the focus to positive avenues of constructive action.

Narrative therapists point to what they consider toxic and oppressive systems of belief in our culture that are internalized by family members. By making culture the culprit they lift families out of the layers of guilt and recrimination that often surround problems and help them unite to fight insidious sources of cultural repression.

The Function of Symptoms

Early family therapists described the identified patient as serving a critical function in disturbed families by detouring conflict and thus stabilizing the family. Vogel and Bell (1960) portrayed emotionally disturbed children as "family scapegoats," singled out as objects of parental projection on the basis of traits that set them apart. Thereafter, their deviance promotes cohesion. Communication theorists thought that symptoms were fraught with meaning—functioning as messages—and consequence—controlling other family members.

Today, many family therapists deny that symptoms have either meaning or function. Indeed, narrative, solution-focused, and psychoeducational therapists are so diametrically opposed to the idea that symptoms serve a function in families that these approaches can be seen as inspired to counter that idea. Narrative therapy is built around the metaphor of symptoms as alien entities, and the psychoeducation approach is devoted to exonerating families by teaching them that they aren't responsible for the mental illness of their identified patients.

Behavioral and MRI therapists don't assume symptoms are necessary to maintain family stability, and so they intervene to block the symptom without being concerned about restructuring the family. Behaviorists have always argued against the idea that symptoms are a sign of underlying pathology or that they serve any important function. Behavioral family therapists treat problems as skill deficits and as the uncomplicated result of faulty efforts to change behavior. Restricting their focus to symptoms is one of the reasons they're successful in discovering the contingencies that reinforce them; it's also one of the reasons why they aren't very successful with cases where a child's behavior problems function to stabilize a conflicted marriage or where a couple's arguments protect them from dealing with unresolved personal problems. MRI therapists recognize that symptoms may serve a purpose but deny that it's necessary to consider that purpose when planning therapy. Members of this school take the modest position that if they help free families from their symptoms, then the families can take care of themselves.

Richard Schwartz's internal systems model maintains that there may sometimes be parts of family members that fear change, but the parts of them that want relief often can be activated without having to confront the fearful parts.

Some schools of family therapy do continue to believe that symptoms signal deeper problems and that they can function to maintain family stability. In families that can't tolerate open conflict, a symptomatic member may serve as a smokescreen and a diversion. Just as symptomatic behavior preserves the balance of the nuclear family, so may problems in the nuclear family preserve the balance in the extended family. In psychoanalytic, Bowenian, and structural formulations, a couple's inability to form an intimate bond may be ascribed to the fact that one or both of them are still being used to mediate the relationship between their parents. In this way symptomatic behavior is transmitted across generations and serves to stabilize the multigenerational family system.

Sometimes it's possible to see how symptoms function to motivate a depressed or disengaged parent to become more involved in the family. Two examples will illustrate this observation. The first is from Jay Haley's (1976) *Problem-Solving Therapy.* According to Haley, a child's misbehavior is often part of a repetitive cycle that serves to keep the parents involved. In a typical sequence, father becomes unhappy and withdraws; the child misbehaves; mother fails to discipline the child; father steps in, reinvolving himself with the mother through the child. The second example is from an interview conducted by Harry Aponte (a noted structural family therapist), quoted in Hoffman (1981).

> The interview is with a poor black family that fully answers to the description "multiproblem." Everybody—the mother, six grown or nearly grown children, and two grandchildren—is at risk, from breakdown, illness, nerves, violence, accident or a combination of all these factors. In addition, the family members are noisy, disruptive, and hard to control.
>
> At a certain point Aponte asks the mother, "How do you handle all this?" The mother, who has been apathetic and seemingly unconcerned as the therapist tries to talk with the children, says, "I put on my gorilla suit." The children laugh as they describe just how terrible their mother is when she puts on her gorilla suit.
>
> An incident occurs shortly after this conversation which suggests that a circular causal sequence is at work, one of those redundancies that may have to do with family balance. Mother is still apathetic and looks tired, and the therapist begins to ask about her nerves. At first the children are somewhat quiet, listening. As she begins to admit that she has had bad nerves and that she is taking pills, they begin to act up. One boy pokes the baby; another boy tries to restrain the baby from kicking back; the baby starts to yell. The therapist asks the twenty-year-old daughter (the baby's mother) if she can control him; she says no. At this point the mother gets up and smacks her daughter's baby with a

> rolled-up newspaper, rising out of her lethargy like some sleeping giant bothered by a gnat. She sits the baby down with a bump, and he makes no further trouble. During this sequence the rest of the children jump and shriek with joy, causing their mother to reprimand them, after which they calm down and the mother sits back, more watchful now and definitely in control. (p. 83)

Here a mother overwhelmed by stress becomes depressed; as she describes her depression the children become anxious and misbehave; the misbehavior triggers a reaction in the mother, rousing her from withdrawal to control the chaos. The children's symptomatic misbehavior functions as cause and cure of the mother's depression, in a recurring cycle.

Underlying Dynamics

In the 1950s family therapists challenged the psychoanalytic belief that symptoms are only surface phenomena and that the real problems are internal. Instead, they showed how observations limited to the surface of family interactions were sufficient to understand and treat most problems.

Today there are still many family therapists who deny that it's necessary or valid to look for underlying dynamics in order to explain or treat symptomatic behavior. These clinicians believe that it's sufficient to observe patterns of interaction in the family. Some strategic therapists, like the MRI group, confine the field of focus to interactions around symptomatic behavior; others, like the Milan group, take a broader view of the whole family. Behaviorists maintain that in order to account for unwanted behavior it's necessary only to observe its reinforcing consequences.

Despite the tradition of explaining problem behavior without bringing in underlying dynamics, many family therapists believe that neither the presenting symptoms nor surrounding interactions are the real problem; the real problem is some form of underlying family dysfunction. When families come in, these therapists look beneath—or beyond—behavioral sequences for some basic flaw in the family. Minuchin's notion of family structure is the leading example of such a concept. Structural therapists pay attention to the problems families bring in, but their real focus is on underlying structural pathology to explain and resolve these problems.

Structural pathology is conceptually different from the intrapsychic conflict in psychodynamic theory. Intrapsychic conflict is an inferred psychological concept; structural pathology is an observed interactional concept. Nevertheless, in practice, structural family therapists shift their attention from the family's complaints to a different level of analysis.

Family structure is now one of the central concepts in family therapy, and the field can be divided into those who do or don't include structure in their analyses. Haley (1980) does, and for this reason many people consider him a structuralist as much as a strategist. Selvini Palazzoli and Lynn Hoffman bring in structural concepts in terms of systemic conflict and "too richly cross-joined systems" (Hoffman, 1981). John Weakland of the MRI group emphatically denied the need to include structural concepts in family assessment, and he considered doing so a return to discredited psychodynamic theorizing. Others, whose focus is more on here-and-now interactions, including behaviorists (Patterson) and some experientialists (Whitaker), eventually came to accept the usefulness of structural concepts.[2] Their doing so was one of the early signs of a growing convergence among competing systems.

[2]Not incidentally, both Patterson and Whitaker came to the Philadelphia Child Guidance Clinic to study with Minuchin at a point in their careers when they felt the need for a more systemic understanding of the families they worked with.

The postmodern revolution, discussed in Chapter 10, is also poststructural in the sense that conceptions of an underlying structure are viewed as modernist (falsely absolutist) and therefore problematic. Postmodern family therapists like Michael White, Steve de Shazer, and Harlene Anderson all avoid structural speculations.

Neither psychoanalytic nor Bowenian therapists make much use of Minuchin's structural concepts; both schools have their own concepts of underlying dynamics.[3] Psychoanalysts originated the idea of underlying dynamics; present-day psychoanalytic family therapy practitioners use this idea in concepts of intrapsychic structural conflict (id, ego, superego); developmental arrest; internal object relations; and interlocking psychopathological structures among family members. According to the psychoanalytic model, problems may develop in interaction, but it's the interacting individuals who have the basic flaws.

In Bowen's theory the major concepts describing family dynamics are fusion, family projection process, and interlocking triangles. So much are these underlying issues emphasized that Bowenians probably spend less time than anyone else dealing directly with presenting symptoms or even with symptom-bearers.

Bowenian theory uses a *diathesis-stress* model of psychological problems. This is a model from genetic research in which a person develops a disorder when a genetic flaw is triggered by stress in the environment. In Bowenian theory, people who develop symptoms in the face of anxiety-arousing stress have low levels of differentiation and are emotionally cut off from support systems, especially in the extended family. The diathesis may not be genetic, but it is passed from one generation to the next.

Psychoeducational therapists brought the diathesis–stress model into family therapy through their view of schizophrenia as a disease that's powerfully affected by environmental (family) stress. The goal becomes to reduce stressful "expressed-emotion" in families. Richard Schwartz, by extending systems thinking into the realm of internal process, offers a solution to the question of whether internal (intrapsychic) or external (interactional) dynamics underlie problems: He sees problems embedded in imbalances at both levels, each affecting the other. Because both are important, therapists can effectively address either.

Pathological Triangles

The double-bind theory was a landmark shift from an individual to a systems unit in the analysis of behavior disorder. Current concepts of pathology sometimes refer to individuals—fusion of emotion and intellect, repressed affect, problem-saturated stories—and sometimes to dyads—fusion in a relationship, mystification, unresolved symbiotic attachment. However, the most sophisticated thinking in the field is triadic.

Pathological triangles are at the heart of several family therapy explanations of behavior disorder. Among these, Bowen's theory is perhaps the most elegant. Bowen explained how when two people are in conflict, the one who experiences the most anxiety will "triangle in" a third person. This model not only provides a beautiful explanation of systems pathology, but also serves as a warning to therapists. As long as a therapist remains tied to one party in an emotional conflict, then he or she is part of the problem, not part of the solution.

In psychoanalytic theory, oedipal conflicts are considered the root of neurosis. Here the triangle is triggered by family interactions, but formed and maintained in the individual psyche. Mother's tenderness may be seductive and

[3]There are apparent exceptions to this rule, like Michael Nichols, whose book *The Self in the System* introduced psychoanalytic ideas to a systemic audience, and Mary-Joan Gerson, whose *The Embedded Self* introduced structural family therapy to her psychoanalytic colleagues. However, both of these advocates of cross-fertilization practice a fairly orthodox version of structural family therapy.

father's jealousy threatening, but the wish to destroy the father and possess the mother is a figment of fantasy. Pathological fixation of this conflict may be caused by developments in the outer space of the family, but the conflict is harbored in the inner space of the patient's mind.

The psychoanalytic model of the individual is that of a divided self at war within. But psychoanalytic family practitioners treat family problems as disorders in relationships. The cause of the problem may be a function of individual personalities, but the result is in the interaction. *Pathological need complementarity* is the core psychoanalytic concept of interlocking pathology in family relationships. A person with a strong need to be submissive, for instance, will marry someone with a strong need to dominate. These needs are based on early identifications and introjections. The husband who has a sense of himself as a victim has internalized pathogenic introjections that revolve around aggressive conflicts, but his needs are acted out in pathological relationships; that is, his unconscious need for an aggressor will lead him to select a mate who can act this role, allowing him to project his repressed or split-off aggression onto his wife. Divided selves thus become divided partners.

Structural family theory is based on triangular configurations where a dysfunctional boundary between two people or subsystems is a reciprocal product of a boundary with a third. Father and son's enmeshment reflects father and mother's disengagement; a single mother's disengagement from her children is the counterpart of her overinvolvement outside the family. Structural theory also uses the concept of pathological triangles to explain *conflict-detouring triads*, where parents divert their conflict onto their child. Minuchin, Rosman, and Baker (1978) have even demonstrated that physiological changes occur when parents in conflict transfer their stress to a psychosomatic child. Therapy is designed to disengage the child from the parents' struggle and to help the parents work out their conflicts directly.

Most strategic therapists work with a dyadic model, in which one person's symptoms are maintained by others' efforts (taken as a single group) to resolve them. Haley and Selvini Palazzoli, however, use a triangular model in the form of *cross-generational coalitions*. These "perverse triangles," as Haley (1977) calls them, occur when a parent and child, or a grandparent and child, collude to form a bastion of covert opposition to another adult. Failure to recognize these cross-generational coalitions dooms to failure any attempt to help parents resolve "their" problems with a symptomatic child. That's why behavioral parent training usually doesn't work when there's significant conflict between the parents. Teaching a father how to reinforce respect from his son won't get very far if the mother subtly encourages disrespect.

Triangular functioning is less central to the newer models because they're less concerned with how families develop problems than with helping them solve them. It might even be argued that ignoring family dynamics is one of the strengths of narrative and solution-focused approaches, if doing so helps these therapists zero in on the constricting habits of thought they're interested in. But it might also be said that ignoring family dynamics is one of the weaknesses of these approaches, especially in cases where conflict in the family isn't just going to go away because family members work together to solve a common problem.

When things go wrong in our lives, it's tempting to look for someone to blame. Your partner never talks about his feelings? He must be from Mars. Families often drop out in the first couple of sessions? They must be resistant. Before we get too judgmental, let's recognize that it's perfectly natural to give other people credit for our problems. Because we look out at life from inside our own skins, we're most aware of other people's contributions to our mutual problems. But therapists, we'd hope, aren't handicapped by this egocentric bias. No, they're handicapped by another bias.

Whenever we hear one side of an unhappy story, it's only natural to sympathize with the person doing the telling. If a friend tells you her boss is a jerk, your sympathy for her puts you automatically on her side. Experience suggests that most stories have two sides. But when your impulse is to show solidarity with someone who's telling you his or her troubles, the temptation is to look abroad for villains. Among professional helpers, this temptation is too often these days not resisted.

One reason for blaming family problems on easily vilified influences—men, racism, mothers—is that it's hard to see past individual personalities and their feelings to the structural patterns that make them a family, unless you see the whole group and see them in action. That's why family therapy was invented in the first place.

Family therapists, who are supposed to see these connections, have lately gotten farther and further away from the idea that families who seek therapy have something wrong with them. Rejecting what they see as the judgmental stance of their predecessors, many family therapists today espouse a more democratic, "nonhierarchical," form of therapy in which clients and therapists are considered partners in a joint enterprise. Some issues to consider are: What's gained and what's lost by avoiding thinking of families who seek therapy as having something wrong with them? Is there a difference between thinking of families as having something wrong with them versus thinking of them as *doing* something wrong—something that isn't working? How can you distinguish between a compassionate therapist who avoids blaming and one who's so anxious to be liked that he doesn't dare confront clients for fear that they might get mad?

Goals of Therapy

The goal of all psychological treatment is to help people change in order to relieve their distress. This is true of individual therapy, group therapy, and family therapy. Why then is so much written about the differing goals of various schools of therapy? Some of it has to do with different ideas about how people change, some of it merely with alternate vocabularies for describing change. When Bowenians speak of "differentiation of self" and psychoanalytic therapists speak of "increased ego strength," they mean pretty much the same thing.

If we strip away the semantic differences, there are two major dimensions of goals on which the schools of family therapy vary. First, schools differ with respect to their intermediate goals; they seek change through different aspects of personal and family functioning. Second, schools differ in terms of how much change they seek. Some are content with symptom resolution, others aspire to transform the whole family system.

Variations in intermediate goals are based on theoretical differences about which aspects of personal and family functioning are most important to change. For instance, one of the goals of experiential family therapy is to help families become more emotionally expressive. Experientialists believe that emotional stagnation is a primary problem and that increased expressiveness will make people more alive and happy. To a large extent, therefore, differences in intermediate goals among different schools reflect differences of opinion about how behavior change is best accomplished. We will discuss these distinctions more fully below in Conditions for Behavior Change.

The second difference in goals—how much change—has to do with the way schools differ with respect to their aims about the resolution of presenting problems or the overhauling of family systems. All therapists are interested in resolving problems. But they vary from being concerned exclusively with symptom resolution to being more concerned with the health of the entire family system. Strategic, solution-focused, and behavioral therapists are least concerned with changing the whole system;

psychoanalytic and Bowenian therapists are most concerned with systems change.

The goal of structural family therapy is both symptom resolution and structural change. But the structural change sought has the modest aim of reorganizing that part of the family that's failed to adjust to meet changing circumstances. Structural therapists don't have the more ambitious goal of remaking the whole family. Narrative, communications, and experiential therapists also aim midway between symptomatic improvement and systematic family reorganization. Practitioners from these schools focus neither on presenting complaints nor on the overall family system. Instead they pay special attention to discrete processes that they believe underlie symptoms: cognitive constructions, patterns of communication, and emotional expressivity. Improvements in these processes are thought to resolve symptoms and promote growth, but neither symptom resolution alone nor systems change per se is the goal.

The focus of strategic therapy and its solution-focused offshoot is on problem solving. The goal is simply to resolve whatever problems clients present. Narrative therapists, many of whom rebelled against the mechanistic aspect of their own strategic practices (cf. Freedman & Combs, 1996), aim to help clients solve the problems they come in with; but they also hope to have them leave with an enhanced sense of personal agency.

In our view, the primary goal of family therapy must be to resolve the presenting problem. If a family asks for help with a specific problem and the therapist helps them express their feelings better but doesn't help them solve the problem, then he or she has failed the family in an important way. One of the virtues of behavioral and strategic therapists is that they don't fool themselves or their clients about whether these problems get solved. Some of the approaches with grander aspirations run the risk of losing sight of this first responsibility of a professional helper. If success is defined as accepting the therapist's point of view and working toward his or her conceptual goal, then therapy becomes a power struggle or an indoctrination. To some extent this happens in all therapies, but it's justified only when achieving the therapist's conceptual goals also meets the family's goals.

The advantage of working toward symptom change is that it's directly responsive to the family's request and eliminates much obfuscation about whether or not therapy is successful. The disadvantage of working *only* at the level of symptomatic or symptom-maintaining behavior is that it may produce change that doesn't last.

As a final note on goals, resolving problems has been family therapy's trademark, emblematic of the optimism of its practitioners. Now, however, by embracing the disease model (Yes, Virginia, there is such a thing as schizophrenia), some family therapists, notably those who practice psychoeducation, advocate coping with, rather than curing, serious psychopathology as a worthy goal. This modest but realistic goal has been hard for some family therapists to accept. What's at stake is a question of which is more powerful, family therapy or certain entrenched conditions—psychopathology, arrested psychodynamics, poverty and despair, or even failures of nerve that make it so very difficult for some people to risk change.

Conditions for Behavior Change

Once it was necessary to contrast family therapy with individual therapy in order to establish family treatment as a distinct and innovative approach. Family therapists began by emphasizing their differences with individual therapists; later they emphasized differences among themselves. Today there is much cross-fertilization among the schools—and even more talk about integrating perspectives. But although most schools share a broad consensus about principles of change, they still differ on many specific issues. In this section we will compare and contrast models in terms of action or insight, change in the session or change at home, duration of treatment, resistance, family–therapist relationship, and paradox.

Action or Insight

One of the early distinctions between family therapy and individual therapy had to do with insight. Individual therapists stressed intellectual and emotional insight; family therapists stressed action. Although they emphasized action in their writing, many of the techniques of early family therapists were designed to affect action through understanding. Actually, since people think, feel, and act, no form of therapy can succeed without influencing all three aspects of the human personality. Different approaches may concentrate on different modes of experience, but they all inevitably deal with the total—thinking, feeling, and acting—person.

Action and insight are the primary vehicles of change in family therapy. Most family therapists use both mechanisms, but some schools emphasize either action (strategic, behavioral) or insight (psychoanalytic, narrative).

The case for action is based on the observation that people often don't change even though they understand why they should. The truth of this is familiar to anyone who's ever tried in vain to lose weight, stop smoking, or spend more time with the kids. Behaviorists make the case for action by pointing out that behavior is often reinforced unwittingly; explanations, they say, don't change behavior, reinforcement does. Parents are taught to modify their children's behavior by rewarding desired actions and ignoring or punishing undesirable actions. Likewise, married couples are taught that actions speak louder than words; it doesn't matter so much what you tell your spouse; what matters is that you reward pleasing behavior. Behavior therapists don't, however, practice what they preach. They tell clients that reinforcement is the way to change behavior, but they rely on simple explanations to bring about those changes. Action may be the message, but understanding is the medium.

Like behaviorists, strategic therapists focus on behavior and aren't concerned with insight. However, they differ from behaviorists in one important respect: Behaviorists rely on the power of rational instruction; strategic therapists eschew understanding altogether. They don't believe in insight and they don't believe in teaching; instead they believe that the way to change behavior is through manipulation. They box stuck families into a corner, from which the only way out is to become unstuck.

The case for insight is based on the belief that if people understand themselves they'll be free to act in their own best interests. Psychoanalytic clinicians believe that people are blind to their real motives and feelings. Without insight into hidden conflicts, action can be self-defeating, even dangerous. Unexamined action can be self-defeating because symptomatic relief without insight fosters denial and repression; it can be dangerous if repressed impulses are acted on precipitously.

Many actions are regarded in the psychoanalytic school as symptomatic—protective devices designed to bind the anxiety that signals impulses whose expression might lead to punishment. Only by understanding their impulses and the dangers involved in expressing them can people change. Moreover, since the important conflicts are unconscious, only methodical interpretation of the unconscious brings about lasting change. In psychoanalytic therapy, unanalyzed action initiated by families is called "acting out"; unanalyzed action initiated by therapists is considered manipulation. Insight can only be achieved if families verbalize their thoughts and feelings rather than act on them, and therapists interpret unconscious meaning rather than suggest or manipulate action.

Discussions of insight are often divisive, because insight is a buzzword; proponents glorify it, opponents ridicule it. Advocates of insight endow it with pseudomedical properties: Insight, like medicine, cures. Actually, insight doesn't cure anything; it's something through which cure occurs. To say that a family acquires insight means that family members learn what they intend by their actions and what they want from each other; how they act on their insight is up to them.

Do people change when they're propelled into action or when they develop understanding? Both. People change for a variety of reasons; the same person may change one day because of being forced into action and another day because of some new understanding. Some individuals may be more or less responsive to either action or insight, and these people will be more or less successful in therapies that emphasize one or the other. People change when they are ready and when the right stimulus is applied.

In contrast to the polar positions taken by some schools, others work with action *and* insight. In structural family therapy, change is initiated in action and then supported by understanding. According to Minuchin (Minuchin & Nichols, 1993), family structure and family beliefs support and reinforce each other; the only way to achieve lasting change is to challenge both. Action comes first because it leads to new experiences that then make insight possible. In Bowen systems theory, interventions also affect both levels—action and understanding; but the order of effect is reversed. Bowenians begin by calming people down, so that they'll stop blaming each other and start reflecting on the relationship processes they're caught up in. Once family members begin to see their role in triangles and polarized patterns like the pursuer–distancer dynamic, they're encouraged to carry out relationship experiments in which they practice stopping their participation in these automatic patterns.

The Milan model and the later work of Cecchin, Boscolo, and Hoffman elevated the importance of working with systems of meaning. Thus, systems-oriented family therapists became less tied to behavioral analyses and action-oriented interventions. Taking into account the "externalizing" technique of Michael White and David Epston, the therapy as conversation model of the late Harry Goolishian and Harlene Anderson, the popularity of social constructionism, and the reemergence of psychodynamic influence (as well as the revival of hermeneutics), the trend in the field is definitely away from action and toward, if not insight, at least cognition.

A growing number of family therapists would reject the notion of insight as tied to outmoded beliefs in objective truth. Being good postmodernists, they prefer the idea of "narrative reconstruction" to "insight" and to see the therapist as helping clients construct newer and more hopeful stories rather than excavating some buried truth. However, regardless of whether we speak in declassé terms of insight or in more contemporary terms of co-constructing reality, the fact is that the contemporary interest in narrative and the popularity of reflecting teams are symptoms of family therapy's drift from action to insight (or meaning, if you prefer).

This contemporary emphasis on meaning is especially attractive to therapists who favor a collaborative approach, but while the individuals who make up families are certainly feeling, thinking, and acting beings, we wonder if what ties them most strongly together in creating and maintaining problems isn't that their actions are coordinated and interlocking. Helping people reconsider the way they perceive their dilemmas may help them see new ways to address them. But all too often seeing what we need to do somehow doesn't quite get us to do it. Perhaps working with meaning *as well as* action would be a better idea for family therapists than trading in one for the other.

Change in the Session or Change at Home

All family therapists aim to transform interactions among family members, but they differ as to where they expect these transformations to take place. In structural family therapy, transformation occurs in the session, in the present, and in the presence of the therapist. Action is brought into the consulting room in the form of enactments, and change is sought then and there. The same is true in experiential therapy; emotional breakthrough comes in session, in response to the therapist's provocations. In both of these therapies, changes wrought in the session are believed to transfer to the family's life outside.

Other family therapists promote changes they expect to occur not in the session but at home. Strategic therapists are relatively inactive in the session. They use sessions to gather information to formulate interventions, often delivered in the form of directives to be carried out at home. Bowenians also plan changes that will take place outside the consultation room. Family members are encouraged to return to their families of origin and coached to respond in new and more productive ways. Most forms of behavior therapy are planned to influence interactions that take place elsewhere. Parents are sent home to reward their children's positive behavior; spouses are taught to please each other or to have sex without anxiety. Some behaviorists, however, supervise parents playing with and disciplining their children in the session, usually behind a one-way mirror.

The primary impact of narrative therapy occurs in sessions, through persistent questioning of self-defeating points of view. However, to fortify changes begun in therapy when clients terminate and life's narrative again takes over, clients are encouraged to reach out to people who will be sympathetic to their new and preferred ways of being. Such "communities of concern" (Madigan & Epston, 1995) or "nurturing teams" (White, 1995) may actually be invited to sessions to witness and support changes the client is making, though more typically contact with these supportive audiences would be encouraged among the client's friends and colleagues. In an even more structured version of "communities of concern," David Epston has taken the lead in developing "leagues" of successful ex-clients to support people struggling with similar problems (White & Epston, 1990). The most famous of these is the Anti-Anorexia/Anti-Bulimia League of New Zealand.

The goal of family therapy is to solve problems so that people can live better. The ultimate test of success comes at home after therapy is over. But since therapists take on the job of creating change, utilizing the context of the session first to promote interactions and then to observe and change them gives maximum impact. Just as live supervision is preferred because it teaches therapists what to do while they do it, so supervised change in the session seems more effective than unsupervised change at home.

Duration of Treatment

Family therapy has always tended to be brief. That's because with most families change takes place rather quickly or not at all. But even "brief" might mean several weeks in a typical structural family therapy case or several months in a Bowenian treatment. With managed care now calling the shots, therapy is often constrained to as few as five or ten sessions. Some, like solution-focused therapists, attempt to make a virtue out of this necessity, but many therapists feel condemned to applying Band-Aids. However, rather than despair or limit therapy entirely to behavioral problem solving, therapists can focus on a single, primary structural problem, for example, the most salient of a network of interlocking triangles, and then give clients the choice of continuing or not—and of determining how to pay for more sessions if they wish to work on additional issues.

Some strategic therapists limit treatment to about ten sessions and announce this at the outset as a means of motivating families to get to work. Haley (1976) says that change occurs in stages and plans therapy accordingly, but many strategic therapists believe that change occurs in sudden shifts (Hoffman, 1981; Rabkin, 1977). Strategists don't reason with families, they give them a sudden jolt. These jolts, in the form of directives, provoke families stuck in dysfunctional homeostasis to change with or without their willing cooperation. Success in this operation requires that lasting change be achieved on the impact of a few interventions, and that it can occur without any understanding on the part of the family.

Solution-focused treatment tends to be briefer still, but here time limits aren't announced or used as leverage. The brevity of this approach is a product of the fact that the search for straightforward solutions is often easier than attempting to deal with systemic problem-maintaining interactions. Small change might be the watchword of this approach.

Other schools of family therapy believe that lasting change requires understanding, and that it occurs gradually over the course of many weeks. The duration of therapy is related both to the goal of treatment and the question of who's considered responsible for change. Strategists and behaviorists limit their goals to solving the presenting problem, and they assume responsibility for change. Psychoanalytic and experiential practitioners seek profound personal changes in their clients, and they place the responsibility for change with the clients. These therapists take responsibility only for providing a therapeutic atmosphere in their sessions; change is up to the clients.

Structural family therapists are interested in solving problems, not in personal growth; however, the problems they're most concerned with are structural. They believe that it's necessary to restructure dysfunctional families for lasting benefit to occur. MRI therapists, on the other hand, say that it's not necessary to change the whole family; all that's required is to interrupt the vicious feedback cycles that maintain presenting symptoms.

Bowenian therapy can be a life-long enterprise. The goal is personal growth *and* change in the entire extended family system. Since change is the responsibility of the client and occurs during visits home, the process may take years.

If the family's goal is growth and enrichment, therapy must be protracted; but if the goal is relief, then therapy should be brief. Problems arise when therapists try to hold on to families. The motives for doing so are many and complex, including pursuit of utopian goals, money, guilt over not having done more, and unresolved emotional attachments. For some mental health professionals being in therapy is a way of life. These therapists may convey exaggerated expectations of improvement, with the result that family members are bound to suffer disillusionment. Fortunately, therapy is expensive, time-consuming, and stressful, which puts pressure on families to get it over with and get on with their lives.

In brief prescriptive therapy, termination is initiated by the therapist when there's improvement in the presenting complaint or when the agreed-upon number of sessions is up. With compliant families, strategic therapists acknowledge progress and give the family credit for success; with defiant families, they express skepticism and predict a relapse. (The idea of giving families credit for success may have a hollow ring when families have no idea what they did to bring it about.) In longer, elicitory therapy, termination is initiated by the clients, either directly or indirectly. It's time to consider termination when family living becomes more enjoyable, when family members run out of things to talk about in therapy, or when they begin to complain about competing obligations. Part of successful termination is helping families accept the inevitability of the normal problems of everyday life. Successful therapy partly changes behavior and partly changes expectations. Therapy *can* go on forever, but by keeping it brief, therapists prevent families from becoming dependent on outside help and teach them to rely on their own resources.

Resistance

Families are notoriously resistant to change. In addition to the combined resistances of individual family members, the system itself resists change—or, to bring this abstraction down to earth, the structure that holds them together is supported by the actions of every one of the family members. Where there is resistance, therapy cannot succeed without overcoming it.

Paradoxically the same device that gives family therapy it's greatest leverage—bringing all the players together—also carries with it the seeds of resistance. With all parties to a problem present, it's hard to resist the temptation of finding someone else to blame—or at least of waiting for that person to change first. Even when a therapist conscientiously points out each person's contribution, it's only human nature for people to hear best what they already believe: "It isn't me; it's them."

It's popular these days to speak of "the death of resistance," and many of the newer schools claim that resistance isn't a problem in their "nonhierarchical, collaborative" approaches. This is partly true, partly posturing. While it's true that resistance is more to be expected to the highly visible and dramatic confrontations of a Minuchin or a Whitaker, resistance, or reluctance to change, is still an issue even for today's persuasive, cognitive approaches. Narrative therapists neither argue with clients nor confront them about their contribution to family conflicts, but what they describe as "externalizing" and "deconstructive conversations" are part of an effort to impose a clearly defined narrative shape on clients' stories. Resistance may not be overt, but people do not as readily give up their "problem-saturated stories" as you might think.[4]

[4]People come to therapy not just to solve problems but also to complain. They want to talk about their troubles, and, because they aren't at home, they expect someone to listen.

Behavior therapists minimize the importance of resistance and succeed only where their clients are willing to follow instructions. Other schools of family therapy consider resistance a major obstacle to treatment and have devised various ways to overcome it.

Psychoanalytic practitioners believe that resistance is motivated by unconscious defenses, which first must be made manifest and then resolved through interpretation. This is an intrapsychic model, but it doesn't ignore conscious and interactional resistances. Instead, psychoanalytic therapists believe that interactional problems—among family members or between the family and therapist—have their roots in unconscious resistance to basic drives. Experiential therapists have a similar model; they see resistance to emotional expression, and they blast away at it using personal confrontations and emotive exercises. Experientialists believe that breaching defenses automatically releases natural, healthy strivings; change occurs from the inside out.

People do avoid knowing painful things about themselves, but even more strenuously conceal painful truths from other members of the family. It's one thing to tell a therapist that you're angry at your partner; it's another thing to tell your partner. Therapies that are more interactive and systems-oriented focus on conscious withholding and on the system's resistance to changing its rules.

Minuchin's solution to the problem of resistance is straightforward: He wins families over by joining and accommodating to them. This gives him the leverage to utilize powerful confrontations designed to restructure family interactions. Resistance is seen as a product of the interaction between therapist and family; change is accomplished by alternately challenging the family and then rejoining them to repair breaches in the therapeutic relationship.

Strategic therapists expect resistance but avoid power struggles by going with resistance rather than opposing it head on. They assume that families don't understand their own behavior and will oppose attempts to change it. In response, some strategic practitioners try to gain control by provoking families to resist. Once the family begins to respond in opposition to therapeutic directives, the therapist can manipulate them to change in the desired direction. In practice, this can result in doggedly pursuing reverse psychology or in creative forms of therapeutic jujitsu. The creative response to resistance is illustrated by the Milan group, who, for example, routinely ask a third person to describe interactions between two others ("gossip in the presence") in order to minimize defensiveness.

Steve de Shazer denies the existence of resistance, saying that it's the family's way of cooperating and that it's up to the therapist to learn to use it. Richard Schwartz sees resistance as a proper reaction of protective parts of family members whose job it is to not allow anyone into the family until it's clear that the person won't harm or humiliate them. Schwartz goes to great lengths to respect and reassure those protective parts.

Finally, under the heading of resistance, we should consider the phenomenon of *induction.* Induction is what happens when a therapist is drawn into the family system—and abides by its rules. When this happens the therapist becomes just another member of the family; this may stabilize the system, but it reduces therapeutic mobility and prevents systems change. A therapist is inducted when he or she is sucked in to fulfill a missing family function, such as disciplining children when the parents don't or sympathizing with a husband whose wife doesn't, or when the therapist does what everybody else does, such as avoids challenging the fragile patriarch or minimizes a drinking problem.

Minuchin described the danger of induction and taught structural family therapists how to recognize and avoid it (Minuchin & Fishman, 1981). Part of the value of live supervision is helping to avoid induction. Working with colleagues helps to avoid induction, either with cotherapists (Whitaker) or with a team (Selvini Palazzoli). Bowenians avoid induction by remaining calm and objective; they stay in contact but keep themselves detriangled and outside of the family projection system.

Induction is so subtle that it's hard to see, so seductive that it's hard to resist. As helpers and healers, therapists are especially prone to take over for people, doing for them what they don't do for themselves. But taking over—being inducted—precludes real change. As long as families have someone to do for them, they don't have to learn to do for themselves.

One reason early family therapists encountered so much resistance was that they were too eager to change people and too slow to understand them. It turns out that families, like you and me, resist efforts to change them by people they feel don't understand and accept them. Family therapists learned to see nagging and withdrawal as circular, but they were slow to see them as human. Only later did therapists come to see through the nagging to the pain behind it, and to understand the anxiety that motivates withdrawal.

Rigidly stuck families are run by their fears, and therapists, eager to be liked, are vulnerable to those fears. Families quickly teach therapists what's safe and what's threatening: "Don't look in there"; "Don't ask *him* about *that.*" The art of therapy is understanding and sympathizing with those fears, but avoiding induction enough to be able to challenge them. As in so many things, progress sometimes means doing what you're afraid to do.

Family–Therapist Relationship

While individual therapists have long believed that the fundamental pillar of treatment was the bond between patient and therapist, early family therapists, who were more technically oriented, minimized the importance of the therapeutic relationship. As long as the dominant metaphor was the family as a cybernetic machine, therapists were seen as technocrats of change. In recent years the wind has shifted 180 degrees, and the prevailing view of the therapist is anything but a technologist.

The first shift occurred in the 1980s, when the cybernetic model was rejected because it placed the therapist outside and above the family. "Second-order cybernetics" was the term used to emphasize that the therapist was part of the system in treatment and therefore incapable of detached objectivity. Family therapists stopped talking about mechanical feedback systems and started talking instead about biological and ecological systems. An even more fundamental shift occurred in the 1990s when family therapists began to reject the role of expert in favor of a more collaborative model.

Unlike the distinction between first- and second-order cybernetics, which was largely academic, the shift to a collaborative model was a major turning point in how family therapy is practiced. What was rejected was the medical model, an authoritarian role model, with the clinician playing the expert-in-charge to whom the patient turned for answers. Early practices were seen as ranging from benign paternalism to an extreme emphasis on power and control, and secrecy. Harlene Anderson and Harry Goolishian called their alternative a "collaborative language-systems approach." Lynn Hoffman adopted a shortened version of the same idea in what she called "collaborative therapy." This shift from a directive, hierarchical position to a collaborative one was consistent with Maturana and Varela's (1980) idea that systems are self-creating and cannot be manipulated like machines. The ultimate example of this attempt to demystify therapy and break down its hierarchical structure was Tom Andersen's reflecting team, in which the clinical team came out from behind the mirror to join the family in equal and open dialogue.

The advocates of a collaborative model have provoked something of a backlash from those who say that while it's fine to renounce authoritarianism, it's not so fine if this means abdicating leadership (e.g., Nichols, 1993). But while the idea of therapy as collaboration has become almost a cliché, what may be more important than whether therapists describe themselves as experts or "co-participants" is whether they act to manipulate or empower people.

In thinking about the stance a therapist takes in treatment, it's important to realize that what the therapist does reflects not only what he or she believes, but also who he or she is. No matter what model a therapist subscribes to, personal style will have a large impact on his or her posture with families. John Weakland's "one-down" stance with families was as consistent with his own shy and unassuming character as Betty Carter's bluntness was with her outspoken nature. Therefore, in trying to classify models of the patient–therapist relationship, we'll consider not only how therapists describe themselves, but also how they come across in action.

The variations of patient–therapist relationships—including subject–object, interpersonal, phenomenological, and encounter—are a function of individual practitioners, but they also tend to characterize different schools of treatment. The hallmark of the *subject–object* paradigm is the therapist's objective observation of the family. In this model the therapist is a natural scientist, who makes observations and carefully tailored interventions. Personal and emotional reactions are regarded as confounding intrusions. The assumption is that therapist and family are separate entities. This isn't a popular conception, and few family therapists would describe themselves in these terms; nevertheless, aspects of behavioral, psychoanalytic, Bowenian, strategic, solution-focused, and structural therapy fit this model.

Behavioral therapists think of themselves as objective observers and rational scientists; without a doubt they fit this paradigm. Psychoanalytic practitioners operate within this model when they think of themselves as neutral and objective, as blank screens on whom patients project distorted perceptions and fantasies. Although many psychoanalytic clinicians still maintain this assumption, it's not consistent with current psychoanalytic thinking. No therapist is neutral and objective; the blank screen is a metaphor and a myth. Therapists reveal themselves in a thousand ways, and patients' reactions are always influenced by the reality of the therapist's behavior as well as by personal distortions. Bowenians think of themselves as objective, even scientific, observers who act as teachers or coaches to help clients overcome their emotionality. The strategic school has produced some of the most sophisticated concepts of the intricate relationship between therapists and families (Hoffman, 1981). The subject–object paradigm isn't a basic feature of this school, but it creeps in when therapists think of themselves as outsiders, locked in contest with families. The adversarial stance of some therapists in this system assumes that the therapist and family can and should be separate. Solution-focused therapists talk about being collaborative but come across like sales agents, aggressively promoting visions of a bright future. The structural emphasis on mapping a family's organization can lead some therapists to see themselves as simply mapmakers, rather than mapmakers who are also part of the territory they map.

The *interpersonal* paradigm treats therapy as a two-way interaction. This model acknowledges that therapists and families are related and that they constantly influence each other. Psychoanalytic clinicians employ this idea in their concepts of transference/countertransference, projective identification, and introjection; the model of influence here is interactive and transversal. In fact, this paradigm describes most family therapists most of the time. However, the constructivist movement in the 1980s represents an even more explicit attempt on the part of some systems-oriented thinkers to include the effects of the therapist's presuppositions and behavior on the families they treat. Most of the newer therapies adopt this language—they favor "generative conversations"—though whether individual practitioners remain open may be more a matter of personal sensitivity than professional identity.

The *phenomenological* paradigm is one in which the therapist tries to adopt the patient's frame of reference. It's what happens when psychoanalytic practitioners try to identify with their patients, when structuralists join families, when narrative therapists try to empathize with clients' stories, and when therapists of any persuasion try to understand and accept that families are doing the best they can. Stanton and Todd (1981) used this concept in their technique of "ascribing noble intention" to families. This tactic fits the phenomenological model when it's done sincerely but not when it's used merely as a strategic ploy—for example, in most reframing. Selvini Palazzoli's positive connotation is far more effective when done with sincerity. (Although the idea of positive connotation seems supportive, it was often experienced as patronizing, especially when delivered by the same therapists who held secret discussions behind a one-way mirror.) Boszormenyi-Nagy's recognition that symptomatic behavior is an act of unconscious loyalty to the family definitely represents a sincere position. Experientialists speak of accepting the patient's frame of reference, but sometimes they follow an encounter paradigm, in which they loudly proclaim their own honest feelings and challenge families to do the same.

The *encounter* paradigm calls attention to the direct engagement between the therapist's total personality and that of the client. It involves mutual sharing, honesty, openness, and self-disclosure, and its use in family therapy is primarily restricted to experientialists. During an encounter the therapist becomes a full participant, which is something that most family therapists don't let happen. However, it's possible to let yourself go and confront a family if you do so with clear therapeutic indications and not simply because you feel like it. Minuchin engages in genuine encounters from time to time, but he shows good timing and an ability to do so without sacrificing his professional objectivity. Honest encounters are perhaps useful when done occasionally, for a good reason, and by someone with enough experience and insight to keep from losing perspective.

Ultimately, the relationship you form with clients will depend on your view of human nature. If you believe that people have problems because they lack something, whether that something is information, good-enough parenting, ego strength, serotonin, or self-reflective awareness, you may feel obliged to take a hierarchical, expert position to fill the void. To really collaborate with clients, therapists must trust that family members already have the capacity to handle their problems themselves but that for some reason that capacity is blocked. With this view, therapists will work with clients to help them find and release whatever's constraining their abilities rather than trying to give them something they lack. It's this abiding faith in the human capacity for self-healing that characterizes the best therapists, whether from old schools or new.

Paradox

The use of paradox was once a central and controversial issue in family therapy. Paradoxical instructions encourage rather than attack objectionable behavior. They're designed to block or change dysfunctional sequences using indirect and seemingly illogical means. Paradoxical interventions were favored by therapists who assumed that families couldn't or wouldn't comply with direct advice or persuasion.

Paradoxical techniques were associated with the strategic forms of therapy in the 1970s, but they weren't confined to this group and they weren't new. Behavior therapists have used paradoxical methods for over fifty years, as negative practice (Dunlap, 1928) or conditioned inhibition (Kendrick, 1960). Frankl's (1960) "paradoxical intention" was an early version of what communications therapists later called "prescribing the symptom." In all of these applications the idea was basically the same: If you deliberately practice a symptom, it will go away.

Strategic therapists used paradox in two ways: as directives and as reframing. Reframing not only gives a new label for behavior, it also acts as an indirect message to change. Strategic therapists think of symptoms as part of self-reinforcing sequences, where symptoms are maintained by attempts to suppress them. Paradoxical directives provoke change by altering the attempted solutions and thus resolving the symptoms.

Hoffman (1981) cites an example of a wife whose constant jealous questioning of her husband only reinforced his reticence, which in turn reinforced her jealousy. The strategy to disrupt this sequence was to use a paradoxical directive to the wife to redouble her jealous questioning. The expected result was that the wife would rebel against the task and the problem would be solved.

There are two problems with provoking people to change by telling them not to. The first is obvious. This paradoxical device implies that families are oppositional, and while some are, many aren't. The second problem is that intervening only around a symptom neglects the broader family context.

Because disturbed families sustain their pathology through an intricate network of paradoxes, Selvini Palazzoli (1978) reasoned that the best way to break these pathological networks was through therapeutic counterparadox. The Milan group not only prescribed the problem behavior, but also the whole configuration of interactions surrounding it. Usually this took the combined form of "positive connotation" and a paradoxical family ritual. In this way, they tried to deal with the problem and its larger context at the same time.

Paradoxical directives can break a family pattern, but such changes will last only if they also effect a change in the total family structure. Many examples of paradoxical instructions are insulting. (Madanes's [1980] pretend techniques avoid this insulting quality and allow the therapist to avoid emotionally distancing himself or herself from the family.) Hoffman (1981), for example, describes a therapist's telling a depressed wife to become more subservient to her husband. Not surprisingly, the woman rebels and defies the therapist. According to Hoffman, this technique worked because the paradoxical directive unbalanced a complementary equilibrium, which then became symmetrical. Previously, the husband and wife were balanced in a relationship where he was one-up and she was one-down. By trying to push her further down, the therapist provoked a rebellion and the couple then established a relationship based on equality. Why that should happen isn't at all clear. Why don't they simply reestablish the same complementarity they had before?

Paradoxical techniques were so intriguing that they seemed like a magic solution to entrenched family problems. Actually, the way to resolve problems is to understand their context. In structural terms, this means understanding the family's dysfunctional structure; in systemic terms, it means understanding the circular patterns and relational context. The real key is the understanding; whether the therapist intervenes directly or indirectly is far less important. Indeed, it's possible to make paradoxical remarks in the form of honest skepticism about people's ability to change.[5] "I don't know, you've been operating this way for a long time, perhaps you won't be able to change." The family who hears such a comment may try to change or may not; either way they're likely to feel understood, not manipulated.

Techniques

Comparing techniques by reading about them is difficult because clinicians often describe techniques as abstract concepts rather than concrete actions. Modeling, for example, is a concept invoked by behaviorists for showing parents how to speak to their children; by experientialists for talking about their own feelings; and by structural family therapists for speaking sharply to family members who interrupt. Are all these techniques the same? Actually, modeling isn't a technique; it is a hypothetical construct to emphasize that people learn through observation. Often, techniques are described in the jargon of a particular school—restructuring, unbalancing, externalizing, differentiating—and it's not clear precisely what's meant. In this section, we'll treat issues of technique as a series of practical questions about how to conduct therapy, and we'll describe techniques as specific actions.

[5]The truth is, most of us don't change much, in therapy or out.

Who to Invite

Most family therapists invite everyone living under the same roof to the first session. This reflects the belief that everyone in the family is involved in any problem (or can at least contribute to its solution), even if the symptom is manifest in only one member. It also reflects the principle that in order to change the presenting complaint it's necessary to change the family interactions that create or sustain it.

Inviting the whole family for a consultation is a powerful restructuring and reframing move in itself. Whether or not it's explicitly stated, including the whole family in the assessment of a problem implies that they're all involved. In many cases the act of assembling the entire family to discuss a problem is the single most effective step toward solving it. Most experienced family practitioners are convinced of this, and they don't waste much time worrying about how to get the family in. They know that it's essential; they know that's how they work; and so they calmly state this to the family. When the request that the whole family attend at least once is put forth in a straightforward, matter-of-fact way, most families comply. Occasionally it's necessary to explain that the therapist would like everyone to attend in order to get all their points of view, but if the therapist is comfortable with the idea, most families will also accept it.

Sometimes, however, one or two family members won't attend the consultation. When this happens most therapists work with whoever is available. In such cases the failure of key family members to participate in treatment seems like a problem; it may be *the* problem. If a father, for instance, refuses to participate in a therapy designed to help his daughter overcome her moodiness, his nonparticipation is probably significant. Working with the mother and children to get the father involved may be the most important step in solving the presenting problem. On this matter, sensitive family therapists are like psychoanalysts who consider resistance not as an impediment to treatment, but as the object of treatment.

Members of some schools rarely insist on seeing the entire family. Practitioners of behavioral parent training focus on teaching the parents—usually the mother—how to deal with the identified patient. For this reason, some invite only the parents and child to the first session, while others (Gordon & Davidson, 1981) recommend interviewing both parents in the child's absence. Strategic therapists vary as to whom they include. Haley (1976) recommends seeing the whole family, but many of his MRI colleagues will see individuals, parents, or couples alone as the situation seems to require. This determination is based on who in the family is "the customer"—who asks for help and who seems to be unhappy enough to do something about the problem.

Bowenians usually work with individuals or couples. If a child is presented as the problem, members of this school see the parents; if a couple complains of marital problems, Bowenian therapists will see them together; and if only one person is willing to attend, the Bowenian therapist will see that person alone.

Because both the solution focused and narrative approaches avoid consideration of family dynamics and instead attend to the stories family members carry about their problems, therapists using these models feel less compelled to bring in the whole family for assessment. They often seem quite content to work with individuals or whatever family configuration would be most helpful in creating new and more productive stories.

Finally, most family therapists (whether they specialize in couples therapy or not) will see a marital couple without their children if the couple complains of problems in their relationship. This isn't, however, universally true. Structural, experiential, and psychoanalytic therapists often ask that the children attend the first session, and exclude them only if and when the couple needs to discuss private matters, such as their sexual relationship. Milan therapists often find they get the most useful information from family members who are most peripherally involved, because they can speak the most openly.

Rather than seeing less than the whole family, some therapists insist on seeing more. Network therapists convene large groups of family and friends; some therapists try to include grandparents. Inviting members of the extended family is a practice that cuts across the different schools. Many family therapists invite grandparents if they live in the household or if they seem particularly involved; some—for example, Whitaker and Selvini Palazzoli—invited grandparents as a matter of course. Another variant on the composition of therapy is seeing several families or couples together in a group. We have some reservations about this procedure. Group therapy with strangers is useful because it creates an imitation of life. In family therapy there's no need to imitate life; inviting the family brings life itself into the treatment room. However, group therapy with couples and families can be useful after they've made progress in overcoming their difficulties, in the focused way that private therapy allows. Then, meeting with other families or couples can be useful by helping them see how others deal with similar problems.[6]

Although each of these variations on who is invited into treatment is supported by a rationale, we believe that the best practice is to include all members of the same household in the first meeting. Later there may be good reasons for meeting with a subset of the family, but at the outset it's best to see everyone. (Encouraging everyone in the family to attend doesn't, however, mean that it's necessary or useful to convert them to a family therapy point of view. In fact, it may not even be a good idea for therapists to call what they do "family therapy," a term that unnecessarily advertises what many families aren't ready to accept.) Sometimes deviations from this format may be due more to anxiety than to good clinical judgment. Families are anxious about meeting together and airing their problems, and so, naturally, many are reluctant to come as a whole group. This is understandable and should be dealt with calmly by urging everyone to attend. Therapists, too, are anxious about convening families, particularly when the family indicates that one of its members doesn't want to come. The therapist's anxiety is sometimes the real reason for meeting with less than the whole family; in other words, some of the variations in composition of family meetings are probably due more to avoidance than to sound principles of family treatment.

There are times when it makes sense to work with a subset of the family, when, for example, absolutely only some will attend or when the therapist thinks some people should be excluded. The main thing is not to be pressured into such a decision and certainly not to drift into it without thinking.

[6]An excellent example of the group format is Virginia Goldner and Gillian Walker's use of couples groups as an adjunct to their work with domestic violence. After couples have achieved a certain amount of stability in private sessions, they're invited to share experiences and support each other's progress in the group setting.

Treatment Team

Under the pressure of managed care, working with colleagues has become a luxury many therapists can no longer afford. However, treatment teams continue to be a vital and useful resource in family therapy, especially in clinics and training programs. Family interactions are so complex that it's hard for one person to see everything, and they stir up so much emotion that it's hard to remain objective. When parents start shouting and kids start crying, or a wife demands while her husband withdraws, it's easy to be drawn in, to take sides and lose balance. Working with colleagues provides additional perspectives and makes any loss of objectivity more apparent. In general, cotherapy seems to be favored by those schools that emphasize intense emotional involvement (especially the experiential school); observation teams are favored by those who emphasize tactical planning (strategic, Milan, narrative) or who train therapists through live supervision (structural).

Carl Whitaker took a strong position in favor of cotherapy. Because his brand of experiential therapy was so intensely personal and interactive, he advocated (Whitaker & Keith, 1981) using cotherapists to counterbalance one another. While one is actively involved in a freewheeling interchange with the family, the other acts to limit partiality and to counteract the intrusion of countertransference-based interventions.

Both Minuchin and Haley have argued that solo therapists are able to act more decisively. Haley's position is consistent with his directive style, and it's shared by most strategic therapists (with the notable exception of the original Milan therapists who worked in mixed-gender teams of cotherapists). Minuchin, on the other hand, is controlling but less central and directive. His goal is to change families by manipulating their interactions in the session. To this end he uses family members as cotherapists. If a small child is shy, Minuchin will prod someone in the family to draw the child out; if a teenager is disobedient, Minuchin will goad the parents to become disciplinarians. By using family members as cotherapists, structural family practitioners avoid being inducted to take over a function that's missing in the family.

In settings where there are more trainees than families, cotherapy may be a way to give everyone a chance to participate. Although having a cotherapist may ease a beginner's initial anxiety, it can lead to confusion about who is in charge and where to go.

A solution favored by many family clinicians is to work alone backed up by a team of observers behind a one-way mirror. Teams of observers are most commonly used by structural, narrative, Milan, and strategic therapists; the observers comment after a session is over and also may enter or consult while the session is in progress. This is done programatically by the MRI group and by the Milan Associates. The advantage of this format is that observers can provide additional information, advice, and feedback. By contacting the family either by entering and speaking directly to them, or by sending a message through the therapist, observers can say something provocative or critical without the therapist's having to share responsibility for their statements. Reflecting teams make this whole process more open, more collaborative, and—we hope—more constructive. But regardless of whether or not they talk openly with families, effective teams, like effective therapists, must offer something more than superficial support.

The use of videotape adds another dimension to the treatment team. It enhances the observers' ability to see small movements and repetitive patterns, and it enables therapists to observe themselves in action.

Entering the Family System

Family clinicians think of the family as a system, a collection of parts interacting as a single entity. Whether or not they realize it, therapists themselves are part of a larger system that includes the family and the therapist. This is true for therapists who keep their emotional distance (Bowenian, behavioral) as well as for those who become more emotionally involved (experiential). All schools of family therapy have a more or less consistent style of making contact with families and of maintaining a particular therapeutic stance.

In structural family therapy the process of entering families is considered crucial. It has been described more fully by this school than by any other. The highly visible and dramatic confrontations that Minuchin became famous for turned out to be possible because he first established a close bond with families. This connection, which he later called *joining* (Minuchin, 1974), is a prerequisite to the challenge of restructuring.

Joining means hearing and acknowledging family members' points of view and accommodating to the family's organization and style. Most families come to treatment anxious and mistrustful; they expect to be challenged and worry about being blamed. Fearing criticism and apprehensive about having to change, they are set to resist. Recognizing this, structural therapists begin by trying to put the family at ease: They greet each member of the family separately; ask each for his or her point of view; and accept what each has to offer, even if at first it's only angry silence.

In addition to joining, therapists gain leverage by establishing their status as experts. Although leading therapists don't emphasize this point, when they're introduced as specialists they are immediately established as experts, figures of authority. Not all therapists have impressive credentials, but most make some effort to establish themselves as trustworthy, whether by hanging diplomas on the wall or demonstrating competence through their actions.

Among strategic therapists, Haley has written the most about entering the family system. His position (Haley, 1976) is similar to Minuchin's;

he describes the therapist as a host who must make the family comfortable and put them at ease, while at the same time maintaining a businesslike demeanor. He also uses the idea of accommodating to the family's organization by suggesting that therapists speak first to the parents. But his recommendation that the less-involved parent be addressed first isn't consistent with accommodating, and it's a clue to Haley's stance as a strategic therapist.

Like most strategic therapists, Haley is an expert manipulator. Members of this school relate to families from an emotionally distant position; they don't say what they really think and feel, but speak for calculated effect, depending on the nature of resistance encountered. Whether they take a one-up or one-down position, their stance is that of experts who coolly assess family problems and prescribe solutions.

In sharp contrast to the strategic approach, experiential therapists enter fully into the emotional life of the family and work from a stance that's open and close. Experientialists begin by greeting families and getting acquainted. In the process, they're likely to speak of their own feelings and attitudes and attempt to develop a warm, empathic relationship. Such intimate engagement makes it difficult to be objective; it's hard to understand the patterns in the whole systems when you're actively engaged in emotional dialogues with individual family members. This was one reason Whitaker insisted on working with a cotherapist.

Psychoanalytic practitioners scrupulously refrain from active involvement with their clients. They do so by design, to avoid directing or becoming actors in a drama that they believe should unfold spontaneously. In psychoanalytic work the therapist's stance is considered the most important ingredient in the method. Not interpretation, not analysis of the unconscious, but silent observation is the key to getting at hidden issues in the family.

The father of psychoanalytic family therapy, the late Nathan Ackerman, was an exception; he engaged in active dialogue with families, aggressively confronting them, "tickling their defenses," and sharing his own feelings. He did so in part because he was more of a psychoanalyst inventing family therapy than a practitioner of psychoanalytic therapy with families. He followed the dictates of his own personality, even though it meant going against what he was taught. It's a thing innovators do.

Bowenians take a position midway between the emotional intimacy of experientialists and the controlled technical mastery of strategists. Their byword is objectivity; their goal is to make contact with families but to remain detriangled. Learning is thought to occur in a calm atmosphere, so Bowenian therapists try to reduce anxiety and create a climate of rational understanding. They begin by inquiring about symptoms and their clinical course. Once this is done the therapist begins to act as a teacher, explaining family systems theory, and as a coach, encouraging family members to make contact with the rest of the family and to work toward defining a self.

Behavioral therapists assume the role of expert. Their stance is that of teachers; they take a central position, ask questions, explain principles, and assign homework. Their centrality, activity, and directiveness make it difficult for them to observe the natural and spontaneous interactions of the families they work with. It's an approach that controls and limits the field of observation. They can thus bring a great deal of technical expertise to dealing with part of the problem, but they run the risk of isolating that part from the totality of the family context.

When communications family therapy began, the family was treated like the opposition—a confused and confusing opponent whose power to destroy meaning had to be countered from the outset. Members of this school paid a great deal of attention to the structure and management of sessions; they were afraid to let things unfold naturally, because they thought they'd never be able to regain control. They began with explicit statements of their belief that the whole family was involved in the patient's symptoms, and they laid down rules for how therapy would be conducted: "Speak for yourself"; "Don't interrupt."

As they gained experience, communications therapists realized that families tend to resist so direct an approach. They began to use more indirect means of establishing control, largely through paradoxical interventions, and so morphed communications therapy into strategic therapy. But the general model was still a cerebral attempt to outwit families. Therapists were considered to be well motivated and rational; families were considered stuck and liable to resist. The result was an emotionally distanced stance and a treatment imposed on families for their own good.

The contemporary emphasis on collaborative relationships is a reaction against this kind of manipulative distance. Harry Goolishian and Harlene Anderson rejected the role of expert in favor of that of a concerned conversationalist, genuinely curious and as free as possible from preconceptions. Narrative therapists listen attentively to clients' stories, but soon begin an active interrogatory designed to open up alternative perspectives. Solution-focused therapists quickly steer conversations with clients toward exceptions to their problems. These postmodernists see themselves as forming more collaborative therapeutic relationships than their structural and strategic forebearers because they mainly ask questions. But while asking questions is undoubtedly an effective way to engage clients, there are questions and there are questions. When therapists listen only to impose a clearly defined narrative shape on what they hear, they are forcing their perspective, regardless of what they say. These days when it comes to being collaborative, most therapists talk the talk but don't always walk the walk.

Assessment

Systems of family therapy vary in their emphasis on assessment and in the methods they use to make assessments. Each school has a theory about families that determines where they look for problems and what they see. Some look at the whole family (Milan, structural, Bowenian); some look at individuals and dyads (psychoanalytic, experiential); some focus narrowly on sequences that maintain symptoms (strategic, behavioral); and some pay very little attention to what causes problems, preferring instead to mobilize people to work against them (solution-focused, narrative).

Behavior therapists place the greatest importance on assessment and use the most formal and standardized procedures. Assessment is separated from treatment and is usually the first order of business. The great advantage of the behavioral emphasis on assessment is that it provides clear baseline data, definite goals, and a reliable way to determine whether therapy succeeds. The disadvantage is that by using standardized interviews and questionnaires, behaviorists don't see the family in natural interaction. By looking only at part of the family (mother and child, or marital couple), they miss the total context; by structuring the assessment, they learn only what the family reports.

Strategic therapists also make careful assessments but in a more naturalistic fashion. They begin by inquiring about problems, then listen for how the problems are maintained by attempted solutions. The critical questions in this approach are: What is the problem? Who is involved? What are people doing that perpetuates their problems? These questions are answered by what the family reports; there's less emphasis on observing actual interactions than in the experiential or structural schools. On the other hand, strategic practitioners are quite sensitive to the interactions between themselves and families. They frequently give directives in the first session to discover whether families are compliant or resistant. This emphasis is consistent with the centrality of the patient–therapist relationship and with the limited utilization of in-session interactions among family members.

Structural therapists also emphasize assessment, but their evaluations are based on observation. Interactions among family members take place spontaneously and at the therapist's direction. Enactments give the therapist a chance to observe patterns of enmeshment and disengagement, principal components of a structural diagnosis. The positive aspects of this school's assessment procedure are that it utilizes the family's patterns of interaction among themselves, it includes the entire family, and it's organized in simple terms that point directly to desired changes. If discussion between parents is frequently interrupted by their children, the structural evaluation would be that the boundary around the marital subsystem is too diffuse. The goal of therapy in such a case would be to increase the parents' involvement with each other, while strengthening the boundary between them and the children. A potential disadvantage to structural assessment is that it may lose sight of individuals while focusing on their roles in the family. This doesn't necessarily happen, but it's an error made by many beginning family clinicians.

The Bowenian school also does an excellent job of considering the whole family in its assessment procedure. Unlike structuralists, however, Bowenians rely on what they're told, and they are interested in the past as well as the present. Their evaluations consist of extensive clinical interrogatories, guided by Bowenian theory. The theory says that symptoms are a function of anxiety-provoking stressors, the level of differentiation of family members, and the degree of emotional cutoff from support systems, especially the extended family.

An extended family systems assessment begins with a description and history of the presenting problem. Exact dates are noted and later checked for their relationship to events in the extended family life cycle. Next comes a history of the nuclear family, including information about when the parents met, what their courtship was like, their marriage, and childbearing. Particular attention is paid to where the family lived and when they moved, especially in relation to where members of their extended families live. The next part of the evaluation is devoted to the history of both spouses' births, sibling positions, significant facts about their childhood, and about the past and current functioning of their parents. All of this information is recorded on a genogram, covering at least three generations. This assessment provides a panoramic view of the whole family and its history; it also provides detailed information about the individuals in the family.

The psychoanalytic and experiential schools also pay a good deal of attention to individuals. Their assessments focus on individual family members and their dyadic relationships within the family. Evaluations in these two schools are unstructured and take place in the ongoing process of treatment. An exception to this rule is that some psychoanalytic clinicians (Nadelson, 1978) meet with each spouse separately before proceeding to evaluate the family together. As in other approaches, the data that psychoanalytic and experiential therapists examine aren't always the same as those that they're ultimately interested in. Behaviorists are interested in behavior, but they accept verbal reports; psychoanalysts are interested in latent ideas and experientialists are interested in latent feelings, but they both look carefully at behavior in the sessions for clues as to what's being withheld.

Although the form of evaluation is similar in psychoanalytic and experiential therapy, the content is quite different. These two schools occupy extreme ends on a continuum of the elaborateness of theory. Psychoanalytic theory is extensive and complex; experiential theory is limited and simple. The breadth of psychoanalytic theory enables practitioners to theorize well ahead of their data; a little information suggests a great deal. The advantage is that the theory organizes the data and provides valuable leads to uncovering hidden meanings. The danger is that the theory may distort the data, leading clinicians to see only what they expect to see. Experientialists have neither these advantages nor disadvantages. Their evaluations are guided by a simple theory about feelings and how they are suppressed; they tend not to uncover much that's hidden, but they also tend not to see things that aren't there.

Two of the newer schools, narrative and solution-focused, eschew any form of assessment. Solution-focused therapists believe that dwelling on problems and their causes undermines the kind of positive thinking they want to generate. They also believe that solutions aren't necessarily related to the ways problems come about, so they turn immediately to a search for solutions. Narrative therapists believe that looking within families for problems to correct perpetuates the therapist-as-expert stance they want to get away from. By personifying problems as external oppressors and talking about their effects rather than their causes, they circumvent the kind of finger-pointing that usually accompanies family discussions of how problems got started. The danger is that by disregarding how problems arise they may overlook real conflicts among family members. And conflict, as you may have noticed, doesn't necessarily go away because you ignore it.

Just as there are many ways to conduct therapy, there are many assessment procedures; what works in one system may not work in another. We believe, however, that there are two general principles of assessment that are valid for all family therapists. First, it's best not to rely on formal, structured evaluation procedures. The introduction of this much structure early in treatment produces an artificial atmosphere; instead of learning how a family behaves naturally, the clinician who makes a formal assessment learns what they say and how they interact with him or her. Moreover, once a therapist becomes a formal evaluator, it's difficult to move into a decentralized position and become an observer of family dynamics. Furthermore, once a family submits to the structure of a formal assessment, they may forever resist freely interacting in therapy.

Although it seems to contradict our first point, we also believe that most family practitioners pay too little attention to assessment. There's a tendency to treat all families the same, especially by therapists with powerful techniques but limited conceptual schemes. For example, paradoxical directives may be useful but aren't necessary with compliant, well-motivated families. "Speak for yourself" is a good suggestion for enmeshed families, but not necessarily for disengaged ones. Quid-pro-quo contracts may not be appropriate for couples with a complementary structure. Asking the Miracle Question before clients feel that their problems have been sufficiently heard and appreciated can turn treatment into "solution-forced therapy."

We all have war stories to tell. While it may be productive to turn our attention from complaining to finding solutions, from pessimism to optimism, some people may feel more patronized than empowered by aggressive attempts to recast their experience into sunnier narratives. Using pet techniques unguided by an assessment of the whole family may do some good, but without an evaluation of the family's structure such techniques are unlikely to change the basic configuration that creates and maintains family problems.

Once a therapist has assembled the family, joined with them, established a therapeutic stance, and assessed their structure and functioning, the stage is set for the powerful techniques that constitute the decisive interventions of family therapy.

Decisive Interventions

Members of every school of family therapy use a wide variety of techniques; some are dictated by the approach, others by the therapist's personality and experience. Even if we limit our attention to the techniques common to all members of each of the schools, the list would be long and confusing. Some techniques are used by virtually everyone who practices family therapy—

reflecting feelings, clarifying communication—and this common list has been growing as the different approaches have become more integrated. Each approach, however, relies on one or two techniques that are unique and decisive. In this section we will highlight and compare these definitive interventions.

In psychoanalytic family therapy there are two decisive techniques. The first of these, *interpretation,* is well known but not well understood. Properly used, interpretation refers to elucidating unconscious meaning. It doesn't include statements of opinion—"You need to express your feelings to each other before you can really be close"; advice—"As long as you continue writing to him the affair isn't over"; theory—"Some of the reasons you were attracted to him are based on unconscious needs"; or confrontations—"You said you didn't care, but you were really angry." Interpretations are statements about the unconscious meaning of certain behavior or utterances. "You've been talking about your son's unpleasant habit of arguing with you all the time. Based on what you've said previously, I think that some of this anger is deflected from your husband. He does the same thing, but you're afraid to tell him so, and that's why you get so mad at your son."

By refraining from asking questions, giving advice, or directing what people should talk about, the psychoanalytic practitioner maintains a consistent stance of listening and fostering understanding. By limiting interventions to interpretations, the therapist makes it clear that treatment is designed for learning; whether families take advantage of this atmosphere and change their behavior as a result of what they learn is up to them.

The second decisive technique in psychoanalytic family treatment is *silence.* The therapist's silence permits him or her to discover what's on the patient's mind and to test a family's resources; it also lends force to the eventual interpretations. When the therapist is silent, family members talk, following their own thoughts rather than responding to the therapist's. If they know that the therapist won't interrupt, they react and respond to each other. This produces a wealth of information that wouldn't otherwise emerge. If a father begins the first session by saying, "The problem is my depression," and the therapist asks, "How long have you been depressed?" he or she may not discover what thoughts are associated in the man's mind with his depression or how the man's wife responds to his complaint.

The therapist's silence prolongs the dialogue among family members. This enables the therapist to learn more about how they talk, and it forces family members to find constructive ways to resolve their own interactional impasses. With an active therapist, families get in the habit of waiting for suggestions when they get stuck; with a silent therapist, they struggle to get themselves unstuck. The therapist's silence also enhances the impact of his or her interventions. Words weigh more when they're punctuated by long silences. (Unfortunately, with chaotic and extremely emotional families, therapists can't always afford the luxury of silence, but must intervene actively to keep things under control.)

Family group therapists use a number of active and manipulative techniques, including giving advice and making suggestions. The essence of this approach, however, is encouraging free and open discussions so that family members can improve their ability to communicate and learn to solve their own problems. The decisive technique in this approach is *confrontation;* family group therapists confront quiet family members and prod them to open up; they confront domineering members and encourage them to be quiet and listen.

Confrontation is also a decisive technique in experiential therapy. In this school, confrontations are designed to provoke emotional reactions and are often aggressively blunt. It isn't unusual for experiential therapists to tell clients to shut up or to mock them for being insincere. Confrontations are often combined with *personal disclosure* from the therapist, the second primary technique of this school. Experientialists use themselves as spontaneous, emotionally expressive, freewheeling models. Finally, most experiential therapists make use of a number of *structured exercises.* These include role playing, psychodrama, sculpting, and family drawings. The rationale for these techniques is that they are a quick way to provoke emotional experiencing in the session; their obvious drawback is that, because they're artificial, the reactions they provoke may be divorced from ordinary family experience. Family members may get something off their chests in a structural exercise, but may not transfer this to their everyday interactions at home.

Most people associate reinforcement with behavior therapy, but reinforcement isn't a technique used in behavioral family therapy; *observation* and *teaching* are the major techniques in this approach. Behavioral family practitioners begin by observing very carefully the contingencies of reinforcement in the families they work with. Their aim is to discover the antecedents and consequences of problem behavior. Once they've completed a functional analysis of behavior, they become instructors, teaching families how they inadvertently reinforce undesirable behavior. As teachers their most useful lesson is how to use positive control. They teach parents that it's more effective to reward good behavior than to punish bad behavior; they teach married couples to substitute being nice to each other for their usual bickering.

Positive control—rewarding desirable behavior—is one of the most useful principles in family therapy. It's a valuable lesson for families, and for therapists. Therapists, like parents, tend to chide their charges for mistakes; unfortunately, if you're told that you're suppressing your feelings, spoiling your children, or using coercive control, you're apt to feel picked on and inadequate. Although it may be necessary to point out people's mistakes, it's more effective to concentrate on praising the positive aspects of their behavior. Among practicing family therapists this point seems best understood by structuralists, who speak of working with the family's strengths; by strategists and Milan therapists, who use reframing and positive connotation to support families' efforts to do the right thing; and of course by solution-focused and narrative therapists, who raised the power of positive thinking to an art form.

Bowen systems therapists are also teachers, but they follow a different curriculum. They teach people to be responsible for themselves and how by doing so they can transform their entire family system. Being responsible for yourself means getting clear about what you think and feel—not what your mother says or what you read in the *New York Times* but what you really believe—and then being true to your beliefs in your dealings with other people. You don't have to change others or even wish they were different; you do have to speak for yourself and maintain your own values. The power of this position is tremendous. If you can accept that you are you, and that other people are different and themselves, then you no longer have to approach relationships with the idea that either you or the other person has to change. This enables you to be in contact with people without becoming unduly upset or emotionally reactive.

In addition to teaching differentiation, Bowenian therapists have two corollary lessons: avoiding triangulation and reopening cut-off family relationships. Taken together these three lessons enable one person to transform the whole network of his or her family system. If your spouse nags, if your kids are disobedient, if your mother never comes to visit, *you* can create a change. Other schools of therapy exert leverage for change by including the entire family in treatment sessions; Bowenians teach individuals to be themselves, to make contact with others, and to resolve conflicts with the people they are in conflict with. This gives a person a leverage for change that is portable and lasting.

Communications family clinicians contributed so much to the theoretical base of family therapy that it's difficult to separate out their techniques or to single out their principal interventions. Perhaps their greatest achievement was to point out that communication is multilayered and that often the most important things being said are said covertly. Therapy was designed to make the covert overt. Initially this was done by pointing out hidden messages; when this direct approach met with resistance, therapists began using directives to make the rules of family functioning explicit and to provoke changes in the rules.

Strategic therapy is an offshoot of communications theory, and the techniques used by strategists are refinements of those used by communicationists. Principal among these are *reframing, directives,* and *positive connotation.* Strategic practitioners begin by getting detailed descriptions of problems and attempts to solve them. In the process, they pay particular attention to the family's language and expectations. They try to grasp the family's point of view and acknowledge it—which is positive connotation; then they use reframing to shift the family's point of view and directives to interrupt their problem-maintaining behavior. Using this outline, members of this school plan a general method; but they tailor their intervention to fit each case.

In most cases the single most powerful intervention is probably the use of a directive. These directives are designed to break up rigid homeostatic patterns, they are assigned to be carried out when the family is at home, and they are often paradoxical. Although strategic therapists emphasize fitting the treatment to the patient, they generally assume that indirect interventions are necessary to outwit resistance. This is sometimes but not always true. It's not so much that some families are resistant and others aren't, but that resistance isn't a property *in* families; it's a quality of interaction between therapist and family. A therapist who proceeds on the assumption that families are unable and unwilling to follow advice is likely to encounter the expected resistance.

Structural family therapy is also a therapy of action, but in this approach the action occurs in the session. The decisive techniques in this system are *enactments* and *boundary making.* Rigid boundaries are softened when the therapist gets people to talk with each other and blocks attempts to detour or interrupt them. Diffuse boundaries are strengthened when the therapist works to realign boundaries in the whole family. Blocking a parent's intrusion into the children's functioning won't last unless that parent is helped to get more involved with the spouse.

Several promising techniques emerged in the 1980s around which whole models of therapy were built. Steve de Shazer and his colleagues expanded the technique of *focusing on successful solutions* to problems that family members had already tried but abandoned. The result was solution-focused therapy. Michael White did the same with the technique of *externalizing* problems—personifying problems and attributing oppressive intentions to them, which is a powerful device for getting family members to work together against a common enemy.

Actually, externalization is a concept, not a technique. The decisive technique of narrative therapy is a persistent and forceful series of *questions*—questions that begin by acknowledging and trying to understand the client's experience of suffering, but then switch from understanding to prodding them to think about their problems as malevolent agents. Narrative therapists also use a relentless series of questions to challenge negative images and convince clients that they have reason to be proud of themselves and that their fates are in their own hands.

In reaction to the techniquism and schoolism that reached a peak in the early 1980s, family therapists today borrow freely from other approaches and deemphasize technique in favor of a less hierarchical and more respectful quality of therapist–family relationship. Both trends are healthy, but we would like to leave this section with two questions. When is cross-fertilization enriching, and when does eclecticism rob separate approaches of their muscle by watering down their distinctive elements? And how best can family therapists get away from a mechanical and distanced emphasis on technique without losing leverage altogether by practicing a more congenial but less effective form of treatment?

Context and Applicability of the Schools of Family Therapy

The predominant influence of social context, emphasized in family therapy, also applies to family therapists themselves and to the systems of treatment they develop. The pioneers of family therapy worked in diverse settings and with different patient populations. They didn't set out to invent family therapy. They were working on other problems—analyzing communication, exploring the etiology of schizophrenia, treating delinquent children—and family therapy emerged as part of the solution. But, as we have seen, "family therapy" isn't one approach, it's many. The variations in setting, population, and intent of the developers combined to influence the nature of the various family therapies, and also help to determine the type of patients for which each method is best suited. In this section we will briefly examine the context from which the different sects of family treatment emerged and then consider which approaches may be best for which problems.

The contextual roots of psychoanalytic family therapy are less easy to locate than those of other systems. Ackerman was certainly the originator of this approach, but his death in 1971 left this school without a leader. Since then contributing influences have come from many different quarters. Until recently most of the major figures in this school, including Ackerman himself, were psychoanalytically trained clinicians who abandoned psychoanalysis for family therapy; their analytic training was reflected in their theoretical papers, but not in their clinical methods. These early psychoanalytic family practitioners worked in a variety of settings—child guidance, social welfare, and marriage and family clinics—but for the most part, the families they worked with were members of the middle class and had mild to moderate problems.

Today more and more psychoanalytically trained clinicians are practicing family therapy using methods consistent with their training (Nadelson, 1978; Nichols, 1987). These practitioners tend to work in the same settings and with similar patients as do individual psychoanalytic therapists, namely medical school outpatient clinics and private practices, with verbal, intelligent, middle-class patients who aren't seriously disturbed. Psychoanalytic treatment, individual or family, is a method of self-discovery that relies heavily on words; and it works best with verbal patients motivated to learn about themselves. The more educated and sophisticated, the more readily they accept this approach.

The specific methods of family group therapy were developed by John E. Bell, but the general model of group therapy was used by most practitioners who treated families before family systems models were available. For this reason it isn't possible to describe a specific context in which this approach was developed. On the contrary, since this approach was developed for treating groups of strangers, it's probably more applicable to such groups than to families.

Carl Whitaker, the most prominent experiential family therapist, worked with delinquents and schizophrenics early in his career; later he shifted toward less seriously disturbed patients. This transition, from more to less serious psychopathology, tends to come with experience as a psychotherapist. Poverty and problems go together. The most seriously troubled people are usually treated by young clinicians in public clinics.

The concepts and methods of experiential psychotherapy were developed in the human potential movement to treat people with problems of everyday life. The cathartic techniques of this approach may not be as useful for people struggling with serious psychopathology or chaotic living conditions; but for those for whom life has become something more to be endured than enjoyed these techniques may help to release them from anxiety and apathy and open the possibility of human happiness.

Behavioral couples therapy was developed in university departments of psychology and applied primarily to members of the academic community. These couples tend to be young educated professionals, whose relationships are symmetrical and whose problems aren't severe. They're usually well motivated and accustomed to an educational format. Behavioral parent training was also developed in academic training centers, but it has been applied to seriously disturbed children in institutions as well as to mildly disturbed children in university clinics. The concrete symptomatic focus of this treatment makes it a popular approach for dealing with severely symptomatic children. For this reason, behavior therapy is often used as an adjunct to other forms of treatment for hospitalized children (Minuchin, Rosman, & Baker, 1978). In hospital settings, behavior treatment is usually applied by staff rather than by parents.

Murray Bowen developed his ideas about therapy while studying schizophrenic families. This may account for two of the main emphases in his work: differentiation of self and working with extended families. In psychotic families there's often a blurring of boundaries, or what Bowen called the undifferentiated family ego mass. These families exhibit an intense clinging interdependence in which individual identities are diffused in amorphous togetherness. Bowen concluded that this lack of differentiation, or fusion, is the underlying source of pathology in all families. His goal was to help family members differentiate themselves, which in turn would have a beneficial effect on the entire system. The process of differentiation began with the therapist, who remained emotionally neutral to avoid being drawn into the emotional quicksand of these undifferentiated families. Bowen wasn't unsympathetic, but he held himself aloof to avoid being engulfed by the chaotic emotions of psychotic families.

Bowen was more successful at understanding schizophrenic families than he was at treating them. He eventually gave up the idea that family therapy was effective with these difficult families (though Michael Kerr, who followed Bowen as director of the Georgetown Family Center, believes that family therapy is useful to reduce anxiety in *any* family), and most of his later work was with middle-class professional families.

Bowenian therapy may be most useful for young couples who haven't yet successfully separated from their original families, including not only those who are obviously still dependent on their parents, but also those whose apparent independence is based on reactive distance. While Bowenian therapy may be ideally suited for middle-class couples in their twenties and thirties, its applicability is certainly not limited to this group. Bowen had an exquisite appreciation of triangular processes, and his therapeutic concepts are useful in any situation where two people form a coalition against a third.

Communications therapists were scientists first, healers second. Their original intent was to study communication in schizophrenic families; only later did they decide to treat these unhappy people. At first they saw patients as victims and tried to protect them from relatives who scapegoated them. Later they realized that there are no victims or victimizers in families. Under stress, the whole faltered, parts malfunctioned and became conspicuous. But the real problem was the disharmonious system.

The feature of family life that captured the attention of communication therapists was the strange and puzzling ways in which families with schizophrenic members communicate. Conversation in these families is permeated with paradoxes, disqualifications, and double binds. It's a tribute to their optimism that they thought schizophrenia might be cured by bringing together patients with their families and somehow talking them out of their strange and destructive patterns of communication. When they found that the direct approach didn't work, they developed an indirect one. In place of interpretation they began to use manipulation. When communications therapists became strategists, they took up an emotionally distanced position, conducting therapy like generals outside the fray.

Jackson and Haley were the pivotal figures in the transition from communications theory to strategic therapy. Haley took the core concept of communications theory—that messages cannot be taken at face value because they are always qualified by other messages on different levels—and derived the notion that all communication is part of a struggle for power in relationships. This position reflected both Haley's personality and the context within which he was working. Haley is an intellectual and an outsider; some of his sharpest contributions have been critiques—of psychoanalysis, the human potential movement, and experiential family therapy. His therapy is about power and control—how to wrest power in order to gain control of families through ingenious manipulation. Psychiatric symptoms are seen as perversions of the normal struggle for control. Instead of openly fighting for control, families of psychiatric patients deny that there is any conflict. They don't refuse to participate; they "can't" because they're "sick." Strategic therapy forces patients into a corner from which they can escape only by giving up their symptoms. Haley's concept of ordeal therapy, derived from Milton Erickson, illustrates this way of thinking.

Emotional distance, struggle for power, manipulation—none of this sounds very nice. To understand *how* these positions were developed it's necessary to consider *where* they were developed. Communications therapists worked with acute schizophrenics whose families, they thought, were capable of driving people crazy with baffling responses and maddening double binds. Perhaps conducting therapy from a distance seemed to be the only way to avoid getting entangled in such families. Perhaps if therapists don't struggle for power, they will be defeated by these families; and if they don't use manipulation, they will be manipulated. Today's strategic therapists still work with seriously disturbed cases, many of whom have tried and failed with other straightforward approaches. But today's therapists are rarely as combative as in the past and are likely to be genuinely sympathetic to the problems of living with a seriously disturbed member.

Structural family therapy was first developed with families of delinquents from the inner city. These families were poor and often disorganized. Some were enmeshed—chaotic and tightly interconnected; others were disengaged—isolated and seemingly unrelated. Both types lacked clear hierarchical structures. Creating functional structures by differentiating subsystems and realigning their boundaries became the object of structural family therapy.

Another characteristic of the inner-city families Minuchin worked with at Wiltwyck is that they were outside the mainstream of American culture and felt alienated from middle-class helping professionals. To work with these families it was first necessary to get their attention, then to gain their confidence. This set of circumstances may help to account for Minuchin's active, directive style and for his emphasis on joining.

Structural family therapy's focus on the whole family is different from some of the other approaches that tend to work with subsets of the family. Strategic and Bowenian practitioners, for instance, move quickly to the adults, even when the presenting problem is about a child. Minuchin, however, was trained as a child psychiatrist, and he's always believed that it's important to include children in treatment.

Many of the leading narrative and solution-focused therapists turn out to be refugees from strategic therapy. They were attracted to the ideology but, eventually, repelled by the calculated shrewdness. In Erickson, Haley, and Selvini Palazzoli they found tactics that were clever, but cold. And so they turned away from what they felt to be an impersonal and manipulative approach. But in rejecting the mechanism of their own strategic model, they turned their backs on systems theory altogether. They may have put their money on the wrong horse.

The protest against paternalism, emphasis on collaboration, and interest in looking beyond the family are all useful correctives. But, in rejecting systems theory because they didn't like one version of it, narrative and solution-focused therapists may have thrown the baby out with the bath water.

Understanding the contexts in which the various systems of family therapy were developed makes it easier to see why they took the forms they did. However, it doesn't tell us which therapy to use with which problem. Unfortunately, there's no proof that any one system is more effective than another, nor do we know which is best with any particular problem.

There are, however, a growing number of researchers beginning to contribute hard evidence to long-standing debates, which in the past were thought to be primarily matters of opinion and personal choice. In increasing number and sophistication, research studies, some of which relate to specific models, others that deal with meta-analyses, are beginning to shed light on crucial questions about which approaches work best with specific problems and under what circumstances. To become a mature and fully respected discipline, family therapy must be able to authenticate its efforts with solid, scientific research. To become mature and fully informed clinicians, family therapists must have some knowledge and appreciation of this burgeoning empirical literature. For a comprehensive summary of the research picture in family therapy, refer to Chapter 15.

In the final analysis, however, the best treatment is given by the best therapist. If the best therapist in town is a structural family therapist, the best therapy in town is structural. If the best therapist happens to be Bowenian, the best therapy is Bowen family systems therapy.

Selection of a Theoretical Position: Rational and Irrational Factors

How do students go about selecting a therapeutic orientation? Or more to the point, how should they? Deliberate choice probably exerts less influence than the personality and values of the student, as well as what's emphasized in the training milieu. Having selected and been selected by a graduate program, students are usually pressured to conform to the models offered by their teachers and supervisors. While the idea of conformity may not be appealing, it's probably a good idea to embrace the model offered by your teachers. Learning whatever you can from every teacher or supervisor doesn't destroy your independence any more than oppositionalism protects it.

Except in the most homogeneous settings, students are liable to be exposed to a variety of different approaches during their graduate education; their interests are based on a series of fluid identifications with faculty members. While this may be confusing, it helps inoculate beginning clinicians against dogmatic thinking. Moreover, it provides the necessary breadth of information on which to later base an informed choice of a specialty. Once you leave academic course work to begin practical training, it's too late to shop around. During your clinical training, you should concentrate on learning one method well, becoming thoroughly immersed in it. It may seem more creative to pick and choose elements from a variety of systems in a personal integration, but this is better postponed until after you've mastered one single approach.

Selecting a system of family therapy to specialize in isn't simply a question of determining which one is best. For one thing, we still don't know which is the best form of treatment for any particular person.[7] The choice depends on what's available, what suits your clientele—and what suits you. The tactics of therapy are never wholly separate from the qualities of the person applying them. Therefore, it's wise to choose an approach that's congruent with your personal style.

Far too many people discontinue their training before they've mastered their craft. Training is expensive. Job offers beckon. Nobody wants to be a student forever. Because most people discontinue their training before they become expert, the field is filled with many so-called family therapists who are equipped with minimal understanding of systems theory and a rudimentary knowledge of techniques.[8]

After training (whether it's pursued diligently or gotten through in a hurry), there's a transition from student to full-fledged therapist. This can be a very gratifying time. Free from the watchful eyes of supervisors, therapists become more spontaneous and fluid. Instead of being anxious about following a model or pleasing a supervisor, the clinician is free to get more involved with families and to incorporate some of his or her natural style along with techniques that by now have become almost second nature. After you've gained experience in applying your model of therapy to the treatment of families, you're liable to start experiencing the limitations of the model or of your skill as a therapist, or both. Many people then take refresher courses or look for workshops in new treatment approaches. Although we do believe strongly in mastering one particular model of therapy, we don't think it matters whether an experienced practitioner returns for a brushup in the original model or seeks out fresh ideas. Experienced practitioners will be able to—will have to—integrate whatever they learn with their personal styles.

However, being able to integrate a variety of family therapy models with your own personality works for only those people who have a thorough background of training and supervision in some form of family therapy. Therapists who substitute periodic attendance at workshops and conferences for a protracted period of indoctrination and training in one particular school of therapy tend not to be competent family therapists. A series of workshops can stimulate and enhance the skills of experienced practitioners, but it cannot substitute for the necessary apprenticeship.

[7]Several reports have been published in *The Journal of Marital and Family Therapy*, by Hetherington in 1987, Kolevzon and Green in 1982, and Kolevzon and Sowers-Hoag and Hoffman in 1989, that deal with therapist selection of orientation.

[8]You can usually spot these novices by the way they learn one or two formulaic techniques and beat them into the ground.

Summary

The theme of the first edition of this book was the proliferation of competing schools, each portrayed as unique and uniquely effective. That was how family therapy entered the 1980s. Now, as family therapy moves toward the twenty-first century, the theme is integration. So many dedicated family therapists have been working for so long that the field has accumulated a significant number of useful ways of looking at and treating families. Today, it no longer makes sense to study one and only one model and to neglect the insights of the others. Family therapists are not only cross-fertilizing across models of family therapy, they are also adding concepts and methods from psychology and individual psychotherapy.

When the field was young we often got by on enthusiasm and promise. But that may not work in maturity. Now when we promise a therapy that works, we're expected to deliver. An important aspect of this will be empirical research demonstrating what we claim to accomplish—and justifying its cost effectiveness to the managed care industry. If family problems cause psychological problems, we should be able to demonstrate it; and, perhaps more important, if we say we can resolve problems with family therapy, we'll probably have to prove it.

Underlying each approach is a view of human nature. Differences among schools in their view of what it means to be human account for many of the differences in concepts and methods that we have discussed. If people are power-game players, therapists will devise indirect strategies to outwit them. If the feelings and behavior of people depend primarily on the web of relationships (or family structure) in which they're embedded, therapists will use their influence on these relationships to restructure families. If people are undifferentiated because of irrational emotionality, therapists will use their own rationality and knowledge of how systems work to teach people how to differentiate. If people contain untapped inner resources, therapists will collaborate with them to bring out those strengths. We're pleased to see this last way of thinking gaining ground.

In the past, each of the rival systems of family therapy proclaimed its unique way of understanding and treating families. However, as we've seen, the differences are more sharply drawn in theory than in practice. The success of new developments in one school often leads to their adoption by others, shrinking the gaps among the various therapeutic orientations. The trend toward convergence was the story of family therapy in the 1990s. In what follows we will offer some very subjective comments about picking and choosing some of the more useful concepts and methods that have proven themselves classics of family therapy.

Theories of family functioning have both a scientific and a practical purpose. The most useful theories treat families as systems; have concepts to describe forces for stability and change; consider the past but concentrate on the present; treat communication as multileveled and complex; recognize the process underlying the content of family discussions; recognize the triadic nature of human relationships; remember to consider the context of the nuclear family, rather than viewing it as a closed system isolated from its environment; and recognize the critical function of boundaries in protecting the cohesiveness of individuals, subgroups, and families.

Clinicians are more concerned with pathology and change than with normality, but it's useful to have a conception of normal family functioning, both to mold treatment goals and to distinguish what is pathological and needs changing from what is normal and doesn't. Some of the most useful concepts of normal family functioning are: Minuchin's structural model of families as open systems in transformation; the communications theory model of direct, specific, and honest communication in a family system with rules clear enough to ensure stability and flexible enough to allow change; the behavioral model of equitable exchange of interpersonal costs and benefits, the use of positive control instead of coercion, and mutual and reciprocal reinforcement between spouses; the family group theory, which points out that groups function best when they are cohesive, when there is a free flow of communication, and when members' roles are clearly defined and appropriate to their needs; the strategic model of systemic flexibility, which allows adjustment to changing circumstances and the ability to find new solutions when old ones don't work; and the Bowenian model, which explains how differentiation of self enables people to be independent at times, intimate at others.

Most family therapy concepts of behavior disorder focus on systems and interactions, but Schwartz's parts model and the psychoanalytic, Bowenian, narrative, and experiential models add psychological depth to the interactional view, bridging the gap between private, inner experience and public, outward behavior. The fact that many divorced people repeat the mistakes of their first marriages supports these schools' position that some of what goes on in families is a product of individual character. Some of the most valuable concepts of personality dysfunction in families are: Bowen's concept of fusion; the experiential concepts of repressed affect and fear of taking risks; and psychoanalytic concepts of developmental arrest, internal object relations, instinctual conflict, and hunger for appreciation. These concepts of individual psychopathology are useful adjuncts, but the guiding ideas in the field explain behavior disorder in terms of systems theory. The most influential of these are about inflexible systems, too rigid to accommodate to individual strivings or to adjust to changes in circumstances; symptomatic family members promoting cohesion by stabilizing the nuclear and extended families; inadequate hierarchical structure; families too tightly or too loosely structured; and pathological triangles.

The broad goals of family therapy are to solve presenting problems and to reorganize families. Behaviorists, strategists, and solution-focused therapists concentrate on the former; Bowenians and psychoanalysts concentrate on the latter; most of the other schools aim for both. As we've seen, some practitioners expect therapy to be prolonged, others keep it brief. These differences reflect differences of opinion about how much change families need to accomplish. In our opinion, that question should be left to the family. Therapists should accept the family's goal to solve their immediate problems and should design therapy to reorganize only that aspect of the family that isn't working. If families want more, they should say so.

Some of the goals of family therapy are practically universal—clarifying communication, solving problems, promoting individual autonomy—and some are unique. Some of the schools take presenting problems at face value, while others treat them as metaphors and signs. In either case, goals shouldn't be so broad as to neglect symptom resolution, nor too narrow to ensure the stability of symptom resolution. Incidentally, values are seldom discussed in the family therapy literature, the notable exception being Boszormenyi-Nagy. There has been too little consideration of practicing therapists' ethical responsibilities, including the possibility of conflicting responsibilities to individuals, families, and the larger community.

If narrative therapists have tended to ignore family dynamics and conflict in order to emphasize the ills of the culture, perhaps this will turn out to be one of those swings of the pendulum that inevitably corrects itself. There's surely no need to neglect systems theory in order to introduce an ethical dimension to working with people in context.

Some of the major differences among family therapists about how behavior is changed are focused on the following issues: action or insight; change in the session or change at home; duration of treatment; resistance; family–therapist relationship; paradox; and the extent to which it's important to work with the whole family system, part of it, or just motivated individuals. Even though there has been general consensus about some issues—for example, once most family therapists believed that action is primary and insight is useful but secondary—there have always been divergent opinions on every one of these points. Strategic therapists, for example, flatly denied that insight is necessary or useful.

We have looked at some of the major methodological issues and tried to separate out the decisive techniques of the different systems. As is always the case when a number of variables are involved in a final result, it's not easy to know to what degree each variable contributes to that result or how important each one is. Furthermore, the more we talk about techniques, the greater the danger of seeing family therapy as a purely technological enterprise. Studying families is like solving a riddle; the art of treating them is to relieve suffering and anguish. The job of the theoretician is to decode or decipher, which requires theory and ingenuity. The job of the therapist is healing, which requires theory but also conviction, perseverance, and caring. Treating families isn't only a matter of theory and technique; it's also an act of love.

References

Bowen, M. 1966. The use of family theory in clinical practice. *Comprehensive Psychiatry, 7*:345–374.

Dunlap, K. A. 1928. A revision of the fundamental law of habit formation. *Science, 67*:360–362.

Frankl, V. 1960. Paradoxical intention: A logotherapeutic technique. *American Journal of Psychotherapy, 14*:520–535.

Freedman, J., and Combs, G. 1996. *Narrative therapy: The social construction of preferred realities.* New York: Norton.

Goldner, V. 1985. Feminism and family therapy. *Family Process. 24*:31–47.

Gordon, S. B., and Davidson, N. 1981. Behavioral parent training. In *Handbook of family therapy.* A. S. Gurman & D. P. Kniskern, eds. New York: Brunner/Mazel.

Haley, J. 1963. *Strategies of psychotherapy.* New York: Grune & Stratton.

Haley, J. 1976. *Problem-solving therapy.* San Francisco: Jossey-Bass.

Haley, J. 1977. Toward a theory of pathological systems. In *The interactional view,* P. Watzlawick and J. Weakland, eds. New York: Norton.

Haley, J. 1980. *Leaving home: The therapy of disturbed young people.* New York: McGraw-Hill.

Hare-Mustin, R. T. 1978. A feminist approach to family therapy. *Family Process. 17*:181–194.

Hoffman, L. 198l. *The foundations of family therapy.* New York: Basic Books.

Imber-Black, E. 1988. *Families and larger systems: A family therapist's guide through the labyrinth.* New York: Guilford Press.

Jackson, D. D. 1965. Family rules: The marital quid pro quo. *Archives of General Psychiatry. 12*:589–594.

Jasnow, A. 1978. The psychotherapist—artist and/or scientist? *Psychotherapy: Theory, Research and Practice. 15*:318–322.

Kagan, R., and Schlosberg, S. 1989. *Families in perpetual chaos.* New York: Norton.

Kendrick, D. D. 1960. The theory of "conditioned inhibition" as an explanation of negative practice effects: An experimental analysis. In *Behavior therapy and the neuroses,* H. J. Eysenck, ed. New York: Pergamon.

Madanes, C. 1980. Protection, paradox and pretending. *Family Process. 19*:73–85.

Madigan, S., and Epston, D. 1995. From "spy-chiatric gaze" to communities of concern: From professional monologue to dialogue. In *The reflecting team in action,* S. Friedman, ed. New York: Guilford Press.

Mahler, M. S., Pine, F., and Bergman, A. 1975. *The psychological birth of the human infant.* New York: Basic Books.

Maturana, H., and Varela, F. 1980. *Autopoesis and cognition: The realization of living.* Boston: D. Reidel.

Minuchin, S. 1974. *Families and family therapy.* Cambridge, MA: Harvard University Press.

Minuchin, S., and Fishman, H. C. 1981. *Family therapy techniques.* Cambridge, MA: Harvard University Press.

Minuchin, S., and Nichols, M. P. 1993. *Family healing: Tales of hope and renewal from family therapy.* New York: The Free Press.

Minuchin, S., Rosman, B., and Baker, L. 1978. *Psychosomatic families: Anorexia nervosa in context.* Cambridge, MA: Harvard University Press.

Nadelson, C. C. 1978. Marital therapy from a psychoanalytic perspective. In *Marriage and marital therapy,* T. J. Paolino and B. S. McCrady, eds. New York: Brunner/Mazel.

Nichols, M. P. 1987. *The self in the system.* New York: Brunner/Mazel.

Nichols, M. P. 1993. The therapist as authority figure. *Family Process. 32*:163–165.

Paul, W. L. 1967. The use of empathy in the resolution of grief. *Perspectives in Biology Medicine. 11*: 153–169.

Pierce, R., Nichols, M. P., and DuBrin, J. 1983. *Emotional expression in psychotherapy.* New York: Gardner Press.

Rabkin, R. 1977. *Strategic psychotherapy.* New York: Basic Books.

Selvini Palazzoli, M., Boscolo, L., Cecchin, G., and Prata, G. 1978. *Paradox and counterparadox.* New York: Jason Aronson.

Stanton, M. D., Todd, T. C., and Associates. 1981. *The family therapy of drug addiction.* New York: Guilford Press.

Thibaut, J. W., and Kelley, H. H. 1959. *The social psychology of groups.* New York: Wiley.

Vogel, E. F., and Bell, N. W. 1960. The emotionally disturbed child as the family scapegoat. In *The family,* N. W. Bell & E. F. Vogel, eds. Glencoe, IL: Free Press.

Whitaker, C. A., and Keith, D. V. 1981. Symbolic-experiential family therapy. In *Handbook of family therapy,* A. S. Gurman and D. P. Kniskern, eds. New York: Brunner/Mazel.

White, M. 1995. *Re-authoring lives: Interviews and essays.* Adelaide, Western Australia: Dulwich Centre Publications.

White, M., and Epston, D. 1990. *Narrative means to therapeutic ends.* New York: Norton.

15

Family Therapy Research: Science into Practice, Practice into Science

Myrna L. Friedlander, Ph.D.[1]

University at Albany, State University of New York

A couple sought your help six months after the birth of their first child. Having been separated for three months, the "Alexanders" wanted to get back together for the sake of their son. Both felt scared and vulnerable. Five months later, at the end of therapy, they were once again living together as a family. Husband and wife were, however, still hurt and wary of one another.

Eight years later you run into the Alexanders at a youth league soccer game. There are now three children in tow, and the couple is thrilled to see you again. They spontaneously and enthusiastically praise the work you did together and express much gratitude. You watch the oldest child running spiritedly up and down the soccer field. He was an infant when the Alexanders first came to your office. In awe, you gaze at the two little ones, happy babes in arms. This chance encounter has made your day!

Most experienced therapists can tell stories like this one, and the feeling of accomplishment

[1]The assistance of Meredith Lyon and Teresa Tuason in locating and reviewing material for this chapter is gratefully acknowledged.

from these successes goes a long way toward keeping us engaged in learning, doing, teaching, and supervising psychotherapy. But, more often than not, we have little information about the long-term effects of our work. We may try for months to help a man and woman stop hurting one another. Slowly they start to get along better and even learn to cherish one another. Then at some point they follow their own path without us. What happens to them months or years later we may never know.

If we could look back and scrutinize our treatment of every successful and unsuccessful family, we might be able to tease out the most important ingredients. More than likely, however, we would be unable to do so. Indeed, when the Alexanders' therapy ended, it wasn't an unqualified success. It was only with the passage of time that its benefits became apparent.

As therapists, we need another way to be certain that we're on the right track. When making recommendations to families and planning treatment strategies, we need to embark on a course of action with reasonable assurance that it can be successful. Doing so requires a knowledge base, and here is where research comes into play.

In this chapter, two general questions are addressed: "How effective is couples[2] and family therapy?" and "What makes family therapy effective?" As you review the research findings,[3] bear in mind that what we don't know about the practice of family therapy can be as informative as what we do know.

[2]By and large, the term *couples therapy* is used in this chapter rather than *marital therapy* so as not to exclude unmarried heterosexual couples and gay and lesbian couples. When *marital therapy* is used, it is because the research under discussion included primarily married or engaged couples. Clearly treatment outcome and prevention research is needed to generalize the findings to other couples.

[3]The research reviewed in this chapter is representative, but not exhaustive, of the family therapy literature.

How Effective Is Family Therapy?

It should not be surprising that, compared with the voluminous literature on individual psychotherapy, the available research on couples and family therapy is sparse. After all, family systems theories emerged some 60 years after the earliest psychoanalytic literature was published.

When the empirical study of conjoint treatment began in the 1970s and 1980s, individual therapy researchers were scrambling to demonstrate the relative effectiveness of different theoretical approaches. The impetus for this horse race approach was twofold. First, the rapid development and increased availability of psychotropic medications made it urgent for psychotherapists to demonstrate the efficacy of their costlier treatments. Second, researchers were eager to respond to the British behaviorist Hans Eysenck (1952), who challenged the assumption that undergoing psychotherapy is better than not doing so. By 1980, researchers claimed substantial evidence that individual therapy is indeed effective for roughly 75 percent of those who seek help (Smith & Glass, 1977).

Being the new kids on the block, family therapy researchers felt a need to demonstrate that family systems approaches were at least as effective as traditional, individual approaches. At present, direct and indirect consumers of all mental health services are primarily concerned with issues of client satisfaction and cost containment (Newman & Tejeda, 1996). For these reasons, the majority of family therapy studies reflect the medical model, addressing the linear questions "Does family therapy work?" and "How effective is family therapy for various disorders?"

In the first subsection below, literature on the general efficacy of conjoint therapy is summarized. The second and third subsections review research on the effectiveness of family therapy for adults and children with various emotional and behavioral problems. In the fourth subsection, the systemically informed studies are reviewed—research on interpersonal difficulties and the prevention of family problems. Finally, implications of the outcome research are presented, including suggestions for future studies.

Overall Efficacy of Family Therapy

In a review of the outcome literature through mid-1996, Pinsof, Wynne, and Hambright (1996; Pinsof & Wynne, 1995) concluded that (1) sufficient data exist supporting the efficacy of family therapy, and (2) there is no evidence indicating that families are harmed when they undergo conjoint treatment. In other words, family therapy treatment groups fare, on average, significantly better than no-treatment controls.

A meta-analysis of 163 randomized clinical trials (Shadish, Ragsdale, Glaser, & Montgomery, 1995) indicated that the effect size for couples and family therapy is comparable to those of other psychotherapy modalities. (A meta-analysis is a statistical analysis of a group of studies in which each investigation is considered to be one subject. In a meta-analysis, the *effect size* refers to the standard difference between treatment and comparison groups.) For the seventy-one studies in which family therapy was compared with a no-treatment control group, Shadish and associates (1995) found an effect size substantially greater than those reported in pharmaceutical, medical, and surgical studies. For the twenty-three studies in which family therapy was compared with individual therapy, the meta-analytic results showed no substantial differences, but there were several studies in which individual child therapy was superior, particularly for children with conduct problems (Shadish et al., 1995). With respect to marital therapy, Dunn and Schwebel's (1995) meta-analysis indicated that three approaches were significantly and substantially superior to no treatment. These included behavior therapy, cognitive-behavioral therapy, and insight-oriented therapy (a category that includes emotionally focused therapy).

At this point, you might well question the need to continue to show that family therapy "works." Indeed, a number of reviewers have reached the same conclusion (e.g., Pinsof et al., 1996), and studies are beginning to accumulate in which one form of conjoint therapy is tested against another. At present, however, there are few comparative family therapy studies. The evidence to date suggests that, like the comparative studies of individual therapy, no one approach is better than the others (Shadish et al., 1995), particularly if we only consider well-designed investigations (Pinsof et al., 1996). On the other hand, because of methodological limitations, it's unwise to assume that different family therapy approaches *don't* have different success rates (Pinsof et al., 1996). To the contrary, it's quite likely that different approaches "work" for different reasons, with different kinds of families, and for different individual or family problems.

These considerations were taken into account by the authors of the studies reviewed next. When you consider the following outcome data, you should be aware that, for the most part, the conjoint treatments *weren't* the family systems approaches described in this text. Many were psychoeducational (i.e., emphasizing information and support), and many were but one component in a larger treatment package including medication and individual and group sessions. Combination treatments are used in residential settings because serious disorders like schizophrenia, substance abuse, anorexia, and autism tend to require a multimodal approach (Pinsof et al., 1996).

Family Therapy for Adult Disorders

Serious Mental Disorders. Many of the early systems theorists became interested in family therapy when they discovered that the seemingly erratic behavior of disturbed young adults had meaning in the context of family interactions. Excited by the possibility of finding a noninvasive treatment for psychosis, these pioneers (Murray Bowen, Lyman Wynne, and Jay Haley, among others) conducted the first family-based research on serious mental illness.

At present, there is strong outcome evidence for treating adults with bipolar depression (Clarkin et al., 1990) and schizophrenic disorders (Goldstein & Miklowitz, 1995) in a psychoeducational family context that includes training in coping skills, reducing blame, improving communication, and crisis intervention. Indeed, it's widely believed that family psychoeducation is more effective than individual therapy for people with psychotic symptoms (e.g., Falloon, Boyd, & McGull, 1982; Falloon et al., 1985; Randolph et al., 1984). Well-designed outcome studies (Falloon et al., 1982, 1985; Leff, Kuipers, Berkowitz, Eberlein-Fries, & Sturgeon, 1982) suggest that structured family programs can reduce the potential for relapse, are more effective than maintenance on antipsychotic medication alone, even for patients from high-risk families (Goldstein & Miklowitz, 1995), and are more cost-effective than standard inpatient care (Pinsof & Wynne, 1995). Leff and colleagues (1982), for example, developed a social intervention program that includes education about schizophrenia, a relatives' support group, and in-home family sessions. Falloon and coworkers' (1985) behavioral family management program includes education, communication skills, and problem-solving training.

Having demonstrated the efficacy of psychoeducation for schizophrenia, researchers began to test the relative importance of various components in multimodal treatment models. Taken together, the literature suggests that the combined effectiveness of family intervention and medication depends on the type of intervention, the setting, and the standard level of care provided in that setting (Goldstein & Miklowitz, 1995). Unfortunately, the data don't provide clear-cut answers about the effective ingredients in the family programs. Linszen (1993), for example, found that family treatment didn't improve on a well-designed educational program for the individual patient, and Keith and associates (1989) found no advantages of active family intervention over a family support program.

The research in this area is impressive. The studies are methodologically sound and programmatic. Not only have they significantly improved the standard of care for seriously disturbed young adults, but they have also contributed to moving the psychiatric community away from blaming the family for the patient's illness.

Depression and Anxiety. Inasmuch as many people suffering from depression relapse within one year, researchers have increasingly become interested in the familial context of depression (Prince & Jacobson, 1995). Results from a substantial number of studies indicate that (1) family relationships play a major role in the onset and maintenance of affective disturbance and (2) the effectiveness of family therapy for depressive disorders depends on severity and the contribution of marital problems.

Whereas people with bipolar disorders respond well to family psychoeducation, these programs tend to be less effective than individual treatment for those with unipolar depression (Clarkin et al., 1990). There are, however, no data indicating whether this difference reflects differences in the disorders, in the individuals diagnosed with the disorders, or in the families' motivation to learn about the disorder. It may well be that many family members view mania as an illness requiring medical care but consider depression to be a personality problem or a moral failure.

In a recent review of literature, Prince and Jacobson (1995) concluded that family interventions for hospitalized adults with major depression have not been shown to be effective, and inpatient family therapy without follow-up can be risky. Not surprisingly, it's difficult to maintain a relational focus when one spouse is actively suicidal (O'Leary, Sandeen, & Beach, 1987). On the other hand, psychoeducation and support seem to have definite benefits when combined with individual treatment. There are, however, no data on the effectiveness of family therapy for depressed inpatients who are specifically experiencing major marital or family problems (Prince & Jacobson, 1995).

For depressed outpatients, there's little research on family therapy (Prince & Jacobson, 1995), but a number of studies have shown that couples treatment is effective for those who perceive their depression to be linked to marital problems (Foley, Rounsaville, Weissman, Sholomaskas, & Chevron, 1989; O'Leary, Risso, & Beach, 1990). Indeed, when problems in the marital relationship are not addressed, treatment may be detrimental (Prince & Jacobson, 1995). On the other hand, marital therapy tends not to be effective for depressed individuals in happy marriages (Jacobson, Fruzzetti, Dobson, Whisman, & Hops, 1993). For some couples, brief treatments don't eliminate either the depression or the marital distress. Longstanding depression related to early trauma or neglect can be maintained in an intimate relationship when the couple's interactions mirror the original trauma. Overcoming such difficulties requires more time in therapy than can reasonably be tested empirically.

Despite the fact that anxiety is the most frequently reported mental health problem in the United States, no research was located on family therapy for adults with generalized anxiety or panic disorder. There is, however, evidence suggesting that individuals with agoraphobia who are also experiencing marital distress are most successful when their spouses are involved in treatment. In a series of studies, Barlow and colleagues (e.g., Barlow, O'Brien, & Last, 1984; Cerny, Barlow, Craske, & Himadi, 1987) demonstrated that spouse-involved, behavioral group treatment for clients with agoraphobia was more effective than non–spouse-involved treatment, and the gains were maintained at 1- and 2-year follow-ups. This positive result wasn't obtained, however, by another group of researchers (Cobb, Mathews, Childs-Clarke, & Blowers, 1984). It may be that when the agoraphobia functions to stabilize the marital relationship, the removal of symptoms is too threatening.

Alcoholism and Substance Abuse. The treatment of alcoholism is one of the best researched areas of family therapy for adult disorders. The major questions include: Does partner involvement motivate alcoholics to stop drinking? Does it enhance treatment effectiveness and/or prevent relapse? What variables, if any, predict family therapy's effectiveness for alcohol-related problems? (Edwards & Steinglass, 1995).

The available research suggests that the most important role for family members is in the initial stage of recovery from alcoholism (Edwards & Steinglass, 1995). Various studies indicate that spouses' willingness to confront their partners (e.g., Liepman, Silvia, & Nirenberg, 1989) and to educate themselves about drinking and its consequences (e.g., Sisson & Azrin, 1986) can be powerful motivating influences, not only to encourage alcoholics to seek treatment but also to begin altering their drinking patterns prior to starting therapy.

On the other hand, the research on marital and family involvement in the treatment itself is less impressive (Edwards & Steinglass, 1995). Family treatments include systemic as well as behavioral approaches. Whereas several studies have demonstrated the superiority of family therapy over individual therapy for achieving sobriety in the short run (e.g., Corder, Corder, & Laidlaw, 1972), other studies show no differences (e.g., Longabaugh, Beattie, Noel, Stout, & Malloy, 1993) with respect to abstinence or marital functioning (Edwards & Steinglass, 1995). Furthermore, the amount of partner involvement varies considerably across investigations, with no indication that greater involvement is more effective (e.g., McCrady, Noel, & Abrams, 1986).

More troubling are the studies suggesting that over time family treatment loses its edge. Indeed, the gains of *all* treatment approaches, not only family treatments, diminish in the years following treatment (Edwards & Steinglass, 1995). While spouse involvement in after-care programs enhances treatment attendance, there is no evidence that therapeutic gains last longer than two years, and there is limited research on the efficacy of the most popular after-care program, Al-Anon (Edwards & Steinglass, 1995).

There are numerous flaws in these studies. Methodological problems include wide variability in the kinds of programs studied, a lack of accurate, long-term follow-up data, and the absence of family assessments (Edwards & Steinglass, 1995). Another problem is the uniformity assumption, that is, that all alcoholics are similar. Research on variables that moderate treatment effectiveness suggest that (1) behavioral couples therapy (BCT) with a relapse prevention component is superior to BCT alone (O'Farrell, Choquette, Cutter, Brown, & McCourt, 1993), (2) couples treatment tends to be less successful for women alcoholics (Wiens & Menustik, 1983) and for people who are very unhappy in their marriages, and (3) alcohol treatment is more effective when family members are also committed to abstinence (Edwards & Steinglass, 1995).

Compared with the substantial body of research on alcoholism, the research on adult drug abuse is sparse and limited in a number of ways. Also in contrast to the alcoholism literature, the substance abuse literature doesn't consistently support the use of family interventions to motivate adults to seek treatment (Liddle & Dakof, 1995). While many studies suggest that family involvement is more effective than drug-counseling-as-usual (e.g., Stanton, 1995), others indicate that family therapy approaches aren't superior to the traditional, individual approaches (Liddle & Dakof, 1995). Some promising research suggests that a combination of pharmacological and psychotherapeutic approaches is most effective (Liddle & Dakof, 1995). Due to a lack of adequate follow-up data, however, the long-term influence of family-based treatments for adult substance abuse remains unknown (Liddle & Dakof, 1995).

A recent, well-designed study of couples treatment for drug abuse (Fals-Stewart, Birchler, & O'Farrell, 1996) yielded some impressive results. Eighty cohabiting or married men, most of whom were referred by the courts for drug offenses, were randomly assigned to either a standard individual and group treatment program or a combination of the standard program with BCT. Results supported the relative effectiveness of the combined program for relationship enhancement at four follow-up points in a twelve-month period. While the individual outcomes (reduced drug use, fewer drug-related hospitalizations and arrests) did not differ significantly during treatment, they did so at post treatment. Over time, however, the differences in drug use in the two groups were not maintained. The authors speculated that BCT reduces the potential for relapse in the months immediately following treatment if the men continue to use the interpersonal skills they learned in the couples sessions.

Drug and alcohol abuse are two of the most intractable problems of our day, and the toll they take on family members is enormous. Despite this, some substance abuse professionals who adhere strictly to a disease model of addiction exclude family members from treatment, and some family systems therapists who reject the disease model refuse to acknowledge the individual's contributions to addiction. Fortunately, in recent years the debate has become less polarized, and experts in each camp have begun to appreciate the efforts of one another. By providing empirical evidence about the interactive influence of individual and family variables, researchers can promote a less political, more productive alliancc of substance abuse professionals and mental health providers.

Medical Problems. Family treatments for cardiovascular and neurological problems (Campbell & Patterson, 1995) are the most consistently studied areas of adult medical problems. Interest in researching interventions for these and other health problems from a systemic perspective arose from evidence indicating that (1) family interaction patterns influence the health status of people of all ages, (2) acute and chronic health problems have a powerful impact on spouses and other family members, and (3) spouse and family support and involvement can enhance medical compliance and prolong life (Campbell & Patterson, 1995). Data on the effectiveness of family therapy in this area are not impressive, however. In a 1995 review, Campbell and Patterson found no controlled trials of family systems therapy for the chronic illnesses of adults. Rather, the treatments have been psychoeducation and family support.

With respect to hypertension, cardiovascular disease, and rehabilitation, studies have demonstrated a link between the patient's physical status and the spouse's level of stress, anxiety, depression, and marital satisfaction (Campbell & Patterson, 1995). Consistent support has been found for the importance of family involvement in treating hypertension. Morisky and associates (1983), for example, found that counseling the spouse during home visits not only improved patient compliance and blood pressure levels but actually increased survival rates.

The focus of research on neurological impairments (dementia and stroke) has been the mental health concerns of family caretakers. Results of several studies suggest that psychoeducational interventions are more effective than either family support groups or respite care, which are nonetheless appreciated by family members (Campbell & Patterson, 1995). Evans, Matlock, Bishop, Stranahan, and Pederson (1988), for example, found that psychoeducational counseling influenced family members' interactions more so than providing them with support and information about the illness. Unfortunately, the intervention studies, like those in the area of cardiac rehabilitation, tend to be designed for only one family member, and they don't reflect a systems perspective on family functioning (Campbell & Patterson, 1995).

Risk reduction has also been the focus of several promising investigations. In a large prevention study, for example, family counseling improved the dietary habits of men with high cholesterol levels (Knutsen & Knutsen, 1991). Two other health problems, obesity and smoking, have been studied from a family perspective.

With respect to obesity, there have been a number of controlled studies of cognitive-behavioral couples therapy. Unfortunately, like the studies of alcoholism and drug abuse, the gains at post-treatment often diminish over time (Black, Gleser, & Kooyers, 1990). Not surprisingly, marital satisfaction and family cohesiveness contribute to a positive outcome (Campbell & Patterson, 1995). One curious finding is that the outcome of treatment tends to be more favorable when wives support their husbands' weight loss efforts than the reverse (Campbell & Patterson, 1995). Overall, results indicate that initial weight loss is greater when the spouse is involved in therapy (Campbell & Patterson, 1995) but refrains from actively participating in the weight loss effort itself (Pearce, LeBow, & Orchard, 1981). This is, of course, not an easy role to play, especially when the spouse's previous efforts to help have been rebuffed.

By and large, smoking cessation programs have been less successful than the weight loss programs, despite the fact that smoking is clearly influenced by the attitudes and behavior of family members (Campbell & Patterson, 1995). Spouse-involved treatment programs have been tested many times, with results showing no systematic benefits (Campbell & Patterson, 1995).

While these programs don't seem to enhance spouse support, the data suggest that (1) people with supportive partners tend to be more successful, and (2) it is more important for the partner to avoid giving criticism than to provide active encouragement (Campbell & Patterson, 1995).

Finally, despite the fact that sex therapists commonly use a couples context, there are few controlled outcome studies on conjoint treatment for sexual dysfunction, and most of the research on individual behavior therapy is uncontrolled (Hogan, 1978). This is not to say that sex therapists discount the importance of the couple's relationship in the onset, maintenance, and resolution of sexual problems. Couples treatment routinely involves encouraging partners to communicate their most intimate desires. Such openness leads, in turn, to the increases in trust and closeness that are necessary for sexual experimentation (Kaplan, 1974).

In one recent investigation, women with inhibited sexual desire were offered emotionally focused couples therapy (EFT; MacPhee, Johnson, & van der Veer, 1995). Although the participants in the study did not report marital distress as a concern, results showed that the more successful women were relatively more satisfied with their marriages prior to therapy. Possibly for this reason there were only modest gains for the treatment group. Compared with wait-list controls, women who received EFT reported less depression and greater sexual desire post-treatment, but there were no differences in sex frequency.

An overview of the research in this area suggests that family intervention is most successful when there is a clear and present medical threat. Unfortunately, with few exceptions, only behavioral approaches that focus explicitly on the medical or physical problem have been subjected to empirical tests. Problems like smoking and obesity occur within a familial context that maintains them, and experienced therapists often find that clients voluntarily reduce their health risks when their interpersonal difficulties are alleviated.

Family Therapy for Children's Disorders

Most adults who seek help do so voluntarily, but children tend to be referred for psychological services by others who find their behavior problematic. Thus, it's not surprising that, relative to the literature on childhood depression and anxiety, there are far more studies on children's behavior problems. The following subsections summarize the outcome research on family interventions for conduct and behavior problems, emotional problems, physical problems, eating disorders, and substance abuse.

Behavior Problems. Parent management training (PMT) is the predominant treatment approach for children's behavioral problems. It typically involves teaching parents—through modeling, role playing, and home practice—to use behavioral management principles with their children. PMT has an impressive amount of data supporting its effectiveness for children under age fourteen years with oppositional and conduct disorders, and results from a few studies show that PMT may be more effective than conventional family therapy for changing the problem behaviors of antisocial children (Estrada & Pinsof, 1995).

Overall, PMT has shown positive results in reducing targeted behavior problems at home and at school in post-treatment and follow-up assessments (Forehand & Long, 1988), up to fourteen years later (Estrada & Pinsof, 1995). Furthermore, controlled studies have demonstrated PMT's potential for reducing family conflict, increasing cohesiveness and expressiveness (e.g., Sayger, Horne, & Glaser, 1993), changing parents' behaviors, and alleviating distress (e.g., Peed, Roberts, & Forehand, 1977; Sayger et al., 1993). PMT isn't successful, however, for a substantial number of families. Not surprisingly, children whose parents are highly stressed or depressed tend to fare poorly (Webster-Stratton, 1990). The drop-out rate tends to be high, especially among disadvantaged and isolated families (Miller & Prinz, 1990), and the treatment gains for those who complete the program successfully aren't always maintained in the long term (Estrada & Pinsof, 1995).

Adjunctive treatments have also been tested. Research suggests that interventions focusing on marital communication can increase the effectiveness of PMT for dysfunctional families (Dadds, Schwartz, & Sanders, 1987). Treatments for the child—training in problem solving, for example—also tend to be effective in combination with PMT (e.g., Kazdin, Esveldt-Dawson, French, & Unis, 1987), and gains tend to be maintained long term (Estrada & Pinsof, 1995).

Whereas PMT has been the treatment of choice for the behavior problems of young children, several family therapy models have been used with adolescents and pre-adolescents. Three approaches have been assessed for their efficacy in treating adolescent conduct disorders and delinquency: social learning (e.g., Patterson, 1982), structural family therapy (Alexander & Parsons, 1982), and multitarget ecological treatments (Chamberlain & Reid, 1991). The success of the family interventions has been clearly documented (e.g., Kazdin, 1987), with outcomes like behavioral improvement (Szapocznik et al., 1989) and decreased rates of incarceration (Bank, Marlow, Reid, Patterson, & Weinrott, 1991) and hospitalization (Chamberlain & Reid, 1991). Like the PMT programs for young children with conduct disorders, the family interventions are less effective for adolescents with multiple symptoms from disadvantaged, highly stressed families, and efficacy rates are best for children under 12.5 years of age (Chamberlain & Rosicky, 1995). It is unfortunate that the neediest families seem to be the most difficult to reach. For children who have never experienced a stable, thriving environment, the lure of the streets may simply be too powerful when they reach adolescence.

Another common childhood disorder, attention deficit hyperactivity disorder (ADHD), has been studied extensively. In a recent review, Estrada and Pinsof (1995) concluded that PMT can improve family relationships and reduce parental stress. PMT tends to affect the aggressiveness and other behavior problems of children with ADHD, but not the defining features of the disorder—distractibility, impulsivity, and excessive activity. Results that compare PMT with other treatments, either alone or in combination, aren't conclusive (Estrada & Pinsof, 1995). Some studies have supported the use of stimulant medication in combination with PMT (Horn et al., 1991), while others have not (Ialongo et al., 1993). Among the more promising studies, Barkley, Guevremont, Anastopoulos, and Fletcher (1992) found no differences between PMT, family systems therapy, and training in parent–child problem solving, and Satterfield, Satterfield, and Cantwell (1981) reported improvements over three years for a combination of multimodal family therapy and stimulant medication. It may be that medication helps children attend to the therapy enough to benefit from it, and parents are more willing to modify their own attitudes and behavior once they see their children's behavior start to improve.

Finally, only one developmental disorder, autism, has been widely studied from a systems perspective (Estrada & Pinsof, 1995). Programs typically involve intensive treatment for the child and a component to teach parents educational and therapeutic techniques based on principles of social learning and operant conditioning. Lovaas (1987), for example, trained parents in a home-based apprenticeship program, and subsequent researchers have replicated and extended this model program (e.g., Birnbrauer & Leach, 1993).

In all of these family training programs, the treatment models empower the parents, who become part of the therapeutic team. Such empowerment seems to be an effective ingredient of these programs, possibly because it reverses the demoralization and helplessness parents feel when they are faced with serious problems in their children.

Emotional Problems. Until the early 1980s, many theorists doubted that children could experience significant emotional problems. To date there has been far less research on the treatment of childhood anxiety and depression relative to other disorders, despite the present consensus that these are major mental health problems for many children and adolescents (Estrada & Pinsof, 1995). Most children referred for depression or anxiety tend to be offered individual psychotherapy or cognitive-behavioral therapy, the same approaches most commonly taken with depressed and anxious adults. This is a curious state of affairs since it is widely believed that family problems are the most salient contributors to children's emotional difficulties.

Recognizing the need to treat children with internalizing disorders (anxiety, phobias, and depression) in a family context, researchers have recently begun to develop and test new treatment models. At present, however, there's only limited evidence to support the family approaches for children with these problems (Estrada & Pinsof, 1995).

In several studies, parent training combined with individual cognitive therapy for the child has been shown to reduce simple phobias (Dadds, Heard, & Rapee, 1991), particularly school avoidance (e.g., Mansdorf & Lukens, 1987), but flawed designs in many of these studies suggest caution (Estrada & Pinsof, 1995). A recent, well-designed study of childhood anxiety (Barrett, Dadds, & Rapee, 1996) tested the efficacy of an extensive family management program combined with cognitive behavioral therapy for anxious children aged seven to fourteen. Family management empowers parents and children in a therapeutic partnership to (1) reward the child's courageous behavior and extinguish excessive complaining through contingency management, (2) help parents become aware of and handle their own anxious responses, and (3) teach parental communication and problem-solving skills. Results indicated substantial gains for the combined individual and family approach relative to the individual approach alone. The combined treatment was most effective for girls and younger children.

Currently, some exciting new work is taking place on family treatment for depressed adolescents at the University of Pennsylvania Medical School and Philadelphia Child Guidance Clinic. Diamond and Siqueland (1995) are gathering outcome data on a brief (ten to twelve sessions) family approach to adolescent depression based on theories of structural therapy, cybernetics, and attachment. Their model differs from the cognitive/behavioral treatments described earlier because it explicitly aims to enhance the emotional connection between parent and teen. If successful, this program has the potential to change the way we do family therapy with teenagers. Too frequently therapists think of adolescents struggling against authority and overlook their very real needs for closeness and nurturance.

Physical Problems and Eating Disorders. Caring for children with chronic physical problems is difficult and emotionally draining for parents and siblings. Research suggests that the most resilient families are cohesive, use active methods for coping, communicate effectively, relate well with medical professionals, make use of social supports, and balance the needs of individuals by establishing boundaries and maintaining flexibility (Patterson, 1991).

Studies testing the effectiveness of family therapy for psychosomatic disorders such as superlabile diabetes and severe asthma (e.g., Liebman, Minuchin, & Baker, 1974) are promising, but the lack of control groups and standardized outcome measures is problematic (Campbell

& Patterson, 1995). Researchers have also tested the efficacy of psychoeducational programs that provide support and information and teach specific ways to cope with chronic medical conditions (e.g., Satin, LaGreca, Zigo, & Skyler, 1989) and physical disabilities. Results suggest that in-home programs are most beneficial for those families with fewer social, economic, and emotional resources (Campbell & Patterson, 1995). While these studies are limited methodologically, several programs have demonstrated positive results, not only for increasing medical compliance, but also for improving the child's physical status and sense of independence and the parents' ability to cope with the stress, frustration, and anxiety common to intensive caregiving (Campbell & Patterson, 1995).

The outcome literature on eating disorders isn't extensive. With respect to obesity, several studies suggest that parental involvement, when matched with the child's developmental level, is important (Campbell & Patterson, 1995). Although the findings aren't consistent, weight loss for preadolescents tends to be greater when their parents are involved in treatment (e.g., Brownell, Kelman, & Stunkard, 1983).

In contrast to cognitive-behavioral treatments of obesity that focus exclusively on the child's eating and weight reduction, family systems approaches, particularly structural therapy, are used to treat anorexia and bulimia. The early structural therapy studies of anorexia were uncontrolled but included a close examination of family interactions and long-term follow-ups (Minuchin, Rosman, & Baker, 1978). In general, for adolescents with anorexia of fewer than three years' duration, family therapy seems to be more effective than individual therapy, but this isn't the case for those with more chronic eating problems (Campbell & Patterson, 1995) or for families with a high level of expressed emotion (Russell et al., 1987). One well-designed, comparative study showed no differences between family and individual treatments for bulimia (Russell, Szmukler, Dare, & Eisler, 1987), but younger children with anorexia fared better with the structural family approach. It may be that older teens do worse in family therapy because parents have less power over their behavior or because their eating problems are more complex due to the emotional, cognitive, physical, and psychosocial changes that adolescents experience.

Substance Abuse. In the adult substance abuse literature, the majority of studies focus on alcoholism, with fewer investigations of drug abuse. The reverse is true for children and adolescents. Since the early 1980s, many studies have demonstrated the positive effects of family therapy for adolescents with drug problems (e.g., Szapocznik et al., 1989). Research suggests that structural approaches, in particular, are effective in engaging youth and their families in treatment (e.g., Liddle & Dakof, 1994; Szapocznik et al., 1988), reducing drug use (e.g., Alexander & Parsons, 1982; Liddle & Dakof, 1994) and associated problems (e.g., Azrin et al., 1994), and improving family functioning (Azrin et al., 1994; Liddle & Dakof, 1994). A particularly impressive program of controlled research conducted by Szapocznik and associates (e.g., 1986, 1988) with Hispanic families indicates that a structural approach can be effective even when only one family member is willing to come for treatment. Unfortunately, many of these studies had small, homogeneous samples, and few included outcomes like prosocial behavior and family functioning (Liddle & Dakof, 1995). While some research suggests positive results in these important areas, none has demonstrated the superiority of family interventions over individual therapy (Liddle & Dakof, 1995).

Family Therapy for Interpersonal Problems

Having read the foregoing review, you can see that family therapy, for the most part, tends to be an adjunct or alternative approach for treating individual problems or disorders. While most people who seek professional help view their problems in individual terms, many others construe their difficulties interpersonally. The literature reviewed in the following subsections concerns the effectiveness of family therapy for (1) relationship problems and (2) the prevention of marital and parent–child problems.

Relationship Problems

Reflecting the common belief that the health of the family system depends on the quality of the marital bond, many studies over the past fifteen years have tested the efficacy of marital therapy. While system-wide outcomes tend not to have been assessed, reviewers repeatedly conclude that (1) couples therapy effectively reduces conflict and increases marital satisfaction, at least in the short run (Bray & Jouriles, 1995) and (2) for marital problems, conjoint treatment is generally superior to individual treatment (Gurman & Kniskern, 1981). The latter point is particularly important since it suggests that, regardless of the therapist's own preference for individual or couples work, troubled relationships tend to do better when treated directly.

Although a recent meta-analysis (Dunn & Schwebel, 1995) found no substantial differences in effectiveness by theoretical approach, behavioral couples therapy has been studied most often in the United States as well as in other countries (Hahlweg & Markman, 1988). Systemic approaches have only recently been investigated, but there is a fair amount of evidence to support their effectiveness (Bray & Jouriles, 1995). Emotionally focused therapy (Johnson & Greenberg, 1985, 1988), in particular, has been the subject of several controlled investigations.

These data are important because they indicate that engaging in couples treatment is more likely to help a relationship than not doing so. Indeed, evidence suggests that couples who engage in therapy are less likely to separate or divorce (Bray & Jouriles, 1995). This conclusion can be misleading, however. While the average couple is likely to improve in couples therapy, the relationship may continue to be distressed (Bray & Jouriles, 1995; Shadish et al., 1995). Estimates of clinical significance suggest that only 50 percent of couples are satisfied with their marriages after therapy (Jacobson & Addis, 1993).

Given this state of affairs, researchers have begun to assess the factors that contribute to successful outcomes for couples. In general, results from several investigations suggest that those who do best in couples therapy are younger, more emotionally engaged with one another, and less distressed at the beginning of treatment; they exhibit less rigidity in their gender roles and greater flexibility in problem solving (Jacobson & Addis, 1993). The research evidence to date suggests that those who view the marriage as contributing to their depression may be helped by a couples approach but that couples therapy may not help individuals who are seriously depressed (Prince & Jacobson, 1995). With time, however, this conclusion may need to be modified. New and exciting couples treatments for major depression are currently being tested at the Ackerman Institute in New York (Papp, 1997).

These studies underscore a point that may be obvious to practicing family therapists: Not all marital distress is similar. Even when two couples score identically on a measure of marital adjustment, their life circumstances can be vastly different. These differences are only beginning to be taken into account by family therapy outcome researchers. In one well-designed study, for example, Walker, Johnson, Manion, and Cloutier (1996) tested the effectiveness of emotionally focused therapy for reducing the marital distress associated with caring for a child with a chronic illness. In contrast to simply providing parents with support and information about the illness itself, Walker and associates focused on relationship dynamics, particularly the emotions aroused by caretaking. Results clearly supported the efficacy of emotionally focused therapy over a no-treatment control group, both at post-test and at a five-month follow-up.

Many believe that conjoint treatment is unwise for violent couples because it implicitly blames the victim, but this point is controversial. Systemic authors maintain that violence is the outcome of emotionally destructive escalations in behavior and that a fundamental change in the couple's relationship can reverse the tide (Minuchin & Nichols, 1993). Many family therapists (e.g., Virginia Goldner and Gillian Walker at the Ackerman Institute) advise a cautious, responsible approach to the treatment of violence. Indeed, it is likely that many couples who are seen together for relationship difficulties have been physically aggressive at some point in their relationship. To date, there is little evidence about the risks or benefits of treating couples in mildly abusive relationships (Prince & Jacobson, 1995).

Data about family therapy for child abuse are also lacking. One uncontrolled case study was located in which parent training and family therapy were part of a comprehensive eight-month outpatient program for sexually abused boys (Friedrich, Luecke, Beilke, & Place, 1992). The primary treatment modality was group therapy. Pre- and post-therapy changes indicated significant improvements for the referred child as well as for maternal depression, sibling behavior problems, and family adaptability and cohesion. Mothers whose sons were most successful in the program were less depressed, offered more support to their children, and reported less family conflict prior to treatment.

In the studies reviewed above, the problems targeted by the treatment were defined interpersonally—marital conflict, for example. Although we assume that the family members also view the problem that way, this isn't necessarily the case. One mediating variable may be the individual's construction of the problem. Let's say that one spouse views the problems as relational but the other sees them entirely as the fault of the first. This therapy will be rough going.

Ideally, we would like to help family members before their views of the problem become polarized. The studies reviewed next deal with the prevention of relationship difficulties.

Prevention of Relationship Problems

Two areas of family functioning, marriage and parenting, have been targeted by prevention researchers. The marital programs have either focused on enrichment or on prevention of conflict and divorce. The parenting programs include parent effectiveness training and psychotherapy to improve parent–infant attachment.

With respect to marital enrichment, the findings are substantial. Meta-analyses have consistently shown that (1) these programs enhance relationships and (2) behavioral changes are observed when couples are taught new skills (e.g., Giblin, Sprenkle, & Sheehan, 1985). With respect to divorce prevention, the long-term evidence is limited, but some data suggest that these programs have important short-term outcomes such as enhanced communication skills (Bray & Jouriles, 1995).

One well-designed prevention program by Markman and colleagues (e.g., Markman & Hahlweg, 1993), PREP (Premarital Relationship Enhancement Program), combines behavioral therapy, communication skills training, and relationship enhancement. A 5-year assessment of PREP for engaged couples indicated the program's success in (1) preventing dissolution of relationships before marriage, (2) enhancing satisfaction and communication skills, and (3) reducing domestic violence (Markman, Renick, Floyd, Stanley, & Clements, 1993). It should be noted, however, that only 25 couples completed the program. Since many couples declined to participate, level of motivation may be an important moderating variable (Bray & Jouriles, 1995).

Over sixty studies have been published on the efficacy of Gordon's (1970) parent effectiveness training (PET), an eight-week prevention program that emphasizes active listening and other communication skills. A recent meta-analysis (Cedar & Levant, 1990) of the twenty-six better-designed studies in this group showed an effect size for PET that was larger than the alternative treatments to which it was compared but somewhat smaller than marital enrichment programs. In these studies, PET had a notable effect on parental attitudes, with lesser effects on parenting behavior and children's self-esteem, and virtually no effects on children's behavior. Whereas outcome wasn't related to the parent's marital status or age, post-hoc tests indicated that the more successful programs took place in suburban communities and targeted parental relationships with older children and with learning-disabled rather than delinquent children (Cedar & Levant, 1990).

Over the past 10 years, several theorists and researchers have been interested in influencing the early bonding process between infants and their parents. The assumption is that intervening in the child's primary relationship early in life can prevent long-term emotional disorders. Not surprisingly, many of those working in this area have a psychoanalytic perspective on human behavior. As described by Daniel Stern (1995) in his recent book, *The Motherhood Constellation,* these approaches aim to change harmful behaviors and attitudes toward the baby that are projections from the parents' own intrapsychic history (Cramer et al., 1990; Lieberman, Weston, & Pawl, 1991).

Outcome research on these interventions has only recently begun to be published. One particularly well done study (Lieberman et al., 1991) compared the treatment of anxiously attached mother–infant dyads with two control groups, a matched wait-list group of anxious dyads and a comparison group of securely attached dyads. Participants were Spanish-speaking families in the lower socioeconomic group of San Francisco. After a one-year combination of individual and conjoint sessions, results showed impressive gains for both infants and their mothers. At post-treatment the mothers' empathy scores and interaction levels with their children were significantly better than those of the anxious control group. More importantly, their scores on these variables were comparable to those of the secure group.

By and large, the prevention studies are heartening, particularly those that suggest long-term effects. The reality is, however, that many more people come for help once a problem has become intolerable than before it has surfaced. While we need to continue to study preventive efforts, we also need to identify ways to motivate families to seek our services before their lives become unmanageable.

Implications

Having read this section on outcome, you may be overwhelmed with the wealth of data on treating individuals within a couple or family context. The following conclusions can guide you in planning treatments for clients who present with the disorders or problems discussed above.

First, the better designed studies and reviews of family therapy literature suggest that (1) there are few outcome differences by theoretical approach, and (2) the efficacy of systemic, behavioral, emotionally focused, and insight-oriented family therapy is most clearly established for marital problems and adolescent delinquency and substance abuse. To a more limited extent, systemic family therapy has been shown to be effective for adult drug abuse (Liddle & Dakof, 1995) and children's anorexia and psychosomatic disorders (Campbell & Patterson, 1995). Second, psychoeducation and other kinds of family support programs have had notable success in motivating alcoholics to seek treatment (Edwards & Steinglass, 1995) and in helping adults with serious mental disorders (Goldstein & Miklowitz, 1995) and people of all ages who are coping with physical illnesses and disabilities (Campbell & Patterson, 1995). Third, behavior management programs that involve family members tend to be effective for adults with agoraphobia (Barlow et al., 1984) and children with oppositional and conduct disorders, simple phobias, anxiety disorders, and autism (Estrada & Pinsof, 1995). Fourth, communication-based approaches have the potential to improve parent–child relations (Cedar & Levant, 1990; Stern, 1995), prepare couples for marriage, enrich satisfactory relationships, and prevent separation and divorce (Bray & Jouriles, 1995). On the other hand, family therapy approaches have *not* been supported for unipolar depression (Prince & Jacobson, 1995), chronic eating disorders (Campbell & Patterson, 1995), or the core features of ADHD (Estrada & Pinsof, 1995). Finally, with respect to the maintenance of treatment gains, the empirical literature is most supportive of family education for schizophrenia and parent management training for children's behavior problems. There has been limited long-term success for programs that target major depression (Prince & Jacobson, 1995) and compulsive and addictive problems—alcoholism, substance abuse, overeating, and smoking (Campbell & Patterson, 1995).

Data on the cost effectiveness of successful programs for preventing divorce and reducing the need for residential treatment, incarceration, and hospitalization are impressive. Whereas this information is important for health-care managers and policymakers (Pinsof & Wynne, 1995), the most valuable outcome studies for the practicing therapist are those that identify factors influencing treatment effectiveness. After all, when you are deciding whether to recommend individual, couples, or family treatment, you need to consider a host of individual and relational variables. In general, the literature suggests that (1) couples therapy is more effective than individual therapy for relationship problems, particularly for depressed women (Prince & Jacobson, 1995); (2) for some disorders—conduct problems and eating disorders, in particular—younger children tend to do better in a family context than adolescents; and (3) family therapy tends to be less effective for families that are disorganized, socially isolated, and disadvantaged (Chamberlain & Rosticky, 1995). This last point is not true across the board, however. When family treatment is responsive to the cultural context of the problem, it can be quite effective for high-risk individuals and families (e.g., Santisteban et al., 1996; Szapocznik et al., 1988).

These conclusions can be misleading, however, for a number of reasons. Many outcome studies lack adequate sample sizes, control or comparison groups, validated instruments, or accurate long-term follow-up. Furthermore, because many of the family therapy programs have been tested only in combination with other treatments, their unique contributions are unknown (Pinsof & Wynne, 1995). More importantly, like the research methods and analyses, most of the treatments themselves are linear in design. When the therapist, the family, and the researcher construe the presenting problem as residing within one family member, the systemic treatment is handicapped from the outset (Shadish et al., 1995). For these reasons, family treatments may actually be effective for more difficulties than researchers can claim at present.

It's also clear from the foregoing review that outcome researchers have *not* studied some very important family problems—sexual problems, acculturation difficulties, in-law conflicts, child and spouse abuse, and posttraumatic stress, to name a few. Nor have most researchers paid adequate attention to variability that is attributable to family structure and dynamics, life stage, ethnic and cultural diversity, sexual orientation, and so forth. When a single man is seen in "family therapy" with his parents, for example, his experience is very different from that of the married man who is seen with his wife and children. Including both families in the same treatment group introduces error variance that can affect the study's validity.

Understanding how the experience of therapy differs for each family is an important concern. It is a concern that does not lend itself easily to scientific inquiry, however. Nonetheless, investigators have begun to identify some of the specific mechanisms—within and across different theoretical approaches—that characterize effective couples and family therapy. Relative to the outcome research, the family therapy process literature is sparse (Friedlander, Wildman, Heatherington, & Skowron, 1994). To date, fewer than 50 process studies have been published.

What Makes Family Therapy Effective?

Imagine, if you will, interviewing a white, Protestant couple in their mid fifties. "Sheila" and "Brian Henderson" are seeking therapy because of long-standing bitterness between them that has grown progressively worse since Brian was laid off from his job three years ago. Sheila, who holds an administrative position, is depressed about her marriage and her parents' deteriorating health. Brian complains about Sheila's work, which averages 60 to 70 hours per week. He himself has become increasingly inactive, spending most of his time hanging around the local firehouse with friends or drinking beer in front of the television. The Hendersons' only child, Jessica, died of a cocaine overdose five years ago at age eighteen.

In the first session you, the therapist, gathered a fair amount of information about this (fictitious) couple. You realize that you can conceptualize the work before you as either a treatment for marital problems or as therapy for Sheila's depression and/or Brian's alcohol abuse. You realize, further, that (1) the psychosocial stress on this couple is severe, and (2) the fact and manner of their daughter's death are likely to play a major role in their problems.

When you begin working with the Hendersons, you have some general treatment goals in mind. You want to help them increase their marital satisfaction and their emotional and physical intimacy, reduce Brian's dependence on alcohol, and alleviate Sheila's depression. In working toward these goals, you expect to explore with them the impact of Jessica's death and the stressors they are currently experiencing—employment problems and their parents' failing health.

You are familiar with the outcome research that's relevant for your work with the Hendersons. First, since Sheila sees her relationship with Brian as the major cause of her distress, marital therapy is likely to be effective for her depression (Prince & Jacobson, 1995). Second, since Brian has little to motivate him toward sobriety other than his relationship with Sheila, conjoint treatment is more likely to help him than individual therapy. Third, there's no reason to believe that one therapeutic approach is superior to any other for the kinds of problems of either spouse, or for couples in their stage of life, or for parents who have suffered the loss of a child.

Unfortunately, there is little in the outcome literature to help you choose a specific approach or plan interventions to achieve the goals you identified for the Hendersons. If you conclude that there's no scientific evidence to guide your work with this couple, you rely on your training, on your personal and professional experience, on the help of colleagues and supervisors, and on books about therapeutic technique.

You should, however, be aware that there is a small but growing body of empirical literature on the therapeutic process of family therapy, and conclusions from some of these studies can indeed inform your work with the Hendersons. The process of family treatment has been investigated using single case as well as group data and qualitative as well as quantitative methods. While some researchers have focused on identifying the techniques of theorists like Minuchin,

Bowen, Whitaker, and Selvini Palazzoli, others have sampled practitioners in actual clinic settings. While the earlier studies were largely descriptive, present-day researchers are attempting to identify specific mechanisms of change in family work.

In the studies reviewed in this section, the observations were either actual in-session behaviors or the participants' self-reported perceptions of those behaviors. Since arguably the fundamental aspect of any therapy is the relationship, the research on this topic is reviewed first, followed by a summary of the literature on effective interventions with couples and families.

The Therapeutic Relationship

In individual psychotherapy, the quality of the therapeutic relationship has been shown to be the most important contributor to treatment success (Orlinksy & Howard, 1986). While many studies of individual treatment have addressed the therapist's empathy for the client and the client's perception of mutual collaboration with the therapist, there are few comparable studies of family therapy. One reason for this state of affairs may be the general lack of attention paid to the relationship on the part of theorists. Rather than considering the quality of the emotional bond with the family, theorists tend to emphasize the strategic and systemic postures therapists take with the family, postures that range from joining (Minuchin, 1974), to expressing strict neutrality (Selvini Palazzoli, Boscolo, Cecchin, & Prata, 1978), to deliberately forming coalitions (Sluzki, 1975), to coaxing or tricking the family into changing (Haley, 1984).

When we pause to consider the therapeutic relationship in family therapy, we realize that we need to account for the therapist's relationship with each family member, with each subsystem, and with the family as a whole. This process can be quite complex from a clinical perspective, let alone a research perspective. Consider your work with the Hendersons. If you support Brian's complaint that Sheila isn't available, you risk alienating her. If you express empathy with the couple as grieving parents, you risk losing Brian because Sheila holds him responsible for Jessica's death.

While family therapy researchers haven't yet studied the relationship in all its complexity, there is some evidence to suggest that the therapist's warmth, support, and general responsiveness are necessary ingredients in effective family therapy. Shapiro (1974), for example, asked therapists to rate their emotional responses to the family as a whole after the initial evaluation. Families rated unfavorably by their therapists were less likely to engage in treatment after the evaluation period. In a more recent study (Heatherington & Friedlander, 1990c) family members rated the emotional bond with the therapist. Stronger bonds characterized sessions that clients perceived as relatively smoother and easier.

Most of the research on the therapeutic relationship deals less with the emotional aspect and more with the sense of collaboration between family and therapist. Results from several studies suggest that a perceived sense of engagement, cooperation, and collaboration increases over time in treatment (Kuehl, Newfield, & Joanning, 1990; Sigal, Rakoff, & Epstein, 1967) and predicts couples' evaluations of the depth or value of a session (Heatherington & Friedlander, 1990c), posttreatment marital satisfaction (Bourgeois, Sabourin, & Wright, 1990; Holtzworth-Munroe, Jacobson, DeKlyen, & Whisman, 1989), and therapist-rated outcome (Pinsof & Catherall, 1986).

The family's alliance with the therapist doesn't develop uniformly, however. Not surprisingly, the possibility of a split alliance is greater when working with families rather than with couples (Heatherington & Friedlander, 1990c). One study suggests that, among couples, a strong alliance with the therapist may be more important for husbands than for wives

(Bourgeois et al., 1990). While this is not true for all couples, in most cases it is the woman who seeks help for the marriage. In this situation, if the husband does not establish a strong sense of collaboration with the therapist early on, the likelihood of drop-out is increased.

But how, exactly, do therapists behave in order to establish a sense of collaboration? In a recent qualitative study, Sells, Smith, and Moon (1996) evaluated perceptions of treatment using an ethnographic research method. (In ethnographic research, an effort is made to fully understand the experiences of people in a single setting, and generalization to other settings is not a consideration.) Analyzing the transcripts of interviews with families and therapists at a university-based training clinic, the authors identified themes underlying the informants' descriptions of effective therapy. Supporting the theory that a strong alliance develops when therapist and client work collaboratively (e.g., Pinsof & Catherall, 1986), Sells and coworkers (1996) found that participants stressed the importance of clear goals, and dissatisfied family members reported a lack of direction from the therapist. Interestingly, whereas family members emphasized the importance of rapport and a warm, trusting relationship with an "informal" and "down-to-earth" therapist, the therapists emphasized the importance of interventions like "joining, unbalancing, and reframing" (Sells et al., 1996, p. 337). This inconsistency isn't surprising when you consider that family theorists have traditionally shown greater concern for the specific (technical) than for the nonspecific (relational) aspects of treatment.

To date, only one study has tested the relation between clients' perceptions of the therapeutic alliance and actual in-session behavior. Using the Family Relational Control Communication Coding System (FRCCCS; Friedlander & Heatherington, 1989; Heatherington & Friedlander, 1987), Heatherington and Friedlander (1990b) found that complementary interactions in which the family member was "one-up" (↑) and the therapist "one-down" (↓) predicted poorer client ratings of the alliance early in treatment. (One-up messages reflect attempts to gain control by, for example, interrupting, asking closed questions, instructing or ordering, disconfirming, and changing the topic, whereas one-down messages reflect relinquishing control by, for example, agreeing or complying.) While this result only approached statistical significance, it's understandable that clients would be less comfortable when the therapist is one-down. Indeed, FRCCCS results repeatedly show that the predominant relational pattern is therapist ↑ and client ↓ (Friedlander, Heatherington, & Wildman, 1991; Heatherington & Friedlander, 1990b; Raymond, Friedlander, Heatherington, Ellis, & Sargeant, 1993). Consistent with these findings, Stevenson (1993) reported, in a qualitative study of one of his own cases, that in the most successful sessions he was in a one-up position with the family and tended to align with either the symptom-bearer or a peripheral family member. Stevenson observed that aligning with the most powerful family member put him in a one-down position. Possibly this dynamic reinforced dysfunctional interactions in the family or was demoralizing for the other family members.

Taken together, this handful of studies suggests that the effective family therapist behaves like a nurturant, authoritative parent or grandparent, fostering a sense of "we're all in this together." While the importance of the therapeutic relationship has been fairly well established, little is known about how, exactly, a strong emotional bond and a sense of mutual collaboration develop in family therapy. Relatively more is known about what actually goes on in family sessions to bring about change. The observational studies of change processes in family therapy are summarized next.

The Process of Change

It is all well and good, you may think, to know that a caring, collaborative relationship with the Hendersons, individually and as a couple, will give them the foundation they need for change, but what *exactly* should take place in your sessions with them? The answer to this question can be approached from several directions. The first has to do with the kinds of interventions you should make. The second has to do with the kinds of changes you should observe over the course of treatment. The third is more complex. It has to do with how you should handle specific dilemmas that might arise in the course of therapy—overcoming resistance, for example. The available literature in each of these areas is summarized below.

Effective Interventions. One way to determine what interventions are most effective is to observe the work of leading family therapists. In a series of descriptive studies, Friedlander and colleagues (Friedlander, Ellis, Raymond, Siegel, & Milford, 1987; Friedlander et al., 1991; Friedlander & Highlen, 1984; Friedlander, Highlen, & Lassiter, 1985; Heatherington, Marrs, & Friedlander, 1995) conducted linguistic content analyses of videotaped sessions by some of the pioneers in family therapy: Nathan Ackerman, Don Jackson, Murray Bowen, Salvador Minuchin, Mara Selvini Palazzoli, and Carl Whitaker, among others. Similarities as well as differences were observed, not only among therapists but also within schools of thought. Although caution is advised because many of the sessions were conducted long ago, the results provide a perspective on the unique characteristics of each approach as well as on their commonalities.

Overall, these comparative studies suggest remarkable similarities across approaches. In the sessions conducted in the 1960s and 1970s (Friedlander & Highlen, 1984; Friedlander et al., 1985, 1987), therapists spoke more with problem children and their parents than with other family members, and they focused more on individuals and dyads, particularly the parental subsystem, than on triangles or the family as a whole. Interventions tended to be present-oriented and informative, with the therapists relying more on questioning and providing information and instructions than on clarifying, reflecting feelings, encouraging, or interpreting. One notable finding was that these expert therapists frequently used indirect interventions to make a point to one family member while addressing another (e.g., "Why doesn't your father want you to grow up?").

Differences among therapists clearly reflected their theoretical divergence. In the studies of the Hillcrest Family Film Series (Friedlander & Highlen, 1984; Friedlander et al., 1985), interviews of Nathan Ackerman, Murray Bowen, Don Jackson, and Carl Whitaker with the same family were compared and contrasted. Results showed, for example, that Bowen made more references to the past and to family-of-origin issues than did the other therapists. Nathan Ackerman's psychodynamic approach was reflected in his focus on individuals, and Carl Whitaker's experiential approach was reflected in his self-disclosures and frequent references to the here-and-now (Friedlander et al., 1985). These findings suggest that various family therapy approaches are not as dissimilar from one another as one might think from reading the theories. On the other hand, the approaches are not identical, and the differences among them are observable, quantifiable, and meaningful.

Interestingly, remarkable consistency has been observed in the kinds of interventions the same therapists make with different families. In a study of Carl Whitaker and Salvador Minuchin, each of whom saw six families, the greatest within-therapist variability was activity level (Friedlander et al., 1987). Other differences were the extent of (1) references to the here-and-now, (2) directness or indirectness, (3) information offered to the family, and (4) focus on the parental subsystem. The authors suggested that the variability was related to the therapist's judgment about how ready and open each family was to change. With a guarded family, the therapist might be more indirect, offer less information, and avoid highlighting immediate interactions or parent–child relations. The opposite pattern might be the case when working with a more open and motivated family.

In a more recent study (Friedlander et al., 1991), six interviews conducted in the 1980s were compared for differences in relational control patterns. The work of three expert Milan systemic therapists was constrasted with that of three leading structural therapists. While the predominant FRCCCS relational pattern in both groups was complementary (therapist ↑ / client ↓), the observed differences were consistent with theory. Compared with the structuralists, the systemic therapists used more neutral indirect messages. In their sessions there were more question-and-answer sequences, and family members spoke less frequently among themselves. The structuralists, on the other hand, used more overtly controlling and unbalancing messages, ordering, interrupting, and praising or supporting family members directly and indirectly.

Finally, in the most recent study, videotaped sessions of seven constructivist theorists were analyzed (Heatherington et al., 1995). In these sessions there was an abundance of therapist questioning, reflecting, and providing information, with relatively little evidence of systematic or direct attempts to change clients' constructions by challenging, confronting, or reframing. These therapists seemed to be most effective when they followed the client's description of the problem or its causes with a slightly altered construction of their own (Heatherington et al., 1995). When blame was evident, for example, the therapists tended to intervene by redirecting the conversation or reinterpreting the family member's construction of the problem.

Researchers have used other methods to identify effective interventions. One method involves contrasting the behaviors of more and less experienced family therapists. In one creative design, Pinsof (1979, 1986) compared the work of family therapy trainees and their supervisors by asking the supervisor to conduct the second half of the session after having observed the trainee for 20 minutes behind a one-way mirror. Results showed that the supervisors worked more interpersonally than the trainees, focusing more on family communication patterns and using a greater repertoire of techniques. In particular, the supervisors were more active, explicit, interpretive, supportive, and more focused on the here-and-now.

Another method for identifying effective interventions involves studying cases with successful outcomes. In an early process–outcome investigation, Postner, Guttman, Sigal, Epstein, and Rakoff (1971) found that therapists addressed fathers more often in the good outcome cases and mothers more often in the poor outcome cases. This result, which is consistent with recent findings (Bourgeois et al., 1990) about the importance of creating a strong therapeutic alliance with husbands in couples therapy, suggests that therapists often reinforce traditional sex role stereotypes.

In a more recent study, Shields, Sprenkle, and Constantine (1991) reported that structuring by the therapist during family disagreements discriminated "completer" from "non-completer" cases in a "structural-strategic" treatment for children's problems. Contrary to the authors' predictions, no differences were observed in the extent of therapist joining or solution focusing in the two groups. In a more detailed, qualitative case study of solution-focused techniques (Gale & Newfield, 1992) therapist Bill O'Hanlon used a high degree of control and structure along with humor to shortcircuit blame and move the couple toward change. Excerpts from the transcript show that O'Hanlon doggedly pursued his own agenda, refusing to permit any problem-focused talk on the part of the couple. It would be interesting to study the couple's private reactions to strategies of this kind.

With respect to family members' behavior, two studies have been conducted of emotion-focused therapy (Greenberg, Ford, Alden, & Johnson, 1993; Johnson & Greenberg, 1988) for couples. In the first study, Johnson and Greenberg (1988) investigated the best sessions, as rated by the therapists, in better and worse outcome cases. Results supported the authors' hypothesis that "softening" characterizes successful cases of EFT. Softening occurs when a domineering, blaming spouse shows vulnerability and asks for closeness or comfort from the other spouse, who—until that point—had been distant. In the more recent study of EFT (Greenberg et al., 1993), the value of "intimate self-disclosure" was demonstrated in sessions rated positively by both the couple and the therapist. In "peak" sessions (rated by the clients) Greenberg and colleagues observed deeper emotional experiencing and more "disclosing, expressing, approaching, and enjoying" (1993, p. 83).

In most of the studies reviewed above, observations were made at only one point in treatment, and in many cases the sessions were demonstration interviews rather than ongoing therapy cases. Because differences in the process are likely to be observed as therapy progresses, a number of family therapy researchers charted changes over time. These studies are reviewed below.

Change Over Time. Two case studies (Laird & Vande Kemp, 1987; Raymond et al., 1993) have been conducted of expert structural therapists (Salvador Minuchin and John Sargent, respectively) working with successfully treated anorexic families at the Philadelphia Child Guidance Clinic, and several group studies have been conducted in other clinical settings. Therapist and client behavior has been observed, as well as their sequential interactions.

First, several investigations suggest ways in which family members' behaviors change over time. Chamberlain, Patterson, Reid, Kavanagh, and Forgatch (1984) reported that the highest levels of client resistance tend to occur in the middle phase of behavioral treatment and that high resistance predicts premature termination. With respect to emotion, Postner and associates (1971) found that family members tend to demonstrate more emotional involvement with each other and to disclose more "emergency emotions" (fear, anger, anxiety, sadness, and dependence) over time, with the greatest change in emotional expression occurring between the second and sixth sessions. Likewise, Greenberg and colleagues (1993) found that, in successful EFT, couples tend to be more supportive, affirming, and understanding and less hostile and controlling in later sessions. On the other hand, in a case study of family therapy (Raymond et al., 1993), greater conflict (defined as an exchange of ↑ messages) was observed between the parents over the course of treatment, but there was less conflict between each parent and the problem child as therapy progressed.

Other researchers have focused on cognitive change in therapy. In a study of couples seen in a group by Murray Bowen, Winer (1971) observed a greater proportion of "I" statements made by each spouse over time, possibly reflecting increases in differentiation of self. In a larger study of successful and unsuccessful cases, Munton and Antaki (1988) reported that, relative to families with poor outcomes, those with good outcomes viewed their problems as less "stable" as therapy progressed.

Second, with respect to changes in therapist behavior, Postner and coworkers (1971) found that successful therapists spoke more over time. In contrast to less successful therapists, they also used fewer "drive" (authoritative) responses relative to "interpretive" responses as treatment progressed. In a large-scale marital outcome study (Cline, Mejia, Coles, Klein, & Cline, 1984), effective therapist behavior differed on the basis of family socioeconomic status (SES). For middle SES couples, movement toward less directiveness predicted increases in clients' emotional expressiveness and positive behaviors like acceptance, agreement, approval, and accepting responsibility. The opposite pattern was observed for lower SES couples, who seemed to fare better when the therapist was increasingly directive. According to Cline and associates, the lower SES husbands benefited from understanding the dynamics in the marriage without actually changing how they communicated with their wives. The middle SES husbands, on the other hand, learned to express their feelings, with the communication patterns of the couple gradually improving as therapy progressed.

Finally, in two successful cases seen at the Philadelphia Child Guidance Clinic, actual moment-by-moment interactions were observed. In the earlier study (Laird & Vande Kemp, 1987), the therapist responded to family members with greater interpersonal complementarity in the early and late phases than in the middle phase of treatment. Complementarity, operationally defined by the Structural Analysis of Social Behavior (Benjamin, 1974), refers to reciprocal, rewarding interactions like leading/following, whereas noncomplementarity refers to interactions that are more challenging. Similar results were reported by Raymond and coworkers (1993), who defined complementarity as a ↑ / ↓ relational control pattern on the FRCCCS (Friedlander & Heatherington, 1989). Although the predominant control pattern was therapist ↑ / family member ↓ throughout treatment, this pattern decreased in frequency between the therapist and the adolescent during the middle, restructuring stage of therapy.

While the research reviewed above is informative because it suggests what takes place in effective therapy, it is nonetheless limited. In none of these studies was the immediate therapeutic context taken into account. In working with an actual family or couple like the Hendersons, the therapist needs to know how to proceed when faced with a specific clinical dilemma. What should you do, for example, when Sheila and Brian avoid talking about a painful topic—their daughter's death, let's say—even though they recognize the need to do so? The research reviewed in the next section addresses the process of change within specific, identifiable therapeutic contexts.

Change Mechanisms. In recent years family therapy process researchers have turned their attention to immediate therapeutic outcomes and away from global measures of treatment success like symptom reduction or marital adjustment. Prompting this shift was increasing evidence that problematic behavior occurring in sessions has identifiable antecedents. In a case seen by Salvador Minuchin, for example, Crits-Christoph and associates (1991) discovered that an adolescent became emotionally labile whenever other family members described her in a pathologizing manner.

Immediate outcomes are of special interest because they reflect the practitioner's concern with evaluating the impact of specific interventions. As one example, Patterson and Forgatch (1985) found that mothers of troubled boys were less resistant when therapists were supportive than when they were didactic or confrontive. As another example, Robbins, Alexander, Newell, and Turner (1996) found that the attitude of delinquent adolescents became less negative after therapist "reframes" but not after other kinds of therapist messages.

Two programs of change process research have sought to identify effective ways to engage families in systemic treatment. The assumption is that many people come for professional help when they define problems as the attitudes or behavior of others. A related assumption is that the clients' individual, linear perspective on problems needs to be modified right away for family therapy to be effective.

In a well-designed program of research, Szapocznik and colleagues (Santisteban et al., 1996; Szapocznik et al., 1988) developed Strategic Structural Systems Engagement (SSSE) to motivate "hard-to-reach" families during the very first telephone contact. The assumption underlying SSSE is that because the problematic interpersonal dynamics that maintain the problem also impede the family from engaging in therapy, the therapist must intervene as soon as a family member calls for help. SSSE interventions include not only demonstrating empathy and concern but also joining; establishing alliances; using reframing, advice, and negotiating; and making home visits to resistant family members when necessary.

In the first study of SSSE, Szapocznik and colleagues (1988) sampled Cuban families with drug abusing adolescents in south Florida. In the second study (Santisteban et al., 1996), Cuban families were compared with non-Cuban Latino families from the same community. Results from both studies demonstrated the effectiveness of SSSE over "engagement-as-usual" family therapy (Santisteban et al., 1996, p. 37). Furthermore, an analysis of those who failed to engage in treatment suggested that more acculturated Cuban parents tended to hold onto their individual perspective on the problem. Attempting to shift their view too quickly was less effective than a more gradual restructuring after extensive joining (Santisteban et al., 1996).

Indeed, helping family members to deal with their problems systemically is the *sine qua non* of family therapy. Seeking to identify how family members' constructions of their presenting problems are "transformed" (Sluzki, 1992), Coulehan, Friedlander, and Heatherington (1996) identified four successful and four unsuccessful intake sessions from the questionnaire responses of therapists, observing staff members, and an independent panel of clinicians. The successful interviews were those in which the parent's construction of the problem shifted from an intrapsychic focus on one child to a more relational or interpersonal view. A qualitative comparison of the successful and unsuccessful transformations suggested a three-stage sequence of change. In the first stage, family members offer their individual constructions of the problem, and interpersonal dynamics and differences or exceptions to the problems are explored. In the second stage, positive aspects of the problem child are acknowledged, as are contributing factors (e.g., family history or structure) and family strengths. In this stage there is a gradual shift in the emotional tone of the session, from a position of blaming the child to a softer, more nurturant or supportive position. In the third stage, family members express hope or recognize that change is possible.

Of course, seeing the problem systemically and being willing to engage in treatment does not ensure smooth sailing. It's understandable—indeed, expected—that moments of resistance will be encountered as the therapist tries to move the family toward change. Several researchers have set about to study sequences of interventions that effectively reduce resistance.

In one program of study, the concern was how to move a family from disengagement, defined as resistance to discuss a specific topic, to engagement in problem solving (Friedlander, Heatherington, Johnson, & Skowron, 1994; Heatherington & Friedlander, 1990a). A qualitative comparison of four successful and four unsuccessful engagement sessions identified a series of interrelated steps in the process of moving from disengagement to sustained engagement. First, family members acknowledge their individual contributions to the interpersonal impasse. Next, they communicate thoughts and feelings about the impasse. This disclosure is validated by others, leading family members to form new constructions of one another's behavior and to recognize the value of engagement.

A similar but larger-scale study was recently reported by Diamond and Liddle (1996), who investigated impasses in parent–child relationships. All families were seen by therapists trained and supervised in multidimensional family therapy (MDFT), an approach specifically designed for adolescent drug abuse. Although similar in many ways to structural therapy, MDFT focuses on intrapersonal processes, emotion, and cognition, as well as interpersonal behaviors.

In this study a "shift intervention" (Diamond & Liddle, 1996, p. 482) followed a phase in the interview where the parents expressed frustration and hopelessness and the adolescents expressed anger and resentment. The successful resolution of the impasse occurred when the family began to engage in a meaningful, mutually respectful discussion about the parent–child relationship. A qualitative comparison of four successful and four unsuccessful shift interventions suggested that the adolescents became less resistant and more cooperative when their parents stopped trying to control them and began trying to understand them. Interestingly, the shift intervention seemed to be most effective with higher functioning families, possibly because it requires parents to be flexible and comfortable with relinquishing control (Diamond & Liddle, 1996).

Implications

In contrast to the abundant outcome research, to date relatively little attention has been paid to the process of family treatment. While many researchers have made careful, detailed analyses of the work of master therapists, few have defined treatment success in terms of client outcome. Most of the studies are descriptive and focus either on therapist behavior or on client behavior, with few investigations of therapist–family sequences of behavior within identifiable episodes of change.

Nonetheless, a body of literature exists from which we can draw some meaningful conclusions about what takes place in effective family therapy. In general, the available research indicates that changes in family members are *intra*personal as well as *inter*personal and involve the emotional and cognitive as well as the behavioral realm of experience. Furthermore, while effective therapists tend to be active and in charge, using a wide range of interventions focused on interpersonal relations, therapy needs to be conducted in a warm, nonthreatening atmosphere in which there is a sense of mutual respect and collaboration. Interestingly, these conclusions do not offer unqualified support for either structural-strategic theorists who stress the need for taking an expert, authoritative position with the family or for narrative theorists who insist that new solutions to old problems unfold with minimal therapist direction. Until future process research sheds more light on this controversy, we should assume that the effective therapist is *both* authoritative *and* collaborative rather than "either . . . or."

In a recent review of published process research, Friedlander and coworkers (1994) outlined several directions for future investigations in this area. First, not only is little known about how clients behave in effective family therapy, but we know little about how they view the therapeutic process, how their values, attitudes, and belief systems change over time, or how they come to feel differently about themselves and their family members. Relatedly, we know little about how therapeutic interventions affect different family members simultaneously. We know that the therapeutic alliance can be split and that some clients, by virtue of their family roles, respond more positively than others to various therapeutic interventions. Yet we have little information about how effective therapists meet the conflicting needs and demands of individuals, subsystems, and the family as a whole. Finally, we know little about how issues of diversity affect the process of treatment. Not only are gender, SES, and racial and ethnic issues important, as shown by some of the studies described earlier, but there are numerous other variables (e.g., age, life stage, religion, type of community) that have yet to be considered. Indeed, diversity needs to be broadly construed to include, for example, remarried families, adoptive families, gay and lesbian families, three-generation families, and so forth. The concept of *family* is changing rapidly, perhaps more so in our culture than in our theories or research (Friedlander et al., 1994).

Practice Into Science

If we return for a moment to the Hendersons, we can see that there is indeed a fair amount of research to guide our work. We can be reasonably certain that couples therapy will be successful for a distressed marriage such as this one, and any number of approaches have the potential to alleviate Sheila's depression and motivate Brian to stop drinking to excess. The process literature offers guidelines about the importance of establishing a balanced, nurturing therapeutic alliance, about the kinds of interventions that can be useful at different points during treatment, and about the cognitive, emotional, and interpersonal changes the Hendersons should experience in therapy.

But it's what we *don't* know about working effectively with the Hendersons that points the way for future scientific endeavors, endeavors that can, in turn, guide therapists working with similar couples. We might speculate, for example, that the loss of the Hendersons' daughter needs to be explored in some depth for therapy to be successful. It might also be important for the Hendersons to work with a therapist who the couple view as having enough life experience to understand the long-standing, destructive patterns in their marriage. These are two considerations that could be translated into clinically meaningful research questions. Indeed, the uniqueness of every family suggests numerous questions deserving of scientific attention, as do the commonalities we observe across families.

In 1995 *Consumer Reports* published the results of a random survey of its readership. Although the return rate was small, most of the 4,000 respondents who had experienced psychotherapy rated the services they received favorably. While the survey and its conclusions have generated some controversy among researchers, it's clear that psychotherapy is here to stay.

Despite this optimistic outlook, we cannot assume that therapy is effective for all who seek it. Nor can we assume that our therapeutic efforts are effective for the reasons we think they are. Looking beyond the obvious artistry of the experts featured in this text, we can find themes, patterns, and regularities in their work (and our own) to observe, measure, and teach to others. In our consulting rooms we must think like scientists—make predictions that can be disconfirmed, test and revise our hypotheses, modify our behavior based on the outcome of our interventions, and so forth. With continued research, formal and informal, we will be better able to anticipate the immediate and long-term effects of our work with families. We won't have to rely on chance encounters with them on soccer fields!

References

Alexander, J. F., and Parsons, B. V. 1982. *Functional family therapy*. Monterey, CA: Brooks/Cole.

Azrin, N. H., Donohue, B., Besalel, V. A., Kogan, E. S., and Acierno, R. 1994. Youth drug abuse treatment: A controlled outcome study. *Journal of Child and Adolescent Substance Abuse. 3*:1–16.

Bank, L., Marlowe, J. H., Reid, J. B., Patterson, G. R., and Weinrott, M. R. 1991. A comparative evaluation of parent training interventions for families of chronic delinquents. *Journal of Abnormal Child Psychology. 19*:15–33.

Barkley, R. A., Guevremont, D. C., Anastopoulos, A. D., and Fletcher, K. F. 1992. A comparison of three family therapy programs for treating family conflicts in adolescents with ADHD. *Journal of Consulting and Clinical Psychology. 60*:450–462.

Barlow, D. H., O'Brien, G. T., and Last, C. G. 1984. Couples treatment of agoraphobia. *Behavior Therapy. 15*:41–58.

Barrett, P. M., Dadds, M. R., and Rapee, R. M. 1996. Family treatment of childhood anxiety: A controlled trial. *Journal of Consulting and Clinical Psychology. 64*:333–342.

Benjamin, L. S. 1974. Structural analysis of social behavior. *Psychological Review. 81*:392–425.

Birnbrauer, J. S., and Leach, D. J. 1993. The Murdoch early intervention program after 2 years. *Behaviour Change. 10*:63–74.

Black, D. R., Gleser, L. J., and Kooyers, K. J. 1990. A meta-analytic evaluation of couples weight-loss programs. *Health Psychology. 9:*330–347.

Bourgeois, L., Sabourin, S., and Wright, J. 1990. Predictive validity of therapeutic alliance in group marital therapy. *Journal of Consulting and Clinical Psychology. 58:* 608–613.

Bray, J. H., and Jouriles, E. N. (1995). Treatment of marital conflict and prevention of divorce. *Journal of Marital and Family Therapy. 21:*461–474.

Brownell, K. D., Kelman, J. H., and Stunkard, A. J. 1983. Treatment of obese children with and without their mothers: Changes in weight and blood pressure. *Pediatrics, 71:*515–523.

Campbell, T. J., and Patterson, J. M. 1995. The effectiveness of family interventions in the treatment of physical illness. *Journal of Marital and Family Therapy. 21:*545–584.

Cedar, B., and Levant, R. F. 1990. A meta-analysis of the effects of parent effectiveness training. *American Journal of Family Therapy. 18:*373–384.

Cerny, J. A., Barlow, D. H., Craske, M. G., and Himadi, W. G. 1987. Couples treatment of agoraphobia: A two-year follow-up. *Behavior Therapy, 18:*401–415.

Chamberlain, P., Patterson, G., Reid, J., Kavanagh, K., and Forgatch, M. 1984. Observation of client resistance. *Behavior Therapy. 15:*144–155.

Chamberlain, P., and Reid, J. B. 1991. Using a specialized foster care treatment model for children and adolescents leaving the state mental hospital. *Journal of Community Psychology. 19:*266–276.

Chamberlain, P., and Rosicky, J. G. 1995. The effectiveness of family therapy in the treatment of adolescents with conduct disorders and delinquency. *Journal of Marital and Family Therapy. 21:*441–460.

Clarkin, J. F., Glick, I. D., Haas, G. L., Spencer, J. H., Lewis, A. B., Peyser, J., DeMane, N., Good-Ellis, M., Harris, E., and Lestelle, V. 1990. A randomized clinical trial of inpatient family intervention, V: Results for affective disorders. *Journal of Affective Disorders. 18:*17–28.

Cline, V. B., Mejia, J., Coles, J., Klein, N., and Cline, R. A. 1984. The relationship between therapist behaviors and outcome for middle- and lower-class couples in marital therapy. *Journal of Clinical Psychology. 40:*691–704.

Cobb, J. P., Mathews, A. M., Childs-Clarke, M. G., and Blowers, C. M. 1984. The spouse as co-therapist in the treatment of agoraphobia. *British Journal of Psychiatry. 144:*282–287.

Consumer Reports. 1995, November. Mental health: Does therapy help? 734–739.

Corder, B. F., Corder, R. F., and Laidlaw, N. C. 1972. An intensive treatment program for alcoholics and their wives. *Quarterly Journal of the Study of Alcohol. 33:* 1144–1146.

Coulehan, R., Friedlander, M. L., and Heatherington, L. 1996, June. *Transforming narratives: A change event in constructivist family therapy.* Paper presented at the annual conference, Society for Psychotherapy Research, Amelia Island, FL.

Cramer, B., Robert-Tissot, C., Stern, D. N., Serpa-Rusconi, S., DeMuralt, M., Besson, G., Palacio-Espasa, F., Bachmann, J.-P., Knauer, D., Berney, C., and D'Arcis, U. 1990. Outcome evaluation in brief mother–infant psychotherapy: A preliminary report. *Infant Mental Health Journal. 11:*278–300.

Crits-Christoph, P., Luborsky, L., Gay, E., Todd, T., Barber, J. P., and Luborsky, E. 1991. What makes Susie cry? A symptom-context study of family therapy. *Family Process. 30:*337–345.

Dadds, M. R., Heard, P. M., and Rapee, R. M. 1991. Anxiety disorders in children. *International Review of Psychiatry. 3:*231–241.

Dadds, M. R., Schwartz, S., and Sanders, M. 1987. Marital discord and treatment outcome in behavioral treatment of child conduct disorders. *Journal of Consulting and Clinical Psychology. 55:* 396–403.

Diamond, G., and Liddle, H. A. 1996. Resolving a therapeutic impasse between parents and adolescents in Multidimensional Family therapy. *Journal of Consulting and Clinical Psychology. 64:*481–488.

Diamond, G., and Siqueland, L. 1995. Family therapy for the treatment of depressed adolescents. *Psychotherapy. 32:*77–90.

Dunn, R. L., and Schwebel, A. I. 1995. Meta-analytic review of marital therapy outcome research. *Journal of Family Psychology. 9(1):*58–68.

Edwards, M. E., and Steinglass, P. 1995. Family therapy treatment outcomes for alcoholism. *Journal of Marital and Family Therapy. 21:*475–510.

Estrada, A. U., and Pinsof, W. M. 1995. The effectiveness of family therapies for selected behavioral disorders of childhood. *Journal of Marital and Family Therapy. 21:*403–440.

Evans, R., Matlock, A. L., Bishop, D. S., Stranahan, S., and Pederson, C. 1988. Family intervention after stroke: Does counseling or education help? *Stroke. 19:*1243–1249.

Eysenck, H. 1952. The effects of psychotherapy: An evaluation. *Journal of Consulting Psychology. 16:* 319–324.

Falloon, I. R. H., Boyd, J. L., and McGill, C. W. 1982. Family management in the prevention of exacerbations of schizophrenia: A controlled study. *New England Journal of Medicine. 306:*1437–1440.

Falloon, I. R. H., Boyd, J. L., McGill, C. W., Williamson, M., Razani, J., Moss, H. B., Gilderman, A. M., and Simpson, G. M. 1985. Family management in the prevention of morbidity of schizophrenia: Clinical outcome of a two-year longitudinal study. *Archives of General Psychiatry. 42:*887–986.

Fals-Stewart, W., Birchler, G. R., and O'Farrell, T. J. 1996. Behavioral couples therapy for male substance-abusing patients: Effects on relationship adjustment and drug-using behavior. *Journal of Consulting and Clinical Psychology. 64:*959–972.

Foley, S. H., Rounsaville, B. J., Weissman, M. M., Sholomaskas, D., and Chevron, E. 1989. Individual versus conjoint interpersonal therapy for depressed patients with marital disputes. *International Journal of Family Psychiatry. 10:* 29–42.

Forehand, R., and Long, N. 1988. Outpatient treatment of the acting-out child: Procedures, long-term follow-up data, and clinical problems. *Advances in Behavior Research and Therapy. 10:*129–177.

Friedlander, M. L., Ellis, M. V., Raymond, L., Siegel, S. M., and Milford, D. 1987. Convergence and divergence in the process of interviewing families. *Psychotherapy. 24:*570–583.

Friedlander, M. L., and Heatherington, L. 1989. Analyzing relational control in family therapy interviews. *Journal of Counseling Psychology. 36:* 139–148.

Friedlander, M. L., Heatherington, L., Johnson, B., and Skowron, E. A. 1994. "Sustaining engagement": A change event in family therapy. *Journal of Counseling Psychology. 41:*438–448.

Friedlander, M. L., Heatherington, L., and Wildman, J. 1991. Interpersonal control in structural and Milan systemic family therapy. *Journal of Marital and Family Therapy. 17:*395–408.

Friedlander, M. L., and Highlen, P. S. 1984. A spatial view of the interpersonal structure of family interviews: Similarities and differences across counselors. *Journal of Counseling Psychology. 31:*477–487.

Friedlander, M. L., Highlen, P. S., and Lassiter, W. L. 1985. Content analytic comparison of four expert counselors' approaches to family treatment: Ackerman, Bowen, Jackson, and Whitaker. *Journal of Counseling Psychology. 32:*171–180.

Friedlander, M. L., Wildman, J., Heatherington, L., and Skowron, E. A. 1994. What we do and don't know about the process of family therapy. *Journal of Family Psychology. 8:*390–416.

Friedrich, W. N., Luecke, W. J., Beilke, R. L., and Place, V. 1992. Psychotherapy outcome of sexually abused boys: An agency study. *Journal of Interpersonal Violence. 7:*396–409.

Gale, J., and Newfield, N. 1992. A conversation analysis of a solution-focused marital therapy session. *Journal of Marital and Family Therapy. 18:*153–165.

Giblin, P., Sprenkle, D. H., and Sheehan, R. 1985. Enrichment outcome research: A meta-analysis of premarital, marital, and family interventions. *Journal of Marital and Family Therapy. 11:*257–271.

Goldstein, M. J., and Miklowitz, D. J. 1995. The effectiveness of psychoeducational family therapy in the treatment of schizophrenic disorders. *Journal of Marital and Family Therapy. 21:*361–376.

Gordon, T. 1970. *P.E.T.: Parent effectiveness training.* New York: Peter H. Wyden.

Gordon Walker, J., Johnson, S., Manion, I., and Cloutier, P. 1996. Emotionally focused marital intervention for couples with chronically ill children. *Journal of Consulting and Clinical Psychology. 64:*1029–1036.

Greenberg, L. S., Ford, C. L., Alden, L., and Johnson, S. M. 1993. In-session change in Emotionally Focused Therapy. *Journal of Consulting and Clinical Psychology. 61:*78–84.

Gurman, A. S., and Kniskern, D. P. (1981). Family therapy outcome research: Knowns and unknowns. In *Handbook of family therapy,* A. S. Gurman and D. P. Kniskern, eds. New York: Brunner/Mazel.

Hahlweg, K., and Markman, H. J. 1988. Effectiveness of behavioral marital therapy: Empirical status of behavioral techniques in preventing and alleviating marital distress. *Journal of Consulting and Clinical Psychology. 57:*440–447.

Haley, J. 1984. *Ordeal therapy.* San Francisco: Jossey-Bass.

Heatherington, L., and Friedlander, M. L. 1987. *The Family Communication Control Coding System: Coding Manual.* Unpublished manual. (Available from L. Heatherington, Department of Psychology, Williams College, Williamstown, MA 01267.)

Heatherington, L., and Friedlander, M. L. 1990a. Applying task analysis to structural family therapy. *Journal of Family Psychology. 4:*36–48.

Heatherington, L., and Friedlander, M. L. 1990b. Complementarity and symmetry in family therapy communication. *Journal of Counseling Psychology. 37:*261–268.

Heatherington, L., and Friedlander, M. L. 1990c. Couple and family therapy alliance scales: Empirical considerations. *Journal of Marital and Family Therapy. 16:*299–306.

Heatherington, L., Marrs, A., and Friedlander, M. L. 1995, June. *Toward an understanding of how clients' constructions change in family therapy.* Paper presented at the annual conference of the Society for Psychotherapy Research, Vancouver, BC.

Hogan, D. R. 1978. The effectiveness of sex therapy: A review of the literature. In *Handbook of sex therapy,* J. LoPiccolo and L. LoPiccolo, eds. New York: Plenum Press.

Holtzworth-Munroe, A., Jacobson, N. S., DeKlyen, M., and Whisman, M. A. 1989. Relationship between behavioral marital therapy outcome and process variables. *Journal of Consulting and Clinical Psychology. 57:*658–662.

Horn, W. F., Ialongo, N. S., Pascoe, J. J., Greenberg, G., Packard, T., Lopez, M., Wagner, A., and Puttler, L. 1991. Additive effects of psychostimulants, parent training, and self-control therapy with ADHD children. *Journal of the American Academy of Child and Adolescent Psychiatry. 30:*233–240.

Ialongo, N. S., Horn, W. F., Pascoe, J. M., Greenberg, G., Packard, T., Lopez, M., Wagner, A., and Puttler, L. 1993. The effects of a multimodal intervention with attention-deficit hyperactivity disorder children: A 9-month follow up. *Journal of the American Academic of Child and Adolescent Psychiatry. 32:*182–189.

Jacobson, N. S., and Addis, M. E. 1993. Research on couples and couple therapy: What do we know? Where are we going? *Journal of Consulting and Clinical Psychology. 61:*85–93.

Jacobson, N. S., Fruzzetti, A. E., Dobson, K., Whisman, M., and Hops, H. 1993. Couple therapy as a treatment for depression: II. The effects of relationship quality and therapy on depressive relapse. *Journal of Consulting and Clinical Psychology. 61:*516–519.

Johnson, S. M., and Greenberg, L. S. 1985. Emotionally focused couples therapy: An outcome study. *Journal of Marital and Family Therapy. 11:*313–317.

Johnson, S. M., and Greenberg, L. S. 1988. Relating process to outcome in marital therapy. *Journal of Marital and Family Therapy. 14:*175–183.

Kaplan, H. S. 1974. *The new sex therapy: Active treatment of sexual dysfunctions.* New York: Brunner/Mazel.

Kazdin, A. E. 1987. *Conduct disorders in childhood and adolescence.* Newbury Park, CA: Sage.

Kazdin, A. E., Esveldt-Dawson, K., French, N. H., and Unis, A. S. 1987. Effects of parent management training and problem-solving skills training combined in the treatment of antisocial child behavior. *Journal of the American Academy of Child and Adolescent Psychiatry. 26:*416–424.

Keith, S., Schooler, N., Bellack, A., Matthews, S., Mueser, K., and Haas, G. 1989. The influence of family management on patient stabilization. *Schizophrenia Research. 2:*224.

Knutsen, S. F., and Knutsen, R. 1991. The Tromso survey: The family intervention study—the effect of intervention on some coronary risk factors and dietary habits, a 6-year follow-up. *Preventive Medicine. 20:*197–212.

Kuehl, B. P., Newfield, N. A., and Joanning, H. 1990. A client-based description of family therapy. *Journal of Family Psychology. 3:*310–321.

Laird, H., and Vande Kemp, H. 1987. Complementarity as a function of stage in therapy: An analysis of Minuchin's structural family therapy. *Journal of Marital and Family Therapy. 13:* 127–137.

Leff, J., Kuipers, L., Berkowitz, R., Eberlein-Fries, R., and Sturgeon, D. 1982. A controlled trial of social intervention in the families of schizophrenia patients. *British Journal of Psychiatry. 141:*121–134.

Liddle, H. A., and Dakof, G. A. 1994, February. *Effectiveness of family-based treatments for adolescent substance abuse.* Paper presented a the 1994 Society for Psychotherapy Research Conference, Sante Fe, NM.

Liddle, H. A., and Dakof, G. A. 1995. Efficacy of family therapy for drug abuse: Promising but not definitive. *Journal of Marital and Family Therapy. 21*:511–544.

Lieberman, A. F., Weston, D. R., and Pawl, J. H. 1991. Preventive intervention and outcome with anxiously attached dyads. *Child Development. 61:* 199–209.

Liebman, R., Minuchin, S., and Baker, L. 1974. The use of structural family therapy in the treatment of intractable asthma. *American Journal of Psychiatry. 131*:535–540.

Liepman, M. R., Silvia, L. Y., and Nirenberg, T. D. 1989. The use of family behavior loop mapping for substance abuse. *Family Relations. 38*:282–287.

Linszen, D. 1993. *Recent onset schizophrenic disorders: Outcome, prognosis and treatment.* Unpublished doctoral dissertation, University of Amsterdam, The Netherlands.

Longabaugh, R., Beattie, M., Noel, N., Stout, R., and Malloy, P. 1993. The effect of social investment on treatment outcome. *Journal of the Study of Alcohol. 44*:465–478.

Lovaas, O. I. 1987. Behavioral treatment and normal educational and intellectual functioning in young autistic children. *Journal of Consulting and Clinical Psychology. 55*:3–9.

MacPhee, D. C., Johnson, S. M., and van der Veer, M. M. C. 1995. Low sexual desire in women: The effects of marital therapy. *Journal of Sex and Marital Therapy. 21*:159–182.

Mansdorf, I. J., and Lukens, E. 1987. Cognitive-behavioral psychotherapy for separation anxious children exhibiting school phobia. *Journal of the American Academy of Child and Adolescent Psychiatry. 26*:222–225.

Markman, H. J., and Hahlweg, K. 1993. The prediction and prevention of marital distress: An international perspective. *Clinical Psychology Review. 13*:29–43.

Markman, H. J., Renick, M. J. H., Floyd, F. J., Stanley, S. M., and Clements, M. 1993. Preventing marital distress through communication and conflict management training: A 4- and 5-year follow-up. *Journal of Consulting and Clinical Psychology. 61*:70–77.

McCrady, B. S., Noel, N. E., and Abrams, D. B. 1986. Comparative effectiveness of three types of spouse involvement in outpatient behavioral alcoholism treatment. *Journal of Studies on Alcohol. 47:* 459–467.

Miller, G. E., and Prinz, R. J. 1990. The enhancement of social learning family interventions for childhood conduct disorder. *Psychological Bulletin. 108:* 291–307.

Minuchin, S. 1974. *Families and family therapy.* Cambridge, MA: Harvard University Press.

Minuchin, S., and Nichols, M. P. 1993. *Family healing: Tales of hope and renewal from family therapy.* New York: The Free Press.

Minuchin, S., Rosman, B., and Baker, L. 1978. *Psychosomatic families: Anorexia nervosa in context.* Cambridge, MA: Harvard University Press.

Morisky, D. E., Levine, D. M., Green, L. W., Shapiro, S., Russell, R. P., and Smith, C. R. 1983. Five year blood pressure control and mortality following health education for hypertensive patients. *American Journal of Public Health. 73*:153–162.

Munton, A. G., and Antaki, C. 1988. Causal beliefs amongst families in therapy: Attributions at the group level. *British Journal of Clinical Psychology. 27*:91–97.

Newman, F. L., and Tejeda, M. J. 1996. The need for research that is designed to support decisions in the delivery of mental health services. *American Psychologist. 51*:1040–1049.

O'Farrell, T. J., Choquette, K. A., Cutter, H. S. G., Brown, E. D., and McCourt, W. 1993. Behavioral marital therapy with and without additional couples relapse prevention sessions for alcoholics and their wives. *Journal of Studies on Alcohol. 54*:652–666.

O'Leary, K. D., Sandeen, E., and Beach, S. R. H. 1987, November. *Treatment of suicidal, maritally discordant clients by marital therapy or cognitive therapy.* Paper presented at the 21st annual meeting of the Association for Advancement of Behavior Therapy, Boston, MA.

O'Leary, K. D., Risso, L. P., and Beach, S. R. H. 1990. Attributions about marital discord/depression link and therapy outcome. *Behavior Therapy. 21:* 413–422.

Orlinsky, D. E., and Howard, K. I. 1986. Process and outcome in psychotherapy. In *Handbook of psychotherapy and behavior change,* S. L. Garfield and A. E. Bergin, eds. New York: John Wiley & Sons.

Papp, P. 1997. Listening to the system. *Family Therapy Networker. 21* (1):52–58.

Patterson, G. R. 1982. *Coercive family process.* Eugene, OR: Castalia.

Patterson, G. R., and Forgatch, M. S. 1985. Therapist behavior as a determinant for client noncompliance: A paradox for the behavior modifier. *Journal of Consulting and Clinical Psychology. 53:* 846–851.

Patterson, J. M. 1991. Family resilience to the challenge of a child's disability. *Pediatric Annals. 20:* 491–499.

Pearce, J. W., LeBow, M. D., and Orchard, J. 1981. Role of spouse involvement in the behavioral treatment of overweight women. *Journal of Consulting and Clinical Psychology. 49:*236–244.

Peed, S., Roberts, M., and Forehand, R. 1977. Evaluation of the effectiveness of a standardized parent training program in altering the interaction of mothers and their noncompliant children. *Behavior Modification. 1:*323–350.

Pinsof, W. M. 1979. The Family Therapist Behavior Scale (FTBS): Development and evaluation of a coding system. *Family Process. 18:*451–461.

Pinsof, W. M. 1986. The process of family therapy: The development of the Family Therapist Coding System. In *The psychotherapeutic process: A research handbook,* L. S. Greenberg and W. M. Pinsof, eds. New York: Guilford Press.

Pinsof, W. M., and Catherall, D. R. 1986. The integrative psychotherapy alliance: Family, couple and individual therapy scales. *Journal of Marital and Family Therapy. 12:*137–151.

Pinsof, W. M., and Wynne, L. C. 1995. The efficacy of marital and family therapy: An empirical overview, conclusions and recommendations. *Journal of Marital and Family Therapy. 21:*585–614.

Pinsof, W. M., Wynne, L. C., and Hambright, A. B. 1996. The outcomes of couple and family therapy: Findings, conclusions, and recommendations. *Psychotherapy. 33:*321–331.

Postner, R. S., Guttman, H. A., Sigal, J. J., Epstein, N. B., and Rakoff, V. M. 1971. Process and outcome in conjoint family therapy. *Family Process. 10:*451–474.

Prince, S. E., and Jacobson, N. S. 1995. A review and evaluation of marital and family therapies for affective disorders. *Journal of Marital and Family Therapy. 21:*377–401.

Randolph, E. T., Eth, S., Glynn, S. M., Paz, G. C., Leong, G. B., Shaner, A. L., Strachan, A., van Vort, W., Escobar, J. I., and Liberman, R. P. 1994. Behavioural family management in schizophrenia: Outcome of a clinic-based intervention. *British Journal of Psychiatry. 164:*501–506.

Raymond, L., Friedlander, M. L., Heatherington, L., Ellis, M. V., and Sargent, J. 1993. Communication processes in structural family therapy: Case study of an anorexic family. *Journal of Family Psychology. 6:*308–326.

Robbins, M. S., Alexander, J. F., Newell, R. M., and Turner, C. W. 1996. The immediate effect of reframing on client attitude in family therapy. *Journal of Family Psychology. 10:*28–34.

Russell, G. F. M., Szmukler, G. I., Dare, C., and Eisler, I. 1987. An evaluation of family therapy in anorexia nervosa and bulimia nervosa. *Archives of General Psychiatry. 44:*1047–1056.

Santisteban, D. A., Szapocznik, J., Perez-Vidal, A., Kurtines, W. M., Murray, E. J., and LaPerriere, A. 1996. Efficacy of intervention for engaging youth and families into treatment and some variables that may contribute to differential effectiveness. *Journal of Family Psychology. 10:*35–44.

Satin, W., LaGreca, A. M., Zigo, M. A., and Skyler, J. S. 1989. Diabetes in adolescence: Effects of multifamily group intervention and parent simulation of diabetes. *Journal of Pediatric Psychology. 14:*259–275.

Satterfield, J. H., Satterfield, B., and Cantwell, D. P. 1981. Three-year multimodality treatment study of 100 hyperactive boys. *Journal of Pediatrics. 98:*650–655.

Sayger, T. V., Horne, A. M., and Glaser, B. A. 1993. Marital satisfaction and social learning family therapy for child conduct problems: Generalization of treatment effects. *Journal of Marital and Family Therapy. 19:*393–402.

Sells, S. P., Smith, T. E., and Moon, S. 1996. An ethnographic study of client and therapist perceptions of therapy effectiveness in a university-based training clinic. *Journal of Marital and Family Therapy. 22:*321–342.

Selvini Palazzoli, M., Boscolo, L., Cecchin, G., and Prata, G. 1978. *Paradox and counterparadox: A new model in the therapy of the family in schizophrenic transaction* (translator, E. V. Burt). New York: Aronson.

Shadish, W. R., Ragsdale, K., Glaser, R. R., and Montgomery, L. M. 1995. The efficacy and effectiveness of marital and family therapy. A perspective from meta-analysis. *Journal of Marital and Family Therapy. 21*:345–360.

Shapiro, R. J. 1974. Therapist attitudes and premature termination in family and individual therapy. *Journal of Nervous and Mental Disease. 159*: 101–107.

Shields, C. G., Sprenkle, D. H., and Constantine, J. A. 1991. Anatomy of an initial interview: The importance of joining and structuring skills. *American Journal of Family Therapy. 19*:3–18.

Sigal, J. J., Rakoff, V., and Epstein, N. B. 1967. Indicators of therapeutic outcome in conjoint family therapy. *Family Process. 6*: 215–226.

Sisson, R. W., and Azrin, N. H. 1986. Family-member involvement to initiate and promote treatment of problem drinkers. *Journal of Behavior Therapy and Experimental Psychiatry. 17*:15–21.

Sluzki, C. 1975. The coalitionary process in initiating family therapy. *Family Process. 4*:67–77.

Sluzki, C. 1992. Transformations: A blueprint for narrative changes in therapy. *Family Process. 13*:593–618.

Smith, M. L., and Glass, G. V. (1977). Meta-analysis of psychotherapy outcomes studies. *American Psychologist. 32*:752–760.

Stanton, M. D. 1995, May. *Family therapy for drug abuse.* Paper presented at the National Conference on Marital and Family Therapy Outcome and Process Research: State of the Science, Philadelphia, PA.

Stern, D. N. 1995. *The motherhood constellation: A unified view of parent–infant psychotherapy.* New York: Basic Books.

Stevenson, C. 1993. Combining quantitative and qualitative methods in evaluating a course of family therapy. *Journal of Family Therapy. 15*: 205–224.

Szapocznik, J., Kurtines, W. M., Foote, F. H., Perez-Vidal, A., and Hervis, O. 1983. Conjoint versus one-person family therapy: Some evidence for the effectiveness of conducting family therapy through one person. *Journal of Consulting and Clinical Psychology. 51*:889–899.

Szapocznik, J., Kurtines, W. M., Foote, F. H., Perez-Vidal, A., and Hervis, O. 1986. Conjoint versus one-person family therapy: Further evidence for the effectiveness of conducting family therapy through one person with drug-abusing adolescents. *Journal of Consulting and Clinical Psychology. 54*:395–397.

Szapocznik, J., Perez-Vidal, A., Brickman, A. L., Foote, F. H., Santisteban, D., Hervis, O., and Kurtines, W. 1988. Engaging adolescent drug abusers and their families in treatment: A strategic structural systems approach. *Journal of Consulting and Clinical Psychology. 56*:552–557.

Szapocznik, J., Rio, A., Murray, E., Cohen, R., Scopetta, M., Rivas-Vazquez, A., Hervis, O., Posada, V., and Kurtines, W. 1989. Structural family versus psychodynamic child therapy for problematic Hispanic boys. *Journal of Consulting and Clinical Psychology. 57*:571–578.

Walker, J. G., Johnson, S., Manion, I., and Cloutier, P. 1996. Emotionally focused marital intervention for couples with chronically ill children. *Journal of Consulting and Clinical Psychology. 64*: 1029–1036.

Webster-Stratton, C. 1990. Long-term follow-up with young conduct problem children: From preschool to grade school. *Journal of Clinical Child Psychology. 19*:144–149.

Wiens, A. N., and Menustik, C. E. 1983. Treatment outcome and patient characteristics in an aversion therapy program for alcoholism. *American Psychologist. 38*:1089–1096.

Winer, L. R. 1971. The qualified pronoun count as a measure of change in family psychotherapy. *Family Process. 10*:243–248.

APPENDIX A
Recommended Readings

Note: Recommended readings are listed first by chapters in this book; then a second list gives our overall recommendations.

Chapter 1 The Foundations of Family Therapy

Nichols, M. P. 1987. *The self in the system.* New York: Brunner/Mazel.

Nichols, M. P. 1992. *The power of family therapy.* New York: Gardner Press.

Chapter 2 The Evolution of Family Therapy

Ackerman, N. W. 1958. *The psychodynamics of family life.* New York: Basic Books.

Boszormenyi-Nagy, I. 1962. The concept of schizophrenia from the point of view of family treatment. *Family Process. 1:*103–113.

Bowen, M. 1960. A family concept of schizophrenia. In *The etiology of schizophrenia,* D. D. Jackson, ed. New York: Basic Books.

Greenberg, G. S. 1977. The family interactional perspective: A study and examination of the work of Don D. Jackson. *Family Process. 16:*385–412.

Haley, J. 1959. The family of the schizophrenic. *American Journal of Nervous and Mental Diseases. 129:*357–374.

Haley, J., and Hoffman, L., eds. 1968. *Techniques of family therapy.* New York: Basic Books.

Jackson, D. D. 1957. The question of family homeostasis. *The Psychiatric Quarterly Supplement. 31:* 79–90.

Jackson, D. D. 1965. Family rules: Marital quid pro quo. *Archives of General Psychiatry. 12:*589–594.

Lidz, T., Cornelison, A., Fleck, S., and Terry, D. 1957. Intrafamilial environment of schizophrenic patients. II: Marital schism and marital skew. *American Journal of Psychiatry. 20:*241–248.

Weakland, J. H. 1960. The "double-bind" hypothesis of schizophrenia and three-party interaction. In *The etiology of schizophrenia,* D. D. Jackson, ed. New York: Basic Books.

Whitaker, C. A. 1958. Psychotherapy with couples. *American Journal of Psychotherapy. 12:*18–23.

Wynne, L. C., Ryckoff, I., Day, J., and Hirsch, S. I. 1958. Pseudo-mutuality in the family relationships of schizophrenics. *Psychiatry. 21:*205–220.

Chapter 3 Early Models and Basic Techniques: Group Process and Communications Analysis

Bell, J. E. 1961. *Family group therapy.* Public Health Monograph No. 64, Washington, DC: U.S. Government Printing Office.

Bell, J. E. 1975. *Family therapy.* New York: Jason Aronson.

Bion, W. R. 1961. *Experience in groups.* London: Tavistock Publications.

Haley, J. 1963. *Strategies of psychotherapy.* New York: Grune & Stratton.

Hoffman, L. 1971. Deviation-amplifying processes in natural groups. In *Changing families,* J. Haley, ed. New York: Grune & Stratton.

Jackson, D. D. 1961. Interactional psychotherapy. In *Contemporary psychotherapies,* M. T. Stein, ed. New York: Free Press of Glencoe.

Jackson, D. D. 1967. *Therapy, communication and change.* Palo Alto, CA: Science and Behavior Books.

Lederer, W., and Jackson, D. D. 1968. *Mirages of marriage.* New York: Norton.

MacGregor, R., Richie, A. M., Serrano, A. C., Schuster, F. P., McDonald, E. C., and Goolishian, H. A. 1964. *Multiple impact therapy with families.* New York: McGraw-Hill.

Satir, V. 1964. *Conjoint family therapy.* Palo Alto, CA: Science and Behavior Books.

Sluzki, C. E. 1978. Marital therapy from a systems theory perspective. In *Marriage and marital therapy,* T. J. Paolino and B. S. McCrady, eds. New York: Brunner/Mazel.

Speck, R. V., and Attneave, C. A. 1971. Social network intervention. In *Changing families,* J. Haley, ed. New York: Grune & Stratton.

Watzlawick, P., Beavin, J. H., and Jackson, D. D. 1967. *Pragmatics of human communication.* New York: Norton.

Chapter 4 The Fundamental Concepts of Family Therapy

Bateson, G. 1971. *Steps to an ecology of mind.* New York: Ballantine.

Bateson, G. 1979. *Mind and nature.* New York: E. P. Dutton.

von Bertalanffy, L. 1950. An outline of General System Theory. *British Journal of the Philosophy of Science. 1*:134–165.

von Bertalanffy, L. 1967. *Robots, men and minds.* New York: George Braziller.

Breunlin, D. C., and Schwartz, R. C. 1986. Sequences: Toward a common denominator of family therapy. *Family Process. 25*:67–88.

Carter, E., and McGoldrick, M., eds. 1989. *The changing family life cycle: A framework for family therapy,* 2nd ed. Boston: Allyn and Bacon.

Davidson, M. 1983. *Uncommon sense: The life and thought of Ludwig von Bertalanffy.* Los Angeles: J. P. Tarcher.

Dell, P. F. 1982. Beyond homeostasis: Toward a concept of coherence. *Family Process. 21*:21–42.

Falicov, C. J., ed. 1988. *Family transitions.* New York: Guilford Press.

Haley, J. 1985. Conversations with Erickson. *Family Therapy Networker. 9*(2):30–43.

Hoffman, L. 1981. *Foundations of family therapy.* New York: Basic Books.

Simon, R. 1982. Reflections on family therapy: An interview with Jay Haley. *Family Therapy Networker. 6*(5):18–26.

Simon, R. 1984. Stranger in a strange land: An interview with Salvador Minuchin. *Family Therapy Networker. 8*(6):21–31, 66–68.

Sluzki, C. 1983. Interview on the state of the art. *Family Therapy Networker. 7*(1):24.

Weiner, N. 1948. *Cybernetics or control and communication in the animal and the machine.* Cambridge, MA: Technology Press.

Chapter 5 Bowen Family Systems Therapy

Anonymous. 1972. Differentiation of self in one's family. In *Family interaction,* J. Framo, ed. New York: Springer.

Bowen, M. 1978. *Family therapy in clinical practice.* New York: Jason Aronson.

Carter, E., and Orfanidis, M. M. 1976. Family therapy with one person and the family therapist's own family. In *Family therapy: Theory and practice,* P. J. Guerin, ed. New York: Gardner Press.

Fogarty, T. F. 1976. Systems concepts and the dimensions of self. In *Family therapy: Theory and practice*, P. J. Guerin, ed. New York: Gardner Press.

Fogarty, T. F. 1976. Marital crisis. In *Family therapy: Theory and practice*, P. J. Guerin, ed. New York: Gardner Press.

Guerin, P. J., Fay, L., Burden, S., and Kautto, J. 1987. *The evaluation and treatment of marital conflict: A four-stage approach.* New York: Basic Books.

Guerin, P. J., Fogarty, T. F., Fay, L. F., and Kautto, J. G. 1996. *Working with relationship triangles: The one-two-three of psychotherapy.* New York: Guilford Press.

Guerin, P. J., and Pendagast, E. G. 1976. Evaluation of family system and geogram. In *Family therapy: Theory and practice*, P. J. Guerin, ed. New York: Gardner Press.

Kerr, M. E., and Bowen, M. 1988. *Family evaluation.* New York: Norton.

Chapter 6 Experiential Family Therapy

Duhl, B. S., and Duhl, F. J. 1981. Integrative family therapy. In *Handbook of family therapy*, A. S. Gurman and D. P. Kniskern, eds. New York: Brunner/Mazel.

Duhl, F. J., Kantor, D., and Duhl, B. S. 1973. Learning, space and action in family therapy: A primer of sculpture. In *Techniques in family therapy*, D. A. Bloch, ed. New York: Grune & Stratton.

Greenberg, L. S., and Johnson, S. M. 1988. *Emotionally focused therapy for couples.* New York: Guilford Press.

Kaplan, M. L., and Kaplan, N. R. 1978. Individual and family growth: A Gestalt approach. *Family Process. 17*:195–205.

Keith, D. V., and Whitaker, C. A. 1977. The divorce labyrinth. In *Family therapy: Full length case studies*, P. Papp, ed. New York: Gardner Press.

Kempler, W. 1981. *Experiential psychotherapy with families.* New York: Brunner/Mazel.

Laing, R. D., and Esterson, A. 1970. *Sanity, madness and the family.* Baltimore: Penguin Books.

Napier, A. Y., and Whitaker, C. A. 1978. *The family crucible.* New York: Harper & Row.

Neill, J. R., and Kniskern, D. P., eds. 1982. *From psyche to system: The evolving therapy of Carl Whitaker.* New York: Guilford Press.

Satir, V. M. 1988. *The new peoplemaking.* Palo Alto, CA: Science and Behavior Books.

Satir, V. M., and Baldwin, M. 1983. *Satir step by step: A guide to creating change in families.* Palo Alto, CA: Science and Behavior Books.

Whitaker, C. A. and Bumberry, W. M. 1988. *Dancing with the family: A symbolic experiential approach.* New York: Brunner/Mazel.

Whitaker, C. A., and Keith, D. V. 1981. Symbolic-experiential family therapy. In *Handbook of family therapy*, A. S. Gurman and D. P. Kniskern, eds. New York: Brunner/Mazel.

Chapter 7 Psychoanalytic Family Therapy

Ackerman, N. W. 1966. *Treating the troubled family.* New York: Basic Books.

Boszormenyi-Nagy, I. 1972. Loyalty implications of the transference model in psychotherapy. *Archives of General Psychiatry. 27*:374–380.

Boszormenyi-Nagy, I. 1987. *Foundations of contextual therapy.* New York: Brunner/Mazel.

Dicks, H. V. 1967. *Marital tensions.* New York: Basic Books.

Meissner, W. W. 1978. The conceptualization of marriage and family dynamics from a psychoanalytic perspective. In *Marriage and marital therapy*, T. J. Paolino and B. S. McCrady, eds. New York: Brunner/Mazel.

Nadelson, C. C. 1978. Marital therapy from a psychoanalytic perspective. In *Marriage and marital therapy*, T. J. Paolino and B. S. McCrady, eds. New York: Brunner/Mazel.

Nichols, M. P. 1987. *The self in the system.* New York: Brunner/Mazel.

Sander, F. M. 1989. Marital conflict and psychoanalytic theory in the middle years. In *The middle years: New psychoanalytic perspectives*, J. Oldham and R. Liebert, eds. New Haven: Yale University Press.

Scharff, D., and Scharff, J. S. 1987. *Object relations family therapy.* New York: Jason Aronson.

Stern, D. N. 1985. *The interpersonal world of the infant.* New York: Basic Books.

Vogel, E. F., and Bell, N. W. 1960. The emotionally disturbed child as the family scapegoat. In *The family*, N. W. Bell and E. F. Vogel, eds. Glencoe, IL: Free Press.

Zinner, J., and Shapiro, R. 1976. Projective identification as a mode of perception of behavior in families of adolescents. *International Journal of Psychoanalysts.* 53:523–530.

Chapter 8 Structural Family Therapy

Colapinto J. 1991. Structural family therapy. In *Handbook of family therapy*, vol. II, A. S. Gurman and D. P. Kniskern, eds. New York: Brunner/Mazel.

Minuchin, S. 1974. *Families and family therapy.* Cambridge, MA: Harvard University Press.

Minuchin, S., and Fishman, H. C. 1981. *Family therapy techniques.* Cambridge, MA: Harvard University Press.

Minuchin, S., Lee, W-Y., and Simon, G. M. 1996. *Mastering family therapy: Journeys of growth and transformation.* New York: Wiley.

Minuchin, S., Montalvo, B., Guerney, B., Rosman, B., and Schumer, F. 1967. *Families of the slums.* New York: Basic Books.

Minuchin, S., and Nichols, M. P. 1993. *Family healing: Tales of hope and renewal from family therapy.* New York: The Free Press.

Minuchin, S., Rosman, B. L., and Baker, L. 1978. *Psychosomatic families: Anorexia nervosa in context.* Cambridge, MA: Harvard University Press.

Chapter 9 Cognitive-Behavioral Family Therapy

Barton, C., and Alexander, J. F. 1981. Functional family therapy. In *Handbook of family therapy*, A. S. Gurman and D. P. Kniskern, eds. New York: Brunner/Mazel.

Bornstein, P., and Bornstein, M. 1986. *Marital therapy: A behavioral-communications approach.* New York: Pergamon.

Dattilio, F. M. 1997. *Integrative cases in couples and family therapy: A cognitive-behavioral perspective.* New York: Guilford Press.

Dattilio, F. M., and Reinecke, M. 1996. *Casebook of cognitive-behavior therapy with children and adolescents.* New York: Guilford Press.

Epstein, N., Schlesinger, S. E., and Dryden, W. 1988. *Cognitive-behavioral therapy with families.* New York: Brunner/Mazel.

Falloon, I. R. H. 1988. *Handbook of behavioral family therapy.* New York: Guilford Press.

Falloon, I. R. H. 1991. Behavioral family therapy. In *Handbook of family therapy*, vol. II, A. S. Gurman and D. P. Kniskern, eds. New York, Brunner/Mazel.

Gordon, S. B., and Davidson, N. 1981. Behavioral parent training. In *Handbook of family therapy*, A. S. Gurman and D. P. Kniskern, eds. New York: Brunner/Mazel.

Jacobson, N. S., and Margolin, G. 1979. *Marital therapy: Strategies based on social learning and behavior exchange principles.* New York: Brunner/Mazel.

Kaplan, H. S. 1979. *The new sex therapy: Active treatment of sexual dysfunctions.* New York: Brunner/Mazel.

Masters, W. H., and Johnson, V. E. 1970. *Human sexual inadequacy.* Boston: Little, Brown.

Patterson, G. R. 1971. *Families: Application of social learning theory to family life.* Champaign, IL: Research Press.

Sanders, M. R., and Dadds, M. R. 1993. *Behavioral family intervention.* Needham Heights, MA: Allyn and Bacon.

Stuart, R. B. 1980. *Helping couples change: A social learning approach to marital therapy.* New York: Guilford Press.

Weiss, R. L. 1978. The conceptualization of marriage from a behavioral perspective. In *Marriage and marital therapy*, T. J. Paolino and B. S. McCrady, eds. Brunner/Mazel.

Chapter 10 Family Therapy Enters the Twenty-First Century

Andersen, T. 1991. *The reflecting team.* New York: Norton.

Anderson, C. M., Reiss, D., and Hogarty, B. 1986. *Schizophrenia and the family: A practitioner's guide to psychoeducation and management.* New York: Guilford Press.

Anderson, H., and Goolishian, H. A. 1988. Human systems as linguistic systems. *Family Process.* 27:371–393.

Avis, J. M. 1992. Where are all the family therapists? Abuse and violence within families and family therapy's response. *Journal of Marital and Family Therapy. 18*:225–232.

Bograd, M. 1992. Values in conflict: Challenges to family therapists' thinking. *Journal of Marital and Family Therapy. 18*:245–256.

Doherty, W. 1991. Family therapy goes postmodern. *Family Therapy Networker. 15*:36–42.

Fowers, B., and Richardson, F. 1996. Why is multiculturalism good? *American Psychologist. 51*: 609–621.

Gergen, K. 1985. The social constructionist movement in modern psychology. *American Psychologist. 40*:266–275.

Goldner, V. 1985. Feminism and family therapy. *Family Process. 24*:31–47.

Goldner, V. 1988. Generation and gender: Normative and covert hierarchies. *Family Process. 27*:17–33.

Goodrich, T. J., ed. 1991. *Women and power: Perspectives for family therapy.* New York: Norton.

Hare-Mustin, R. T. 1994. Discourses in the mirrored room: A postmodern analysis of therapy. *Family Process. 33*:19–35.

Hare-Mustin, R. T., and Marecek, J. 1988. The meaning of difference: Gender theory, postmodernism and psychology. *American Psychologist. 43*: 455–464.

Held, B. S. 1995. *Back to reality: A critique of postmodern theory in psychotherapy.* New York: Norton.

Keeney, B. P. 1983. *The aesthetics of change.* New York: Guilford Press.

Kellner, D. 1991. *Postmodern theory.* New York: Guilford Press.

Krestan, J., and Bepko, C. 1980. The problem of fusion in the lesbian relationship. *Family Process. 19*:277–289.

Laird, J., and Green, R. J. 1996. *Lesbians and gays in couples and families: A handbook for therapists.* San Francisco: Jossey-Bass.

Luepnitz, D. 1988. *The family interpreted: Feminist theory in clinical practice.* New York: Basic Books.

McDaniel, S., Hepworth, J., and Doherty, W. 1992. *Medical family therapy.* New York: Basic Books.

McGoldrick, M., Anderson, C., and Walsh, F., eds. 1989. *Women in families: A framework for family therapy.* New York: Norton.

McGoldrick, M., Giordano, J., and Pearce, J. 1996. *Ethnicity and family therapy,* 2nd ed. New York: Guilford Press.

Rolland, J. 1994. *Helping families with chronic and life-threatening disorders.* New York: Basic Books.

Schwartz, R. C., and Perrotta, P. 1985. Let us sell no intervention before its time. *Family Therapy Networker. 9*(4):18–25.

Walsh, F., ed. 1993. *Normal family processes,* 2nd ed. New York: Guilford Press.

Chapter 11 From Strategic to Solution-Focused: The Evolution of Brief Therapy

Cecchin, G. 1987. Hypothesizing, circularity and neutrality revisited. *Family Process. 26*:405–413.

de Shazer, S. 1988. *Clues: Investigating solutions in brief therapy.* New York: Norton.

de Shazer, S. 1991. *Putting difference to work.* New York: Norton.

Fisch, R., Weakland, J. H., and Segal, L. 1982. *The tactics of change: Doing therapy briefly.* San Francisco: Jossey-Bass.

Haley, J. 1973. *Uncommon therapy.* New York: Norton.

Haley, J. 1976. *Problem-solving therapy.* San Francisco: Jossey-Bass.

Haley, J. 1980. *Leaving home.* New York: McGraw-Hill.

Hoffman, L. 1976. Breaking the homeostatic cycle. In *Family therapy: Theory and practice,* P. J. Guerin, ed. New York: Gardner Press.

Madanes, C. 1981. *Strategic family therapy.* San Francisco: Jossey-Bass.

Madanes, C. 1984. *Behind the one-way mirror.* San Francisco: Jossey-Bass.

Madanes, C. 1990. *Sex, love and violence: Strategies for transformation.* New York: Norton.

Miller, S., Hubble, M., and Duncan, B. 1996. *Handbook of solution-focused brief therapy.* San Francisco: Jossey-Bass.

Price, J. 1996. *Power and compassion: Working with difficult adolescents and abused parents.* New York: Guilford Press.

Rabkin, R. 1972. *Strategic psychotherapy.* New York: Basic Books.

Selvini Palazzoli, M., Boscolo, L., Cecchin, G., and Prata, G. 1978. *Paradox and counterparadox.* New York: Jason Aronson.

Tomm, K. 1987. Interventive interviewing: Part 1. Strategizing as a fourth guideline for the therapists. *Family Process. 26*:3–14.

Watzlawick, P., Weakland, J., and Fisch, R. 1974. *Change: Principles of problem formation and problem resolution.* New York: Norton.

Chapter 12 Narrative Therapy

Bruner, J. S. 1986. *Actual minds, possible worlds.* Cambridge, MA: Harvard University Press.

Dickerson, V. C., and Zimmerman, J. 1992. Families with adolescents: Escaping problem lifestyles. *Family Process. 31*:341–353.

Eron, J., and Lund, T. 1996. *Narrative solutions in brief therapy.* New York: Guilford Press.

Freedman, J., and Combs, G. 1996. *Narrative therapy: The social construction of preferred realities.* New York: Norton.

Gilligan, S., and Price, R. 1993. *Therapeutic conversations.* New York: Norton.

White, M. 1989. *Selected papers.* Adelaide, Western Australia: Dulwich Centre Publications.

White, M. 1995. *Re-authoring lives: Interviews and essays.* Adelaide, Western Australia: Dulwich Centre Publications.

White, M., and Epston, D. 1990. *Narrative means to therapeutic ends.* New York: Norton.

Zimmerman, J., and Dickerson, V. 1996. *If problems talked: Adventures in narrative therapy.* New York: Guilford Press.

Chapter 13 Integrative Models

Breunlin, D. C., Schwartz, R. C., and Mac Kune-Karrer, B. 1992. *Metaframeworks: Transcending the models of family therapy.* San Francisco: Jossey-Bass.

Eron, J., and Lund, T. 1996. *Narrative solutions in brief therapy.* New York: Guilford Press.

Jacobson, N. S., and Christensen, A. 1996. *Integrative couple therapy.* New York: Norton.

Pinsof, W. M. 1995. *Integrative problem-centered therapy.* New York: Basic Books.

Schwartz, R. C. 1987. Our multiple selves. *Family Therapy Networker. 11*:25–31.

Schwartz, R. C. 1994. *The internal family systems model.* New York: Guilford Press.

Chapter 14 Comparative Analysis

Gurman, A. S. 1978. Contemporary marital therapies: A critique and comparative analysis of psychoanalytic, behavioral and systems theory approaches. In *Marriage and marital therapy,* T. J. Paolino and B. S. McCrady, eds. New York: Brunner/ Mazel.

Madanes, C., and Haley, J. 1977. Dimensions of family therapy. *Journal of Nervous and Mental Diseases. 165*:88–98.

Piercy, F. P., Sprenkle, D. H., and Wetchler, J. L. 1996. *Family therapy sourcebook.* 2nd ed. New York: Guilford Press.

Sluzki, C. E. 1983. Process, structure and world views: Toward an integrated view of systemic models in family therapy. *Family Process. 22*: 469–476.

Sluzki, C. E. 1987. Family process: Mapping the journey over 25 years. *Family Process. 26*:149–153.

Chapter 15 Family Therapy Research: Science into Practice, Practice into Science

Consumer Reports. 1995, November. Mental health: Does therapy help? 734–739.

Dunn, R. L., and Schwebel, A. I. 1995. Meta-analytic review of marital therapy outcome research. *Journal of Family Psychology. 9*:58–68.

Friedlander, M. L., Wildman, J., Heatherington, L., and Skowron, E. A. 1994. What we do and don't know about the process of family therapy. *Journal of Family Psychology. 8*:390–416.

Jacobson, N. S., and Addis, M. E. 1993. Research on couples and couple therapy: What do we know? Where are we going? *Journal of Consulting and Clinical Psychology. 61*:85–93.

Journal of Marital and Family Therapy. 1995. *21* (Special Issue on Research in Family Therapy).

Newman, F. L., and Tejeda, M. J. 1996. The need for research that is designed to support decisions in the delivery of mental health services. *American Psychologist.* 51:1040–1049.

Pinsof, W. M., Wynne, L. C., and Hambright, A. B. 1996. The outcomes of couple and family therapy: Findings, conclusions, and recommendations. *Psychotherapy.* 33:321-331.

The following are among the best and most useful books about families and family therapy.

General Principles of Family Systems

Carter, B., and McGoldrick, M. 1988. *The changing family life cycle: A framework for family therapy*, 2nd ed. Boston: Allyn and Bacon.

Guerin, P. J., Fogarty, T. F., Fay, L. F., and Kautto, J. G. 1996. *Working with relationship triangles: The one-two-three of psychotherapy.* New York: Guilford Press.

Hoffman, L. 1981. *The foundations of family therapy.* New York: Basic Books.

Imber-Black, E., ed. 1993. *Secrets in families and family therapy.* New York: Norton.

Kerr, M. E., and Bowen, M. 1988. *Family evaluation.* New York: Norton.

Minuchin, S. 1974. *Families and family therapy.* Cambridge, MA: Harvard University Press.

Paolino, T. J., and McCrady, B. S., eds. 1978. *Marriage and marital therapy.* New York: Brunner/Mazel.

Watzlawick, P., Beavin, J., and Jackson, D. 1967. *Pragmatics of human communication.* New York: Norton.

Culture and Family Therapy

Boyd-Franklin, N. 1989. *Black families in therapy: A multisystems approach.* New York: Guilford Press.

Davis, L., and Proctor, E. 1989. *Race, gender, and class: Guidelines for practice with individuals, families and groups.* Englewood Cliffs, NJ: Prentice-Hall.

Pedersen, P. 1987. The frequent assumptions of cultural bias in counseling. *Journal of Multicultural Counseling and Development.* 15:16–24.

Pinderhughes, E. 1989. *Understanding race, ethnicity, power: The key to efficacy in clinical practice.* New York: The Free Press.

Sue, D. W., and Sue, D. 1990. *Counseling the culturally different: Theory and practice,* 2nd ed. New York: Wiley.

Marriage

Dicks, H. V. 1967. *Marital tensions.* New York: Basic Books.

Guerin, P. J., Fay, L., Burden, S., and Kautto, J. 1987. *The evaluation and treatment of marital conflict: A four-stage approach.* New York: Basic Books.

Lederer, W., and Jackson, D. 1968. *The mirages of marriage.* New York: Norton.

Lerner, H. G. 1985. *The dance of anger: A woman's guide to changing patterns of intimate relationships.* New York: Harper & Row.

Scarf, M. 1987. *Intimate partners: Patterns in love and marriage.* New York: Random House.

In-Laws and the Extended Family

Guerin, P. J., ed. 1976. *Family therapy: Theory and practice.* New York: Gardner Press.

Lerner, H. G. 1989. *The dance of intimacy: A woman's guide to courageous acts of change in key relationships.* New York: Harper & Row.

McGoldrick, M., and Gerson, R. 1985. *Genograms in family assessment.* New York: Norton.

Families with Babies and Small Children

Brazelton, T. B. 1983. *Infants and mothers: Differences in development.* Rev. ed. New York: Dell.

Combrinck-Graham, L. ed. 1988. *Children in family contexts: Perspectives on treatment.* New York: Guilford Press.

Faber, A., and Mazlish, E. 1974. *Liberated parents, liberated children.* New York: Grosset & Dunlap.

Ginott, H. 1969. *Between parent and child.* New York: Macmillan.

Patterson, G. 1975. *Families: Application of social learning theory to family life.* Champaign, IL: Research Press.

Families with Older Children

Bank, S., and Kahn, M. 1982. *The sibling bond.* New York: Basic Books.

Blos, P. 1979. *The adolescent passage: Developmental issues.* New York: International Universities Press.

Faber, A., and Mazlish, E. 1987. *Siblings without rivalry.* New York: Norton.

Fishel, E. 1979. *Sisters: Love and rivalry inside the family and beyond.* New York: Quill/William Morrow.

Schlaadt, R., and Shannon, P. 1986. *Drugs of choice,* 2nd ed. Englewood Cliffs, NJ: Prentice-Hall.

Divorce, Remarriage, and Stepparenting

Ahrons, C., and Rodgers, R. 1987. *Divorced families: A multidisciplinary developmental view.* New York: Norton.

Isaacs, M. B., Montalvo, B., and Abelsohn, D. 1986. *The difficult divorce.* New York: Basic Books.

Vaughan, D. 1986. *Uncoupling: Turning points in intimate relationships.* New York: Oxford University Press.

Visher, E., and Visher, J. 1988. *Old loyalties, new ties: Therapeutic strategies with stepfamilies.* New York: Brunner/Mazel.

Leaving Home and the Postchildrearing Years

Levinson, D. 1978. *The seasons of a man's life.* New York: Ballantine.

Nichols, M. P. 1987. *Turning forty in the eighties.* New York: Fireside/Simon & Schuster.

Viorst, J. 1986. *Necessary losses.* New York: Simon & Schuster.

Family Therapy Technique

Anderson, C., and Stewart, S. 1983. *Mastering resistance: A practical guide to family therapy.* New York: Guilford Press.

Gerson, M-J. 1996. *The embedded self: A psychoanalytic guide to family therapy.* New York: Analytic Press.

Guerin, P. J., Fay, L., Burden, S., and Kautto, J. 1987. *The evaluation and treatment of marital conflict: A four-stage approach.* New York: Basic Books.

Isaacs, M. B., Montalvo, B., and Abelsohn, D. 1986. *The difficult divorce: Therapy for children and families.* New York: Basic Books.

Minuchin, S., and Fishman, H. C. 1981. *Family therapy techniques.* Cambridge, MA: Harvard University Press.

Minuchin, S., and Nichols, M. P. 1994. *Family healing: Tales of hope and renewal from family therapy.* New York: Touchstone/Simon & Schuster.

Taibbi, R. 1996. *Doing family therapy: Craft and creativity in clinical practice.* New York: Guilford Press.

White, M., and Epston, D. 1990. *Narrative means to therapeutic ends.* New York: Norton.

APPENDIX B

Glossary

accommodation Elements of a system automatically adjust to coordinate their functioning; people may have to work at it.

anorexia nervosa Self-starvation leading to loss of 25 percent or more of body weight, hyperactivity, hypothermia, and amenorrhea (in females).

aversive control Using punishment and criticism to eliminate undesirable responses; commonly used in dysfunctional families.

basic assumption theory Bion's concept that group members become diverted from the group task to pursue unconscious patterns of *fight–flight*, *dependency*, or *pairing*.

behavior exchange theory Explanation of behavior in relationships as maintained by a ratio of costs to benefits.

black box metaphor The idea that because the mind is so complex, it's better to study people's input and output (behavior, communication) than to speculate about what goes on in their minds.

blended families Separate families united by marriage; stepfamilies.

boundary A concept used in structural family therapy to describe emotional barriers that protect and enhance the integrity of individuals, subsystems, and families.

bulimia An eating disorder characterized by bouts of excessive eating followed by self-induced vomiting, purging with laxatives, strenuous exercise, or fasting.

circular causality The idea that events are related through a series of interacting loops or repeating cycles.

circular questioning A method of interviewing developed by the Milan Associates in which questions are asked that highlight differences among family members.

classical conditioning A form of respondent learning in which an unconditioned stimulus (UCS), such as food, which leads to an unconditioned response (UCR), such as salivation, is paired with a conditioned stimulus (CS), such as a bell, the result of which is that the CS begins to evoke the same response; used in the behavioral treatment of anxiety disorders.

coalition An alliance between two persons or social units against a third.

communications theory The study of relationships in terms of the exchange of verbal and nonverbal messages.

complementary Relationships based on differences that fit together, where qualities of one make up for lacks in the other; one is one-up while the other is one-down.

concurrent therapy Treatment of two or more persons, seen separately, usually by different therapists.

conjoint therapy Treatment of two or more persons in sessions together.

constructivism A relativistic point of view that emphasizes the subjective construction of reality.

Implies that what we see in families may be based as much on our preconceptions as on what's actually going on.

contingency contracting A behavior therapy technique whereby agreements are made between family members to exchange rewards for desired behavior.

countertransference Emotional reaction, usually unconscious and often distorted, on the part of the therapist to a patient or member of a family in treatment.

cross-generational coalition An inappropriate alliance between a parent and child, who side together against a third member of the family.

customer De Shazer's term for a client who not only complains about a problem ("complainant") but is motivated to resolve it.

cybernetics The study of control processes in systems, especially analysis of the flow of information in closed systems.

deconstruction A postmodern approach to exploring meaning by taking apart and examining taken-for-granted categories and assumptions, making possible newer and sounder constructions of meaning.

detriangling The process by which an individual removes himself or herself from the emotional field of two others.

differentiation of self Psychological separation of intellect and emotions, and independence of self from others; opposite of fusion.

disengagement Minuchin's term for psychological isolation that results from overly rigid boundaries around individuals and subsystems in a family.

double bind A conflict created when a person receives contradictory messages on different levels of abstraction in an important relationship, and cannot leave or comment.

dyadic model Explanations based on the interactions between two persons or objects: Johnny shoplifts to get his mother's attention.

emotional cutoff Bowen's term for flight from an unresolved emotional attachment.

enactment An interaction stimulated in structural family therapy in order to observe and then change transactions that make up family structure.

enmeshment Minuchin's term for loss of autonomy due to a blurring of psychological boundaries.

entitlement Boszormenyi-Nagy's term for the amount of merit a person accrues for behaving in an ethical manner toward others.

epistemology The branch of philosophy concerned with the study of knowledge. Used by Bateson to mean worldview or belief system.

exception De Shazer's term for times when a client is temporarily free of his or her problem. Solution-focused therapists focus on exceptions to help clients build on successful problem-solving skills.

expressive role Serving social and emotional functions; in traditional families, the wife's role.

extended family All the descendants of a set of grandparents.

externalization Michael White's technique of personifying problems as external to persons.

extinction Eliminating behavior by not reinforcing it.

family drawing An experiential therapy technique where family members are asked to draw their ideas about how the family is organized.

family group therapy Family treatment based on the group therapy model.

family homeostasis Tendency of families to resist change in order to maintain a steady state.

family life cycle Stages of family life from separation from one's parents to marriage, having children, growing older, retirement, and finally death.

family structure The functional organization of families that determines how family members interact.

family myths A set of beliefs based on a distortion of historical reality and shared by all family members that help shape the rules governing family functioning.

family of origin A person's parents and siblings; usually refers to the original nuclear family of an adult.

family projection process In Bowenian theory, the mechanism by which parental conflicts are projected onto the children or a spouse.

family ritual Technique used by Selvini Palazzoli and her Milan Associates that prescribes a specific act for family members to perform, which is designed to change the family system's rules.

family rules A descriptive term for redundant behavioral patterns.

feedback The return of a portion of the output of a system, especially when used to maintain the output within predetermined limits (negative feedback), or to signal a need to modify the system (positive feedback).

first-order change Superficial change in a system that itself stays invariant.

first-order cybernetics The idea that an outside observer can study and make changes in a system while remaining separate and independent of that system.

functional analysis of behavior In operant behavior therapy, a study of a particular behavior, what elicits it, and what reinforces it.

function of the system The idea that symptoms are often ways to distract or otherwise protect family members from threatening conflicts.

fusion A blurring of psychological boundaries between self and others, and a contamination of emotional and intellectual functioning; opposite of differentiation.

general systems theory A biological model of living systems as whole entities that maintain themselves through continuous input and output from the environment; developed by Ludwig von Bertalanffy.

genogram A schematic diagram of the family system, using squares to represent males, circles to indicate females, horizontal lines for marriages, and vertical lines to indicate children.

group dynamics Interactions among group members that emerge as a result of properties of the group rather than merely their individual personalities.

hermeneutics The art of analyzing literary texts or human experience, understood as fundamentally ambiguous, by interpreting levels of meaning.

hierarchical structure Family functioning based on clear generational boundaries, where the parents maintain control and authority.

homeostasis A balanced steady state of equilibrium.

identification From psychoanalytic theory, not merely imitation, but appropriation of traits of an admired other.

identified patient The symptom-bearer or official patient as identified by the family.

instrumental role Decision-making and task functions; in traditional families, the husband's role.

intensity Minuchin's term for changing maladaptive transactions by using strong affect, repeated intervention, or prolonged pressure.

internal family systems A model of the mind that uses systemic principles and techniques to understand and change intrapsychic processes, developed by Richard Schwartz.

introjection A primitive form of identification; taking in aspects of other people, which then become part of the self-image.

invariant prescription A technique developed by Mara Selvini Palazzoli in which parents are directed to mysteriously sneak away together.

invisible loyalties Boszormenyi-Nagy's term for unconscious commitments that children take on to help their families.

joining A structural family therapy term for accepting and accommodating to families to win their confidence and circumvent resistance.

linear causality The idea that one event is the cause and another is the effect; in behavior, the idea that one behavior is a stimulus, the other a response.

live supervision Technique of teaching therapy whereby the supervisor observes sessions in progress and contacts the therapist to suggest different strategies and techniques.

managed care A system in which third-party companies manage insurance costs by regulating the terms of treatment. Managed care companies select providers, set fees, and control who receives treatment and how many sessions they are entitled to.

marital schism Lidz's term for pathological overt marital conflict.

marital skew Lidz's term for a pathological marriage in which one spouse dominates the other.

metacommunication Every message has two levels, report and command; metacommunication is the implied command or qualifying message.

miracle question Asking clients to imagine how things would be if they woke up tomorrow and their problem was solved. Solution-focused therapists use the miracle question to help clients identify goals and potential solutions.

mirroring Expression of understanding and acceptance of another's feelings.

modeling Observational learning.

monadic model Explanations based on properties of a single person or object: Johnny shoplifts because he is rebellious.

morphogenesis The process by which a system changes its structure to adapt to new contexts.

multigenerational transmission process Murray Bowen's concept for the projection of varying degrees of immaturity to different children in the same family; the child who is most involved in the family emotional process emerges with the lowest level of differentiation, and passes problems on to succeeding generations.

multiple family therapy Treatment of several families at once in a group therapy format; pioneered by Peter Laqueur and Murray Bowen.

multiple impact therapy An intensive, crisis-oriented form of family therapy developed by Robert MacGregor; family members are treated in various subgroups by a team of therapists.

mystification Laing's concept that many families distort their children's experience by denying or relabeling it.

narcissism Self-regard. The exaggerated self-regard most people equate with narcissism is pathological narcissism.

network therapy A treatment devised by Ross Speck in which a large number of family and friends are assembled to help resolve a patient's problems.

neutrality Selvini Palazzoli's term for balanced acceptance of family members.

nuclear family Parents and their children.

object relations Internalized images of self and others based on early parent–child interactions that determine a person's mode of relationship to other people.

object relations theory Psychoanalytic theory derived from Melanie Klein and developed by the British School (Bion, Fairbairn, Guntrip, Winnicott) that emphasizes relationships and attachment, rather than libidinal and aggressive drives, as the key issues of human concern.

open system A system that exchanges information or material with its environment, as opposed to a closed system that does not. Living systems are, by definition, open systems.

operant conditioning A form of learning whereby a person or animal is rewarded for performing certain behaviors; the major approach in most forms of behavior therapy.

ordeals A type of paradoxical intervention in which the client is directed to do something that is more of a hardship than the symptom.

paradox A self-contradictory statement based on a valid deduction from acceptable premises.

paradoxical directive A technique used in strategic therapy whereby the therapist directs family members to continue their symptomatic behavior. If they conform, they admit control and expose secondary gain; if they rebel, they give up their symptoms.

parental child A child who has been allocated power to take care of younger siblings; adaptive when done deliberately in large or single-parent families, maladaptive when it results from unplanned abdication of parental responsibility.

positive connotation Selvini Palazzoli's technique of ascribing positive motives to family behavior in order to promote family cohesion and avoid resistance to therapy.

postmodern Contemporary antipositivism, viewing knowledge as relative and context-dependent; questions assumptions of objectivity that characterize modern science. In family therapy, challenging the idea of scientific certainty, and linked to the method of deconstruction.

Premack principle Using high-probability behavior (preferred activities) to reinforce low-probability behavior (nonpreferred activities).

prescribing the symptom A paradoxical technique that forces a patient to either give up a symptom or admit that it is under voluntary control.

pretend techniques Madanes's playful paradoxical intervention in which family members are asked to pretend to engage in symptomatic behavior. The paradox is if they are pretending to have a symptom, the symptom cannot be real.

process/content Distinction between how members of a family or group relate and what they talk about.

projective identification A defense mechanism that operates unconsciously, whereby unwanted aspects of the self are attributed to another person and that person is induced to behave in accordance with these projected attitudes and feelings.

pseudohostility Wynne's term for superficial bickering that masks pathological alignments in schizophrenic families.

pseudomutuality Wynne's term for the facade of family harmony that characterizes many schizophrenic families.

psychoeducation A type of therapy developed in work with schizophrenics, which emphasizes educating family members to help them understand and cope with a seriously disturbed family member.

quid pro quo Literally, "something for something," an equal exchange or substitution.

reflecting team Tom Andersen's technique of having the observing team share their reactions with the family following a session.

reframing Relabeling a family's description of behavior to make it more amenable to therapeutic change; for example, describing someone as "lazy" rather than "depressed."

regression Return to a less mature level of functioning in the face of stress.

reinforcement An event, behavior, or object that increases the rate of a particular response. A positive reinforcer is an event whose contingent presentation increases the rate of responding; a negative reinforcer is an event whose contingent withdrawal increases the rate of responding.

reinforcement reciprocity Exchanging rewarding behaviors between family members.

resistance Anything that patients or families do to oppose or retard the progress of therapy.

restraining A strategic technique for overcoming resistance by suggesting that a family not change.

role-playing Acting out the parts of important characters to dramatize feelings and practice new ways of relating.

rubber fence Wynne's term for the rigid boundary surrounding many schizophrenic families, which allows only minimal contact with the surrounding community.

scapegoat A member of the family, usually the identified patient, who is the object of displaced conflict or criticism.

schemas Cognitive constructions, or core beliefs, through which people filter their perceptions and structure their experience.

schizophrenogenic mother Fromm-Reichmann's term for aggressive, domineering mothers thought to precipitate schizophrenia in their offspring.

sculpting, family A nonverbal experiential technique in which family members position themselves in a tableau that reveals significant aspects of their perceptions and feelings.

second-order change Basic change in the structure and functioning of a system.

second-order cybernetics The idea that anyone attempting to observe and change a system is therefore part of that system.

selfobject Kohut's term for a person related to not as a separate individual, but as an extension of the self.

separation–individuation Process whereby the infant begins, at about two months, to draw apart from the symbiotic bond with mother and develop his or her autonomous functioning.

shaping Reinforcing change in small steps.

social constructionism Like constructivism, challenges the notion of an objective basis for knowledge. Knowledge and meaning are shaped by culturally shared assumptions.

social learning theory Understanding and treating behavior using principles from social and developmental psychology as well as from learning theory.

solution-focused therapy Steve de Shazer's term for a style of therapy that emphasizes the solutions that families have already developed for their problems.

structure Recurrent patterns of interaction that define and stabilize the shape of relationships.

subsystem Smaller units in families, determined by generation, sex, or function.

symmetrical In relationships, equality or parallel form.

system, closed A functionally related group of elements regarded as forming a collective entity that does not interact with the surrounding environment.

system, open A set of interrelated elements that exchange information, energy, and material with the surrounding environment.

systems theory A generic term for studying a group of related elements that interact as a whole entity; encompasses general systems theory and cybernetics.

three-generational hypothesis of schizophrenia Bowen's concept that schizophrenia is the end result of low levels of differentiation passed on and amplified across three succeeding generations.

time-out A behavioral technique for extinguishing undesirable behavior by removing the reinforcing consequences of that behavior. Typically, making the child sit in a corner or go to his or her room.

token economy A system of rewards using points, which can be accumulated and exchanged for reinforcing items or behaviors.

transference Psychoanalytic term for distorted emotional reactions to present relationships based on unresolved, early family relations.

triadic model Explanations based on the interactions among three people or objects; Johnny shoplifts because his father covertly encourages him to defy his mother.

triangle A three-person system; according to Bowen, the smallest stable unit of human relations.

triangulation Detouring conflict between two people by involving a third person, stabilizing the relationship between the original pair.

unconscious Psychoanalytic term for memories, feelings, and impulses of which a person is unaware. Often used as a noun, but more appropriately limited to use as an adjective.

undifferentiated family ego mass Bowen's early term for emotional "stuck-togetherness" or fusion in the family, especially prominent in schizophrenic families.

unique outcome Michael White's term for times when clients acted free of their problems, even if they were unaware of doing so. Narrative therapists identify unique outcomes as a way to help clients challenge negative views of themselves.

APPENDIX C

Careers and Training

Becoming a Family Therapist

There are many paths to becoming a family therapist. Not all of them involve going through an academic program in marital and family therapy, although that's the most direct path. Many people who have a state marital and family therapy (MFT) license or certificate graduated with a more traditional degree—master's or Ph.D. in clinical psychology, an MSW from a social work program, or a master's in counseling or nursing. Depending on their state's requirements, these therapists, after completing their non-MFT degree, have to take some additional MFT course work and receive extensive supervision in order to be able to call themselves marital and family therapists (see section on licensing, below).

Which path you choose should depend on what you want to do in your career. For example, if you hope to teach or do research in family therapy, you would do well to go through a Ph.D. program. If, on the other hand, you primarily want to do clinical practice, either in an agency or in private practice, you may not need a Ph.D. and could go to one of the many master's programs in MFT (for a list of approved MFT academic programs, contact the American Association for Marriage and Family Therapy, described below).

If you're interested in studying an aspect of mental health not thoroughly covered in MFT programs, for example, psychological testing, social policy, individual psychotherapy, or psychopharmacology, you could get a non-MFT degree and then pick up the required courses and supervision from one of the many nonacademic family therapy institutes described in the last section of this appendix.

Professional Organizations

The *American Association for Marriage and Family Therapy* (AAMFT), located in Washington, DC, was organized in 1942 by Lester Dearborn and Ernest Graves as a professional organization to set standards for marriage counselors. In 1970 it was expanded to include family therapists and has become the major credentialing body for the field. Through its requirements for membership, standards have been set for becoming a family therapist that are used by the various states that regulate the profession. AAMFT also lobbies state and federal governments for the interests of family therapists, such as state licensing.

AAMFT's membership has grown enormously, reflecting the growth of the field. The organization has more than doubled since 1982 and now represents 23,000 marital and family therapists. This kind of membership and the money generated from it has made AAMFT a powerful player in mental health politics and has aided in public and governmental recognition of family therapy as a distinct field.

AAMFT has a code of ethics that covers the following issues: responsibility to clients; confidentiality; professional competence and integrity; responsibility to students, employees, supervisees, and research subjects; financial arrangements; and advertising. AAMFT can be contacted at 1133 15th Street NW, Suite 300, Washington, DC 20005-2710; telephone: 202-452-0109; web site: http://wow.aamft.org.

Although the AAMFT has a presence in California, the dominant organization for MFTs there is the California Association of Marriage and Family Therapists (CAMFT). With 29 regional chapters and 25,000 members, CAMFT's size has given it a strong voice in the state legislature. CAMFT sponsors an annual conference and publishes the *California Therapist.* For further information, contact CAMFT, 7901 Raytheon Road, San Diego, CA 92111; telephone: 619-292-2638; web site: http://wow.camft.org.

The *American Family Therapy Academy* (AFTA) was organized in 1977 to serve the needs of the field's senior researchers, clinicians, and trainers who wanted a smaller, more intimate context for sharing ideas and developing common interests. Despite high standards for membership regarding years of teaching and clinical experience, and an interest in remaining small, AFTA's membership has doubled since 1983, from 500 to over 1,000. AFTA is a high-level think tank focused around its annual conference, described below, and its newsletter. For more information, contact AFTA, 2020 Pennsylvania Avenue NW, #273, Washington, DC 20006; telephone: 202-994-2776.

The *International Family Therapy Association* (IFTA) was begun in 1986 as a way for family therapists around the globe to connect. Each year IFTA sponsors the World Family Therapy Congress in a different country. So far the countries that have hosted the congress include Finland, Greece, Holland, Ireland, Israel, Hungary, Mexico, and Poland. In addition, IFTA biannually publishes a newsletter, *The International Connection.* IFTA can be reached at the Akron Child Guidance Center, 312 Locust Street, Akron, OH 44302.

Conferences

Besides the multitude of workshops or conferences privately sponsored or put on by local chapters of AAMFT, there are four main national meetings. The largest is AAMFT's annual conference each October. With over 200 presentations on various family therapy topics to select from, there is usually something for everyone.

The second largest (over 2,000) is the Family Therapy Network Symposium held each March in Washington, DC. Sponsored by the *Family Therapy Networker* magazine (described below), all presenters are invited so that quality throughout the 80 workshops is ensured. Each year the symposium has a theme, and invited plenary speakers are often famous for work done outside the field of family therapy. For information, telephone: 202-829-2452.

AFTA's annual meeting deliberately has a flavor different from that of other conferences. Because of its small size (usually around 300—it's not open to nonmembers), it's the one place where leaders of the field can gather in a relatively informal setting to discuss ideas. Rather than workshops, the meeting is organized around interest groups and brief presentations designed to promote dialogue and debate.

The other conference where many family therapists can be found isn't devoted exclusively to family therapy. The American Orthopsychiatric Association is a multidisciplinary organization whose annual conference usually contains a sizable percentage of presentations devoted to family therapy and issues of interest to systems-oriented clinicians.

Publications

The first book devoted entirely to the diagnosis and treatment of families was Nathan Ackerman's the *Psychodynamics of Family Life*, published in 1958. The field's first journal, *Family Process*, was founded in 1961. Since these early publications, the family therapy literature has proliferated to the point where it is virtually impossible to stay on top of it. We count over twenty journals or newsletters devoted to some aspect of family therapy published in the United States, with many other countries publishing their own journals. The number of books is equally overwhelming, so we refer the reader to Appendix A, *Recommended Readings* for a selective guide to some of the most useful books and articles in the field. We describe some of the major periodicals in the following discussion.

Family Process continues to exert a powerful influence on the field. Many of the debates and developments described in earlier chapters of this book appeared first in its pages. Founded in 1961 by Don Jackson and Nathan Ackerman, its editors have included Jay Haley, Don Bloch, Carlos Sluzki, and, since 1990, Peter Steinglass. The *Journal of Marital and Family Therapy* is also quite influential and, as the official journal of AAMFT, has a large readership. Under the editorship of Alan Gurman during the 1980s and Douglas Sprenkle in the 1990s, it increased its focus on research and improved its standards. Current editor, Froma Walsh, is balancing the research and clinical foci.

The *Family Therapy Networker*, a magazine devoted to issues related to family therapy and psychotherapy in general, also has a strong influence. Its large readership (over 70,000) has been won through tackling provocative issues with high-quality writing. Rich Simon has turned what began as a small newsletter into the most widely read publication on psychotherapy and, in so doing, has introduced many of family therapy's ideas to therapists throughout the country. In 1993, the *Networker* won the American Magazine Award for feature writing, the highest honor possible for a magazine.

There are a number of other well-established journals that, like *Family Process* and *Journal of Marital and Family Therapy*, are devoted to general issues in the field. These include the *American Journal of Family Therapy*, *Journal of Family Psychotherapy*, *The International Journal of Family Therapy*, *Contemporary Family Therapy*, and *Family Therapy Collections*. In addition, a number of specialized journals have emerged. For example, the *Journal of Systemic Therapies* (formerly the *Journal of Strategic and Systemic Therapies*) is widely read by therapists who use those adjectives to describe themselves, while Bowen systems therapists read *Family Systems* and those interested in Michael White's work subscribe to the *Dulwich Centre Review* and *Family Therapy Case Studies*.

The cross-fertilization of family therapy with other fields is represented by *Family Systems Medicine*, a journal devoted to the collaboration between medicine and family therapy; by the *Journal of Family Psychology*, published by a division of the American Psychological Association; and by *Feminism and Family Therapy*, which reflects the growing influence of feminist thought on the field.

News within the field and digests of important developments are conveyed through AAMFT's newsletter, *Family Therapy News*, and through the *Marriage and Family Review* and the *Brown University Family Therapy Newsletter*. Those interested in the branch of sociology called family studies have much in common with family therapists and read *Family Relations* and the *Journal of Marriage and the Family.*

Licensing

Thirty-seven states currently regulate MFTs, and several other states are currently considering licensing bills. The number of states licensing or certifying MFTs has more than tripled in the past decade. Most state requirements for licensure are comparable to the standards for Clinical Membership in AAMFT. Common requirements include graduation from an accredited marital and family therapy program, two years of post-degree supervised clinical experience, and passing the state exam (18 states require this) or the national exam for MFTs, which is conducted by the Association of Marital and Family Therapy Regulatory Board and used by the remaining 19 states.

Training Centers

As discussed earlier, family therapy developed primarily outside academia. There are, however, a handful of doctoral programs and a larger number of master's degree programs specializing in marital and family therapy in universities around the country. The American Association for Marriage and Family Therapy accredits 29 master's programs and 10 doctoral programs and can provide a list of them. Because we are aware of no comparable list of the major nonacademic training centers we will describe some of the best-known centers in the United States here. Although other major centers exist throughout the world, our space is too limited to list them here. The reader may notice that the majority of the centers described are clustered in the Northeast where family therapy is most strongly rooted. We will begin there and move west.

The *Family Institute of Cambridge* in Massachusetts was founded in 1976. Now located in Watertown, it is a nonprofit center of training and research in applied systems theory. Faculty members include such notable therapists as Michele Bograd, Laura Chasin, Richard Chasin, Terry Real, Kathy Weingarten, and Sallyann Roth. The institute offers four training sequences: (1) narrative approaches, (2) family systems theory, (3) couples therapy, and (4) women's group process. The institute also offers a wide variety of long- and short-term courses, group supervision, and conferences; it has some research stipends for its students. For more information, contact Suzanne Bourque, 51 Kondazian Street, Watertown, MA 02172.

The *Kantor Family Institute,* in Somerville, Massachusetts, was founded by David Kantor after he left the Family Institute of Cambridge in 1980, and is informed by his structural/analytic model of therapy, as well as by psychodynamic and other family therapy influences. This institute offers a sequence of three one-year training programs that build on each other but can be taken independently. They also offer a specialized program in couples treatment and in organizational consultation, as well as a variety of apprenticeships, internships, and courses. For more information, contact Ulrike Dettling, Kantor Family Institute, 7 Sheppard Street, Cambridge, MA 02138.

The *Minuchin Center for the Family* is a small, private training institution in New York City, founded in 1981 by Salvador Minuchin. The faculty also includes Ema Genijovich, David Greenan, Richard Holm, Wai-Yung Lee, and George Simon. Special programs are designed for on-site training and consultation with agencies that work with poor families, foster care, substance abuse, the homeless, and children in psychiatric facilities. The year-long extern training program is at three levels: beginning family therapists, more experienced therapists, and administrators and supervisors. The orientation emphasizes structural family therapy but has been influenced by feminism and multiculturalism. Inquiries may be directed to George Simon, 114 East 32nd Street, 4th Floor, New York, NY 10016.

The *Ackerman Institute for Family Therapy* in New York City was founded as the Family Institute by Nathan Ackerman in 1965. Following Ackerman's death in 1971, the center was renamed in his honor and the directorship was assumed by Donald Bloch, who recently passed the baton to Peter Steinglass, current editor of *Family Process.* In addition to Bloch and Steinglass, the institute has such noted family therapists and theorists as Peggy Penn, Peggy Papp, Jorge Colapinto, Olga Silverstein, Marcia Scheinberg, Virginia Goldner, Peter Fraenkel, and Gillian Walker. The institute offers training in systemic family therapy. It offers a two-year clinical externship program for more experienced family therapists and weekend workshops throughout the year. For further information contact Marcia Sheinberg, Director of Training, 149 East 78th Street, New York, NY 10021.

The *Family Institute of Westchester* recently moved from Mount Vernon to White Plains, New York, and is directed by Betty Carter. The institute teaches the multicontextual approach, which includes aspects of structural and strategic techniques, and is based on the Bowenian model. The institute has been in operation since 1977 and is primarily known for its training program, which usually takes three years to complete. There is also a two-year externship that meets weekly. Specialized training programs are offered in multicultural family therapy and therapy with gay and lesbian couples and families. Additional information is available from Lillian Fine, Director of Administration, Family Institute of Westchester, 7-11 South Broadway, Suite 400, White Plains, NY 10601.

The *Center for Family Learning* in Rye Brook, New York, was founded in 1973 by Philip Guerin, who was trained by Murray Bowen. The center provides a three-year training program in family systems therapy, which includes a clinical externship year for experienced clinicians, followed by a fellowship year with center faculty working on the Child and Adolescents Project. The third year is another fellowship, studying marital conflict. The center also offers a variety of seminars and workshops and a Community Education Program, which is taped for cable television. For additional information, contact Eileen Guerin Pendagast, Director of Post Graduate and Community Education, 16 Rye Ridge Plaza, Rye Brook, NY 10573.

The *Family Therapy Training Program at the University of Rochester* was established in 1983 by Judith Landau-Stanton and M. Duncan Stanton. This program teaches the Rochester Model, an integration of structural, strategic, transgenerational, experiential, and ecosystemic approaches in a series of externships and seminars. Special areas of interest are cultural transition and medical family therapy. Cases are provided for trainees. The faculty includes Lyman Wynne, Susan McDaniel, David Seaburn, and the founders. For more information, contact David Seaburn, Family Therapy Training Program, Department of Psychiatry, University of Rochester, 300 Crittenden Boulevard, Rochester, NY 14642–8409.

The *Family Institute of New Jersey* was founded in 1992 by its director, Monica McGoldrick. It is committed to training, research, and service in support of cultural diversity and the empowerment of those voices our society silences. In addition to a three-year certificate program, the institute offers a variety of workshops, free lectures to the community, and consultation to schools and other organizations. Minority scholarships are available. Faculty includes notable therapists such as Nydia Garcia Preto, Rhea Almeida, and Paulette Moore Hines. For further information, contact Monica McGoldrick, 312 Amboy Avenue, Metuchen, NJ 08840.

The *Family Therapy Institute of Washington, DC,* is the training center and clinic codirected by Jay Haley and Cloe Madanes, until recently when Haley retired. Faculty members teach, supervise, and conduct therapy emphasizing the strategic, problem-focused approach. The institute clinic offers treatment by a multidisciplinary staff, all of whom have previously trained with Haley and Madanes. Inquiries may be made to James Keim, Family Therapy Institute of Washington, DC, 5850 Hubbard Drive, Rockville, MD 20852.

The *Georgetown Family Center,* located in Washington, DC, exists to refine, test, extend, and define Bowen systems theory. Murray Bowen founded and directed this center until his death in 1990. The current director is Michael Kerr. Training programs include a weekly postgraduate program and a special program for out-of-towners that meets for three consecutive days, four times a year. Other learning opportunities include the monthly Clinical Conference Series and the annual Main Symposium. Descriptions of these programs are available from Daniel Papero, Director of Training, Georgetown Family Center, 4380 MacArthur Boulevard NW, Washington, DC 20007.

The *Family Therapy Practice Center of Washington, DC,* was founded in 1980 by Marianne Walters, after she left the Philadelphia Child Guidance Clinic. The center has a strong structural family therapy base and offers a postgraduate externship. In addition, the center develops programs for dealing with a at-risk populations and changing family structures such as their adolescent foster care project, family violence assistance project, and runaway youth/multiple family group project. For more information, contact Director of Training, 2153 Newport Place NW, Washington, DC 20037.

The *Philadelphia Child Guidance Center,* now known as the *Child Guidance Center of the Children's Hospital of Philadelphia,* became one of the leading centers of family therapy in the world during the 1970s. It was here that Salvador Minuchin and his colleagues defined and promulgated the concepts of structural family therapy. It provides the full range of children's services: outpatient, home-based, day hospital, and inpatient. The outpatient specialty services include early childhood intervention, sexual abuse (victims and offenders), divorce and remarriage, and preadjudicated youth. Three home-based programs serve children and adolescents at risk for placement and provide specialized foster care. The inpatient service includes family apartments so that families are maximally involved in the treatment process.

Unlike most of the other centers of family therapy training, which are located in small clinics and old houses, the center is a large, modern, well-equipped facility affiliated with the Departments of Psychiatry and Pediatrics of the University of Pennsylvania School of Medicine. The center probably has trained more family therapists than any other in the world. The training programs include internships and externships for psychology, social work, and child psychiatry postgraduate students. Additional information can be obtained by writing to Marion Lindblad-Goldberg, Director, Family Therapy Training Center, 34th Street and Civic Center Boulevard, Philadelphia, PA 19104-4322.

The *Brief Family Therapy Center* (BFTC) of Milwaukee is known for its specialization in the research, training, and clinical practice of brief, solution-focused therapy. BFTC provides short- and long-term training in solution-focused therapy that attracts practitioners from across North America, Europe, and Asia. The staff includes Steve de Shazer and Insoo Kim Berg, who have presented workshops and seminars in more than 30 countries and have written extensively on solution-focused therapy. For further information, contact Brief Family Therapy Center, 13965 West Burleigh Street, Brookfield, WI 53005.

The *Family Institute* (formerly of Chicago) was founded in 1968 by Charles Kramer to provide training, research, and clinical services. William Pinsof is the president of the institute, which probably has the largest full-time faculty in the country, including notable family therapists Douglas Breunlin, Cheryl Rampage, and Richard Schwartz. They offer a variety of training programs grounded in a multilevel, integrative approach. Elements of the approach include integrative problem-centered therapy, the metaframeworks perspective, the internal family systems model, feminism, and multiculturalism. They offer a two-year certificate program that is accredited by AAMFT, a master's program in family therapy in affiliation with Northwestern University, and a one-year clinical training practicum, a psychology internship, and a postdoctoral fellowship. In 1994 the institute opened a spacious new facility in Evanston, Illinois. For more information, contact Therese Smith, 618 Library Place, Evanston, IL 60201.

The *Chicago Center for Family Health* (CCFH) was begun in 1991 by codirectors John Rolland and Froma Walsh. Affiliated with the University of Chicago, the center's orientation integrates systems theory with a multigenerational family life-cycle framework. In addition to general training in family therapy, CCFH offers specialized training in couples therapy, divorce mediation, and medical family therapy. Training programs include a two-year certificate program, workshops and courses, and consultation groups. Faculty also include other notable family therapists such as Gene Combs, Jill Freedman, Jay Lebow, John Schwartzman, and Tom Todd. For more information, contact John Rolland, CCFH, North Pier, Suite 651, 445 E. Illinois Street, Chicago, IL 60611.

The *Houston Galveston Institute*, a private, nonprofit organization, was founded in 1977 by Harlene Anderson and the late Harry Goolishian. The orientation of the institute is a "collaborative language systems approach" that emphasizes openness, sharing of clinical experiences, live consultation, and observation of faculty work. Programs include (1) residential (fellowships, internships, and apprenticeships), (2) external programs (externships, seminars, supervision, and workshops), and (3) international visitor study programs. For more information, contact Susan Levin, 3316 Mount Vernon, Houston, TX 77006.

The *Mental Research Institute* (MRI) in Palo Alto, California, was founded in 1969 by the late Don Jackson and is considered one of the birthplaces of family therapy. The MRI is best known for its brief therapy approach to families. Its faculty includes such notable names as Paul Watzlawick, Richard Fisch, and Arthur Bodin. The MRI offers a wide variety of training programs, including workshops, continuing seminars, four- or six-week residency programs, and programs in brief therapy or in Michael White's approach. A program for on-site training has also begun recently. For further information, contact Karin Schlanger, Director of Training, 555 Middlefield Road, Palo Alto, CA 94301.

The publisher gratefully acknowledges permission from the following sources to reprint materials in this book:

For material on pages 112, 113, and 115: Copyright © 1983 by M. Davidson. From the book *Uncommon Sense* and reprinted with permission from Jeremy P. Tarcher, Inc., Los Angeles, CA.

For material on pages 122 and 123: From *Family Therapy in Clinical Practice*, by Murray Bowen, M.D., copyright © 1985, 1983, 1978 by Jason Aronson Inc. Reprinted with permission of the publisher.

For material on pages 382 and 384: From *In Search of Solutions, A New Direction in Psychotherapy*, by William Hudson O'Hanlon and Michele Weiner-Davis, by permission of W. W. Norton & Company, Inc. Copyright © 1989 by William Hudson O'Hanlon and Michele Weiner-Davis.

For material on pages 191 and 192: From Steve Andreas, *Virginia Satir: The Patterns of Her Magic*. Reprinted by permission of the author and publisher. Available through Science & Behavior Books, Inc., Palo Alto, California (800) 547-9982.

For material on pages 337, 338, 340, and 341: From *Schizophrenia and the Family*, by C. Anderson, D. Reiss, and B. Hogarty. Copyright © 1986. Reprinted by permission of The Guilford Press.

For material on pages 415 and 416: From *Selected Papers*, by Michael White, Copyright © 1989 by Michael White. Reprinted with permission of the author.

Author Index

Page numbers in italics refer to reference citations.

Subject Index